The Order of Public Reason
A Theory of Freedom and Morality in a Diverse and Bounded World

In this innovative and wide-ranging work, Gerald Gaus advances a revised, and more realistic, account of public reason liberalism, showing how, in the midst of fundamental disagreement about values and beliefs, we can achieve a moral and political order that treats all as free and equal moral persons. The first part of the book analyzes social morality as a system of authoritative moral rules. Drawing on an earlier generation of moral philosophers such as Kurt Baier and Peter Strawson as well as current work in the social sciences, Gaus argues that our social morality is an evolved social fact, which is the necessary foundation of a mutually beneficial social order. The second part considers how this system of social moral authority can be justified to all moral persons. Employing the tools of game theory, social choice theory, experimental psychology, and evolutionary theory, Gaus shows how a free society can secure a moral equilibrium that is endorsed by all, and how a just state respects, and develops, such an equilibrium.

Gerald Gaus is the James E. Rogers Professor of Philosophy at the University of Arizona. He was previously professor of philosophy and political economy at Tulane University. He is the author of a number of books, including *On Philosophy, Politics, and Economics* (2008); *Contemporary Theories of Liberalism* (2003); and *Justificatory Liberalism* (1996). His essay "On Justifying the Moral Rights of the Moderns" won the 2009 American Philosophical Association's Kavka Award.

The Order of Public Reason

*A Theory of Freedom and Morality in a Diverse and
Bounded World*

GERALD GAUS

University of Arizona

 CAMBRIDGE
UNIVERSITY PRESS

CAMBRIDGE UNIVERSITY PRESS
Cambridge, New York, Melbourne, Madrid, Cape Town,
Singapore, São Paulo, Delhi, Mexico City

Cambridge University Press
32 Avenue of the Americas, New York, NY 10013-2473, USA

www.cambridge.org
Information on this title: www.cambridge.org/9781107668058

First published 2011
Reprinted 2011 (thrice), 2012
First paperback edition 2012
Reprinted 2012

A catalog record for this publication is available from the British Library.

Library of Congress Cataloging in Publication Data
Gaus, Gerald F.
The order of public reason: a theory of freedom and morality in a diverse and
bounded world/Gerald Gaus.
        p.   cm.
Includes bibliographical references and index.
1. Political ethics. I. Title.
JA79.G38   2010
172–dc22   2010036917

ISBN 978-0-521-86856-3 Hardback
ISBN 978-1-107-66805-8 Paperback

To Andrea

The enemies of liberty have always based their arguments in the contention that order in human affairs requires that some should give orders and others obey.

F. A. Hayek, *The Constitution of Liberty*

We need not, perhaps, insist upon just the same answer for all; but, if we take the question seriously, we must insist on *some* answer for all.

P. F. Strawson, "Social Morality and Individual Ideal"

[A] society's morality is the joint product of the moralities of its individual members. As far as its content is concerned, individual members are its joint makers, not merely its subjects.

Kurt Baier, *The Rational and the Moral Order*

Contents

Preface

"The fox knows many things, but the hedgehog knows one big thing." Perhaps by now, invoking Isaiah Berlin's famous distinction risks banality, but it is more than just an interesting contrast. Philip Tetlock, in his wonderful book *Expert Political Prediction*, has shown that it has a genuine basis in different cognitive styles. Overall, and of course with many important exceptions, moral, social, and political philosophy is the clash of the hedgehogs. Often political philosophers actually characterize themselves as defending one supreme value – "I'm an egalitarian" or "I'm a libertarian." But even when hedgehogosity is not quite so blatant, moral, social, and political philosophy is often the clash of well-defined schools with well-defined programs: Aristotelians, virtue theorists, perfectionists, Kantians, Humeans, utilitarians, deontologists, expressivists, realists, intuitionists, naturalists, moral sense theorists, and on and on. And when philosophers are dissatisfied with the current state of philosophy and seek to advance a new view, they almost always see the need to ensure that it qualifies as a fully fledged hedgehog view. Thus many moral philosophers who have been impressed by the need to take empirical evidence seriously go on to insist that moral philosophy really is simply cognitive psychology. One experimental moral philosopher once objected to me: "I have no idea what people are talking about when they invoke the idea of rationality." All that old rationality talk is out, and now it is just the study of cognitive processes. Philosophy as the clash of the hedgehogs is central to our pedagogy. The standard philosophy course is a confrontation of the Great Hedgehog views on a topic – a tour of theories that assert a simple truth and seek to fit all moral, social, or political phenomena into that single truth. The outcome of the course is typically that all have some insight and all fall short. But the next semester we begin, once again, with the clash of the Great Hedgehogs.[1]

A fox approach to moral, social, and political philosophy might appear necessarily antitheoretical. Bernard Williams was a foxy philosopher (well, in our sense, at least), and he was also generally against theorizing about morality. But to appreciate the diversity of a phenomenon, and the ways that different schools and methods have contributed to our understanding of it, is not to abandon the idea that we may develop a unified and coherent account of it. A foxy theory will be complex, and it will draw on a variety of approaches. It will be sensitive to the relevance of new data, and so it must allow that its conclusions are revisable (at the same time it will resist turning the study of empirical phenomena into the new hedgehog truth of philosophy). A foxy theory need not take everything on board, singing the bland refrain that "everything is beautiful in its own way." But it will be sensitive to the fact that the complexity of the moral and social world cannot be captured by one value, one method, or one school. Its theory will not be a deduction from one core truth or insight, but a piecing together of many truths that leads to a bigger and, one hopes, true picture. It may even have a central concern or worry. A fox is not one who cannot be moved to answer a single question; it is one who sees the complexity of the answer.

The attentive reader may well have guessed that I aim to present a foxy account of social and political philosophy in this work. This work advances a theory that forms a unified picture of what I call "social morality," and the ways that it relates to the political order. We shall see, though, that unity does not imply simplicity; along the way we will have to grapple with the insights of, among many others, Hobbes, Hume, Kant, Rousseau, J. S. Mill, T. H. Green, P. F. Strawson, Kurt Baier, S. I. Benn, R. M. Hare, F. A. Hayek, David

---

[1] Of course it will be objected that we include Hume – a fox! But is he just turned into the "empiricist" hedgehog, to be contrasted with the great rationalist one?

Gauthier, Alan Gewirth, Kenneth Arrow, John Rawls, James Buchanan, and Amartya Sen. We will draw on game theory, experimental psychology, economics, sociological theories of cultural evolution, theories of emotion and reasoning, axiomatic social choice theory, constitutional political economy, Kantian moral philosophy, prescriptivism, and the concept of reason and how it relates to freedom in human affairs. I am convinced that until philosophy turns away from its obsession with clashing schools and approaches, it will be caught in an eternal circle of covering the clash of the hedgehogs but will never advance in grasping complex truths. I am aware, though, that because hedgehogosity is so firmly ingrained in philosophers' minds, unless one's work fits into a hedgehog category, it is unlikely that anyone will pay much attention to it. (How can it be taught? Where do we put it in our syllabus? Is it really philosophy?) My work is often categorized under the "libertarian" label since I argue that human freedom is terribly important, that coercive interferences infringe freedom and so must always be justified to the person being coerced. Scanning over the available hedgehog categories, the philosopher's mind stops at "libertarian." That most of my views on freedom and coercion were learned from Stanley Benn, a traditional Labor Party social democrat, never makes much of a difference to the categorization. To this worry one can only quote the great Doris Day: "Que sera, sera."

Perhaps I am a bit of a hedgehog too, for this book is motivated by one central concern: can the authority of social morality be reconciled with our status as free and equal moral persons in a world characterized by deep and pervasive yet reasonable disagreements about the standards by which to evaluate the justifiability of claims to moral authority? My worry, which I try to show should be yours too, is that claims of social morality may be simply authoritarian. One demands that others must do as he instructs because he has access to the moral truth; another admits that she has no access to any moral truth, but nevertheless employs morality as a way to express (or, to use an older language, emote) her own view of what others must do. But what if reasonable moral persons deny the purported truth or are unimpressed by the expressive act? And what if, in spite of that denial, one goes ahead and makes demands, blames, punishes, is indignant, and so on at their refusal to comply? In this case, I shall argue, one is just being a small-scale authoritarian. And authoritarians do not respect the moral equality of their fellows. A social order that is structured by a nonauthoritarian social morality is a free moral order: a moral order that is endorsed by the reasons of all, in which all have reasons of their own, based on their own ideas of what is important and valuable, to endorse the authority of social morality. Such a social and moral order is what I shall call "an order of public reason" – it is endorsed by the reasons of all the public. Only if we achieve an order of public reason can we share a cooperative social order on terms of moral freedom and equality. Only in an order of public reason is our morality truly a joint product of the reasons of all rather than a mode of oppression by which some invoke the idea of morality to rule the lives of others.

The idea that morality can itself be authoritarian strikes many as odd. We all know the first line of section 1 of *A Theory of Justice* – "Justice is the first virtue of social institutions, as truth is of systems of thought." Isn't morality a wonderful thing? And can we have too much of it? Kurt Baier is less enamored of moral discourse. Consider how he begins his great work, *The Moral Point of View*: "Moral talk is often rather repugnant. Leveling moral accusations, expressing moral indignation, passing moral judgment, allotting the blame, administering moral reproof, justifying oneself, and, above all, moralizing – who can enjoy such talk? And who can like or trust those addicted to it?" Morality does not directly speak to us; it is other people who speak to us, asserting their views of morality as demands that we act as they see fit. Baier's morality is not an "ideal morality" shorn of all blame, reproof, and guilt. It is our real practice, which makes your activities your neighbor's business; he calls on morality to tell you what to do, and he will not simply shrug his shoulders and walk away if you ignore his demands. Confronting this actual practice – in which "imperfect compliance" is a central feature – we have to ask "why do we need it?" and "when can its claims to authority be freely recognized by all?" These are the questions I seek to answer in this work.

Of course, many have sought to answer these questions, from Hobbes to Rousseau and Kant, from Gauthier to Rawls. I build on their great work, but I also believe that these famous proposals ultimately flounder on one or the other of two main obstacles. Some, such as Hobbes and Gauthier, recognize that the authority of social morality is a prerequisite for social life and so suppose that instrumentally rational individuals could reason themselves into acknowledging such authority as a means to secure their aims and goals. In Part One I show that this enticing proposal fails. Moral rules are required if we are to advance our ends, but they are not merely servants of our ends. Others, such as Kant and Rawls, hold that individuals committed to treating each other as free and equal could, under conditions of impartiality, agree on, or will, a common authoritative social morality. This gets us much nearer the truth, but it fails to take account of the pervasiveness of rational disagreement about the correct impartial morality. There is no compelling way to generate rational agreement on a specific morality in anything approaching the diverse and bounded social world we inhabit. We are left confronting the problem of the indeterminacy of rational justification. In Part Two I analyze and defend several ways in which free and equal persons can cope with this real and deep problem of moral disagreement.

As the reader has no doubt noticed, this is a long book. It is long partly because I seek to integrate empirical and formal work with normative social and moral philosophy, and so almost every reader will find much unfamiliar. Because different disciplines are drawn upon, I seek to explain things carefully as I proceed. I have also found that more compressed presentations of these ideas tend to leave readers a bit disoriented. The crux of the account, taking very seriously instrumentalist reasoning, rule-based reasoning, the moral emotions, actual psychological and social facts while providing a Kantian-inspired framework for normative evaluation that admits the importance of the social evolution of norms, runs against the current of much contemporary social and political philosophy which, as I have said, tends to package up views into fairly neat, identifiable schools. Unless things are developed systematically, readers understandably revert to their existing interpretive frames (e.g., Hobbesian, libertarian, economic-not-moral, empirical-not-normative, Darwinist, Rawslian) and so (at least in my view) tend to misinterpret the analysis. As useful as it would have been, I have not been able to devise clear abridged paths through the book for readers with different interests. I have, though, provided extensive cross references so that those picking the book up at one place can find where they should look for earlier and later relevant discussions. I have also tried to provide an index that is useful for such readers.

In formulating these ideas over the last decade I have benefited from conversations – usually in the form of lively disagreements – with a number of colleagues and students. My great and longtime friend Fred D'Agostino has consistently encouraged my line of inquiry and has offered wonderful advice on how to (and how not to) proceed. Kevin Vallier has provided invaluable insights and has discussed the manuscript with me, as has John Thrasher. My deep thanks to both. Kevin was also kind enough to organize a reading group at the University of Arizona on the manuscript (to which I was periodically invited if I bought the beer). Thanks so much to the members of that group, especially Michael Bukowski, Keith Hankins, John Thrasher, Kyle Swan and Kevin – for spurring me to think more deeply about some important issues. Jon Anomaly, Fred D'Agostino, Peter de Marneffe, and Jon Quong also read a draft of the book; my deep thanks for their comments, questions, and suggestions. I am also grateful for discussions with my terrific fellow political philosophers at Arizona, Tom Christiano and David Schmidtz; Chris Maloney has not only been the best department chair in the world, but a wonderful and supportive friend. Many of the ideas in this book are the result of great conversations with Shaun Nichols over a couple of IPAs. I have learned a tremendous amount from Shaun; this book would have been entirely different if it weren't for those beers. Many others have commented on various parts of the project. I hope they will not be offended if I simply list them; to fully note my appreciation for their specific help would make this very long book considerably longer. So, my sincere appreciation, and thanks for pressing and assisting me, to Robert Berman, Pete Boettke, Jim Bohman, Geoffrey Brennan, Bruce Brower, Shane Courtland, Rich Dagger, Derrick Darby, Christopher Eberle, David Estlund, Steffen Ganghof, Michael Gill, Bill Glod, Thomas E. Hill, Brad Hooker, John Horton, Rachana Kamtekar, Julian Lamont, Charles Larmore, David Lefkowitz, Andrew Lister,

Sharon Lloyd, Steve Macedo, Eric Mack, Kirstie McClure, Chris Maloney, Rex Martin, Fred Miller, Michael Moehler, Jim Nichols, Julinna Oxley, Ellen Paul, Jeff Paul, Guido Pincione, Tom Powers, Jon Riley, Andy Sabl, Debra Satz, Geoff Sayre-McCord, Hillel Steiner, Jim Sterba, John Tomasi, Pilvi Toppinen, Piers Turner, Peter Vallentyne, Peter Vanderschraaf, Steve Wall, Will Wilkenson, Andrew Williams, Shaun Young, Enrico Zoffoli and Matt Zwolinski.

I was fortunate enough to be able to present these ideas in a variety of conferences and colloquia, in which the comments and questions of the audience were immensely valuable. My thanks to the Arizona State University Committee on Law and Philosophy and the members of seminars on rights at the University of Arizona and the University of Kansas in the fall of 2008; the Dutch-American Symposium on Public Reason in Amsterdam in 2008; the Research Triangle Ethics Circle; the Workshop on Equal Respect for Persons held at the University of Genova in 2007; the Political Theory Project at Brown University; the Murphy Institute conference on rights; the seminar on public reason at the University of Arizona in 2007; the Manchester Centre for Political Theory; the Philosophy Departments at the University of Reading, North Carolina State University, Vanderbuilt, and the University of Georgia; the UCLA/CATO Institute conference on a common liberalism; the Social Philosophy and Policy Center; the UCLA Political Theory Workshop; the workshop in Philosophy, Politics and Economics at George Mason University; and various meetings of the American Philosophical Association and the American Political Science Association. My special thanks to all my colleagues and students at the University of Arizona, who make it the best place in the world for me to work and to learn. The penultimate draft of this book was written while I was a Distinguished Visiting Research Professor at the Murphy Institute at Tulane University; I am deeply grateful to the Institute's former director, Rick Teichgraeber III, for his friendship and support for my work over the last decade. Last, and by no means least, I would like to express my gratitude to my Cambridge editor, Beatrice Rehl, who not only encouraged this project, but who was patient and supportive through far too many delays.

For better or worse, my essays are often initial attempts to work out ideas – attempts that often have significantly evolved by the time I am ready to write it all down in a book. A number of essays have been a part of this project. I have employed parts – but seldom large parts – of these essays at various points in this book. They always have undergone significant changes. The papers that have been most important to this project are "The Place of Autonomy in Liberalism" (in *Autonomy and the Challenges to Liberalism*, edited by John Christman and Joel Anderson); "Liberal Neutrality: A Radical and Compelling Principle" (in *Perfectionism and Neutrality*, edited by George Klosko and Steven Wall); "On Justifying the Moral Rights of the Moderns" (*Social Philosophy and Policy*); "Recognized Rights as Devices of Public Reason" (*Philosophical Perspectives: Ethics*); "The Demands of Impartiality and the Evolution of Morality" (in *Partiality and Impartiality*, edited by Brian Feltham and John Cottingham); "Reasonable Utility Functions and Playing the Cooperative Way" (*Critical Review of International Social and Political Philosophy*); "Coercion, Ownership, and the Redistributive State," (*Social Philosophy and Policy*); and "On Two Critics of Justificatory Liberalism" (*Politics, Philosophy and Economics*).

The epigraphs in this book from F. A. Hayek, *The Constitution of Liberty* and *Rules and Order*, are used with the permission of the Estate of F. A. Hayek. Epigraphs from Kurt Baier's *The Rational and the Moral Order* are used with permission of Open Court Publishing Company, a division of Carus Publishing Company, Chicago, IL, and are reproduced from *The Rational and the Moral Order: The Social Roots of Reason and Morality* by Kurt Baier copyright © 1995 by Open Court Publishing. Epigraphs from P. F. Strawson, "Freedom and Resentment" are used with the permission of the British Academy, and are reproduced from *The Proceedings of the British Academy*, vol. 48, 1959. Epigraphs from P. F. Strawson, "Social Morality and Individual Ideal" are used with the permission of Cambridge University Press, and are reproduced from *Philosophy*, vol. 36, 1961. The epigraph from Benjamin Constant, "The Liberty of the Ancients Compared with that of the Moderns" is used with permission of Cambridge University Press and is reproduced from the *Political Writings of Benjamin Constant*, edited and translated by Biancamria Fontana, Cambridge University Press, 1988.

I

The Fundamental Problem

> The problem is to find a form of association which will defend and protect with the whole common force the person and goods of each associate, and in which each, while uniting himself with all, may still obey himself alone, and remain as free as before. This is the fundamental problem of which the Social Contract provides the solution.
>
> Rousseau, *The Social Contract*

In this chapter I provide an overview of the main ideas and problems that I shall address in this work and sketch some approaches to their solutions. Section 1 introduces the idea of a "social morality." Social morality, I argue in Part One, constitutes the basic framework for a cooperative and mutually beneficial social life. Social morality provides rules that we are required to act upon and that provide the basis for authoritative demands of one person addressed to another. Section 2 analyzes this authority relation, and its apparent tension with understanding others as free and equal moral persons. How can free and equal moral persons claim authority to prescribe to other free and equal moral persons? A general solution to this problem, advanced by Rousseau and Kant, is that authority and freedom can be reconciled if each freely endorses the authority of morality. As I argue, a publicly justified morality – one that the reason of each endorses – allows each to remain free while subject to moral authority. Although Rousseau and Kant, and later Rawls, point the way to a solution to the

1

fundamental problem of a free social order, their solutions flounder on the core idea of reasonable pluralism. Individuals with very different values, conceptions of the good life, and other normative commitments are unlikely to have good reasons to endorse the same moral rules; the application of the ideal of public justification under these conditions is indeterminate. How to cope with this indeterminacy is one of the main concerns of Part Two.

1 Social Morality

1.1 A MORAL ORDER AMONG FREE AND EQUAL PERSONS

My aim in this work is to provide a general account of social morality that reconciles freedom and the demands of public order in a society in which individuals, exercising their reason about the best thing to do, deeply disagree. Showing how this is possible, I shall argue, is not just fundamental for our understanding of a free political order, but it is also the basic task for seeing how a moral order among free and equal persons is possible. The question that has occupied liberal political theory – whether free and equal persons can all endorse a common political order even though their private judgments about the good and justice are so often opposed – is the fundamental problem of a free moral order. A recurring theme throughout this work is the continuity of the problems of political philosophy and what I shall call "social morality." This is by no means to say that the solutions to this fundamental problem are the same in these two spheres. The moral and political orders provide, as we shall see, different but complementary solutions to this fundamental problem.

1.2 SOCIAL MORALITY AS THE FRAMEWORK OF SOCIAL LIFE

By "social morality" I mean the set of social-moral rules that require or prohibit action, and so ground moral imperatives that we direct to each other to engage in, or refrain from, certain lines of conduct. Much of what we call "ethics" – including visions of the good life and conceptions of virtue and vice – lies outside social morality so understood. Social morality and its limits are the focus of Mill's great *On Liberty*: the subject of "Civil" or "Social Liberty" involves the nature and limits of the moral authority of society over individuals to insist that they refrain from speaking, acting, and living as they wish.[1] It is important to stress that social morality is but one aspect of morality, or the realm of the ethical.[2] P. F. Strawson certainly understood the plurality of our moral practices. In his important (though underappreciated) paper, "Social Morality and Individual Ideal," he distinguished the broad "region of the ethical" – which includes visions of what makes life worth living and what constitutes a noble or virtuous life – from a system of moral rules that structures social interaction. As Strawson saw it, individuals are devoted to a vast array of individual ideals: "self-obliterating devotion to duty or to service to others; of personal honour and magnanimity; of asceticism, contemplation, retreat; of action, dominance, and power; of the cultivation of 'an exquisite sense of the luxurious'; of simple human solidarity and cooperative endeavour; of a refined complexity of social existence."[3] Pursuit and achievement of these ideals, Strawson argued, presupposes an organized social life, and for such a life there must be a system of shared expectations about what must and must not be done in our interactions with each other. What philosophers such as Strawson and Kurt Baier called "social morality" has its roots in this requirement of social life.[4] As Strawson and Baier understood it, the rules of social morality structure social interaction in ways that are beneficial to all and make social existence possible; social morality lays down requirements (including prohibitions) that are to direct people's social interactions. Of course Strawson and Baier stressed that not all such social rules constitute moral rules: to constitute bona fide moral requirements, social rules must meet further conditions. Most important, they must in some way be verified from the requisite moral point of view.

---

[1] See John Stuart Mill, *On Liberty*, p. 217 (chap. 1, ¶1).
[2] This is an important point; I address it in some detail in Appendix A.
[3] P. F. Strawson, "Social Morality and Individual Ideal," p. 1.
[4] Kurt Baier, *The Moral Point of View: A Rational Basis for Ethics*, chap. 10, and his *The Rational and the Moral Order*, p. 157, chap. 6.

This Baier–Strawson analysis of social morality has been shared by many in the history of moral philosophy. Hobbes certainly understood the study of laws of nature as the "true Moral Philosophy"; they are rules that, if followed, promote "peaceable, sociable, and comfortable living."[5] Despite his many disagreements with Hobbes, Hume too saw the rules of justice as necessary to secure the advantage of social life and social cooperation.[6] Sometimes these views are understood as insisting that moral rules are nothing but conventional rules, conformity to which promotes cooperative social relations, but no such radical constitutive claim is required. Crucial to this tradition is the more modest claim that a necessary function of one type of moral practice (i.e., social morality) is that it serves these social purposes. As we shall see, this is consistent with a number of views about the ultimate character of such rules, for example, whether they are discovered or constructed. (Recall that Hobbes allows that the laws of nature may be commands of God.)[7] In recent moral philosophy, I believe, focus on this crucial notion of social morality has been overshadowed by, on the one hand, more theoretical questions, such as the ultimate sources of normativity and the ontological status of moral properties and, on the other, more applied questions, such as the justice of various social institutions.[8] Nevertheless, the social function of morality is in the background; certainly one of the things morality must do is allow us to live together in cooperative, mutually beneficial, social relations.

Some traditions of moral theorizing, especially those influenced by Hobbes and Hume, have understood that the first step in understanding a free social morality is to understand the necessity of social morality for social existence. Hobbesians such as David Gauthier thus start out with the insight that morality has a role to perform, and there is no point analyzing what "morality requires of us" or "what we owe each other" if we do not grasp why a system

---

[5] Hobbes, *Leviathan*, p. 100 (chap. 15, ¶40).

[6] Hume, *A Treatise of Human Nature*, Book III, Part II, §§1–2.

[7] Hobbes, *Leviathan*, p. 100 (chap. 15, ¶41).

[8] Thus Baier's great 1995 book, *The Rational and the Moral Order: The Social Roots of Reason and Morality*, has been largely ignored.

– and what sort of system – of requirements and "owings" is necessary to human social life. In a very general way, we might call this a naturalistic understanding of social morality; although its demands are verified by reason, they are rooted in the conditions for human social life and cooperation, and so we cannot understand the requirements of morality without understanding the conditions of human social life and the capacities of its participants – and their limitations. I believe this is a fundamental insight that those in the broadly "Kantian" tradition have often overlooked, or at least have not sufficiently appreciated. Often contemporary moral theory seems to suppose that there is some well-defined set of reasons called "morality," which instruct us what to do, and it is never precisely clear why – indeed, whether – we need it. Unless we can explain why humans need social morality, we might wonder whether we would be better off without it. In our post-Nietzschean world it will not do to start from the assumption that social morality merits our allegiance. Maybe it just is, as Nietzsche would have it, a ploy of the priestly class (which is now headed by moral philosophers) to control hoi polloi. "Even apart from the value of such claims as 'there is a categorical imperative in us,' one can always ask: what does it tell us about a man who makes it?"[9] Just as political philosophers are rightly skeptical of political authority and insist that it be justified, so too should moral philosophers critically examine the authority of social morality. As Baier recognized, social morality sometimes requires people to sacrifice what they deeply care about, and, indeed, often seeks to frighten them into complying with its demands. As participants in social morality we blame others if they fail to do what is required; indeed we think violators ought to punish themselves by feeling guilt.[10] One better have good reasons for inflicting all of this on one's fellows and oneself. And, I will argue, one does: it is fundamental to large-scale human cooperation and social life.

What I shall call the "Baier–Strawson View" of social morality focuses on the relation between, on the one hand, personal values, ideals, or interests and, on the other, social-moral rules that

---

[9] Friedrich Nietzsche, *Beyond Good and Evil*, p. 99 (§187).
[10] Baier, *The Moral Point of View*, pp. 1ff.

structure the interaction of individuals whose lives are planned around the pursuit of these ideals or interests. The relation is complex; social-moral rules both provide the conditions for the successful pursuit of these ideals and simultaneously constrain our choices about how to pursue them. Once we acknowledge that social morality has a job to perform, the question that immediately arises is whether it is no more than an instrument – no more than a tool to achieve our goals and ends. Those who have most stressed the functions of social morality such as Gauthier have seen it as, in the end, simply a construct of our instrumental rationality. And if so, it has seemed to many that its rules are not categorical imperatives but instructions about how each of us is to best achieve her goals. In the history of moral and social philosophy this has been a deeply attractive idea: if social morality secures our ends, our reasons to obey it must be contingent on it doing so. One of the main aims of Part One is to show that this enticing view is erroneous. Morality has a function, but our reasons to obey it are, to a significant degree, autonomous of its ability to promote our ends and goals. To understand the relation of human ends, goals, and values to the rules of the moral order is one of the most perplexing questions of moral and social philosophy. I hope to make some progress on it in Part One.

1.3 THE AUTHORITY OF SOCIAL MORALITY

(a) Social Morality as Imperatival

Social morality is imperatival: it is the basis for issuing *demands* on others that they *must* perform certain actions. Like the law (again, note the continuity between political and moral philosophy), it instructs us how to act regardless of our personal aims and desires. Charles Larmore has argued that this is a distinctively modern, juristic, view of ethics. Following Sidgwick, Larmore contrasts this modern conception of ethics, founded on the notion of the right, to the view of the ancients, according to which the good is the foundation of ethics:

If the notion of right is replaced by that of good at the foundations of ethics . . . then the moral ideal will no longer be imperative, but rather attractive.

His [i.e., Sidgwick's] point was that ethical value may be defined either as what is binding or obligatory upon an agent, whatever may be his wants or desires, or as what an agent would in fact want if he were sufficiently informed about what he desires. In the first view, the notion of right is fundamental, in the second the notion of good.[11]

As Sidgwick saw it, "[a]ccording to the Aristotelian view – which is that of Greek philosophy generally, and has been widely taken in later times – the primary subject of ethical investigation is all that is included under the notion of what is good for man or desirable for man; all that is reasonably chosen or sought by him, not as a means to some ulterior end, but for itself."[12] Ancient ethics was teleological, a science of ends; it concerned what a person properly desires or what a proper, virtuous, person desires, or finds attractive. In contrast, modern ethics concerns what we must do – what we are required to do even if we are not attracted by it.[13] As Mill stressed, morality concerns what can be demanded of one:

This seems the real turning point of the distinction between morality and simple expediency. It is part of the notion of Duty in every one of its forms, that a person may rightfully be compelled to fulfill it. Duty is a thing which may be *exacted* from a person, as one exacts a debt. Unless we think it may be exacted from him, we do not call it a duty. . . . There are other things, on the contrary, which we wish people to do, which we like or admire them for doing, perhaps dislike or despise them for not doing, but yet admit that they are not bound to do; it is not a case of moral obligation.[14]

Utilitarianism too is a science of duties. Moralities justifying imperatival notions of right and wrong are part and parcel of the modern condition, in which we constantly confront others whom

---

[11] Charles Larmore, *The Morals of Modernity*, p. 20. See Henry Sidgwick, *The Methods of Ethics*, 7th edition, pp. 105–6; Sidgwick, *Outlines of the History of Ethics for English Readers*, pp. 1–10.

[12] Sidgwick, *Outlines of the History of Ethics*, p. 2.

[13] Cf. H.A. Prichard's "Does Moral Philosophy Rest on a Mistake?" p. 13.

[14] J. S. Mill, *Utilitarianism*, p. 246 (chap. V, ¶14). Rashdall and Sidgwick realized that this imperatival conception of morality is characteristic of consequentialist as well as Kantian views. See Hastings Rashdall, *The Theory of Good and Evil*, vol. I, pp. 102ff.

we do not know and who typically entertain notions of what is good and desirable that differ markedly from our own. Our moral relations with such strangers must be centered on what actions and forbearances we owe each other and, as Mill says, what we can *exact* from each other. Thus the notions of right, wrong, duty, and obligation become the core of social morality. Seen against this background, neo-Aristotelian virtue ethics is a rejection of modernity rather than a solution to its problems.

(b) The Authority Relation in Social Morality

At the heart of social morality is a fundamental claim to authority over others. This is nicely brought out in R. M. Hare's work (which, alas, like so much good philosophy has fallen victim to current fashions). Hare's approach is enlightening because it focuses not on the general imperatival nature of social morality but on imperatival utterances, and more generally, imperatival relations between individuals. For Hare, the core of moral utterances is the illocutionary act of telling another what to do: that is, issuing an imperative.[15] Morality is, of course, much more than telling others what to do; it gives us *standing* to tell them what to do. I might "issue" an imperative to you to "Drink better wine!" but even if I have good reason to insist that you should drink better wine, you may dismiss my imperative by telling me that your wine drinking habits are none of my business — I have no standing to instruct you. As Margaret Gilbert observes:

To say that someone has the standing to do something means simply that he is in a position to do it. If someone lacks standing to do it, the question whether he is justified in doing it does not arise. For he cannot do it. One who lacks the standing to make a certain demand or issue a rebuke can, of course, utter a purported rebuke or make a purported demand. He can speak in a rebuking or demanding tone. His target, meanwhile, may have little interest in this if it is possible to question his standing to rebuke or

[15] R. M. Hare, *Sorting Out Ethics*, p. 16. Hare is drawing here on J. L. Austin's distinction between the illocutionary and perlocutionary functions of speech acts. As Hare puts it, "the first being what we are doing *in* saying something" while the latter is "what we are doing *by* saying something" (*Sorting Out Ethics*, p. 13). Perlocutionary aspects of speech acts are related to their pragmatic force.

demand. His target may well respond in some such words as these: "It's none of your business, so . . . forget it!'[16]

Morality makes my action your business, and so gives *you* standing to *tell me* what *I* must do (§11.2). I cannot reply to your moral imperative "Keep your hands to yourself!" by saying it is none of your business where I put my hands. Your moral position is that you have standing to issue demands to which I must conform. This constitutes a claim to authority to direct my actions. You believe that morality prohibits ϕ and so I must not ϕ, even if I would rather like to, and indeed even if I do not now see anything especially wrong with it. Stephen Darwall has recently stressed the way in which such interpersonal morality involves "authority relations that an addresser takes to hold between him and his addressee."[17] When you make this moral claim on me, Darwall points out, you are not making a request that I refrain from ϕ, or calling attention to your view of morality according to which ϕ is immoral: you are issuing an imperative that I must not ϕ.[18]

There is an obvious rejoinder. You may insist that you are not demanding that I submit to *your* authority but only to the *authority of morality*. Morality, you might say, provides you *standing* to make my actions your business, but this only involves the authority of morality, not your authority over me. Both Hobbes and Kant recognized the inadequacy of this response – at least in their political philosophy. Despite the common interpretation of Hobbes as concerned only with the clash of self-interest, his analyses of the roots of disagreement and conflict are much more subtle and wide ranging. *Leviathan* focuses on problems of rationality and disagreement that arise when individuals rely on their private judgment of what reason requires. The exercise of our rationality is fallible; "no one man's reason, nor the reason of any one number of

---

[16] Margaret Gilbert. *Theory of Political Obligation*, p. 147. See also pp. 103ff, 147ff, 245ff. Gilbert stresses the close relations between the concepts of standing, authority, command, and obligation (p. 46).

[17] Stephen Darwall, *The Second-Person Standpoint: Morality, Respect and Accountability*, p. 4.

[18] Ibid., pp. 10–11, 76.

men, makes the certainty."[19] Rational people aim at what Hobbes calls "right reason" – true rationality, which reveals the truth. However, because everyone's exercise of rationality is fallible, we often disagree about what is right reason; the private use of reason leads to disagreement and, thought Hobbes, conflict. Although in such controversies each person claims that the use of his own private reason is "right reason," these claims only exacerbate the conflict: "when men that think themselves wiser than all others clamour and demand right reason for judge, yet seek no more but that things should be determined by no other men's reason but their own, it is . . . intolerable in the society of men." Indeed, Hobbes insists that those who claim that their reason is correct reason betray "their want of right reason by the claim they lay to it."[20] Someone who insists that *his* reason is right reason and so *his* reason should determine the resolution of disputes is not only a danger to society, but because he sees "every passion" of his as an expression of "right reason," he is *irrational*; he demonstrates the lack of right reason by virtue of the claim he lays to it. And Hobbes applies this to the interpretation of the basic rules of social morality:

All laws, written and unwritten, have need of interpretation. The unwritten law of nature, though it be easy to such as without partiality and passion make use of their natural reason, and therefore leaves the violators thereof without excuse; yet considering there be very few, perhaps none, that in some cases are not blinded by self-love, or some other passion, it is now become of all laws the most obscure, and has consequently the greatest need of able interpreters.[21]

When we employ our "private reason" there is, says Hobbes, great dispute about the laws – both the laws of nature and civil laws.[22] Kant agrees; the insecurity of the state of nature arises from

---

[19] Hobbes, *Leviathan*, p. 23 (chap. 5, ¶3).

[20] Ibid., p. 23 (chap. 5, ¶3). See further David Gauthier, "Public Reason," p. 27. This same point was made earlier, and in more detail, by R. E. Ewin, *Virtues and Rights*, chap. 2.

[21] Hobbes, *Leviathan*, p. 180 (chap. 26, ¶20).

[22] Ibid., p. 98 (chap. 15, ¶30), emphasis in original.

disagreement about what the good and justice require: "individuals, nations, and states can never be certain that they are secure
against violence from one another, because each will have his own
right to do what seems good and just to him, entirely independent
of the opinion of others."[23]

   When you assert your demand as authoritative – something that
overrules my view of the matter – our private reason leads us to
disagree on what morality requires. Morality does not fax its
demands down from above; you are asserting your interpretation
of the demands of morality as that which should be followed by me
over my own interpretation. In your eyes, your demand that I must
ϕ is not undermined simply because I reply that on my view of
morality, I have no duty to ϕ. My reply may lead you to pause and
reconsider, but if on reflection you determine that you were correct
on this matter, you will go ahead and press your demand. But that
means that, in the end, you are asserting that my action must conform to your judgment even though you cannot get *me* to accept
that it should – you are overriding what I see as the thing to do and
claiming that your private judgment is authoritative over me. You
are staking a real claim to authority over me: your judgment on this
matter is to preempt mine.

   To begin to understand moral authority we must distinguish
two senses of authority. If Alf has *moral authority qua moral power*
over Betty, Alf possesses moral Hohfeldian powers such that he can
alter her moral rights, claims, duties, and liabilities.[24] This is the
"common view" that an authority can *impose* (in the sense of create)
a moral duty.[25] I shall argue later (§18) that moral rights involve
such moral authority. At this point, however, I am calling attention
to *moral authority as a claim to deference in judgment*. To issue a moral
imperative based on a moral rule or principle is to hold that one's
judgment of the rule's justifiability and its proper interpretation
must be deferred to by the other. To see the importance of this

---

[23] Kant, *Metaphysical Elements of Justice*, p. 116 [Akademie, 312].

[24] See Wesley Hohfeld, *Fundamental Legal Conceptions as Applied in Judicial Reasoning*.
   For an excellent recent analysis in the Hohfeldian tradition see Leif Wenar, "The
   Nature of Rights." I am using "power" here in Hohfeld's technical sense, as a
   moral status that allows one to alter the moral status of others.

[25] For a discussion, see Joseph Raz, *The Morality of Freedom*, pp. 28ff.

claim, suppose it was not made. That is, assume one appeals to a moral rule L and makes a demand that another ϕs, but when the other informs you that, using her own judgment, she has concluded that L does not call for ϕ, this itself leads you to renounce any claim that she should conform to your directive. "Well," you say, "if she doesn't agree, who am I to tell her what to do?" If one takes this attitude, one no longer believes that morality gives one standing to demand actions of another. One can advise, or request, but not demand. Perhaps one might take a more subtle tack and detach making a demand on another from thinking she must pay any attention to your demand. "I can still demand that she ϕ," one might say, "but I don't claim that she should defer to my view of what I think she should do, so I don't think it is untoward of her to ignore me." But it *is* unacceptable to ignore moral demands. Moral demands are not simply prescriptions that you decide to give others that they are free to ignore; they are prescriptions that are made on the basis of a claim to have standing to direct the actions of others, and so cannot be blamelessly ignored.

One might think that all this simply shows that issuing moral imperatives is not a nice way to act, since you are taking on the job of commanding others. There is a temptation to retreat into what might be called a "purely first-personal" view of ethics.[26] On this view, Betty's moral judgments are only about how she evaluates others, and what *she* decides *she* must do. She may judge them as "having done wrong," she may express disapproval, she may decide to intervene, but the aim of her deliberations is to determine her own judgments, attitudes, and actions. In effect, Betty only makes private judgments that purport to have no public standing; they are in no way authoritative for others. Much of Part One of this book is devoted to showing the inadequacy of this first-personal view of morality. Chapters II and III demonstrate the social functions of morality and how it can perform crucial tasks only if it has authoritative public standing, and if each of us can appeal to its public standing in our disputes with others. Chapter IV shows that the first-personal view of one's moral judgments

---

[26] See further section 12.4 in this volume.

undermines a great deal of our current understanding of our moral practices and how we see our moral relations with others.

Still, the advocate of the first-personal account of moral judgment may insist that the imperatival view of social morality simply cannot be correct. Indeed, sometimes when I have remarked on the value of Hare's prescriptivism, listeners have thought this was pretty much a sufficient self-refutation. (If one wants to be a non-cognitivist one should at least be up-to-date and be an expressivist!) Surely, they say, Hare's prescriptivism was simply an early and not very convincing form of non-cognitivism. If, however, one is a realist, one thinks that moral judgments report truths about what should be done and so one rejects non-cognitivism and, so, prescriptivism. Of course moral truths are, like all truths, truths everyone should endorse, but one's own deliberative activity is always first-personal in the sense that one is deciding for oneself what the truth about moral action is.

This simply misconstrues Hare's ethical theory. Hare is wary of the "realist/anti-realist" and "cognitivist/non-cognitivist distinctions."[27] He rightly points out that it is not clear how they relate; the former is an ontological dispute, the latter an epistemological one.[28] As did the objector in the previous paragraph, going back and forth between these claims manifests confusion. To a large extent Hare seeks to avoid these ways of framing the issues in moral theory rather than seeking to take sides on them. His preferred terms are "descriptivist/non-descriptivist," which he takes to identify two positions about the primary point of moral judgments: are they primarily intended as descriptions of certain properties of actions, or prescriptions about how to act? Hare defends non-descriptivism.[29] But his ultimate position is complex. Although he thinks that the primary point of moral statements is to prescribe, not describe, action, he also believes that (*i*) moral judgments have significant descriptive components and (*ii*) they not only can be justified/unjustified but, true/false. In the end Hare thinks that "moral statements are a hybrid, sharing characteristics of both pure

---

[27] Hare, *Sorting Out Ethics*, pp. 47ff.
[28] Hare, *Essays in Ethical Theory*, chap. 6.
[29] Hare's views on these matters is the subject of *Sorting Out Ethics*, Part II.

descriptions and pure prescriptions."[30] In any event, I am not defending Hare's metaethics in this book, although I do follow him in putting aside ontological issues about the nature of morality. Hare was importantly right that (some) ethical relations are centered on issuing prescriptions to our fellows, and so he was able to appreciate fundamental aspects of social morality that many have overlooked. As Hare pointed out, this does not mean that morality is simply prescriptive, that moral judgments are not truth-apt, and so on.

2 Moral Authority among Free and Equal Persons

2.1 MORAL FREEDOM AND EQUALITY: SOME PRELIMINARY COMMENTS

For Locke, "the natural liberty of man is to be free from any superior power on earth, and not to be under the will or legislative authority of man, but to have only the law of Nature for his rule."[31] To be morally free is to have *only* the law of nature as one's rule. This implies, though, that one is not also ruled by the judgment of others as to what the law of nature is. As a morally free person one employs one's reason to understand the requirements of the law of nature, and one submits to rule by that law, which is the rule of reason. Lockean moral freedom is not freedom from morality, but freedom to directly employ one's reason to determine what morality requires. If one is, in addition, under the authority of another, it is her reasoning about the law of nature to which one is subject. The crux of the social contract is that, because we are all naturally free to interpret the moral law, this submission of one to the reason of another always requires special justification.

The idea of moral freedom can be divorced from natural law theory and, indeed, any specific ethical theory. A Kantian-inspired conception of social morality such as I develop here seeks to respect

---

[30] Hare, *Essays in Ethical Theory*, p. 95.
[31] Locke, *Second Treatise of Government*, §21.

the status of all as free and equal moral persons, but we need not also endorse the details of Kant's own conception of the nature of morality.[32] To respect another as a free moral person is to acknowledge that her reason is the judge of the demands morality makes on her. In Locke's terms, she understands herself as ruled only by morality, not the reasoning of others about what that morality is.

The idea of moral freedom is closely related to Kant's idea of moral autonomy; we must, though, distinguish two interpretations of that idea. Susan Wolf distinguishes what she calls a "Reason View" from an "Autonomy View" of moral responsibility. Whereas an Autonomy View locates moral freedom and responsibility in one's option to do or not do one's moral duty, for the Reason View "[w]hat matters is rather the availability of one very particular option, namely the option to act in accordance with Reason."[33] The idea of moral freedom as it is employed here is closely related to the Reason View: a free moral person is one who acts according to her own reasoning about the demands of morality (and, as we shall see, it is her access to these reasons that is crucial for judgments of moral responsibility, §12.3). Whether or not the "Autonomy" or "Reason" view is the preferred interpretation of Kantian autonomy is not my concern.[34] At present the point to be stressed is that "moral freedom" as it is understood in this book does not imply that one is free to ignore the demands of morality, or that there is no morality prior to public justification. *The claim to freedom is not made in relation to the demands of morality but the interpretation of those demands by others.* And that is why the idea of moral freedom is so intimately bound to moral equality; moral persons are all equally authoritative interpreters of the demands that morality places on one. This, of course, is not to say that they are all equally correct, or that one person's judgment is as good as the next. The claim is about the lack of authority of another's judgment over one's view of the demands of morality. As Rawls says, qua free persons who

---

[32] John Rawls, "Kantian Constructivism in Moral Theory," p. 309.
[33] Susan Wolf, *Freedom Within Reason*, p. 68.
[34] I suspect that both are involved in Kant's doctrine. See my essay "The Place of Autonomy in Liberalism."

recognize their fundamental equality we claim no moral authority over each other.[35]

A moral order of free persons rejects appeal to the natural authority of some people's private judgments over those of others. A social morality that allows the (self-appointed?) "enlightened" to make moral demands on others that as free and equal moral persons those others cannot see reason to acknowledge is *authoritarian*. Just as authoritarians in politics hold that they should rule over others who are too unenlightened or corrupt to see the wisdom of their laws, so too do these "enlightened" moralists hold up their "right reasoning" about morality as the standard that warrants their demands about how others should live, even when those others, exercising their rational moral autonomy, cannot endorse the imperatives to which they are subject. Jeffrey Reiman puts the worry in a dramatic way: the assertion that one "has a higher authority" over how another should act raises the specter of "subjugation" – that "the very project of trying to get our fellows to act morally" may be "just pushing people around."[36] This insight – that social morality may oppress in ways similar to political regimes – was central to Mill's *Liberty*:

Like other tyrannies, the tyranny of the majority was at first, and is still vulgarly, held in dread, chiefly as operating through the acts of the public authorities. But reflecting persons perceived that when society is itself the tyrant – society collectively, over the separate individuals who compose it – its means of tyrannizing are not restricted to the acts which it may do by the hands of its political functionaries. Society can and does execute its own mandates: and if it issues wrong mandates instead of right, or any mandates at all in things with which it ought not to meddle, it practises a social tyranny more formidable than many kinds of political oppression, since, though not usually upheld by such extreme penalties, it leaves fewer means of escape, penetrating much more deeply into the details of life, and enslaving the soul itself.[37]

[35] John Rawls, "Justice as Fairness," p. 55.
[36] Jeffrey Reiman, *Justice and Modern Moral Philosophy*, p. 1.
[37] Mill, *On Liberty*, pp. 219–20 (chap. 1, ¶5).

As I understand it, to conceive of another as a free and equal moral person is simply to acknowledge a fundamental constraint on the justification of claims to moral authority over her.[38] Because we recognize other moral persons as free and equal, having authority – perhaps we should say "moral sovereignty" – to interpret their own moral obligations for themselves, our claims to have standing to command that they comply with our view of the demands of morality appears to manifest disrespect for them as equal interpreters of morality. Dissolving the suspicion that moral authority is nothing more than a disguise for "social control" whereby some order others about on the basis of unjustified claims to superiority is a core task of Part Two of this book.

Now it is important at the outset to distinguish the idea of freedom and equality presented here from (what I shall call) T. M. Scanlon's widely shared "Expansive View" of freedom and equality: that is, that the "recognition" of others as free and equal requires that we only act toward others according to principles that they could not reasonably reject. "The contractualist ideal of acting in accord with principles that others . . . could not reasonably reject is meant to characterize the relation with others the value and appeal of which underlies our reasons to do what morality requires. . . . This relation . . . might be called a relation of mutual recognition."[39] Thus interpreted, recognizing others as free and equal immediately implies a formula for what actions are morally permissible; the very ideas of freedom and equality imply a sort of categorical imperative regulating interpersonal action to treat others only in ways they cannot rationally reject. Darwall also endorses this Expansive View, holding that the very idea of human dignity implies that we possess authority to "demand certain treatment": "The fundamental idea of the dignity of persons . . . is mutual accountability as equals. And this commits us to regulating our conduct by principles that are acceptable, or not reasonably

---

[38] My thoughts on these matters owe a great deal to discussions with Eric Mack and Robert Berman.

[39] T. M. Scanlon, *What We Owe Each Other*, p. 162. Cf. Charles Larmore, *The Autonomy of Morality*, p. 147.

rejectable, to each as free and rational agents."[40] The Expansive
View maintains that the recognition of others as free and equal implies a commitment to a morality whereby we treat others only in
ways they reasonably can be expected to endorse, or not reject. On
this view both the commitment to morality as well as the general
structure of that morality follow from the core commitment to seeing others as free and equal moral persons. The canonical form of
argument on the Expansive View is that a moral requirement to ϕ is
demanded by our respect for the freedom and equality of others,
for ϕ follows from principle P that is required by interpersonal
relations in which we recognize each as free and equal, and the test
for this is, say, universalization or reasonable rejectability.

What is striking about the Expansive View is how an analysis
that begins with a denial of any "default" moral authority of one
person over another so seamlessly yields a comprehensive claim to
moral authority over others, so that Alf now has moral authority
over all others to demand that any action that constitutes a "treatment" of him is one that must conform to a principle that he
reasonably endorses (or does not reasonably reject) or else they do
wrong. This is indeed a wide-ranging authority: Alf now has a
moral standing to demand action of which he reasonably approves
(or that he does not reject) whenever a person engages in a
"treatment" of him. We might well wonder how the lack of moral
authority has been transformed into such a comprehensive authority. For Darwall the crucial link between the necessity of justifying
moral authority to possessing an authority over others is human
dignity.[41] Respect for the dignity of others seems the fount of
morality. Perhaps there is some way to seamlessly make the transition from showing how problematic moral authority is among free
and equal persons to the justification of a comprehensive authority
to demand certain treatment from others. I am skeptical, and I
suspect that many who are not already committed to some sort of
Kantian project will think that too much of morality ends up being
packed into the seemingly innocuous ideas of "freedom and equality." In any event, I take a different route here. Why we should

[40] Darwall, *The Second-Person Standpoint*, pp. 13, 300.
[41] Ibid., pp. 244ff.

reject the claim of others to have a natural moral authority over us is one issue; under what conditions we should all endorse moral authority, I will argue, leads us to a very different set of issues concerning the necessity of moral rules for human cooperation and social life and under what conditions they might be endorsed by all. I thus shall argue for only a Restricted View of moral freedom and equality. This Restricted View has both a positive and a negative dimension. The positive element is an account of what constitutes moral personhood. Although Kantian-inspired accounts of moral personhood are often deeply moralized – for example, being based on a robust conception of human dignity – the Restricted View holds that moral personhood consists in the capacity to care for moral rules in such a way that one recognizes a compelling reason to abide by the rule even when such conformity does not promote one's wants, ends, or goals (§12). The negative dimension is constituted by the idea that to respect others as free and equal moral persons is to refrain from claiming moral authority over them to demand that they do what they do not themselves have reason to endorse. The Restricted View says nothing whatsoever about what treatments or actions morality allows us to demand of others but places a fundamental constraint on claims to moral authority. It thus is a principle that regulates our moral practices, not directly our actions or "treatments."

The contrast is better brought out, perhaps, by noting that on the Restricted View it would be (in principle, and leaving out any further argument) possible to respect each as free and equal by abandoning all moral claims on them and acting simply on one's own first-person view of morality. Suppose Alf comes to the (as we will see, erroneous) conclusion that respecting others as free and equal moral persons is inconsistent with ever making moral demands on them, so he entirely abjures advancing such demands. He has his own first-person view of morality – suppose this is a strongly perfectionist view – and he seeks to be true to it, but he never issues moral prescriptions to others. Sometimes he interferes with others and tries to arrange things so that these others end up (as he sees it) more perfect people, even if they hold well-grounded anti-perfectionist views. On the Expansive View he disrespects the moral freedom and equality of others; on the Restrictive View he does not. Because freedom and equality is about claims to moral authority, and he makes no such claims, he does not run afoul of respecting this feature of moral persons. He makes other errors, to be sure, but there is no reason to think that all of morality reduces to one supreme moral principle, or all moral mistakes end up being the same mistake.

Now it may seem that this cannot be right: it would seem to follow on this view that one could treat another as "free and equal" while acting horribly to her, say killing her, so long as one did not make any moral claims on her.[42] Now once we have completed the account of a justified social morality we will see why, indeed, a moral person who treats another immorally does indeed fail to treat her with respect. But that, as it were, is what we want an account of morality to show us: we want to see why this attack on the agency of others is wrong, and why those who see others as free and equal moral persons typically have overriding reasons not to engage in such action. But the aim is not to build all of that into the very meaning of what it means to treat another as free and equal – as if all of morality was really a sort of conceptual analysis of the idea of "treating another as a free and equal moral person." The aim is to commence with minimal ideas of moral personhood, freedom, and equality that do not at the outset give us all we seek at the end of the day. I hope at the end of the day to show that the firmest substantive intuitions of the Expansive View can be publicly justified as part of the conclusions of an account that commences with the Restricted View. But if some of the substantive intuitions of a friend of the Expansive View cannot be so justified, we have reason to think that these are overly controversial: they are substantive moral demands that all devoted to public justification could not endorse. If some of the substantive intuitions underlying the Expansive View cannot be justified commencing with the Restricted View, the Expansive View fails to justify those substantive claims of moral authority to some who are devoted to the idea that all exercises of moral authority must be justified.

---

[42] I am grateful to Jon Quong for pressing this point on me.

2.2 WHY SHOULD WE SUPPOSE THAT MORAL PERSONS ARE FREE AND EQUAL?

Still, some advocates of the Expansive View may insist that we must begin with their more full-blooded conception of what it means to treat others as free and equal, because that is what human dignity is all about. But we must press: why must we all accept, as the very supposition of the moral enterprise, this strong conception of what is involved in the very idea of a morality? To be sure, to those in the Kantian tradition this will appear to be an uncontroversial starting point, but, alas, the Kantian tradition has itself proven to be a controversial starting point. In many ways the Kantian approach has become sectarian: some see it as obvious, and others see all this as obscure and implausible. Some may think that that it is good or even obligatory, other things equal, to treat others as free and equal, but one's own first-person moral convictions may sometimes justify one in not treating them as equals but as subject to one's superior wisdom (that is, authoritarianism sometimes may be justified).[43] Others may think that it is simply nonsense to suppose that all moral persons are one's equals and are morally free: most are simply patients to be treated, not persons to be respected. And yet others will insist that all this talk of respecting persons is just so much Kantian nonsense and distracts us from the important problem of constructing a rational morality that promotes the interests of all.[44]

The Restricted View of the freedom and equality of others is, I will argue in Chapter IV, internal to our practice of social morality. Once we understand the tasks that social morality must perform, and the practices of responsibility and the attendant moral emotions, we shall see that these practices suppose that others have reasons to conform to our exercises of moral authority – and that is precisely what the Restricted View requires. We thus shall see that the hard work of Part One – which shall involve examining a good deal of empirical work about the nature of morality and moral

---

[43] See, e.g., Christopher Eberle, *Religious Conviction in Liberal Politics*, pp. 132ff.
[44] See Ken Binmore, *Natural Justice*; Louis Kaplow and Steven Shavell, *Fairness versus Welfare*.

reasoning – has an important reward. The Restricted View of freedom and equality, so far from being a Kantian extravagance, is embedded in our moral practices. This gives us, I think, a decisive reason to endorse the Restricted over the Expansive View of freedom and equality; the latter can be justified only by appealing to a controversial moral ideal, while the former should not only appeal to those already convinced by the importance of freedom and equality but also those who take seriously our social morality as an ongoing social practice that is necessary for a cooperative social life.

2.3 TWO PUZZLES ABOUT MORAL AUTHORITY

Moral authority is a puzzling – perhaps an inherently contradictory – idea. If I am to respect another as a free and equal moral person, I cannot claim that my private judgment about the demands of morality is authoritative for her; if she is to respect me, she cannot claim that her private judgment is authoritative for me. Yet, as soon as we participate in social morality we claim authority over (qua deference from) others (§1.3). When I make a moral claim on her, I issue an imperative that tells her what to do. How can I coherently claim a moral authority to instruct a moral equal how to act? Relations of authority are relations of superiors to inferiors, yet our supposition is that there is no such inequality. Call this *the puzzle of the assertion of authority over an equal*. It is important to realize that the puzzle is not simply about whether the illocutionary act of issuing an order to an equal makes sense. The fundamental issue is not about speech acts but about claims to authority over another. The problem is how one justifiably assumes the mantle of a moral authority, issuing orders to which one normally expects the other to defer while claiming that you and she are moral equals. It is both a question about the grounds for you taking the role of commander and the grounds of the other for complying. This second feature of a moral demand is crucial: we are not just saying things to other people but morally demanding that they conform to our judgment. And we do not just insist that they comply; we think that they have good reason to.

This is intimately related to a second puzzle, *the puzzle of mutual authority*. There is no puzzle for one such as Robert Filmer, who attacked the "dangerous opinion" of the "natural freedom of man-kind" and insisted some are naturally the moral superiors of others, or for Thomas Carlyle, who held that the wise deserve to be the masters of others.[45] If there is some mark of this natural authority (such as, in Filmer's case, that one is the father), then we can easily see how moral authority works. Those with the mark of natural moral authority are superiors who should receive deference from their inferiors. However, among free and equal persons, none pos-sess a mark of authority denied to others: if I have authority over you, then you have precisely the same authority over me. But how can *that* be? I issue a prescription that you must φ regardless of whether your ends are promoted by φ-ing, or whether you agree that morality requires that of you. You then invoke your authority to deny this: you assert that you have no duty to φ and, indeed, I have an obligation to mind my own business. Mutual authority, it would seem, can only yield a standoff. I have my reasons to insist that you φ, you have reasons not to. But then our private judgments are in conflict. As Hobbes, Locke, Rousseau, and Kant all insisted, the whole point of authority is to resolve the conflict of private judgment by some submitting to a public authority. Where there is no submission, there is no authority. A puzzle indeed.

2.4 A SOCIAL MORALITY OF FREE AND EQUAL PERSONS: INSIGHTS OF ROUSSEAU AND KANT

(a) The Idealized and the Actual
There seems to be a basic tension between a conception of moral persons as free and equal and the authoritative claims that each advances as a participant in social morality. The social contract theories of Hobbes and Locke cannot help much in solving these puzzles. Both solve the disagreement in private judgment by insti-tuting an arbitrator or umpire (*i*) to which the private reason of each person endorses submission and (*ii*) which possess a mark of authority and a unique right to command. The upshot is that we all

---

[45] Robert Filmer, *Patriarcha*, p. 53; Thomas Carlyle, *Past and Present*, p. 212.

alienate some of our freedom, and accept the status of subject and
so an unequal status. Wrote Locke:

> If man in the state of nature be so free, as has been said; if he be absolute
> lord of his own person and possessions, equal to the greatest, and subject
> to nobody, why will he part with his freedom? *Why will he give up his em-*
> *pire, and subject himself to the dominion and control of any other power*? To
> which it is obvious to answer, that though in the state of nature he hath
> such a right, yet the enjoyment of it is very uncertain, and constantly
> exposed to the invasion of others; for all being kings as much as he, every
> man his equal, and the greater part no strict observers of equity and justice,
> the enjoyment of the property he has in this state is very unsafe, very unse-
> cure. This makes him willing to quit a condition, *which, however free, is full*
> *of fears and continual dangers*: and it is not without reason, that he seeks out,
> and is willing to join in society with others, who are already united, or
> have a mind to unite, for the mutual preservation of their lives, liberties,
> and estates, which I call by the general name, property.[46]

For Locke (as well as Hobbes), except in the most extreme of circumstances the only resolution of the clash of private judgments
about morality is a procedural-political resolution, which creates an
umpire who is the voice of public reason: "all private judgment of
every particular Member" must be excluded in determining the
demands of morality.[47] It is the task of government to serve as the
umpire and the voice of public reason about what morality
requires. Public reason, as it were, is the authorized private reason
of some people. Thus the Hobbesian and Lockean solutions are
inherently political and so politicize the resolutions of all moral
disputes.[48]

In grappling with this problem, Rousseau reformulates the very
idea of public reason. For Hobbes and Locke, public reason is the

---

[46] Locke, *Second Treatise*, §123. Emphasis added.

[47] Ibid, §88. As I note in the text, Locke holds that there are exceptional
circumstances when the umpire no longer possesses moral authority. If the
majority becomes convinced "in their consciences, that their laws, and with them
their estates, liberties, and lives are in danger, and perhaps their religion too,"
they may employ their private conscience and its authoritative claims to reject the
government's claim to authority. Ibid., §§208, 209, 225, 230.

[48] As did my Lockean-inspired account in *Justificatory Liberalism*. See further section
22.1*a* in this volume.

reason of the umpire to which we have consented to abide. For both, we bracket our private judgment and defer to the reason of public authority. In contrast, for Rousseau, public reason as expressed in a rule-governed social order harmonizes with individual reason:

It is to law alone that men owe justice and liberty. It is this salutary organ of the will of all which establishes, in civil right, the natural equality between men. It is this celestial voice which *dictates to each citizen the precepts of public reason, and teaches him to act according to the rules of his own judgment, and not to behave inconsistently with himself*. It is with this voice alone that political rulers should speak when they command; for no sooner does one man, setting aside the law, claim to subject another to his private will, than he departs from the state of civil society, and confronts him face to face in the pure state of nature, in which obedience is prescribed solely by necessity. [49]

Thus his statement of the fundamental problem in the epigraph to this chapter: "The problem is to find a form of association which will defend and protect with the whole common force the person and goods of each associate, and in which each, while uniting himself with all, may still obey himself alone, and remain as free as before." Rousseau's solution identifies two roles that each occupies, as a member of the sovereign and as subject. As a member of the sovereign, we legislate on the basis of our reason; as subjects, we are "under the laws of the State" and must obey.[50] Rousseau, however, remained focused on social authority as political authority. It is only with Kant's ideal of the realm of ends that Rousseau's solution is applied to nonpolitical moral demands. "A rational being belongs to the realm of ends as a member when he gives universal laws in it while also himself subject to these laws. He belongs to it as sovereign when he, as legislator, is subject to the will of no other."[51] Kant insists that for morality to be consistent with "the dignity of a rational being," a rational being must obey no law other than that which he gives himself. For morality to exist, the

---

[49] Rousseau, *A Discourse on Political Economy*, pp. 256–7. Emphasis added.
[50] Rousseau, *The Social Contract*, p. 16 (Book I, chap. 6).
[51] Immanuel Kant, *Foundations of the Metaphysics of Morals*, p. 52 [Akademie, 433–4].

individual must be a subject; for it to be consistent with her moral freedom, she must be the legislator.

We must not confuse members of the realm of ends with actual persons. As we all know, actual people are subject to biases and selfishness, employ heuristics that can lead them astray, and may be simply pig-headed.[52] As I will argue in Chapter V, we must abstract away from obvious failures of impartiality and rationality; our aim is not to induce the consent of actual persons but to appeal to the reasons of all moral persons seeking to legislate for (i.e., give imperatives to) other moral persons. As Kant stressed, it is legislation among the members of the realm of ends that is the benchmark of a morality among free and equal moral persons. Because the idea of a "realm of ends" is so tightly bound with Kant's own thought, and because it is apt to suggest that all moral justification must be universal and cosmopolitan (theses I shall question; see §§14.3, 15.2*e*), I shall use as a term of art (that, I'm afraid, has considerably less literary appeal and is unlikely to be the title of anyone's book) "Members of the Public." I will argue that a Member of the Public is an *idealization* of some actual individual; a Member of the Public deliberates well and judges only on the relevant and intelligible values, reasons, and concerns of the real agent she represents and always seeks to legislate impartially for all other Members of the Public. The moral rules (giving rise to imperatives)[53] that a Member of the Public endorses are the ones that as a moral person she has sufficient reason to endorse. That is, we characterize a Member of the Public by reflecting on *her* reasons as a specific moral person with her own reasonable values and aims, and who seeks in good faith to legislate moral rules for all. Our characterization of a Member of the Public is only as sound as our account of what her real counterpart's evaluative reasons are. At this juncture, we have only the bare idea that such a distinction can be drawn; just how it is to be drawn will occupy us in Part Two.

Now qua Members of the Public, each must be guided by her own reasoning about the demands of morality if all are to be

---

[52] I consider these in some depth in *Justificatory Liberalism*, pp. 54–62.

[53] On Hare's view, which I shall follow, moral imperatives are grounded in moral rules. See R. M. Hare, *Essays in Ethical Theory*, chap. 2.

respected as free and equal. In the end, we will see that we can relax Kant's and Rousseau's self-legislation requirement, for what is crucial is not that each legislates – devises moral rules – but that each endorses the rules under which she lives (§15.1). Thus, rather than a principle of universal self-legislation, a moral demand that respects all as free and equal moral persons must conform to what I shall call the *Deliberative Public Justification Principle*:

> *L* is a bona fide rule of social morality only if each and every Member of the Public endorses *L* as binding (and so to be internalized).

Authoritative moral prescriptions, I shall argue, are based on such justified rules. The heart of Part Two is to explicate and defend this principle and explore its applications and implications. For now the point to be stressed is that the Deliberative Public Justification Principle specifies a requirement for bona fide demands of social morality such that morality and moral freedom are reconciled. Private reason and public reason are thus harmonized. The force of the Deliberative Public Justification Principle depends on, first, the account of social morality, which shows the importance of rules and requirements to social life, and second, the importance of respect for the moral freedom of all, which will be stressed in Chapter IV. This second feature is the most important. If one disputes the account of social morality in Chapters II and III, one can reformulate the Deliberative Public Justification Principle in a way that does not appeal to the idea of a rule – perhaps an account might focus on abstract "principles." I hope to show that this would be mistaken, but the core idea of public justification would be preserved so long as the rational endorsement of all free and equal Members of the Public is required. Those who reject *that* requirement advocate a social morality that is not endorsed by the reasoning of some moral persons. To reject that requirement is to maintain that some people are subject to authoritative claims by some others that their reason does not validate.

Kant says that as members of the realm of ends we are subject to our own legislation. Although this is certainly true, in one sense Members of the Public would never have to actually advance moral demands against each other – that is, to insist that another φs even if the other does not see a reason to φ. As Members of the Public they all endorse the moral rules requiring ϕ in circumstances C, and so their own reason leads them to act in accordance with morality (see Chapters III and IV). The most they would have to do is remind each other of the relevant moral requirements. When I have promised my wife that I will buy coffee on the way home from work, she might remind me on the phone "Don't forget the coffee," but she would hardly say "Get the coffee on the way home!" Unless, of course, I tend to ignore my promises when I am tempted to stop and have a beer with a colleague on the way home – then she is indeed apt to make a point of insisting that I perform them. Actual people do not always act on their sound and overriding reasons. As Peter J. Richerson and Robert Boyd observe, "we are imperfect and often reluctant, though often very effective cooperators."[54] We need authoritative moral rules because we are a complex combination of selfish and moral creatures: the moral system, we might say, has developed on top of an earlier selfish set of motivations. In less psychological terms, we are often tempted to put aside our normative commitments and cheat, even when we accept that this violates a rule we have good reason to endorse and internalize. Thus others must have authority to insist that we live up to our moral commitments. We must actually make moral demands, and advance imperatives that we insist upon, because actual others are not their counterpart Members of the Public.

(b) On Solving the First Puzzle: Authority Claims among Equals

We can now see how the first of our two puzzles about moral authority might be solved (although, of course, all the details need to be filled in). Understood as Members of the Public, we are free and equal, and none has moral authority over any other. Morality is "self-legislated" by all in the sense that, consulting her own (private) reason, each Member of the Public endorses the relevant moral rule as binding on all, and so on herself. Public reason in the form of social morality comes from all and applies to all, and so it is an expression of moral autonomy. But too often actual people do

---

[54] Peter J. Richerson and Robert Boyd, "The Evolution of Free Enterprise Values," p. 114.

not live up to their own rational commitments. When I confront another who is violating a requirement that meets the Deliberative Public Justification Principle, I demand that she conform to what, on her own view, she has reason to do, as I might demand that she keep a promise she has made. If a person makes a promise, one of the things she does is to give me standing to demand that she keep it: the act of promise making is one that recognizes the standing of others to make demands. In a similar way, a rule that is publicly justified is one that, on the reasoning of each Member of the Public, gives others standing to make authoritative demands.

As an actual person participating in social morality, when I make a demand on you to conform to a publicly justified rule, I am claiming that I have standing to direct your actions because your own reason has accorded me that standing, though you are now failing to see, or refuse to concede, that you must conform to the rule. As Rousseau put it (in the passage quoted in §2.4*a*), I am dictating to you the precepts of public reason, and calling on you to act according to the rules of your own judgment, and not to behave inconsistently with yourself. A real inequality between actual persons is, of course, now being asserted. I claim that you are failing to live up to your own rational moral commitments: you are acting wrongly by your own lights as well as mine. My demand is based on appeal to your own reasons and your own rational moral autonomy. It is your failure to exercise your rational moral capacities to which I object; I am not seeking to override them. In this way a moral equal can make moral demands, and so claim moral authority over another.

In the end, then, when I make a moral demand on another I do claim an epistemic or practical inequality between us; I claim that I have understood the publicly justified moral rule and you have not, or else you refuse to do what you know is right. If, however, it disrespects the freedom and equality of other moral persons to advance moral demands that cannot be justified to them, isn't it equally disrespectful to insist that they really do have reasons to endorse one's demand even in the face of their disagreement?[55] If

---

[55] This objection is considered more fully in section 11.4.

we must, in the end, advance moral claims that others resist, then isn't the idea of respecting each as a free and equal moral person an impossible aspiration? In the end, what is important about showing that all Members of Public endorse the rules of social morality? The importance is the distinction between justified authority and authoritarianism: justified authority is not "browbeating," whereas unjustified authority is.[56] If I claim simply that you must ϕ, because my use of reason leads me to conclude that ϕ is required though you do not have access to reasons that show why it is required, I am simply insisting that you must believe what I believe, or you must act as I would have you act. Even on my own view, the demand has no normative authority accessible to you. Because, as far as you can see, my demand has no normative authority – you cannot see reasons to comply – doing as I say must be simply giving in to me. If, on the other hand, my demand is rooted in your reasons as a free and equal person – reasons that are accessible to you (§13) – the normative authority to which I appeal, even when you disagree, is rooted in your own evaluative point of view. Although I am insisting that you have made an error, your error is in failing to see the normative authority that your own view – your own normative commitments – grants to my demand. Again, think of a promise. In demanding that you keep your word I appeal to the authority you have granted me, even if you are now refusing to comply. I am not browbeating you when I insist on your performance.

(c) Morality and Positive Freedom

Still, it may be insisted, when "actual Alf" demands that "actual Betty" ϕs, he is not treating her as free: his demand limits her freedom. It is easy to think that his claim to authority over her must be limiting her freedom, for his moral claim is that she is not free to refrain from ϕ-ing. Treating idealized Members of the Public as free appears very different from treating actual people as free. We confront here the relation between reason and freedom (a question

---

[56] For a more complete discussion of browbeating and normative authority, see *Justificatory Liberalism*, pp. 123ff.

that will occupy us in Chapter IV). I shall argue in this book that both negative and positive conceptions of freedom are important in understanding the morality and political philosophy underlying a society of free individuals; it is unfortunate that so many have seen the task of political philosophy to be defending a favored conception of freedom, and so denying the force of the others.[57] The real problem is to get clear in what contexts one or the other is compelling.[58]

Now it may seem that in the most important way of all morality is inherently a constraint on our freedom. "From the standpoint of the agent," writes David Gauthier, "moral considerations present themselves as constraining his choices and actions, in ways independent of his desires, aims, and interests."[59] A condition in which each person acted simply to advance her personal aims and goals would result in mutual frustration. The lesson of the Prisoners' Dilemma is clear: to better advance our interests we require moral norms that restrict the pursuit of interest (§§5–6). Morality thus conceived is a mutually beneficial restraint on our freedom. It may make our remaining freedom more valuable, but in itself it is a restraint. In one respect this is undeniable. Moral rules provide grounds for others to demand that you refrain from doing what best advances your aims, or to demand that you perform acts that do not best advance your own aims; moral rules are *strong rules* (§9.2*a*). Such rules are the ground of demands on us, and these demands are not contingent on showing that our aims and desires will be best satisfied – even in the long run – if we accede to them. We are obligated. And as Hobbes observed, obligation and liberty

---

[57] It is no doubt true that different theories put the emphasis in different places (see my *Political Concepts and Political Theories*, especially chaps. 2 and 4). But we should avoid the idea that, say, classical liberals only endorse negative liberty, and so positive and "republican" liberty are alien to the classical tradition.

[58] As Stanley Benn shows in *A Theory of Freedom*. Both liberty as noninterference and freedom as rational self-direction play basic roles in Benn's analysis of a free person. Recall that even T. H. Green, the most famous proponent of positive liberty, held that "it must be of course admitted that every usage of the term [i.e., freedom] to express anything but a social and political relation of one man to other involves a metaphor. . . . It always implies . . . some exemption from compulsion by another." "On the Different Senses of Freedom," p. 229. See also Bernard Bosanquet, *The Philosophical Theory of the State*, p. 147.

[59] David Gauthier, "Why Contractarianism?" p. 16.

are opposed: in "one and the same matter [they] are inconsistent."[60] Moreover, moral obligation certainly can feel like a restraint. All this must be granted and, indeed, in Chapters II and III we shall see that it is a crucial insight about the social basis of morality.

Contrast, though, two ways in which a person may confront these restraints. He may see them as socially useful, but in consulting his "all things considered" reasons, conclude that in a specific case he can see no reason to accede to the demands of morality. He admits that it is wrong to steal or cheat, but cheating or stealing would certainly advance his fundamental goals. Why shouldn't he cheat? Suppose that his only good answer is that he fears external sanctions, or he feels coerced by a sense of duty that presents itself as an internalized voice of an alien other, commanding him to obey.[61] The demands of morality confront such a person as a manifest restraint on his freedom – an action that he is compelled to perform, either by the disapproval of others or his own guilt. Such a person could not help but think that, at least in this case, he – that is, his complete system of aims and values – would be better off if he could only avoid these sanctions. They limit him from achieving his aims.

Compare such a person to one who, consulting her own total set of values and concerns, sees that her own reasons imply that, in this case, she has most reason not to pursue her self-interests but to conform her action to a rule that her own values endorse. To be sure, such a woman sees that in this case some of her cherished goals ought not to be pursued, but she sees that they ought not because of her recognition of other fundamental reasons, which are just as much a part of her as are her personal aims and concerns. She may feel constrained, just as she may feel constrained when the dictates of prudence instruct her not to make an attractive purchase – but there is no doubt that in the end she is acting on what her total set of values and reasons requires. When she feels guilt it is an emotional reaction to her awareness that she has failed to live up to her

---

[60] Hobbes, *Leviathan*, pp. 79–80 (chap. 14, ¶3).

[61] Think here of Freud's concept of the superego, the internalized voice of others, which the self acknowledges but with which it does not fully identify. See Jennifer Church, "Morality and the Internalized Other," esp. p. 215.

own standards – standards that she has not only internalized, but which she freely endorses (§11.4).

Indeed – and this is a core claim of positive liberty views – she would be less, not more, free if she ignored the demands of prudence and gave in to the desire to make the purchase, or ignored her moral reasons and pursued her own ends. "The claim to obey only yourself is a claim essential to humanity; and the further significance of it rests upon what you mean by 'yourself.'"[62] The insight of positive liberty theorists is that not every action a person chooses is a true expression of her overall aims and values. One sense (it is not the only sense) of a free person is one whose actions and beliefs are based on her reason.[63] We may think that with more information, a person would appreciate reasons that would cause him to act differently – as in the case of John Stuart Mill's man crossing an unsafe bridge he mistakenly thinks to be sound, his ignorance prevents him from appreciating *his own* reasons. Even Mill did not think stopping this person interfered with his freedom.[64] As I will argue later, this person has an accessible reason not to cross the bridge, and that is why stopping him from crossing is compatible with respecting him as a free person (§13).

All this implies that not only is our second agent free when she sees moral imperatives as the demand of her own reason, but it is no disrespect to her status as a free agent when another demands that she do what her own reason demands, even if she does not see it. This leads us straight to Rousseau's apparently illiberal claim that when we are forced to obey the general will (or public reason) we are "forced to be free."[65] Isaiah Berlin famously argues that any such "positive liberty" view, which identifies freedom with rational action, rather than avoiding authoritarianism is quintessentially authoritarian. If someone with superior access to reason – a sage – induces, or even forces, the less rational to act according to reason and morality, the less rational are "forced to be free":

[62] Bosanquet, *The Philosophical Theory of the State*, p. 151.

[63] See Benn, *A Theory of Freedom*, p. 170.

[64] Mill, *On Liberty*, p. 294 (chap. V, ¶5). Bosanquet saw this admission by Mill as the first step to a conception of positive freedom as rational action. See *The Philosophical Theory of the State*, pp. 96–7.

[65] Rousseau, *The Social Contract*, p. 18 (Book I, chap. 7).

The sage knows you better than you know yourself, for you are the victim of your passions, a slave living a heteronomous life, purblind, unable to understand your true goals. You want to be a human being. It is the aim of the state to satisfy your wish. "Compulsion is justified by education for future insight." The reason within me, if it is to triumph, must eliminate and suppress my "lower" instincts, my passions and desires, which render me a slave; similarly (the fatal transition from individual to social concepts is almost imperceptible) the higher elements in society – the better educated, the more rational, those who "possess the highest insight of their time and people" – may exercise compulsion to rationalize the irrational section of society. For, so Hegel, Bradley, Bosanquet have often assured us, by obeying the rational man we obey ourselves – not indeed as we are, sunk in our ignorance and our passions, sick creatures afflicted by diseases that need a healer, wards who need a guardian, but as we could be if we were rational; as we could be even now, if only we would listen to the rational element which is, *ex hypothesi*, within every human being who deserves the name.[66]

In Berlin's eyes this tendency to authoritarian corruption is at the heart of all conceptions of positive freedom, certainly including Kant's.[67] Whenever we tell another what her reason requires, and thus claim that she would be free if she were to do as we say, we are on the slippery slope to despotism. We should question this. Berlin's essay, though rhetorically powerful, is not philosophically nuanced. His indictment is most persuasive against those who claim that the reason of some is so superior to that of others that the inferior would be rational, and so free, to simply obey, though the use of their reason could not allow them to grasp the underlying rationality of what they do. As Berlin rightly stresses, in this case the authority of reason becomes the mere authority of some over others; and those subject to such authority, and perhaps forced to conform, are further insulted by being called "free." To claim that the auxiliaries or tradesmen are free in Plato's republic because they are induced to live in accordance with the reason of the guardians, which they cannot grasp, is indeed an abomination.

[66] Isaiah Berlin, "Two Concepts of Liberty," pp. 149–50.
[67] Ibid., p. 153.

Berlin, however, does not distinguish freedom qua acting *in accordance* with reason from freedom qua acting *on one's reasons*. The noble lie, Plato might have thought, could induce the auxiliaries and tradesmen to act in accord with what reasons there are, but they surely do not act on *their* reasons. As I shall argue (§13) that for a person to "have" a reason – for a reason to be hers – it must not simply apply to her, but in some way it must be such that, should she exercise her rationality, it actually can ground her action. But a reason that one could not possibly grasp could not possibly be the rational grounds of one's action. Nor could a reason one could not possibly grasp be the rational grounds for one's belief. There must be some not-too-difficult bridge to cross connecting what reasons a person can be said to possess and what the exercise of her rational faculties can lead her to. To be free as a rational agent and believer is to act on, and believe on the basis of, one's good reasons – as revealed by the exercise of one's own rationality. One whose actions and beliefs are not grounded on her reasons cannot be free as a rational agent and believer, even if somehow she is induced to perform the act required by reason or believe that which reason requires.

I take it Berlin would deny that positive freedom as acting on one's reasons is, ultimately, any less authoritarian than freedom as action in accordance with reason. Indeed, I suspect that he would have insisted that the difference between the views is illusory. It is this claim that I shall seek to undermine in this work. *Pace* Berlin, when we confront someone "sunk in ignorance and passions," we do not take her current set of her acknowledged reasons as definitive about what reasons she has, and what reasons a person has is relevant to what she does as a free person. Think again of the man in Mill's "bad bridge" case: although in one way we are definitely interfering with his choice, we do not think his status as a free person is infringed by stopping him from crossing. The relevant freedom contrast we have been exploring is not between the unconstrained and the constrained, but between the self-directed and those who fail to achieve self-direction either because they are other-directed (think of our man who sees morality as only constraints, or Plato's auxiliaries) or because of failures of self-direction (such as the man in Mill's bad bridge case).[68] If we think of a free person as one whose life is guided by her own values, commitments, and goals, advocates of positive liberty are quite right to point out that demanding that she live up to her own values is not disrespecting her freedom.

3 Evaluative Diversity and the Problem of Indeterminacy

3.1 THE FUNDAMENTAL PROBLEM WITH THE PROPOSED SOLUTION TO THE FUNDAMENTAL PROBLEM

We seem to have come full circle. Our original problem was that the judgments of good-willed persons competently employing their human reason will diverge, but the Kantian proposal only reconciles freedom and authority if all Members of the Public converge on the same rules of social morality. How can we achieve the requisite agreement among Members of the Public given the disagreement in judgments? In describing the realm of ends Kant tells us that

By "realm" I understand the systematic union of different rational beings through common laws. Because laws determine ends with regard to their universal validity, if we abstract from the personal differences of rational beings and this from all content of their private ends, we can think of the whole of all ends in systematic connection, a whole of rational beings in themselves as well as of the particular ends which each man may set himself. This is a realm of ends. . . .

---

[68] "This, then, we may take as the practical starting-point in the notion of freedom. It is what, with reference to a formed society, we may call a status; the position of a freeman as opposed to a slave; that is, of one who, whatever oppression he may meet with *de facto* from time to time, or whatever specified services he may be bound to render, normally regards himself and is regarded by others as, on the whole, at his own disposal, and not the mere instrument of another mind." Bosanquet, *The Philosophical Theory of the State*, pp. 144–5.

A rational being belongs to the realm of ends as member when he gives universal laws in it while also himself subject to these laws. He belongs to it as sovereign when he, as legislating, is subject to the will of no other.[69]

Kant's method for determining moral laws as universal laws of freedom involves an individual decision procedure: each individual is to propound universal laws. Of course, as universal laws of morality regulating the realm of ends to which all free persons are subject, these laws are to be the same for all. How are different individuals, each acting as moral sovereign, to arrive at the same set of laws? Often Kant is seen simply as a formalist, as if the mere universal form of the law guarantees convergence of legislation. There are well-rehearsed objections to any such purely formal account of moral legislation. As we see in this passage, Kant suggests a rather more subtle procedure: we must abstract from our differences and "private ends." For this abstraction strategy to succeed, we must have good reasons to bracket the considerations that set us apart (our private ends), and having done this, we must still have available to us some common considerations that can serve as the basis of individual deliberations about what laws to legislate. As Rawls suggests (in his discussion of the universal law formulation of the categorical imperative), we might appeal to a notion of our common "true human needs" that are not mere private ends.[70]

Rawls' argument from the original position can be understood as a formalization of this two-step bracketing procedure. First (via the veil of ignorance), we abstract away "private ends" that would lead us to legislate different universal laws.[71] One excludes "knowledge of those contingencies which set men at odds."[72] Second, we attribute to the parties a concern with primary goods that provide a basis for their common deliberation. These primary goods are to be understood as akin to "true human needs." Insofar as we consider

---

[69] Kant, *Foundations of the Metaphysics of Morals*, pp. 51–2 [Akademie 33–4]. Emphasis added.
[70] John Rawls, "Themes in Kant's Moral Philosophy," pp. 501ff.
[71] See Fred D'Agostino, *Incommensurability and Commensuration: The Common Denominator*, p. 100.
[72] John Rawls, *A Theory of Justice*, p. 17.

ourselves as agents devoted to some ends, they are what we need. When abstracted to the common status of agents devoted to their own (unknown) evaluative standards (values, comprehensive conceptions of the good, and so on),[73] because "everyone is equally rational and similarly situated, each is convinced by the same arguments."[74] So although the original position begins by posing a problem of collective choice, the problem is reduced to the Kantian problem of public legislation by one person.[75] The result is a unanimous choice on a specific conception of justice:

> The restrictions on particular information in the original position are, then, of fundamental importance. Without them we would not be able to work out any definite theory of justice at all. We would have to be content with the vague formula stating that justice is what would be agreed to without being able to say much, if anything, about the substance of the agreement itself. . . . The veil of ignorance makes possible a unanimous choice of a particular conception of justice. Without these limitations on knowledge the bargaining problem of the original position would be hopelessly complicated.[76]

Rawls, then, explicitly argues that allowing diversity of evaluative judgments in the original position would render the choice among idealized persons indeterminate. It is only by abstracting away from our diversity that free and equal persons can legislate common rules.

3.2 FREE-STANDING AND OVERLAPPING CONSENSUS JUSTIFICATIONS

The Kantian-Rawlsian solution to the problem of universal legislation under diversity of private judgment depends on the claim that public agreement can be insulated from deep disagreement on fundamental issues about how to live. We can put aside the matters

[73] See further section 17.2 in this volume.
[74] Rawls, *A Theory of Justice*, p. 120.
[75] Ibid., pp. 120–1.
[76] Ibid., p. 121.

on which we disagree, and reason simply on the basis of what we share. For this solution to succeed it must be the case that our reasoning from what we share can somehow be insulated from our disagreements. It is sometimes held that we share certain fundamental values or interests in successfully pursuing our plan of life, and by bracketing our disagreements about many private matters (say, religion), we can focus on our agreement about these common concerns.[77] As Rawls says, justice as fairness expresses "shared reason."[78] So in the view of many followers of Rawls, only shared reasons can form the basis for public justification.[79] However, while this insistence that only shared reasons can be appealed to in public justification may yield determinate principles, it does not show us that what we share is significant enough to justify all things considered endorsement of the public principles that the procedure yields. Fundamental to Rawls' liberalism (and to any defense of a free society) is the question of "how it is possible that there may exist over time a stable and just society of free and equal citizens profoundly divided by reasonable though incompatible religious, philosophical, and moral doctrines?"[80] This question is so fundamental because liberals suppose that "a plurality of reasonable yet incompatible comprehensive doctrines is the normal result of the exercise of human reason within the framework of free institutions of a constitutional regime."[81] Under these conditions, a social order that respects the freedom and equality of all must show that individuals who care deeply about their divergent conceptions of value nevertheless have strong reason to endorse and abide by shared moral rules. Now to say that they have strong reason to endorse such shared rules only when they reason on the basis of shared

---

[77] Ibid., p. 120. This was basic to Locke's case for toleration. "I esteem it above all things," Locke argues, "necessary to distinguish exactly the business of civil government from that of religion, and to settle the just bounds that lie between the one and the other. If this be not done, there can be no end put to the controversies that will be always arising between those that have, or at least pretend to have, on the one side, a concernment for the interest of men's souls, and, on the other side, a care of the commonwealth." Locke, "A Letter Concerning Toleration," pp. 9–10.

[78] Rawls, *Political Liberalism*, p. 9.

[79] See, e.g., Jonathan Quong, *Liberalism Without Perfection*, chap. 9. See §14.4d.

[80] Rawls, *Political Liberalism*, p. xviii.

[81] Ibid., p. xvi.

concerns and are unaware of their divergent conceptions is not an especially compelling conclusion. In reply to the conclusion "If you bracket most of what you care about, you will reason as others do, and will endorse these shared rules," the reasonable query is "And what will be my view of these rules when I *do* know what I deeply care about?"[82]

A bracketing or insulation strategy that takes this rejoinder seriously must stress the *robustness* of public justification in light of the full range of people's diverse values, concerns, and ends. Rather than insisting that these diverse evaluations remain bracketed because they are irrelevant to public justification, the robustness approach holds that even when they are considered, the conclusions of public reason are not affected. Rawls came to accept that diverse "comprehensive conceptions of the good" are indeed relevant to the public justification of a conception of justice. Unlike Kant, who apparently saw "private ends" as simply irrelevant considerations that are appropriately entirely put aside in moral legislation, Rawls' commitment to the importance of evaluative pluralism prevents him from simply dismissing different conceptions of the good as irrelevant to moral justification. Rawls maintains that the argument from the original position is *free standing*: it is based on an abstract conception of persons as reasonable and rational, free and equal – a conception that is said to be implicit in our democratic society, and so *shared* by all reasonable citizens.[83] Rawls thus maintains that justice as fairness is a justified political conception because it articulates the requirements of the concepts of the person and society that all reasonable citizens in our democratic societies share. However, Rawls does not believe that this exhausts justification. Indeed, he says that this is simply a *pro tanto* (so far as it goes) justification.[84] In what he refers to as "full" justification citizens draw on their full range of evaluative criteria

---

[82] Some defenders of the shared reason view seek to show the irrelevancy of non-shared reasons to public justification by disputing their status as bona fide reasons; actual people may hold them but idealized Members of the Public would not. The very concept of "a reason," it is argued, demands that all justification must take the form of consensus. I consider this objection in section 13.

[83] Rawls, *Political Liberalism*, p. 10.

[84] Ibid., p. 386.

and find further reasons for endorsing the political conception. At this stage, Rawls tells us, the *pro tanto* abstract justification "may be overridden by citizens' comprehensive doctrines once all values are tallied up."[85] What was simply "freestanding" justification based on a shared view must, if it is to be fully justified, serve as a "module" that fits into each free and equal rational moral person's full set of diverse evaluative considerations – in which case the shared justification would be robust in the face of our disagreements.[86] Whereas the freestanding stage of justification appeals to *shared* reasons, full justification appeals to a *convergence* of different conceptions of the good,[87] which for different reasons[88] confirm and "fill out" the results of the freestanding justification.[89] Rawls believes (or, perhaps, hopes) that even after a reasonable person reasons on the basis of her own comprehensive conception of the good in full justification, the results of the freestanding justification will be stable – the "private" concerns initially excluded will not overturn the *pro tanto* justification. The conclusion of the freestanding argument will be robust in the face of knowledge of our comprehensive schemes of value.

In Chapter VI we shall see that for a restricted set of abstract principles a "freestanding" argument is enlightening. However, once this "freestanding" (or, as I shall describe it, "abstracted") justification is achieved, we are faced with two remaining problems. First, this abstract justification may not be stable under full justifi-

---

[85] Ibid., p. 386.

[86] Many commentators mistakenly identify these two ideas. Rawls employs the idea of a "module" when explaining "overlapping consensus" (*Political Liberalism*, pp. 12–13; 144–5) whereas "freestandingness" applies to the appeal to shared conceptions of the person and lack of metaphysical and other commitments in the abstract argument for the two principles (*Political Liberalism*, pp. 10, 40, 133, 144). The crucial passage that confuses many readers is on pages 144–5 of *Political Liberalism* where Rawls argues that because the political conception is freestanding it can serve as a module; many readers suppose that Rawls is simply equating the two ideas.

[87] On the difference between justifications based on shared reasons, and convergence justifications, see Gaus and Vallier, "The Roles of Religious Conviction in a Publicly Justified Polity: The Implications of Convergence, Asymmetry, and Political Institutions."

[88] Rawls, *Political Liberalism*, p. 171.

[89] Ibid., p. 286.

cation: once free and equal individuals are aware of their full range of relevant values and concerns, they may conclude that the abstract justification is defeated. In this case, the abstract justification is not robust. Second, however, even when it is robust these justifications occur at a high level of abstraction, and so do not provide justification of moral rules that are sufficiently fine-grained to serve as the basis of our actual social life. The problem then is how to continue on to the justification of more specific moral rules. At this stage, comprehensive conceptions and the freestanding justification are apt to interact in complex ways. Once people are aware of their full range of values, religious convictions, and other views, even if they continue to affirm the conclusions of the freestanding argument they are apt to disagree on how its abstract principles are to be interpreted. We thus are faced with a neglected problem of contemporary theories of public reason: how do we get from general principles of public morality to the justification of an actual social morality?

3.3 PUBLIC JUSTIFICATION UNDER INDETERMINACY

(a) The Limits of Impartial Reason

The Kantian legislation procedure is caught in a dilemma. If we follow Kant in entirely excluding that which sets us apart as mere "private ends" irrelevant to moral legislation, we may get a shared result, but only because we have ignored fundamental evaluative diversity. Rational evaluative diversity is not about mere private conflicts that are irrelevant to what moral rules agents have reason to endorse; they are fundamental to what a person sees as rational social-moral rules to live by. Remember, our goal is for each to follow her own reason while seeing herself as a member of the "realm of ends"; by declaring irrelevant so much of what a person understands as basic to her evaluative outlook, she can see these rules as rationally endorsed only in an extremely attenuated sense. Rawls saw this, and so insisted that the abstract justification is only *pro tanto* – full justification must admit the full range of relevant evaluative considerations, which might override the abstract justification. But then, as I will argue, only a limited set of freestanding arguments (or arguments from abstraction) for moral rules is stable under full justification.

Because, at least in their strong forms, both the shared reasons and robustness approaches are ultimately implausible, evaluative diversity about conceptions of the good, values, and so on – all of which I group under the label "evaluative standards" – must characterize plausibly described Members of the Public (Chapter V). Rawls (§3.1) believed that this would make the "bargaining problem" too complex to yield a determinate result. I conclude that Rawls was entirely correct: unless we employ highly controversial choice procedures, allowing diversity of evaluative standards into the reasoning of Members of the Public renders their choice indeterminate (§16.3). Rawls appeared to believe that this itself was a strong justification for restricting deliberations to a common set of concerns: to achieve determinacy we must radically restrict the information available to the parties to the original position. I disagree. In light of the implausibility of the strong versions of the shared reasons and robustness approaches, the best response is to give up on the hope that we can construct a compelling description of the deliberations of members of the "realm of ends" that will lead them to agree on the same rule. The most we can achieve, I shall argue, is a compelling description that selects, as Rawls put it in his later work, a set of reasonable rules. Or, as I shall describe it, we are left with a (nonempty, nonsingleton) set of *optimal eligible proposals*: the disagreement in our private judgment is extensive but is bounded within a set. Within this set, Members of the Public will differ in their ranking of proposed rules. The problem is how, as free and equal moral persons, we are to select from this set given that our reasoning has led us to disagree. I argue in Chapter V that the Rousseauean–Kantian ideal of rational, impartial legislation among free and equal persons cannot itself solve this problem. Unless we appeal to controversial mechanisms to solve Rawls' "complex bargaining problem," the reasoning from the perspective of the "realm of ends" yields a set of acceptable requirements, all of which are evaluated as giving everyone reasons to endorse every rule within the set, but none of which dominates the other. That we can identify such a set, I shall argue, is a moral result of the first importance. But it still leaves us facing moral indeterminacy. Kantian theory has set itself a problem it cannot solve.

It might help to express the problem I have been considering in a more general way. Robert Talisse has argued that at bottom public reason defenses of a free society succumb to a fatal tension. On the one hand, such views stress that our society is characterized by a deep, reasonable, pluralism concerning evaluative standards while, on the other, they insist that only some sort of reasonable consensus could justify authority – political or moral. He concludes that such an approach is ultimately inconsistent. "Liberal theory is inconsistent with the pluralism that is the result of liberal practice. If liberals really stress reasonable pluralism, they will be unable to find any consensus on which to build political legitimacy; if they allow for enough agreement to justify the state, pluralism is qualified."[90] More dynamically, Talisse argues that liberalism encourages a pluralism that undermines consensus on principles of right. I shall argue that Talisse is wrong that this is a fatal incoherence in liberalism, but it is certainly true that it cannot be resolved by public reason approaches as they have developed thus far. We need to look elsewhere.

(b) Hume's Helping Hand

In ethical theory Kantian views of morality as self-legislation among members of the realm of ends are typically seen as fundamentally at odds with the line of theorizing about morality that extends from Hobbes through Ferguson, Hume, and Smith to F. A. Hayek and contemporary game theorists. According to this second tradition, moralities are social facts with histories. The social morality we have ended up with is, to some extent, a matter of chance. In some places at some times, adultery has been considered a great wrong; in other places and other times, it may be a minor personal failing or even encouraged. In some places, restricting marriage to male–female couples is considered right and proper, while in other places it is considered a basic injustice. In some

---

[90] Robert B. Talisse, *Democracy after Liberalism: Pragmatism and Deliberative Politics*, p. 37.

places it is considered morally crucial that everyone be provided health care; in other places it is considered wrong for those who refuse to work to receive such benefits. The social morality we end up with is partially *path dependent*; only because our social morality started somewhere, and has changed in response to certain problems, can we explain why we ended up where we have, with different social moralities.

The proponents of the broadly "Kantian" and the broadly "Humean" approaches typically seek to discredit or dismiss the other. Those who conceive of morality as the demand of reason as specified by members of the realm of ends often simply insist that "positive morality" (the social morality that people actually follow) should not be confused with justified or "true morality," which is revealed by impartial reason. The former, they say, tells us nothing very significant about the latter. For every issue mentioned above there is a correct moral answer, regardless of the differences in moral beliefs or convictions. More ecumenically, some such as James Rachels insist that differences in practices are local applications of general moral principles.[91] Less sophisticatedly, some simply insist that the evolutionary view exemplifies the dreaded "undergraduate cultural relativism," and so dismiss the whole idea.

In this book I set out on a reconciliation project of these two traditions.[92] Part One seeks to reconcile the Hobbesian–Humean insight that our devotion to social morality must derive from its usefulness to human life with the Kantian insight that its rules are

[91] James Rachels, *The Elements of Morality*, chap. 2. Recall the explorer Kund Rasmussen's discoveries that so shocked Europeans: an Eskimo woman he met had borne twenty children, ten of whom she killed at birth; female babies were especially apt to be killed by their parents, with no condemnation by other members of the community; and he reported an Eskimo practice of leaving old, ill people on the snow to die. Rachels insists that all of these are different responses to environmental challenges: underlying the diversity of specific practices is an impartial rational principle – the importance of arranging social practices so that the general welfare is advanced. Peter J. Richerson and Robert Boyd persuasively argue that cultural variation – including variation in norms – cannot be satisfactorily explained simply by environmental variation. See their *Not by Genes Alone*, chap. 2.
[92] Alas, as Strawson observed of his own reconciliation project in "Freedom and Resentment" (p. 187), this may mean that it seems wrongheaded to everyone.

not properly seen as simply instrumental to this end. Part Two seeks to show that, as Kantians observe, morality is the dictate of impartial public reason *and* that Humeans are correct that it has a history and so is path dependent and indeed in a significant sense a society chooses its morality. Without appeal to social evolutionary processes, the Kantian ideal of common self-legislation is either hopelessly controversial or indeterminate; without appeal to the critical perspective of the Deliberative Public Justification Principle, the evolutionary view cannot distinguish authoritarian from non-authoritarian evolved positive moralities. An adequate account of morality needs both Kant and Hume. This should have always been apparent to those of us who teach the insights of these two giants of moral thinking, yet, as happens far too often, our peda-gogical method of depicting them as sharp rivals hinders our efforts to integrate their insights.

The precise social morality with which we end up, I shall show, is a matter of the rise of a complex coordination and selection process among a large number of people. As Hume observed, a rule of social morality rises through "a slow progression, and by our repeated experience of the inconveniences of transgressing it."[93] Although free and equal Members of the Public reasoning simply on their own evaluative standards will seldom converge on a specific rule of social morality as unequivocally the best, free and equal persons acting on their own evaluative standards neverthe-less can and often do freely converge on some member of the optimal eligible set. A publicly justified morality, I shall show, con-stitutes an equilibrium solution among free and equal moral persons seeking to select from the optimal eligible set revealed by the reasoning of the idealized Members of the Public. The result is a specific social morality that achieves the goal to which those in the tradition of Rousseau and Kant aspire. Each is subject to the authority of social morality while still acting on her full set of rele-vant evaluative standards – following her own reason and conceiving of herself as a member of the realm of ends.

[93] Hume, A *Treatise of Human Nature*, p. 490.

3.4 THE SECOND PUZZLE ABOUT MORAL AUTHORITY

Recall the puzzle of mutual moral authority (§2.3): if I have authority to interpret social morality and issue imperatives to you, and
you have a similar authority to issue counterimperatives to me, the
authority of each seems to negate the other's. Thus the worry that
countervailing authority, in which the authority claim of one person
is checked by the authority claim of the other, is no authority at all.

As the classical social contract theorists realized, the usefulness
of the mutual authority of social morality does have its limits.
Hobbes, Locke, and Kant all stressed the way that moral disputes,
in which each acts on his own judgment of the demands of morality, can end up in the political arena, adjudicated by the state. As I
will argue in Chapter VIII, a flaw in Hobbes' and Locke's analyses
was that there seems to be no effective nonpolitical method to
resolve disagreement of private judgment about morality. Moral
disputes, as it were, push us immediately into politics. This was an
error: morality is in itself an important source of social order, and it
could not perform that function if it did not have internal mechanisms to resolve disputes. But this is not to say that moral disputes
are never intractable; when they are we typically need to resort to
political authority (Chapter VIII).

I shall argue that we can solve the puzzle of mutual authority
within social morality by abandoning the dyadic perspective of
thinking of justification as essentially between pairs of agents, and
instead appreciating the "Humean" insight that the development of
a social morality involves large-scale coordination among moral
agents. Rather than focusing on the two-person case, the social
evolutionary view leads us to think of the selection of a specific
morality as a many-person problem. The problem is not mutual
authority but dispersed authority. Once a society of free and equal
persons has coordinated on specific moral rules and their interpretation, the point of invoking moral authority is to police this equilibrium selection against "trembling hands" – individuals who make
mistakes about what rule is in equilibrium – and those who otherwise fail to act on their best reasons. In these cases the overwhelming social opinion concurs in criticizing deviant behavior. An individual who violates the social equilibrium will not simply

be able to check demands on her, for she will meet the same demand from almost all others. In Mill's terms, the deviant will not simply confront the opinion of other individuals but the judgment of "society." This, I shall argue, renders decentralized authority effective in inducing compliance with social morality.

CONCLUSION

This chapter has introduced the core ideas of social morality, free and equal moral persons, authority claims based on the rules of social morality, public justification, and public reason. Social morality, I have argued, raises problems similar to the traditional problems of liberal political philosophy: how can free and equal moral persons accept the authority of others to command them? Are we to alienate our freedom for the sake of social order, or, as Rousseau claimed, can freedom and social order be reconciled through public reason? In politics it is often thought that the Hobbesian and Lockean bargain, trading some liberty for greater security, makes sense: we submit to the authority of the state to achieve public order and justice. Rousseau rejects such a bargain: it is exchanging liberty for chains. It is natural to think that Rousseau and those influenced by him simply refuse to learn the lesson of opportunity costs. In order to get something of value, we must give up something of value; to achieve order and security we must alienate our freedom. Rousseau's rejection of the Hobbesian–Lockean bargain is far more difficult to dismiss, though, once we appreciate that the problem of authority also applies to social morality. Here the alienation of freedom for the sake of order is much more worrisome. To whom do we alienate liberty and grant control over our lives? Everyone? Is everyone, or the majority, to be our moral sovereign, dictating what we must do? As Mill recognized, although social morality is not backed up by the "extreme penalties" of the requirements of the legal system, "it leaves fewer means of escape, penetrating much more deeply into the details of life." If social life requires moral authority, and if authority requires renouncing one's freedom, then social life may constitute a much greater renunciation of freedom than Locke and others have supposed. Rousseau's worry that it constitutes a bad bargain starts to

gnaw. Kant's notion of the realm of ends points to a broad reconciliation of the pervasive authority of social morality and moral
freedom: if each is legislator as well as subject, the rules of social
morality reflect rather than restrict moral freedom. However, I have
argued that the Kantian solution to this expanded version of
Rousseau's problem supposes that our reasoning about public
morality can be insulated from the diversity of private judgment
about conceptions of the good, values, and so on. Because such insulation cannot be achieved, and so the problems of pluralism of
private judgment "infects" reasoning about public moral norms,
Kantian and Rawlsian deliberative models cannot produce determinate results.

Rawls seeks to avoid the indeterminacy looming in the Kantian
public reason view by introducing powerful philosophical devices:
the veil of ignorance and maximin reasoning. Others resort to bargaining theory or some form of social aggregation. I will consider
these responses as we proceed, but I shall argue that we should
look elsewhere – to the social evolutionary tradition suggested by
Hume and his followers. At this point, though, we have exhausted
the usefulness of prolegomena and précis. If we are to solve our
puzzles we must begin assembling the pieces in a careful way.

PART ONE

SOCIAL ORDER AND SOCIAL MORALITY

II

The Failure of Instrumentalism

> We must ask whether societies could exist without more or less severely sanctioned rules, such as are embodied in the law, custom, and in social morality, and if so, whether it would be desirable to do away with at least the most intrusively coercive ones, as the anarchists believe.
>
> Kurt Baier, *The Rational and the Moral Order*

> Like all other values, our morals are not the product but a presupposition of reason, part of the ends which the instrument of our intellect has been designed to serve.
>
> F. A. Hayek, *The Constitution of Liberty*

To begin our understanding of social morality, we must see why it is necessary: why human social life confronts us with situations in which each individual relying on her own reasoning about her ends can lead to results that are bad for all. This chapter considers instrumental reasoning in "mixed motive games" in which although all benefit from cooperation, all are tempted to cheat, but if they do so, all will be worse off. In the history of social and moral philosophy, those who have taken this problem most seriously, and from whom we have the most to learn, are Hobbes and his contemporary followers such as David Gauthier. Rational individuals, they argue with great sophistication, can reason themselves out of such situations by agreeing to social morality; social morality is a tool of rational individuals who are seeking to promote their values and ends. In this chapter I show that instrumental reasoning is unable to provide the basis of social morality; as Hayek indicates in the epigraph, morality is not, and cannot be, the construction of human reason as a way to solve the basic problems of social life. The instrumentalist analysis of the problems of social cooperation is correct: its solution fails. In the last twenty years a large body of theoretical and empirical findings has arisen that demonstrates that instrumentally rational individuals could not achieve effective social order in large groups. There is, I think, a widely held but mistaken view that recent developments in iterated game theory (tit-for-tat) and evolutionary psychology (kin altruism) show that instrumental reason can secure large-scale social cooperation. I shall show why this is not so.

4 The Instrumentalist Approach to Social Order

4.1 THE CRISIS OF SOCIAL MORALITY

In an important essay, David Gauthier worries that morality is undergoing a foundational crisis, in many ways similar to that of religion. Morality advances constraints on action: it tells each to set aside her aims, interests, and desires, and do as it commands. "But," Gauthier asks, "what justifies paying attention to morality, rather than dismissing it as an appendage of outworn beliefs? We ask, and we seem to find no answer."[1] Just as religious modes of justification have been supplanted by the sciences, so too in the modern world moral justification seems supplanted by each deliberating on the basis of her own ends, affections, and desires. Instrumental reasoning and moral justification are directed at the same things – a person's choices – and appear to be competing modes of deliberation. But, Gauthier presses, the rational basis of the moral is increasingly difficult to accept; compared to instrumentalist reasoning its basis is obscure, its ontology suspect. We are threatened with skepticism and nihilism; it would seem that only a childlike belief in moral properties can sustain moral practices, but

---

[1] David Gauthier, "Why Contractarianism?" p. 16.

what are adults to do?[2] A clearly attractive option is to derive the system of constraints that we call social morality from instrumentalist reasoning itself:

The key idea is that in many situations, if each person chooses what, given the choices of others, would maximize her expected utility, then the outcome will be mutually disadvantageous in comparison with some alternative – everyone could do better. Equilibrium, which obtains when each person's action is a best response to the other's action, is incompatible with (Pareto-)optimality, which obtains when no one could do better without someone doing worse. Given the ubiquity of such situations, each person can see the benefit, to herself, of participating with her fellows in practices requiring each to refrain from the direct pursuit of her own utility, when such mutual restraint is mutually advantageous. . . . We may represent such a practice as capable of gaining unanimous agreement among rational persons who were choosing the terms on which they would interact with each other. And this agreement is the basis of morality.[3]

This is an enormously attractive proposal. Surely social morality must be important as a way to structure human interaction so that it leads to cooperation rather than conflict, benefit rather than loss. And surely all rational persons would agree to a practice that secures these great benefits. If all of this can be derived simply from the most basic notion of rationality – that people prefer more over less of what they value, and will act to achieve it – we will have explained how all free and equal rational moral persons can embrace the system of restraints that we call "social morality." In response to the query "Why should I do as you demand?" one can answer: "Because doing so best promotes your own values and concerns." No recourse to the special rationality of rule following, or a special notion of moral justification, is required. This was Hobbes' great ambition, as it has been Gauthier's.

This enticing proposal, I believe, conclusively fails. This chapter is devoted to demonstrating this failure. I examine its problems at some length for three reasons. First, of course, it continues to have

[2] Gauthier describes his work as "moral theory for adults." See Robert Sugden "The Contractarian Enterprise," p. 2.
[3] Gauthier, "Why Contractarianism?" pp. 22–3.

wide appeal, especially among those, such as myself, who think that *of course* social morality has a point – providing the foundations for social life – and this fact must shape our understanding of it. I wish to show that those who share this conviction must look elsewhere for an account of social morality. Second, for all its shortcomings, the problems the instrumentalist project seeks, but fails, to resolve are indeed the core problems of social cooperation. For all its failures, the instrumentalist project has clearly focused on the core problems in achieving social cooperation among agents whose lives are primarily devoted to pursuing their own aims. To understand its failures is to better understand these problems. And third, a good deal of the attraction of the rule-based analysis that I defend in Chapter III is that it provides the solutions to the problems that have so vexed instrumentalism since Hobbes.

There is, though, a danger with beginning with the instrumentalist case. Two thoughts may lead people to reject the instrumentalist analysis as too misguided to even warrant serious attention, and so too my analysis, since it takes instrumentalism so seriously. First, many think that instrumentalism depends on the view that social morality is simply a way to advance individual self-interest, and since this is deeply mistaken, there is no point in thinking through the instrumentalist analysis. Instrumentalists have encouraged this conception, often stressing their lineage to Hobbes and his doctrine of self-interest. And often the general instrumentalist approach is conflated with *"Homo Economicus"* – "economic man" – although the latter is a much more specific model of human action.[4] These are misconceptions. The instrumentalist analysis supposes that each individual is devoted to her own ends, goals, values, and aims, and that her rational action is aimed at securing these. There is no supposition that these aims must be self-interested. In a world of deep pluralism in which individuals are devoted to different ends, the instrumentalist problem is "how do people with different, and sometimes competing, ends manage to cooperate and avoid conflict?" Surely this is a question that must interest any

---

[4] I distinguish these in some detail in *On Philosophy, Politics, and Economics*, chap. 1.

philosopher who believes that reasonable pluralism is a basic problem of modern social life.

Many also think that the instrumentalist seeks to answer the question "why be moral?" and this question either need not, or cannot be, answered. As H. A. Prichard insisted, any answer to the question of why I should be moral and perform my duty in terms of my interests simply would be the wrong sort of answer: it would not tell us why we are obligated to do what morality requires, regardless of our interests.[5] I think Prichard was exactly right; as we shall see, the instrumentalist does give the wrong sort of reason for a person to conform to specific moral demands made on her (§11.1*a*). But as Gauthier stresses, there is another worry that the instrumentalist seeks to answer: it is not a worry about why *I* should now do what morality requires of *me*; it is a worry that morality itself may be simply a confused, nasty, or obsolete practice.[6] Social morality gives us authority to "boss others around," to be indignant when they do not conform to our demands on them, to publicly chastise them, and often to punish them. Why should *we* accept this way of relating to each other? Some will say that a well-developed or well-functioning person will just "see" that this is of course the way she should relate to her fellows. But once we appreciate that this means that she claims that *of course* she has authority to command others, we cannot help but wonder whether this is such an obvious way to relate to others. A feature of the modern world has been to interrogate authority claims that have previously been upheld as natural or in the nature of things; the crisis of social morality is that it too is now subject to such interrogation. Contemporary expressivists (and "hybrid expressivists")[7] proclaim that they can make sense of the semantics and psychology of morality, but *should* we make sense of this practice, or should we rid ourselves of it? One can imagine a wonderful expressivist analysis of Santa Claus discourse; but we do not wish to know whether Santa Claus discourse expresses our approval of the idea of rotund elves bearing presents but whether we would do best just to grow up

[5] H. A. Prichard, "Does Moral Philosophy Rest on a Mistake?"
[6] For such a case, see Walter Kaufmann, *Without Guilt and Justice.*
[7] See Mark Schroeder, "Hybrid Expressivism: Virtues and Vices."

and stop talking of Santa. For all their problems, the instrumentalists refuse to take social morality as given in the nature of things, and so to simply suppose its claims on us are beyond interrogation. And even if social morality is somehow in the nature of things, we need to inquire whether this part of nature has authority over free persons.

4.2 INSTRUMENTAL RATIONALITY

There are numerous instrumentalist solutions to the problem of securing mutual benefit in, as Gauthier puts it, situations in which "if each person chooses what, given the choices of others, would maximize her expected utility, then the outcome will be mutually disadvantageous in comparison with some alternative." Before considering these in detail, however, we need to get clearer about the idea of instrumental rationality.[8] Gauthier refers to "utility maximization" but that is simply a formal way to represent consistent choice; we shall see that in an important sense even Kantians are utility maximizers (§9.4). What is really at the heart of Gauthier's account is the idea that practical reason is "strictly instrumental."[9] "Instrumental rationality," says Robert Nozick, "is within the intersection of all theories of rationality (and perhaps nothing else is). In this sense it is the default theory, the theory that all can take for granted, whatever else they think. . . . The question is whether it is the whole of rationality."[10] Indeed, Nozick thinks "it is natural to think of rationality as a goal-directed process. (This applies to both rationality of action and rationality of belief)." So according to the basic "instrumental conception, rationality consists in the effective and efficient achievement of goals, ends, and desires. About the goals themselves, an instrumental conception has little to say."[11]

---

[8] This section draws on my *Philosophy, Politics, and Economics*, chap. 1.

[9] Gauthier, *Morals by Agreement*, p 25.

[10] Nozick, *The Nature of Rationality*, p. 133. Cf., however, Scanlon, *What We Owe Each Other*, p. 69.

[11] Nozick, *The Nature of Rationality*, p. 64.

The most obvious interpretation of instrumental rationality might be called *Rationality as Effectiveness:*[12]

Alf's action φ is instrumentally rational if and only if φ-ing is an effective way for Alf to achieve his desire, goal, end, or taste, G.

However, Rationality as Effectiveness is both too narrow and too broad. To see how it is too narrow, suppose that Alf is a loyal viewer of the Weather Channel, which forecasts a clear day today. Alf, though, is very cautious, so he compares this with the forecasts of the National Weather Service with the Weather Underground. They concur; it is going to be a gorgeous day. On the basis of all this information, Alf goes out without an umbrella, gets soaked in a freak thunderstorm, ruins his Converse high-tops, and comes down with pneumonia. According to Rationality as Effectiveness, Alf's decision not to carry an umbrella was not rational; it was anything but an effective way to achieve his goals. More generally, Rationality as Effectiveness deems "not rational" any action that harms one's goals, no matter how diligent the agent was in getting information and hedging against risks. So any risky action – such as an investment – that turns out badly runs counter to rationality: it is irrational.

This cannot be right. Whether a risky action that turns out badly is irrational depends on, say, whether the agent took care to inform himself about the risk, whether he sought to minimize the risks, and so on. Rationality, including instrumental rationality, is a concept that concerns a person's cognitive processes and her choices about what to do, and so it cannot be reduced to simple effectiveness of action. This becomes even clearer when we consider the way in which Rationality as Effectiveness is too broad. Suppose Betty never bothers with weather forecasts of any sort but consults her Ouija board. On the day that Alf gets soaked, Betty's Ouija board instructed her to carry an umbrella, so she kept dry. Rationality as Effectiveness deems her action rational; after all, carrying the umbrella was an effective way to achieve her goal (of staying dry). But this really seems a case of dumb luck, not

---

[12] For another treatment of the issues I discuss here, see G. W. Mortimore, "Rational Action," pp. 96ff.

instrumental rationality. As Amartya Sen reminds us, the concept of rationality focuses on the relation of goals to choices among options: it asks, given your goals, "what is the rational course of action to choose?"[13] Our concern is the quality of the choice about what to do, not simply the effectiveness of what is done. Of course, to choose an option is still to do something; it is to buy the Honda rather than the Ford, or to go out to dinner rather than order a pizza to be delivered. But when we evaluate the rationality of what is done, our focus is not on the actual consequences of what is done (whether, in the end, the action secured the person's goals), but whether, when she chose that action over the alternatives, it was the one that, given her beliefs, had the best prospects for satisfying her goals. To say that action ϕ had the best prospects for satisfying a person's goals is not to say that in the end it did satisfy them best, but at the time of choice, given what the person believed, it was her reasonable expectation that ϕ was the best action available to her.

The inadequacies of Rationality as Effectiveness have led some to adopt a purely subjective test of rational choice, as in Subjective Rationality:

Betty's action ϕ is instrumentally rational if and only if when she chose ϕ

(*i*) her choice was based on her beliefs (β);

(*ii*) *if* β were true beliefs, ϕ-ing would have best satisfied her desire, goal, end, purpose, or taste, G.

Alf believed that it would not rain, so Subjective Rationality deems Alf's action instrumentally rational even though he was soaked despite all his precautions; *if* he was right that it was not going to rain, *then* his action would have achieved his goals. So Subjective Rationality absolves Alf from irrationality, and that seems correct. But Subjective Rationality also implies that Betty was rational when she consulted her Ouija board; indeed, according to Subjective Rationality, Betty would be instrumentally rational even on those days when she consults her Ouija board and it tells her *not* to carry an umbrella – and she gets thoroughly soaked. After all, *if* her beliefs about the accuracy of Ouija boards were true, then doing

[13] Amartya Sen, "Choice, Orderings and Morality," p. 55.

what they say *would be* an effective way to pursue her goals. Despite this rather odd implication, subjectivist theories of rationality have appealed to many. And we can see why. If we take Betty's beliefs as given, then we can see her *reasons* for carrying an umbrella, even though they are not *good* reasons for doing so. Insofar as our only concern is to make Betty's choice to carry her umbrella intelligible,[14] we can understand her action as displaying a sort of "instrumental rationality." We can see what she was trying to accomplish in acting as she did.

Although thoroughly subjective theories of instrumental reasoning have their attractions in social scientific explanation, almost all attempts to develop the idea of rational action have sought to justify some constraints on what constitutes reasonable beliefs that underlie an instrumental choice.[15] An account of instrumental rationality must build in some reference to the well-groundedness of the beliefs on which the agent acts.[16] Consider one of Sigmund Freud's most famous cases – that of "Little Hans." Little Hans "refused to go out into the street because he was afraid of horses."[17] He believed that if he went out into the street, horses would bite him. Now *if* Little Hans' beliefs were correct, then his choice not to go on to the street would seem instrumentally rational – it makes sense to avoid getting bitten by horses. But Little Hans strikes us, as he did Freud, as not being rational, since Little Hans had no good reason to believe that horses *would* bite him if he went on to the street. Thus Freud set out to uncover why Little Hans believed such an odd thing. (Freud's conjecture was that Little Hans, desiring his mother, feared retribution from his father; Little Hans transferred his fear that his father would castrate him on to horses: they would, thought Little Hans, "bite" him.) If there is something irrational

[14] On the importance of intelligibility to economic explanations, see Alexander Rosenberg, *Philosophy of Social Science*.

[15] This is true even regarding those decision theorists who describe themselves as "subjectivists." As one of the most eminent subjectivists insists, "your 'subjective' probability is not something fetched out of the sky on a whim." Richard Jeffrey, *Subjective Probability*, p. 76.

[16] See further Jon Elster, "The Nature and Scope of Rational-Choice Explanation," pp. 60–72.

[17] Sigmund Freud, "Inhibitions, Symptoms and Anxieties," p. 254.

about Little Hans' choice not to go on to the street, there is something amiss with a purely subjective theory of instrumental rationality.

In our rather more mundane cases, Alf seems instrumentally rational when he does not wear a raincoat, even though he fails to achieve his goals, because his beliefs about the weather (on which he acted) were well grounded; Betty, even though she succeeds in achieving her goals, is not instrumentally rational because her beliefs about the weather are, from an epistemic point of view, terrible. And Little Hans is irrational because the horses will not bite him; and if he is afraid that his father will castrate him, avoiding horses will not help much. An adequate characterization of *Instrumental Rationality*, then, must go something like this:

> Alf's action ϕ is instrumentally rational only if Alf soundly chooses ϕ because he believes it is the best prospect for achieving his goal, values, end, *G*.

An agent who is instrumentally rational acts in light of his goals; his decision must be based on at least minimally sound beliefs (ones that are not grossly defective from an epistemic viewpoint), and the deliberation leading to action must not be grossly defective. I shall employ the admittedly vague ideas of a "good reason" and a "sound choice" to cover these minimal epistemic requirements.[18]

---

[18] Some resist this: they would like the theory of rational action to be independent from an account of rational belief (or at least they would like the account of rational action not to depend on an independent theory of what constitutes rational belief). Thus it is argued that rational belief is simply belief that advances one's ends. Little Hans' beliefs are irrational because avoiding horses is a singularly ineffective way to avoid being castrated by his father. Note that this proposal simply revives Rationality as Effectiveness by applying it to belief: the act of adopting a belief ϕ is rational if and only if it effectively achieves one's goals. This proposal, however, seems unappealing. It still is apt to identify the rational with dumb luck: suppose Little Hans' refusal to go out on the street so upset his father that his father left town, and left Little Hans alone with his mother. His beliefs about horses would turn out to be rational after all. Moreover, we seem to confront a troublesome regress. An instrumental reason to perform act ϕ presupposes a notion of sound (or rational, or justified) belief (β). Now, as a way of explaining rational belief, we simply are treating "believing β" as another rational action. But then, to evaluate the rationality of this "action" ("believing β") we still require some notion of a rational belief – we need to know whether it is rational to believe that believing β would advance one's goals. So suppose we accept φ –

4.3 THREE FUNDAMENTAL FEATURES OF INSTRUMENTAL
RATIONALITY

The canonical passage for the theory of instrumental rationality comes from Hume:

'Tis not contrary to reason to prefer the destruction of the whole world to the scratching of my finger. 'Tis not contrary to reason for me to chuse my total ruin, to prevent the least uneasiness of an Indian or person wholly unknown to me. 'Tis as little contrary to reason to prefer even my own acknowledg'd lesser good to my greater, and have a more ardent affection for the former than the latter.[19]

For Hume, our reason cannot tell us what to desire, so no desire can ever be against reason. Contemporary philosophers, however, often hedge Hume's thesis. Although Nozick acknowledges that "we have no adequate theory of the substantive rationality of goals and desires, to put to rest Hume's statement, 'It is not contrary to reason to prefer the destruction of the whole world to the scratching of my finger,'" he still seeks to take "a tiny step beyond Hume"[20] by identifying some rational limits on desires, goals, and so on. Others have more ambitiously maintained that there is room within a Humean account for a theory of rational ends.[21] I shall put aside this well-rehearsed debate.[22] For our purposes, three other features of an intuitively appealing account of instrumental rationality are of importance.

---

the belief that believing β advances one's goals. Then, however, we must consider the rationality of embracing φ – does believing it effectively advance one's goals? Further appeals to the general criterion of effectively advancing one's goals will merely lead to new levels of regress of rational justification. For a strenuous recent defense of this view, see Guido Pincione and Fernando Tesón, *Rational Choice and Democratic Deliberation: A Theory of Discourse Failure*, chap. 2.

[19] David Hume, *A Treatise of Human Nature*, Book II, Part iii, §3.

[20] Nozick, *The Nature of Rationality*, pp. 63, 148.

[21] See, for example, David Schmidtz' notion of a "maieutic end." *Rational Choice and Moral Agency*, pp. 60–6.

[22] I consider some of the proposals in *Philosophy, Politics, and Economics*, chap. 1.

(a) More Is Better than Less

In Hume's canonical passage, he not only indicates that reason cannot select goals, he tells us that "'Tis as little contrary to reason to prefer even my own acknowledg'd lesser good to my greater, and have a more ardent affection for the former than the latter." To be sure, this remark is open to different interpretations, but if we take it to mean that, when choosing between quantity p of one's goal, or good, G and quantity q of G, where $p > q$, then Hume's preference does look irrational. As Russell Hardin puts it, "[t]he simplest definition of rationality . . . is that one should choose more rather than less value."[23] If G is one of Alf's goals or ends, and he is faced with a simple choice between the satisfaction of G to degree p or the satisfaction of a G to level q, and p is greater than q, to choose qG would be to choose less value over more.

More is better than less is closely related to the idea of *dominance* reasoning. If option A includes all the goods or goal satisfaction of option B, plus additional goods, then it must be instrumentally rational to choose A, and irrational to choose B. Imagine that Betty is an instrumentally rational agent; she values Australian wine of a certain winemaker and vintage, and she is confronted with a choice: for $25 she can have either one bottle or two bottles of that wine and vintage. And suppose she chooses one bottle over two. We can think of a variety of reasons she might do this. Perhaps she is drinking too much wine these days, and knows that she'll drink both bottles right off, something of which her doctor might not approve. Or perhaps she is riding her bike home and really can't carry a second bottle. Note, though, that explanations like these appeal to some other goal (health) or constraints (the second bottle cannot be transported, and so cannot be consumed). These other considerations make sense of what seems to be an irrational choice: a choice for less rather than more of a something she values. Imagine, though, that confronted with the choice between one or two bottles of her favorite wine she simply chooses the one, saying she desires less of what she values to having more of it. A sign that we are confronting an irrational desire here is that it seems

[23] Russell Hardin, *Indeterminacy and Society*, p. 16.

unintelligible why someone would want that; we need to tell more of a story to make her choice sensible to us.

(b) Modular Rationality

On the standard, intuitively compelling, formulation of the instrumental theory, actions are understood as causal routes to goal satisfaction. Hobbes presents a picture of human thoughts and action as regulated by "some desire and design." On his view we possess two capacities for causal reasoning that allow us to reason instrumentally in achieving our ends. First, we share with animals an ability to imagine an effect or result that we seek and then infer the causes that will bring it about; second, we have a distinctive human capacity to take a thing and imagine all the effects it can produce (and so we can understand something as an instrument to produce various effects).[24] Now what this means is that because an instrumentally rational agent views her actions as routes to the satisfaction of goals, her reasoning is inherently forward-looking; at any point in time she has a set of goals, and employs her reasoning to see what causal paths are open to her to satisfy them. Deliberation appears to be not about what occurred in the past, but about how the desired results can be brought about in the future.

I say "appears" because this is not quite right. We must allow that an instrumentally rational person sometimes ϕs at time t because doing so directly right here and now satisfies her goals. Say, for example, that Betty is eating ice cream and she explains her behavior by proclaiming "I like ice cream." Now a hedonist – someone who believes that all action is aimed at producing pleasant mental states – might explain Betty's action by saying that it was an instrumentally effective way of achieving pleasure, and the pleasure came a wee bit after the ice cream was eaten. If pleasure is the sole end, and if we are constructed in ways such that we always pursue pleasure and avoid pain, then indeed all action is instrumental to experiencing the mental state of pleasure or avoiding that of pain. However, if we reject hedonism and allow that an instrumentally rational agent may entertain a wide variety of goals,

[24] Hobbes, *Leviathan*, p. 13 (chap. 3, ¶¶4–5).

this interpretation of Betty's ice cream eating is strained. In general, what we might call "direct consumption" activity is noninstrumental; if ϕ is a consumption activity, it is not usefully understood as a way to achieve some goal that is distinct from ϕ. This is an important, but often ignored, point. Suppose a person has a desire for an ice cream cone; she ate one. We do not want to say that her decision to eat the ice cream cone *aimed* at "satisfying her desire for an ice cream cone" as if there was a distinct thing called a "desire to eat the ice cream cone" which her eating somehow assuaged – as if it was a itch that she sought to get rid of.[25] On this "itch" theory of desires, we perform acts that satisfy desires because we actually have the aim of getting rid of the desire. But the itch theory seems wrong, at least as a general account of desiring. Perhaps, if she is on a diet, Betty would prefer to buy a pill for $1, which eliminated her itch (her desire for ice cream), rather than spend $2 for an ice cream cone. But if desires were simply itches, then an "itch elimination pill" that was less costly than obtaining the good that would assuage the desire would, generally, be the best option. But in almost all cases, what we want is the *desired thing*, not the elimination of the itch for it. In the overwhelming run of cases, Betty does not eat the ice cream cone to get rid of her "itch" to eat the ice cream cone: she ate the ice cream cone because she likes ice cream cones. The "aim" of her eating the ice cream cone was, well, to eat an ice cream cone.

This, however, raises the specter of entirely vacuous explanations of people's actions. We see Betty ϕ-ing (eating the ice cream cone) and we "explain" it by saying that "Betty's goal is to ϕ (eat the ice cream cone), so ϕ-ing (eating the ice cream cone) satisfies her goal." But now that which is doing the explaining (Betty has a goal to ϕ) and that which is to be explained (Betty ϕ-ed) look as if they are the same thing. The worry is that this ends up as a vacuous explanation: we observe that someone does something and we explain it by saying it is her goal to do that, and the very action which is the goal satisfies the goal. This looks far too much like

---

[25] I consider the inadequacies of this account of desire in some depth in *Value and Justification*, pp. 85–8.

saying that she does it just because she wants to do it. But since it is generally thought to be an analytic truth that if one does something, one wants to do it, it doesn't look like we have explained anything at all.

Although it is tempting to revert back to a thoroughly instrumentalist account and say that the "aim" of our action is to "satisfy" our desire to perform that very action (so it is not really the action we value, but the satisfaction of a desire to which performing the action is a mere causal route), we can solve the problem without resorting to the implausible itch theory of desires. Betty's specific act, ϕ, can be genuinely *explained* (as opposed to merely restated) if it is an instance of a general disposition to Φ, or engage in Φ-type acts – that is, a disposition, or goal, to engage in actions of a certain *type*. Thus, for instance, when Betty explains eating ice cream cones by saying, "I like them," this counts as an explanation if Betty is generally disposed to eat ice cream cones – if her goal is to generally eat ice cream, and this is a case of doing so. The explanation here is one of token and type, or specific instance and general kind. Now this sort of explanation is not altogether empty. Consider:

Explanandum: (1) Betty ϕs.

Explanans: (2) Betty's reason for ϕ-ing (in this instance) is that she likes Φ-type.

In this case what is doing the explaining is not a restatement of the thing to be explained; the specific act is explained by showing it to be *an instance of a general type*. Again, one may be tempted to reduce this to an instrumental explanation: Betty ϕs as a way to bring about her goal of Φ-typing. But this really is to get the relation of the specific act and the general type wrong: ϕ-ing is not a means to Φ-typing, it is an instance of it. We must, then, complement the idea of instrumental rationality with what I shall call *Direct Consumption Rationality*:

Betty's action ϕ is "consumptively rational" only if it is an instance of Φ-type – a general desire, value or end of hers.

With this necessary amendment we can say that the instrumentally rational agent is concerned with her options from *right now and into the future*. At each moment in time she confronts a world offering the possibilities for goal satisfaction, and employs her reasoning to determine the preferred paths to it (though she may now be exactly at a point to engage in a bit of direct consumption).

We can formalize this basic idea in terms of the requirement that the plans of an instrumentally rational actor must conform to *modular rationality*.[26] We can think of a person confronting a large decision tree as she moves through her life; at time t_0 she may form a plan P about future decisions. Now a constraint on P is that at t_1 it does not commit her to choosing paths that violate the principle that "more is better than less" from t_1 onward. Once she has reached t_1 her sole concern is to choose actions that, from t_1 onward yield the most goal satisfaction; what happened at t_0 is irrelevant to her choice except insofar as it affects her prospects at t_1. Once she reaches t_2, her sole concern is to choose a course of action that, from t_2 onward, best satisfies her goals. Since she knows all of this at t_0, she will not adopt a plan at t_0 that requires her to choose less rather than more at t_1 or t_2. The upshot of this is that a rational plan must be modular: at every point the plan must instruct the agent to perform the instrumentally rational act. A quintessential nonmodular plan was the nuclear strategy of Mutually Assured Destruction. At t_0 the plan looks attractive; if one threatens total destruction of the world, then it is likely the other side will not attack, and so there will be peace, which satisfies one's goals. But should the other side attack at t_1 the plan commits you at t_2 to launching your bombs with no prospects of doing any good (since the sole good from the threat was deterrence, which at t_1 failed). At t_2 one would be choosing (far) less over more value if one launched. Thus Mutually Assured Destruction was not modularly rational.

(c) Consistency

Once we accept that an instrumentally rational agent is one who chooses more value over less, we begin to see her as an intelligent and intelligible pursuer of value. But unless her instrumental choices are consistent in some very basic ways, we cannot view her in this light.

---

[26] See Brian Skyrms, *Evolution of the Social Contract*, pp. 24ff.

Since we are talking about the relation between choices, we can usefully employ the idea of *preference*. The core preference relation is the general or weak preference relation, *R*, where *xRy* is to be read as "*x* is at least as good as *y*." We can say that if *xRy* and not *yRx*, then *xPy* – *x* is strictly preferred to *y*. If *xRy* and *yRx*, then *xIy* – *x* is indifferent to *y*. Now if Alf is even the most minimally consistent chooser, it must be the case that if, say, he strictly prefers shiraz to cabernet sauvignon, it must be the case that he does *not* strictly prefer cabernet sauvignon to shiraz. If someone strictly prefers a shiraz to cabernet sauvignon *and* cabernet sauvignon to shiraz we cannot even understand what his preferences are.[27] Alf's strict preferences thus must be *asymmetric*: ¬[i.e., not] (*xPy* & *yPx*). In contrast, if Alf is indifferent between cabernet sauvignon and shiraz, he is also indifferent between shiraz and cabernet sauvignon; indifference, therefore, must be *symmetric*: (*xIy*) if and only if (*yIx*). Even more basically, if Alf is any sort of consistent chooser his preferences must be *reflexive*: shiraz must be at least as good as shiraz (*xRx*). More interesting but more controversial, there is a strong case that Alf's strict preferences must be transitive. If Alf prefers shiraz (*x*) to cabernet sauvignon (*y*), and cabernet sauvignon to merlot (*z*), then it would seem that a consistent chooser of more value over less must prefer shiraz to merlot. So *xPy*, *yPz* implies *xPz*. (Many also hold that indifference should also be transitive: [*xIy*] & [*yIz*] implies [*xIz*].)

The transitivity requirement has been subject to debate.[28] Perceptual judgments, for example, do not always conform to the

---

[27] Benn and Mortimore, "Technical Models of Rational Choice," p. 163.

[28] See, for example, Stuart Rachels, "Counterexamples to the Transitivity of Better Than"; Alex Voorhoove, "Heuristics and Biases in a Purported Counterexample of the Acyclity of 'Better Than.' "In their "Technical Models of Rational Choice," S. I. Benn and G. W. Mortimore argue that rationality does not require transitivity. For a discussion of the weaker requirement of "quasi-transitivity," see Amartya Sen, *Collective Choice and Social Welfare*, pp. 14–16. Some have responded to doubts about the transitivity requirement by invoking once again the idea of instrumental rationality, providing an instrumental justification for the transitivity axiom via the "money pump" argument. Suppose Betty has the following preferences: (shiraz *P* cabernet sauvignon), (cabernet sauvignon *P* merlot), (merlot *P* shiraz). Suppose she starts out with a bottle of merlot. If she strictly prefers cabernet sauvignon to merlot, she must be willing to trade her merlot and some amount of money (say, 1¢) for the cabernet sauvignon. She makes the trade. Since

transitivity of indifference; I may not be able to tell the very tiny difference between x and y, or the tiny difference between y and z, but I might be able to tell the difference between x and z, and so we may get (xIy) & (yIz) but also (xPz). Transitivity of strict preference is much more compelling, although there are deep philosophical issues involved in distinguishing intransitive preferences from fine-grained or conditional preferences.[29] Along with more is better than less, the asymmetry of strict preference and the reflexivity of strict preference are constitutive of our conception of a fully rational agent. Failure to recognize relations of transitivity is characteristic of schizophrenics;[30] those disposed to blatantly ignore transitivity are unintelligible to us; we cannot understand their pattern of actions as sensible ways to promote their values.

5 Revisionist Theories

5.1 THE PRISONERS' DILEMMA AS A MODEL

Suppose Alf and Betty are purely instrumentally rational agents, each committed to his or her own scheme of values, goals, ends,

---

she strictly prefers shiraz to cabernet sauvignon, she must be willing to trade her new bottle of cabernet sauvignon (and, 1¢) for the shiraz. She makes this trade too. But since she prefers merlot to shiraz, she must be willing to trade her shiraz and 1¢ for the merlot. Note that she has back her original bottle of merlot, but is three cents poorer. And of course she can be made to go around and around, ending each cycle with her original merlot (poor thing) but always a little poorer for it. So, it is said, we can see an instrumental or pragmatic justification for the transitivity axiom: agents who reject it could not possibly achieve their goals. The money pump argument depends on the "more is better than less" axiom: more money is better than less. If one is committed to "more is better than less," then one should endorse transitivity of strict preference. Rather than, as it is often put, being a "pragmatic" argument that shows people why they should endorse transitivity, it shows that transitivity is closely bound to more is better than less: if one rejects transitivity one may end up choosing less over more.

[29] If a person chooses x over y, and y over z, and then chooses z over x, this seems manifestly intransitive, but only if we specified the preferences with just the correct degree of precision. Suppose "choosing x when y is the alternative" and "choosing y when z is an alternative" are discrete preferences; in this case choosing z over x need not be intransitive. For a subtle discussion see Broome, "Rationality and the Sure-Thing Principle."

[30] Michael Argyle, *The Psychology of Interpersonal Behavior*, third edition, p. 211.

and so on. These schemes may or may not be focused on promoting his or her interests. What is important is that each pursues his or her own goals and does not seek directly to promote those of the other, and that based on these goals, each can rank the outcomes that can be brought about through his or her own choices conjoined to the other's. Alf and Betty face a *strategic* situation: what she should choose depends on his choices and vice versa. Each seeks to make the best response to the choice of the other. The most famous (perhaps at this point infamous) strategic situation in philosophy is, of course, the Prisoners' Dilemma, presented in ordinal form (high numbers indicate most preferred outcomes) in Display II-1.[31]

Betty

		Cooperate	Defect
Alf	Cooperate	3 3	4 1
	Defect	1 4	2 2

DISPLAY II-1 THE PRISONERS' DILEMMA IN ORDINAL FORM

[31] To recount the all-too-familiar story: Two suspects, Alf and Betty, have been arrested by the police. The police have enough evidence to convict both on a relatively minor charge. If convicted of this charge – and the police can obtain a conviction – each will get two years in prison. The police, however, suspect that Alf and Betty acted together to pull off a bigger crime but the police have inadequate evidence. They make the following offer to Alf (the same offer is made to Betty). "Turn state's evidence against Betty, and we'll let you go free; we'll demand the maximum penalty for Betty, so she will get twelve years. If Betty confesses too, we're not going to let you both free: you'll each get ten years. However, if you keep quiet and she confesses, we'll let her go free, and you will be the one to get twelve years. But if neither of you confesses to the bank job, we won't have enough evidence to prosecute. We will then proceed with the lesser charge, and you'll get two years each." Alf reasons: "If Betty confesses, and I keep quiet, I'll get twelve years; if Betty confesses and I confess too, I'll get ten years; so I know one thing: if Betty confesses, I better confess too." What if Betty keeps quiet? Alf reasons: "If Betty keeps quiet and I keep quiet too, I get two years; if Betty keeps quiet and I confess, I go free. So if Betty keeps quiet, I do best by confessing." But now Alf has shown that confessing is a dominant strategy: no matter what Betty does, he does best if he confesses. And Betty will reason in a parallel way; she will conclude that no matter what Alf does, she does best by confessing. So they will both confess, and get ten years. Hence the (sole) equilibrium outcome is strongly Pareto-inferior to the nonequilibrium outcome {keep quiet/keep quiet}.

The Prisoners' Dilemma is the quintessential case in which faultless individual reasoning leads to outcomes that are worse for each
than some other alternative. Given their ordering of the outcomes,
for each the best response to any choice of the other is to defect.
Defecting is the *dominant strategy*: no matter what the other does, it
is one's best response. If Alf and Betty each pursue their dominant
strategy, both will defect, giving each his or her third highest (i.e.,
second-worst) outcome. *In the Prisoners' Dilemma, what is rational to
do leads to a strictly Pareto-inferior result*: both could be better off by
adopting some other strategy. This, though, means that two fully
rational people with complete knowledge of their situation will
both fail to best pursue their goals, values, and so on. Note that
according to Rationality as Effectiveness (§4.2), two fully rational
individuals under full information simply could not reason
themselves to this outcome: it does not effectively promote their
ends. So tight is the connection between being rational and best
achieving your goals that many insist that there is a more comprehensive notion of instrumental rationality that would direct us to
cooperate in the Prisoners' Dilemma. (I take up two such proposals
in §§5.2–5.3.)

Prisoners' Dilemmas are a model of precisely the type of social
interactions that, in Gauthier's eyes, requires the practice of morality.[32] Each has a reason to defect, and defecting is the best response
to the defecting of others (indeed, it is the best response to the
cooperation of others), yet if all defect everyone will do worse than
if no one defects. It is important to stress that the Prisoners'
Dilemma does not present us with a paradox. Given these
orderings, the assumption that the agents choose independently,
and there are no binding agreements,[33] there is one unequivocally
rational response to the choice of another: do not cooperate. As
Philip Pettit notes, "one of the firmest intuitions around is that
cooperating in a one-shot prisoners' dilemma is irrational."[34] Some
have denied this; the history of the Prisoners' Dilemma is filled
with attempts to show that it can be "solved" – that is, to show that

[32] As he notes in "Why Contractarianism?" p. 23n.
[33] It need not be assumed that the parties do not communicate.
[34] Pettit, "The Prisoner's Dilemma Is an Unexploitable Newcomb Problem," p. 123.

somehow faultless reasoning by individuals under these conditions will lead them to cooperate. The remainder of this section reviews the most important proposals. Throughout I stress two points. (*i*) Although they often proclaim their devotion to the ideal of instrumental rationality, each seeks to modify it by abandoning at least one of the fundamental features of instrumental rationality (§4.2). (*ii*) Each is ultimately implausible.

5.2 "VOODOO DECISION THEORY"

The heart of the problem with the Prisoners' Dilemma is *dominance* reasoning (§4.3*a*): Alf looks at Betty's possible choices and concludes that no matter what choice she makes, he would do best by defecting. So if one can somehow undermine dominance reasoning as the rational thing to do, one can perhaps show that cooperation is rational even given the payoffs in Display II-1. Thus the relevance of the debate on whether the Prisoners' Dilemma is really a Newcomb problem; here too people have seen a case against causal-dominance reasoning.[35] In the Newcomb problem an agent confronts a situation with two boxes. The first box is clear, and the agent can see that it contains one thousand dollars; the second is opaque. The agent can choose to take the contents of one box or both. So far it is an easy choice – rely on dominance reasoning and take both boxes, so assuring oneself of at least a thousand dollars, plus whatever is in the opaque box. However, the agent also knows that an extremely reliable predictor has put the money in the boxes. She has put a million dollars into the opaque box if and only if she predicts you will choose it alone; if she predicts that you will choose both, she has left the opaque box empty.

According to Nozick's important analysis,[36] if one employs a simple principle of expected utility the agent will just calculate the utility of each option's possible outcomes, weighted by their likelihood, and then add these up. Since, however, the outcomes are

---

[35] See David Lewis, "Prisoner's Dilemma Is a Newcomb Problem," and Philip Pettit, "The Prisoner's Dilemma Is an Unexploitable Newcomb Problem."

[36] See Nozick, *The Nature of Rationality*, pp. 43ff; Robert Nozick, "Newcomb's Problem and Two Principles of Choice."

not necessarily probabilistically independent of the action the agent performs (this is the real sticking point), a more adequate evidentially expected utility principle calculates the expected utility of actions by taking account of the conditional probabilities of the outcomes, given that the agent performs that action. Now, Nozick famously argued, an agent employing an evidentially expected utility principle will reason that given the information about the predictor, the probability of getting a million dollars conditional on choosing both boxes (the dominant choice) is extremely low, whereas the evidential expected utility of taking only the opaque box is high, so the evidentially expected utility principle recommends choosing only the opaque box. This seems counterintuitive to those moved by dominance reasoning; after all, at the time of choice, the million dollars is either in the opaque box or not, and so the agent's decision to take one or two boxes at that time cannot affect what is in them. So why not still take both? We seem to be torn between two different ways of connecting outcomes and actions: a causal connection supports dominance reasoning and taking both boxes, and evidential connection indicates that one ought to take only one box.

David Lewis argued that the Prisoners' Dilemma has the same structure. (It seems that some, not all, Prisoners' Dilemmas are truly Newcomb problems, but this need not detain us here.)[37] Lewis advances a version of the Prisoners' Dilemma/Newcomb problem, which, he thinks, shows them to be the same problem:

You and I, the "prisoners," are separated. Each is offered the choice: to rat or not to rat. . . . Ratting is done as follows: one reaches out and takes a transparent box, which is seen to contain a thousand dollars. A prisoner who rats gets to keep the thousand. (Maybe ratting is construed as an act of confessing and accusing one's partner, much as taking the Queen's shilling was once construed as an act of enlistment – but that is irrelevant to the problem.) If either prisoner declines to rat, he is not at all rewarded; but his partner is presented with a million dollars, nicely packed in an opaque box. (Maybe each faces a long sentence and a short sentence to be served consecutively; escape from the long sentence costs a million, escape from the

---

[37] Jorden Howard Sobel, "Not Every Prisoner's Dilemma Is a Newcomb Problem."

shorter sentence costs a thousand. But it is irrelevant how the prisoners propose to spend their money).[38]

Thus we have Display II-2 (again, high numbers indicate most preferred outcomes). Note the ordering of the payoffs (in square brackets) is the same as in Display II-1: we have a Prisoners' Dilemma. As Lewis sees it, each player in a Prisoners' Dilemma is in a Newcomb problem. On the one hand, in both the standard Newcomb problem and its Prisoners' Dilemma version, Alf has no causal control over what Betty will do, so no matter what she does Alf does best by taking both boxes/ratting. But Alf has strong rea-

		Betty	
		Cooperate *(keep quiet)*	*Defect* *(confess)*
Alf	*Cooperate* *(keep* *quiet)*	[3] Betty gets 1,000,000 Alf gets 1,000,000 [3]	[4] Betty gets 1,001,000 Alf gets 0 [1]
	Defect *(confess)*	[4] Betty gets 1,001,000 Alf gets 0 [1]	[2] Betty gets 1,000 Alf gets 1,000 [2]

DISPLAY II-2 THE PD AS A NEWCOMB PROBLEM

on to suspect that if he takes the dominant strategy, he will do worse than he would by just taking one box/cooperating. After all, Alf has strong reason to suspect that Betty will reason as he does, so his conclusion that he should defect is evidence that Betty will, and this affects his conditional probabilities concerning possible

---

[38] Lewis, "Prisoner's Dilemma Is a Newcomb Problem," pp. 251–2.

outcomes. Alf takes his own reasoning as showing something about what Betty, his replica, will do, and he sees this as evidence about what will happen. It seems that Alf will not defect.

Brian Skyrms accurately, if not charitably, describes this as "voodoo decision theory": if Alf and Betty do cooperate, "their cooperation appears to be based on magical thinking, because each knows that his act cannot *influence* that of the other."[39] By Alf's supposing that (*i*) the probability of Betty's cooperating conditional on his cooperating is higher than simply (*ii*) the probability that Betty will cooperate, this solution to the Prisoners' Dilemma denies that the choices are truly independent: if I suppose that the other will do what I do, I thus can eliminate asymmetric outcomes as impossible.[40] But they *are* independent choices. Even if there is a correlation between what Alf and Betty do, this correlation is, as Skyrms says, "spurious": when Alf comes to make his decision it will have no effect on Betty's choice. His choice does not alter the probability that Betty will choose one way or the other because there is no causal connection between them.

5.3 REJECTING MODULAR RATIONALITY: ON BEING TIED TO THE PAST

(a) Instrumental Rationality as Effectiveness, Again

Let us continue analyzing one-play games with Prisoners' Dilemmas characteristics – games in which Alf's reasoning leads him to defect and pursue his own gains, and so produces a situation that makes him (and others) worse off. David Gauthier and Edward McClennen have been insistent that the Prisoners' Dilemma poses a problem only for the flawed, "orthodox," theory of rational choice,

---

[39] Brian Skyrms, *Evolution of the Social Contract*, p. 50.

[40] Christopher McMahon also advances a "solution" to the Prisoners' Dilemma that, roughly, involves eliminating asymmetric outcomes, though I think this is largely what I shall call a "preference-transforming solution" (§6.3). See his *Collective Rationality and Collective Reasoning*, chap. 1. Still, certain aspects of McMahon's "Principle of Individual Rationality" allow for Newcomb-problem-like reasoning to enter in, though he does not exploit this. See my "Once More Unto the Breach, My Dear Friends, Once More: McMahon's Attempt to Solve the Paradox of the Prisoner's Dilemma."

which accepts modular rationality (§4.3*b*). Once we see that the correct theory of instrumental rationality does not include a commitment to modular rationality, we will see that instrumental rationality alone can solve the problems of social cooperation. Gauthier tells a tale adapted from Hume to highlight the problem with the orthodox view:

My crops will be ready for harvesting next week, yours a fortnight hence. Each of us will do better if we harvest together than if we harvest alone. You will help me next week if you expect that in return I shall help you in a fortnight. Suppose you do help me. Consider my decision about helping you. I have gained what I wanted – your assistance. Absent other not directly relevant factors, helping you is a pure cost to me. To be sure, if I were to help you I should still be better off than had I harvested alone and not helped you, but I should be better off still if having received your help, I did not return it. This calculation may appear short sighted. What about next year? What about my reputation? If I do not help you, then surely I shall harvest alone in future years, and I shall be shunned by our neighbors. But as it happens I am selling my farm when the harvest is in and retiring to Florida, where I am unlikely to cross paths with anyone from our community.

Being rational persons, we both know this, the scenario I have sketched is one each of us can sketch – and each of us knows it to be true. It would be pointless of me to pretend otherwise. So you know that I would not return your help, and being no sucker, will therefore leave me to harvest my crops alone. Neither of us will assist the other, and so each of us will do worse than need be. We shall fail to gain the potential benefits of cooperation.[41]

The problem can be depicted as in Display II-3. My neighbor chooses at the diamond, I choose at the ovals; payoffs are ordered from 4 (best) to 1 (worst), first my neighbor's, then mine. The problem is that my neighbor knows the decision tree, and that I am modularly rational; once it is my turn to choose I will look to what decision will be best for me from here on into the future. If my neighbor helps, I do best by not helping (getting 4 rather than 3). If

---

[41] David Gauthier, "Assure and Threaten," p. 692. See Hume, *Treatise of Human Nature*, Book III, Part ii, §5.

my neighbor doesn't help, I do best by not helping (getting 2 rather than 1). As in the Prisoners' Dilemma my dominant strategy is not to help. My neighbor knows this, and so will not help; once again we are both stuck at a Pareto-inferior outcome.

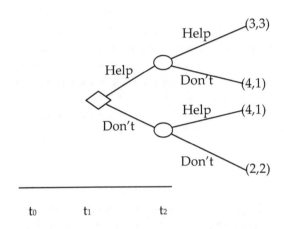

DISPLAY II-3 THE HUME–GAUTHIER ONE-PLAY HARVESTING GAME

Gauthier is convinced that an adequate conception of instrumental rationality cannot lead to this result. The aim of instrumental rationality is that one's life goes "as well as possible," but here it instructs one to do what does not make one's life go well. He writes:

> If a person's reasons take their character from her aim, then it is surprising and troubling if acting successfully in accordance with her reasons, she must sometimes expect to do less well in relation to her aims than she might. If my aim is that my life go as well as possible, and I act successfully in accordance with the reasons determined by that aim, then should I not expect my life to go as well as possible? If the orthodox account of the connection between the aim and reasons were correct, then sometimes I should not expect success in acting on my reasons to lead to my life going as well as possible.[42]

Notice that Gauthier is invoking a version of instrumental rationality as effectiveness (§4.2). For Gauthier, an action is "successful if

---

[42] David Gauthier, "Assure and Threaten," p. 694.

and only if at the time of performance it is part of a life that goes as well as possible for the agent." And he is clear that "an agent is primarily concerned with the outcome, and not the manner of her deliberations."[43] If someone follows what she sees as instrumental rationality and it is quite clear that in doing so she will not effectively achieve her goals, this shows that this was not truly the instrumentally rational thing to do. "[D]eliberative procedures are rational if and only if the effect of employing them is maximally conducive to one's life going as well as possible."[44] More important, perhaps, on this view it simply cannot be shown that fully and purely instrumentally rational people under full information may end up pursing a less desirable option, which makes their lives go less well. If they chose such an option when they were aware of the better one, it simply shows that they have not conformed to instrumental rationality.

(b) Intention-Action Consistency and the Pull of the Past

As Gauthier understands it, the problem in the Harvesting Game is that I want to be able to assure my neighbor that I will help him after he has helped me, for then he will help me, and I can get my harvest in. So (in Display II-3) I wish at time t_0 to form the intention to help him time t_2; if I do, I can give him a sincere assurance at t_0 that I will help him at t_2, and so he will help me at t_1. The problem is that at t_2 the rational thing for me to do (according to the standard view) is not to help him. But if I accept the standard view, I cannot form an intention at t_0 to help my neighbor at t_2, for I cannot at t_0 intend to do at t_2 what I know at t_0 I will not do. As I stressed above (§4.3*b*), modular rationality is a constraint on what plans it is rational to adopt. Consequently, I cannot offer my neighbor a sincere assurance, and so I cannot gain the fruits of cooperation.[45]

---

43 Ibid., pp. 700–701.
44 Ibid., p. 700.
45 Some readers will recognize, as does Gauthier, that this is Gregory Kavka's "Toxin Puzzle." See ibid., pp. 707–9. See also his "Rethinking the Toxin Puzzle" as well as Kavka's classic essay on "The Toxin Puzzle."

It seems, though, that I can form the sincere intention if I reject modular rationality. Suppose in Display II-3 I choose not at each node, but over courses of action "taken as a whole"[46] – in this case, I make one choice at t_0 for how I am to navigate the entire tree. If at t_0 I select help/help, I can form the intention to help at t_2; you know this, and will help me at t_1. Suppose at t_2 you have helped. Why should I now help you?

My reason [at t_2] cannot be that helping you will be part of a life that thenceforth will go best, for that is not the case. . . . My reason for helping you, it may therefore be proposed, is that helping you is part of the best course of action that I can choose to follow – part of the course of action that makes my life go as well as possible.[47]

Gauthier, though, is worried by an objector who presses why, at time t_2, should I actually act on the intention formed at t_0? If I am lucky enough to have received help at t_1, even if forming the sincere intention at t_0 was part of a plan to make one's life go as well as possible, surely what would make my life go as well as possible is *now* not to help (we can think of this as the resurgence of modular rationality).[48] Although it is often overlooked, Hobbes suggests a way out of this problem: if there are relations of consistency between the will at t_0 and the action at t_2, and if this consistency relation itself can provide a reason to act, then it is rational to act at t_2 in accord with one's intention at t_0. In Chapter V (on "Reason in General") of *Leviathan*, Hobbes characterizes theoretical reason in terms of a reckoning of the "consequences of general names"; irrationality involves "absurdity" – senseless speech arising out of a contradiction in the use of names. In Chapter XIV, Hobbes draws on this idea in explaining why one should keep one's word: an injustice arising out of a broken contract

is somewhat like to that in which in the disputations of scholars is called absurdity. For as it is there called an absurdity to contradict what one

---

[46] Gauthier, "Assure and Threaten," p. 695.
[47] Ibid., p. 695. Emphasis added, paragraph breaks deleted.
[48] Ibid., p. 695.

maintained in the beginning, so in the world it is called injustice and injury voluntarily to undo that from the beginning he had voluntarily done.[49]

Hobbes thus suggests a conception of rational action as intention–action consistency. If at time t_0 I will to help my neighbor at t_2 in return for his help at t_1, then I should help at t_2. If I do not help, it is as if my action at t_2 contradicted my will at t_0 and so I committed a sort of absurdity – declaring at t_0 my will to help at t_2 and then by my action at t_2 declaring that was not my will. If I did not understand my words at t_0 to indicate the state of my will at t_2, I "should not have let them run."[50] (Notice that Hobbes thus links this sort of absurdity in action to absurdity in speech, and so back to his core doctrine of reason.) To be sure, if there is some intervening event that greatly alters the situation, then my will can rationally change between t_0 and t_2, but if no new information arises between t_0 and t_2 such that, if I had the information at t_0 I would not have declared my will to help at t_2, then I am rationally bound by my declaration at t_0. "For that which would not hinder a man from promising, ought not to be admitted as a hindrance to performing."[51] By appealing to the criterion of intention–action consistency, Hobbes seeks to show the rationality of performing one's part of a covenant in the state of nature when the other party has already has done his part (another often overlooked doctrine of Hobbes).[52]

Although he takes Hume as his inspiration (and does not cite Hobbes' discussion), Gauthier provides a sophisticated development of Hobbes' (almost entirely neglected) proposal. The rationality of what I do now is tied to what I did in the past via some consistency or compatibility relation – what in the past I assured others I would do now. Now as Hobbes recognized, if rationality is tied to past decisions in this way, it is crucial to determine foolish from reasonable assurances: we would not want the rationality of our actions now to be tied to previous foolish assurances or

---

[49] Hobbes, *Leviathan*, p. 81 (chap. XIV, ¶7).
[50] Ibid., p. 83 (chap. XIV, ¶15).
[51] Ibid., p. 85 (chap. XIV, ¶20).
[52] See ibid., pp. 84–5 (chap. XIV, ¶¶18–20; see also ¶27).

statements about my future will.[53] Gauthier first suggests *The No Assurance Would Have Been Better Test*:

"[A]n assurance is foolish if the agent could expect to do better (though not necessarily best) were he to offer no assurance at all."[54]

In our One-Play Harvesting Game (in Display II-3) this seems like an obvious test. If I have been helped at t_1 and am trying to decide whether to act on my previous assurance, I realize that I would not have been in the position to get my second-best payoff had I not given the assurance, so giving the assurance made my life go better than it would have otherwise, and so was not a foolish assurance.

Consider, though, Gauthier's probabilistic Helping Game in Display II-4. You act at the diamond nodes, I act at the ovals (the lightning indicates a chance event); your utility is first, mine is second. The core of this game is that chance determines whether mutual assistance is advantageous to me. Ex ante, the expected utilities indicate that mutual help is advantageous to me. If we both help and the .8 event occurs, my expected utility[55] is 6.4 (8 × .8); if we both help and the .2 event does occur, my expected utility is 0 (0 × .2), for a total expected utility of 6.4. My utility when not giving the assurance is 5, so the expected utility calculations indicate that my life will go best if I give the assurance to help (6.4 > 5). But assume that the .2 event occurs; I receive zero utility, so my assurance fails The No Assurance Would Have Been Better Test as I would have received 5 had I made no assurance. Perhaps I should only have made a conditional assurance to help – only if the .8 event occurs do I assure you I will help. But that will not do, for then your expected utility from helping (10 × .8 = 8) is less than the utility you receive by not helping (9), so it is not rational for you to help. For you, helping is the rational thing to do only if I assure you

[53] Hobbes insists that the object of voluntary acts is good to oneself; if the assurance is harmful to oneself, we do not suppose that a person intended it. *Leviathan*, pp. 82ff (chap. XIV, ¶¶8ff.).
[54] Gauthier, "Assure and Threaten," p. 704.
[55] The expected utility of an act is the utility of its occurring times the probability that it will occur. Utility must be measured in cardinal terms to generate expected utility.

that I will help regardless of which event occurs (for then your total expected utility is 8 + [10 × .2] = 10). So it is rational ex ante for me to give an unconditional assurance, even though that can commit me (should the .2 event occur) to doing something that will make my life go worse than if I had not made an assurance.

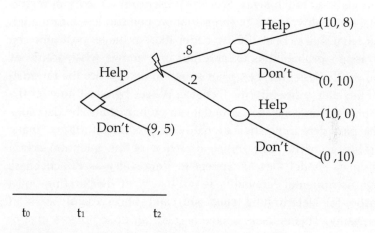

DISPLAY II-4 A PROBABILISTIC HELPING GAME[56]

Did I make a foolish assurance? Ex ante, it was an assurance that made my life go as well as possible; ex post, my life would have gone better if I had not made the assurance. Gauthier believes that we should be tied to ex ante reasoning. He is attracted to what might be called the *Ex Ante Rationality Test* to distinguish foolish from nonfoolish assurances:

When I come to consider whether or not to honor my assistance, I simply refer back to my previous deliberation; if I reaffirm my judgment that in the circumstances as I then knew them, it was rational for me to issue an assurance, then I conclude that I should honor it, even if the circumstances as I now know them are such that I should have in fact done better never to have given the assurance.[57]

[56] From Gauthier, "Assure and Threaten," p. 714.
[57] Ibid., p. 715.

As Gauthier realizes, this test can have somewhat odd consequences, from which he draws back at least in the case of threats.[58]
It could justify – on instrumental grounds – the destruction of the
world in the case of a failed deterrence threat, if at the time the
threat was issued it had the highest expected utility. But it is hard
to see how that would make one's life go better! It is odd for the
past to have so much sway over the present for a theory of instrumental rationality. In the ex ante situation, one had less information
about what makes one's life go better than in the ex post (one can
only assign probabilities ex ante but one knows what occurs ex
post), yet the less informed prior situation determines the rationality of the later, more informed, choice. We see here just how far the
intention–action consistency model can go in making the decisions
of the past determine the rationality of present efforts to "make
one's life go well." The initial attraction of the intention–action
consistency model was an appeal to Rationality as Effectiveness
(§4.2): instrumental rationality is not a way of deliberating but a
criterion for determining successful and unsuccessful ways of
deliberating. This is itself, I have argued, an unacceptable idea of
reasoning instrumentally. Indeed, it is not really a theory of
reasoning at all, but a criterion of goodness of action and reasoning:
that which best secures one's goals. Now, however, we see how
difficult it is for me to rationally achieve "mastery over my future
choices that enable me to give assurances" without committing me
to ignoring new and better information, the consideration of which
would, in the end, make my life go better. Upon reflection, though,
we see that ignoring information is fundamental to the entire
project of formulating the intention–action consistency model. It
must require us to ignore some current information – for example,
whether the other person has already done his bit. If we do not
ignore any current information about how to best promote our
ends we move back toward modular rationality.

Perhaps Gauthier just made the wrong choice – perhaps, that is,
he should have concluded that in the Probabilistic Helping Game it

---

[58] Gauthier ultimately recommends a theory in which assurances and threats are
treated differently.

is foolish to give an assurance because there is a possible assured helping outcome such that if it eventuates, one's life would have gone better if one had given no assurance at all. This suggests the *Ex Post Guaranteed Better Life Test*:

> An assurance is foolish if there is some outcome that can be produced by the assurance that is worse than some outcome the agent could have achieved if she offered no assurance at all.

The problem with this test is that, in a world where many outcomes have some nonzero chance of occurring, it is nearly equivalent with acting on the standard view of instrumental rationality (never giving assurances that rationally commit). Consider:

1. There is almost always some nonzero chance that the helping behavior will turn out badly. For example, when my neighbor helps me harvest, he may accidentally cut off some valued body part with his sickle. A bad assurance outcome.
2. There is almost always some nonzero chance that I can achieve what I wish without giving an assurance. Perhaps my neighbor is a closet Kantian, or he has mistakenly assumed that I gave him an assurance. A good nonassurance outcome.

Given (1) and (2) it will almost always be the case that there is some outcome that is produced by giving an assurance that is worse than an outcome that would have been achieved by not giving an assurance. To be sure, we can develop other tests of foolish assurances (e.g., a maximin test according to which the worst outcome produced by an assurance must be better than the worst outcome produced by not giving an assurance). We can see, though, that there is no obvious notion of what constitutes a foolish assurance once we abandon strict reliance on the ex ante perspective. But then we face the problem of being tied to a past in which we had less information about how to promote our ends than we now have.

I have considered Gauthier's proposal at length because some version of intention–action consistency rationality lies behind the most plausible attempts to show that following rules and pure instrumental rationality are consistent: we adopt rules ex ante as effective policies or plans to promote our ends, and then follow them because such a commitment to prior intentions is rational.[59] On the basis of instrumental rationality alone, we allow our ex ante intentions to override later deliberations based on modular rationality. The deep problem with such views is that locking us into ex ante choices, though designed as a way to overcome later temptations to cheat, also commits us to acting on less information than we presently possess in the pursuit of our goals.[60] That we made a great choice back then is not a good reason to follow through now when we know more. Gauthier's long project of developing an unorthodox theory of instrumental rationality floundered because he could not find a convincing way of tying our goal-promoting choices to the past without tying us to making our lives go less well than they might go.

The idea of "forming a plan" or "adopting policies" is to some extent a philosophical abstraction that often does not track well our efforts to promote our ends. We do not adopt a plan at one point, but form it slowly and constantly revise it, and there is seldom a clear distinction between an action that falls under a plan (and, so we are tied to past intentions to forgo modular rationality) and a choice outside of a plan (where, apparently, we can reason in the standard instrumental way). Adequate accounts of planning focus on the tentative and fuzzy nature of plans, but such plans are not good vehicles for resolute choices that insist that the intentions of the past must override clear opportunities to advance our ends now.[61]

---

[59] See, e.g., Edward F. McClennen, "The Rationality of Being Guided by Rules." See also David Gauthier, "Commitment and Choice: An Essay on the Rationality of Plans."

[60] For an insightful recent criticism of planning accounts of instrumental rationality, see Heath, *Following the Rules*, pp. 52–7.

[61] My comments here should not be read as applying to all theories of planning, especially those that have a more adequate account of intentions and when it is rational to reconsider them, as, for example, Michael Bratman's *Intentions, Plan and Practical Reason*. Compare Bratman's account of the Toxin problem (pp. 101–6) with Gauthier's (see note 45, this chapter).

6 Orthodox Instrumentalism

6.1 THE FOLK THEOREM

Thus far I have focused on attempts to show that an adequate conception of instrumental rationality can show that even in one-play Prisoners' Dilemma-like games, instrumentally rational individuals can achieve a cooperative, mutually beneficial, outcome. The interest of these attempts at "solving" one-play games is that they lead us to foundational issues concerning the nature of instrumental rationality. They seek to show that instrumentally rational agents could achieve cooperative results in these games because instrumental rationality is not what the orthodox view thinks it is. In understanding these attempts at revision, we come to better appreciate the core elements of instrumental rationality. I believe it is clear that these revisionist proposals have grave problems and offer no plausible way out of the noncooperative outcome of the Prisoners' Dilemma. I now turn to a more modest way of trying to solve problems of such mixed motive games in a world of instrumentally rational agents: repeated game analysis. The interest of this approach is just the opposite of our single-play analysis. Here the theorist adopts the standard analysis of instrumental rationality but holds that when we focus on repeated interactions, instrumentally rational people can achieve cooperation.

Robert Axelrod is widely understood to have shown that cooperation can emerge among "egoists" playing repeated Prisoners' Dilemmas.[62] To see this, assume that although you are in a Prisoners' Dilemma with Alf, both of you know that every day from here on in you will play one Prisoners' Dilemma after another. Axelrod has shown, using a computer simulation, that you often would do best by adopting a very simple strategy: tit-for-tat. According to tit-for-tat, your first move is the cooperative move. But if Alf defects rather than cooperates, the next time you meet Alf you will be uncooperative too. In short, except for the first move of the game, you decide whether to cooperate or act aggressively with

---

[62] See Robert Axelrod, *The Evolution of Cooperation.*

respect to any person by a simple rule: "I'll do to him this move whatever he did to me the last time we met." Essentially, a tit-for-tat player says to others, "If you defect on me in this game, you will get away with it, but I guarantee that in the next game I will defect, so that we will both be losers. But I am forgiving: if you start cooperating again, I'll begin cooperating again on the move after your cooperative move." Axelrod constructed a computer program specifying a game with hundreds of moves and a variety of actors employing different strategies. Some always act cooperatively no matter what others do, while some always defect. Each strategy played a 200-move game with each other strategy, making for over 100,000 moves: tit-for-tat won.

Many believe that tit-for-tat is somehow the correct strategy for all repeated Prisoners' Dilemmas, but this is not so.[63] Whether tit-for-tat is the correct strategy depends on the strategies of the other players. There is no single solution to an infinite (or indefinite) series of Prisoners' Dilemmas; indeed repeated Prisoners' Dilemmas have infinitely many equilibrium "solutions."[64] Two tit-for-tatters are, at least trivially, in a Nash equilibrium when cooperating in such a series. Remember, tit-for-tat cooperates on the first game in a series of Prisoners' Dilemmas, and then will do to its opponent on the nth game whatever its opponent did to it on the $n - 1$ game. So if one tit-for-tatter defects on the $n - 1$ game, the other tit-for-tatter responds by "punishing" the defector in the nth game. If one tit-for-tatter unilaterally defects from cooperation, the other tit-for-tatter will punish, and so lower the payoffs of the defector. Knowing this, neither tit-for-tatter can gain by unilateral defection, so they are in a Nash equilibrium. But it is not just two tit-for-tatters that are in equilibrium. Consider "the Grim strategy." Grim

[63] See Ken Binmore, *Natural Justice*, pp. 78ff.
[64] If the games are played for a definite number of times, such that we can know the end points of the trees, we can solve the game via the standard method of backward induction, in which case mutual noncooperation (mutual defection) strategies are the only strategies in equilibrium. There is controversy about whether backward induction and the associated idea of subgame perfection should be employed here. See my *On Philosophy, Politics, and Economics*, chap. 4. Russell Hardin argues that backward induction is a "cute" argument that leads to perverse results. *Indeterminacy and Society*, p. 25.

cooperates on the first move, but if its opponent defects, Grim will punish for every move after that – forever. Two Grim players are also in equilibrium: neither would benefit from defection. The important thing here is that punishing strategies can achieve equilibrium: if I can punish you from defecting from a cooperative interaction, repeated Prisoners' Dilemmas allow what are essentially "self-policing contracts" to cooperate. Since we are playing infinitely or indefinitely many games, I can afford to punish you to bring you around, and you will see that, and will not unilaterally defect. Indeed, any cooperative outcome that gives each player more (or, more formally, at least as much) as the minimum he might receive if the other player acted in the most punishing way can be an equilibrium: if we are each above this minimum point, then one party still has room to inflict punishment on the other for a deviation from the "contract." Thus the "minimax payoff" is the baseline: it is the payoff a person could get if her opponent treated the game as a zero sum game in which he was intent on making sure she got as little as possible. As long as the agreement (the coordinated payoffs) is above this minimum there is room for punishment, and so unilateral defection will not pay. Thus there will be a Nash equilibrium. This result is known as "the folk theorem."

Note we have "solved" the (one-play) Prisoners' Dilemma by turning it into a different game. Now the payoffs for the first Prisoners' Dilemma game with Alf include probabilities of future beneficial or costly interactions with him. Suppose Alf and Betty play a series of games with each other. It would seem that in the first game they have two concerns: (*i*) what is my best response to the other in this game and (*ii*) will my move in this game affect future prospects with this player? The second question shows us that their concern in deciding their present move is not focused simply on payoffs from this game. Alf's (and Betty's) present decision is affected by what some have called "the shadow of the future." But this means that they are not playing a straightforward Prisoners' Dilemma at all; that is why there is the possibility of cooperation among standard instrumentally rational agents.

6.2 REPUTATIONS

If instrumentally rational individuals, concerned simply with the best pursuit of their own goals, are to achieve social order and cooperation via the folk theorem, it is of the first importance for us to track what individuals have done to us in the past. While computers can be programmed to have perfect memories, when actual agents interact we face three problems. (*i*) We may forget what the person's past actions were. (*ii*) We may have misunderstood what the individual was seeking to do in the past; it is not always easy to distinguish a person who sought to cooperate but failed, or looked like she failed, from the genuine noncooperator. Or again, if we do not have many interactions with the same individual, her last interaction with us may be atypical, and so a poor guide to the future. Thus our individual information about the past behavior of others may be subject to mistakes, biases, and sampling error. (*iii*) Last, as society expands we are constantly meeting many people for the first time. In a large number of our interactions with others for the first time, a strategy such as tit-for-tat, which employs initial charity, may be quite risky. Saying "I'll cooperate now, but if you do not reciprocate I'll punish you next time" is less attractive if we are unsure whether there will be a next time. Sophisticated models indicate that tit-for-tat-like reciprocity allows the development of cooperation in small groups but not in larger ones.[65]

Because relying on our own individual tracking of others' cooperativeness has these serious drawbacks, an effective "iterated game" response to cooperation requires that we have more general knowledge of people's reliability as cooperators. Knowledge of people's reputations is essential for what we might call the practical application of the folk theorem. If you have a reputation for being untrustworthy I can punish you by declining (for a time) to cooperate with you. If there is general social knowledge of a per-

---

[65] See Peter J. Richerson and Robert Boyd, *Not by Genes Alone: How Culture Transformed Human Evolution*, pp. 199-201. For an analysis showing the difficulty for reciprocity developing when larger groups face iterated *N*-person Prisoners' Dilemmas, see Robert Boyd and Peter J. Richerson, *The Origin and Evolution of Culture*, chap. 8.

son's reliability, then our three problems of individual tracking can be mitigated; we need not keep track of all our own past interactions but simply know the person's overall reputation; our own biases and misunderstanding can be corrected by a much larger information pool that provides a larger sampling of a person's past interactions; and we have an idea whether to "punish" by refraining from cooperation even the first time we encounter a person. This is sometimes put as the contrast between "direct" and "indirect" reciprocity.[66] With direct reciprocity we keep track of our own interactions, and cooperate with those who have cooperated with us; with indirect reciprocity, we cooperate with those who have reputations as cooperators, even if we they have not yet cooperated with us. Indirect reciprocity demands far less tracking of past interactions, and so it seems applicable to larger groups.

Experimental evidence indicates that people do engage in indirect reciprocity. In one recent experiment people were randomly assigned the roles of donor and recipient; it was found that regardless of whether being a donor affected the person's own reputation, subjects donated more to those who were known as donors.[67] More interesting, perhaps, is Natalie Henrich's ethnographic research among the Chaldeans, a non-Arabic, Christian, ethnic group that emigrated from Iraq to the Detroit metropolitan area. The Chaldeans are a fairly large group – about 100,000 Chaldeans live in the Detroit area. Henrich's research indicates that intragroup cooperation is sustained both by direct and indirect reciprocity. Funeral expenses, for example, are paid for by mourners leaving money in envelopes with their names. Chaldeans keep records of these contributions; when the mourner herself dies, families will consult their records to determine how much she has contributed to funerals in their family, and leave the equivalent amount at her funeral.[68] This clearly brings out the demanding tracking requirements of direct reciprocity. Aside from weddings

---

[66] See Natalie Henrich and Joseph Henrich, *Why Humans Cooperate*, pp. 116–8. See also Richard Joyce, *The Evolution of Morality*, pp. 31–3.

[67] Dirk Engelmann and Urs Fischbacher, "Indirect Reciprocity and Strategic Reputation Building in an Experimental Helping Game."

[68] Henrich and Henrich, *Why Humans Cooperate*, pp. 118–20.

and funerals, keeping track of individual cooperative interactions is generally too difficult, so Chaldeans rely a great deal in their interactions on indirect reciprocity and reputations. As one subject reported:

> Everyone knows which families are good or bad, and you just do business with people who come from good families – I go by family name. If I don't know someone, I call people and ask about his family. People just mention who they are and [if they have a good reputation], they get credit.[69]

(I will return in point 6 below to the use of "markers" such as family and ethnicity in determining reputation.) Because the Chaldeans have social networks in which almost everyone is heavily enmeshed (family businesses, clubs, organizations, and churches), and because they have "a fondness for gossip," only a few calls are required to get information about the reputation of any potential participant in a business deal.[70] The costs of a bad reputation are quite severe. "Among Chaldeans, a person with a bad reputation is less likely to be given credit, to be hired, to be desired as a business partner, or be lent money. People will also not want to date or marry a person with a bad reputation and if they do so people will gossip about them."[71] The Chaldeans, then, are a case of a reasonably large group in which cooperation is to a large extent sustained by indirect reciprocity and knowledge of reputations.

Henrich and Henrich's analysis, however, also displays a number of pathologies and inefficiencies of social cooperation sustained through indirect reciprocity.

1. *Establishing a reputation: costs.* Individuals have an incentive to spend a great deal of time establishing their reputations as cooperators. It is not simply something that accrues from past behavior: it is an important goal to be advanced and shapes behavior. Henrich and Henrich report that at meetings in Chaldean organizations it is often impossible to accomplish much because most time is taken up by participants trying to show that they are responsible for successes

---

[69] Ibid., p. 123.
[70] Ibid.
[71] Ibid., p. 124.

and accomplishments. "During the meeting, the men self-aggrandized, repeatedly calling out their accomplishment and making certain that they would get credit from the group for everything that they had done."[72]

2. *Establishing a reputation: cooperation with noncooperators.* Because it is important that a person establish a generalized reputation as a cooperator, there is a significant incentive to ratchet up one's reputation in public arenas with a show of cooperative behavior even with noncooperators.[73]

3. *Establishing a reputation: conflict.* Conflict arises because of competition among individuals within groups, and between groups, to claim credit for accomplishments to bolster reputations. Groups and individuals are relatively less concerned with producing benefits that will not be publicly acknowledged, or cooperating with others when this will dilute reputational advantages.[74]

4. *Establishing a reputation: faking it.* Individuals exploit opportunities to gain reputations without contributing. If they join large groups in which it is impossible to track individual contributions, there is a tendency to free ride while claiming credit for group accomplishments. Individuals will also exploit opportunities to establish a reputation by public acts of generosity but refrain from private helping behavior (when this cannot be tracked).[75]

5. *Reputations are general.* To have a reputation as a cooperator is not simply about one's past tendencies to engage in certain well-defined cooperator behavior but is closer to a reputation as being a good group member, who conforms to the group's customs and norms. Thus one gains a "bad reputation" through divorce or letting one's children (let alone oneself) marry an African American. Because the bad reputation attaches to the entire family (see 6 below), there is a strong incentive for all members of the family to enforce

[72] Ibid., p. 128.
[73] Ibid., p. 126.
[74] Ibid., pp. 129–31.
[75] Ibid., pp. 125–31.

the requirements for a "good reputation." "[C]ooperation maintained through reputation (indirect reciprocity) can also maintain other costly norms – that have nothing to do with cooperation – once reputation is generalized beyond what happens in the indirect-reciprocity encounters."[76]

6. *The use of markers.* To reduce information costs in identifying character traits of individuals, there is strong evidence that an efficient response is to employ "markers" – overt characteristics that an individual possesses that have evidential value that he or she possesses a less easily observed trait (such as reliability). We saw that family membership may serve as such a marker; those who are members of families with good reputations are treated as having good reputations. And those in families with historically bad reputations are treated as having bad reputations, even if they have no such individual history. These markers are particularly apt to be associated with ethnic characteristics: overt public traits that one is a member of an in-group that, presumably, shares values with other members of that group.[77] Thus Chaldean cooperation is focused on other Chaldeans: there is considerable distrust of outgroup members. Chaldeans prefer to do business with co-ethnics, even at significant costs to themselves.[78]

All these are significant costs to social cooperation through indirect reciprocity. More important, though, it is unclear to what extent indirect reciprocity actually can sustain cooperation within large groups without intense social networks conveying reliable information.[79] Even among the Chaldeans, when real trust is required – for example, in hiring an employee whom you can trust "won't steal" – many tend to employ close kin. Overall, Chaldeans appear less trusting of their nonkin than do typical Europeans and North Americans.[80] The core problem remains: getting sufficient

---

[76] Ibid., p. 124.
[77] See Boyd and Richerson, *The Origin and Evolution of Culture*, Part 2.
[78] Henrich and Henrich, *Why Humans Cooperate*, pp. 193–6.
[79] See Robert Boyd and Peter J. Richerson, "The Evolution of Indirect Reciprocity."
[80] Henrich and Henrich, *Why Humans Cooperate*, p. 99.

reliable information about the trustworthiness of strangers. Peter Vanderschraaf has formally analyzed the conditions under which reputation alone enforces performance in covenants. Vanderschraaf focuses on what he calls "the covenant game," seeking to model Hobbes' and Hume's proposal that rational agents would not cooperate with those who have reputations as defectors, and this knowledge should itself provide a sufficient incentive for would-be defectors to refrain from double-crossing on covenants.[81] In his iterated "covenant game," one has a choice to (*i*) boycott the other party by refusing to make an agreement, (*ii*) promising-and-performing or (*iii*) promising-and-double-crossing; as in the Prisoners' Dilemma (which forms a subgame of Vanderschraff's more complex game), there is an incentive to double-cross rather than perform. The parties know that they would gain in the present stage by double-crossing but also may gain a bad reputation by double-crossing, and those with bad reputations would be boycotted in future stages of the game, and so would not gain in those stages the fruits of social cooperation. The novel and insightful idea in Vanderschraff's analysis is modeling types of information available to the parties. The folk theorem and many invocations of indirect reciprocity assume something like accurate common knowledge of the trustworthiness of potential partners; under this assumption, reputation effects can indeed secure cooperation. But public, accurate, common knowledge is seldom available – certainly it would not be in the state of nature! Vanderschraaf thus models information produced by gossip – individuals letting other individuals know what they think of certain parties. Vanderscraaf takes account of the effects of false gossip as well as true gossip. As we saw with the Chaldeans, there are strong incentives to exaggerate and fake one's cooperative history. Once we model information as gossip (true and false) and allow "Fooles" to adopt slightly more sophisticated strategies (such as only double-crossing half the time rather than always), Vanderschraaf shows that "Fooles can fare better than Humeans in a community that must rely upon private information or 'gossip' only to spread information." In a

[81] Peter Vanderschraaf, "Covenants and Reputations."

world of such imperfect information Vanderschraaf concludes that "Rationality alone does not explain reciprocal cooperation."[82]

6.3 PREFERENCE TRANSFORMATION ACCOUNTS

One final "solution" to the Prisoners' Dilemma must be considered. A long train of thought has tried to show that individuals in a Prisoners' Dilemma situation could reason in a way that, somehow, their deliberations would actually conform to a Stag Hunt (Display II-5) or an Assurance Game (Display II-6). Payoffs are given in ordinal utility, with 4 being the best result. In each of these games, there are two Nash equilibria: cooperate/cooperate and defect/defect. What strikes many as attractive about such games is that they indicate a preference for conditional cooperation: if Alf cooperates, then Betty prefers to cooperate, but if he does not cooperate, then she prefers not to cooperate (and, of course, vice versa). So we now have people who rank conditional cooperation most highly. I shall put aside the question of how individuals might reason their way into conceiving of the payoffs of a Prisoners' Dilemma as if it was one of these two games, or whether there is any sense in which individuals are still relying on instrumental rationality when they do so.[83] Rather, let us go directly to the heart of the matter: how much would it help if individuals were transformed such that what was once a Prisoners' Dilemma-type interaction becomes one with such conditional cooperators?

Betty

		Hunt Stag	Hunt Hare
Alf	Hunt Stag	4 / 4	3 / 2
	Hunt Hare	2 / 3	3 / 3

DISPLAY II-5 A STAG HUNT

---

[82] Ibid., p. 185.
[83] In my "Reasonable Utility Functions and Playing the Cooperative Way" I consider Nozick's similar "solution" to the Prisoners' Dilemma.

Betty

		Cooperate	Defect
Alf	Cooperate	4 / 4	3 / 1
	Defect	1 / 3	2 / 2

DISPLAY II-6 AN ASSURANCE GAME

Less than many think. Consider the Stag Hunt, suggested by Rousseau.[84] If Alf and Betty hunt together, they can catch a stag and have lots of meat; if each hunts hare alone, each can catch a hare and have enough to survive. But if Alf hunts stag and Betty "defects" by hunting hare, Alf goes hungry. When people first look at the Stag Hunt, they are apt to suppose that, of course, Alf and Betty will both hunt stag, for it is obviously best for each. How can two rational individuals not choose to do what is best for both? Rational individuals, however, are pulled in two directions: mutual benefit points to cooperating, but risk aversion points to hunting hare. Under some conditions it is remarkably easy to end up in social states in which everyone is hunting hare. Suppose first a very simple iterated game in which individuals randomly encounter each other, and suppose (cardinal payoffs) such that hunting hare has a payoff of 3 and getting a stag 4, but hunting stag alone gives a 0 payoff. If less than 75 percent of the population begins with hunting stag, the population will gravitate over time to all hare hunters; only if the initial stag hunting population is over 75 percent of the total will the group evolve into all stag hunters. To be sure, more sophisticated models that allow individuals to copy their successful neighbors can lead us reliably to an all stag-hunting population, though other strategies, such as making the best strategic response to one's neighbors, can still lead to a population of all hare hunters. The point is that while stag hunting may evolve, it

---

[84] See Brian Skyrms, *The Stag Hunt and the Evolution of the Social Structure*, p. 1. This paragraph follows Skyrms' analysis.

is by no means a forgone conclusion that it will, even if we all have been transformed into agents with Stag Hunt preferences.

If the conversion process is incomplete – if most but not all of us have adopted preferences such as those in Displays II-5 and II-6, so some remain unreformed Prisoners' Dilemma players – the prospects for social cooperation seem quite dim. Gregory Kavka introduced the game of an "Assurance Dilemma" to model interactions in a Hobbesian state of nature, according to which some agents have unreformed Prisoners' Dilemma orderings while others are reformed, more cooperative, Assurance Game orderings (as in Display II-7).[85] Assume that parties do not have perfect information about each other's preferences. When Alf encounters another, the question facing reformed Alf is whether he is playing another reformed, "nice," person (in which case he will be playing the game in Display II-6), or whether he is playing an unreformed "nasty" person as in Display II-7. Vanderschraaf has recently developed a far more sophisticated version of this game in which players have a range of possible payoffs (rather than just two types), and ways of estimating (based on past performance) what the payoffs of the other player are. Players are uncertain about the payoffs of others but have ways of learning and updating their probability estimate that the others are prone to attack. In computer simulations of anarchy under these conditions, Vanderschraaf finds that "[t]he presence of only a few 'nasty' individuals gradually drives all, including those inclined to be 'nicer,' to imitate the 'nasty' conduct of these few. This dynamic analysis suggests that the Hobbesian war in anarchy is indeed inevitable in most realistic circumstances."[86] Under conditions of imperfect information and a range of parties' preferences, the uncertainty created by the presence of a few unreformed agents (i.e., with Prisoner Dilemma-like preferences) leads to universal war (or defection).

---

[85] Peter Vanderschraaf reports this is Kavka's view on the basis of the latter's unpublished 1989 manuscript on "Political Contractarianism." See Vanderschraaf, "War or Peace? A Dynamical Analysis of Anarchy."
[86] Vanderschraaf, "War or Peace?," p. 245.

Charlie

(Unreformed)

		Cooperate	Defect
Alf(Reformed)	*Cooperate*	3 4	4 1
	Defect	1 3	2 2

DISPLAY II-7 THE ASSURANCE DILEMMA

Vanderschraaf's analysis is important as it illustrates a deep flaw in a long line of theorizing that has supposed that social cooperation emerges from people reasoning themselves into, or adopting, more cooperative preferences. It has often been thought that the core task in explaining the rise of cooperation is to show the reasonability of preferences for conditional cooperation. That is, at best, only the first step. Having a large majority of the population with preferences for conditional cooperation (such as in the Assurance Game) by no means guarantees social cooperation, or even makes it likely. Although we began with the Prisoners' Dilemma, with "nasty" preference orderings, we now see that the problem is not so much the character of the preferences but uncertainty about what others' preferences are. Even interactions that are "objectively" cooperative (i.e., under perfect common knowledge we would all see that we are conditional cooperators) may easily end up at noncooperative equilibria. Indeed, even under full common knowledge and cooperative preferences, cooperative equilibria are by no means certain; as Cristina Bicchieri stresses, first-order firm expectations about what others will do are required.[87] The problem of social cooperation cannot be resolved by individual instrumental rationality: a crucial element of the rise of social cooperation is a reasonable expectation that others will act in the cooperative manner. Social cooperation, as we are about to see, requires the firm social expectations provided by social rules issuing strong requirements.

---

[87] Cristina Bicchieri, *The Grammar of Society*, p. 37.

CONCLUSION

Instrumentalists have had two great insights: (*i*) that the very idea of a system of restraints needs to be justified and cannot be simply taken as given in the nature of things, and (*ii*) that this system can be justified on the grounds that it provides the framework for a mutually beneficial and cooperative social order, allowing us to overcome the temptation to defect in interactions that have Prisoners' Dilemma features. Their elegant idea was that all this could be done simply by appeal to the basic concept of instrumental rationality. If social morality allows us to better achieve our ends, it must follow that individuals concerned only with achieving their ends could reason their way to it. This elegant proposal has failed. Gauthier and others tried to implement it by revising the very concept of instrumental rationality, but in so doing the elegance and plausibility of their solutions was undermined. Those who sought to achieve it without abandoning the core elements of the instrumental idea had a variety of interesting ideas, but more sophisticated analysis shows that they are unable to support large-scale human cooperation. Instrumentalism has proposed a problem that it cannot solve in its own terms. As we are about to see, "deontological," rule-based reasoning that does not derive from instrumental reasoning – the bête noire of the instrumentalists – is required to solve the problem that they posed.

III

Social Morality as the Sphere of Rules

> [I]t is a condition of the existence of any form of social organization, of any human community, that certain expectations of behaviour on the part of its members should be pretty regularly fulfilled: that some duties, one might say, should be performed, some obligations acknowledged, some rules observed. We might begin by locating the sphere of morality here. It is the sphere of the observance of rules.
>
> P. F. Strawson, "Social Morality and Individual Ideal"

> Man is as much a rule-following animal as a purpose-seeking one.
>
> F. A. Hayek, *Rules and Order*

The instrumentalists have shown that social life among individuals devoted to diverse ends and values is permeated by interactions in which, if each person seeks to best promote her own goals, all will be worse off. It is again worth pointing out that for all its problems, the instrumentalist project is based on the insight that we no longer can be complacent that, of course, the restraints of morality are worthy of our respect, and, of course, we should submit to the authority of morality. Gauthier and his fellow instrumentalists grapple head-on with the foundationalist crisis of morality (§4.1). Social morality has a fundamental task to perform; unless we can put aside our instrumentalist optimization strategies, we cannot achieve a cooperative social life. But, we have seen, the instrumentalist cannot show (to use a currently popular phrase) how we can "bootstrap" effective constraints out of our goal-promoting reasoning. In this chapter I shall argue that social life requires social rules of a certain sort – moral social rules. My aim in this chapter is primarily to dispel what many have seen as the mystery about rule following, especially a case for rule following that seeks to show that it is necessary for a social life that benefits all. Some think it is mysterious how those who are devoted to their own ends could come to be devoted to rules that can thwart their ends. I will seek to dispel this mystery by showing how a society of rule followers may arise out of a group of individuals who are concerned only with promoting their own goals, without anyone trying to reason herself into being a rule follower. Others think it is a mystery how we could actually reason deontically, and how this way of thinking could pass muster as rational; I also seek to dispel these mysteries. I close the chapter by discussing the relation of moral rules to social rules.

Much of this chapter, then, is devoted to dispelling a pervasive skepticism about rule following, especially by those friendly to the instrumentalist project. But it also seeks to address those already convinced that "deontological" reasoning is fundamental to morality. Many of those who have broad sympathies with Kantian analyses of morality as fidelity to maxims capable of passing a test of impartiality often seek to take what might be called the "high road," of insisting that the correct analysis of morality has nothing to do with its social function, and recent experimental work in moral psychology can only tell us how people actually think about morality, not how they ought to. (The "is/ought" distinction comes heavily into play here.) Thus they seek to insulate their moral view from the messy empirical world of what morality does and how people think about it. I believe this is unfortunate. Kantian-inclined philosophers often give the impression of being unworldly, and making grand pronouncements about respecting others and following principles that are alien to human morality as we know it. In fact, I think just the opposite is the case; as Joseph Heath has recently argued in his excellent book, *Following the Rules*, actual moral reasoning as we know it is broadly "deontological" and the Kantian emphasis on fidelity to rules is central to it. The giants of the Kantian tradition, such as Kant himself and Rawls, were well aware that the beginning point of understanding "true morality" is "actual morality." It is that insight that I seek to develop in the next two chapters.

7 The Evolution of Rule-Following Punishers

7.1 WHAT RULES DO FOR US

In cooperative social orders, individuals obtain mutual benefits because they can generally count on each other to refrain from opportunistic cheating (such as defecting in Prisoners' Dilemma-type situations) and preemptive defection (as can easily occur in Stag Hunts, Assurance Games, and Assurance Dilemmas) in the face of great uncertainty about the character of others' ends, and how much they value cooperative behavior. Gauthier was entirely correct that social cooperation requires us to be confident that rational others will refrain from opportunistic cheating on cooperative arrangements.

Cristina Bicchieri has recently stressed the way that acceptance of social rules transforms mixed motive interactions such as the Prisoners' Dilemma into types of coordination games.[1] If we develop, as she puts it, a conditional preference to act on social rule L that instructs us to cooperate in a mixed motive game, we can achieve a stable equilibrium on following L: so long as I can be assured that enough others are following L, I too will follow it (since I non-derivatively prefer to do so), and thus I will not defect on it even when, all things considered, doing so would better advance my aims and goals. But how could rational individuals develop an independent "preference" or reason to follow a rule? They could not, we have seen in the previous chapter, reason themselves into it as a way of advancing their values, for this independent devotion to rules leads them to follow rules even when doing so does not best promote their values. Perhaps we must simply posit that we have such a preference, following Max Weber in taking as basic that humans engage in both instrumental and norm-

---

[1] See Bicchieri, *The Grammar of Society*, chap. 1. Bicchieri talks of "social norms" rather than "social rules." See section 10.2 below.

based reasoning.[2] While in one sense this is, as we shall see, ultimately the case, since norm-based reasoning cannot be reduced to instrumental reasoning, we still need to explain the fundamental insight of the instrumentalists: communities of humans who follow cooperative norms better promote their individual goals than do communities who do not (and so who are stuck playing Prisoners' Dilemmas). Surely it is not just an accident that all human communities are devoted to rule following, and that rule following has this attractive property. We are confronted by yet another puzzle: although the instrumentalist project of deriving cooperative reasoning from individual instrumental reasoning fails, it remains that the quintessential function of social rules is to allow individuals to better advance their ends. How can we explain the puzzling relation between social rules and individual value promotion — the devotion to social rules cannot be reduced to goal promotion, indeed limits it, yet the core function of social rules is to effectively advance it?

7.2 THE EVOLUTION OF COOPERATION

Instrumentalists such as Gauthier tried to show that the best way to achieve our ends is to reason ourselves into being the sorts of instrumental reasoners who do not reason about the best way to achieve our ends. Although I have shown why this project comes to naught, the core idea needs to be explored: rule-based, cooperative, reasoning is best for us, and it tells us not to always decide on the grounds what is best for us. As Brian Skyrms has demonstrated so well, although rationality cannot explain this uniquely human characteristic, an evolutionary account can do so.[3] Rationality, we have seen, must be a respecter of modularity and dominance reasoning (§4.3), but evolution is not. Evolution can select strategy T on the grounds that those employing T outperform those who do not employ T in terms of how well they achieve their goals and yet

---

[2] For Weber's contrast between instrumental and norm-based action, see his *Economy and Society*, vol. I, pp. 29ff. See also the distinction between substantive and formal rationality, pp. 85ff, and on norm-based action, pp. 217ff, and on ethical norms, pp. 325ff.

[3] Brian Skyrms, *The Evolution of the Social Contact*, chap. 2.

T constitutes an instruction to those employing it not to perform some acts that would best achieve their goals. The important lesson that Skyrms has taught us is that evolutionary selection can do for us what our reason cannot.

A compelling current hypothesis, endorsed by many sociologists, cognitive psychologists, and anthropologists is the cultural–biological co-evolution of strong reciprocity, namely, the tendency of individuals to cooperate when enough others are cooperating and to punish those who transgress on social rules (or norms).[4] Especially important in this regard is the path-breaking work of Peter J. Richerson and Robert Boyd.[5] Let us suppose that, in an obvious sense, a norm or rule requiring cooperative behavior is beneficial from the group's perspective. If we think back to the Prisoners' Dilemma (§5.1), we see that groups in which individuals always play the cooperative strategy will achieve much higher levels of goal satisfaction (assuming for the moment that "utility" here is defined simply in terms of a person's satisfaction of her own goals; see further §9.4*d*). It is of some importance that early discussions of game theory tended to distinguish "group" (or "collective") rationality, which concerned Pareto-optimality, from "individual" rationality; if the collectivity could make a choice qua collective, it would certainly choose mutual cooperation.[6] If we compare the total utility of groups in which individuals defect in Prisoners' Dilemmas with those in which they do not, everyone in the latter will have higher utilities. And, we have seen (§§6.2–6.3), even in a variety of more cooperative interactions, public signaling of the expected behavior and public knowledge of an adequate level of conformity seem necessary for cooperation.

Social rules requiring cooperation are clearly useful to the group. Suppose that rule followers have emerged in a group – that is, for

---

[4] For a general account of strong reciprocity, see Herbert Gintis, Samuel Bowles, Robert Boyd and Ernst Fehr, "Moral Sentiments and Material Interests: Origins, Evidences and Consequences."

[5] For a formal and highly mathematical treatment of the core issues, see Robert Boyd and Peter J. Richerson, *Culture and the Evolutionary Process*; for a much more accessible treatment see Peter J. Richerson and Robert Boyd, *Not by Genes Alone; How Culture Transformed Human Evolution*.

[6] See R. Duncan Luce and Howard Raiffa, *Games and Decision*, p. 193. David Schmidtz refers to collective rationality in his *Rational Choice and Moral Agency*, chap. 8.

whatever reason some people have arisen in a population who
have a non-derivative commitment to following rules (we can say
that devotion to rules is part of their utility function).[7] Let us start
with a simple model, according to which these people are Unconditional Rule Followers: they are unconditionally disposed to
follow rules that dictate cooperation in mixed motive games such
as the Prisoners' Dilemma regardless of the strategy of other actors.
Now a group with a preponderance of Unconditional Rule Followers will outperform a group of purely instrumental agents: as we
saw in the last chapter, the instrumentally rational agents will act
on their dominant strategy and so defect, getting their third-ranked
payoff in a Prisoners' Dilemma, while a population of Unconditional Rule Followers will receive their second highest payoffs. The
problem is that Alf's being an Unconditional Rule Follower easily
detracts from his overall fitness, at least if we think that his fitness
is well correlated with his achieving his own individual goals.
Although individuals in groups dominated by Unconditional Rule
Followers will on average do better than individuals in groups
where everyone is a Defector, groups of Unconditional Rule
Followers could always be invaded by Defectors,[8] each of whom

[7] See here See David Schwab and Elinor Ostrom, "The Vital Role of Norms and
Rules in Maintaining Open Public and Private Economies," 126ff; Hartmut
Kliemt, *Philosophy and Economics I: Methods and Models*, p. 139.

[8] That is to say such rule following would not be an evolutionarily stable strategy
(ESS) in relation to non-cooperation. A strategy S is an ESS when it cannot be
invaded. Let us say that S is an evolutionarily stable strategy if and only if, with
respect to a mutant strategy S^* that might arise either (1) the expected payoff of S
when playing itself is higher than the expected payoff of S^* playing S, or (2) even
if the expected payoff of S playing itself is equal to the expected payoff of S^*
playing S, it is also the case that the expected payoff of S playing S^* is greater than
in the expected payoffs S^* playing itself. The idea is this. Suppose that we have an
S population in which one or a few S^* types are introduced. Because of the pre-
dominance of S types, both S and S^* will play most of their games against S.
According to the first rule, if S does better against S than S^* does against S, S^* will
not get a foothold in the population. Suppose instead that S^* does just as well
against S as S does against itself. Then S^* will begin to grow in the population,
until there are enough S^* players such that both S and S^* play against S^* reasonably often. According to the second rule, once this happens, if S does better
against S^* than S^* does against itself, S will again grow at a more rapid rate. To
say, then, that S is an ESS is to say that an invading strategy will, over time, do
less well than will S. The core idea was introduced by John Maynard Smith in
"The Evolution of Behavior." For a helpful discussion, see Herbert Gintis, *Game
Theory Evolving*, chap. 7.

would do better than the group average (they would receive the group benefits of social cooperation but the individual advantages of cheating in all their personal interactions). In the Hume-Gauthier Harvesting Game in Display II-3 (§5.3*a*), a helpful society of Unconditional Rule Followers would have an average payoff of 3, but an invading Defector would have an average payoff of 4.

Because Unconditional Rule Followers can be so easily taken advantage of by narrowly instrumentally rational agents, many who analyze the evolution of rule following focus on the ability of rule followers to discriminate fellow rule followers from unconstrained instrumentally rational agents. It is certainly the case that if rule followers are Discriminating Rule Followers (i.e., they can discriminate such that they reliably follow cooperative rules when interacting with other rule followers but act like simple instrumental agents when interacting with nonrule followers), they can do well and perhaps dominate the population.[9] The problem, though, is that the ability of Discriminating Rule Followers to evolve under these conditions depends crucially on their ability to discriminate, and so on the quality of their information about others.[10] If it is difficult to get reliable information about the propensities of potential partners, simple instrumental reasoning easily takes over for everyone. The problems of the indirect reciprocity solution to cooperation (§6.2) reappear: in large relatively anonymous groups with many one-off interactions, and with strong incentives of nonrule followers to deceive rule followers, the information requirements are demanding and expensive. Under realistic constraints on information in large anonymous societies, rule following seems apt to be abandoned by Discriminating Rule Followers in favor of simple instrumental reasoning.

Let us, then, reconsider our Unconditional Rule Followers, who possess a disposition to follow cooperative rules without knowing whether their partners are also rule followers. Unconditional rule following obviously has far less informational demands, and has great advantages for the group as a whole, but can it survive in the

[9] See, e.g., Brian Skyrms, *Evolution of the Social Contract*, esp. chaps. 1, 3.
[10] See Kliemt, *Philosophy and Economics I: Methods and Models*, chap. 6.

face of opportunistic instrumentally rational agents? Following Boyd, Gintis, Bowles, and Richerson, suppose that the benefit to the group of each act of cooperation through following norms is b and a contributor incurs a cost of c to produce these benefits. Defectors in the group produce no benefits and incur no costs, though by living in a cooperative group they enjoy the group benefits of cooperation. To simplify matters, assume that all the benefits of each act of cooperation accrue to the entire group. Whatever a person gains by her own b production – contribution to the group's welfare – is less than c; otherwise there would be no temptation to defect. If there are x Unconditional Rule Followers in the group (where x is less than the total population of the group), the expected benefits to an Unconditional Rule Follower is $bx - c$: the total benefits of x number cooperative acts minus the cost of her own cooperation. The expected benefit to Defectors is simply bx, and so the Defector will always have a higher expected payoff than the average in any group of Unconditional Rule Followers. So far it seems that while groups with large numbers of Unconditional Rule Followers will thrive, within those groups they will always be less fit – do less well – than Defectors. This need not be a story about genetic fitness and natural selection. There is considerable evidence that copying the activities of the more successful members of one's group is fundamental to culture.[11] Given this, Defectors would provide a model of someone "doing better," and so imitators would tend to copy them, spreading defection throughout the group.[12]

Now suppose that "Rule-following Punishers" enter the population. As the name indicates, Rule-following Punishers unconditionally follow cooperative rules and punish those who do not. Again following Boyd, Gintis, Bowles, and Richerson, we can say that a punisher reduces the benefit of an act of defection by punishment p at a cost of k to the punisher. Suppose that there are y punishers, who punish each act of defection. We have

1. The expected benefits to an x-type person, i.e., a non-punishing, Unconditional, Rule Follower (to stress this non-

---

[11] Boyd and Richerson, *The Origin and Evolution of Cultures*, chap. 2.

[12] Boyd, Gintis, Bowles, and Richerson, "The Evolution of Altruistic Punishment," p. 217.

punishing feature, let us call these "Easygoing Rule Followers") are: $b(x + y) - c$. Each Easygoing Rule Follower gets the full advantages of cooperative acts performed by both her own x-types as well as the Rule-following Punishers (y-types) and, in addition, she receives the social advantages of punishment of Defectors by Rule-following Punishers, and incurs only the cost of her own cooperative act.

2. The expected benefits to a Defector are $b(x + y) - yp$. A Defector still receives the full benefits of cooperation generated by x and y types, but incurs a punishment of p from each of the y punishers.

3. The expected benefits for being a Rule-following Punisher (a y-type) are: $b(x + y) - c - [k(1 - x - y)]$. Each y receives the full benefits of cooperation generated by x and y types, and like Easygoing Rule Followers, each incurs the costs of cooperation. In addition, each punisher must incur a cost of k for punishing each Defector; if there are x Easygoing Rule Followers, and y Rule-following Punishers in a group, then the number of Defectors is $1 - x - y$.

If the costs of being punished are greater than the costs incurred in cooperating – that is, if $yp > c$ – Defectors will decline in the population. The problem is that Rule-following Punishers have a fitness disadvantage relative to Easygoing Rule Followers. Groups of Rule-following Punishers can be invaded by Easygoing Rule Followers, who reap all the benefits of cooperation but do not incur the costs of punishment.[13] On the face of it, just as the superior fitness of Defectors within the group undermined Unconditional Rule Followers, the superior fitness of Easygoing Rule Followers undermines the Rule-following Punishers. However, as Boyd, Gintis, Bowles, and Richerson show, the crucial difference between the two cases is that in the first, because the cooperators incur a constant cost c they are always less fit by c in relation to defectors. They can never, as it were, close the gap. However, the gap in fitness between Easygoing Rule Followers and Rule-following Punishers reduces to zero when Defectors are eliminated from the

---

[13] Ibid., p. 216.

population; it is only the punishing of Defectors that renders Rule-following Punishers less fit than Easygoing Rule Followers. We would not expect the fitness gap to reduce to zero – mutations, errors in determining defection, and immigration from other groups will result in above zero rates of punishing. Nevertheless, under a large range of values of the relevant variables, the discrepancy in relative fitness is small enough so that Rule-following Punishers remain a high proportion of the population and defection thus declines.[14] However, it is certainly possible that a group may evolve to a "mixed" or polymorphic equilibrium, composed of Rule-following Punishers (or what are sometimes called "moralistic punishers"), Easygoing Rule Followers, and perhaps Defectors as well.[15]

It is important that in such group selection models the survival of a strategy depends on two factors: (*i*) its individual fitness within the group and (*ii*) its inclusion in a group that has groupwide advantages over competing groups. In pure individual fitness accounts, only the first factor is relevant. In our first group selection account with simply Unconditional Rule Followers and Defectors, the former enhance group fitness, but their serious individual deficit drives them to extinction within the group; the result is that Defectors take over. Interestingly, though Defectors take over and, indeed, a group of all Defectors cannot be invaded by Unconditional Rule Followers (Defection is an evolutionarily stable strategy), the group would be driven to extinction in a competition with cooperating groups.[16] In the case of Easygoing Rule Followers, Defectors, and Rule-following Punishers, Rule-following Punishers reduce Defectors; during an initial period they are less fit than Easygoing Rule Followers, but as punishers succeed in eliminating Defectors, their fitness converges with their more easygoing comrades, and the group's overall fitness is enhanced. The more the Rule-following Punishers must punish (say, because of high rates of mutation that constantly reintroduce Defectors into the population), the greater will be the gap between the fitness of the punish-

---

[14] See ibid.; Boyd and Richerson, *The Origin and Evolution of Cultures*, chap. 10.
[15] See Boyd and Richerson, *The Origin and Evolution of Cultures*, chap. 9. In this model, Rule-following Punishers were rarer than more easygoing strategies.
[16] Ibid., chaps. 10-11.

ers and the Easygoing Rule Followers. As I noted, under some configurations of payoffs, equilibria of mixed punishing/easygoing cooperative strategies emerge.[17] However, if there is (*i*) second and *n*-order punishing – punishing Easygoing Rule Followers when they fail to punish Defectors, and punishing those who fail to punish those who fail to punish, and so on – and (*ii*) a weak tendency to copy the majority,[18] the population of Rule-following Punishers can stabilize and so stabilize group cooperation; again, once cooperation is stable within a group, it can spread through group selection.[19]

Our punishers are genuinely "altruistic" agents in the sense that they engage in activities that do not best maximize their own goals, but are advantageous for the group. Purely instrumental agents could never reason themselves into being strictly altruistic, that is, performing acts that, all things considered, set back their own values, goals, and ends. We thus have a powerful model for one of the most perplexing of evolutionary phenomena: the selection of altruistic traits that, by definition, reduce the individual fitness of those who possess them.[20] Punishing violators is a public good; because the Easygoing Rule Followers share it, they do better by cooperating but never punishing. And of course an agent solely devoted to her own goals will defect if she is not punished; Rule-following Punishers will not. Thus, if we focus on simply instrumental rationality in terms of promoting one's goals, Rule-following Punishers are not instrumentally rational.

This discussion has been rather complex — but the core point is straightforward. In Chapter II we examined the failure of the instrumentalist case that rational individuals could reason themselves into constrained action as a strategy to pursue their goals. But then we are faced with a worry: if we are basically instrumen-

---

[17] See Skyrms, *Evolution of the Social Contract*, chap. 2.
[18] Note the importance of imitation to the development of culture.
[19] Boyd and Richerson, *The Origin and Evolution of Cultures*, chap. 10.
[20] Elliot Sober and David Sloan Wilson strenuously argue for group selection accounts of altruistic behavior in their *Unto Others: The Evolution and Psychology of Unselfish Behavior*. After a long period of disfavor, group – or more generally, multilevel – selection is again respectable in genetic evolutionary theory. For a helpful analysis, see Samir Okasha, *Evolution and Levels of Selection*. It is *more* than respectable in accounts of cultural evolution.

tally rational agents devoted to our own goals, how could we ever become rule followers? Does becoming a rule follower make one less "fit" – less able to pursue one's own goals, survival, and welfare? The sociological model we have been examining shows how such individuals often could be more fit – more apt to satisfy their own goals – than agents solely devoted to their own ends. The groups populated by such individuals do much better than groups without them (they are bad news for Defectors), and within these groups the Rule-following Punishers may be nearly as fit as the cooperative free-riders. And they can pretty much eliminate Easygoing Rule Followers by punishing those who fail to punish Defectors. To be a member of a society dominated by Rule-following Punishers is the most effective way to advance one's ends.[21]

7.3 COMMON RULES AND EFFICIENT COOPERATION

(a) Rules as the Unit of Justification

Note that I have called the punishers "Rule-following Punishers" rather than simply (as is often the case .in the literature), "cooperating punishers" or "altruistic punishers." The evolution of cooperation is, as we have seen, closely tied to the evolution of groups with punishers, but the stability of the population of punishers is threatened when punishing is costly. The more costly is punishment, the greater the advantage of Easygoing Rule Followers; but they are a threat to group cooperation because, should they come to dominate, the group can be invaded by Defectors, driving down overall group cooperation (and, so, fitness). In the evolution of cooperation, then, it is crucial that the costs of punishment be minimized as far as possible. Now the costs of punishment are increased when it is unclear what constitutes an infraction – a punishment-worthy act. To punish ill-defined "uncooperative" behavior will result in a great deal of mistaken punishment, which will not only drive up the costs of punishment

---

[21] Of course this is a simplification: individuals do not fall neatly into simple categories, but fall on a continuum as to the degree to which they internalize rules, and degree they are willing to punish. See Henrich and Henrich, *Why Humans Cooperate*, p. 155.

but, simultaneously, drive down the benefits of being a cooperator (as you might be mistakenly punished even if you do cooperate). Consequently, group cooperation requires norms or rules that are specific enough in their requirements that cheater detection is highly reliable within the group. Cooperative rules must be sufficiently general so that they provide guidance in unforeseen future circumstances while, at the same time, it is reasonably clear to the great majority of group members (*i*) when the rule applies and (*ii*) what the rule calls for. Because punishment seems so fundamental to the evolution of cooperative orders, and because these two desiderata are so important to the emergence of effective punishment, it appears less important that rules be fine-tuned to get the "correct cooperative result" than that these desiderata be fulfilled.

This helps us see that, as it were, what we might call the "unit of justification" in social morality is not an arbitrary commitment of a particular moral theory. Some, for example, argue that the main concern of moral theory should be the justification of abstract principles, while others focus on specific acts. Insofar as we conceive of social morality as a device to allow individuals with diverse ends to live together in a fair and mutually beneficial way, our concern will be the justification of what we might think of as "middle-level social-moral objects" – that is, social rules. We require guidance that is general enough to apply to unforeseen future circumstances while specific enough that we have common understandings of what the rule requires.

(b) The Evolution of Agreement

The social contract tradition in political philosophy has been deeply skeptical that individuals will be able to coordinate on their interpretation of social and moral rules. Social contract theorists always recognized that moral judgment is an exercise of private reason and, consequently, widespread and intractable dispute about the claims of morality are inevitable. "All laws, written and unwritten," Hobbes tells us,

have need of interpretation. The unwritten law of nature, though it be easy to such as without partiality and passion make use of their natural reason, and therefore leaves the violators thereof without excuse; yet considering there be very few, perhaps none, that in some cases are not blinded by self-love, or some other passion, it is now become of all laws the most obscure, and has consequently the greatest need of able interpreters."[22]

Locke agrees: "though the Law of Nature be plain and intelligible to all rational Creatures; yet men being biassed by their Interest, as well as ignorant for want of studying it, are not apt to allow of it as a Law binding to them in the application of it to their particular Cases."[23] And to Kant, the root of conflict in the state of nature is that "individual men, nations and states can never be certain they are secure against violence from one another because each will have the right to do what seems just and good to him, entirely independently of the opinion of others." Kant goes on to insist that justice is absent in the state of nature because each relies on his own judgment, and thus "when there is a controversy concerning rights (*jus controversum*), no competent judge can be found to render a decision having the force of law."[24] For Hobbes, Locke, and Kant a social order in which real justice obtains necessitates that individuals abandon reliance on their private judgments of equity and justice and accept the public judgment of an umpire or judge.

Hobbes, Locke, and Kant trace the problem of social disorder to conflicting claims of private conscience about morality, and all see the solution to be establishing the state as the final umpire as to the demands of justice.[25] In their analyses of interpretive disagreements, though, Hobbes, Locke and Kant all paid insufficient attention to our evolved ability to coordinate our actions on common interpretation of norms. The tendency of our natural reason to produce divergent interpretations is countered by our tendency to converge on a common understanding of the norms that structure social life. To see how such convergence may evolve, let us start with a common and simple model of the development of property rights: the classic Hawk-Dove game given in Display III-1.

---

[22] Hobbes, *Leviathan*, p. 180 (chap. 26, ¶20).
[23] Locke, *Second Treatise of Government*, §124.
[24] Kant, *Metaphysical Elements of Justice*, pp. 116–119, 146.
[25] This is not to say that citizens must believe that the state is always correct about these matters. While Hobbes perhaps flirts with this view (and in some ways Rousseau did so as well), Locke and Kant are clear that the state can be wrong, and the citizen may conclude that it is. The core question is about the social authority, not truth.

Suppose Hawks and Doves are types of individuals in the population. A Hawk always battles for a territory until either it is injured or its opponent retreats. A Dove engages in display battle: if it meets a Hawk it quickly retreats without injury; if it meets another Dove, there is a .5 probability that it will retreat – in no case does it sustain injury. Let v be the value of the territory (and suppose it is positive); and w be the cost of injury that is sustained by the loser in a fight over a territory (and suppose that $w > v$); then let $z = (v - w)/2$. Display III-2 provides a specific set of payoffs.

	Hawk	Dove
Hawk	z z	0 v
Dove	v 0	$v/2$ $v/2$

DISPLAY III-1 GENERALIZED HAWK–DOVE GAME[26]

	Hawk	Dove
Hawk	-5 -5	0 10
Dove	10 0	5 5

DISPLAY III-2: A SPECIFIC HAWK–DOVE GAME

Let us view this as an evolutionary game. Players do not change strategies, but play their strategy against whomever they meet. The expected payoff of a Hawk playing another Hawk is –5; the expected payoff of a Hawk meeting a Dove is 10; the expected payoff of a Dove meeting a Hawk is 0; and the expected payoff of a Dove meeting a Dove is 5. Though the players do not vary their strategies (and so they cannot make "moves" in the sense of traditional game theory), we can understand the population as

---

[26] I am drawing here on Herbert Gintis' analysis in *The Bounds of Reason: Game Theory and the Unification of the Behavioral Sciences*, pp. 39–40, 201ff. For the classic analysis, see John Maynard Smith, "The Evolution of Behavior."

"moving" in the sense that, if being a Hawk has a higher expected payoff than being a Dove, the population will move towards more Hawks and less Doves. In evolutionary terms we can think of this as a *replicator dynamic* in which those strategies that tend to have higher average payoffs increase in the population and so displace lower payoff strategies.[27] So as the Hawks and Doves play each other repeatedly over long periods of time, the percentage of Hawks and Doves in the population from generation to generation will vary with how many points they gather in our Hawk/Dove game (points, let us say, indicate relative fitness). It is immediately obvious that neither all-Hawk nor all-Dove is an evolutionarily stable strategy. For a population of all Hawks the average expected payoff of the population is –5; since a mutant Dove would have a payoff of 0 it would outperform the population average and increase. For a population of all Doves, the average population payoff is 5; a mutant Hawk would receive a payoff of 10, thus again outperforming the average of the Dove population. In the case of Display III-2 an evolutionarily stable equilibrium would be a mixed population evenly split between Doves and Hawks. At that mix the average Hawk and average Dove payoffs are the same (2½), and so neither population can grow at the expense of the other.[28]

While this population mix is stable, it is inefficient: our Hawks and Doves have arrived at a stable equilibrium, but this includes the cost of injury to losing Hawks.[29] (And remember that a population of peaceful Doves can always be invaded by Hawks.) Now suppose a new type of person arises, the Correlated Agent. Correlated Agents correlate their response to each other: they act aggressively to protect their territory, but are easily deterred from taking that of others. In short, the Correlated Agent acts like a Hawk on its own territory and a Dove on that of others. Suppose that our

[27] See Skyrms, *Evolution of the Social Contract.*
[28] In an evenly split Dove/Hawk population, a Dove will play half its games against other Doves, and in each game it receives 5 (so ½ × 5 = 2½), while it plays the other half of the time against Hawks, for an average payoff of 0 (½ × 0 = 0); thus a Dove's overall expected payoff against the entire population is 2½. Hawks play Doves half the time, and in each game receive 10 (so ½ × 10 = 5); the other half the time a Hawk plays against other Hawks, with an expected payoff each time of –5 (so ½ × –5 = –2 ½) – thus (5) + (–2½) = 2½.
[29] Gintis, *The Bounds of Reason*, p. 135.

Correlated Agents have half of their encounters on their own territory, and half on that of others; the expected payoff of Correlated Agents thus interacting is 5; half the time a Correlated Agent playing another Correlated Agent will get 10, and half the time 0 (notice that because they are correlated, they never fight each other). Our Correlated Agents can invade pure Hawk or pure Dove populations, as well as our mixed population in equilibrium. Recall that the average payoff of a Dove against a Dove is 5; but a Correlated Agent playing a Dove will get 10 the half the time it is on its own territory ($10 \times \frac{1}{2} = 5$) and will receive the Dove payoff the half the time it is on another's territory ($5 \times \frac{1}{2} = 2\frac{1}{2}$), for a total expected payoff of 7½, thus outperforming the Dove. In a population of all Hawks, the average payoff is –5; the Correlated Agent will also receive the –5 payoff the 50 percent of the time it is on its own territory, but will receive the 0 payoff when it is off its territory, giving it a total expected payoff against Hawks of –2½, again outperforming the Hawk population. And neither can the Correlated Agent population be invaded by either Hawks or Doves.[30] Correlated Agents are evolutionarily stable, and have hit upon an efficient equilibrium.[31]

Of course the advantage of Correlated Agents depends on the costs and benefits of predation and defense; if preying on others is very easy and beneficial, Hawks may have an advantage. If preying is exceptionally difficult or yields little returns, Correlated Agents may have relatively little advantage over pure Doves. But societies filled with Hawks and Doves (without enough Doves to prey on, a society of predators does badly indeed), tend to reach inefficient equilibria over a wide range of values (concerning the variables in Display III-1). If we add to our analysis competition between

[30] The expected payoff of Doves against Correlated Agents is 2½ (half the time a Dove gets nothing, half the time 5); the expected payoff of Hawks against Correlated Agents is 2½ (i.e., –5 half the time for –2½, and 10 half the time for an average of 5, so –2½ + 5 = 2½). Recall that the expected payoff of Correlated Agents against themselves is 5, so they cannot be invaded. Correlated Agents can also invade the mixed population in equilibrium.

[31] It constitutes what Robert Aumann called a "correlated equilibrium," which is more efficient here than the Nash equilibrium characterizing our simple Hawk-Dove mixed population. See Skyrms, *Evolution of the Social Contract*, chap. 4. For a sophisticated treatment see Peter Vanderschraaf, *Learning and Coordination: Inductive Deliberation, Learning, and Convention*.

groups, societies of Correlated Agents overall have a distinct advantage. And as Richerson and Boyd have demonstrated in their impressive body of work, cultural variation shows strong group selection processes.[32] Groups with fundamentally more efficient forms of organization tend to expand, and to be copied by others. Within broad parameters what Gintis calls the "property equilibrium"[33] is fundamental to social life, and over the long term we can expect social convergence on some type of Correlated Agents.

All this is standard evolutionary game theory. Note, however, that we can redescribe "Hawks" as those who are assertive in their private judgments about the interpretation of proper social rules, "Doves" as those who are deferential to the private judgments of others about what rules call for, and Correlated Agents as those who have achieved a common interpretation of the rules.[34] Locke thought the state of nature would be populated by Hawkish interpreters of the law of nature: each asserts, and employs force to defend, her own view of the rules with a strong bias towards self-interest.[35] If Locke was right about this – if the state of nature would be a world of interpretive Hawks – then indeed they would do well to abandon all private judgment and abide by the umpire (the state) to avoid destructive war (a payoff of –5). Over the long term, however, successful and efficient social orders would heavily favor our correlated interpreters, who tend to converge on a common understanding of their shared norms.

7.4 SUPPORT FROM EXPERIMENTAL DATA

Do we have any reason to think that we – or at least most of us – are Rule-following Punishers? Recent experimental data provide

---

[32] See, for example, Peter J. Richerson and Robert Boyd, "The Evolution of Free Enterprise Values," p. 114.

[33] Gintis, *The Bounds of Reason*, 210ff.

[34] Following Brian Skyrms, we can think of this as the development of a signaling system. See *The Evolution of the Social Contract*, chaps 4 and 5; *The Stag Hunt and the Evolution of Social Structure*, Part II.

[35] Recall that according to Locke "though the Law of Nature be plain and intelligible to all rational Creatures; yet men being biassed by their Interest, as well as ignorant for want of studying it, are not apt to allow of it as a Law binding to them in the application of it to their particular Cases." *Second Treatise of Government*, §124.

strong support for the claim that subjects are apt to punish those who are norm violators even at net costs to themselves.[36] Consider, for example, experiments involving the ultimatum game. An ultimatum game involves two subjects, Proposer and Responder, who have X amount of some good (say, money) to distribute between them. In the simplest version of the game, Proposer makes the first move, and gives an offer of the form, "I will take n percent of X, leaving you with $100 - n$ percent," where n is not greater than 100 percent. If Responder accepts, each gets what Proposer offers; if Responder rejects, each receives nothing. If players cared only about the amount of X that they received and were instrumentally rational, it would be rational for Proposer to, say, take 99 percent, offering Responder 1 percent. Responder would be faced with a choice between 1 percent of X and nothing, and since an instrumentally rational agent must choose more over less (§4.3a), she will accept the offer. Since Proposer knows this, and since Proposer also will not choose less over more, Proposer will make that offer.

This is not the observed outcome. In the United States and many other countries, one-shot ultimatum games result in median offers of Proposers to Responders of between 50 percent and 40 percent with mean offers being 30 percent to 40 percent. Responders refuse offers of less than 20 percent about half the time.[37] This is normally taken to show that most individuals are not simply acting as purely instrumentally rational agents.[38] A responder who rejects an offer of 30 percent in a one-shot game seems to be choosing less rather than more: she goes away with nothing rather than 30 percent of the good. Consider two possible hypotheses about why Responders refuse offers:

[36] Ernst Fehr's work on these problems has been especially influential. See Ernst Fehr and Urs Fischbacher, "The Economics of Strong Reciprocity"; Ernst Fehr and Simon Gächter, "Cooperation and Punishment in Public Goods Experiments"; Ernst Fehr and Simon Gachter, "Fairness and Retaliation: The Economics of Reciprocity"; Ernst Fehr and and Klaus M. Schmidt, "A Theory of Fairness, Competition, and Cooperation."

[37] Bicchieri, *The Grammar of Society*, p. 105. For a classic study, see Richard H. Thaler, "The Ultimatum Game."

[38] Shmuel Zamir objects that investigators have rushed to this conclusion, and we have no clear game theoretical prediction as to what fully rational agents would do in ultimatum games. See "Rationality and Emotions in Ultimatum Bargaining."

Equal Outcomes: Responders prefer roughly equal outcomes.

Norm Violation: Responders punish Proposers who choose to violate perceived norms of fair division.

Both may tell a part of the story but, I believe, overall the data indicate that *Norm Violation* is the fundamental explanation.[39] Consider a modified ultimatum game conducted by Armin Falk et al. in Display III-3:[40]

	Proposer's Options		
	Pair 1	Pair 2	Pair 3
	80/20 50/50	80/20 20/80	80/20 0/100
Responder's Rejection Rate of 80/20 offer	44.4%	27%	9%

DISPLAY III-3 REJECTION RATES DEPEND ON THE CHOICES MADE BY PROPOSERS

In each version of this game the Proposer has only two possible choices. The first is always to take 80 percent and offer 20 percent; in different versions the paired option is (*i*) a fifty–fifty split, (*ii*) take 20 percent and offer 80 percent, and (*iii*) give everything to the Responder. The Responder knows the Proposer's options. Under pair 1, rejection rates of the 20 percent offer are 44 percent. Note that rejection rate of 20 percent offers drops dramatically when the only option of the Proposers is either to take 80 percent and give 20 percent, or take 20 percent and give 80 percent. If those are the Proposer's options, it does not seem unfair to take the 80 percent for oneself, though the unfairness of the outcome is the same as under pair 2. And Responders are almost always willing to live with 20 percent given Pair 3, though again the overall outcome is just as unfair as in pair 1.

---

[39] For a sustained analysis of the data in relation to these two hypotheses, concluding that it endorses the Norm Violation hypothesis, see Bicchieri, *The Grammar of Society*, chap. 3. See also Cristina Bicchieri and Alex Chavez, "Behaving as Expected: Public Information and Fairness Norms."

[40] Reported by Bicchieri, *The Grammar of Society*, pp. 121–2.

A study conducted by Falk, Fehr, and Fischbacher again shows the importance of punishment for norm violation.[41] In this study in the first round subjects played a Prisoners' Dilemma, which was depicted as contributions to a cooperative enterprise with the possibility of free riding. In the second round, subjects were informed of others' choices (identities of participants remained anonymous) and were given the opportunity of punishing others for their play in the previous round. In the low-punishment treatments, subjects could spend up to y unit of money to punish the defectors up to a y amount (a payment of y yielded a punishment of y); in the high-punishment treatments, y unit spent in punishment could reduce another's gains by up to $2.5y$ or $3y$. Here one can expend money to reduce others' gains by a multiplier. Falk, Fehr, and Fischbacher found:

1.   When cooperators punished, they only punished defectors. In both treatments, 60–70 percent of the cooperators punish.
2.   In the high-punishment treatment, defectors also chose to "punish." When they did so, they punished other defectors and cooperators randomly. We might call this "spiteful punishment." Such defectors thus will punish if doing so increases their relative position vis-à-vis the punished.
3.   Cooperators by far imposed higher punishments.
4.   In low-punishment treatments (where a unit spent punishing could not reduce the relative payoffs of the punishers and the punished), only cooperators punished.

After reviewing their data, Falk, Fehr, and Fischbacher conclude that "theories of inequality aversion cannot explain why cooperators punish in the low sanction condition. Despite this, 59.6 percent of the cooperators punished the defectors. . . . This suggests that the desire to retaliate, instead of the motive of reducing unfair payoff inequalities, seems to be the driving force of these sanctions."[42] To be sure, debate continues – some continue to hold that inequality

[41] Armin Falk, Ernst Fehr, and Urs Fischbacher, "Driving Forces behind Informal Sanctions."
[42] Ibid., p. 15. This conclusion is of special significance as Fehr and Schmidt originally proposed the inequality-reduction hypothesis.

aversion, rather than punishment, is a significant factor explaining much of the data.[43] It does, though, seem quite clear that punishment is at least a significant factor in explaining these findings.

To sum up: there is considerable experimental evidence that those who cooperate also tend to punish.[44] Subjects' behavior in ultimatum games is not best interpreted as a taste for equal or fair distributions, or avoiding unequal ones. The best explanation of the results, I believe, indicates that individuals – at least in market societies (§22.4a) – endorse norms about fairness in certain sorts of interactions and are willing to forgo material benefits to punish those who do not comply.

8 Deontic Reasoning

8.1 RULES: REGULATING THE SPECIFIC THROUGH THE GENERAL

Thus far I have employed the rather vague idea of a social rule and what it means to follow one. Moral rules, customary rules, social norms, social mores, and in some societies the rules of etiquette all qualify as social rules (§10). All human, and probably some non-human primate, social groups are structured by social rules.[45] As we have just seen, there is good reason to think that human society depends on people conforming to, and enforcing, moral rules. H. L. A. Hart observed that "[i]n any large group general rules, standards and principles" are the primary mode of regulating social life; the rules identify general classes of action and require or prohibit particular acts falling under these general descriptions.[46] We have compelling reason to think that social life depends on a

---

[43] See, e.g., Christopher T. Dawes et al, "Egalitarian Motives in Humans" and James H. Fowler, Tim Johnson, Oleg Smirnov, "Egalitarian Motive and Altruistic Punishment." See the response by Ernst Fehr and Simon Gächter in the same number of *Nature*.

[44] For a good review of the data supporting this conclusion, see Henrich and Henrich, *Why Humans Cooperate*, chaps. 7 and 8.

[45] See Denise Dellarosa Cummins, "The Evolutionary Roots of Intelligence and Rationality," pp. 132–6 and her "Evidence for the Innateness of Deontic Reasoning," pp. 167ff.

[46] Hart, *The Concept of Law*, p. 121.

rule-based social morality; we now need to better understand what rules are, and how people act on them.

Hart's basic insight that regulation by rules involves regulation of particular actions by reference to general categories can be interpreted in two ways. If we adopt a *set/subset* analysis, rules identify a certain set of actions. The rule then states that for all actions in the set, a certain type of actor must, must not, or may perform them.[47] Consider, for example, Denise Dellarosa Cummins' important research on deontic reasoning in children. In one of her experiments she presented three- and four-year-old children with ten rubber mice, five of which squeaked when squeezed, and five of which did not. The children were presented with a large cardboard box, painted so as to clearly indicate an indoor and outdoor area. The rubber mice were placed at various places inside and outside the box. The children were presented with the prescriptive rule: "All squeaky mice MUST stay inside the house."[48] Children readily understood the rule in terms of universal quantifiers over sets of action: all mice of a certain description must stay inside the house. Moreover – and this is a point to which I shall return (§8.2) – they were excellent at detecting whether the rule was violated by any of the squeaky mice.

Nevertheless, as a general analysis, understanding rules as employing universal quantifiers over a set of actions is objectionable. Rules do not pick out a set of particulars: they identify certain general characteristics or properties, and issue directives for actions with these properties.[49] A fully specified social rule identifies (*i*) a set of persons to whom the prescription is addressed, (*ii*) a property of actions, (*iii*) a deontic operator such that actions with that property may, must, or must not be performed and (*iv*) a statement of the conditions under which the connection between (*ii*) and (*iii*) is relevant. Contrast, for example, two rules:[50]

---

[47] Nozick provides a set interpretation of individual principles in *The Nature of Rationality*, pp. 14ff. I analyze Nozick's account in "Principles, Goals, and Symbols: Nozick on Practical Rationality."

[48] See Denise Dellarosa Cummins, "Evidence for the Innateness of Deontic Reasoning in 3- and 4-Year-Old Children," p. 824.

[49] See, e.g., Frederick Schauer, "Rules and the Rule of Law," pp. 647ff.

[50] My discussion here draws on Laurence Fiddick, "Adaptive Domains of Deontic Reasoning," p. 109. Studies of children's moral reasoning show that from a very

Hand Raising: "In our school, you should not speak without first raising your hand."

No Hair Pulling: "In our school, you should not pull other children's hair."

One interesting finding is that children distinguish *Hand Raising* as a purely conventional rule from *No Hair Pulling*, which they see as a moral rule. Consequently, in *Hand Raising* they understand the "in our school" qualifier as actually stating the condition under which the rule holds (point *iv*): children accept that other schools may not have such a rule and so only in our school does it apply. In contrast, in the case of *No Hair Pulling* they do not see this as stating the conditions of application. *No Hair Pulling* is conceived as a moral rule, and so it could not be the case that in other schools it is permissible. Children, then, distinguish moral and conventional rules, implicitly invoking the conditionality of the rule *(iv)* as a criterion.[51]

Even something as apparently specific as hair pulling is a property of a great many actions. *No Hair Pulling* applies a deontic operator to all actions possessing the property of hair pulling. At the base of reasoning about social prescriptive rules[52] is a type-to-token relation. The rule identifies a type of action by its possession of some property or properties, and then employs a deontic operator indicating what is to be done with all tokens instantiating this

---

early age children make the moral/conventional distinction, although children over eight make it more consistently. Elliot Turiel, Melainie Killen, and Charles C. Helwig, "Morality: Its Structure, Functions and Vagaries," p. 177.

[51] Joseph Heath, criticizing Shaun Nichols, has argued that "there is an inclination among philosophers to draw a sharp distinction between 'moral' and what are called 'conventional obligations' such as rules of etiquette, or 'social norms' more generally. I reject this distinction" (Heath, *Following the Rules*, p. 10; Nichols, *Sentimental Rules*, pp. 5–8). Much depends here on what we mean by a "sharp" distinction: I argue here that moral rules are a subset of social rules. Overall Nichols' position is well-confirmed by research – it is by no means simply the view of philosophers. This is not to deny that there is some controversy. For research indicating that the moral/conventional distinction is stronger in Western than in some other cultures, see Richard Schweder, Manamohan Mahaptra and Joan G. Miller, "Culture and Moral Development," and Carolyn Pope Edwards, "Culture and the Construction of Moral Values." But cf. Turiel, Killan, and Helwig, "Morality: Its Structure, Functions and Vagaries."

[52] Again I do not wish to claim this is a general account of all rule following. An important result of experiments in rule reasoning is that it differs by domain. Here, as elsewhere, the aim of giving a single account of diverse phenomena tends to lead many philosophers astray.

property. We need to be careful here. Although I will argue that social-moral rules are a subset of social rules (§10.4), I am not concerned here with a concept of moral rules as instantiating moral properties.[53] At this point the idea is simply that social rules identify certain natural or social properties of actions and state prescriptions regarding acts that instantiate those properties. An act falls under a rule if, under certain condtions, the act instantiates a property to which the rule identifies as grounding a prescription. Thus, at the base of social rule reasoning is the

> *Instantiation Relation*: An act may/must not/must be/ performed by persons *P* in conditions *C* if it instantiates property *T*.

Because social rules issue prescriptions for acts that instantiate a natural or social property (e.g., being old enough to drink, coercing a person),[54] and because such properties are often continuous, social rules typically identify some threshold level of *T* above which the prescription holds and below which it does not. Stanley Benn and I noted this with the concept of the public and private.[55] Although in many ways publicness and privateness are continuous concepts (one's sex life is more private than one's tastes in literature), when they form the basis of, say, rules of privacy, the requirement that we generate prescriptions often forces us to dichotomize this continuous variable. A rule of privacy, for example, identifies some information as "private"; once that threshold is passed, actions that instantiate that level of privateness provide the basis for prescriptive rules. The same holds true for pulling hair. There is a continuum from gently pulling a single hair to ripping out a handful. Because so many social rules are based on dichotomizing continuous properties, we have recurring disputes about "where to draw the line" from everything from the age of purchasing alcohol to rules about offensive speech. Nevertheless, some general agreement about where to draw the line is necessary if we are to share a social rule. I return to this problem below.

---

[53] "A moral rule states or expresses a relation claimed to obtain between a moral property and other, grounding properties that are correlated with its instantiation." Russ Shafer-Landau, "Moral Rules," p. 584. See section 9.2*b*.

[54] Sometimes coercion is seen as a moral property. See sections 17.3*c*, 23.1.

[55] See Benn and Gaus, "Public and Private: Concepts and Action."

8.2 SOCIAL RULES AND DEONTIC REASONING

There is immense skepticism of the rationality of rule following in the philosophic literature on practical reasoning – unless, somehow, following rules can be seen as aligned with one's goals (or, more generally, instrumental rationality). I will turn to these skeptical arguments in section 9. We should begin, though, by noting that while philosophers often continue to see rule following as mysterious and often straightforwardly irrational, the psychological literature paints the opposite story. Social rule following capacities develop sooner than general reasoning abilities, and we constantly do better at following social rules and understanding them than in many general reasoning tasks. One of the striking findings of recent investigations of moral reasoning is how good we are at deontic reasoning and how easy it is for us to do it. In a series of important experiments, P. C. Wason, P. N. Johnson-Laird, and others investigated people's ability to test "if, then" rules.[56] Consider an example from Cummins, depicted in Display III-4.

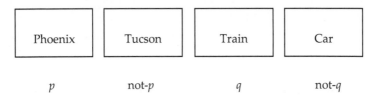

DISPLAY III-4 A SELECTION TASK

Suppose Alf says to you, "In Arizona, if you travel to Phoenix, you go by train." You are faced with the four cards in Display III-4, and you are told that on one side is a person's destination, and on the other side is her means of transport. Your task is to decide which cards you need to turn over to test whether Alf's claim is correct. In most experiments the overwhelming response is "p" and "q." That is, most people follow a *confirmation* strategy, seeking to confirm whether $p{\to}q$. It is standardly thought that the correct strategy in testing such conditionals is to seek *falsification*: to see whether p has

---

[56] See P. C. Wason, "Reasoning about a Rule," and P. C. Wason and P. N. Johnson-Laird, *The Psychology of Reasoning: Structure and Content.* For a review, see K. I. Manktelow and D. Over, "Deontic Reasoning."

not-*q* on the other side and whether not-*q* has *p* on the other side (so the person should turn over *p* and not-*q*).[57] Remarkably, however, what is in many ways the same practical problem is solved correctly by the overwhelming majority when the issue is rephrased in deontic terms.[58] Rather than asking whether Alf's statement is correct, imagine you are told that, as an employee of the Arizona Department of Transportation, you are to enforce the new rule that travel to Phoenix must be by train. Now most people choose to turn over *p* and not-*q*.[59]

This result holds for subjects from young children to adults. In experiments such as the "squeaky mouse" rule (§8.1), 82 percent of the four-year-olds and 64 percent of the three-year-olds make the correct choice about which mouse to test if the problem is put in terms of a deontic requirement. On the other hand, if the problem is posed as an indicative, only about 33 percent of the children choose the correct testing strategy.[60] Not only do children perform better, but they appear to better understand deontic rules.[61] These are comparable to the figures in studies of adult reasoners. There is convincing evidence that when these problems are put in terms of deontic requirements, people of all ages perform well because they immediately see the relevance of a *cheater detection strategy* (which is, roughly, equivalent to a falsification strategy for testing conditionals). [62]

---

[57] Jesse Prinz is "unconvinced," insisting that this is indeed a "confirmation problem," and so the best inductive rule is to employ the confirmation strategy. "It's like trying to determine whether all ravens are black. To do that efficiently, it's a good idea to check the ravens we encounter, but a total waste of time to check all things that aren't black" (*The Emotional Construction of Morals*, p. 265). However, efforts to consistently model Wason task subjects as following a plausible inductive strategy have not been promising. See Branden Fitelson, "The Wason Task(S) and the Paradox of Confirmation."

[58] This is not to say that these are precisely the same logical problems such that one formulation can be deduced from the other. The concern here is their practical similarity.

[59] For a summary of findings, see Cummins, "Evidence for the Innateness of Deontic Reasoning," pp. 162–4.

[60] Ibid., p. 171.

[61] Paul L. Harris and María Núñez, "Understanding of Permission Rules by Preschool Children."

[62] Cummins, "Evidence for the Innateness of Deontic Reasoning," p. 171. See also Cummins, "Evidence for the Innateness of Deontic Reasoning" in 3- and 4-Year-Old Children."

Two observations are appropriate in light of these findings.

First, if we understand social morality as a subset of social rules, Hare's claim that morality is prescriptive rather than descriptive is supported (§1.3*b*). We have difficulty in understanding normative–descriptive propositions such as "If you are a good (or virtuous) student, you don't pull other children's hair;" we readily understand "Students must not pull other children's hair!" If we suppose that the ability to understand social morality is a widely distributed human capacity (and it would be most odd if it wasn't), because a prescriptive social morality better conforms to human cognitive capabilities, it seems a better way to conceive of the social morality than an account that stresses conditional descriptive truths.

Second, deontic reasoning about social morality generally occurs in a social setting, and this is necessary for any explanation of how we go about it.[63] Most researchers in this area hold that deontic reasoning about social rules is *domain specific*.[64] The evidence indicates that reasoning about social rules is not simply an instance of a general capacity to follow rules; it is not even the same as the capacity to follow prudential rules.[65] Humans appear to have specific domains of rule-based reasoning, and one of the domains is social-moral rules. Leda Cosmides and her co-authors have especially stressed that under the influence of evolutionary forces, reasoning about moral obligations and entitlements is a distinct domain of reasoning with its own competencies and "mental logic."[66] There is evidence, for example, that reasoning about prescriptive social rules takes place in a different part of the brain than thinking about prudential rules. One of Cosmides' co-workers,

---

[63] See K. I. Manktelow and D. Over, "Deontic Reasoning," p. 92.

[64] Ibid., p. 103. This provides empirical support for the moral pluralism thesis advanced in Appendix A. Philosophers often resist this empirical claim. Heath claims that it is implausible to think that rule following in different domains employs different "modules" (*Following the Rules*, p. 9). Prinz also strenuously denies this hypothesis – he sees it as a threat to his defense of cultural relativism, and so propounds rival hypotheses (*The Emotional Construction of Morals*, pp. 263ff). Heath's and Prinz's skepticism notwithstanding, there is sound evidence for this view.

[65] Fiddick, "Deontic Reasoning," p. 108. Again, Prinz resists this idea. *The Emotional Construction of Morals*, pp. 266–7.

[66] Leda Cosmides, "The Logic of Social Exchange: Has Natural Selection Shaped How Humans Reason? Studies with the Wason Selection Task," p. 232.

Laurence Fiddick, conducted functional magnetic resonance imaging studies that indicate that deontic rules relating to social interactions are processed in parts of the brain having to do with social and emotional understanding.[67] Cosmides and John Tooby have argued that social rules arose in contexts of possible reciprocal benefits with the possibility of cheating through which one party can gain additional illicit benefits or reduced costs for herself.[68] Cosmides' hypothesis is that the domain of moral deontic reasoning is shaped by "social contract" reasoning: cooperation between two or more individuals for mutual benefit.[69] In game theoretic terms, her hypothesis is that deontic reasoning has been shaped by the demands of cooperation in mixed-motive games: all can gain by following cooperative rules, but there is an incentive to cheat. (Hence the relevance of the discussion of such games in Chapter II.)

In section 7.2 I argued that a compelling model of social evolution indicates that cooperation requires not only following rules but cooperators punishing those who violate them. We already considered (§7.4) some experimental evidence for the tendency to punish cheaters. A striking support for the idea that social morality depends on Rule-following Punishers is provided by the findings in moral psychology that indicate that our understanding of social rules is tightly bound to our ability to detect cheaters in mixed-motive social interactions.[70] The wealth of data supporting this hypothesis not only supports the claim that reasoning about social rules is domain specific, being closely tied to understanding social interactions, but, in addition, it provides important insight into the

---

[67] Fiddick, "Adaptive Domains of Deontic Reasoning."
[68] See Leda Cosmides and John Tooby, "Evolutionary Psychology and the Generation of Culture, Part II"; Cosmides, "The Logic of Social Exchange"; Fiddick, "Adaptive Domains of Deontic Reasoning."
[69] Cosmides, "The Logic of Social Exchange," p. 193. For a critical discussion of Cosmides, see Patricia W. Cheng and Keith J. Holyoak, "On the Natural Selection of Reasoning Theories." Joseph and Natalie Henrich – in my view rightly – point out that although Cosmides and her colleagues are correct to tie deontic reasoning to the social contract, they put too much weight on reciprocity and not enough on social rules. *Why Humans Cooperate*, pp. 142-43.
[70] Although cheater detection is plausibly understood as based on solving these games, it is quite clear that we can follow, and detect cheaters on, any social rule. See Henrich and Henrich, *Why Humans Cooperate*, p. 143.

nature of an adequate social rule. As I have stressed, if the rules are to solve the problems of mixed-motive games, then they must (*i*) provide determinate enough guidance that we can gain the benefits of cooperation through coordinating our activities, and (*ii*) be determinate enough that we can detect cheaters without incurring great costs (thus confirming the analysis of §7.3). We understand social deontic rules so readily and see that a "falsification" rather than a "confirmation" strategy is appropriate because the rules are, first and foremost, about cooperation under incentive to defect, and so looking out for cheaters is of the first importance.

These findings should make us wary of accepting the common supposition that there is a general unified account – one applying to all rules – of what is involved in following a rule. Many, for instance, think that Wittgenstein's account of rule following gives rise to a fully general analysis of the place of rules in thinking.[71] Others hold that prudential-rule–based reasoning is the model for other practical rules.[72] This seems most unlikely. We have reason to suppose that our cognitive structure is such that reasoning about indicatives, prudential-rule following, and social-rule following are processed in different parts of the brain, with different ties to emotional states, that humans have very different competencies in these types of reasoning that develop at different ages, and that understanding social rules is fundamentally related to cheater detection while, say, this plays no part in prudential rules. Our best philosophy of mind and our best account of practical rationality is a reflective and rationalized understanding of actual human capacities and activities. As we come to know more about these, and as we come to see that what, given our folk psychology, we have treated as a unitary phenomenon actually involves different cognitive domains, our philosophical analysis must adjust. If this is correct, the Baier–Strawson View, which identifies social morality as a discrete phenomenon based on social-rule following, is certainly bolstered. The suspicion that the Baier–Strawson View arbitrarily hives off one area of morality is undermined: there is good reason to conceive of social morality as a discrete area of inquiry.

[71] See, e.g., Philip Pettit, *Rules, Reasons, and Norms*, Part I.
[72] See, e.g., Scott J. Shapiro, "The Difference That Rules Make."

9 The Rationality of Following Rules

9.1 DOES EVOLUTION BLIND US TO THE WISDOM OF THE FOOL?

Richerson, Boyd, the Henrichs, and others maintain that the development of humans as Rule-following Punishers has been a process of cultural, and to some extent also biological, evolution: culture has itself provided an environment in which natural selection has occurred, so that the evolution of culture and genes has had important interactive effects.[73] In section 7.4 I indicated that experimental data about punishing non-cooperators in mixed motive games endorses this analysis. An even more important source of empirical support derives from findings in moral psychology that we have examined in section 8. There is very strong evidence that from a very early age humans excel at deontic reasoning, and this reasoning is intimately related to cheater detection abilities concerning social rules. A compelling hypothesis is that much of our cognitive structure concerning the processing of moral social rules has been formed in environments in which reproductive success depended on being in groups of Rule-following Punishers, and being such rule followers was a viable individual survival strategy within a cooperative group. Our thinking about social morality is, to a large extent, the thinking of Rule-following Punishers – the sort of thinking upon which social cooperation depended. The convergence of sociological models of cooperation and studies of deontic reasoning is striking: following deontic rules and detecting cheaters seems absolutely fundamental to understanding humans as social creatures. The analyses of sections 7 and 8 are thus strongly reinforcing.

Thus – *pace* the view of many moral and social philosophers – the appeal to moral rules to make good the failures of instrumental rationality to explain cooperation (Chapter II) is by no means ad hoc. Yet we have not addressed the rationality of following rules. Perhaps, though rule following is necessary to social order and so the evolution of rule followers is necessary for such order, being

---

[73] Richerson and Boyd, *Not by Genes Alone; How Culture Transformed Human Evolution*; Henrich and Henrich, *Why Humans Cooperate*, chap. 2.

such a rule follower is nevertheless irrational: by a sort of cunning of evolution, most of us are induced to deliberate and act irrationally for the sake of social order. Perhaps Hobbes' fool really saw through the confusions of our evolutionary baggage to perceive the truth: that reason can only tell us how to achieve our own goals and, so, reason can never instruct us to set aside our concerns to conform to social rules. Prominent philosophers have been convinced that the apparent irrationality of rule following is so deep a problem that, in the end, they worry that following social rules may ultimately rest on a sort of mistake or deception.[74] Hayek is, I think, ultimately correct that this hypothesis makes little sense insofar as it appears to suppose that there is a faculty called "rationality" that was not itself formed by our evolution. When Hayek tells us that "individual reason is a product of interindividual relationships,"[75] he is arguing that our conception of rationality is itself a product of social life. Mind is at least partly a product of the social order in which it has evolved.[76] Successful social orders evolve ways of reasoning that make sense of following social rules:[77] hence Hayek's often-quoted remark that reason not only shapes culture but is shaped by it.[78] Still, this only suggests that an adequate account of rationality should end up making sense of something so basic to human culture as following social rules and detecting cheaters; it does not tell us how to do it. We need to turn from sociological and psychological studies to a more traditional question of social philosophy: what is a rule of social morality, and how do such rules relate to the goals, ends, and purposes of individuals?

9.2 THREE BROADLY INSTRUMENTAL PROPOSALS

(a) Rational Conditional Policies as Weak Rules

I begin by examining accounts of rule following that seek to redeem its rationality by, in some more complex way, tying it to a sort of instrumental reasoning thus, as it were, resurrecting the basic idea

---

[74] See Larry Alexander and Emily Sherwin, *The Rule of Rules*, pp. 86–91.
[75] Hayek, The Counter-Revolution of Science, p. 91.
[76] Hayek, *Rules and Order*, p. 17.
[77] Hayek, "Notes on the Evolution of Systems of Rules of Conduct," p. 72.
[78] Hayek, *The Political Order of a Free People*, p. 155.

of instrumentalism as being the heart of rational action. Joseph Raz advances an account of "mandatory norms" that appears to show the rationality of following rules that instruct one to set aside one's goals. According to Raz, "[a] person follows a mandatory norm if and only if he believes that the norm is a valid reason for him to do the norm-act when the conditions for application obtain and that it is valid reason for disregarding conflicting reasons and if he acts on those beliefs."[79] Raz requires both that one has a first-order reason to act on the norm and that one takes the norm as "exclusionary" in the sense that it is a reason to disregard some reasons not to act on the norm. It thus follows that in some cases one will act against one's "balance of reasons": the norm instructs one to ignore some considerations that, if considered, would have mandated a different action. Consider an example discussed by Raz:

> Jill has made a rule to spend her holidays in France. . . . Jill faces many conflicting considerations, but she has no intention to act on the balance of reasons. She has adopted a rule to spend her holidays in France and she did so precisely in order to spare herself the necessity of deciding every year what to do during her holidays. She adopted the rule in order not to have to act on the balance of reasons on each occasion. Having the rule is like having decided in advance what to do. When the holidays come she is not going to reconsider the matter. Her rule is for her an exclusionary reason.[80]

Raz holds that this is a genuine case of a rule based on an exclusionary reason. Jill has a standing policy, we might say, of taking her vacations in France, and this policy precludes her from considering year-by-year where, on the basis of all her reasons, is the best place to vacation. So there can be a case in which Jill, reasoning on the basis of her standing policy, goes to France whereas, if she had deliberated on her full set of reasons, she would have gone to Greece; nevertheless, she is thought to have reason to act on the rule. It looks like in individual cases one's reasons to act as determined by the rule need not align with the reasons that follow from

---

[79] Raz, "Reasons for Actions, Decisions, and Norms," p. 140. See also Raz, *Practical Reason and Norms*, chap. 2.

[80] Raz, "Facing Up: A Reply," p. 1156.

one's goals, and so on. Still, we would expect this policy to align with her overall values and concerns over the long run. Jill may think that the extra time involved in rethinking the issue each year would not be worth it: she would usually go to France anyway, and the alternatives are not really much better. Or perhaps she is anxious about such deliberations and is happier if she has a policy of not deliberating. If the policy is to be rational, though, surely it must, overall, align with her total set of aims and concerns over the long run. Suppose Jill became aware that the policy of always vacationing in France was, overall and all things considered, less conducive to her concerns than a policy of alternating every other year between France and Greece. The alternating policy now seems to be the rational one to adopt. Faced with a choice between incompatible Policies A and B, where B better satisfies all one's concerns and goals, Jill has more reason to adopt B. Of course she could still continue on with A, her France-only policy, but now this looks to be rationally suspect. As an economist would say, the opportunity costs of continuing with policy A exceed its benefits; the opportunity costs of staying with A is to forgo the greater benefits of B. Perhaps Jill has a meta-policy against reconsidering policies, and that is her reason not to reconsider. But the same point can be made with meta-policies: if there are two meta-policies, A^* and B^*, where B^* better satisfies all one's aims and goals, one has more reason to adopt B^*. Rational policies must in the end align with one's overall concerns.

I cautioned against assuming that prudential rules enlighten us about social rules (§8.2) but there is a long tradition in social and political philosophy that depicts social rules as conditional policies that enhance long-term goal pursuit. On this view, "to accept a rule and be guided by it is to put oneself in a position in which the balance of reasons could turn out, if only one had deliberatively explored them, to favor reconsideration."[81] Consider again Hobbes' laws of nature. These are typically understood as rules the following of which, if adhered to by others, will best promote one's values. The idea is that *if* others follow these rules that sometimes instruct us not to follow our immediate self-interest, then one's

<hr />

[81] Edward McClennan, "The Rationality of Being Guided by Rules," p. 232.

own following them is in one's own long-term interest. Although the laws of nature are in the enlightened self-interest of each, Hobbes thought that people tend to be biased and passionate. More important, in some situations one would do better by violating them. Because Hobbes believed that people are short-sighted, they pay far too much attention to these short-term gains.[82] Consequently, adopting a policy of acting on the laws of nature and not considering the balance of reasons in each case may be the most rational course of action – the one that best aligns with our goals.

An account of moral rules as rational conditional policies has been tremendously appealing in the history of moral and political thought. To many it promises the best possibility of explaining the nature of rule-governed social life. Yet its problems are clear. Although Raz's version is not concerned simply with instrumental rationality qua goal pursuit but with the best way to act on one's all-things-considered reasons, the problems with such an account are remarkably similar to those we explored in relation to instrumental rationality (§4.1). (*i*) Following Gauthier, one may seek to abandon any commitment to modular rationality (§4.3*b*), so that one should follow the rule at time t_2 even though one knows that, at this time, acting on it will fail to do what one has most (non–rule-based) reason to do. But then it looks irrational: even if Jill knows that, from here on out, the balance of reasons supports dropping her policy, she sticks with it because in the past at t_1 she has made it her policy. Again, it seems irrational to be so tied to the past. Alternatively, (*ii*) modular rationality may be affirmed, but then the policy will be dropped when it no longer is an effective way to act on one's all-things-considered reasons. However, on this view, rule following is rational only in the sense of a conditional policy: a rule should be dropped when doing so would better serve our other, non–rule-based, reasons.

Rules that are simply means to secure action on one's overall, non–rule-based reasons, are *weak rules*.[83] They can enter into deliberations, but they never can override one's all-things-considered reasons to do what, putting aside the rule, one thinks is

---

[82] See Hampton, *Hobbes and the Social Contract Tradition*, chap. 3.

[83] Cf. the account of weak rules and strong rules in Goldman, *Practical Rules*. I borrow these terms from him.

best.[84] Rules understood as conditional rational policies are weak rules. A person can adopt a policy to obey the rule, but the rationality of the policy depends on the rule aligning, at least over the long term, with one's non–rule-based reasons. As soon as one discovers that such a policy no longer is an effective way to act on one's overall reasons, its justification withers and continuing on with it looks irrational. The rules of social morality are not weak rules of this sort. They do not depend on the claim that they are simply (even broadly) instruments for acting on one's best (non–rule-based) reasons. We are open to criticism for violating a social rule;[85] the claim that following the rule did not serve our purposes or our other reasons, or is not the best way to do so in the long run, by no means is guaranteed to silence appropriate criticism. As Frederick Schauer has stressed, the way in which rules are distinct from goal or end-based reasoning is manifest when we must follow them even in the face of such "recalcitrant experiences" – where following the rule does not achieve our end, or the aim of the policy.[86] Let us call rules that demand compliance even when one realizes they do not best promote one's goals *strong rules*.

Strong rules may seem *too* strong: it would appear that they simply instruct one to engage in Φ-type acts with no concern for, or

---

[84] Especially with regard to prudential rules, the alignment of the rules and ends may be complex (that is the reason the rule is necessary). Consider what might be called the "bolstering" role of rules – that is, bolstering our reasons to do what we already have adequate reason to do. Nozick argues that an important function of prudential rules, policies, and principles is to help us get past "temptations, hurdles, distractions, and diversions" and so help us better achieve our ends. Suppose I wish to work after dinner, and always have good reason to drink only one glass of wine. Nozick suggests that on any single night it may seem that an extra glass of wine makes sense – I can always work tomorrow, and the payoff of working is in the future, but the payoff of drinking wine is now. If I discount the future, it may always seem that the best thing to do is to have the extra glass, and so I never get work done after dinner, though doing so would best promote my goals. A rule never to drink more than one glass might be seen as bolstering my reasons to refrain and helping to overcome my discounting of the future. In this case, the rule is aligned with one's all-things-considered goals against one's immediate goals. See Nozick, *The Nature of Rationality*, pp. 14ff. I raise doubts about the details of Nozick's account in "Goals, Symbols, Principles," pp. 199–214. See also Shapiro, "The Difference That Rules Make" for an account that stresses the way rules bind future selves.

[85] See Hart, *The Concept of Law*, pp. 54ff.

[86] Schauer, *Playing by the Rules*, chap. 3.

relation to, one's values, goals, and so on. Whereas the obvious appeal of rules as rational conditional policies is their linkage of rule conformity to efficiently promoting one's overall goals and concerns, strong rules appear to "avoid" these problems by abandoning all attempt to align a person's goals and her overall reasons. However, it does not follow from the definition of a strong social rule that it makes no connection between its range of application and promotion of a person's values. To see this, contrast two views:

> *The Common Good View*: According to B. J. Diggs "Following Rousseau and Kant, there is a fundamental requirement that binds one, in matters that concern the common good, to seek a consensus to which all can reasonably agree." According to Diggs, this is another way of understanding Kant's idea of the "Original Contract."[87]

> *The Moral Realist View*: According to Russ Shafer-Landau, moral realists "believe that there are moral truths that obtain independently of any preferred moral perspective, in the sense that *the moral standards that fix the moral facts are not made true by virtue of their ratification from within any given actual or hypothetical perspective.*"[88]

As stated, both the Common Good View and Moral Realist View can endorse strong rules. For the Common Good View, L can strongly require Φ-type acts in the sense that while L advances everyone's good to a "reasonable" extent (and, of course, that needs to be explicated), for at least some persons in society L does not constitute a rational conditional policy. Given their expectation that the rest will follow L, some people may do better to adopt some policy Y, which would better promote their good, or better track their overall reasons. Given that, L is not a rational policy for them, but the Common Good View nevertheless may hold that Φ is required of them. That is, L is still a strong rule: it requires Alf's conformity in cases in which following it manifestly does not best advance his goals: L advances a deontic requirement on Alf to engage in Φ-type acts even if over the long term such acts are not the best way to advance his overall (non–rule)-based reasons. This,

---

[87] B. J. Diggs, "The Common Good as a Reason for Political Action," p. 293.
[88] Russ Shafer-Landau, *Moral Realism*, p. 15. Emphasis in original.

though, does not mean that L is in no way aligned with his goals. According to the Common Good View, unless L had some level of "ratification" from everyone's perspectives – it must promote their good to a "reasonable" extent – it could not be a valid strong requirement. So the Common Good View of strong rules requires what we might call "minimal alignment" of the strong rules with one's good, evaluative commitments, ends or values. In contrast, as the Moral Realist View is stated, it seems that there could be some who, consulting simply their perspectives and their evaluative standards or perspectives, see no reason to ratify L, and yet L nevertheless is held to identify or imply requirements to which they must conform. In Chapter V I shall defend the Social Contract/Common Good View of strong rules. [89]

(b) Rules as Generalized and Abstracted Statements of Moral Reasons

Closely related to the rational conditional policy approach is viewing social rules as generalized and abstracted statements of moral (or other normative) reasons to act. Suppose there is a set of reasons $\{r_1...r_n\}$ such that they typically all relate to the moral thing to do in circumstances of type C. Suppose also that when we consider C-type circumstances and $\{r_1...r_n\}$, we conclude that Φ-type acts are generally the best or the moral thing to do in these circumstances (§8.1). We thus might formulate a rule, "In C, Φ!" Why? Larry Alexander and Emily Sherwin analyze the question from the perspective of Lex, a law giver:

Lex's rules respond to a variety of reasoning errors [of those to whom the rule is directed]. Perhaps the simplest type of error results from lack of information or expertise. In this case, the function of the rule is to require uniform conduct when this is the best course of action for most of those subject to the rule. If, among the sum of actions governed by the rule, more harm would result from mistaken judgment that from compliance with the rule, the rule is justified.[90]

Lex has reason to think that overall and given people's errors, biases, information problems, and so on, general conformity to the

---

[89] We might call this the "weak interpretation of strong rules."
[90] Alexander and Sherwin, *The Rule of Rules*, p. 55.

rule "In C, Φ!" would be the best way for subjects to act on $\{r_1...r_n\}$ when they are applicable, and to do the rational thing in C-type circumstances. This shows the close tie to Raz's approach, for the rule is still justified as instrumental to getting people to act on their best reasons. If we all act on "In C, Φ!" then generally we will best track the reasons we have in C circumstances – reasons that are in some sense prior to the rule.

The clear problem that has plagued this view is that because the rule is a generalization of the reasons that apply in C-type circumstances, there are bound to occur token instances of C where a person could best track her reasons to act by not performing a Φ-type action. Rules abstract from contexts, and there may be something about this particular context such that a person has reasons not to φ (a token of Φ) but, instead, to γ.[91] If in this case she recognizes this, then the rational thing for her to do must be to γ, since that it what is recommended by her all-things-considered reasons in this case, and it must be rational to act on one's all-things-considered reasons.[92] So just as a straightforwardly instrumentally rational agent will have no reason to follow a rule when doing so does not best promote his ends, an all-things-considered rational agent does not have reason to follow such rules when doing so does not best reflect her full set of reasons in a particular context. "[I]ndividual actors may endorse Lex's rule, believing that it does more good than harm. Yet . . . actors faced with particular problems may also conclude that the rule's prescription is not the best answer to the question what to do. If so, it is not rational, and arguably not morally acceptable, for them to follow the rule."[93]

(c) Goldman's Resolution of the Paradox of Rule Following

If one is convinced that social rules are in this broad sense instrumental, and if one recognizes that particular contexts are bound to occur in which these generalized guides are not effective in producing the correct result, it is very hard to see how such rules can

---

[91] See Schaefer, *Playing by the Rules,* chap. 2, and Frederick Schauer, "Rules and the Rule of Law;" Russ Shafer-Landau, "Moral Rules;" Alexander and Sherwin, *The Rule of Rules,* chap. 4.

[92] Unless Raz is correct about the nature of rational policies (§6.2).

[93] Alexander and Sherwin, *The Rule of Rules,* p. 60.

give compelling reasons to comply even when they clearly are not effective routes to our ends, or devices for acting on our "on balance" reasons. Alan H. Goldman has recently argued that the "paradox" of seeing rules as both instrumental and strong can be resolved.

The situation defined here is one in which (1) a rule is justified by the fact that universal compliance with it produces better consequences than those produced by all acting on their own, (2) each individual can produce better consequences (as measured by ordinary moral considerations absent the rule) by deviating from the rule, (3) the rule itself does not constitute a reason for following it, (4) only ordinary consequential reasoning (in the broad sense) counts, (5) each individual ought to produce the best consequences in her actions, and (6) each individual ought to follow the rule. These six propositions seem mutually incompatible but are all true in some circumstances. Hence, the paradox.[94]

Goldman's solution has several steps. First, he argues quite correctly that general conformity to rules is often necessary to a group's securing collective goods, such as public goods. Goldman further argues, however, that it many cases there is a collective moral obligation for the group to provide such goods – "the group itself has an overriding obligation to achieve the collective outcome at which the group aims . . . education, police, national security, and transportation, among others . . . are of such vital importance that the opportunity to produce them amounts to a moral obligation."[95] The next step is to argue that the group cannot fulfill its obligations unless individual members do so:

each member of the group shares the obligation to contribute . . . so as to achieve the needed collective outcome. The obligation of the group entails an obligation on the part of its individual members to do their part to contribute to the fulfillment of the obligation. Otherwise, it could make no sense to speak of an obligation on the part of the group. The implication is a simple consequence of the fact that the group consists of its individual

---

[94] Alan H. Goldman, "The Rationality of Complying with Rules: Paradox Resolved," p. 455.
[95] Ibid., p. 462.

members. . . . A group cannot have an obligation if the members of which it is composed do not share individual obligations to fulfill it.[96]

At this last stage something like a principle of fair play is invoked: if there is a collective obligation which others are doing their part to fulfill, then fairness requires that one does one's part, and so complies with rules. [97]

While inventive, this line of analysis is ultimately misconceived. To explain as rational so fundamental a phenomenon as following strong moral rules in terms of (*i*) a group obligation to provide goods and (*ii*) a principle of fairness about acting on individual obligations needed to discharge group obligations is a little like explaining the rationality of exchange for mutual benefit in terms of a shared commitment to maximizing the general welfare, and the belief that exchange will do that. The problem is not that the argument is invalid, but the order of explanation is wrong: the basic is being explained in terms of the quite refined and indeed highly disputable (i.e., that group obligations, or the general welfare, are obviously the basis of reasons to act). There is in fact good reason to think that a concern for fairness is itself a manifestation of a certain sort of strong reciprocity (§7.2), and so the development of rule following and a concern for fairness may be intimately related.[98] If so, explaining following social rules by invoking the rationality of acting fairly seems to beg the real question: what makes fairness rational is plausibly intimately related to what makes rule following rational.

9.3 DISSOLVING THE FIRST MYSTERY OF SOCIAL RULES: HOW RULES CREATE REASONS

(a) The Modest Version of the Rules Create Reason Thesis
Goldman believes two great virtues of his rather complex proposal are, first, that "there is no mysterious appeal to the rule as itself creating or nullifying moral reasons for actions. Only ordinary

---

[96] Ibid., pp. 463–4. Paragraph breaks deleted.
[97] Ibid., p. 464.
[98] See Ernst Fehr and Urs Fischbacher, "The Economics of Strong Reciprocity."

consequentialist reasoning suffices when consequences are taken broadly. . . . Second, this sufficiency obviates the need for a mysterious opposition between different and irreconcilable principles of rationality."[99] In Goldman's eyes, in order to avoid this double mystery, we must show that "consequentialist reasoning suffices" to explain rule following.

Let us turn to the first apparent mystery, namely, that the rule itself might "create" a reason to act or, let us say, provide a reason to act that cannot be reduced to the rule's instrumental value in securing some outcome. What does it mean to say that a rule can "create" a reason? One modest way of answering this question certainly does not invoke any mysterious property of rules. According to Philip Pettit, a consequentialist believes that "the proper way to respond to any values recognized is to promote them: that is, in every choice set to select the option with prognoses that mean it is the best gamble with those values."[100] In contrast:

The deontological approach takes a certain universal value – say, the respecting of such and such rights – as given and argues that institutions should be shaped in a way that bears witness to this value, honoring it punctiliously in the treatment they give to different human beings. In particular, institutions should be shaped to honour the value even if this means, as a result of various side-effects, that there is less of the value overall: even if it means that in general other agents respect people's rights less well than they might have been brought to.[101]

In a similar vein, S. I. Benn distinguished responding to value by maximizing or promoting it from respecting it. As Benn argued, someone who professes to value, say, a great art work, but saw no reason to refrain from ridiculing it or using it to weigh down garbage, would not be respecting the value. If to respect something is to give "appropriate consideration or recognition to some feature" of it in our deliberations about what to do, it seems inappropriate to treat a valued work thus, and so is disrespectful.[102]

---

[99] Goldman, "The Rationality of Complying with Rules," pp. 467–8.

[100] Philip Pettit, "Consequentialism," p. 233.

[101] Philip Pettit, *The Common Mind*, p. 303. For a similar understanding of deontology, see Robert Nozick, *Philosophical Explanations*, p. 499.

[102] Stanley I. Benn, "Personal Freedom and Environmental Ethics," p. 414.

A somewhat different view distinguishes acting on rules (or, more broadly, principles) from pursuing values not in terms of different ways of responding to a common notion of "value" but in different ways of responding to fundamentally different normative concepts. Writes Benn:

A contrast familiar in the philosophical literature is that between deontological theories of ethics, with their corresponding reasons for action, and teleological theories and their corresponding reasons. I shall work with a related but somewhat different distinction, between reasons of respect and reasons of concern, the former being *person-centered*, the latter *value-centered*. Reasons of concern look primarily to the good consequences of an action, to whether it will bring about or preserve some valued and valuable state of affairs, sustain some valued and valuable activity, or promote the survival and well-being of some valued and valuable object. Such objects, which I call *axiotima* (things to be valued), may be animate or inanimate.[103]

Although Benn allowed that in some cases we might distinguish respecting a value from promoting it, his position was that, by and large, maximization is the appropriate response to value. However, while values are normally best promoted, persons are to be respected. "Person-centered reasons have to do with principles, such as freedom, justice, equal respect for a person's rights, and fidelity to truth inasmuch as we are committed to these principles in our dealings with any other person, simply in virtue of that person being a person. . . . The notion of a natural person is fundamental to such principles."[104] Our reasons for action differ, argued Benn, because they are based on different sorts of normative concepts.

I deem these "modest" versions of the "rules create reasons thesis" as rules do not in any deep sense "create" reasons. The reasons characteristic of rules and principles, we might say, each flow from distinct normative notions (values, persons).[105] The characteristics of the reasons identified by rule- or principle-based responses differ from promoting responses, but in both cases the

---

[103] Ibid., pp. 7–8. Emphasis in original.
[104] S. I. Benn, *A Theory of Freedom*, pp. 7–8.
[105] I have examined this "flow model" of reasons for action in detail in "Goals, Symbols, Principles."

reasons ultimately derive from the normative concepts of value or personhood. Why might someone think this is mysterious? Apparently because, though it is easy to see that one can have reason to *promote* a value, there is something odd about the instantiation relation at the heart of respecting and honoring (and, we have seen, also rule following). To remind ourselves, we saw in section 8.1, rules suppose the following:

> *Instantiation Relation*: An act may/must not/must be performed by persons *P* under conditions *C* if it instantiates property *T*.

Much of the skepticism about following rules is, I think, traceable to worries that the instantiation relation cannot be at the root of practical rationality. Nothing is more common than to be confronted with an example in which the agent is confronted with a choice between an act that instantiates a property and one that achieves goals. How you can have reason to advance your goals is obvious; how you can have reason to perform an act that instantiates a property seems odd. Or so it is often thought. However, as we saw in section 4.3, ultimately a theory of instrumental rationality must endorse consumption rationality, and consumption rationality itself presupposes the instantiation relation. I have a goal of drinking good beer, and this is an instance of a good beer, so I have a reason to drink it. Unless we resort to hedonism or to the "itch" theory of desire satisfaction – in which my *aim* in drinking the beer is to rid myself of the desire, or to achieve a state of satisfaction – I must say that I drink this particular beer because it is a good beer, and I value good beer. That is, this is an instance of the stuff I value. More generally, the very idea of promoting values or ends implies consistency requirements (§4.3c), and these are themselves rules, and so following them implies recognition of instantiation relations.[106] The instantiation relation, then, cannot be

---

[106] It might be argued that while instrumentally rational agents must *conform* to such rules, they do not *follow* them. Conforming to them, we might say, defines a rational agent, but rationality does not consist in actually recognizing their requirements and taking them as guidelines (see §§4.3, 10.2). However, rational agents must be able to recognize mistakes and reasoning; those who make mistakes are not irrational, but those who fail to respond to errors may well be. As John Pollock points out, rationality is best understood as norms about how to cognize (*Thinking about Acting*, p. 10). On the relation between performance and competence errors, see Edward Stein, *Without Good Reason: The Rationality Debate*

the source of the special mystery about rule following for it is basic to instrumentalist reasoning as well.

(b) The More Ambitious Version

The modest version of the "rules create reason" thesis is not mysterious. The problem for this view is, rather, practical. When stated in terms of abstract principles – such as "Respect persons!" – it captures the heart of deontological views of ethics; it is much more difficult to see how this can ground social rules that provide the sorts of specific requirements for action that are necessary (§7.3). The problem here is basically that which we have already considered in relation to Alexander and Sherwin's analysis of rules (§9.2b). With any rule specific enough to provide guidance to solve the problems of cooperation in social life, there will be some contexts in which the rule's requirements ("Φ in circumstances C!") do not properly instantiate the relevant moral property or concept. Although there is no great puzzle with the principle "Respect persons!" it is not clear how this could lead to a strong social rule such as "Do not interfere with adults purchasing pornography!" Perhaps this rule usually instantiates respect, but it is also plausible that sometimes violating it might better instantiate respect for personhood. If we wish to uphold the rationality of following strong social rules rather than abstract principles, we need to defend a more ambitious version of the "rules create reasons" thesis: strong social rules themselves provide us with reasons to act. Rather than showing that the instantiation relation is a rational response to the recognition of some normative property, we must show that people place value directly on following rules of social morality.

Normal socialized individuals care about the rules of social morality.[107] "Caring," is, I think, especially apt in this context, since there is strong evidence that moral rule following is closely associated with emotional-social cognitive capacities. Perhaps the most robust finding in contemporary moral psychology is the intimate

---

in *Philosophy and Cognitive Science,* esp. chaps. 1 and 2. I have greatly benefited from discussions on these matters with Jonathan Anomaly.

[107] Heath, *Following the Rules,* p. 85.

relation of moral rules and the emotions.[108] There is a great deal of evidence that reasoning about quintessentially moral questions such as whether to kill one to save five takes places in the social-emotional parts of the brain.[109] And there is an impressive body of evidence that the violation of moral rules is firmly linked to emotional reactions.[110] People typically feel "moral anger" – resentment and indignation – when others violate moral rules, and tend to feel guilt at their own violations.[111] Importantly, Paul Rozin has identified a "process of moralization" by which behavior becomes moralized: that is, it comes to be socially censured. This moralization seems accompanied by an "emotionalization" of people's reactions: at least in some cases disgust is generated.[112] Overall, there is impressive evidence that as the norms and their violation become emotionalized, they become widely seen as moral.[113] On the other hand, psychopaths, though they are instrumentally rational, do not care at all about moral rules: there is good reason to believe that their amoralism comes from a lack of emotional investment in moral rules (see §§11.2, 12.1).

Social creatures care about many things involved with living with others, such as families, friends, and moral rules.[114] It is no part of my claim that agents must, qua agents, care about moral rules, but rather that there is nothing at all mysterious in humans caring about them in a way that does not derive simply from their usefulness as ways to pursue goals, or as instruments to act on one's other reasons. As we saw in Chapter II, purely instrumentally rational agents cannot reason themselves into being rule followers

---

[108] Chapter IV is largely devoted to the place of the emotions in our moral practice; what I say here is merely a sketch.

[109] This is true, at least, when the agents are reasoning about moral rules rather than simply cost–benefit calculations. See, for example, Joshua D. Greene et al., "The Neural Bases of Cognitive Conflict and Control in Moral Judgment"; Joshua D. Greene et al., "An fMRI Investigation of Emotional Engagement in Moral Judgment"; Joshua D. Greene, "The Secret Joke of Kant's Soul." See also §8.2.

[110] For excellent discussions directed to philosophers, see Jesse J. Prinz, *The Emotional Construction of Morals*, pp. 21ff; Shaun Nichols, *Sentimental Rules*, chap. 1; Jesse J. Prinz and Shaun Nichols, "Moral Emotions."

[111] For an especially nice account, see Shaun Nichols, "After Incompatibilism: A Naturalistic Defense of the Reactive Attitudes."

[112] See Paul Rozin, "The Process of Moralization."

[113] Shaun Nichols, "Emotions, Norms, and the Moralization of Fairness."

[114] None of which psychopaths care much about.

and yet rule following seems absolutely critical to social life. What reason cannot achieve on its own, cultural (and biological) evolution has: normal humans have evolved into social creatures who care about following moral rules. So far from being mysterious, our best understanding of the evolution of social cooperation strongly endorses the conclusion that Rule-following Punishers – agents who care about following moral rules and ensuring that others follow them too – are a prerequisite of a cooperative social order. Thus Hayek rightly points out that our reason presupposes morality (and our caring for it) as much as it presupposes our goals; it does not construct either.[115] This is not to say that none of our reasons to care about a social rule derive from our goals. That our concern with rules is not simply derivative of our goals does not mean that their impact on our goals, values, and ends is irrelevant to our all-things-considered reasons to follow rules. On the Common Good View (§9.2*a*), while moral rules provide normal humans with a reason to conform to them even when, all things considered, following the rule will not best advance one's goals, values, and ends, if the rule is deeply hostile to one's goals and other evaluative criteria, one will not have reason to follow it. These important matters will concern us later. For now, the core point is that there is nothing mysterious about social beings such as humans seeing moral rules as providing them with reasons to act that are not simply derivative of their ends, values, and so on.

Could it be that the mystery surrounding our devotion to moral rules is not that we care for them but that such a caring for them could give us a reason to act? Recall, though, that the standard instrumental view does not provide significant rationality conditions on what ends a person may endorse (§4.2); whatever "mystery" surrounds the idea that rules "create reasons," it cannot be that a "caring for" can ground a reason, for that is at the heart of the instrumentalist theory. So the "mystery" must be that while we can see why a rational person can care about her goals in a way that yields reasons, we cannot see why she should care about moral rules, except, derivatively, as a way to promote her own goals. Fundamental to being an agent is to have goals and to pursue them;

---

[115] Hayek, *The Constitution of Liberty*, p. 63.

but, it may be thought, it is not fundamental to being an agent that one cares about social rules. But by now we have seen that this atomistic and asocial conception of an agent in a large-scale society – as one who has ends and cares only derivatively about her cooperative relations with others – is a philosophic myth. If there ever were such humans (and that is most doubtful), societies composed of them would never have grown larger than the relatively small groups that can be organized by indirect reciprocity (§6.2).

9.4 DISSOLVING THE SECOND MYSTERY OF SOCIAL RULES: THE MULTIDIMENSIONALITY OF PRACTICAL RATIONALITY

(a) The Conceptual Unity Argument
Recall that, according to Goldman, the second reason for preferring an instrumentalist or consequentialist account of rule following is that it "obviates the need for a mysterious opposition between different and irreconcilable principles of rationality" (§9.2c). This complaint against rule-based reasoning is widespread, so it would do well for us to consider it carefully. We can distinguish two different formulations of it: (*i*) an argument about conceptual unity and (*ii*) an argument about indeterminacy. Both insist that allowing different types of reasons into rational deliberations leads to "different and irreconcilable demands of rationality."

The conceptual unity argument holds that we must possess a single coherent notion of what it means to be rational. To allow that fidelity to rules, as well as value promotion, counts as rational would be to admit "different" principles of – in the sense of different concepts of – rationality, and we would have no way then to decide what rationality is (hence the charge of irreconcilability). In appendix A, I argue that our concept of morality is pluralistic, in the sense that there is no obvious unified account of what is a "moral judgment." Social morality is very different from, say, the morality of individual ideals or virtue. Pluralistic accounts of a concept are often superior to a monistic theory that insists on squeezing a complex idea into a simple mold. However, even if we accept that our concept of rationality must be monistic, two considerations lead us to doubt that endorsing a direct reason to act on rules introduces significant pluralism. First, we have seen that the instantiation relation is basic both to instrumental rationality (§4.2) and to rule-based reasoning (§8.1), so there *is* a deep unity to both types of reasoning. It is not as if we are calling two entirely different things "rational"; we are explicating two different ways in which a person can see that cared-for general objects can be instantiated in her actions. Second, we should not suppose that the unity of rationality must be understood in terms of the principle "maximize value." An alternative, suggested by the work of Joseph Raz, is that the unity of rationality is the principle that we should always act on the "balance of reasons" or "the best reason overall." The unity of rationality, then, is not that there is only one sort of reason (promote greater over less value!), but that there is one sort of best response to one's reasons (act on one's best reasons!).

(b) Complex Decision Problems

This brings us to the second worry. If we admit multiple types of reasons, it appears we will be unable to determine what *is* the single best thing to do, so we will not be able to act on our best reasons: hence the objection from indeterminacy. How can we compare and trade off different sorts of reasons? This is indeed a problem for theories of rationality, but it arises within purely consequentialist theories as well as in those that combine nonconsequentialist and consequentialist reasoning. Ralph Keeney and Howard Raiffa contrasted "simple" and "complex" value problems.[116] Value problems in which a person is choosing different options ranked according to the same value are simple; every branch of one's decision tree has outcomes characterized by the same value. Under certainty – if the chooser knows the relative amounts of the value associated with each option – the choice is trivial; under risk one needs to perform expected utility calculations, but then the rational choice again is relatively straightforward. In contrast, in complex value problems different branches in one's decision tree are characterized by different values, so before one can make any decisions one must find how to consistently

---

[116] Ralph L. Keeney and Howard Raiffa, *Decisions with Multiple Objectives: Preferences and Value Tradeoffs*, pp. 14–19.

trade off different values. This "commensuration"[117] problem can be avoided only by adopting a monistic value theory, according to which there is only one value, thus making all choices simple value problems. When there are genuinely different and multiple values that cannot all be reduced to a third master value, problems of commensuration confront a theory: how is a certain amount of liberty to be compared with a certain amount of welfare? Many of the problems of commensuration are formal; they do not simply concern commensurating values but, more generally, trying to find some way to make consistent choices based on multiple evaluative criteria. These problems are certainly complex but by no means unsolvable. For present purposes the important point is that they confront pluralistic value consequentialism as well as a deeper pluralistic reasons theory.

So any complex theory of reasoning, whether based on complex values within a consequentialist framework or complex criteria within a broader theory, will have to consistently relate different desiderata. The complex theory will have to develop a trade-off rate between the different values. Let us suppose that this problem can be solved in the case of a complex value problem, in the sense that a person can order these different values. We should not think of this as a simple ordering of gross values (justice, liberty, equality, welfare) but as orderings of different bundles of value satisfaction.

One way to think of this is in terms of an indifference map between different amounts of value satisfaction, as in Display III-5, where the chooser is indifferent between satisfying liberty to degree A (and so no equality) and equality to degree B (and so no-liberty). The line A–B is thus an indifference curve.[118] As we travel "northeast" from the origin, the person prefers value combinations on higher indifference curves, any value combination on the line C–D is strictly preferred to one on A–B. Similarly, combination F is strictly preferred to G. We must remember that "preference"

---

[117] See Fred D'Agostino's insightful study, *Incommensurability and Commensuration: The Common Denominator*.

[118] It does not have the inward-sloping shape of the normal indifference curve as I am not supposing decreasing rates of marginal substitution (or, roughly, decreasing marginal utility). That may well be a characteristic of value trade-offs, in which case the curves would have the normal shape. Nothing turns on the point here.

simply describes an ordered pair. A preference always and necessarily relates two options (or bundles) and compares them in terms
of choice worthiness. To prefer x to y is not a special sort of reason
to rank x as more choice worthy: it simply *is* the ranking in terms of
choice worthiness. We define preference as the "P" relation, such
that xPy means "x is preferred to y," and that simply means that x
is more choice worthy than y. "Preference" thus understood is a
technical term in decision theory describing pairwise rankings, and
not the basis of any ranking.[119]

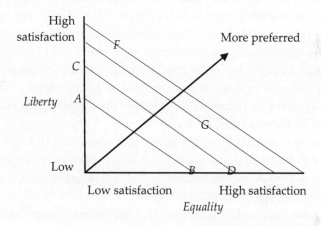

DISPLAY III-5 A TRADE-OFF RATE BETWEEN TWO VALUES

[119] Even those who know better sometimes slip into the error of supposing that we
rank x as better than y *because* we prefer it. The equation of the technical idea of a
"preference" with the folk psychology notion of a "desire" has caused endless
confusions. A closely related error is to suppose that we prefer x to y *because* x
gives us more utility. Unless we are appealing to some nontechnical sense of utility (such as welfare), this too literally makes no sense: a utility function is simply
a mathematical representation of one's preferences. It would be most odd to have
a preference because it promotes the maximization of a mathematical representation of one's preferences. But the error is easy to commit. John C. Harsanyi
writes: "If one individual prefers situation X to situation Y, while another prefers
Y to X, is this because the former individual attaches a *higher* utility to situation
X, or because he attaches a lower utility to situation Y, than does the latter?" To
prefer something just *is* to attach a higher utility; it cannot explain the higher
utility. "Cardinal Welfare, Individualistic Ethics, and Interpersonal Comparisons
of Utility," p. 16.

There is no reason preventing us from developing the same sort of trade-off rate between two rules, so long as several conditions are met. (*i*) A person must be able to judge that the satisfaction of any rule L_1 is more important, less important, or just as important, as any other L_2; (*ii*) her rankings must be consistent and transitive.[120] (*iii*) A rule can be implicated to different degrees in different situations or, I shall say, can vary in *salience*. Consider H. L. A. Hart's famous example of a rule that forbids vehicles in a park. Even if a bicycle rider places great weight on this rule, if she is uncertain whether it applies to bicycles, the rule will be less salient for her than in cases where its requirements are clear. Another type of variation in salience occurs in cases where a rule is relevant, and one knows how an action impacts it, but the extent of this impact is modest. I may endorse a property rule and believe it is wrong to trespass; but I may also hold that a quick shortcut across my neighbor's lawn to retrieve my newspaper does not impact very much on her property rights. (*iv*) In addition to recognizing degrees of salience, to have a constant trade-off rate a person's system of rules must be continuous in the sense that there will always be some point in which she is willing to trade-off small satisfaction of Rule L_1 for a greater satisfaction of L_2.[121] If these assumptions are met, then for any rules L_1 and L_2, we can develop a rule-indifference map along the lines of Display III-6. This indifference map has the same features as the value map in Display III-5: the person is indifferent between rule satisfactions on the *A–B*. And strictly prefers that she act on rule satisfactions on *C–D*.

---

[120] *Mutatis mutandis*, the conditions discussed in section 4.3c obtain.

[121] If the person's trade-off rates are not entirely continuous in the sense that she will never sacrifice any satisfaction of L_1 for any degree of satisfaction of L_2, we will get an indifference map with "chasms" that cannot be crossed. Benn considers these in *A Theory of Freedom* (pp. 56ff). My aim here is simply to show that rule trade-offs can be modeled the same as value trade-offs if they meet parallel conditions, and so invoking rule rationality into a pluralistic theory need not add great complications. Of course if the rules (or values) have special features, then the modeling becomes more complex.

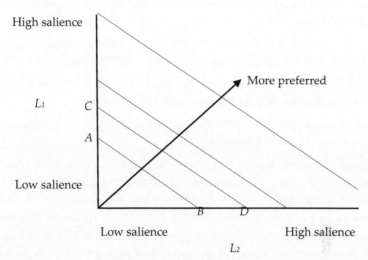

DISPLAY III-6 A TRADE-OFF RATE BETWEEN TWO RULES

If we can develop trade-off rates between values and between rules, there is no special problem with developing them between rules and values. Stanley Benn has done this. His preferred example was the case described by the Roman historian Livy, of the Roman consul Lucius Junius Brutus, who acted in accordance with his civic duty by sentencing his rebellious son to death. Let us understand this as a conflict between reasons of fidelity to the rules of his judicial office and his valuing the welfare and happiness of his family. Now Benn stressed that even though in this famous case (let us call it Case 1) Brutus acted on his reasons based on the rules of his office rather than his family values, it does not follow that a rational Brutus must do so in every case of conflict. For just as the family values may be either marginally or critically affected in a given situation – the "amount" of the good to be had may vary – as we have seen, so too rules are implicated to different degrees in different situations. For example, Benn considers another possible situation in which Brutus' civic duty and family concerns may clash. In Case 2, on his way to a Senate Committee meeting Brutus sees that one of his sons (not a rebellious one) is drowning in the Tiber and needs his assistance. If he saves him, Brutus will be a few minutes late for the meeting. Brutus thus confronts two choice situations, each with two options.

Case 1, option A (*1A*): act on the consular rule and sentence his son to death.

Case 1, option B (*1B*): promote his family values and so violate the duties of his office by pardoning his rebellious son.

Case 2, option A (*2A*): act on the duties of his office, get to the meeting in time, and let his innocent son drown in the Tiber.

Case 2, option B (*2B*): promote family values by saving his innocent son, and so be late for the meeting.

As Benn observes, Brutus may take an "ultra-Kantian view, that since his reason for [consular] action is that it is a duty and not, for example, a consequentially valuable action, any dereliction would be just as bad as any other."[122] But, as Benn says, "this would be an extreme and somewhat austere judgment."[123] In Case 2, Brutus may well choose to save his son (*2B*) instead of acting on his consular duty (*2A*) even if in Case 1 he chooses acting on his civic duty (*1A*) over saving his son's life (*1B*). Some may think this shows that he acts inconsistently, since at first he holds that *A* is preferred to *B*, then that *B* is preferred to *A*. But no inconsistency need be involved. In the second situation, the consular commitments are less "at stake" than in the first, historically famous, case. Brutus may reasonably hold that a consul who ignores proof of guilt and allows his son to go free would demonstrate contempt for his judicial duty, whereas being late for a meeting to save a son from drowning is a minor infraction, one that is consistent with taking his duty seriously.   Once again we can analyze Brutus' preferences in terms of indifference curves. Brutus must compare his value and rule systems, and determine his trade-offs between the two. Again, in this case Brutus' choice will depend on both the relative importance of the value and the rule, and the extent to which they are implicated in the choice. Brutus, for example, may know that it is his civic duty to attend consul meetings, and he also knows that saving his son will definitely impact on it by making him late; but being a few minutes late for a meeting does not greatly impact his duty, so the demands of duty will be less salient in his decision. Display III-7 gives Brutus' indifference map.

---

[122] Benn, *A Theory of Freedom*, p. 51.
[123] Ibid., p. 52.

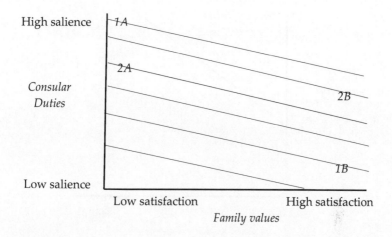

DISPLAY III-7 BRUTUS' INDIFFERENCE MAP

As we can see, Brutus tends overall to rank consular duties as more
important than family values. In the famous Case 1, sentencing his
son to death (*1A*) is on a higher indifference curve than letting his
rebellious son go free (*1B*). On the other hand, in Case 2, acting on
family values and saving his son (*2B*) is on a higher indifference
curve than arriving at the meeting on time (*2A*). So we see that he is
rational to choose *1A* over *1B*, but *2B* over *2A*.

Display III-8 provides an alternative way of representing
Brutus' reasons for action. We can map any conflict between
reasons based on rules and values in this space. The curve divides
Brutus' decision space into essentially two parts: above and to the
left of a curve he has most reason to act on his values; below and to
the right his reasons indicate that he should act on the rule. (If a
case falls exactly on a curve Brutus will be indifferent.) As in the
account of Livy, this Brutus heavily favors reasons of fidelity over
family values; he begins to take family values seriously only when
reasons of fidelity to rules are not much at stake. We thus see that
even Brutus, who is so strongly committed to reasons of duty, can,
given his trade-off rate, consistently act to save his son and ignore
his consular reasons in Case 2 while in Case 1 condemning his son
because it is demanded by reasons of duty.

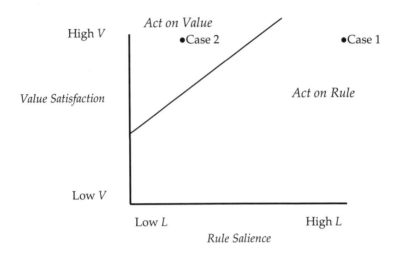

DISPLAY III-8 BRUTUS' RULE-VALUE TRADE-OFFS

Our analysis suggests that measuring personal consistency in decision-making, although certainly possible, is apt to be more difficult than personality theorists have sometimes thought. Students of personality have long sought to measure traits such as "honesty," for example, in measuring children's resistance to theft or lying. As is well known, considerable controversy exists as to whether such personality traits allow prediction from one situation to the next; some have insisted that they have very low predictive value.[124] We can now see, though, that personal consistency can obtain even if Brutus sometimes chooses to save his son, and sometimes chooses to condemn one, and this even when the same rule/value conflict occurs. Behavioral "inconsistency" can emanate from consistent trade-off rates.

(c) Do We Simply Value Following Rules?
It might be thought that, after all, a reason based on caring for rules can be folded back into instrumental rationality and so we can in

---

[124] Lee Ross and Richard E. Nisbett, *The Person and the Situation,* esp. chap. 4. Cf. Derek Wright, *The Psychology of Moral Behaviour,* pp. 51ff.

the end achieve a monistic theory of practical reason. Suppose one takes as a goal "that rule L be instantiated by me." That is, one cares that the rule be followed by you and so it becomes one's goal that it will be followed by you. So it may seem that, after all, we can merely employ instrumentalist or, as Goldman says, "consequentialist" reasoning. Many think that this must be the uniquely rational view: if one has reason to conform to a rule, surely one wishes to maximize conformity over, say, a lifetime.[125] As soon as we put the issue in this way the problem is clear. Basic to instrumental rationality is that "more is better than less" (§4.3a): rational agents always have some reason to choose more value over less. If rule conformity is a value, agents have reason to choose more rule conformity over less and, so, say, would have reason to place themselves in circumstances C in which they have an opportunity to conform to social rule L and so achieve a valued goal. That is, just as I, a valuer of beer, have a reason to bring about a situation in which I can act to obtain a beer, as a rule follower I would have a reason to act to bring about situations in which I can act on rules. Suppose a rule follower knows at time t that if he engages in act ϕ, this will produce circumstances C, and if C obtains, he will be able to instantiate rule L. If acting on L were a value, this would give him reason to ϕ. But it doesn't. Compare: when ϕ is a trip to the microbrewery, a valuer of beer has a reason to ϕ, which will put him in C; when C is an opportunity to make another promise, a rule follower does not have a reason to ϕ in order to put himself in C. If a rule follower was now in C, he would have reason to act on rule L (keep his promise), but he has no reason at all to bring about C.[126] None of this is to deny that, in addition to a rule-based reason, one might also have a value-promoting reason to bring about circumstances in which, say, rights violations by others will be reduced; perhaps one aspect of being a moral person is to have

---

[125] For this strategy, see Philip Pettit, "Non-consequentialism and Political Philosophy."

[126] This concerns perfect duties. Imperfect duties are another matter: one may have reason to seek out an opportunity to perform an imperfect duty. I considered these issues in relation to a specific theory of instrumental rationality, *Homo Economicus*, in "Why All Welfare States (Including Laissez-Faire Ones) Are Unreasonable." For differences in modeling perfect and imperfect duties, see Mark D. White, "Can *Homo Economicus* follow Kant's Categorical Imperative?"

such a valuing. Too much ink has been spilled on this issue because philosophers typically insist that our reasons to abide by moral rules can only be of one or the other sort.[127]

(d) Utility Functions and Rule Following

Once we see that a person can form a trade-off rate between the satisfaction of rules and values, we see that allowing rules into decision theory as a distinct category (distinct, that is, from consequential value) need not lead to indeterminacy as to what constitutes the rational thing to do. Indeed, we now can see that it is in principle possible to devise for any individual a cardinal utility function that integrates both her value-based considerations and her rule-based reasons. So far from being committed to a mysterious indeterminacy of practical reasoning, one of the most elegant systematizations of the idea of rational choice – that a rational person always possesses a utility function such that her rational action can be represented as maximizing it – is fully consistent with rules as a basic desideratum for choice.[128]

Most see decision theory as an account of instrumental or a goal-oriented reasoning, and so find the idea of a rule-based utility function contradictory. Those who believe that all reasons are to promote value typically embrace decision theory because they think it is essentially a formalization of their view. Just as an instrumentally rational agent aims to maximize the satisfaction of her goals, it is thought, an agent who corresponds to the axioms decision theory seeks to maximize the satisfaction of her preferences or her utility.[129] And if "goals" and "preferences" are the same thing, decision theory is simply a formal version of instrumental rationality. This, I think, is a serious mistake, albeit a

---

[127] See Amartya Sen, "Rights and Agency."

[128] I show more formally how this can be done in "Reasonable Utility Functions and Playing the Cooperative Way," and *On Philosophy, Politics and Economics*, chap. 2. For other approaches upholding the same result, see Heath, *Following the Rules*, chap. 3; White, "Can *Homo Economicus* Follow Kant's Categorical Imperative?"

[129] For an extremely insightful if contentious analysis, see Hampton, *The Authority of Reason*, chap. 7. David Gauthier makes the error of conceiving of decision theory as instrumental in *Morals by Agreement*, chap. 2. James Morrow presents a typical interpretation: "Put simply, rational behavior means choosing the best means to gain a predetermined set of ends." *Game Theory for Political Scientists*, p. 17.

common one. Decision theory allows us to model choice based on one's notion of the overall ordering of outcomes based on *whatever criteria one thinks appropriate*. What is required to generate a utility function is that one has some way to determine what is the best outcome, what is the next best outcome, and so on – but "best" need not be that which leads to the highest satisfaction of one's goals. A rational person always can be modeled as selecting the option that, according to a utility function, has the highest value, though that may not be the act that best promotes her values.[130] As we have seen, the actions may also be ordered by one's system of rules. There is no reason whatsoever to suppose that Alf's set of evaluative criteria are all about Alf's *goals, welfare,* or *goods* that he wishes to pursue.[131] Although decision theory does rank the choice worthiness of an act by the ranking of its "outcomes," we should not confuse this sort of formal decision-theoretic "consequential-ism" with what is called "consequentialism" in philosophy, or with the theory of instrumental action.[132] As Peter Hammond stresses, *anything* of normative relevance for choice is part of the conse-quence domain, and this includes the normative significance of performing a certain action that is called for by a rule.[133] One of Alf's preferences over outcomes may be that he performs act ϕ, say, "telling the truth when under oath today." If in his current set of options, one action-option is to tell the truth under oath, he will rank that act highly. Given this, the action of telling the truth under oath has "high utility" – that is, the action he has most reason to perform.[134] If, then, one's practical criteria include moral rules, and these lead to ranking outcomes in ways that meet the basic axioms of utility theory, then a person acting on her moral principles can be modeled as maximizing a mathematical cardinal function.[135]

130 Thus on a rule-based account, there is never a "preference for choosing less than the best option available." Cf. Goldman, "The Rationality of Complying with Rules," p. 461.
131 Cf. Morrow, *Game Theory for Political Scientists*, p. 17.
132 As Paul Anand recognizes. Foundations of Rational Choice under Risk, p. 84n.
133 Hammond, "Consequentialist Foundations for Expected Utility," p. 26.
134 Benn has modeled deontological requirements in this way. See *A Theory of Free-dom*, chap. 3.
135 As John Rawls notes: "A utility function is simply a mathematical representation of households' or economic agents' preferences, assuming these preferences to satisfy certain conditions. From a purely formal point of view, there is nothing to

To see how utility theory and instrumental rationality are distinct, consider again the "ultimatum game" (§7.4). In this game, it will be remembered, there is a good (say, an amount of money) to be divided between two players: in order for either player to get the money, both players have to agree to the division. In ultimatum games, the players make their moves sequentially. It seems that the Responder, if she is instrumentally rational, would take an offer of 1 percent. After all, as an instrumentally rational agent, she sees that 1 percent will achieve some of her goals, and 0 percent will not; so once the 99:1 offer has been made, as she is an instrumentally rational person, it looks as if she must take it (more is, after all, better than less). And, as an instrumentally rational person, Proposer should see that it will better advance his ends to insist on 99 percent. But we have seen that in experiments this does not happen: if Responder is offered 1 percent, or 10 percent, or even 20 percent, it is very likely she will reject. And Proposer tends to demand between 50 and 60 percent or so. But this does not mean that people are acting against their preferences or irrationally, even if they are acting against their goal of having more money rather than less. The best explanation is that the players' utility functions are not simply about getting funds to best advance their goals but about acting according to some rules of fair play. But acting according to rules of fair play is not a goal (§9.4c): it is a norm to which a person wishes to conform. There is, then, no inherent problem precluding us from specifying "deontological" utility functions, or formally modeling agents who act on strong reciprocity.[136] Utility theory – the development of a mathematical function such that an individual always chooses the option with the most value – is by no means closed to us if we abandon a purely consequentialist theory of practical reason.

---

prevent an agent who is a pluralistic intuitionist from having a utility function." *Political Liberalism*, p. 332n.

[136] See Armin Falk and Urs Fischbacher, "Modeling Strong Reciprocity."

9.5 CAN RATIONAL AGENTS SEE MORAL RULES AS OVERRIDING?

Some moral philosophers may object that an account that allows a rational trade-off rate between one's devotion to rules and the pursuit of goals is not *really* an account of rule-following at all. To many, Raz's exclusionary account is the proper model: rules tell us to ignore our other concerns, and so are not themselves to be included in the "balance of reasons" (§9.2a). Such philosophers appear to suppose precisely the "austere" trade-off rate which Benn rejects (§9.4b): duty must always come first if we are to be genuine rule followers. If that is what rule following is taken to require, it is little wonder many see it as unreasonable and myopic. The only way to make such extreme views plausible is to build numerous exceptions into the rules – otherwise one is committed to acting on even relatively minor moral rules regardless of the cost in terms of one's values and goals.[137] But if the rules of social morality are to perform their core function of generating shared expectations of cooperative action they cannot be overly complex (§7.3): we must have a pretty firm idea of what is expected of us, and what constitutes cheating behavior. Building in numerous exceptions thus seems inconsistent with properly functioning moral rules.

But this seems to pose a deep problem: to achieve social cooperation the rules of social morality must be generally overriding: it must typically be the case that, when I call on the authority of a social rule, I suppose that other moral agents take it to have overriding importance (§11.2). But we have seen that unless one has a very austere notion of duty, one inevitably weighs one's reasons of value against one's rule-based reasons. Once we understand the nature of a rational agent, we come to see that moral and social philosophy cannot simply proclaim that she *must* act on social rules and forgo the pursuit of her values, regardless of the costs to her. A successful social morality must have overriding rules while, at the same time, devotion to the rules must not suppose an austerely Kantian devotion to duty, and a refusal to ever compare rules and one's reasons to advance one's goals. We now see the importance of the contrast between the Common Good and the Moral Realist

---

[137] For a discussion of rule violation in a number of areas, see Robert A. Hinde, *Bending the Rules*.

Views of strong moral rules (§9.2*a*). The latter does not tie a justified rule to being verified by each individual's overall evaluative
perspective, and so has no limit on how much, from the point of
view of any person, justified morality can demand of her. And so
its claims to give overriding reasons is an extraordinarily strong
one. In contrast, the Common Good view holds that a justified
overriding rule must be acceptable from each person's overall
evaluative perspective, and so she only is committed to a rule when
endorsing it as overriding is reasonably favorable to her overall
evaluative perspective. At the core of the Common Good View is
the supposition that morality cannot demand more sacrifice of
one's overall good than normal moral agents can deliver. As Rawls
would say, the "strains of commitment" cannot be overwhelming.[138] A free and equal person cannot endorse a morality that she
cannot live up to, or one that she could honor only with unreasonable sacrifice to what she most deeply cares about. Thus it is
precisely because rational agents are aware of the value costs of
acting of rules, and do not lexically order rules over the pursuit of
values, that a plausible social morality must give each reasons,
based on her own devotion to her values as well as the moral rules,
to take the moral rules as generally overriding. How this can be
done is the subject of Part Two.

Although, generally, moral rules must be overriding – otherwise
they could not perform their key function of inducing cooperation
in mixed motive interactions – there is no reason to think that there
is not some range of overridingness. Moral philosophers may rebel
at the thought of "relatively unimportant" parts of morality, but it
is hard to provide any accurate analyses of our moral practices that
omit such an idea. Suppose it violates a moral requirement to push
to get into a subway, but one has the only opportunity of the year
to see the Buffalo Bills on Monday Night Football. In such a case we
may share no expectation that a person will conform to the rule. At
a minimum, in such cases we are apt to excuse the violation on the
grounds that the harm is very minor, and the costs of observance
greater than we would normally expect people to bear.

---

[138] Rawls, *A Theory of Justice*, pp. 153ff.

10 Moral Rules as Social Rules

10.1 DE JURE MORAL AUTHORITY

In an epigraph to this chapter Strawson tells us that social morality "is the sphere of the observance of rules." Note that he does not simply say that social morality is about an ideally justified set of rules, or a normatively correct set of rules: it is about *the observance of rules*. If moral rules are to provide a framework for a cooperative social life, it is not sufficient that they be normatively justified. They must provide the basis for a common set of understandings of what can and cannot be demanded of one, and they must be widely understood as possessing authority over us, and grounding claims to authority (§1.3). A moral claim on others, we have seen, is a claim to a sort of authority over their actions: it is a claim that they must do as required in this circumstance. Now, as I argued, a moral order among free and equal persons must be one in which this authority is justified to all: to employ Kant's depiction, each must be both legislator and subject. If each has reason to endorse a moral rule, then when others make demands on the basis of such a rule one is requiring the action of oneself. In the terms of political philosophy, the authority of social morality must be de jure, or justified; no simply de facto authority will do. We are concerned with a system of moral authority that meets the test of public justification (§2.4).

It is thus of the first importance to grasp what is implied by the idea of de jure authority or sovereignty. In his *Lectures on the Principles of Political Obligation* T. H. Green resists the idea that de jure sovereignty is simply "rightful authority" that has no practical force, as when appeal is made simply to a "general will, or the mere name of a fallen dynasty exercising no control over men in their dealings with each other."[139] Instead, Green argues, the distinction between de facto and de jure sovereignty "has natural meaning in the mouths of those who, in resisting some coercive power that claims their obedience, can point to another determinate authority to which they not only consider obedience due, but to which

---

[139] T. H. Green, *Lectures on the Principles of Political Obligation*, §105.

obedience in some measure is actually rendered."[140] Green's general point, and he seems entirely right, is that a political authority that has, or is likely to have, no practical effect is no political authority at all, as it cannot perform its main task of sorting out actual disagreements and coordinating activities. To be any sort of authority at all there must be some general recognition of it; only then can it perform its designated tasks. If it is not generally recognized as an authority, we might argue that it *ought* to be an authority, that it alone *could qualify* as a justified authority, but we cannot claim that it now *is* such an authority. The job of moral authority is to regulate and coordinate social interaction; if so, an authority that is not recognized simply is unable to perform the office of an authority, as one who is not socially recognized as a leader is unable to fulfill the position of "group leader." We can say that a person who is not recognized – either explicitly or implicitly – as a leader *ought* to be the leader, that she would be a wonderful leader, or even that she would be the only leader worth having; but we cannot say that a person no one pays attention to is *now* the leader.

To be sure, difficult issues arise here concerning how effective, or potentially effective, a justified authority must be before we can say that it *is* the de jure authority. We might say that it has to have a significant following, or that it has some reasonable prospect of gaining such a following. All these are complicated issues, but the crucial point is that on Green's analysis, that "A is the de jure authority over Φ" is not established simply by a moral or philosophical argument that submitting to the direction of A in Φ-matters is justified, or even uniquely justified. A de jure authority must meet both the (*i*) justification and (*ii*) minimal effectiveness conditions.[141] If, as Green says, we claim that rightful obedience is to be rendered only to some forgotten fallen dynasty, or a fantasized one, exercising no control over men in their dealings with each other, we are claiming that there simply is no de jure authority – no one has sovereignty – since no party has both minimal effectiveness and a justified claim.

---

[140] Ibid., §105.
[141] This is not to claim that a de jure authority must be de facto authority; that is a significantly stronger claim.

10.2 THE EXISTENCE OF SOCIAL RULES

The rules of justified social morality, if they are to be a de jure authority that structure human interaction and so provide the grounds of a society of morally free persons, must also be social rules: they must in some sense exist. In his classic account of social rules H. L. A. Hart argued that for L to be a social rule two conditions must be met:[142]

1. *Social convergence in judgment*: At least some of those in group G "must look upon [and endorse] the behavior in question as a general standard to be followed by the group as a whole." [143]
2. *Observed collective behavior*: Rule L describes a regular course of behavior ϕ among G.

As Hart recognizes in the first requirement, for a rule to actually guide behavior there must be an "internal aspect" such that at least a subset of the population takes the rule as a standard to be followed. Others have put this idea in terms of "internalizing" a rule.[144] Often this crucial idea is left exceedingly vague: it is assumed that somehow we are socialized into rules and they come to guide our behavior, but the mechanism for this is seldom analyzed. Cristina Bicchieri has advanced by far the most sophisticated analysis of rule internalization, drawing on the idea of mental schemata and scripts. As she understands them, mental

schemata are cognitive structures that represent stored knowledge about people, events, and roles. When we apply a schema, our interpretation of the situation is theory-driven, in the sense that prior knowledge heavily

---

[142] Hart saw these as necessary, not sufficient, conditions. I consider below additional features that Hart thought necessary.

[143] See H. L. A. Hart, *The Concept of Law*, pp. 54–6. See also Shapiro, "The Difference That Rules Make," p. 34.

[144] This notion is appealed to in a wide variety of discussions of rule following. See, for example, Talcott Parsons, *The Social System*, pp. 207ff; Viktor J. Vanberg, *Rules and Choice in Economics*, p. 14; Jerome Kagan, *The Nature of the Child*, chap. 4; Heath, *Following Rules*, pp. 66ff. Alan Gibbard distinguishes being "in the grip" of a norm from "accepting it." This crucial contrast will concern us in Chapter IV, and indeed throughout all of Part Two. See his *Wise Feelings, Apt Choices*, pp. 68ff.

influences the way we understand and interpret salient stimulus. I say "theory" because the schema does not represent particular, detailed knowledge, but rather generic knowledge that holds across many instances. A schema is thus concerned with the general case, not the specifics of any situation encountered. . . . Once a schema is activated, there is a demonstrable tendency to conform to it.[145]

A schemata for an appropriate series of events is a script. A script is a "stylized, stereotyped sequence of actions that are appropriate in this context, and defines its roles and actors."[146] On Bicchieri's analysis, "*social norms are embedded into scripts.*"[147] Once a situation is categorized as being of a certain type (condition *iv* is met; see §8.1), a general series of actions is seen as appropriate. When individuals come to share the same scripts (§7.3), they have a shared understanding of the general sorts of actions that are appropriate once they perceive this as a case of "circumstances *C*." Scripts may be quite complicated, and individuals may share the same scripts, and thus rules, without being able to fully articulate them.[148]

Suppose we share scripts, but they are conditional: condition *C* specifies "if enough others endorse rule *L* that requires Φ-type acts, then Φ!" We would still not have social rules unless something like Hart's *second* condition is also met: that is, the rules actually structure social interaction. Insofar as social rules structure social interactions to secure social benefits of cooperation, such benefits will only accrue if the rules are generally followed. If very few people actually follow a rule, then any given individual's following it will be unlikely to yield significant benefit: crucial to social rules performing their function is that there is a sufficient number of people following them such that the benefits of reciprocity are achieved. Hart's second condition requires that the rule be an observed collective behavior within group *G*; we can describe the members of *G* as generally acting in a certain way, and according to the first criterion, at least some of the members of *G* see this way of

---

[145] Bicchieri, *The Grammar of Society*, p. 93. Note and references deleted.
[146] Ibid., p. 94.
[147] Ibid.. Emphasis in original.
[148] Compare Hayek, *Rules and Order*, p. 11.

behaving as required from all members of the group. So for Hart, a convergence by at least a significant subpopulation of the group on the required behavior is necessary for L to be a social rule.

The problem with Hart's second condition is that it simply requires a fact about the overt behavior members of G. This sort of behavioristic characterization of action – which was current when Hart wrote – is problematic. Purely behaviorist descriptions of action are hopelessly indeterminate: any effort to explain Alf's act as ϕ rather than γ necessarily involves an intentional description – a description of his understanding of what he is doing, and the nature of the choices confronting him.[149] "Voting," for example, is not simply a piece of behavior qua movement of a body. A description of an act as a "vote" necessarily turns on the intentions of actors involved. The behavior of "raising an arm" may be the act of asking a question or casting a vote (or innumerable other acts); only reference to the intentions of the agents can distinguish the two. So we can hardly purge the mental from our description of what people are doing. Once we see this, we need to rethink Hart's collective behavior condition.

Bicchieri has formulated an analysis for the existence of a social "norm" that focuses on intentionality. Suppose we have group G divided into subgroups g_1 and g_2. We can say that social rule L exists in G if g_1 is a sufficiently large proportion of G such that for each individual (call such a person Betty) in g_1:[150]

1. Betty recognizes L as rule that applies to C circumstances;
2. Betty typically has a motivating reason to conform to L rather than act simply on her own goals in C circumstances on the condition that
    (*a*) Betty believes that a sufficiently large subset of G conforms to L in C;
    (*b*1) Betty believes that a sufficiently large subset of G expects Betty to conform to L in circumstances C or (*b*2) Betty believes that a sufficiently large subset expects Betty to conform to L in C, prefers that Betty does so, and will sanction Betty for noncompliance.[151]

---

[149] See Alexander Rosenberg, *Philosophy of Social Science*, chap. 3.
[150] I have slightly modified Bicchieri's first and second conditions, as well as replaced her reference to social norms with social rules.
[151] Bicchieri, *The Grammar of Society*, p. 11.

Bicchieri notes that her account of the existence of a social norm does not imply that L is *followed* by the group. Clause 2 builds in a condition: Betty will have reason to conform to L if and only if (*a*), and either (*b*1) or (*b*2) is met. If none of these belief conditions is met for individuals in g_1, but the set of individuals like Betty is sufficiently large, then Bicchieri claims that the social rule exists, but is not followed. The social rule, then, exists and is followed if, given these conditions, a sufficiently large subset of G has a motivating reason to follow the rule.[152] Note that clause 2 not only requires that Betty has some motivation to act on L; she must also have a system of trade-off rates (§9.4*b*) between L and other concerns such that in conditions C it will typically be the case that Betty acts on L.

In an important experiment, Bicchieri and Erte Xiao have studied the importance of empirical expectations (clause *b*1, which connects with Hart's observed behavior condition). They found that, indeed, expectations about what others will do are crucial for norm following. Bicchieri and Xiao found that in dictator games normative ideas about what ought to be done do not have a significant impact on people's decisions once empirical expectations about the expected behavior of others are controlled for, thus supporting the conditionality clause in 2(*b*1).[153] There seems good evidence to support the claim that people act on social norms only when they expect that a sufficiently large subset of others will. The idea that a core function of social morality is to allow for a mutually beneficial social life, I think, helps explain this result: unless the rule actually structures the interactions of a large proportion of the group it fails to secure beneficial social cooperation. Although normative reasoning might lead us to form a conditional intention to follow a

[152] Bicchieri's account of a social norm could, I think, be translated into the idea of a social practice based on collective intentions. Cf. Raimo Tuomela, *The Philosophy of Social Practices*, chap. 2.

[153] Cristina Bicchieri and Erte Xiao, "Do the Right Thing: But Only if Others Do So." In a dictator game, subjects are randomly paired. There is an amount of money to be divided; the player chosen to go first decides on the division for both – hence she is the dictator. In their experimental work on public goods games among the Machiguenga and the Mapuche, Joseph Henrich and Natalie Smith also found that "the primary indicator of what a subject will do is what the subject thinks the rest of the group will do." Henrich and Smith, "Comparative Experimental Evidence from Machiguenga, Mapuche, and American Populations," p. 153. I further examine their findings in section 22.4*a*.

rule, such conditional intentions are not enough to actually produce the benefits of a cooperative order. Unless people form the empirical expectation that cooperation is the "done thing" in a group, individuals do not have sufficient reason to comply with the normative expectations of their fellows. Recall again that to care for a rule does not mean that one will always act on it in the relevant circumstances, for one may possess a system of trade-off rates such that it is often ranked lower than other concerns (§§9.4*b*, 9.5). Consequently, simply being preached to that we should adopt the rule, and even the true reports of others that they endorse it, do not tell us what we really need to know: how important is the rule in their overall system of reasons? Does it actually motivate them in the relevant cases? To know that, we must see to what extent the rule actually determines people's actions in the relevant situations.

Bicchieri and Xiao's experiments are consistent with other findings that indicate that "preaching" or "exhorting" others to, say, donate to charity, has relatively little effect on behavior. One the other hand, when others observe people *being* charitable, they are much more likely to engage in charitable acts.[154] To be sure, these data may be interpreted in several – probably ultimately consistent – ways. One hypothesis is that these experiments show the importance of imitation in human groups; we copy the behavior of others, including giving to charity. It is not clear, though, that copying is the entire story. The data also show that subjects who experience inconsistency between what a person preaches (what she states are the normative expectations) and what she actually does tend to have a harder time recalling the content of the exhortation; those who witness conformity of preaching and action better recall the content of the preaching message. This suggests that statements of normative expectations that do not mesh with observed behavior are washed out, while the congruence of normative expectations with action increases the subjects' awareness of the normative expectations.

---

[154] For a report of a number of studies, see Natalie Henrich and Joseph Henrich, *Why Humans Cooperate*, pp. 29–30.

10.3 AN EXISTING PRACTICE OF RECIPROCAL OBLIGATION

In many ways Bicchieri's "social norms" look like candidates for moral rules: others reasonably expect us to conform to them, and she thinks this itself gives you some reason to conform to them.[155] Moreover, we are subject to criticism for violating them. Studies show that violations of these sorts of social rules induce a sort of anger which, I think, can be best interpreted as a sort of Strawsonian moral resentment (§§11–12).[156] Nevertheless, some are reluctant to describe such "norms" as "moral" because our reason to act on them is conditional upon others' actual conformity.[157] Indeed, Bicchieri herself seems to accept this: "by their very nature moral demands (at least in principle) are an unconditional commitment."[158] If I should conform to *L* only if I benefit from a reciprocal exchange, *L* would appear to fall short of a moral rule.

The "conditionality" of social rules (norms) can be interpreted in two ways. If interpreted to mean that one's obligation to act on the rule is conditional upon thinking others will benefit you in return, this does indeed appear to undermine the plausibility that such rules are moral rules. If, as Bicchieri and Xiao found, notions about what *ought* to be done have no significant effect once expectations about what people *will* do are controlled for, it would seem that people are simply involved in useful rules for mutual benefit, but these cannot be understood as having anything to do with morality.

However, a second interpretation of the conditionality of rule following presents itself. If few are following a rule, then a person may question whether any rule of reciprocal obligation exits. A recurring finding in studies of deontic reasoning on social matters is the supposition of reciprocal obligation. Cummins reports that reciprocity is a common theme in studies of the deontic reasoning of preliterate cultures, "although, interestingly, not in terms of a

---

[155] Bicchieri, *The Grammar of Society*, p. 24.
[156] Fiddick, "Adaptive Domains of Deontic Reasoning," p. 110.
[157] See Shaun Nichols, "Emotions, Norms, and the Genealogy of Fairness." Nichols especially focuses on the way that moral norms are connected with emotional reactions. See section 12.2 below.
[158] Bicchieri, *The Grammar of Society*, p. 20. On the next page, however, she seems to qualify this concerning the moral obligations of justice.

strict accounting of benefits given and received. These men believed that when an item was given in good faith, the receiver was honour-bound to return the favour in the future. . . . This type of reciprocity is evidence of sensitivity to obligation structures – one is obligated to return help one is given in times of need."[159] Cummins notes here that although the content of the practice concerns mutual benefit, the ideas of reciprocity inherent in the subjects' understanding of deontic concepts is not based on straightforward considerations of self-interest, namely, a simple "I will follow the rules if I expect net benefits." The reciprocity of deontic reasoning crucially involves reciprocity within the structure of obligation itself. The core of social rules is to identify reciprocal obligations or, as I have put it, relations of mutual authority (§§2.3, 3.4). Given this, if there is low expectation that others perform as the rule instructs, this undermines the belief that a reciprocal structure of obligation is in fact recognized in the group. If, for example, rules of justice are structures of reciprocal obligation, then when faced with evidence that few act on such obligations, one may conclude that there simply is no practice of justice in one's group. If so, when Bicchieri and Xiao find people ignoring what they are told are the normative expectations of others when these do match up with their empirical expectations of the behavior of others, this indicates that they must think that the others do not see the structure of obligation as reciprocal. Others expect me to act on the rule, but they clearly do not act on it themselves.

I am maintaining, then, that we must distinguish two views:

(*a*) *Conditional compliance*: Alf's compliance with social rule *L* is conditional upon enough others complying such that he expects to benefit from his own observance;

(*b*) *Moral-social rules as practices of reciprocal obligations*: Social rule *L* exists only if there is a practice of reciprocal obligation to conform to *L*.

We may say that rules concerning social cooperation exist in a group only when there is an ongoing recognition of a structure of mutual obligation. And this requires the practice of most actually acting on their obligations. There simply is no practice of justice in

[159] Cummins, "Evidence for the Innateness of Deontic Reasoning," p. 174.

groups where a high percentage of the group fails to act on the rules of justice, even if they all endorse the rules. This was, I think, the important insight in Hart's observed behavior requirement: unless the rule actually structures the way the group behaves, it is not a social rule. And if there is no social rule L in group G such that people should engage in Φ-type acts, people who do not Φ-type are not ignoring a rule. Consequently, if as in the Bicchieri and Xiao experiments, information about what people think they ought to do conflicts with the information about how people actually behave, the conclusion ought to be that there is no social rule in play.

10.4 POSITIVE AND TRUE MORALITY

(a) What Makes a Rule Part of Positive Morality? Some Basic Features
The rules of social morality are a type of social rule. What distinguishes moral rules from other social rules? Philosophers have identified certain formal characteristics, which I consider later (§15.2). Recent work in psychology stresses several features.

1.   All investigators understand moral rules to be emotionally infused. I shall return to the place of emotions in social morality in Chapter IV.
2.   We have seen (§8.1) that even children see moral rules as nonconventional: they are categorically binding in the sense that even authority figures cannot waive them.[160]
3.   The rules of social morality concern interpersonal relations, and should be distinguished from "prudential or "precautionary" rules that concern self-preservation and avoiding self-harm. Again, children distinguish such rules from moral ones.[161] Interestingly, subjects tend to see prudential rules as *more* objective than moral rules, which are seen as depending on a social contract or societal agreement.[162] That something is dangerous is simply a fact, and is seen as

---

[160]   See Elliot Turiel, Melainie Killen, and Charles C. Helwig, "Morality: Its Structure, Functions and Vagaries," p. 170.
[161]   Fiddick, "Adaptive Domains of Deontic Reasoning," p. 109.
[162]   Ibid.

entirely universal. Thus, although moral rules are seen as nonwaivable by those in authority (and so are categorical), their categorical nature does not clearly translate into a conviction that they are universal. Most subjects have different reactions to violation of moral and prudential rules: the former tend to evoke anger, the latter fear.[163]

4. The rules of social morality (or justice) presuppose reciprocal obligations and in many cases mutual benefit. Cosmides and Tooby stress this point, but the work of others, such as Cummins and Bicchieri, also endorses it.

5. Cheater detection seems an especially important aspect of such rules. Several of Hart's additional conditions for the existence of a social rule relate to this feature. A person's deviation from a rule is subject to criticism by others, and indeed is taken as a good reason for criticism; others can demand conformity to it when deviation is actual or threatened; and those who criticize violations are not themselves liable to criticism for doing so (violations, we might say, are everyone's business; §11.2).[164] Among philosophers, Bernard Gert distinguished moral from nonmoral rules by appeal to moral attitudes, especially attitudes about punishment. On his analysis, to endorse a rule as a moral rule is to endorse that "Anyone who violates the rule when no impartial rational person can advocate that such a violation be publicly allowed may be punished."[165]

(b) The Error of Dismissing Positive Morality

We must confront a deep objection: what could all these data about how people *think* about moral rules tell us about what is *truly* moral? As Joseph Heath observes:

Many moral philosophers . . . use the term "moral" to refer to some heavily idealized set of normative judgments, which are presumably timeless and eternal. They then draw an invidious contrast between what is moral and

---

[163] Ibid., p. 110.
[164] Hart, *The Concept of Law*, pp. 54–6
[165] Bernard Gert, *Morality: A New Justification of the Moral Rules*, p. 119.

what people *take* to be moral, or what society *tells us* is moral. This way of talking seems to me to beg a variety of important philosophical questions. . . . Thus my inclination is to use the term "moral" in a quasi-anaphoric sense, to refer to what people themselves take (and have taken) to be moral.[166]

Heath's impatience with the transcendence view, and its too easy dismissal of mere "positive" morality or what people "think" is morality, as basically irrelevant to true morality and real moral theory, is understandable. Unless our analysis of "true morality" connects up with what actual agents see as morality, our philosophical reflections will not address our pretheoretical worries. We come to philosophy worried about the nature of morality, moral relations between free and equal people, and the justification of moral claims. If we develop a philosophical account of morality that tells us what is "right and wrong" that treats moral and conventional rules the same, or sees morality as just another form of prudence, or insists that morality is entirely a matter of reason and so emotion is simply a threat to sound moral judgment – then our account is too far distant from our actual moral concepts to enlighten us about our initial concerns.[167] This is certainly not to say that we seek a philosophical account of morality according to which all current beliefs about morality are confirmed, but our starting point must be what agents think they are doing when they judge and act morally – and our final destination cannot stray too terribly far from this. After all, our "considered judgments" – which so many take as a basic datum of moral theorizing – are the judgments we have formed living a moral life as shaped by our moral practices.[168]

Given that so many contemporary moral philosophers are deeply influenced by the work of John Rawls, one would have thought that the importance of positive morality – the moral status quo – would be more widely recognized. Aaron James has convincingly argued that Rawls' concern throughout his work was to

---

[166] Heath, *Following the Rules*, p. 11. Emphasis in original.
[167] See here Prinz, *The Emotional Construction of Morals*, pp. 16–19.
[168] I am indebted to Kevin Vallier for impressing upon me the importance of this point.

evaluate principles for reform of the status quo. As James understands Rawls, he sought first to "identify an existing social practice,
including its point, or the goods it is meant to realize [and]
[a]ssume circumstances favorable to its continuance" and then
"[i]dentify the practice's participants [and] [a]ssume general
compliance with its terms."[169] The task then was to design a procedure by which free and equal people could evaluate the fairness of
the practice and its distributions. This was manifest in his early
essay on "Justice as Fairness." In this first statement of his contractualist theory, Rawls depicted the parties as confronting an "established practice":

Since the persons are conceived as engaging in their common practices,
which are already established, there is no question of our supposing them
to come together to deliberate as to how they will set the practices up for
the first time. Yet we can imagine that from time to time they discuss with
one another whether any of them has a legitimate complaint against their
established institutions. Such discussions are perfectly natural in any
normal society. Now suppose that they have settled on doing this in the
following way. They first try to arrive at the principles by which
complaints, and so practices themselves, are to be judged.[170]

On James' reading this remained a fundamental feature of Rawls'
work: "Rawls assumes what might be called the *Existence Condition*:
any (fundamental, ideal theory) principle of social justice has as a
condition of its application the existence of some social practice."[171]
Rather than proposing a model of moral theory that aims to
uncover the true morality without any necessary connection with
the moral life and practices in which we are enmeshed, Rawls
insists that, properly understood, moral theory systematizes a type
of reflection of how free and equal persons engage in their practices. Moral theory is not about de novo moral legislation, but a
reflection on free and equal people's evaluations of the practices

---

[169] James, "Constructing Justice for Existing Practice: Rawls and the Status Quo," p.
281.
[170] Rawls, "Justice as Fairness," p. 53.
[171] James, "Constructing Justice for Existing Practice: Rawls and the Status Quo," p.
295. Emphasis in original.

that undergird our social life – "the basic structure." "*A Theory of Justice* follows Hegel . . . when it takes the basic structure of society as the *first* subject of justice. People start as rooted in society and the first principles of justice they select are to apply to the basic structure."[172] At its core, that is the conception of moral theory at the heart of this work.

Some (alas, many) moral philosophers may be tempted to reply that it makes no sense to develop a conception of social morality in terms of the jobs we need it to perform, or its social functions. Morality, they may say, simply *is*. It concerns only a certain sort of authoritative fact about the way we must act; it is not a way in which we seek to ensure that certain jobs necessary to human social life will be accomplished in a manner that respects the moral freedom of all. Now there may be such facts, and perhaps there is "normativity" to which these facts give rise, that are recognized by some. But surely that cannot be the whole story of morality, or even I think the really important part. A theory of morality that does not take seriously the way in which morality makes a cooperative social life possible among human beings would miss the role that social morality has in fact played in all human societies, and so its place in what it means to be human. Such a view threatens to transform this indispensable way that humans relate to each other in a cooperative social life into a somewhat unpalatable practice of judging others, charging them, and criticizing their actions, employed by the high-minded (or, the priestly) who refuse to acknowledge that the facts of our social life can possibly have a fundamental impact on their perception of how the world ought to be.[173] A moral theory that refuses to take seriously an analysis of how morality is necessary to secure cooperative human life is academic in the most pejorative sense.

(c) On Avoiding the Opposite Error – The Moral Point of View and the Testing Conception

Despite the importance of appreciating how people understand morality, we must not give into the temptation of thinking that the

---

[172] John Rawls, *Lectures on the History of Moral Philosophy*, p. 366.
[173] I have in mind, for example, G. A. Cohen's criticism of the Rawlsian approach in "Facts and Principles."

task of philosophical ethics is basically to understand our positive morality and how it relates to our natural sentiments. The wonderful work in moral psychology of the last twenty years has, I fear, tempted some to think that moral philosophy is essentially a sort of systemization of moral psychology and positive morality. In the end, however, we cannot rest content with understanding "moral" in a quasi-anthropological sense to refer to what people themselves take (and have taken) to be moral. As Baier recognized, having understood our positive morality,

it should make sense to ask, "But are these moral convictions true?" or "Is this moral code correct?" or words to that effect. The question implies that the moral rules and convictions of any group can and should be subjected to certain tests. It implies a distinction between this and that morality on the one hand, and true morality on the other.[174]

What Baier calls a "true" morality is one that passes certain tests of impartiality and common acceptability. Testing existing social moralities on the basis of such considerations is to evaluate them from "the moral point of view" – identifying this point of view and analyzing its dictates is the subject of Part Two of this work. For now, it is important to stress that although the rules of social morality must be social rules, and so exist, this is simply a necessary, and by no means a sufficient, condition for a rule to be part of "true social morality." We begin with existing social rules; we do not end there. A main theme of this work is that much of moral and social philosophy, especially in the last thirty years, has gone fundamentally astray, supposing that the starting point of moral theory is appeal to "intuitions" that inform us, not about existing social practices and people's views of them, but directly about the sort of timeless moral truth that rightly worries Heath. But that does not mean that we should embrace the opposite error, of thinking that moral theory is basically about what people think is moral. Moral theory must be rooted in our actual practices but, as Rawls clearly recognized, it must also give us critical leverage on

---

[174] Baier, *The Moral Point of View*, pp. 112–13.

them: it must identify a moral point of view from which we can evaluate the morality with which our society has ended up.

As Baier also stressed, if we start with existing social rules, and seek to evaluate whether they are acceptable, "[t]here is no a priori reason to assume that there is only one true morality. There are many moralities, and of these a large number may happen to pass the test which moralities must pass in order to be called true. It would, therefore, be better to speak of 'a true morality' or of 'true moralities' than 'true morality.'"[175] Strawson agrees: "There is no reason why a system of moral demands characteristic of one community should, or even could, be found in every other."[176] Indeed, any plausible theory that upholds moral rules – rules that are determinative enough to provide the basis for mutual expectations and predictable prescriptive demands – must admit significant variation from society to society. All societies, for example, must have property rules that distinguish mine and thine, but precisely what set of rules define one's property will appropriately vary from society to society: the idea that there is just one morally correct way of resolving all property disputes is implausible. Furthermore, as Thomas Scanlon points out, some moral requirements may suppose conditions not present in every society: appropriate privacy rights, for example, depend greatly on existing communication and other technologies.[177]

Although Scanlon accepts some such variation from society to society in justified morality, he also endorses a "central core" of "judgments of right and wrong that hold everywhere."[178] Such judgments, he believes, concern what a reasonable person in any society would reject. This idea – that no reasonable person in any society could reject some moral rules – is entirely consistent with the Baier-Strawson View. No doubt there are fundamental human concerns that must be reflected in any (justified) social morality. As Strawson noted:

[175] Ibid., pp. 180–1. See also Baier, *The Rational and the Moral Order*, p. 199.
[176] Strawson, "Social Morality and Individual Ideal," p. 11.
[177] Thomas Scanlon, *What We Owe Each Other*, p. 348.
[178] Ibid., p. 348.

It is important to recognize the diversity of possible systems of moral demands, and the diversity of demands which may be made within any system. But it is also important to recognize that certain human interests are so fundamental and so general that they must be universally acknowledged in some form and to some degree in any conceivable moral community. Of some interests, one might say: a system could scarcely command sufficient interest in those subject to its demands for these demands to be acknowledged as obligations, unless it secured to them this interest. Thus some claim on human succour, some obligation to abstain from the infliction of physical injury, seem to be necessary features of almost any system of moral demands. . . . Another interest which is fundamental to many types of social relation and social grouping is the interest in not being deceived. . . . When all allowance has been made, then, for the possible diversity of moral systems and the possible diversity of demands within a system, it remains true that the recognition of certain general virtues and obligations will be a logically or humanly necessary feature of almost any conceivable moral system: these will include the abstract virtue of justice, some form of obligation to mutual aid and to mutual abstention from injury and, in some form and in some degree, the virtue of honesty.[179]

Part Two of this book will concern itself with analyzing what all true social moralities must share, and what can differ from one to the other. This is in many ways the core of our project. At present, the point to be stressed is the refusal of the Baier–Strawson View to embrace either of the extreme conceptions that dominate contemporary moral philosophy: moral philosophy as normative theorizing that is minimally constrained by psychological and social facts, or as a study of our moral psychology and moral practices.

(d) Transcendent Morality
A thesis of this work is that for a society to have a justified social morality, it must possess social rules – rules that are actually followed by its members and so form a basis for an ordered and cooperative social life. As we have seen, not all social rules pass the test of being moral. However, it appears deeply objectionable to say that a society without such rules has no social morality. Think of an

---

[179] Strawson, "Social Morality and Individual Ideal," pp. 11–12. Cf. Baier, *The Moral Point of View*, pp. 114–15.

unordered group in which rules do not exist, or – as most philosophers almost immediately do in any discussion of ethics – a
horribly immoral order such as that of the Nazis. It would seem
that the Baier–Strawson account implies that the oppressed in such
conditions cannot call on social morality to criticize their oppressors and demand moral treatment, because there just is no social
morality on which to ground such demands. I think it is largely on
the basis of such cases that philosophers are drawn to transcendent
conceptions of morality, which free moral claims from grounding
in actual social life and institutions. Morality, we may think, must
provide a perspective that transcends the social order so that we
make claims regardless of that order.

Baier agreed that not all our morality was tied to the social order,
distinguishing "true" from "absolute" morality:

True moralities are actually embedded moralities, those forming part of a
given way of life of a society, or an individual, which would pass a certain
test, if they were subject to it. Absolute morality, on the other hand, is a set
of moral convictions, whether held by anyone or not, which is true quite
irrespective of any particular social conditions in which they might be
embodied. Every true morality must contain as its core convictions
belonging to absolute morality, but it also may contain a lot more that
could not be contained in every other true morality.[180]

Again, Baier's analysis is insightful: although the core tasks that
morality performs require that it be embedded in a social order, we
must be able to stand back from our social institutions and take the
perspective of what, we might say, "morality itself tells us." The
moral principles that transcend the social order are, however,
highly abstract and subject to wide-ranging interpretive controversy. Witness the idea of human rights: prior to attempts at codification in the international order, they functioned primarily as
transcendent moral claims that, while having some content, are
subject to endless controversy about what they are, and what they
require of whom. Contrary to much contemporary moral and social

---

[180] Baier, *The Moral Point of View*, p. 183.

philosophy, such claims are not the heart of our moral life, but abstract and vague demands whose function is more to inform us how our morality fails in fundamental ways to respect all as free and equal rather than telling us what we are now required to do in order to respect them (see §§17.3, 17.6). The relation of these transcendent abstract claims to the rules of a free social order is the subject of Part Two.

CONCLUSION

Social life is a wide-ranging cooperative order among individuals with partly competing, partly complementary ends and goals. This is not at all a truism about social life in general: it applies neither to the social insects (who have a wide-ranging order, but little divergence in ends) nor to social mammals (who do not have anything like the wide-ranging order of humans). An adequate social philosophy must present an account of the conditions under which social arrangements are justifiable. I have argued in this chapter that moral rules are necessary, and that it is entirely unremarkable that normal humans care about them and have reason to follow them. Indeed, the evidence is conclusive: Hayek was entirely right that we are as much rule following as we are purpose pursuing creatures. That so much social philosophy fails to see this has led to innumerable dead-ends.

Although deontologists recognize the importance of rule- (or, at least, principle-) based action, they typically fail to appreciate the social functions of morality: they fail to see the relation of moral rules and social rules. The great strength of what I have called the "Baier–Strawson View" (although, it also might be called, somewhat inelegantly, the "Baier–Strawson-and-certainly-early-and-perhaps-also-later-Rawlsian View") is that it not only appreciates, but focuses on, the relation of moral rules to social practices, including positive morality. Moral rules, considered as social rules, are not simply normatively justified deontic requirements. They are not even normatively justified deontic requirements that a large part of the population has a conditional collective intention to follow; they are justified deontic requirements that a large part of the population intends (at least conditionally) to follow and are actually conformed to by a large part of a group's members. "True morality" must also be a "positive" (existing) morality, although not all positive moralities qualify as true moralities.

IV

Emotion and Reason in Social Morality

> It is far from wrong to emphasize the efficacy of all those practices
> which express or manifest our moral attitudes, in regulating
> behaviour in ways considered desirable; or to add that when certain
> of our beliefs about the efficacy of some of these practices turn out to
> be false, then we may have good reason for dropping or modifying
> those practices. What is wrong is to forget that these practices, and
> their reception, the reactions to them, really are expressions of our
> moral attitudes and not merely devices we calculatingly employ for
> regulative purposes. Our practices do not merely exploit our natures,
> they express them.
>
> P. F. Strawson, "Freedom and Resentment"

At the close of the previous chapter we began to examine the intimate relation between what Baier called "positive morality" and
"true morality." If we are going to understand what an adequate
normatively justified social morality would be, we need to understand our current moral practices and the core claims implicit in
them. Once moral theory abandons the aspiration to construct
social morality from the ground up (or, as it were, to discover it for
the first time), we must understand the fundamental features of our
moral practices, and then we can seek to evaluate them from an
impartial view – a moral point of view of free and equal persons.
This chapter focuses on a fundamental feature of our social morality: the way it integrates the emotions and reason in our moral
relations with others. The sentimentalists stress that morality is

about emotional reactions; the rationalists stress that it is about giving others reasons. We will see that they are both correct, and any adequate understanding of our social morality must see how this is so.

As Strawson indicates in this chapter's epigraph, although it is certainly crucial to understand that social morality fulfills certain necessary functions in all human societies, and if it did not serve these functions we would have reason to alter it, we should not suppose that it is *simply* an instrument to achieve certain social ends. Rather, it is essentially a type of interpersonal relation. In this chapter I examine the interpersonal nature of social morality. In section 11, drawing on Strawson's important essay on "Freedom and Resentment," I argue that at the heart of social morality is an authority relation: others hold themselves to have standing to make my action their business, to demand compliance with social morality, and I acknowledge both their standing and the authority of the moral demands to require that I set aside my goals and abide by their prescriptions. Section 12 then considers the conditions under which this authority relation, and the moral emotions that accompany it, can be maintained. I argue that for our normal moral relations to be maintained, we must hold that others have a sufficient reason of the right sort to endorse moral prescriptions. The upshot of a version of Strawson's analysis, I shall argue, is that our apparently controversial starting point – that we are to understand ourselves and others as free and equal moral persons, and this in turn commits us to conceiving of a justified social morality as one that secures positive freedom for all – is implicit in our everyday moral practices. This, of course, was Kant's own view, but it is often forgotten today, giving rise to the image of Kantian-inspired ethics as unworldly and based on controversial values. Because social morality is a form of interpersonal reason giving, we cannot grasp it without grasping what is involved in giving another the right sort of reason, and so we must understand what is involved in claiming that another has a reason. This is the subject of section 13, in which it is argued that the reasons we attribute to others in a practice presupposes an adequate standard of deliberation for participants, such that if the agent engaged in rational deliberation to that standard, she would affirm this to be her reason. I close by considering the proper standard for our practice of social morality.

11 Moral Demands and the Moral Emotions

11.1 THE INSTRUMENTALIST VIEW, RULE-FOLLOWING PUNISHERS, AND THE PRACTICE OF SOCIAL MORALITY

(a) Why a Purely Instrumental Account of Social Morality Was Doomed to Fail

Suppose, contrary to the analysis of Chapter II, that the instrumentalist project in social morality was successfully completed. That is, assume that the instrumentalist demonstrated that each person's reasons to pursue her ends, goals, and values always indicated that she should conform to some social rule, L. Now the most this could demonstrate is that these instrumentally rational agents could converge on conforming to L, not that they could converge on following social morality. To see this, assume that despite this instrumentalist demonstration Alf failed to conform to L, and that his failure to conform to L seriously set back Betty's goals. What can Betty say to him on this instrumentalist account – what sort of reasons can she give him to show that he ought to conform to L? The only reasons on the instrumentalist account she can cite are his reasons to promote his own goals, ends, and values. Thus Betty may point out that his reputation as cooperator will suffer and he will be boycotted by others in future interactions, or that others will retaliate (as the Folk Theorem shows is rational; §6.1), and so his goals will be set back. Perhaps Betty might be lucky and Alf likes her; she can remind him that since she is a favorite of his one of his goals is the enhancement of her welfare, so the failure to conform to L once again sets back his values (note that we allow that Alf is not necessarily narrowly self-interested but, rather, an instrumental agent with concern for others as one of his values). None of the reasons suppose that Betty has any standing to demand that Alf conform to L; they are reminders that he is harming himself by its violation. As Baier observes, this is not to make a moral criticism:

A person who does not act in accordance with self-concerned reasons gets the reputation of being eccentric, foolish, rash, unwise, or weak-willed. But although this reputation has many disadvantages for him, we regard the question of whether he wants to be foolish or not, as *entirely his business*. We may argue, plead, or reason with him, but we cannot claim that he is obligated not to be foolish and no one is entitled to punish him. This is not true of the mores and laws of a group. Whether a person conforms to the mores and laws of the group is not entirely his own business.[1]

Even if the instrumentalist achieved all she hoped for, she could not account for the fundamental aspect of social morality: what Alf does is the business of others, and they have standing to demand that he complies with social morality's requirements. As Stephen Darwall, following the classic account of Strawson, has recently stressed, those such as our instrumentalist give the wrong sort of reason for morality. They could, at best, show that Alf's goals would be advanced if Betty had standing to complain (that is, if social morality came about), but this could not show that Betty has standing, for ultimately it is Alf's business whether his goals are effectively advanced. For Betty to have standing to demand that Alf conform to L requires that she be able to hold Alf responsible for his failure to conform to L and to punish him for his failure. All the instrumentalist can show is that it would be desirable for each individual if he could be held responsible by others in this way. Strawson replies to our instrumentalist: "But the only reason you have given for the practices of moral condemnation and punishment . . . is the efficacy of these practices in regulating behaviour in socially desirable ways. But this is not a sufficient basis, it is not even the right sort of basis, for these practices as we understand them."[2] In the end, the instrumentalist only "owes himself" fidelity to the rules of morality; even if it would be better for him to owe it to others, he has no reasons available to him to recognize their standing. And it will not do for Alf to say, "Betty, I'll give you standing to hold me responsible for violating L." Unless she has standing to hold him to his word, she is still without the authority

---

[1] Baier, *The Moral Point of View*, abridged edn., pp. xviii–xix. Emphasis in original.
[2] Strawson, "Freedom and Resentment," pp. 189–90. See also Darwall, *The Second-Person Standpoint*, pp. 15–18.

to demand his compliance regardless of his wishes – for his compliance to be genuinely her business.[3]

(b) The Standing of Rule-Following Punishers to Demand Compliance

Now it might seem that the analysis of the necessity of Rule-following Punishers for cooperative social life has precisely the same problem as instrumentalism: it defends social morality in terms of its consequences, so it would appear to give what Strawson and Darwall insist is the wrong sort of reason. It is important to keep in mind the distinction between a defense of morality as instrumentally useful and an evolutionary account of why we care about morality, which shows how a certain practice fulfills a social function. As Skyrms stressed (§7.2), the latter can show how certain sorts of ways of thinking have arisen when we could not, via instrumental rationality, reason our way to those ways of thinking. And that is precisely the case with the practice of morality. In the practice of rule following with punishment that is the heart of social morality, each must take an interest in the rule conformity of others and recognize the appropriateness of others taking an interest in their rule conformity. Whereas mere conditional cooperators are only concerned with whether they should cooperate given the dispositions of others, if Alf is a Rule-following Punisher, the conformity of others to the rules is his business, and he exercises his standing even when this does not best promote his own goals and so on (that is why such agents are often called "altruistic punishers"). Fundamental to a system of rules populated by Rule-following Punishers is (*i*) a concern with the conformity of others, and enforcing conformity and (*ii*) a recognition on one's own part that the rules normally override one's own goals, values, and ends. Sections 11.2–3 consider the first point; 11.4 turns to the second.

---

[3] This is a reason to doubt whether Hobbesian individuals can, in the end, authorize the sovereign's action in the sense of giving him authority over them. They can say to the sovereign "You have authority over us" but unless the sovereign already has standing to insist on the performance of this undertaking, all they really can do is say "It would be good for us if you had authority over us, and we will act as if you did." To use a preferred contemporary phrase, the subjects cannot bootstrap themselves out of their own first-person goal-based reasons to create reasons that give others standing to demand action.

11.2 MORAL VIOLATIONS AS EVERYONE'S BUSINESS

(a) Resentment, Indignation, and Moral Standing

We have seen that moral psychologists display great consensus in linking the violation of moral rules and emotional responses, especially "moral anger" (resentment and indignation; §9.3*b*); on a plausible moral psychology these emotions are central motivating factors in performing the critical task of detecting and punishing moral cheaters (§8.2). Crucial to Strawson's account is that such emotional reactions to the actions of others are not simply psychological correlates of our practice of social morality. Strawson points out that a "central commonplace" of our reflective understanding of social morality is "the very great importance that we attach" to "the non-detached attitudes and reactions of people directly involved in transactions with each other; of the attitudes and reactions of offended parties and beneficiaries; of such things as gratitude, resentment, forgiveness, love, and hurt feelings."[4] We cannot understand the practice of social morality without grasping its interpersonal nature: we experience a wide array of "non-detached" attitudes in response to the morally relevant actions of others, and the inferences we make about their capacities, intentions, and beliefs. In the standard case, when another violates a moral rule and so harms me, I do not experience simply a detached disapprobation; I experience the moral emotion of resentment. When I see some ignoring the basic claims of others, I experience indignation and outrage. Such indignation is especially noteworthy. Neither we nor our near-and-dear need to be harmed; even a moral violation toward a stranger is apt to evoke this moral emotion.

Emotions (as opposed to moods) typically have two features.[5] They are, first, an affective state focused on a certain content and, second, have action implications. (*i*) "[E]motions typically have high cognitive involvement and elaborate content."[6] Consider a basic emotion such as fear. Fear is directed at objects or states of

---

[4] Strawson, "Freedom and Resentment," pp. 190–1.

[5] This is condensed. I consider these matters in more depth in *Value and Justification*, pp. 49–64.

[6] Gordon H. Brower and Joseph P. Forgas, "Affect, Memory, and Social Cognition," p. 89.

affairs: one is afraid of the vicious dog, or that one may be attacked. To be sure we sometimes experience free-floating emotions – it is as if one has an affective state but is not sure about what.[7] We typically find such emotions puzzling; that one is scared, but not about anything in particular, or that one has remorse, but not about any specific act or performance, calls for explanation and investigation – we want to know what is going on. And if we think the fear is just hooking on to any suitable "ideational content" we still are puzzled; the object is not evoking the emotion but almost appears to be a cover, or an excuse, for the emotion. It is as if one is searching around for some suitable content so that the emotion seems to make sense, yet we know that the emotion is not really about *that* content. Think of a father, unhappy and exhausted by his work, who often comes home angry, and finds something one of his children does to be angry about – the anger is really about something else, that which evokes the emotional response. (*ii*) Emotions also typically have implications for appropriate action. If one is afraid of the vicious dog, one should avoid it or seek to protect oneself against it.[8] Again, of course, there are complexities. One might have a project of ridding oneself of a certain instance of an emotion (most typically, if one thinks it is inappropriate; see §12), so one might seek to deny that a particular fear – for example, the fear of academic failure – should lead to avoidance of situations one fears. And again, we might have purely contemplative emotions, such as awe at Niagara Falls. Nevertheless, in the standard case an emotion calls for some sort of response on our part. Emotions are not simply reactions to the world but crucial to our interactions with it.

Resentment and indignation are characteristic emotions in most ways. They certainly have contents – generally violations of social

---

[7] A free-floating fear is perhaps better described as a sort of anxiety. As Freud understood anxiety neurosis, a "quantum of anxiety in a freely floating state is present, which, where there is expectation, controls the choice of ideas and is always ready to link itself with any suitable ideational content." Sigmund Freud, "On the Grounds for Detaching a Particular Syndrome from Neurasthenia under the Descriptions 'Anxiety Neurosis,'" p. 39.

[8] As Nico H. Fridja puts it, "emotions are action tendencies." *The Emotions*, p. 71. See further Richard S. Lazarus, *Emotion and Adaptation*, pp. 226–7; Alain Berthoz, *Emotion and Reason*, chap. 4.

morality, especially those that harm others or treat them unfairly. These emotions are aimed at actions (though perhaps sometimes also the character) of others. And they have action implications for the person who experiences them: as we shall see, they are related to blaming and punishing others (§11.3). However, unlike most emotions, one who holds them insists that *others* take certain appropriate actions. If Alf is indignant at Betty's treatment of another, he will insist that she ceases: Alf's emotion calls for an action on Betty's part. Alf is not simply disapproving of Betty's action, nor is he simply thinking "I had better punish her" (as he would think "I'd better avoid the vicious dog"). His response is that she must stop: he experiences "moral anger" at her action, and if her action is ongoing his moral emotion not only disapproves, but calls for her to cease what she is doing. It would be puzzling if Alf were to say that he was indignant that Betty was immorally harming another but did not think she must stop. Contrast this to someone who, without experiencing a moral emotion, simply reports "I know it is immoral for Betty to take bribes, but everyone does, so I can't see a point in insisting that Betty stop." In this case there is not the immediate unintelligibility (indeed, anyone who has lived in Louisiana will see it as all too intelligible). Here the moral judgment is about a normatively justified rule, but because there is no social conformity – as Bicchieri would say, there are insufficient empirical expectations of conformity (§10.2) – the judgment does not arouse the moral emotions: it remains as a theoretical judgment, but we can make sense of people asserting it, yet refusing to make any demands on others. When the moral emotions are aroused, apathy about whether their targets continue in their behavior is deeply perplexing.

Of course, the reason that Alf thinks Betty should stop is not his emotion but the immorality of her action, just as the reason that Alf should avoid the vicious dog is that it is dangerous, not that he fears it. He fears the dog because it is dangerous, and he is indignant because Betty's action is immoral. The emotions show that the reason – the violation of the moral rule – has engaged one: one cares about it. A moral practice constituted by resentment and indignation is one in which we both care about the actions of others and hold ourselves to have standing to insist on actions on their part (§9.3*b*). The moral emotions of resentment and indignation are constitutive of our claim to have standing to demand actions and forbearances of others. It is not merely that the moral emotions are reactions to the failure of others to comply with the moral demands of the community. As Strawson says, "the making of the demand *is* the proneness to such attitudes"[9] – part and parcel of the moral emotion is that the appropriate action is that the other stops. We make demands on others because we are prone to the moral emotions. The "reactive attitudes" (what I have called the moral emotions), Darwall observes, "invariably involve 'an expectation of and demand for' certain lines of conduct from one another. Reactive attitudes invariably involve concern what someone can be held to, so they invariably presuppose the authority [i.e., standing] to hold someone responsible and make demands on him."[10]

(b) Internal versus External Justification of Our Moral Practice

Strawson's analysis is apt to give rise to the objection that, at best, it shows the nature of a certain sort of moral practice. It analyzes our moral practice from within, considering its presuppositions. But it does not show that this moral practice is correct. It does not establish that we really have standing to make claims on others; it only shows that we suppose we have such standing when we experience these emotions. To demonstrate that the practice was truly correct, it might seem that we need to get outside of it and consider its justifiability from a detached, objective point of view. Now Strawson and those who have followed him have generally insisted that we cannot give such an external justification of our moral practice:

Inside the general structure or web of human attitudes of which I have been speaking, there is endless room for modification, redirection, criticism, and justification. But questions of justification are internal to the structure or relate to modifications of it internal to it. The existence of the general framework of attitudes is something we are given with the fact of

---

[9] Strawson, "Freedom and Resentment," p. 207. Emphasis in original.
[10] Darwall, *The Second-Person Standpoint*, p. 17. The quote within the Darwall quotation is from Strawson.

human society. As a whole, it neither calls for, nor permits, an external "rational" justification.[11]

Strawson does allow, though, that sometimes we can take a purely "objective" view and see others not in transactional terms, but in what we might call social planning terms: in terms of participants in social practices who can be induced to perform actions that achieve our desired ends. If we can sometimes take this objective perspective, in which the reactive attitudes and moral emotions play no part, why can't we try harder and take it more often? Strawson's reply seems to be that even if this were in some sense rational, we simply could not do it; human morality is interpersonal, and we simply could not accept a purely objective view of morality. Is this an adequate reply?

It is more adequate than many suppose. We are embedded in certain sorts of practices, with certain beliefs and emotions. They form part of the reasons from which we must judge, criticize, and propose changes. A practice such as social morality is deeply embedded in our view of the world; it affects our understanding of interpersonal relations, including love and friendship, and so of what sort of life is worth living.[12] If the presuppositions of our moral practices are so deep a part of the way we see the world, then to renounce the practice would be to renounce most of what we care for and value. But how could we have reason to do *that*? How could we survey all that matters to us and come to the conclusion that our reasons lead us to give it up, by renouncing the view of the world on which our reasons depends? Where would *that* reason come from? It is, I think, as difficult to argue a moral person out of her moral practices as it would be to argue the psychopath into them; given who they are, they do not have reasons to change their view of the world (§13).

Still, the worry gnaws: have we simply landed in a confused practice that we cannot reason ourselves out of? That may be a

---

[11] Strawson, "Freedom and Resentment," p. 208. Compare Darwall's notion of a "circle of irreducibly second-personal concepts," Darwall, *The Second-Person Standpoint*, pp. 11–15.

[12] Again, I argue this point more fully in *Value and Justification*, chap. VI. See also Benn, *A Theory of Freedom*, pp. 97ff.

recipe for despair rather than contented resignation, much less justification. We not only wish to know where we have landed but to
have some reassurance that it is a destination worth arriving at, and
not the result of being marooned with no hope of rescue. Our
current moral practice is made intelligible and sensible once we
understand that human society depends on a social morality based
on Rule-following Punishers. For such a system to have arisen, we
must care about the moral actions of others, care about making
demands on them, and hold that we have standing to make these
demands. When Strawson says that the "existence of the general
framework of attitudes is something we are given with the fact of
human society," he presents us with a deeper truth than even he
realizes: human society would not even be possible without this
framework. We can now glimpse at least the beginning of a reconciliation between two apparently conflicting traditions of moral and
social thought. The instrumentalists from Hobbes to Gauthier have
insisted that social morality is necessary for human cooperation
and social life: how can we think that somehow the whole appara-
tus of interpersonal morality is anything but a device that humans
hit upon for cooperative social life? In contrast, those such as
Darwall – inspired by, among others, Kant, Fichte, and Strawson –
insist that our moral relations can never be reduced to their instrumental benefit and must involve recognition of mutual moral
standing on the part of fellow members of the moral community as
moral agents. Both are correct.

11.3 BLAME AND PUNISHMENT

(a) Scanlon's Relationship Account of Blame

When we make a moral demand on another and she fails to comply
– or if she knowingly fails to do what she knows is demanded of
her – we blame her. Blame certainly would appear a central moral
emotion for an analysis of social morality that focuses on Rule-
following Punishers. We must inquire: how does blame relate to
punishment?

Thomas Scanlon contrasts two accounts of blame. In one view –
which I shall call the *enforcing* account – blame is a form of sanction,
and closely related to punishment. On Scanlon's alternative view,

"to blame a person for an action . . . is to take that action to indicate something about the person that impairs one's relationship with him or her, and to understand that relationship in a way that reflects that impairment."[13] In some ways, Scanlon's view follows Strawson's account of the reactive attitudes. Although Scanlon does not stress the role of the reactive attitudes in his account of blame, Strawson maintained that the "reactive attitudes" were, literally, attitudes reacting to the attitudes of others – their perceived good or ill-will.[14] In this sense both Strawson and Scanlon offer what we might call *relationship* accounts of blame.[15] Blame is a response to a failing in an interpersonal relationship. To distinguish the two accounts in this way, of course, is not to say that a relationship account has nothing to say about punishment, or that an enforcing account has nothing to say about the role of insult, or damage to relationships. The issue at stake is what is more central, and what is more peripheral.

Scanlon's model is blame in a relation such as friendship:

Suppose I learn that at a party last week some acquaintances were talking about me, and making some cruel jokes at my expense. I further learn that my close friend Joe was at the party, and that rather than coming to my defense or adopting a stony silence, he was laughing heartily and even contributed a few barbs, revealing some embarrassing facts about me that I told him in confidence.[16]

Scanlon is certainly correct that this raises a question about his relationship with Joe – whether Joe really is his friend. Scanlon, though, argues that such a judgment is at the core of what is involved in blaming Joe: to blame someone *is* just to make a judgment that his action shows him to have attitudes that impair his relations with you (or, more generally, others). "To *blame* the

---

[13] T. M. Scanlon, *Moral Dimensions: Permissibility, Meaning, Blame*, pp. 122–3.

[14] "What I have called the participant reactive attitudes are essentially natural human reactions to the good or ill will or indifference of others towards us, as displayed in *their* attitudes and actions." Strawson, "Freedom and Resentment," p. 195, emphasis in original. Cf. Scanlon, *Moral Dimensions*, p. 128.

[15] Aaron James brings out the importance of relationship in Scanlon's overall contractualism. See his "The Significance of Distributions."

[16] Scanlon, *Moral Dimensions*, p. 129.

person is to judge him or her to be blameworthy and to take your relationship with him or her to be modified in a way that this judgment of impaired relations holds appropriate."[17] These reactive attitudes are varied: they may include an intention to complain, the demand for an explanation, or an apology, but they need not; one response may simply be a reaffirmation that one is in an impaired relation. Fundamental to Scanlon's account is that blame is not a particular attitude or even a specific group of attitudes. Rather, blame constitutes an appropriate revision of one's attitudes toward a relationship upon judging "one's relationship with the person as changed and one's interactions with the person as having different meaning."[18] Blame thus involves a wide variety of attitudinal shifts, including a disposition to not interact with the blamed other than on normal terms, not to trust the other (in the same way), and so on.[19]

The idea of "impairing" a relationship thus is central to the account. We can distinguish two conceptions of impairment:

Present Baseline: At time *t* Alf impairs relationship *H* with Betty if his action φ shows Betty that he entertains attitudes that are inconstant with *H* up to that time. Betty blames Alf if she now holds attitudes that are appropriate in regard to what φ has revealed (that *H* has been impaired).

Relationship Standards: Alf impairs his relationship *H* with Betty if his action φ shows Betty that he entertains attitudes that are inconsistent with the standards for that relationship. Betty blames Alf if she now holds attitudes that are appropriate in regard to what φ has revealed (that *H* has been impaired).

The Present Baseline view holds that an impairment is defined relative to what has been the relationship up to this point. Consider two versions of Scanlon's account of Joe (with Betty replacing TS as the friend).

Joe's Disappointing Performance: Up to this point Joe (at least in the eyes of Betty) has been a paragon of friendship; in every respect he has been the very best friend that one can be. At the cocktail

[17] Ibid., pp. 128–9. Emphasis in original.
[18] Ibid., p. 137.
[19] Ibid., p. 143.

party in which jokes are made about Betty, Joe fails to rise to her defense, but walks away indicating some disapproval of the jokes, though it is not clear to everyone just what is the reason for the disapproval.

Joe's Gratifying Performance: Up to this point Joe has been a somewhat unreliable friend, sometimes stooping to telling tales behind Betty's back. At the cocktail party in which jokes are made about Betty, Joe, though he fails to rise to her defense, walks away indicating some disapproval of the jokes, though it is not clear to everyone just what is the reason for the disapproval.

Although Joe has performed precisely the same action in the two cases, on the Present Baseline view he has impaired the relation in Joe's Disappointing Performance but not in Joe's Gratifying Performance. If Betty appropriately adjusts her attitude in Joe's Disappointing Performance, thinking that the former relationship is not consistent with this lukewarm reaction, it would seem that she thus blames him for the Disappointing Performance, though the only reason he is now blameworthy is that he has excelled in the past. In Joe's Gratifying Performance something like gratitude[20] may be in order; something like the opposite of an impairment has occurred, and the adjustment in her attitude may be significant.

This result is worrisome. It does not seem that the previously exemplary are subject to blame when they, as it were, come down to merely being normally good. Betty is certainly disappointed by Joe's Disappointing Performance, but blaming him for falling short of his usual excellence would be harsh. Of course, if Joe had gone out of his way to encourage her to rely on his superlative performances, we get closer to blame. An important question for the Present Baseline view concerns who sets the terms of the relationship and what constitutes an impairment of it. Perhaps Joe's view of the relationship is that it is a normal academic friendship (though Joe always gives more than this calls for), whereas Betty sees it as deep friendship.[21] Betty might view Joe's action as an impairment, while Joe might see it as entirely consistent with a

---

[20] See ibid., p. 151.
[21] In Scanlon's terms, they differ on the meaning of the friendship.

normal friendship. Under these conditions it would be mistaken for Betty to blame Joe; certainly Betty cannot impose her view of the relationship on Joe. But then we are left wondering whose view is determinative.

Scanlon apparently avoids these complexities and problems by adopting the Relationship Standards view:

> It is important to distinguish, here, between the normative ideal of a relationship of a certain kind, such as friendship, and particular relationships of that kind, which hold between particular individuals. The normative ideal of a particular kind of relationship specifies what must be true in order for the individuals to have a relationship of that kind, and specifies how individuals should, ideally, behave toward each other, and the attitudes that they should have. It thus sets the standards relative to which particular relationships of this kind and (higher) standards relative to which relationships can be better or worse, and seen as impaired. . . .
> . . . Impairment of the kind I refer to occurs when one party, while standing in the relevant relation to another person, *holds attitudes toward that person that are ruled out by the standards of the relationship*, thus making it appropriate for the other party to have attitudes other than those that the relationship normally involves.[22]

The ideal of friendship has certain standards, and those whose attitudes indicate that they fall short of these standards impair that relationship. In his Disappointing Performance, Joe has previously exceeded those standards, but he still meets them, so his actions do not impair the friendship. Thus the problems of the Present Baseline view are avoided. Joe is not held blameworthy for his Disappointing Performance, and we have a nonarbitrary standard for what impairs the relationship: those implied by the ideal of friendship.

A new worry, though, arises: the Relationship Standards view puts a great weight on the distinction between a reactive downgrading of one's attitudes about a relation that results from failing to live up to the relevant standard and a reactive downgrading of the relation which, say, results from finding out that the relationship is not as superlative as one thought it was (as in Joe's

---

[22] Scanlon, *Moral Dimensions*, pp. 133–5. Emphasis added.

Disappointing Performance). Remember, on this account, to blame someone *just is* "to hold attitudes that reflect" an impairment.[23] A blameworthy person, Scanlon says, "gives others good reasons to revise their understanding of their relationship with you."[24] But we now see that others can give us reason to downgrade our attitudes about a relationship without being blameworthy, and we can indeed experience a reactive downgrading of our attitudes without blaming, because only once the standards implicit in the ideal have been violated is the relation "impaired." In Joe's Disappointing Performance, we might say that the relationship has been "diminished" but not "impaired," so our realignment of attitudes does not constitute blame. Yet the phenomenology looks awfully similar in both cases. Scanlon constantly draws our attention to the importance of our relationships and how blame typically simply is an appropriate reactive adjustment to a revised and diminished view of what the relation is. But that occurs in Joe's Disappointing Performance as well. Betty might feel hurt by Joe's lukewarm response, be less likely in the future to rely on Joe in important matters, and be less prepared to go the extra distance for Joe. Indeed, if Joe repeats his disappointing performance, Betty might reasonably become distinctly cool toward him. It is not the case that when a person has been a dear friend and no longer lives up to that, he simply becomes a "normal friend" – he may well become no friend at all. So Joe's Disappointing Performance could lead to a much more drastic revision of Betty's attitudes toward the friendship than in a case where Joe has previously managed to stay just above the minimal standards, but now has dropped a little below. Scanlon must say that in this latter case the friendship is "impaired" and so the slight change of attitudes constitutes "blame" but the more drastic change in Joe's Disappointing Performance is not accurately described as blaming. This could be justified if blame is tied to specific attitudes like complaint and resentment, but as we have seen Scanlon resists tying blame to specific reactive attitudes. If meeting the standards is so crucial, it would seem that what is really doing the work is not the idea that certain sorts of actions impair a person's relationships with others,

23 Ibid., p. 145.
24 Ibid., p. 157.

but those who do not meet the standards fail to do what is required of them.

Even if we accept that the distinction between impairing and (what I have called) diminishing a relationship can bear the necessary weight, to account for moral blame Scanlon must show that there is a distinctive moral relationship that is impaired by wrongful acts. The moral relationship, he tells us, is characterized by "the kind of mutual concern that, ideally, we have toward other rational beings."[25] This, he argues, is the default relation that we assume holds between strangers: this mutual concern sets the standards by which we judge impairment. "It is relatively easy to say what this type of impairment consists in. It occurs when a person governs him- or herself in a way that shows lack of concern with the justifiability of his or her actions, or an indifference to considerations that justifiable standards of conduct require one to attend to."[26] And so, actions that impair our moral relations with others in these ways are blameworthy.

The generalization of the analysis from the core case friendship to morality as another such relationship is, in my view, unconvincing. The focus of friends is on their friendship. Much of the language we use to indicate failures of friendship – betrayal, disloyalty, fickleness, unreliability – are precisely about how the participants react to each other and acknowledge their bonds. Perhaps blame in a friendship is really centered on the way the other has forced you to acknowledge an impaired or diminished relationship. But when a stranger does not do what "justifiable standards of conduct require" of him, it gets things backward to say that the focus of the blame is on the impairment of this moral relation one has with all strangers. The focus is not our diminished relationship but the violation of a justified requirement. This is not to deny that such wrongdoing does affect our moral relationship with the violator, but we blame him because he has failed to honor a requirement of social life. When I blame the radical Hutus for their genocide against the Tutsi, it is verging on the implausible to maintain that my concern is in some basic way really the impaired

[25] Ibid., p. 140.
[26] Ibid., p. 141.

moral relations between myself and the Hutus, or the Tutsis and the Hutus, or the Hutus and the rest of us.[27]

(b) Blame and Enforcement

Recall that Scanlon contrasts his relationship account of blame to an enforcement account according to which blame is a form of sanction and related to punishment. If social morality is a practice based on Rule-following Punishers, we should expect that central to our morality will be punishing and sanctioning. In Scanlon's relationship account, enforcing and sanctioning have little role in the practice of blame. In contrast, Mill understood social morality as centrally about what is to be enforced: "All that makes existence valuable to anyone, depends on the enforcement of restraints upon the actions of other people. Some rules of conduct, therefore, must be imposed, by law in the first place, and by opinion on many things which are not fit subjects for the operation of law."[28] Thus for Mill, to blame others simply is to hold that they are the "proper objects of punishment."[29]

I cannot hope to resolve these long-standing debates about blame and punishment here (or, in fact, anywhere). Two things, though, seem quite clear: (*i*) blame is definitely *not* a quintessential reactive attitude, and (*ii*) it has more intimate ties to negative desert judgments and punishment than do reactive attitudes such as indignation and resentment. Regarding the first point, blame is not a quintessential moral emotion since assigning blame, or holding another blameworthy, need not be emotional at all. Sometimes we conceive of blame as an emotion, but at other times it is a distinctly cool judgment of others. Blame is not a type of moral anger directed at another because she has not acted as she ought, though a judgment of blame may underlie such anger.[30] While

---

[27] I think that the crux of this point also applies to proposals according to which the point of criminal sanctions is restoring a person's good standing in the moral community; the point, rather, is that we punish her because she has done wrong and deserves to be punished. See Geoffrey Sayre-McCord, "Criminal Justice and Legal Reparations as an Alternative to Punishment" and my response, "Taking the Bad with the Good: Some Misplaced Worries about Pure Retribution."

[28] Mill, *On Liberty*, p. 220 (chap. 1, ¶6).

[29] Mill, *Utilitarianism*, p. 247 (chap. 5, ¶16).

[30] Cf. Lazarus, *Emotion and Adaptation*, p. 223, who closely links anger and blame.

"unemotional resentment" seems oxymoronic, a "cool blame" does not. Courts typically, without emotion, apportion blame; sometimes we say that the judge was indignant, but this is a special case – an unemotional assignment of blame is typical. This brings us to the second point: the tie between blame and negative deserts. When we blame another for not doing what she ought to have done, this is often associated with censure, or at least an assignment of negative deserts.[31] Indeed, there is evidence that normal moral agents reason about questions concerning blame and punishment in similar ways, and these may be significantly different from the ways they reason about wrongdoing and permissibility.[32] In civil law, the relation of blame and negative deserts takes the form of determining who should pay the costs of a harmful interaction. And even when there is no sanction, there remains, as Les Holborow put it, the shadow of censure in that "we hold it against" the agent for not doing what she ought to have done.[33] Blame often has the character of a moral bookkeeper's entry of a debit in his moral accounts. "The relevant opposite to blaming in its central use is *giving credit to. Getting the credit* for contrasts with being *blamed for*...."[34]

A person generally deserves credit for some above standard performances or a good bestowed on others, and deserves blame for subpar performances or harm to others. Blame thus typically presupposes some standard of performance to which we hold that the person blamed ought to have lived up to, and we hold this failure against her.[35] "The agent and the action are there for all to see,

[31] I consider the relation between negative desert and punishment in my essay "On Taking the Bad with the Good."

[32] Fiery Cushman, "Crime and Punishment: Distinguishing the Roles of Causal and Intentional Analyses in Moral Judgment." We need to be tentative here. Cushman's results indicate that blameworthiness, like punishment, is more closely tied to the evaluation of consequences than to intentional states; other research indicates that holding another morally blameworthy is indeed closely related to one's evaluation of the justification of their beliefs. See Liane Young, Shaun Nichols, and R. Saxe, "Investigating the Neural and Cognitive Basis of Moral Luck: It's Not What You Do But What You Know." See also Lazarus, *Emotion and Adaptation*, pp. 222-23.

[33] Les Holborow, "Blame, Praise, and Credit," pp. 88-89. See also William Lyons, *Emotion*, pp. 193-95.

[34] Holborow, "Blame, Praise, and Credit," p. 89. Emphasis in original.

[35] Ibid., p. 86.

and the crucial question is whether the performance is such as to make it reasonable to impute fault to the agent. The question is: 'Did the action come up to the expected standard?,' and the blaming ... *consists* in giving a negative answer to this question."[36] In contrast to Scanlon's relationship account, a rule-based analysis makes perfect sense of this central role of standards. In Scanlon's account it was not clear why the minimum standard is so critical: if the crux of the matter is a reevaluation of the attitudes characterizing the relation, a person who reduces his performance from the superlative to the ordinary may spur a fundamental reevaluation of the appropriate attitudes while always meeting the accepted standards. On a rule-based account, it is clear why we fault the agent for failing to live up to the standards (the rules), and why Rule-following Punishers hold it against her by blaming her.

11.4 GUILT, MORAL AUTONOMY, AND MORAL AUTHORITY

Rule-following Punishers do not simply demand that others comply with moral requirements and monitor their actions: they follow the rules themselves. As we saw in Chapter III (§10.2), rule followers do not merely conform to moral rules; they "internalize" them. There is convincing empirical evidence that "cheater detection" (§8.2) and the sort of monitoring that is involved in some types of basic blame judgments develop before rules are internalized. Consider a fascinating series of experiments by Gertrude Nunnar-Winkler and Beate Sodian. Children between four and eight were told a story about two children, both of whom liked candy. The first child was tempted to steal the candy, but did not; the second stole the candy. Even the four-year-old subjects knew that stealing was wrong and could provide reasons why this is so. Thus they could engage in punishing violators. The difference is that the youngest children expected the child who stole the candy to be happy with his violation of the rule, while they (the youngest children) expected the child who resisted temptation to be sad. Older children reversed this; they supposed the child who stole would be sad – guilty – while the child who resisted temptation

---

[36] Ibid. Emphasis added. Note how blame can be seen as a judgment.

would be the happy one. In another experiment four- to eight-year-olds were told stories of two children. In the first story a child wanted to play on a swing and so pushed another child off; in the second, a child pushed another child off the swing just because he desired to push the child to the ground (so he was not aiming at any benefit to himself). In both cases the younger children knew that such infliction of injury was wrong because it caused harm to others, but they expected the violator to be happy that he succeeded at doing what he wanted to do – even if this was simply hurting another. Younger children apparently expect people to be happy when they get what, all things considered, they want, regardless of whether this violates a moral requirement and harms others.[37] Again older children expected the violator to feel unhappy. Nunnar-Winkler and Sodian conclude:

> children may first come to know moral rules in a purely *informational* sense, that is, they know that norms exist and why they should exist. Not until several years later, however, do they seem to treat them as personally binding obligations the intentional violation of which will be followed by negatively-charged self-evaluative emotions or genuinely empathetic concerns.[38]

Young children view moral rules as external facts, and they can appreciate reasons that these rules are important; what they do not grasp is that the rule can function as a requirement in an agent's deliberations and can be seen as "personally binding,"[39] so that the agent will feel guilt for failing to meet this requirement even if by so doing she gets what she wants. What young children do not grasp is, in short, the heart of moral autonomy – that a person cares about moral requirements and so can put aside the things that she wants and, instead, conform to the rule's requirements. Young

---

[37] It is generally thought that young children see harm to others as violating a basic moral requirement. See Elliot Turiel, Melainie Killen, and Charles C. Helwig, "Morality: Its Structure, Functions and Vagaries," p. 174. Guilt is especially associated with violation of rules against harm and the rights of others. Prinz, *The Emotional Construction of Morals*, p. 77.

[38] Nunner-Winkler and Sodian, "Children's Understanding of Moral Emotions," p. 1336. Emphasis in original.

[39] Ibid., p. 1324.

children (and, alas, many moral philosophers) suppose that, in the
end, a person seeks to best fulfill her goals and ends and will be
happy when she succeeds in doing so. They do not grasp the possibility that a person may act autonomously. A person acts autonomously when her action is directed by her internalized *nomos* or
rule, not by what she most wants or what others expect of her. An
autonomous person has made the requirement hers: it is not simply
a bit of "information" about what is required; it is what she accepts
as required. A person who has developed into an autonomous
moral agent will feel remorse should she fail to act autonomously,
even though she achieves her goals when she does so.

Some will object that Nunner-Winkler and Sodian's experiments
are not truly about moral autonomy: autonomy, it is often thought,
is a purely rational attitude of respect for rules that overcomes
selfish "passion," where Nunner-Winkler and Sodian show that
what is crucial for moral behavior is emotional engagement. We
have already rejected this overly rationalistic depiction of rule
following (§9.3b). As Nunner-Winkler and Sodian's experiments
help show, as moral agents mature they become emotionally
invested in moral rules; they come to care for the rules and expect
to feel guilt when they violate them. And importantly, as a person
morally matures she comes to recognize an internalized "ought"
that requires of her that she set aside her goals and conform to the
requirements of morality. Having so matured, she comes to see
others in a more sophisticated light, as also recognizing this internal ought, and so feeling guilt at their own transgressions.

Gabriele Taylor points out that the internalized nature of guilt
presupposes that one accepts the authority of the demand on one:

To feel guilty he must accept not only that he has done something which is
forbidden, he must accept also that it is forbidden, and thereby accept the
authority of whoever or whatever forbids it. The person who accepts the
authority does not merely recognize its power and so thinks it simply
prudent to obey its commands; he also accepts its verdicts as correct and
binding.[40]

---

[40] Gabriele Taylor, *Pride, Shame, and Guilt*, p. 85.

One does not – or, we should say, one should not (§12) – feel guilt when one fails to conform to a demand that one does not acknowledge as correct and binding. To be sure, Taylor stresses, a person may feel guilty at breaking a taboo and yet be doubtful that there is any good reason for the taboo. "Taboos exercise great authority which is often strong enough to survive to some extent and for some time any rational rejection. . . . Taboos will naturally carry varying degrees of weight, and the struggle to free oneself from them may correspondingly be more or less prolonged."[41] For those dominated by taboos, Freud writes, "every sort of thing is forbidden; but they have no idea why, and it does not occur to them to raise the question."[42] Morality is not composed of simply taboos;[43] to see something as merely a "taboo" is to see it as exercising unwarranted authority over us – something from which, in Taylor's words, we struggle to free ourselves.[44] It is not simply philosophers who insist on reasons for accepting this authority over their actions. As Elliot Turiel and his co-authors have shown, from a very early age children provide justifications for their moral judgments based on notions of welfare, justice as well as nonmoral notions such as maintaining team work or class order.[45] But as taboos show, we can find ourselves experiencing an emotion we see as inappropriate: what does it mean to judge that one has inappropriate emotions?

12 Moral Emotions and Moral Autonomy

12.1 EMOTIONS AND APPROPRIATENESS

One of Strawson's great contributions was to show that the moral emotions – the reactive attitudes – can be maintained only if we

---

[41] Ibid., p. 86.
[42] Sigmund Freud, *Totem and Taboo*, p. 21.
[43] Cf. Prinz, *The Emotional Construction of Morals*, pp. 70ff.
[44] Compare Gibbard's idea of being "in the grip" of a norm. *Wise Choices, Apt Feelings*, pp. 68ff.
[45] Elliot Turiel, Melainie Killen, and Charles C. Helwig, "Morality: Its Structure, Functions and Vagaries," p. 180. See also Elliot Turiel, *The Development of Social Knowledge*.

hold certain beliefs about the person at whom they are aimed. In this they are like other emotions, which almost always have certain appropriateness conditions.[46] This was long ago noted by the great psychologist, William McDougall:

Yesterday I was walking alone in an English beech-wood, a place than which none could be safer or more peaceful: suddenly a rabbit, than which no creature could be less dangerous, started up from the undergrowth about my feet; and, absurd as it may seem, I experienced a faint shock of excitement which had quite recognizably the quality of fear.[47]

As McDougall recognized, it does indeed seem absurd to say that one fears something one believes to be utterly harmless. When confronted with a genuinely absurd – totally inappropriate – emotion, we try to make it somehow intelligible. We do not rest content by remarking something like "How unusual to be afraid of things one sees as utterly harmless!" We seek to make sense of the report of the inappropriate emotion by better understanding what is going on. One response we might make to McDougall's report that he was afraid of the rabbit is to suggest to him that he was actually startled and not really afraid at all. We might support our claim that he has misidentified his emotion by pointing out that it is widely agreed that facial expressions differ when experiencing fear and when being startled; and, if we saw him, we might say that his facial expression was akin to the latter rather than the former.[48] Or we might point out that his own description of his state, in which he reports a "faint shock," is characteristic of those describing how it feels to be startled.[49]

But what if McDougall continues to insist he *really* was afraid, and we have no reason for doubting him apart from the object of his fear? The fear would continue to be absurd and puzzling until

---

[46] For a detailed defense of this claim, see my *Value and Justification*, pp. 64–80, 283ff. The remainder of this paragraph draws on that more extensive discussion.

[47] William McDougall, *The Energies of Men*, p. 150.

[48] On emotions and facial expressions, see, Paul Ekman, "Biological and Cultural Contributions to Body and Facial Movement in the Expression of Emotions"; Paul Ekman, Wallace V. Friesen, and Phoebe Ellsworth, *Emotion in the Human Face*; Frijda, *The Emotions*, pp. 60–9.

[49] See Carroll E. Izard, *Human Emotions*, p. 13.

we discover some belief (or, more generally, cognitive state) that showed rabbits to be in some way threatening or perhaps to stand for something that is seen as threatening. That this latter move would help dissolve our puzzlement is one of the attractions of psychoanalysis: it purports to reveal an unconscious belief that, if sound, would make the emotion sensible. Anxious reactions that have no apparent relation to danger, Freud noted, are "quite beyond our comprehension."[50] To render them comprehensible, Freud sought to show that the ego is reacting to a perceived danger situation, such as castration by one's father.[51] Regardless of one's opinion of the success of the psychoanalytic project, its long-standing appeal rests on our conviction that inappropriate emotions are in some way unintelligible and call out for explanation; psychoanalysis renders them intelligible by showing some – though often quite wrong-headed – connection to appropriate beliefs.

Having shown the patient why, say, rabbits are a target or focus of his fear, the analyst aims to undermine the fear by showing its wrong-headed basis. Assume that we discovered that the real target of McDougall's fear is his father, whom McDougall feared would castrate him, and the rabbit is merely serving as a "front" for that "target."[52] In a sense, we have made the fear intelligible; we see what he sees as dangerous and, via the psychoanalytic account, how the rabbit came to symbolize it.[53] However, once the patient sees this, we expect the fear to vanish because he can see that his beliefs about his father are ill-grounded, and the symbolic role of the rabbit was a way to avoid examining his beliefs about his father. And while there is dispute about the matter, there is strong reason to believe that people generally seek to render their beliefs and feelings consistent: they tend not to maintain positive affects (feelings) toward things about which they have negative beliefs (and vice versa). Not only is there evidence that change of belief can change a person's feelings (say, changing them from negative to positive), but in a series of classic experiments Milton Rosenberg

---

50 Sigmund Freud, *Introductory Lectures on Psychoanalysis*, p. 447.
51 Sigmund Freud, "Inhibitions, Symptoms, and Anxiety," pp. 227–33.
52 See Amélie O. Rorty, "Explaining Emotions," pp. 106ff.
53 See further my "Principles, Goals, and Symbols."

induced via hypnosis a change of feelings (say, about racial inte-
gration or foreign aid) and found that people tended to change
their beliefs to align with their new feelings.[54] Having a negative
feeling such as fear toward an object about which one has no negative beliefs is not only rationally objectionable but psychologically
unstable.

Just as we cannot rationally fear something under the description "perfectly harmless," so too are there certain descriptions of
others that undermine the moral emotions. Suppose that we view
an agent under descriptions such as "He was acting under post-
hypnotic suggestion" or "He's only a child."[55] Under those descriptions, Strawson pointed out, we do not think the person is responsible for his actions, and so our moral reactions to his wrongdoing
are undermined. We need to press further, though: why is responsibility undermined by these descriptions? In the case of post-
hypnotic suggestion it seems that, literally, the person does not
know what he is doing. But a young child in some sense knows
what he is doing; he knows, for example, that he has stolen candy,
or that he intentionally pushed another child off the swing. We
might be tempted to say that he does not know that this is wrong,
though this may end up simply begging our question. Young
children, we have seen, are good at knowing the rules and what
constitutes a violation; they know that such-and-such an act breaks
the rule. Indeed, as we have seen, children as young as four identify moral rules (such as the wrongness of theft or causing injury to
others), give reasons for the rule, and why it should be binding.[56]
But, we might say, though the four-year-old knows he has broken
the rule, he does not really *see* that it is wrong. Nunner-Winkler and
Sodian's experiments discussed in section 11.4 point, I think, to the
answer: it is not that the young child (or the psychopath) does not

---

[54] See Milton J. Rosenberg, "An Analysis of Affective-Cognitive Consistency." See
also Milton J. Rosenberg, "Cognitive Structure and Attitudinal Affect," and
Milton J. Rosenberg, "An Analysis of Affective-Cognitive Consistency." More
generally see my *Value and Justification*, chap. II. For skepticism, see Jesse Prinz,
The Emotional Construction of Morals, pp. 29–32.

[55] Strawson, "Freedom and Resentment," p. 193.

[56] Nunner-Winkler and Sodian, "Children's Understanding of Moral Emotion,"
Turiel, Killen, and Helwig, "Morality: Its Structure, Functions and Vagaries," p.
170.

know right from wrong in the sense of knowing the rules and even their justifications, but that he has yet to develop into a rule follower, who has internalized the requirements and holds himself to be obligated by the rule. There is no sense of addressing a moral demand as an authoritative prescription to them, for they have not yet grasped (and in the case of the psychopath, never will) such internalized authority. Being unable to exercise moral autonomy, they cannot grasp that a demand of social morality is authoritative, that they are required to set aside what they most care for and conform to the rule. Being unable to grasp the idea that they can be committed to setting aside what they most want and, instead, genuinely will conformity to the rule, the point of addressing moral prescriptions (§1) to them is undermined. They can see the prescription as an external demand but not one that obligates them and that is verified by their internal point of view. We might say that in their own decision value schema, they only have been able to grasp goal-promoting reasons (§9.4*b*). We can see how such young children share traits with psychopaths, who also seem unable to grasp that moral rules can provide them with reasons to put aside their own ends and concerns.[57] Consequently, it seems clear that psychopaths do not experience significant remorse or guilt.[58] Nor do they tend to experience resentment or indignation, as they do not conceive others as having the ability to set aside their own wants and act on rules.

---

[57] It is important to stress that psychopaths do grasp value-promoting reasons: they can, for example, cooperate in iterated Prisoners' Dilemmas. Cathy Spatz Widom found that "Psychopaths did not behave more selfishly, more egocentrically, show more concern with personal gain, or act less responsively than normal subjects. Psychopaths can and will cooperate with one another over a period of time if the stakes are high enough and if feedback on their performance is immediate" ("Interpersonal Conflict and Cooperation in Psychopaths," p. 33). There is reason, then, to conclude that psychopaths can grasp the instrumental case for social cooperation but not the idea of moral rules, which provides further grounds for thinking that the former cannot explain the latter. It is usually thought that psychopaths cannot defer gratification, and so are not good instrumental reasoners; Widom shows that this may be due to sampling error – psychologists tend to study the psychopaths who have been caught! When one examines psychopaths who have not been caught, the picture is different. See Widom, "A Methodology for Studying Non-Institutionalized Psychopaths."

[58] Derek Wright, *The Psychology of Moral Behavior*, p. 92; Benn, "Freedom, Resentment and the Psychopath."

We do not confront young children and psychopaths as moral persons to whom authoritative moral prescriptions can be sensibly addressed. To be sure, we may still seek to regulate their behavior through social rules by threatening punishment for failure to comply, but it makes no sense to address them as moral agents who can see themselves as committed to acting on strong rules (§9.2a). Because of this our normal moral emotions are undermined in our interactions with them. We can treat them as patients to be helped, potential agents to be trained, or threats to be neutralized, but not as fellow moral persons who are able to grasp the authority of moral prescriptions. To feel resentment toward a four-year-old's violation of a moral rule is akin to being afraid of a harmless rabbit. Given our practices and concepts, these reactions just do not make sense: they are, as McDougall said, absurd.

It may be wondered, though, why it matters that we possess certain practices and concepts, which have presuppositions about their rational employment. Even if our practice of morality supposes that the reactive attitudes are only appropriately targeted at those who are able to exercise moral autonomy, can't one just jettison these social presuppositions and proclaim that "*I* feel resentment – moral anger – toward anyone who violates a moral rule, regardless of whether she can grasp the idea of a moral demand to set aside her wants"? Of course one can define ideas stipulatively, as one may stipulate that one can sensibly be afraid of something under the description "utterly harmless." But, as I have been stressing, morality is not an individual invention but a social practice (though not only that). As Strawson recognized, our understandings of morality, demandingness, and responsibility are embedded in a network of shared concepts: to understand our morality is to understand the form of social life that it constitutes. And, I have argued, a deep presupposition of this form of social life is that we address our moral demands to those who can make sense of the idea of the authority of morality – those who are capable of morally autonomous action.

Acknowledging that we suppose that our moral demands are addressed to those who are capable of moral autonomy, we thus must accept at least:

The Principle of Minimal Autonomy: A moral prescription is appropriately addressed to Betty only if she is capable of caring for a moral rule even when it does not promote her wants, ends, or goals.

To say that a moral prescription is appropriately addressed to Betty only under this condition is to say that unless it is fulfilled, she cannot recognize the authoritative nature – the demandingness – of the prescription, and so resentment and indignation for her failure to acknowledge its authority would be inappropriate. Given the empirical evidence, if one denies the Principle of Minimal Autonomy one seems committed to holding that moral prescriptions can be appropriately addressed to very young children; as I have stressed, in many cases they fulfill most of the other typical requirements for responsibility, such as knowing what is morally wrong and that there are good reasons for holding it to be wrong. Of course there may be some other disability one can point to, but their lack of minimal moral autonomy appears the crucial factor.

12.2 THE CHALLENGE OF THE NEW SENTIMENTALISTS

Throughout the last two chapters I have stressed the findings of moral psychologists over the last twenty years who have shown the importance of emotions in moral deliberation and action. I believe their work has effectively undermined a certain rationalistic picture of morality, in which reason leads us to do the right thing by opposing the passions that incline us toward the things we care for, or the things we hate. It is no longer an open question whether the emotions are fundamental to morality, and an adequate account – such as that pioneered by Strawson – gives them a central role in our reflective understanding of social morality. It is important, though, that we do not become so impressed by the emotions that we come to make the opposite mistake, of relegating reasoning and conceptual thinking to a relatively minor aspect of morality. This, I believe, is the error committed by what we might call the "new sentimentalists" such as Shaun Nichols and Jesse Prinz.[59] Nichols

---

[59] See, e.g., Shaun Nichols, *Sentimental Rules*; Jesse J. Prinz, *The Emotional Construction of Morals*; Jesse J. Prinz and Shaun Nichols, "Moral Emotions"; Shaun Nichols,

argues that accounts of morality and the reactive attitudes that require moral agents to be able to conceptualize the appropriateness of their emotions are overly intellectual. "Moral anger [resentment, indignation], he writes, "is triggered by perceived injustices. . . . Such judgments do not require anything philosophically fancy – no Rawlsian procedure or Kantian reasoning is involved."[60] It is simple: if one recognizes a demeaning offense against "me and mine," one experiences the relevant reactive attitude. Nichols is especially insistent that one need not have the ability to conceptualize the appropriateness conditions of the emotion or make judgments about the cognitive states of the target. Interestingly, he draws a very different conclusion from Nunner-Winkler and Sodian's work than have I. As he sees it, the fact that four-year-olds can make judgments about moral violations, but seem unable to conceptualize when guilt or happiness in others is appropriate, shows that "core moral judgments" do not require that one be able to conceptualize the appropriateness conditions for emotions or understand others' perspectives.[61] For Nichols, the lack of ability of a four-year-old to understand guilt – and apparently the idea that one can feel obligated to put aside one's wants – does not undermine the young child's ability to make "core moral judgments." Such a child apparently has full membership in the moral community.

However, it seems mistaken to understand very young children as making full-fledged moral judgments. As Nunner-Winkler and Sodian themselves conclude from their experiments, very young children do not grasp the "internal ought" involved in moral judgments; they see them as external, and providing information about the rules in play but do not grasp how they are internally binding, and that appears why they cannot grasp the concept of guilt. There is strong reason to think that even slightly older children, as they come to better understand the idea of an internal ought and its authority, come to better understand others' reactions to violation. The moral judgments of very young children fail to

---

"After Incompatibilism: A Naturalistic Defense of the Reactive Attitudes."

[60] Shaun Nichols, "After Incompatibilism: A Naturalistic Defense of the Reactive Attitudes," p. 413.

[61] Nichols, *Sentimental Rules*, pp. 90–1.

qualify as a core case of moral judgment; they are on their way to making full-fledged moral judgments but are not there yet. Observed Strawson of "parents and others concerned with the care and upbringing of young children":

They are dealing with creatures who are potentially and increasingly capable both of holding, and being objects of, the full range of human and moral attitudes, but are not yet truly capable of either. The treatment of such creatures must therefore represent a kind of compromise, constantly shifting in one direction, between objectivity of attitude and developed human attitudes. Rehearsals insensibly modulate towards true performances. The punishment of a child is both like and unlike the punishment of an adult.[62]

As Strawson also emphasized, it is part of our everyday practice of morality not to hold people fully responsible when we know certain things about their capabilities, beliefs, and intentions. One's beliefs about the perspectives of others are manifestly relevant to one's moral reactions. This is by no means a philosophical idealization: studies consistently show that normal moral agents consider the beliefs of others when determining whether those others are morally responsible.[63] Four-year-olds who violate the norms of justice are not fully responsible. We try to teach them not to perform such acts, but moral anger at a violation is undermined by the reminder that "he's just a little kid." It would be odd to think that, simultaneously, we think them fully competent to give core moral judgments but do not expect them to act on them. In fact, we think they are beginning to understand the basics of the moral enterprise, but not really grasp what it is all about (the internal sense of obligation).

Nichols insists that it would be an error to dismiss the moral judgments of four-year-olds as somehow not genuine, arguing that we have no good grounds to suppose "that most adult moral judgment is radically different from core [young children's] moral

[62] Strawson, "Freedom and Resentment," p. 204.
[63] See Young, Nichols, and Saxe, "Investigating the Neural and Cognitive Basis of Moral Luck"; Cushman, "Crime and Punishment: Distinguishing the Roles of Causal and Intentional Analyses in Moral Judgment."

judgment."[64] If one insists that grasping the perspectives of others is really crucial to moral judgment, then, he adds, Lawrence Kohlberg's work suggests that *few adults* are able to fully understand the perspectives of others. In Kohlberg's famous six-stage account of moral development, relatively few reach the sixth stage, in which understanding the perspectives of others is fundamental and well developed.

Display IV-1 summarizes Kohlberg's basic stages.[65] All I have claimed is that in full-fledged moral judgments – judgments based on a competent grasp of the moral enterprise – the agent sees that morality is not simply a matter of external rules. She understands the notion of an internalized ought that is capable, at least normally, of overriding her pursuit of ends, goals, and values. Having this sort of understanding of the perspectives of others is very different from achieving what Kohlberg calls "stage 6" moral reasoning; there is good reason to think that most ten-year-olds grasp the internal ought. Jean Piaget, on whose work Kohlberg's theory is based, distinguished two basic moral orientations: "a morality of constraint or of heteronomy, and a morality of cooperation or autonomy."[66] This distinction, I think, maps more closely on to the issue of whether morality is seen simply as external rules or an internalized sense of justice based on some notion of reciprocity; as Kohlberg notes, Piaget's higher stage commences with his "stage 2" morality; the large majority of adults reason at above or above this stage. Indeed, the majority of adults operate at the higher (4–6); the internal ought is already being grasped at stage 3.[67]

---

[64] Nichols, *Sentimental Rules*, p. 91.
[65] In other works Kohlberg complicates his account, especially when faced with the resurgence of relativistic thinking in late adolescence. See Lawrence Kohlberg and R. Kramer, "Continuities and Discontinuities in Child Development," pp. 109ff. For a useful critical discussion, see James S. Fishkin, *Beyond Subjective Morality*, especially his Appendix A.
[66] Jean Piaget, *The Moral Judgment of the Child*, p. 197.
[67] Kohlberg and Kramer, "Continuities and Discontinuities in Child Development," pp. 93, 104–8.

Stage	Characteristic Attitudes
Pre-conventional 1. Punishment and obedience	The consequences of action determine moral judgment; avoiding punishment and deferring to power are important values in moral action.
Pre-conventional 2. Instrumental exchange	Mutual benefit, exchange and reciprocity are understood in terms of conditional benefit are central to moral judgment.
Conventional 3. Interpersonal conformity	Conformity to accepted or natural social norms is combined with the beginnings of judgment based on the intentional states of others.
Conventional 4. Social system maintenance and one's duties	Authoritative rules are seen as necessary to social order; duty is defined by the rules of the social order. Conscience and an internal sense of duty are developed.
Post-conventional 5. Social contract orientation	Awareness has developed of the relativism of personal values and the importance of individual rights. The person has a moral perspective in terms of a moral point of view which all in society can agree on; legalistic thinking and the "legal point of view" become important to moral thinking.
Post-conventional 6. The universal ethical principle orientation	Right is defined in terms of self-chosen moral principles that can be willed by all; abstract and general principles based on equality and reciprocity replace concrete social rules.

DISPLAY IV-1 KOHLBERG'S BASIC STAGES OF MORAL DEVELOPMENT

Source: Lawrence Kohlberg, *The Philosophy of Moral Development*, pp. xxviii, 17–19.

Nichols, though raises an important point that must be addressed. Kohlberg's work provides strong evidence that there are degrees in sophistication of understanding moral rules and the perspectives of others, and as one becomes more sophisticated one's reasoning about morality changes, and perhaps one's substantive views as well. Kohlberg hypothesized that these stages form a universally invariant sequence of increasing cognitive sophistication; higher stages were more adequate than lower stages, providing solutions to issues left unresolved by lower stages.[68] Kohlberg remained uncertain whether the existence of the sixth stage could be confirmed;[69] at best, less than 10 percent of urban populations reached it, and much less in rural populations. The sixth stage remained an anomaly in Kohlberg's data: among his American subjects, by the age of sixteen, the most common stage reached was the fifth, next the fourth, then the third, then the second, the first, and then, finally, the sixth.[70] Following Piaget, Kohlberg thought higher stages replaced lower: not only must one proceed through the stages in order, but one must leave behind a lower stage as one achieves a higher. Cushman, however, suggests an alternative hypothesis based on the results of his study of attributions of wrongness and blame.[71] His data lead him to the conclusion that the judgments of more mature moral agents combine reasoning at the more mature stages with earlier stage reasoning. When deliberating about whether people did wrong, were blameworthy, or liable to punishment, Cushman's subjects engaged in a lot of "Stage 4 and more" reasoning about internal states of agents: they employed information about the beliefs and desires of agents in making judgments about wrongness, blame and punishment. However, even though the subjects had arrived at the stages in which the beliefs of agents are important in making moral judgments about them, he found that these later stages quali-

---

[68] See Kohlberg, *The Philosophy of Moral Development*, pp. 20, 168ff, chap. 5. See also Fishkin, *Beyond Subjective Morality*, p. 158.

[69] "Continuing empirical work with our longitudinal sample in the United States and Middle East has not allowed us to confirm the existence of, or define, a sixth stage. Thus our sixth stage remains a theoretical hypothesis rather than an empirically confirmed stage." Lawrence Kohlberg, "A Reply to Owen Flanagan and Some Comments on the Puka-Goodpaster Exchange," p. 523.

[70] Kohlberg and Kramer, "Continuities and Discontinuities in Child Development," pp. 103–4.

[71] Cushman, "Crime and Punishment: Distinguishing the Roles of Causal and Intentional Analyses in Moral Judgment."

fied, but did not obliterate, the more objective rule conformity criterion of Kohlberg's earlier stages. Thus we can agree with Nichols that those at this more objective, norm conformity, stage do make some moral judgments characteristic of more mature agents, but there is much in the judgments of more mature agents that they have yet to grasp.

Moral agents, we might reasonably conjecture, are not best understood as simply operating at only one or two (adjacent) stages but are apt to combine simpler and more sophisticated forms of reasoning in different judgments and at different times. To be sure, some achieve more sophisticated reasoning and employ it more often (there would be no point in doing moral philosophy at all if this was not the case), but there is no reason to doubt that normal adults make the crucial step of understanding the relation of belief, desire, and the idea of an internal sense of obligation. Those who also operate at the more sophisticated levels of reasoning develop a greater insight into the beliefs and desires that we can reasonably attribute to others, which we have seen figure into so many of our moral judgments. As with almost any normative performance concept, we must distinguish competency from excellence. To be competent one must grasp the basic concepts involved in the practice – and this certainly involves the internal ought, caring about the rules and putting aside one's goals, guilt, and a general grasp of when the reactive attitudes are and are not appropriate. There is good reason to think that even older children are competent at this. But better moral reasoners may be able to extend reasoning in ways that others cannot. For example, it is widely agreed today that a person with a normal concern for her own welfare and values could not be expected to care for a rule that, say, enslaved her, and so such a rule could never generate a justified internal ought for her: it could not be a binding moral rule. (A four-year-old probably could not see this.) A better moral reasoner, though, may point out that the same considerations show that the slave cannot be bound to show that a similarly reasonable person cannot be bound by an oppressive property regime. Such people may serve us all as moral critics and reformers; they do not disqualify the rest of us from being competent moral agents.

12.3 REASONS AND MORAL AUTONOMY

(a) Systematic Perversion

Moral autonomy, I have argued, is not simply a rational capacity as many have been wont to conceive it, but an affective capacity: a capacity to care for moral rules and feel guilt when one satisfies one's goals and ends by violating a rule. Thus the Principle of Minimal Autonomy refers to a person's emotional ability to care for rules and act on them against her wants. However, I have just been at pains to point out that we should not take the findings of moral psychology over the last twenty years as showing that basic emotional reactions are all there is to moral personality. Giving reasons for one's moral judgments is by no means simply an obsession of philosophers. In this light, consider another type of person against whom, Strawson thinks, the reactive attitudes are inappropriate: one whose mind has been "systematically perverted."[72] Suppose someone has been indoctrinated; while he is able to put aside his wants and act on rules or commands, he has been systematically indoctrinated into a perverted morality. The quintessential instance is Winston Smith in the last pages of *1984* – he has at last overcome his "selfish" ideas and embraced Big Brother. When Smith gives up Julia we do not feel resentment or indignation, but pity, or perhaps loathing. Even if he has minimal moral autonomy, he is insufficiently autonomous because he is unable to evaluate the soundness of the reasons on which he acts. We could hardly feel outraged that he refuses to acknowledge our moral claims; we know that they are now beyond his comprehension. Less dramatically, consider a typical citizen of Oceania, who has been restricted by Newspeak from grasping some reasons; her reasoning process has not been directly perverted as in Smith's terrifying brainwashing, but suppose her range of concepts has been so restricted that she cannot have some thoughts. Again, assume I demand that she ϕs, and she wants to know why she should (assuming that she can still ask this question). I say that it is the moral thing to do, but she doubts that it is; why is it the moral thing to do? Must I answer?

---

[72] Strawson, "Freedom and Resentment," p. 193.

Suppose I deny that I must give an answer. It is the moral thing to do, and that's that. However, I know that she does not see that it is the moral thing to do, and suppose I think her lack of appreciation is quite genuine. I demand "φ!" and she does not see why she is obligated to φ. She is puzzled that anyone would think φ is obligatory. If I think this, then again I cannot reasonably feel resentment or indignation that she fails to φ, any more than I can feel indignation at a four-year-old who is unable to detach himself from what he most wants to do and so steals some favorite candy. She just cannot see how "φ!" has any internal authority over her; she does not understand why I think φ is the thing that must be done. Compare: I am speaking to her in a language she does not really understand, and she replies "I don't know what you are talking about." In the *1984* case I cannot feel resentment or indignation, nor fully blame her for failing to cultivate a more comprehensive moral understanding,[73] for she has been so controlled that the relevant concepts are not available to her. But even if I could be resentful and indignant at her for *that* (as I might in some cases be resentful that she has not bothered to learn my language), what I cannot be resentful or indignant about is her current failure to respond to imperatives that she does not understand as genuinely authoritative over her. Given the way normal reasoners understand the notions of "wrongness" and "permissibility" (§11.3*b*), my judgments about these matters are apt to be undermined by her perverted beliefs and desires.

So I try to give her a reason. If my reply requires her to recognize *R* as a reason to adopt the rule that requires that she φs, but *R* is a reason beyond the pale of her Newspeak conceptual space, resentment and indignation are still undermined. For she still does not understand why I insist that she is obligated to φ; my language is still a foreign and untranslatable language to her, for "*R* is a reason to be obligated to φ" does not translate into Newspeak as a believable proposition (perhaps it barely makes sense). She may view my claim much the way I view the claims of many of Freud's patients,

---

[73] See Young, Nichols and Saxe, "Investigating the Neural and Cognitive Basis of Moral Luck;" and Cushman, "Crime and Punishment: Distinguishing the Roles of Causal and Intentional Analysis in Moral Judgment."

who make fantastic claims about their reasons.[74] She understands that I see such-and-such as a reason, but she can't see it as being a reason. She is not able to grasp my demand as having authority over her, for she is unable to grasp the reason for it. To say that she is unable to grasp it is, of course, not to say that there is no possible world in which she could grasp it (think about the world in which I could reeducate her); it is to say that, given who she now is, the reasons I offer her are beyond her grasp and, so, she cannot acknowledge the authoritative nature of my demand. Or, rather, we should say, my demand has no authority over her.

(b) Moral Authority and Rational Moral Autonomy

We now see, though, that no assumption need be made that the subject of my demand is "systematically perverted": all the previous analysis supposed was that, regarding my demand that she ϕ, she cannot grasp any reason that ϕ-ing is obligatory for her. She cannot see how it falls under a rule she has reason to endorse. Perhaps regarding all my other moral demands she grasps the reasons, so the opaqueness of my reasons is a local phenomenon (regarding ϕ, and the rule it is based on), not global. We still

---

[74] Consider one of his cases – a nineteen-year-old girl with obsessional sleep ceremonies: "The pillow at the top end of the bed must not touch the wooden back of the bedstead. . . . The eiderdown . . . had to be shaken before being laid on the bed so that its bottom became very thick; afterwards, however, she never failed to even out this accumulation of feathers by pressing them apart." At this point the behavior is simply incomprehensible. Freud appeals to reasoning – albeit still odd reasoning – to make some sense of it. In the course of her therapy, "[s]he found out the central meaning of her ceremonial one day when she suddenly understood the meaning of the rule that the pillow must not touch the back of the bedstead. The pillow, she said, had always been a woman to her and the upright wooden back a man. Thus she wanted – by magic, we must interpolate – to keep man and woman apart – that is, to separate her parents from each other, and not allow them to have sexual intercourse. . . . If a pillow was a woman, then the shaking of the eiderdown till all the feathers were at the bottom and caused a swelling there had a sense as well. It meant making the woman pregnant; but she never failed to smooth away the pregnancy again, for she had been for years afraid that her parents' intercourse would result in another child." As Freud notes, these are "wild thoughts." Admittedly, if "wooden bedstead = father," and "pillow = mother," then we can see a crazy sort of reasoning in keeping bedstead and pillow apart. If she was correct in thinking that what she does to the bedstead and pillow affects what her parents do at night, then keeping the bedstead and pillow apart has a certain sort of rationality to it. Freud, *Introductory Lectures on Psychoanalysis*, Lecture 17.

confront the basic problem: I cannot feel morally outraged that she fails to conform to a moral rule that makes no sense to her. Again, I might feel resentment that she somehow put herself in the situation in which she could not grasp my demand (but, again, perhaps I cannot – it all depends on why she is in this situation), but I cannot feel insulted by her action. She has not ignored a moral claim; she does not understand my insistence that I am making one. Indeed, only by denying her rational nature – doing what she cannot see she has reason to do – can she submit to my authority. To advance such a moral claim would be to demand that she puts aside her own reason and submit to mine.

Suppose she does understand my insistence, and even that I have given her a genuine reason to endorse a rule that requires it. My recognition of this still may be insufficient to ground my resentment and indignation. For example, assume that the rule is the norm of the antebellum American South according to which she is my property, and I claim that respect for property rights is necessary for social life, and so she has a reason to accept the rule as a strong requirement. She says, "I know what you are saying, but given all I believe and care about, that cannot possibly be a good enough reason to endorse the current social rule." And to make the case similar to the previous ones, we must also suppose that I am convinced that she is right: "Of course," I say, "I could not expect you to endorse this rule!" I suspect that at this point (though not with this example), some will wish to insist that now I can rationally feel indignant. She sees this as a social rule, sees that it performs an important social purpose, and yet she refuses to give me what I claim as my due. But the problem with our four-year-olds, with Winston Smith, with our "normal" subject of Oceania, and with our "locally perverted" agent resurfaces here: given what we know of our slave, we cannot see how she would be able to endorse this rule as a strong requirement applicable to her. She could not, exercising her rational capacities as well as she can, take this rule as a moral obligation, which she should feel guilt for violating. One should not feel guilt for failing to do what one does not think one has reason to do – we do not wish to confuse moral norms and taboos (§11.4). If so, we must think it is untoward to advance an authoritative demand that she φ: we are still speaking a sort of alien language, a language in which the interest in social stability provides sufficient reason for her to become chattel property. I do not wish to press the language analogy too far; she understands what I am saying, and she may even say "Yes, from your perspective, I can see that this is what you endorse." But what she cannot see is how she has sufficient reason for her to endorse all of this.

If this is right, we must expand the Principle of Minimal Autonomy, giving us:

> *The Principle of Moral Autonomy:* A moral prescription is appropriately addressed to Betty only if she is capable of caring for a moral rule even when it does not promote her wants, ends, or goals and she has sufficient reasons to endorse the relevant rule.

Again, to say that a moral prescription is appropriately addressed to Betty only under these conditions is to say that unless they are fulfilled, she cannot, consistent with her rational and affective nature, recognize the authoritative nature – the demandingness – of the prescription, and so resentment and indignation for her failure to acknowledge its authority would be inappropriate, nor can we fully blame her for her actions. Just what it means for Betty to "have" a "sufficient" reason is, admittedly, a vexed issue, which will occupy us later in this chapter and, in different ways, through most of Part Two. For now I put these important issues aside.

Note that, according to the Principle of Moral Autonomy, if Betty endorses a rule *L*, but does so for bad (insufficient) reasons, and I know this, my resentment and indignation at her failure to comply with *L* is undermined. Return to our slavery case and suppose that the slave endorses her own chattel status – perhaps she has been conditioned into accepting it and is afraid to even think about it – but nevertheless runs away.[75] If otherwise the circumstances are as I described, my resentment will be undermined. Athough she failed to do as she thought she was obligated, I knew that her endorsement of this obligation was a mistake: given all she cared about, she had insufficient reasons to internalize the rule. If so, acts of compliance are mistakes on her part; they are

---

[75] Compare here Benn's analysis of Katherine Mansfield's story "The Daughters of the Late Colonel." *A Theory of Freedom*, p. 165.

called for by a rule she should not have accepted. I cannot be resentful that she failed to act on a mistake. If I say, "How could she fail to act on her mistaken moral commitments!" I am, at best, exasperated that she failed to do as I expected and wanted; I hardly can call her to task for her "error" of violating L.

(c) Free and Equal Moral Personhood as an Endogenous Commitment of Our Morality

For us to rationally maintain the reactive attitudes toward Betty, a moral prescription addressed to her must suppose that the Principle of Moral Autonomy is met. But that is to suppose that we see her as a free and equal moral person. She is a free moral person as she can be guided by her own sense of obligation based on her own reasons; she is equal because her reasons are as definitive about what she can recognize as her obligations as mine are about what I can see as mine. If she and I are to share a common social morality that sustains the reactive attitudes, our reasons must converge: a common morality must in this way be endorsed by all free and equal moral persons. Our initial assumption that we confront others as free and equal persons (§§1.1, 2.1) turns out not to be an exogenous (external) demand on an acceptable social morality based on some foundational moral intuition but a deep presumption of our social morality with rational reactive attitudes. To build an analysis of the moral order denying the fundamental supposition of free and equal moral persons means that either (*i*) the reactive attitudes are pushed to the periphery of moral practice (§11.3) or (*ii*) we must embrace the new sentimentalist's essentially nonrational account of the reactive attitudes and the moral community, with all the problems that involves.

When we confront others as free and equal moral persons who have endorsed moral rule L, we are in a position to demand of them that they act as L requires. Our moral demands have genuine authority; those to whom they are addressed have reasons to comply, and because they do have such reasons we can hold them responsible for their failures, and the reactive attitudes are justified. We are not merely preaching to them or calling them names ("bad person!"). We are engaging in a moral relationship with them in which our prescriptions should be acknowledged by them as authoritative (this is the insight underlying Scanlon's relationship analysis of morality). Such prescriptions are neither primarily expressive nor veiled descriptions ("your act fails to conform to certain standards"); they are practical exercises in which we appeal to others as rational moral persons to induce them to fulfill their obligations, even when this goes against their values, ends, and goals. Our moral claims do not demand that others ignore their rational natures, but that they conform to them.

It is important that while a person must have her reasons to endorse a strong moral rule, the rule directs her to act even at a cost to her own values and goals. On the Common Good View of strong rules although the rules must be endorsed by one's overall reasons and goals, they are not policies for goal pursuit (§9.2*a*). Because strong rules are not simply instruments to optimally securing one's aims, a person does not owe compliance simply to herself: the rules of social morality give others standing to demand compliance. As Darwall stresses, moral rules that give us authority over each other are rules of mutual accountability.[76] When I have authority over you and you fail to respect it, the reactive attitudes come into play. And as Baier emphasized, the violation is other people's business, and because it is their business they have standing to insist on performance and standing to hold the violator responsible for what she has done.

A social morality that grounds the rational moral emotions reconciles moral obligation with freedom: each acts on her own reasons when acting morally. And so each is both constrained by strong moral rules and yet, in the positive sense, is free (§2.4*c*). Contrary to Berlin, positive freedom is not an abstruse and dangerous doctrine of Continental philosophers and Englishmen such as T. H. Green whom they corrupted. It is what our own morality aspires to, and it is achieved when the reactive attitudes are fully justified.

[76] Darwall, *The Second-Person Standpoint*, chap. 5.

12.4 THE FIRST-PERSON PERSPECTIVE ON MORAL TRUTH

(a) An Affirmation of the Centrality of the First-Person Point of View
Steven Wall has criticized the idea that in social (and political) morality we are in some way committed to reasoning from the standpoint of others. "[T]he first-person standpoint," says Wall, is fundamental to . . . morality. Any principle of restraint or any settlement reached from a shared standpoint must be grounded in reasons that speak to the first-person standpoint. . . . But proponents of public justification . . . demand that we adopt a shared or common standpoint rather than rely on our own first person moral convictions. . . . *If the demand is to have a claim on us, it must itself be rooted in first-person moral commitments."*[77] Now this last sentence is manifestly correct; it is of the utmost importance to be clear why an account of morality that emphasizes what Darwall calls the second-person standpoint also affirms the centrality of first-personal commitments. The central message of Strawson's essay is that an understanding of one's own first-personal understanding of the authority of one's moral demands – what is involved in holding others responsible for failure to comply and the associated reactive attitudes – drives one to consider the viewpoint of others. It is not as if, somehow, one starts simply with reasoning from the perspective of others rather than one's own. One reasons about one's own understanding of the authority of social morality and holding others responsible, and this fuller understanding of one's first-person commitments leads one to see that one is committed to making claims on others that can only be well grounded if certain things are true about the viewpoints of others.

One not only must begin, but one must end, with one's own point of view. One starts out examining one's concepts and moral commitments, and one sees that one can advance authoritative prescriptions only if one can confirm that others have certain capacities and reasons. To advance an authoritative prescription presupposes a certain conception of the sorts of agents who can acknowledge such a demand. And so, I have been arguing, one comes to see that one is committed to an interpersonally justified

---

[77] Wall, "On Justificatory Liberalism," p. 140. Emphasis added.

social morality. Given this, one recognizes "first-personal" reasons to provide this sort of justification and consider what reasons others have. Now in the end, of course, this must be based on deliberation from one's first-person perspective about what reasons another has. One never, as it were, gets out of one's first-person perspective; rather, one comes to integrate one's understanding of others' perspectives into it. This is what Piaget called "decentering."[78] Piaget describes as "egocentrism" the idea that one's own perspective is, as it were, the center of the reasons universe: all good reasons are one's own reasons. As she matures and decenters, a person comes to refocus; she does not abandon her perspective (how could she do that?) but comes to model *within it* the perspectives of others. Now this modeling of others must remain her own model of them; it is part of an expanded and more sophisticated first-person perspective, but it is of course nonetheless her own view of the world. In the end, each person must, on the basis of her own reasons, judge whether her authority claims and reactive attitudes conform to the Principle of Moral Autonomy.

Because of this, a person's standard T of what constitutes a good reason R for others need not itself be verified by the reasoning of others; her internal first-person commitments require that R pass the test T. If R passes T, the rational reactive attitudes are maintained. We should thus be skeptical of the so-called reflexivity requirement in public justification – that not only one's moral demands, but one's test T of whether others have reason to accept those demands, must be verified by the reason of others.[79] We never really go outside our perspective, though we must have within our perspective an adequate understanding of the reasons of others. David Estlund, in contrast, has argued that the reflexivity requirement must be endorsed by theories of public reason. The core of Estlund's account of public reasoning is an "Admissibility

---

[78] I consider Piaget's view in more depth in my *Value and Justification*, pp. 198–203. Unsurprisingly, new sentimentalists such as Nichols are skeptical of the importance in morality of seeing things from the viewpoint of others. *Sentimental Rules*, pp. 8–11.

[79] I have argued against this requirement in some detail in *Justificatory Liberalism*, pp. 175–80 and in Fred D'Agostino and Gerald Gaus, "Public Reason: Why, What and Can (and Should) It Be?" Lawrence B. Solum endorses reflexivity in "Constructing an Ideal of Public Reason," p. 735.

Principle" according to which "No doctrine is admissible as a premise in any stage of political justification unless it is acceptable to a certain range of (real or hypothetical) citizens, C, and no one else's acceptance is required."[80] Now, he argues:

The acceptability requirement has a logically interesting feature. It says that political justifications cannot appeal to doctrines that are not acceptable to all qualified points of view, and it itself is a doctrine appealed to in political justification. It says, then, that even it cannot be used unless it is acceptable in that way.[81]

Estlund thus maintains that the Admissibility Principle must apply reflexively: it must apply to itself, and so it must conform to its own requirements. So he advocates the

Reflexivity Requirement: A test T of acceptability in justificatory discourse D, that specifies requirement Q for all admissible arguments in D, must itself (that is, T) conform to Q.

Estlund argues that there is nothing inherently suspicious about reflexive rules. As he says, "in general some requirements apply to themselves."[82] However, he presses further and claims that the Reflexivity Requirement "is indeed a requirement for the coherence of *any* version" of an admissibility principle.[83] I believe this to be clearly mistaken. There are a number of perfectly coherent tests for admissibility of an argument into a discourse D that are not reflexive, such as the Falsification Principle for scientific discourse: an argument must contain a falsifiable empirical premise in order to be admitted into the discourse. Leaving aside whether the Falsification Principle is correct, our question is whether its coherence requires meeting the Reflexivity Requirement. Need *it* contain a falsifiable empirical premise to be coherent? No. It is perfectly sensible to understand the Falsification Principle as a meta-claim, justified in the philosophy of science, about what constitutes a

---

[80] David Estlund, *Democratic Authority*, p. 53.

[81] Ibid.

[82] Ibid. I think Estlund underestimates some of the logical puzzles that arise with self-referential tests. See Fred D'Agostino's and my essay "Public Reason: Why, What and Can (and Should) It Be?"

[83] Estlund, *Democratic Authority*, p. 56. Emphasis added.

normatively sound scientific argument, and advocates of it can without incoherence admit that it contains no falsifiable empirical premises. It is a requirement about the way discourse D is to be conducted which is seen as a norm that structures D, but it is itself justified through a meta-discourse D^*. Thus it seems that, contra the Reflexivity Requirement, a test T about the admissibility of arguments into discourse D can be justified through some non-D discourse, and T may not pass its own test in D discourse.

Requirements of public reasoning and of public admissibility should be understood in a similar way. They are requirements entailed by one's own view of our moral practices and the way public justification is to be conducted. Suppose we have a Baier-like theory of public justification according to which an admissible argument for rule L "at any stage of political justification"[84] must have as an implication of its acceptance that L works to the good of everyone.[85] And suppose we identify an idealized set of individuals Ω that are competent representatives of various viewpoints, so that any argument that is passed by Ω is taken to pass the test. There is no reason to insist that every member of Ω also accepts our common good test. If given my conception of social morality I have compelling reason to adopt the common good requirement as a condition for any bona fide moral rule, my justificatory concern is not that each and every person accepts the requirement (i.e., my conception of morality), but that, given the requirement, each and every person has reason to agree that a moral rule promotes her good. *That* public test would help satisfy me, given my first-person understanding of morality, that moral rule L is acceptable.

(b) The Imperious Private Conscience

It is, then, something of a red herring to cast the dispute between the advocate of the necessity of interpersonal justification and his critic as being about the importance of the first-person point of view. It is about the commitments of a sophisticated first-person

---

[84] I suspect that this is the phrase that Estlund may wish to stress. But if everything depends on this precise phrase, then I think the argument is an artifact of the specific formulation, and is not of much general interest.

[85] See Baier, *The Moral Point of View*, pp. 200-204. I endorse this requirement in section 14.2f.

point of view. Wall's core point is that, first and foremost, moral judgment and action concerning others are based on one's own moral convictions, whether or not they meet the Principle of Moral Autonomy. He thus tells a story of Jack and Jill. Jill believes that voluntary euthanasia is morally wrong. Jack disagrees: he cannot see Jill's considerations as reasons.

Now it is possible that Jill may come to doubt that she is correct. As a result of her interaction with Jack, she might come to think that the reasons she was appealing to in order to ground her judgment that voluntary euthanasia was morally wrong are less compelling than she previously thought. She might change her mind on the issue or she might hold her view with less confidence. But suppose that this does not happen. Does Jill have any reason to revise her view about euthanasia simply because another person cannot rationally accept it? I do not see how it could.[86]

Wall, then, holds that Jack's rational rejection of Jill's reasons is not decisive for Jill's view of the moral truth on this matter; she can continue to believe that Jack does wrong even in the face of his inability to see her case as providing reasons. Perhaps. "Morality" is a pluralistic concept (see Appendix A). An understanding of "morality" entertained by many people is that it refers to a realm of normative facts that in some sense concerns how things "really are" and that are independent of agents' "subjective perspectives." Moral judgments are beliefs about these "objective" facts.[87] On this notion of morality, that "Alf's action ϕ was wrong" is a fact about Alf's action that is independent of what he can see as a reason to hold that it is wrong. Nothing I say in this work is inconsistent with such a view of morality and truth. Those who hold it can continue to make such judgments of others without rejecting the analysis. So long as proponents of the supremacy of private conscience simply assert descriptive statements about right and wrong – and so make no claim to authority over others – there is no conflict between their devotion to their beliefs and a moral order of public reason.

---

[86] Wall, "On Justificatory Liberalism," p. 139.
[87] For Joseph Raz, justification and evaluation are about these facts. *Engaging Reason: On the Theory of Value and Action*, p. 31.

However, many advocates of the first-person conscience do not simply hold that it may insist on its beliefs about what is true, but that these truths should shape social morality, and so our claims to authority over others.[88] Consider how impoverished and inadequate such a conception of morality is as a way to regulate our interactions and social life – that is, as a basis for social morality. The necessary tie between wrongdoing and the moral emotions and responsibility is lost.[89] Consequently, so is the intimate connection between wrongdoing and responsibility. On this view there is nothing remarkable about Alf's violating moral requirements but not being responsible; we should not be indignant or resentful, and it is often thought by its proponents that there would be no point in blaming him. "But this," responds Russ Shafer-Landau, "does not undermine the possible justice of the verdict."[90] Perhaps this is so, but then our just verdicts are without authority over others. For Alf to have justified authority to insist that Betty φ, it is not sufficient for Alf to claim that he must be obeyed, to be convinced in his heart that he knows the truth, or even for him to really have the truth: she must have a reason to comply. Authority must in some way be recognized by those over whom it is exercised (§10.1); otherwise, it is mere power, no matter how benevolently exercised. Wall insists that Alf can have a moral claim even when another moral person Betty, exercising her rationality as well as we could expect, can see no reason to acknowledge the claim. So she does not recognize the authority of his claim. It is a moral claim without moral authority – an assertion that others must do as you would have them do.

This brings us to the deeply objectionable characteristic of a conception of social morality based simply on a first-personal conviction about the moral truth. Social morality, which regulates the social interactions of diverse individuals, would be dictated by the conscience of some, demanding that others simply obey. Social interaction is to be on their terms, directed by their conscience and their convictions about moral truth. Those who do not share this

---

[88] For a view that puts the sanctity of private conscience at the very foundation of social and political morality, see Chandran Kukathas, *The Liberal Archipelago*.

[89] Advocates of this view often accept this implication. See Wall, "On Justificatory Liberalism," Appendix; Wall, *Liberalism, Perfectionism and Restraint*, p. 118; Christopher Eberle, *Religious Convictions in Liberal Politics*, p. 133.

[90] Russ Shafer-Landau, *Moral Realism*, p. 177.

conscience must submit to the truth. It is precisely this imperious claim of private conscience that the social contract-liberal tradition has rejected. Hobbes saw that it was fundamentally hostile to cooperative social life for each conscience to claim not only to know, but in the name of truth assert its authority to impose its view of proper behavior on others (§1.3b). That others such as Jack, employing their reason, disagree with Jill's conviction about the truth, says Wall, ultimately "should not matter" to Jill.[91] She may go ahead and force Jack to comply. To be sure, Wall does not claim that each has the moral standing to impose her view of the moral truth on her fellows: only those who really know the truth have such authority. In the end the reasoning here seems to be essentially what Mill called "the logic of persecutors, . . . that we may persecute others [or force them to comply] because we are right, and that they must not persecute us [or force us to comply] because they are wrong."[92] A social morality on these terms must be one in which power supplants justified authority as the core social moral relation. Given that the free exercise of private judgment leads to disagreement (§3.2), each will claim that her reason is right reason, and so that she is justified (just *because* her reason is right reason) in dictating the terms of social cooperation to her fellows.

The social contract tradition has sought to show how dangerous this attitude is to social cooperation and morality; so far from fulfilling the function of social morality in helping us to live together in a cooperative social order, the social morality of the imperious private conscience endangers it. Moreover, I have tried to show how this conception of morality undermines many of our current moral practices concerning responsibility, guilt, resentment, and indignation. In response to all of this, the imperious private conscience replies that it must act on the truth as it understands it, for is not the truth what we all seek, and which must guide all our actions? How can we *not* act on the truth (as we see it)?[93] But surely the great liberal lesson, first glimpsed in the sixteenth century, is that successful large-scale cooperative social orders are precisely those in which people do come to "bracket" their rationally

[91] Wall, "On Justificatory Liberalism," p. 139.
[92] Mill, *On Liberty*, p. 285 (Chap. IV, ¶15).
[93] See Joseph Raz, "Facing Diversity: The Case of Epistemic Abstinence."

controversial first-personal convictions about the truth when these convictions are about how others must live. Only, if, instead we regulate our common life by public reason can the rational moral emotions, based on authoritative moral claims, be maintained. Thus arises a moral order of public reason.

13 The Reasons One Has

13.1 THE REASONS THERE ARE AND THAT ONE HAS

The analysis I have offered of the authority of social morality may appear to presuppose what is known as an "internalist," as opposed to an "externalist," conception of reasons. It would not, I think, be too much of an exaggeration to say that contemporary analyses of rationality – especially practical rationality – are obsessed with the debate about whether reasons (and/or rationality) are "external" or "internal."[94] Joseph Raz has strenuously upheld what he calls "the classical view" according to which "reasons are facts which endow an action with some good-making properties."[95] Reasons are facts about the properties of action; they are not facts about what one believes, or what one is committed to by one's beliefs. Raz admits that sometimes we employ the term "reason" to refer to those mental entities that enter into reasoning, but these are really "beliefs about reasons," not reasons.[96] Thus an externalist is apt to see rationality as our ability to track these (external) facts.[97] The internalist counters that reasons are part of reason*ing*, and reasoning is a mental event; reasons are "links" in "chains" of reasoning.[98] In his classic essay that spurred the debate, Bernard Williams maintained that a person's reasons are internal

[94] For an excellent overview of the debate, see Brad Hooker and Bart Streumer, "Procedural and Substantive Practical Rationality."

[95] Raz, *Engaging Reason*, p. 25.

[96] Ibid., p. 25. If it held that reasons are external, in the sense of being facts or propositions about the world, then they cannot directly enter into reasoning, which is a mental event: they are just the wrong sorts of entities. There can, though, be mental states that represent them – that is, beliefs.

[97] See Derek Parfit, "Rationality and Reasons."

[98] See Baier's description of the "dominant" conception of reason (which he rejects), *The Rational and the Moral Order*, p. 28.

because they depend on her subjective motivational set – her beliefs and desires.[99] Unless a person has the requisite beliefs and desires that would motivate her to ϕ, or she can deliberate her way to them, there is no reason for her to ϕ.

Initial appearances notwithstanding, nothing I have said commits to the internalist side of this debate. Although, like many enduring controversies in philosophy it is often not clear precisely what the debate really is, at its most fundamental level this controversy is about what *reasons are*: an essentially metaphysical question. The debate also easily translates into a substantive controversy in ethics about what *reasons there are* (which is closely tied to metaphysical questions about what is involved in a reason *existing*). I have not, however, been concerned with what reasons are, or even what reasons there are, but what reasons people can be said to *have*. As Robert Audi makes clear, what reasons there are, and what reasons one can be said to possess, are distinct notions.[100] The analyses of sections 11 and 12 are only inconsistent with externalism if the externalist also adopts:

> *The Externalist View of Having a Reason*: An agent has reason R if and only if R is an external reason that applies to him.

As Schafer-Landau describes the moral rationalist, she appears to accept this view: "Everyone has a reason to regard genocide as evil, because it is true that genocide is evil."[101] I believe the Externalist View of Having a Reason to be implausible: it misconstrues the relation between having a reason and being a rational agent. First consider the Externalist View of Having a Reason applied to

---

[99] Williams, "Internal and External Reasons." It is important to realize that motivational internalism is simply one type of internalism, not the entire set of internalist theories; one can argue that all reasons are internal without basing this on the idea that reasons must motivate. The core of internalism is the idea that reasons are best understood as elements of reasoning; practical reason is not about one's "beliefs about reasons," but about one's reasons. Williams' argument is that the internalist can explain why reasons motivate, but that is a feature of his version of internalism, not of internalism per se. We should not, then, think that internalism is simply a consequence of the view that all reasons require action (and so must motivate it) rather than simply showing action to be permissible. Cf. Joshua Gert, *Brute Rationality*, pp. 57–8.

[100] Robert Audi, *The Architecture of Reason*, pp. 53–5.

[101] Schafer-Landau, *Moral Realism*, pp. 206-7. Schafer-Landau adds that, in addition, application conditions of this fact to the person's action need to be provided.

theoretical reasoning. It implies that Aristotle, when writing on physics, had – possessed – a reason to embrace particle physics, because particle physics is true. But surely he did not have any such reason; to see *R* as a reason is to see it as justificatory, but Aristotle simply could not employ his rationality in a way that could lead him to see the facts supporting particle physics as justificatory (he could not even understand these facts). Only by *not* following the conclusions of his rational deliberation – being irrational – could Aristotle endorse such a "reason," and he could never see it as justifying a belief. Turn now to what would seem the apparently easy, philosopher's knock-down case: everyone having a reason to avoid genocide just because it is evil. Unless one has the concept of an ethnic group or race such that its elimination is a crime in addition to the murder of the discrete individuals (perhaps, unless one has discovered the horrors of the twentieth century), one simply could not see eliminating groups as a crime above and beyond eliminating the constituent individuals. In a world of small-scale societies in which neighboring tribes and ethnic groups are in competition for scarce resources and so regularly eliminate their neighbors, either by destruction or forced assimilation, individuals could not employ their rationality and come to see avoiding genocide as a reason – something that justifies action.[102] Consider the following description of warfare among the Alaskan Eskimos:

The objective of warfare in North Alaska was to annihilate the members of the enemy group, men, women, and children....A fully successful war thus served to terminate inter-regional relations altogether through elimination of the members of one entire group. The typical result, however, was only partial success, some members of both groups being killed, and others

[102] On the justificatory force of practical reason, see J. David Vellman, *The Possibility of Practical Reason,* chap. 1. This raises the distinction between explanatory and justificatory reasons. In section 4.2, we saw that the (explanatory) reason why Betty was not caught in the rain is that she followed the instruction of her Ouija board, though we say that was a bad reason (i.e., not a justificatory reason) for her action. The relation between explanatory and justificatory reasons is rather more complex than many take it to be, but for the present discussion it will suffice to say that our concern is with justificatory reasons.

surviving. Thus warfare tended to perpetuate inter-regional hostilities since survivors were always morally obliged to seek revenge.[103]

To attribute a reason *to* these peoples, to say that they *possessed* a reason not to eliminate other groups, while acknowledging that any justificatory force of this reason is inaccessible to them as reasoning beings is, I think, not only a misuse of language, but undermines the point of discourse about reasons and rationality. It is intelligible enough to insist that there is a reason that applies to their action but is beyond their comprehension; but to say they possess these incomprehensible justifying considerations is close to bizarre. The problem cannot be they do not recognize the reasons they have; it could be that they do not possess the reasons that apply to them. We employ the concepts of reasons and rationality to make others intelligible to us, to grasp how they do, and could, see the world, so that we can interact with, or at least understand them, as fellow agents. But when we ascribe to them reasons that are truly inaccessible to them as agents, to insist that they have a reason φ is simply a way of saying that φ is right, but the rightness is not something that can enter into their agency.

13.2 THE MYTH OF FULL RATIONALITY

(a) The Affirmation Thesis Rejected
It is sometimes thought that the issue between internalists and externalists is whether we can ascribe reasons to a person that she does not recognize.[104] I have been arguing that we cannot ascribe reason R to Alf just because R is a reason that applies to Alf. Now it might be thought that this commits me to

> *The Reason Affirmation Thesis.* Alf has R as a reason if and only if he affirms R as a reason.

To say that Alf recognizes R as a reason is to say that he affirms that R is a reason, or would immediately affirm that R is a reason if another points R out to Alf. The Reason Affirmation Thesis must be rejected: Alf's affirming R as a reason is neither necessary nor

---

[103] Quoted in Azar Gat, *War in Human Civilization*, p. 94.
[104] See Schafer-Landau, *Moral Realism*, p. 177.

sufficient for R to be a reason of Alf's. It is certainly not *sufficient*, since a person can be wrong about the reasons that he has. At a deep level, Freud's understanding of neurosis is centrally about people being mistaken about their reasons. They think they have reasons to avoid horses, when it is their father they are afraid of, or they think they have reasons to keep their pillow from touching their bed, but it is really having a sibling whom they wish to avoid.[105] As we saw in the discussion of instrumental rationality (§4.2), a purely subjective understanding of one's reasons is inadequate: if people have crazy beliefs, they do not have reasons to act as the crazy beliefs indicate, though they may take themselves to have such reasons.

Nor is Alf's affirmation of R *necessary* for R to be a reason of his. Recall Mill's bad bridge case (§2.4c): a person who is about to cross a dangerous bridge has a reason R not to cross it, even if he does not know that it is dangerous and so could not presently affirm R. Not even Bernard Williams, often seen as the paradigm of an internalist, thought that affirmation was necessary to ascribe a reason to a person. "The internalist view of reasons for action," says Williams, "is that this formulation provides at least a necessary condition of its being true that A[lf] has a reason to ϕ: A[lf] has a reason to ϕ only if he could reach the conclusion to ϕ by a sound deliberative route from the motivations he already has."[106] Thus Alf *now* has a reason R to ϕ if there is a sound deliberative route from Alf's present motivational set to R. Alf, then, need not now affirm R as a reason for R now to be a reason of his.

(b) Full Rationality as the Recognition of the Reasons That Apply to One
The rejection of the affirmation thesis implies that any ascription *now* of reasons to the actual person Alf must involve some idealization of actual Alf. To say what reasons actual Alf now has, we have to consider the reasons that Alf would arrive at if he followed certain sound deliberative routes from his present reason set. Whether actual Alf is inclined to follow these deliberative routes is not relevant. Perhaps Alf is neurotic and refuses to contemplate the

[105] On the former case, see §4.2; on the latter case, see note 74 above.
[106] Williams, "Internal Reasons and the Obscurity of Blame," p. 35.

idea that the bridge he is crossing is unsafe. Regardless, if a non-neurotic version of Alf – idealized Alf – soundly reasoned from actual Alf's present set of reasons, including the reason to gather easily obtained relevant information, then this idealized Alf's conclusion affirming *R* would warrant us in ascribing *R* to actual Alf, who refuses to affirm it. Likewise, if idealized Alf examined Alf's presently affirmed set of reasons and concludes that some of these are bad reasons (say, his reliance on political ideology to decide what philosophical doctrines to accept), then actual Alf does not now have the reasons he affirms because they would not be affirmed by idealized Alf.

Now once it has been admitted that any plausible doctrine of the reasons one has must involve some idealization of actual people in this way, the door seems opened for a resurrection of the Externalist View of Having a Reason (i.e., an agent has reason *R* if and only if *R* is an external reason that applies to him). As Wall argues, since some level of idealization is required for any plausible view of what it means for a person to have a reason, if we fully idealize a person – if we suppose her to be fully rational – then she will affirm "the full range of evaluative considerations that apply to the situation at hand."[107] That is, a fully rational person will affirm all, and only, the (external) reasons that apply to her. If so, assuming that full rationality is the right level of idealization (and how could anything *short* of full rationality be adequate?), the Externalist View of Having a Reason appears, after all, correct.

Depending on what is understood by "full rationality," this proposal is either simply (*i*) a restatement of the Externalist View of Having a Reason or (*ii*) a substantive claim. It is (*i*), simply a restatement, if "rationality" is also understood in an externalist manner, as an ability to discern the external reasons that there are. So full rationality would be the ability to discern fully all the reasons that there are, and so, by definition, a fully rational person would affirm all the reasons that apply to her. Like many philosophical victories that come too easily, this one accomplishes little; all the problems that we canvassed in section 13.1 with the External View of Having a Reason persist. People who could not possibly

---

[107] Wall, "On Justificatory Liberalism," p. 138.

reason themselves to affirming a reason as justificatory are now said to now have this reason because if they were fully rational they would affirm the reason, and to be fully rational requires that one affirms this as a reason. Actual Alf may find totally opaque the "reasoning" of his idealized "counterpart" who arrived at R, and no matter how hard he tried or how faultlessly he employed his powers of reasoning, he simply could not reproduce it, or arrive at R himself, but nevertheless R is attributed to him. If one was not already impressed by the External View of Having a Reason, one could not be moved by this notion of what reasons a fully rational person would affirm.

In contrast, the full rationality argument is, (*ii*), a substantive and interesting philosophical thesis if full rationality is characterized independently of recognizing external reasons. In the history of philosophy, many have understood full rationality in terms of one who has the full powers of reasoning, who follows impeccable epistemic norms, who changes his beliefs by making all the inferences from his current set of fully affirmed beliefs,[108] and who employs the fullest possible information set. Given such persons, it then might be argued that they would recognize all the external reasons that apply to them. We would then have an argument that, contrary to what I maintained in section 13.1, there is a sense in which a person can always make sense of, or appreciate, all the external reasons that apply to him if he was this sort of rational Hercules. There would still be the question of whether a rational Hercules is really the best way to idealize a person's reasoning, but the Externalist View of What Reasons We Have would be, as it were, back on the agenda.

In the remainder of section 13.2 I argue, first, that even if we were all rational Herculi we would not agree on the reasons that we have, and secondly, that any even remotely useful ideal of full rationality is indeterminate about what is to be believed.

---

[108] See Isaac Levi, "Commitment and Change of View." This idea of "deductive closure" is far more problematic than it first appears. See Harman, *Reasoning, Meaning, and Mind*, pp. 21–3.

(c) Sensitivity to the Initial Set: The Root of Indeterminacy

Suppose poor actual Alf and poor actual Betty, mired in their cognitive limitations, are suddenly transformed into their rational Hercules counterparts. Each suddenly has the highest possible powers of reasoning (whatever that means), each sees all the inferences from his or her fully held beliefs and can see precisely, and immediately, the maximally coherent and consistent set of beliefs that results.[109] Assume also that each has complete information (again, assuming that we can make sense of this idea). Despite all these not very modest powers, Hercules Alf and Hercules Betty are guaranteed to converge on the same set of beliefs only if either (*i*) they initially believe precisely the same things and had precisely the same values, ends, goals, and so on, or (*ii*) what they initially believed had no effect on their final set of beliefs. We can set aside (*i*), since that would be as rare as their powers, and in any event we are concerned with people in general, not just perfect clones.

Possibility (*ii*), though it has been attractive to many in the history of epistemology, is also implausible. Even the reasoning of Hercules must start from somewhere; Hercules Alf starts out with a set of beliefs that he immediately transforms into a maximally coherent set; Betty starts with her belief set, which she transforms into her maximally coherent set. Will these sets be identical? Many coherence epistemologists have dearly hoped so, though they generally allowed that nonequivalence of maximally coherent beliefs systems was possible.[110] It seems, though, far more than merely possible. Think of it this way: divide Alf's and Betty's belief systems into two parts, those which they share and those which they do not. Call χ the common element; call α the part of Alf's system that is not shared by Betty, and β the part of her system that is not shared by Alf. So Alf's belief set is $\alpha + \chi$ and Betty's is $\beta + \chi$. Suppose our two Herculi first turn their attention to χ; and suppose that they entertain the precise same epistemic norms and ideal of

---

[109] As Levi points out, this would require that there be maximally fine discrimination of beliefs, which he denies is a sensible idea ("Commitment and Change of View," p. 214). However, since rational Hercules is, to use Levi's phrase, itself "philosophical moonshine," this should not deter us here. I consider the relation of consistency and coherence in *Justificatory Liberalism*, pp. 74–84.

[110] See Alan H. Goldman, *Empirical Knowledge*, pp. 80–7.

coherence,[111] so that they are led to the same fully coherent, χ^*. Now the question is, will Alf's perfect "coherentizing" of $\alpha + \chi^*$ lead him to the same outcome as Betty's of $\beta + \chi^*$? Consider three possibilities: (*i*) Alf rejects all of α and Betty rejects all of β; (*ii*) whatever elements of α that Alf retains, Betty adopts and whatever elements of β that Betty retains, Alf adopts; (*iii*) Alf and/or Betty retain some elements of his or her belief set that the other does not adopt. If (*i*) occurs they will end up with the common belief set composed of only χ^*; cases of (*ii*) will lead them to new identical belief sets; any cases of (*iii*) will almost surely lead them to different final belief sets.

Possibility (*i*) may eventuate in some cases, but not generally. Suppose that Alf and Betty start out with very different beliefs sets. Assume that of all the actual persons who are made into rational Herculi, they start out with the least similar belief sets, so χ is relatively small. It has always been stressed that a fully rational, coherent, belief system is not simply consistent, but one that is rich in content: one cannot achieve maximal coherence by whittling one's belief set down into two elements that entail each other. Coherence is more than logical consistency.[112] So if Alf and Betty share little they cannot achieve maximal coherence simply by adopting χ^*: they need more beliefs.[113] Now this would not matter if (*ii*) is universally the case, for they would still end up with the same, fuller, belief set. But (*ii*) will not be universally the case. There will be instances of (*iii*). The reason that there will be instances of (*iii*) is that Alf has more reason to retain any particular element of α than Betty has to adopt it. The principle of conservatism implies that Alf's reasons of whether to reject a member of α (α_1) and Betty's of whether to accept α_1 will differ. Alf now holds α_1: he sees it as having some degree of justification insofar as it is one of the things

---

[111] This is a very strong assumption; we are essentially supposing that all their epistemic norms are in χ, and so none are in α or β.

[112] See Lawrence BonJour, *The Structure of Empirical Knowledge*, chap. 5; Harman, *Reasoning, Meaning, and Mind*, pp. 32–5.

[113] The idea of "more beliefs" is itself hard to really make sense of, for there are many trivial beliefs that one has under deductive closure – if one believes all the implications of one's full beliefs one believes a lot! But much of it may be rather trivial (say, a belief about the square root of 66789.0667).

he believes: he needs some positive reason to *reject* it.[114] Betty, though, needs some reason to *accept* it: they are in different very epistemic positions regarding members of α. Alf can have no reason to reject what Betty has no reason to accept, because Alf's ideal deliberations are based on α + χ*, while Betty's are not. As Harman observes, as a reasoner,

> [y]ou start from where you are, with your present beliefs and intentions. Rationality or reasonableness then consists in trying to make improvements in your view. Your initial beliefs and intentions have a privileged position in the sense that you begin with them rather than with nothing at all or with a special privileged part of those beliefs and intentions serving as data.[115]

It has often been held that fully rational agents who had full information and who believed all the implications of their beliefs would arrive at the same, maximally coherent, belief set. There would not be even one logical inconsistency in any such belief set, and since the truth is consistent, these sets would contain only truths and available truths. Coherence, as we have seen, is more than deductive consistency and closure. As long as our fully rational ideal agents are "coherentizing" over different initial data sets (with relations between beliefs characterized not only by deduction but by various types of inductive relations, and different initial values, and so on), we have every reason to suppose that full convergence would occur only in unusual and rare cases.[116]

(d) Path-Dependency: Indeterminacy Magnified
In any event, the idea of such rational Herculi is utterly fantastic. To see instantaneously and costlessly all the implications of all one's beliefs and to render them maximally coherent is so far beyond human cognitive capacities that it is hard to see such beings as even the most idealized versions of ourselves.[117] Is God an

---

[114] See Gilbert Harman, *Change in View*.
[115] Gilbert Harman, *Reasoning, Meaning, and Mind*, p. 23. See also See William Lycan's defense of the principle of conservation of beliefs, and his criticism of Keith Lehrer's "epistemic anarchism." *Judgment and Justification*, chap. 8
[116] See further Harman, *Reasoning, Meaning, and Mind*, pp. 27–35.
[117] See Christopher Cherniak, *Minimal Rationality*, pp. 76ff.

idealized human agent? Perhaps we can be a wee bit more realistic. When the ideal of full rationality is employed by philosophers, it often is applied to specific choices: what would our fully rational selves decide about what to do in situation C, say, when confronted by a specific option set? We are coming a little more down to earth here, for now our fully rational agents need only do a complete scan of all their beliefs and values regarding choice from the specified set, and only information that is relevant to that set is required.

Suppose we employ this conception of full rationality: we can immediately see that full rationality is now a deeply indeterminate ideal even for a single person. Assume that at time t_1 Alf has to choose from, say, a certain action set (call it Y), and to do that he must decide what are the fully rational beliefs about these options, and what are the relevant fully rational values, so he does a complete, costless survey of all his relevant beliefs and values, as well as all the relevant epistemic norms and obtains all the relevant information (as we can see, Alf is still quite an impressive reasoner). Alf makes his decisions, and decides that beliefs α_1 and α_2 are relevant, but he recognizes a conflict between them and determines that he can make his system more coherent by dropping α_1 and adding α_3 in its place. At time t_2 he confronts another situation Z with the belief set $\{\alpha_2, \alpha_3\}$, and so he chooses option Z_1, which α_2 and α_3 favor. Now consider a different history of Alf's choices. Instead of Y, he first confronted situation X, and the relevant beliefs concerning X were α_1 and α_4; he sees that α_1 and α_4 commit him to also accepting a new belief, α_5.[118] Again Alf confronts the Y situation and again uncovers the conflict between α_1 and α_2. But now he sees that dropping α_2 would make his system more coherent, for α_1 coheres exceptionally well with the newly acquired α_5: in *this* system dropping α_2 would increase coherence. On this history, when he confronts the Z choice situation with a different belief set, the Z_1-favoring α_2 and α_3 are not present, and he may instead have a Z_2-favoring α_1.

---

[118] It might be objected that α_2 must still be relevant here, since it is inconsistent with α_1. I have tried to keep the story reasonably simple to illustrate the basic idea: instead of directly appealing to α_1 at X, we could add a different belief α_x with inferential connections to α_1 and not to α_2, and could generate the same result in a more complex way.

If our slightly more modest "fully rational" individuals make partial belief revisions, their "full rationality" will be *path dependent*: a fully rational choice at one time will depend on the order of fully rational revisions at earlier times. Thus, as in our example, either of two inconsistent beliefs may have been chosen by a fully rational person depending on the path her belief revisions take. Consequently, the criterion of a fully rational choice is indeterminate: depending on the order in which the choice is made, full rationality may lead to a variety of outcomes. This result might tempt some to retreat to the "all-at-once global" conception of full rationalization that we considered above (§13.2c), despite its extraordinary epistemic suppositions. This retreat, though, will be to no avail, for the problem we have uncovered here infects it as well: the time at which the full global rationalization occurs is apt to affect the outcome. The analysis I gave of why Hercules Alf and Hercules Betty will arrive at different fully idealized belief-value sets also shows why Alf-last-month and Alf-this-month may arrive at different fully rationalized belief-value sets: if the initial data sets differ, their full rationalization may also differ.

Full rationality is, then, an indeterminate ideal. And it will not help to switch from asking what a fully rational individual will do to what our fully rational advisor would advise us to do,[119] for our fully rational advisors are a committee of conflicting voices, or else they too can change their advice day by day. All this, I think, gravely undermines the attraction of assumptions about full rationality. To many, the extravagant cognitive-processing and information-set assumptions are warranted because they allow us to identify a determinate rational choice – a single rational thing to do.[120] This, I think, is the myth of full rationality: fully rational persons would choose the same specific morality, or the same principles of justice, or the same government. Once we see that we cannot obtain the hoped-for result, there is little attraction in invoking

[119] See Michael Smith, *The Moral Problem*, pp. 151ff and Michael Smith, "Internal Reasons," pp. 18–20.
[120] If some reasons are seen as merely indicating permissions (i.e., it would be rational to choose φ but not rationally required), then this hoped-for determinacy seems in principle unachievable on yet other grounds. See Gert, *Brute Rationality*; Ronald De Sousa, "Modeling Rationality: Normative or Descriptive?"

such Herculean assumptions as the grounds for moral and social philosophy.

13.3 HAVING A SUFFICIENT REASON

The philosophical tradition appealing to full rationality commences analysis with a highly idealized state, which is seen as providing guidance for real agents. If we conclude that this is ultimately a futile exercise, we might work the other way around: begin with real agents and then see what degree of idealization of their reasoning makes sense. John Pollock has advanced a theory of "real rationality" – one that takes human cognitive limitations as central to understanding what a rational agent will believe and do – as an explicit alternative to "ideal rationality." Pollock distinguishes a justified from a warranted choice:

> A *justified* choice is one that a real agent could make given all the reasoning that it has performed *up to the present time* and without violating the constraints of rationality. A *warranted* choice is one that would be justified if the agent could complete all possibly relevant reasoning.[121]

A justified choice to act, or a justified belief in a proposition, is one that has been arrived at in conformity with the norms of rationality, which are to be understood procedurally.[122] These norms are about the rules of good reasoning. Evidence indicates that basic norms tend to be universally shared by humans (though language may affect the ease at which they are retrieved in reasoning), and we certainly attribute them to others when we interpret their beliefs and actions.[123] A rational agent is one who is competent at

[121] Pollock, *Thinking about Acting*, p. 6. Emphasis in original.
[122] Theories of "real" or "bounded" rationality have long stressed the procedural aspects of rationality; see Herbert Simon, "From Substantive to Procedural Rationality."
[123] See, e.g., Lance Rips, "Cognitive Processes and Propositional Reasoning"; Martin Braine, "On the Relation between the Natural Logic of Reasoning and Standard Logic"; Martin Braine and B. Rumain, "Development of Comprehension of 'or': Evidence for a Sequence of Competencies"; Edward Stein, *Without Good Reason*, chaps. 1 and 2; Cooper, *The Evolution of Reason*. See also Piaget's classic, *Logic and Psychology*. I consider these issues in more depth in *Justificatory Liberalism*, chap.

following a set of norms about how to go about reasoning – epistemic norms. Failures of rationality are "performance errors," and choices based on these sorts of errors are unjustified.[124] A reason R to believe β, or to perform act ϕ, arrived at through following these norms – rational deliberation – is a good reason.

Suppose a person has arrived at the conclusion that R_1 is a reason to believe β by correctly following the norms of reasoning. One thing that this implies is that he has not uncovered a *defeater* of R_1. If R_1 is a reason for Alf to believe β, R_2 is a defeater for this reason if and only if (*i*) R_2 is a reason of Alf's and (*ii*) R_2 is logically consistent with R_1 and (*iii*) (R_1 & R_2) is not a reason to believe β. If, then, Alf believes β on the basis of R_1, but he also believes R_2, which is a defeater of the inference from R_1 to β, the inference is defeated, and the belief β is not justified. For example, suppose that Alf is deliberating whether voluntary euthanasia is justified, and first decides that the temptation for children to convince their parents to commit suicide (in order to get their wealth) is a reason (R_1) against allowing it, and so this leads him to conclude that it is not justified ($\neg\beta$). But then he determines that a more important consideration is the suffering that might be avoided (R_2) such that R_2 *rebuts* the inference that voluntary euthanasia is unjustified – in that case R_2 is a defeater of R_1.[125]

So if Alf has reasoned correctly according to the norms of reasoning, and has not uncovered a defeater for R_1, we might say

---

4.

[124] If we suppose humans are rational, accounting for these performance errors raises puzzles. See Edward Stein, *Without Good Reason,* esp. chap. 3.

[125] See John Pollock, *Contemporary Theories of Knowledge,* p. 38. See also Foley, *The Theory of Epistemic Rationality,* chap. 1. As Pollock notes, defeaters come in two types. Sometimes (as in my example in the text) the defeater rebuts an inference by justifying the opposite belief – i.e., that $\neg\beta$. More formally, then:

> If R_1 is a reason for Alf to believe β, R_2 is a *rebutting defeater* for this reason if and only if R_2 is a defeater (for R_1 as a reason for Alf to believe β) and R_2 is a reason for Alf to believe $\neg\beta$.

In contrast:

> If R_1 is a reason for Alf to believe β, R_2 is an *undermining defeater* for this reason if and only if R_2 is a defeater (for R_1 as a reason for Alf to believe β) and R_2 is a reason for Alf not to hold R_1 is a reason to believe β.

A rebutting defeater can allow that there is a bona fide inference from R_1 to β, but that there is a better or more powerful inference from R_2 to $\neg\beta$; an undermining defeater directly challenges the inference from R_1 to β. See further my *Justificatory Liberalism,* pp. 66–70.

that his belief β is justified. However, this does not seem quite right – at least we would not want to say that Alf *has* a sufficient reason to believe β. To modify an example of Audi's, suppose that there is "equally accessible" to Alf a reason R_2, which defeats R_1.[126] If R_1 and R_2 are equally accessible to him, then it seems unjustified for Alf to believe β. In this case, while he has not reasoned against a norm of good inference, he simply has failed to see that there is a reason, *just as accessible* as R_1, that defeats it. In an obvious sense, at the level of deliberation which he is employing, he really does not have justified reason to hold β. Given this, we should adopt:

> *Sufficient (Justified) Reasons (with the No Equally Accessible Defeaters Criterion)*: Alf has a sufficient reason R (to act or believe) only if he has arrived at R by following the norms of good reasoning and there is no equally accessible (to him) defeater of R.

Let us call this the "No Equally Accessible Defeaters Criterion." It is based on two insights: that, qua rational agents, we seek to avoid basing our beliefs and decisions on defeated reasons, and that the accessibility of a reason to an agent matters. If all that mattered for having sufficient reasons was whether there are defeaters somewhere lurking in our system, we would be driven back to some conception of a full rationality: only ideally rational agents, capable of scanning their entire belief systems for lurking defeaters, could come to have, or know they have, sufficient reasons to believe or to judge. As Pollock observes, though real agents live in a world in which their current beliefs and judgments are defeasible, and they acknowledge that more reasoning and new information might change their minds, they manage to come to justified conclusions about sufficient reasons to believe and to judge right now.[127] That there may be defeaters that are very hard to detect somewhere in our overall system does not mean that we do not now have sufficient reasons R to hold β or to φ.

This is an important point: again we seem to depart from externalist accounts about our reasons. As we saw in section 13.1, we must reject the strong externalist thesis that a person has a

---

[126] Audi, *The Architecture of Reason*, p. 45.
[127] Pollock, *Thinking about Acting*, p. 6.

reason just in case there is a reason that applies to her. If, though, we accept the No Equally Accessible Defeaters Condition, we must also reject a weaker externalist thesis, namely:

Reasons Possessed Must Be Real: Alf can have a reason R only if there is a reason R.

This certainly looks plausible enough: if there is not a reason, you cannot have it. On this thesis, if Alf continued his reasoning to the limit, and if at the limit he would find that there is a defeater for R, then we cannot say that at less reflective levels (where the search for defeaters is less comprehensive) he has a sufficient reason R, for there simply is no reason R, so you could not have a sufficient reason R to ϕ. If it doesn't exist, you can't have it. Since actual agents can never reason to the limit, it may follow that we could never actually know what our sufficient reasons are.

But then, in a world in which we can never reason to the limit, what is rational deliberation and justification? There must be some standard of rational deliberation such that actual agents can have access to sufficient justifications for what they believe and do, even if it turns out that, after much more deliberation (perhaps by others at a later date), they are wrong.[128] In a world of less than perfect information and cognitive capacities, we need some concept to indicate when a person's reasoning about the world is up to acceptable standards and when it is not,[129] and we cannot appeal here to what is true, for it is our approach to making judgments about an elusive truth that is at issue. Whatever one's metaphysics of reasons, one must have some such deliberative performance concept, and some notion of when one's deliberative performance adequately grounds decisions. Henceforth I shall call this a "sufficient reason," though others may wish to translate this as "a sufficiently justified belief that one has a reason." Thus the apparent rejection of the Reasons Possessed Must Be Real thesis may only be semantic, for the heart of this work can be accepted by those who

---

[128] It is interesting that in political philosophy, as distinct from epistemology, the idea of a justified false belief is often thought incoherent. I think this is simply a mistake (perhaps made by those who are overly confident that they track normative truth in all their moral judgments).

[129] As Audi points out, rationality functions here as a virtue concept. *The Architecture of Reason*, pp. 55–6.

accept the Reasons Possessed Must be Real thesis, but also accept (*i*) that one can have justified beliefs that one has a reason to φ even if such a reason does not exist, and (*ii*) what matters in interpersonal justification is the warrant of our beliefs about reasons.

To return to the No Equally Accessible Defeaters Criterion: it applies only to a special case – namely, when the defeater's accessibility is the same as the reason in question. However, even when one has reasoned well to R justifying β, and even if there is no equally accessible defeater of R, one still might not have sufficient reason to hold β. A famous philosopher I knew tended to answer questions by saying "If you thought about that a little more carefully, you'd see that can't be right." This was, admittedly, not a very helpful reply (it certainly did not endear him to his audiences), but it had a point: the defeater was a little harder to access than the obvious error, but not so hard that the agent had sufficient reason to hold the error. Indeed, the questioner had readily available reasons to hold (what the philosopher saw as) the correct view, and, the philosopher was implicitly asserting, no ready defeaters of this correct view were accessible. Audi quite rightly stresses that there must be some internal accessibility condition imposed on epistemic justification, and certainly a defeater must be within the scope of one's understanding,[130] but in order to show that one does not have sufficient reasons to believe R the defeater surely need not be *just as* accessible as the reason it defeats. It is no excuse for making an obvious mistake that the correct answer is a little less obvious.

This begins to move us toward what Pollock calls "warranted" choices: the requirement that to have a sufficient reason to believe or decide, it must be the case that if the agent continued her norm-based reasoning – if she considered less accessible reasons than R –

---

[130] Audi, *The Architecture of Reason*, pp. 43–4. On internal accessibility, see pp. 48ff. Raz appears to advocate not only an externalist theory of the reasons that there are, but also an externalist theory of justification: "Justification and evaluation depend on how things really were at the time. . . . Justifications (at least some kinds of justifications) do not depend on the agents' perspective [*sic*], and do not depend on the reasons for which agents acted" (*Engaging Reason*, p. 31). But even Raz is driven to imply in the parenthetical phrase that *some* sort of justification is internal, for there must, as I argued in the previous paragraph, be some norma-tive deliberative relation between beliefs that warrants some other beliefs.

she would still not uncover a defeater. If we press too far down this road, of course, we are back to ideal rationality. Writes Pollock:

The [fully] warranted choices are those an ideal agent that was able to perform all the relevant reasoning would make on the basis of the information currently at its disposal. One might suppose that [fully] warranted choices are those an agent would want to make. The difficulty is that a real agent cannot complete all the reasoning that might possibly be relevant to a decision . . . reasoning is non-terminating process. Eventually the agent has to act, so we cannot require that it act only on the basis of [fully] warranted choices. The most that we can require is that the agent perform a "respectable amount" of reasoning, and then base the choice on that.[131]

Need we actually require that a "respectable amount" of reasoning has been engaged in before we say that Alf has sufficient reason to believe or act? Suppose that Alf at time t_1 has reasoned according to the norms of rationality and has a sufficient reason R to ϕ as judged by the No Equally Accessible Defeaters Criterion. Now consider two versions of Alf's short-term future: Reflective Alf, who at time t_2 actually does the "respectable amount" of further reasoning and so looks for less accessible defeaters and finds none, and Unreflective Alf, whose initial belief set is the same but does not engage in the further reasoning. We could certainly say, with Pollock, that Reflective Alf at time t_2 has a higher degree of warrant: he has rationally come to appreciate what his reasons at the level of a "respectable amount" of reasoning are; but it also follows that the two versions of Alf *have* the same sufficient reasons to ϕ at time t_1 (and t_2). Reflective Alf will certainly see this ("after I thought a bit, I could see that R was a good reason"); simply because Unreflective Alf didn't think about it for a bit could not make it the case that he has a different set of reasons. Given this, it looks like we should adopt:

Sufficient (Justified) Reasons (with the Less Accessible Defeater Condition): Alf has a sufficient reason R to hold that β is the thing to believe, or ϕ is the thing to do, if, and only if, (*i*) he has arrived at R by following the norms of good reasoning and (*ii*) if Alf

---

[131] Pollock, *Thinking about Acting*, p. 7.

engaged in a "respectable amount" of reasoning, he would not (or did not) discover defeaters for R.

Consider now the possibility that Reflective Alf's "respectable amount" of deliberation revealed a defeater for R_1 (R_2), and showed, at that level of warrant, he had reason R_2 to hold $\neg\beta$. It follows that, on the above principle, neither he nor Unreflective Alf at time t_1 had sufficient reason R_1 to hold β. But we can, I think, say more: that at time t_1 both Reflective and Unreflective Alf had (though they did not know it) sufficient reason R_2 to hold $\neg\beta$. At the appropriate level of accessibility (that which would be considered in a "respectable amount" of rational deliberation), Alf would see that he has an undefeated reason R_2 to hold $\neg\beta$. Thus in Mill's bad bridge case, we can say that the person about to cross the bridge *now* has a reason not to cross because, if he engaged in a reasonable amount of rational deliberation with the available information, he would arrive at an undefeated reason not to cross. There is, in Bernard Williams' terms, "a sound deliberative route" to the conclusion that he ought not to cross. If this is correct, then we should adopt yet a stronger principle along the lines of:

> *The Reasons One (provisionally) Has*: Alf has (provisionally) a sufficient reason R if and only if a "respectable amount" of good reasoning by Alf would conclude that R is an undefeated reason reason (to act or believe).

Let us distinguish two accounts of undefeated reasons. According to the first, which we might call "ties imply mutual defeat," if Alf has equally good justifications for the inference from R_1 to belief β_1 and from R_2 to β_2 (where β_1 and β_2 are inconsistent beliefs), R_1 defeats the inference to β_2 and R_2 defeats the inference to β_1.[132] On this view, both inferences are defeated – an undefeated reason must be your *best* reason on the matter after an adequate amount of deliberation. If there is no best reason, there is no undefeated reason. Alternatively, on the "ties imply a standoff" view, if one discovers two equally good inferences to inconsistent beliefs, we can say that neither defeats the other (as I have put it elsewhere, neither is

---

[132] See Audi, *The Architecture of Reason*, p. 45.

defeated but neither is victorious over the other).[133] At this point one's deliberations are inconclusive about the comparative merits of β_1 and β_2, though further deliberation may show which is defeated. Now in this case, although one certainly does not have reason to believe (β_1 & β_2); one does have reason to believe (β_1 or β_2). As Williams points out, here it is uncertain what the person's reasons to believe or do are. "But," he continues, "this is not a disadvantage of the position. It *is* often vague what one has reason to do."[134] Even here one's reasons are not totally indeterminate on this matter, for one has arrived at the conclusion that one has a reason to believe β_1 or β_2. As we shall see presently (§16.1*a*), when one confronts such indeterminacy one can be understood to have a maximal set about what to hold {β_1, β_2}, but neither can be identified as the best option. While on the first view, because neither belief is justified since the inferences defeat each other one should believe neither; on the second view one should believe one or the other, but not both. I shall henceforth employ the "ties imply standoff view." This view is especially appropriate in the context of moral justification in which we must, say, employ our reason to endorse one or the other candidate rule, L_1 or L_2. Refusing to commit to either (that is, following the first view and holding $\neg L_1$ & $\neg L_2$) is, as we shall see in the next chapter, often the clearly irrational option, leaving us with no rule at all because we could not decide which of two alternatives is better.

13.4 THE PROVISIONALITY OF REASONS, LEARNING FROM OTHERS, AND THE DEMANDS OF RATIONALITY

"The Reasons One (provisionally) Has" principle only identifies reasons "provisionally." Suppose that Philosopher Alf goes beyond the level of accessibility identified by the "reasonable amount" criterion and deliberates either harder or better, such that he canvasses even less accessible reasons, and discovers that at (what I shall call) a "high level" of deliberation, the defeater R_2 leading to

---

[133] I defended this view in *Justificatory Liberalism*, pp. 151–8.
[134] Williams, "Internal Reasons and the Obscurity of Blame," p. 38. Emphasis in original.

¬β is itself defeated by R_3, and so, after all, β is justified at this high level. We need to ask, given Philosopher Alf's discovery, what does this tell us about the reasons that we can ascribe to Unreflective and Reflective Alf?

Suppose Alf is the same person; at time t_1 he had a belief based on less than the reasonable amount of deliberation, at t_2 he engaged in the reasonable amount, and at t_3 he engaged in a high level of reflection. At t_3 he will certainly revoke the claim that he had at time t_2 a sufficient reason R_2 to hold ¬β. Once Alf is aware of this, he will hold that he always had a sufficient reason to hold β, though his early unreflective belief was not well warranted, and his later belief that R_2 defeated the justification of β must now be rejected. In the world of real rationality, our cognitively limited world, ascribing a reason to a person she does not yet recognize must always be provisional, for we must hold that our reason claim would be confirmed at some standard or expected level of deliberation, but since all reasons are defeasible, we always know that any conclusion we make about the reasons of a person (including oneself) could be defeated at a higher level of deliberation. So we confidently say that in Mill's bad bridge case the person does not have a reason to cross the bridge because we are assuming a standard degree of deliberation, which yields a defeasible conclusion. If, however, he was a civil engineer and had just concluded a study showing that the bridge was much safer than it seemed, we will retract our claim. Although there is a sound deliberative route to the conclusion not to cross, there is a more warranted conclusion *to* cross of which we are now aware.

This twist on the basic example from Mill shows the fundamental social dimension to our understanding of what reasons we have, for experts engage in levels of deliberation that most of us do not (they do graduate work, or give a sermon on the mount, for example) and thus help show the rest of us what our reasons are. After the civil engineer has confirmed the safety of the bridge, we all see that we no longer have a reason to avoid crossing. This does not require us to replicate the reasoning of experts. Surely this cannot be so, for few of us would understand the calculations of the engineer, yet all of us would wish to know his conclusions. Expert conclusions show that nonexperts have a reason to do as they advise if, after a "respectable amount" of good reasoning, the nonexperts, consulting their values and beliefs (including beliefs about reliable experts), would arrive at a victorious reason to follow the expert's advice. Again, like all claims about the reasons one has, this would be provisional, but such is our fate in a world of limited rationality.

What, though, if one does not accept the expert advice after a "respectable amount" of rational deliberation? Suppose the expert claims that, as a rational real agent, rationality demands that you accept the conclusions of his much deeper deliberation as reasons for you to believe and to act. Perhaps my philosopher acquaintance, after you have performed your respectable amount of reasoning and still disagree, insists that "if you thought just another little bit more" you would see that you would have this reason R, and so he insists that you do, now, have R. Put aside the possibility that the disagreement is really about what is the respectable amount of reasoning required, and put aside any claim that you have made a mistake, and suppose that our philosopher has presented his case and you still do not understand it to be a sufficient reason to believe or act. The worry about the constant enjoinder to think about things a little more and one will see the light is that there may be no light that you can see. The reasons you have must be accessible to you, and as a real rational agent in a world in which cognitive activity has significant costs, rationality does not demand one keep on with the quest to discover less and less accessible reasons. I have stressed that this is by no means a debilitating limit on the reasons we can acknowledge, and indeed in many ways we move surprisingly close to a highly idealized rationality, for expert advice and the growth of social knowledge allows increasingly sophisticated and complex conclusions to be accessible as reasons to all with simply an adequate amount of deliberation. Think about all the reasons to believe and act that one has after twenty minutes on WebMD.

13.5 "RESPECTABLE" AND "MORE THAN RESPECTABLE"
REASONING IN OUR MORALITY

No doubt by now the reader is getting impatient: all this supposes
that we have some idea of how to determine what constitutes a
"respectable amount" of deliberation, but this may seem a hopelessly indeterminate idea. It is not hopelessly indeterminate, though
it is often vague and always contextual. An adequate amount of
deliberation in a physics seminar is demanding; in that context one
may assume that one's audience has reasons for belief that took
years of deliberation. In a baseball game the standards of deliberation are mixed: on the one hand we suppose the umpires have
reasons to make judgments based on a thorough study of the rules,
yet we also expect an umpire to make a prompt judgment at first
base. "Let me think it over and I'll get back to you" is not acceptable from an umpire, but it is from someone who is about to decide
on a house to buy. To say that an umpire who called the player safe
had a reason to call the runner out because, if he had seen the
replay from another angle he would have done so, is inappropriate;
to say that a homebuyer has a reason to cancel the sale because the
inspection report reported a serious deficiency, though he failed to
read the report, is warranted. To say, further, that he had sufficient
reason to cancel because of a new paper on plate tectonics (of
which he was not aware) showed the house was subject to earth-
quakes, is not.

Our practice of social morality leads to two parameters on what
is an adequate amount of rational deliberation to presuppose,
which help identify a minimum and a maximum. The maximum –
what sets an upper limit on how difficult it can be to access the
reasons which we suppose all participants to have – is that the
practice of morality is not an elite practice such as physics or moral
philosophy, but a basic human practice in which all adults who
have grasped the Principle of Moral Autonomy (§12.3b) are
competent. We cannot ascribe to moral agents reason to accept infinite utility calculations, the noumenal self, or the original position.
These may be elements of philosophical theories that explain or
further justify people's moral reasons, and the philosophers who
advocate them may argue that they are in some way the upshot of

what normal moral agents do believe, but they are the result of specialist constructions based on long deliberations, and even their teaching is difficult (and alas, not convincing to many of our students). Our account of moral reasons cannot suppose that a person must grasp them in order to identify her reasons. In contrast, we can ascribe to normal moral agents reasons to conform to morality, to act on the basic moral convictions, reasons to advance their values, their conception of the good, and their religion, to accept that there is an internal ought, and that morality involves reciprocity and mutual benefit, and the appropriateness of the moral emotions. To say that we can ascribe such reasons to normal moral agents is to say that, given the public debate and the opinions of experts, normal moral agents have accessible undefeated reasons to affirm them. If there are defeaters, they are too inaccessible – even after all the rational deliberation we could expect from normal moral agents, they would not uncover these defeaters. If, for example, a philosopher insists that this only shows that we should expect a lot more, and we must demand a higher degree of warrant, we will end up with a moral practice that is outside the rational grasp of most of its "participants." Given the realities of life, the demands on their time and resources, and differences in the sophistication of their reasoning, most simply would never understand the reasons this practice ascribes to them; it must remain to them an alien form of social life. The social practice judges them incompetent to understand the very reasons that are said to be theirs. Throughout I have stressed the costs of embracing an elitist conception of a basic social practice such as our morality. Social morality is not an esoteric game of philosophers, the revelation a wise elite, a description of a set of correct judgments, or even simply a device we use to criticize others: it is the foundation of social existence, and it requires that its participants grasp, and respond to, what is going on, and what reasons we have to conform to moral demands.

If that was the only desideratum, we would have reason to think that a respectable amount of deliberation is very modest indeed: perhaps we would simply satisfy ourselves with what Pollock calls "justified" choices and beliefs (§13.3). The reasons that are ascribed to one should be easily accessible. But our practice sets the minimum higher. We know that (*i*) we often think that people deliberately do wrong and (*ii*) the reactive attitudes suppose that we hold that they had reasons not to do as they did (§12.3). So getting it wrong – not acting on your best reasons – is a common enough occurrence, and if that is so we must attribute reasons to others that require significant deliberation. "If you had thought about this more, or better, or clearer," we say, "you would have seen that you shouldn't have done that." Our very practice of morality presupposes that the relevant reasons are sometimes not very easily accessible. Moral reasons are not always glaring; it often enough takes some thought to see what is the right thing to do.

Now some would say that I have presented an elegant two-axiom impossibility theorem: both desiderata cannot be met. Any practice that is within the rational grasp of most adults must be too simple to allow claims that one has reasons that are sometimes sufficiently inaccessible that one must think carefully. And so, if the analysis of this chapter has been correct, our social morality is fundamentally incoherent. This skeptical, perhaps cynical, view is not warranted. One of the important revelations of the work of Piaget and Kohlberg is that even children are moral philosophers of a sort: they do not simply reiterate what they have been taught but engage in reflection about morality's bases, its aims, and how it relates to their own concerns.[135] To be sure, individuals differ in the sophistication of their reflection, but almost all come to see our morality as a scheme of mutual benefit, and most Americans arrive at "4 and more" (§12.2) reasoning of considerable complexity.

Of course, in any social practice there will be some who are unable to engage in the sort of reasoning that would allow them to really understand what the practice is about. I said that we wish to avoid a moral practice that most cannot grasp; it is impossible to have one that absolutely everyone grasps. Those adults who are at Kohlberg's stage 1 may not grasp the internal ought at all, and those at the lower stages may find some aspects of moral reasoning elusive. On the bright side, Kohlberg's data about the relative sophistication of moral reasoning of fathers and sons shows some support, as Kohlberg himself notes, for a cultural evolution

---

[135] See, for example, Kohlberg's, "The Child as Moral Philosopher." See also Turiel, Killen, and Helwig, "Morality: Its Structure, Functions and Vagaries."

hypothesis: more sophisticated reasoning is becoming more common.[136] In any event, we have seen (§13.4) that more sophisticated reasoners can assist the less sophisticated in seeing the reasons they have. While, for example, purely conventional reasoners may not themselves have been able to think through cases for basic human rights, more advanced reasoners' advocacy of human rights – sometimes drawing on religious sources as in the case of Martin Luther King, Jr. – can make these reasons accessible to others. That, indeed, is one of the things our moral teachers do. Moral reasoning itself is a social and cooperative enterprise, and so we should not infer that less sophisticated reasoners are unable to access reasons for conclusions originally arrived at by their more sophisticated fellows.

I have insisted that our morality must not attribute reasons to people the warrant for which is beyond that which can be accessed by the amount of deliberation we can expect from the average – or even the somewhat below average – participants. So we cannot ascribe to normal moral agents reasons based simply on sophisticated moral theories. However, our moral practice must also speak to those who have thought about moral matters at these more sophisticated levels (as we saw in section 13.3 the reasons we attribute to participants are provisional and can be overturned by higher levels of deliberation). A social morality that all have reason to grasp must neither presuppose sophisticated reasoning, nor must it ignore it when it occurs. This, I think, is the important upshot of our analysis of what it is to have a reason. We cannot say that we have given a reason to a person when this presupposes a reasoning that is beyond his comprehension, but neither can we deny that more sophisticated reasoners have reasons that differ from those of the average participant. Thus an adequate public justification must give sufficient reasons both to those who are attributed only the basic degree of warrant characteristic of the practice and to those who have given, as it were, more than adequate thought to the matter. This has never been appreciated in discussions of public reason; I shall show in the next chapter how it can be accommodated.

---

[136] Kohlberg and Kramer, "Continuities and Discontinuities in Childhood and Adult Moral Development," p. 106.

CONCLUSION

This chapter has been concerned with the relation of reason and emotion in our social morality. We have seen that it is a complex mixture of both: to be a moral agent is to develop an emotional life that responds to the reasons we see ourselves as having and which we suppose others to have. And only those capable of a certain type of emotional life could come to appreciate the practice of morality. Moral philosophy has recently rediscovered the moral emotions, and that is all to the good, but this should not lead it to the opposite error of forgetting the way in which moral practices appeal to our reasons. Our moral emotions and practices, I have tried to show, affirm the primary role of moral agents as Rule-following Punishers.

Our moral emotions point us to the reasons we suppose others have: the authority we ascribe to our moral claims is based on the supposition that others have reasons to conform to our demands. Thus, I have argued, implicit in our emotion- and reason-based moral practice is a conception of others as free and equal autonomous persons, who act on an internal ought that they have reason to endorse. Kant was basically correct: moral autonomy is the deep premise of our social morality. However, I have argued that we cannot follow Kant and others when they understand autonomous action as that of a fully rational person: full rationality is an extravagant assumption that only disappoints, for it succumbs to the very indeterminacy that it seeks to avoid. A reasonably reflective real rationality is the most we can demand of others, and what is reasonable to demand of others depends on the nature of the social practice in which the appeal to reasons occurs. This is a messy and indeterminate sort of standard – different people will have different reasons, and we may not always be able to say what a person's reasons are. Perhaps if full rationality could deliver its promise of a determinate and noncontextual determination of the reasons we have, its extravagance would be a price worth paying. In any event, we must work with the complexities of a realistic account. And if our account of moral justification can accommodate it, it will be all the stronger.

PART TWO

REAL PUBLIC REASON

V

The Justificatory Problem and
the Deliberative Model

> Suppose we now raise that old philosophical question: What interest
> has the individual in morality? . . . [W]hen we ask what the interest
> of the individual is in morality, we mean to ask about all those indi-
> viduals on whom socially sanctioned demands are made; not just
> about the imaginatively restless and materially cosy. We need not,
> perhaps, insist upon just the same answer for all; but, if we take the
> question seriously, we must insist on *some* answer for all. . . .
>
> We have arrived at the fact that everyone on whom some form of
> socially sanctioned demand is made has an interest in the existence
> of some system of socially sanctioned demands. But this fact seems
> inadequate to answer the question what the individual's interest in
> morality is. . . . A socially sanctioned demand is doubtless a demand
> made with the permission and approval of a society; and backed, in
> some form and degree, with its power. . . . [I]f no interest of mine is
> safeguarded by the system of demands to which I am subject, then,
> in fulfilling a demand made upon me, I may indeed, in one sense, be
> doing what I am obliged to do; but scarcely what I am *morally*
> obliged to do.
>
> P. F. Strawson, "Social Morality and Individual Ideal"

In Part One I analyzed social morality as a system of social rules,
which Rule-following Punishers take as the basis of authoritative
demands on each other. In the last chapter we saw that this practice
is grounded on the supposition that it is not simply socially necessary, but that all individuals have sufficient reason to comply with
these demands. As Strawson says in the epigraph, the mere fact

that a system of social demands is necessary for social life does not show that any specific rule gives each sufficient reason to internalize it and endorse its requirements as moral. For that, we have seen, each must have his or her own sufficient reasons to comply though, as Strawson points out, each may not have the same reason. We thus arrive at the justificatory question: how can we identify social demands that all have sufficient reason to acknowledge as moral demands? This is the problem of public reason.

In the last chapter I criticized conceptions of "full" and "ideal" rationality. Our problem as reasoners is to think things through the best we can in a world in which cognitive capacities are limited, and we cannot think forever. Because fully idealized conceptions of rationality assume away the very context in which reasoning occurs and the problems it addresses, they are useless to us and our real problems as rational agents. We must begin with real rationality. This is not to say that our conception of rationality cannot give us a critical perspective, and even a humanly accessible ideal, but the ideal must start from, and not stray too far from, our real situation and its problem. So too with conceptions of public reason. Conceptions of public reason that identify it with what would be arrived at under conditions of full rational consensus, or what abstract reasoners who shared all the same concerns would agree to, abstract away the very context that directs us to pubic reason; we have limited cognitive capacities, we disagree on the ends of life, and within the limits of our reasoning we never will agree on what is best, even what is the best social morality, yet our morality demands that all have sufficient reason to comply. Just as we need a realistic conception of rationality, so too do we need a realistic conception of public reason. Defending such a conception is the aim of Part Two.

14 On Modeling Public Justification

14.1 THE PRINCIPLE OF PUBLIC JUSTIFICATION

We have arrived at the "Basic Principle of Public Justification":

> A moral imperative "φ!" in context C, based on rule L, is an authoritative requirement of social morality only if each normal moral agent has sufficient reasons to (*a*) internalize rule L, (*b*) hold that L requires Φ-type acts in circumstances C and (*c*) moral agents generally conform to L.

We now have a reasonably good grasp of most of the key ideas: internalizing a rule, demands, social rules, social morality, and the general idea of sufficient reasons. As we have seen, the Basic Principle of Public Justification is not an ideal imposed upon morality by a philosophical commitment to the idea that moral agents are free and equal but is itself grounded in our reflective understanding of a bona fide social morality – one in which the moral emotions are well grounded and for which it is appropriate to feel guilt for violations. Unless each has sufficient reasons to internalize the relevant rule, and unless each has sufficient reasons to see that the rule requires φ in this context, and to typically act on the rule in the appropriate circumstances, the moral emotions that are necessary for social morality cannot be rationally sustained. A social rule that is publicly justified grounds authoritative moral requirements and claims based on them. The rule is one that all have sufficient reasons to internalize and follow. When another demands that you comply with a rule, she is demanding that you do what you have sufficient reasons to do; she is appealing to your rational nature, not demanding that you put it aside. She must be saying: "You have reasons to comply that you are ignoring. My demand is not simply a demand that you live as I see fit, but as you would see fit if you adequately employed your reason." And she says this not just to you, but to any violator whom she comes across. How can she be so confident of her judgment, instructing each of us violators to do as we have reason to do, and thus to perform the morally autonomous action, even though we disagree?

Some are convinced that there simply is no good answer so they abandon the requirement that a person's own reason must confirm the demand, and thus they embrace simple authoritarianism: "You must obey me just because I know better (i.e., I am quite certain in my own mind that I know better). End of story." To some, all morality *is* some people pushing others around. This is to embrace Jeffrey Reiman's nightmare – morality becomes a form of "subjugation" (§2.1). Those who recoil at this frank admission are perhaps more apt to say that *if* you were fully rational you would agree with me that I know better, but since we have no idea what that really means, this claim comes to much the same thing (§13.2). How can we assume moral authority over others without simply giving way to the authoritarian stance? The only good ground we have is confidence that our social morality conforms to the requirements of the Basic Principle of Public Justification. One's claim to authority, rather than being authoritarian, is as sound as the judgment that the rule is publicly justified. In this chapter I consider in some detail how we might go about assuring ourselves of this – or discovering, instead, that we are simply pushing others around in the name of morality.

14.2 THE BASIC IDEA OF THE DELIBERATIVE MODEL

(a) Hypothetical Consent

One of Rawls' fundamental insights was that the justificatory problem – what moral requirements do we all have reason to endorse? – can be translated into a deliberative problem among a certain partly idealized group.[1] Suppose we model every person in society such that each deliberates solely on her relevant reasons, and in some way the group evaluates possible social rules. If we properly specify the model, what the parties to the deliberative model would decide tells *us* as inquirers – as Rawls would say, "you and me" – what moral rules we all have sufficient reasons to endorse as binding.[2] It is tempting to interpret this as a contractual argument: what the parties would agree to shows what we would agree to, and so shows that we are contractually bound. This is surely confused: what my abstract model-self would agree to

---

[1] John Rawls, *A Theory of Justice*, p. 16.
[2] John Rawls, *Political Liberalism*, p. 28.

certainly cannot contractually bind me. This would be not simply a hypothetical contract, but a doubly hypothetical one; *if* we abstract away from certain details of my current beliefs and *if* I reasoned correctly, *then* I would agree to a certain rule.[3] Famously, Ronald Dworkin has objected that a (doubly) hypothetical agreement cannot bind any actual person.[4] After all, the point of the whole device is that, as I actually am, I might not agree to be bound by the rule (otherwise the idealization serves no purpose): so the problem is not simply that I have not actually agreed, but there is reason to think that if asked, I actually might not agree. If we read this as a contractual argument, it seems to be proposed that you can be bound by agreements that others, different from you, would have made. While it might – just – be reasonable to suppose that you can be bound by agreements that you would yourself have entered into if given the opportunity,[5] it seems crazy to think that you can be bound by agreements that, demonstrably, you wouldn't have made if you had been asked.

This criticism is decisive only if the hypothetical social contract is supposed to invoke your normative power to self-bind via consent. That your model-self employs his power to self-bind would not mean that you had employed your power. But the power to obligate oneself is not relevant to a defense of morality as publicly justified; the problem of deliberation is supposed to help us make headway on the problem of public justification. So the question for the deliberative model is whether the hypothetical agreement of your surrogate tracks your reasons – the reasons *you have* – to endorse (and internalize) a moral rule. The agreement, then, is evidence that the Basic Principle of Public Justification is met. The authority of morality derives from conformity to the Basic Principle of Public Justification, and only via it from the Deliberative Model.

(b) Two Perspectives in the Model

When we set up a deliberative model we must always keep in mind the distinction between two perspectives: we might call these the

---

[3] I owe this point to Fred D'Agostino. See our "Contemporary Approaches to the Social Contract."

[4] Ronald Dworkin, "The Original Position."

[5] This also seems most doubtful. See my *Social Philosophy*, pp. 71–2.

perspective of philosophical reflection and the *perspective of real moral agents*. At some point in our reflections on morality, many of us arrive at the point where we come to appreciate our commitment to the Basic Principle of Public Justification, and so we inquire whether our social morality, or some alternative, could satisfy it. This is a reflective and sophisticated enterprise, and the perspective of philosophical reflection may require deep thought about the nature of social cooperation, the idea of rationality, and a philosophic device such as a deliberative model as a guide to judging how the Basic Principle of Public Justification might be met. There is no claim that this is part of the reasoning of ordinary moral agents. Nichols' quip (§12.2), that one doesn't have to understand "anything philosophically fancy" such as Rawls' original position to be a competent moral agent, is entirely right. But this implies no objection to a deliberative model, for such models are intended as a guide to fairly sophisticated reflection about whether our morality warrants our continued allegiance, or whether really, in the end, some people are just pushing others around (and trying to make them feel guilty if they resist) on the basis of their self-confirmed vision of the moral truth. Within deliberative models, in which we seek to reflect on the conditions for a morality to be publicly justified, we must, however, attend to the perspectives of real moral agents; in satisfying our reflective inquiry into whether the Basic Principle of Public Justification is met, we must not attribute to our fellow agents reasons that would not be confirmed if they engaged in the expected amount of rational deliberation (§13.3). The parties to such models are idealizations of real moral agents – they are idealized in the sense that they recognize, and judge on, their sufficient reasons in the deliberative model. They are realistic idealizations of real moral agents (§13.5). One does not have to be a philosopher or a Kolbergian stage 6 reasoner to appreciate that morality is about making demands on others, and that they have good reason to do what is demanded of them. Throughout, it is absolutely crucial to keep these two perspectives distinct.

(c) The Deliberative Principle of Public Justification
We can, I think, make progress in seeing when the Basic Principle of Public Justification is met by translating the problem of what

rules all normal moral agents have sufficient reason to internalize, endorse, and follow into a deliberative problem of idealized "Members of the Public" who deliberate only on their sufficient reasons. We can understand these Members of the Public as the rationalized counterparts of real moral agents. We imagine a deliberative situation in which these Members of the Public are considering possible moral rules, and each must consider which she has reason to endorse, or, more helpfully, which she has more reason to endorse. Thus we can (partly) translate the Basic Public Justification Principle into a deliberative version (§2.4*a*):

> *L* is a bona fide rule of social morality only if each and every Member of the Public endorses *L* as binding (and so to be internalized).

The Deliberative Public Justification Principle concerns itself only with the public justifiability of the rules of social morality. It thus models only one of the requirements of the Basic Principle of Public Justification: it does not consider the context specific claim that we are actually in circumstances *C*, and that the rule does call for φ here. Surely, however, our fundamental philosophical worry is whether the basic structure of our social life can be publicly justified. To make headway on that problem would be gratifying indeed.

14.3 THE TASK OF THE MEMBERS OF THE PUBLIC

Social contract theories typically suppose that the deliberators are members of a common society or a cooperative social order. Critics charge that this is the wrong group; they insist that the proper group is, say, all of humanity – what *it* would agree to reveals a cosmopolitan morality. In thinking about what is the correct deliberative group – or, we might say, the proper bounds of the justificatory public – we should distinguish two cases.

One case, presented by a moral innovator, calls for the establishment of new moral practices and rules – new, either in the sense that at present there is no social-moral rule governing some aspect of social life, or there is an existing social rule but it is proposed that its reach be extended to cover a larger public. Moral innovation is of course of the utmost importance, but it leads to special problems; I defer them until Chapter VII. I shall first concentrate on a case of critical reflection on our current positive morality (§10.4), in which we are confronted by a currently accepted rule and we wish to know whether it is publicly justified, or whether an alternative rule might be publicly justified.

Moral rules, we have seen, are social rules, and social rules exist (§10.2); our social life occurs in the context of existing social rules. Members of the Public are thus defined as the participants in the relevant rule-governed practice. Our analysis of social morality in Chapter IV showed us that we must justify our demands to those on whom we press them. The problem of justification arises when moral authority is claimed: it is our fellow participants in the rule-governed practice on whom we make demands in its name. Our question, confronting a social rule, is whether those whose lives are governed by the rule – those who make demands on each other grounded on the rule – all have sufficient reasons to internalize it and endorse it as binding. Thus the range of the public is determined by the extent of the moral practice governed by the rule. Depending on the rule, this may be a subpopulation such as an ethnic group (recall the Chaldeans, §6.2), a society, a culture, or a cosmopolitan community.[6] In the next few chapters I will focus on moral rules applying to a large-scale moral order in which we often confront others as strangers – what F. A. Hayek called "the Great Society."[7] My focus, then, is the rules that govern our interactions when we know little about the other, except that she is a moral person. I shall assume that this society is embedded in a broadly Western culture of pluralism. Having first analyzed the social morality of such a Great Society, I shall then turn to questions of human rights (§§21.2–3) and problems of international justice (§22.4).

If we are to have a good grasp of the public justifiability of moral demands based on moral rule L, we must have comparative knowledge of how L stacks up against the alternatives we can canvass.

---

[6] For a more detailed discussion of boundaries of justificatory publics, and questions of moral cosmopolitanism and parochialism, see my *Value and Justification*, pp. 367–76.

[7] F. A. Hayek, *Rules and Order*, chap. 2.

Even Members of the Public, who recognize their sufficient reasons, are of limited rationality, and as creatures of limited reasoning powers, when asked whether they have sufficient reason to endorse a rule, they must ask, "what are the alternatives we are deciding between, and what are the costs of refusing to endorse any of them?" Take a prosaic example: someone offers you a new car at a cost of q, and you wish to know whether you have sufficient reason to take up the offer or, as it is sometimes put in moral philosophy, whether it would be reasonable to reject the offer. But how can you deliberate about this without having a good idea of the choice set and the costs of refusing to select any member from it? If there is only one car on the market and it costs q, then you may have good reason to take it; if there is another car that costs less than q you have a different choice problem, and if there is also a third that costs more, then your deliberation will be, again, very different. To ask "what do I have sufficient reason to endorse?" when I do not know the set of options is an ill-formed question. In the terms of economics, one must know the opportunity costs of one's choice – the value of the options that one has passed over – before one can come to any reasonable judgment of what is to be endorsed.

Contrast in this regard the contractualisms of Scanlon and Rawls. "According to contractualism," Scanlon writes, "in order to decide whether it would be wrong to do X in circumstances C, we should consider possible principles governing how one may act in such situations, and ask whether *any* principle that permitted one to do X in those circumstances could, for that reason, reasonably be rejected."[8] The judgment thus begins, apparently, with a consideration of an indefinite set of principles;[9] we must determine whether any can be reasonably rejected. Now although Scanlon does not stress it, he maintains that judgments of reasonable rejectability are indeed comparative: we must not only compare the costs of the permissions and prohibitions implied by a candidate principle but also the costs and benefits of alternatives.[10] The difficulty is that the

---

[8] T. M. Scanlon, *What We Owe Each Other*, p. 195, emphasis added.

[9] Scanlon says that there is an "indefinite number" of valid moral principles (*What We Owe Each Other*, p. 201); it is not clear how many possible principles would allow one to X in C; it would surely be an indefinite, perhaps an infinite, number.

[10] See Scanlon, *What We Owe Each Other*, pp. 195, 196, 205, 213.

comparative judgment is over an indefinite set of options. Now, as
Scanlon suggests, this probably reflects some features of our moral
deliberation,[11] but it seems extraordinarily difficult to say what
principles are not reasonably rejectable when the option set is not
even in theory identified. Different, real individuals will scan their
systems differently, coming up with different candidate principles,
and so they are making choices from different sets. Yet, remarkably, Scanlon seems to believe that this procedure somehow yields
a determinate answer.[12]

Rawls was much more sensitive to the importance of, at least in
principle, tying the choice of the parties to a set of options.[13] In *A
Theory of Justice*, Rawls observed that though "[i]deally of course
one would like to say that they are to choose among all possible
conceptions of justice," he pointed out intractable problems. For
one, there may be no best in set (e.g., there may be a Condorcet
cycle, in which every option is beat by another) and, in any event,
"even if there is a best alternative, it seems difficult to describe the
parties' intellectual powers so that this optimum, or even the more
plausible conceptions, are sure to occur to them."[14] Rawls, as he
says, "handles" these problems by presenting the parties with a
definite list of principles from which they are to choose. In his
initial deliberative model in "Justice as Fairness" the parties themselves generated the choice set: "Their procedure . . . is to let each
person propose principles."[15] In this, and in a number of others
ways, I propose to develop this early and elegant Rawlsian model:
in the Deliberative Model each person may propose either to
continue with moral rule x or to replace it with an alternative, y.[16]
Let us say that y is an alternative to x just in case the central range
of circumstances in which x and y apply are the same, but they

---

[11] Ibid., p. 201.
[12] Scanlon rejects the criterion of "rational rejectability" because it may not generate
a "determinate answer." Ibid., p. 192.
[13] We must be careful here. In contrast to Rawls', Scanlon's contractualism is not a
collective choice problem; as Aaron James nicely brings out, it is based on a series
of individual interactions with an overall bookkeeping by the individual to see
which principles have passed the test. "The Significance of Distribution."
[14] Rawls, *A Theory of Justice*, pp. 105–6.
[15] Rawls, "'Justice as Fairness," p. 53.
[16] To avoid cumbersome notations, henceforth I shall simply employ w, x, y, and z to
designate possible moral rules.

provide incompatible prescriptions. It follows that w is not an alternative to x simply if it sometimes provides incompatible prescriptions: it may be a quite different rule that conflicts. Alternatives must share their central range of application – the core circumstances in which they prescribe actions.

That the task of the deliberators is to select a moral *rule* as opposed to say, an abstract principle, is the upshot of our analysis of Part One. Rules are somewhat out of fashion in moral and social philosophy: the recent debate seems to be between particularists, who insist on an act-by-act evaluation, and proponents of general, abstract principles[17] (though this is changing as philosophers become more empirically sensitive, as in the excellent and innovative recent work of Nichols, Bicchieri, and Heath).[18] Scanlon, for example, insists that contractualism is about the justification of moral principles, "not rules which can easily be applied without moral judgment."[19] In Scanlon's eyes, moral principles are akin to grand constitutional principles such as the First Amendment to the U.S. Constitution, which proclaims that "Congress shall make no law abridging freedom of speech, or of the press," and which has had an intricate and subtle history of interpretation. Now I do not wish to deny that abstract principles have an important role in moral thinking (see §§17, 21.2), but they are inadequate as the grounds of morality for precisely the reason revealed by the history of First Amendment interpretation: they cannot serve the function of adequately regulating social life until they are interpreted, and it will not suffice for each to advance her own, reflective interpretation. As the constitutional scholar Alexander Bickel remarked about "majestic concepts" such as freedom of speech, "men may in full and equal reason and good faith hold differing views about . . . [their] proper meaning and specific application."[20] The Supreme

---

[17] Cf. Jonathan Dancy, *Ethics without Principles*; Sean McKeever and Michael Ridge, *Principled Ethics*; Russ Shafer-Landau, "Moral Rules." An earlier generation of philosophers took rules more seriously; the classic example is Bernard Gert, *Morality: A New Justification of the Moral Rules*.

[18] Nichols, *Sentimental Rules*; Bicchieri, *The Grammar of Society*; Heath, *Following the Rules*.

[19] Scanlon, *What We Owe Each Other*, p. 199.

[20] Alexander Bickel, *The Least Dangerous Branch: The Supreme Court at the Bar of Politics*, pp. 36–7.

Court selects, of the many interpretations being advanced at any one time, a definitive one, which then provides a shared understanding of the amendment's requirements – at least shared enough to provide the basis for relatively firm expectations as to what is protected. Philosophers specialize in judgment and reflecting on hard cases, but social life together requires that the range of judgment be narrowed so that there is a widely shared understanding of what constitutes compliance and noncompliance (think about the importance of cheater detection; §§7.2, 8.2, 10.4). Until the abstract principles are interpreted in a common and more specific way via shared scripts (§§7.3, 10.2) they cannot perform the crucial task of social morality: mutually understood guidelines for social life. The grand questions of constitutional interpretation are more philosophically interesting (and certainly appeal to stage 6 moral reasoners such as Scanlon), but the heart of social morality is more prosaic and is more akin to everyday laws that are generally known and well understood by all. Rule following, of course, is not simply automatic, never requiring judgment. The difference between principles and rules is a matter of degree in their determinacy and the degree of convergence in judgment about (as Wittgensteinians would say) "how to go on." We have disagreements about moral rules too, and in due course I shall consider them (Chapter VIII). But although many philosophers believe otherwise, we do not best understand the nature of an enterprise by examining its most perplexing cases, where the normal features break down (as if a theory of grammar commenced with those utterances that cannot be determined as grammatical or nongrammatical).

Not only should moral justification focus on abstract principles, argues Scanlon, but it must be holistic: "a sensible contractualism, like most other plausible views, will involve a holism about moral justification."[21] The justification of one principle depends on what other principles are justified. If we take holism seriously – if we really cannot evaluate any one principle without knowing what other principles are justified – then the object of evaluation should not be individual principles but entire moral codes.[22] Revealingly,

---

[21] Scanlon, *What We Owe Each Other*, p. 214.

[22] As in David Copp's analysis, in which an entire moral code is justified only if a society would be rational to choose it in preference to any alternative. *Morality,*

although Scanlon maintains that a plausible view must be committed to justificatory holism, his approach is to consider principles one at a time, holding the rest fixed. "This does not mean that these other principles are beyond question, but just that they are not being questioned at the moment."[23] But there is no reason to suppose that this approach will lead to a holistically justified system of principles: it is path dependent. As we saw with the analysis of full rationality (§13.2*d*), the result one ends up with will be a function of the order in which one takes up the examination of the elements. Efforts to mitigate path-dependency will lead us in constant circles. When we look at principle P_1, we evaluate it in light of the other principles held constant, such as P_2; suppose we accept P_1. Now we look at P_2 and we reject it. If we are really committed to holism we must go back and look at P_1, for P_2 was one of the background principles we assumed in deliberating about P_1. But suppose, if holism is correct, we might now reject P_1 since at least one of the background principles we assumed in evaluating it has changed: now the holist requires that we go back and revisit our rejection of P_2, for now at least one of the background principles we assumed in evaluating *it* has changed.

It is no simple matter to square holism with reliance on local justification of specific principles (or rules). Happily, this does not mean that we must resort to holism rather than piecemeal justification; I have argued elsewhere that holism is objectionable as a criterion of justified belief.[24] However, we can put aside the dispute as to what is the correct ultimate standard of justification; for the Deliberative Model, the critical question is the level of deliberation – and so the degree of warrant – that is appropriate. Now regardless of its merits as the ultimate standard of justification, holism is manifestly inappropriate as a guide to deliberation for cognitively limited creatures such as ourselves. Considerations of computational complexity indicate that "an agent could never attempt to make an inference from . . . his entire belief set, or even a large portion of it."[25] Even significantly idealized agents could not reason

---

Normativity and Society, p. 104.
[23] Scanlon, *What We Owe Each Other*, p. 214.
[24] *Justificatory Liberalism*, chaps. 6 and 7.
[25] Cherniak, *Minimal Rationality*, p. 91; see also pp. 65ff.

holistically. Once we give up the illusive ideal of full rationality, and so the ideal of making all the inferences from one's current belief set and achieving "deductive closure," there is no option but piecemeal justification as the norm. We look at the belief in question and the clearly relevant possible justifiers and defeaters; except in unusual cases, that is all the warrant that can be expected of a boundedly rational agent, even an idealized one. To be sure, there is always the possibility of lurking defeaters in far-flung parts of our belief system – which is why we must acknowledge that all our beliefs are defeasible. On the other hand, we should not overestimate the fragility of our justifications given such a possibility: the justification of many of our beliefs is overdetermined, so defeating one supporting reason often does not defeat the belief.[26]

Consequently, it is plausible to suppose that, generally, real rational agents would deliberate about an individual moral rule's justifiability without holistically bringing into the deliberation other rules, just as almost every reader of this book – a pretty reflective group – has deliberated about particular laws such as health care reform without, say, insisting that we must simultaneously deliberate about overall distributive justice, much less about free speech law. Two important exceptions to this must be acknowledged.

(*i*) Some moral rules are tightly bound into a single practice, where it makes no sense to separate their justifiability, and so the deliberations should be about a set of rules. A nonmoral practice such as baseball provides a good example: the set of rules produces a game in which offense and defense are in a type of equilibrium. If we change some rules to favor the defense (say, we decrease the distance between the pitcher and home plate) we may wish to reconsider other rules, to give some compensating advantage to batters (say, reducing the strike zone). But even here it is easy to overestimate the mutual connectedness between rules: the Designated Hitter rule (which permits a substitution in the batting order for the pitcher) was introduced in the American League, giving a significant advantage to offense, without offsetting change for the

---

[26] Audi points this out in relation to perceptual beliefs. *The Architecture of Reason*, p. 14.

defense. Our ability to deliberate rule by rule, even in apparently tightly interconnected practices, should not be underestimated.

(*ii*) Scanlon is entirely correct that our deliberation about the acceptability of one principle (or rule) occurs in the context of supposing others, but this is not, I think, a case of holism but an instance of a moral structure. Consider Scanlon's example of First Amendment interpretation. Americans have spent so much effort interpreting the principle of free speech because, in the United States Constitution, it is identified as basic in the order of justification: in justifying other laws, the free speech principle must be supposed as given, and other laws cannot justifiably conflict with it. It is, I will say, basic *in the order of justification*. All moral orders suppose an order of justification: some things are more or less settled, and that settlement provides a background for further justification. Of course "settled" does not mean that we cannot go back and rethink the answers we have given; if we see that further up the order a basic principle or rule is precluding too much, or giving really unacceptable results, we are apt to go back and rethink the basic principle in this light. Thus, in First Amendment interpretation, it was held that an interpretation of the free speech principle that allowed seditious speech in times of national emergency was clearly unacceptable.[27] This is the truth behind the idea of "reflective equilibrium": we do sometimes revise our basic principles if we are struck by the manifestly unacceptable implication of the current interpretation. Still, this should not blind us to the importance of the First Amendment, which severely constrains the justifiability of other laws. To justify a moral order is not simply to justify a collection of rules but to provide some structure to the order of justification.[28] That is the key insight of Rawls' focus on "constitutional essentials" – once we have justified them, we have a fixed point for further justification.

---

[27] The most famous case here is Schenk v. United States [249 U.S. 47; 39 S. ct. 247; 63L. Ed. 470 (1919)]. For a general discussion, see Frederick Schauer, *Free Speech*, pp. 197–9.

[28] This relates to the idea that a moral order must contain priority rules. See Kurt Baier, "The Point of View of Morality."

14.4 THE EVALUATIVE STANDARDS OF MEMBERS OF THE PUBLIC

(a) A Plurality of Evaluative Standards

We must keep in mind the aim of the Deliberative Model: we are not proposing a definition of wrongness, nor are we seeking to develop a theory of justice. Our concern is whether the rules of our social morality are publicly justifiable to moral agents. Given this regulative concern, it would not help to construct a deliberative situation in which highly idealized parties agreed on the true principles of justice, if actual agents simply do not have reason to endorse those principles. Because of this, we cannot require abstracting too far away from the reasons of normal moral agents. At the end of the day, you and I wish to know whether the morality we live under is publicly justified and so sustains the rational moral emotions; the depiction of the Members of the Public must be such that their deliberations enlighten us about this regulative moral and philosophical worry. The Members of the Public, then, are idealized counterparts of actual members of the public, but they are not so idealized that their reasoning is inaccessible to their real-world counterparts. In judging whether to endorse a proposed rule, our Members of the Public rely only on the reasons they *have* to endorse it (§13). They do not bargain, bluff, or engage in strategic behavior: you and I are not interested in what bargains Members of the Public might strike, but the reasons they recognize, because those are the reasons that actual agents have.

This is a significant but realistic level of idealization. Because it is realistic, we cannot suppose that in deliberating about a proposed rule, Members of the Public will rely on the same considerations. In the public justification of a social morality we must start with Rawls' insight that a wide range of rational disagreement is the "normal result of the exercise of human reason."[29] Any attempt to simply reduce the reasons of the deliberators to a common basis seeks to solve the problem of public justification by denying its fundamental feature: our task of justifying moral rules to all occurs in a world in which people rationally disagree about the reasons they have. Another reason to suppose reasonable disagreement

---

[29] Rawls adds: "within the framework of free institutions of a constitutional regime." *Political Liberalism*, p. xviii.

among Members of the Public is that they differ in the sophistication of their moral reasoning. In Kohlberg's terms, we must suppose that at least stages 3–6 are well represented in the deliberative model. (We have seen that stage 1 reasoners do not grasp the internal ought [§12.2]; grasping it does not seem really complete until stage 4, which is still a "conventional" orientation.) We suppose a basic level of reasoning that is presupposed by participation in the moral practice (§13.5), but we also must allow more sophisticated reasoning. And this must be right: we must justify a public morality not just to normal agents but to Rawlsian-Scanlonian stage 6 agents. We can neither insist that normal agents reason as if they were stage 6 reasoners nor that stage 6 reasoners somehow mimic stage 3 reasoning. We must, then, allow for a great diversity in the reasons that Members of the Public bring to bear on the question, for that is the basic character of the justificatory problem we (you and I) face. Again, we must keep firmly in mind the distinction between the perspectives of real agents and that of philosophical reflection. Real agents differ in the sophistication of their reasoning, and so the descriptions of Members of the Public must model this. But, of course, our philosophical perspective is, in Kohlberg's terms, explicitly "post-conventional": you and I are seeking to answer the post-conventional question of whether our conventional morality can fulfill its promise of adequately grounding our moral practices and the rational moral emotions.

The fact of reasonable pluralism, then, must be at the core of a realistic deliberative model. Suppose, then, that we assume reasonable pluralism in the sense that our characterization of Members of the Public supposes that they bring a wide variety of standards and reasons to bear on the justificatory problem. These will include many (but, as we shall see, not all) of their values, ends, and goals in life: when they are deliberating about whether to endorse a rule, consideration of whether this rule sets back or advances the things for which they care surely is typically relevant. These are, roughly speaking, akin to the sorts of "personal reasons" to which Scanlon appeals in his contractualist theory.[30] Now it is often thought obvious that the reasons drawn upon in public justification cannot

---

[30] Scanlon, *What We Owe Each Other*, p. 219.

include nonpersonal reasons such as moral judgments or intuitions. It is widely held, for example, that a contractualism that allowed as inputs moral intuitions or judgments would be objectionably circular: contractualism aims to arrive at moral judgments as outputs of the contract and so cannot employ them as inputs. Whether or not this is an axiom of contractualist moral theory, it is not apropos to our problem. We are not seeking to generate moral truth but to discover whether social morality is confirmed by the reasons that each has. If a proposal conforms with one's moral judgment – suppose one has engaged in Kohlbergian stage 6 reasoning and has come to the conclusion that this moral rule is the best – one has a reason to endorse it. However, this is still a "personal reason" in the sense that it is a reason that a Member of the Public has to endorse the rule, but she acknowledges that it may be a reason that other Members of the Public do not have (and, we have seen, this is consistent with her believing that it is a reason that applies to all to endorse true morality; §13.1).

Abstracting from the notions of goods, values, moral intuitions, and so on, let us say that Σ is an evaluative standard for Member of the Public Alf if holding Σ (along with various beliefs about the world) gives Alf a reason to endorse rule x over y.[31] Evaluative standards, again, are to be distinguished from justified moral requirements: as I have characterized them they need not meet the test of deliberative public justification but are the reasons Members of the Public draw on to devise proposals and rank proposed moral requirements. Evaluative standards are prior to justified moral claims only in the sense that they are the bases of public justification. This priority does not imply, though, that they are logically prior, or developmentally prior, to moral codes and convictions, as if evaluative standards are somehow formed independently of the moral environment in which one lives. To some extent, a person's evaluative standards are the result of moral convictions that she has gained through living in a community. But until these moral convictions are publicly justified they are merely her own view of

[31] I leave aside here whether Σ is itself a belief about the world, or supervenes on one, as ethical naturalists would have it. Nothing in the analysis precludes moral realism as a meta-ethical or metaphysical thesis. The rationality-based constraint on justificatory reasons is the crucial principle on which the analysis rests.

morality, or her moral intuitions, which cannot form the bases of demands that treat others as free and equal.

(b) The Mutual Intelligibility of Evaluative Standards

A realistic account of public reason, then, must presuppose wide pluralism in the evaluative standards employed by Members of the Public in their deliberations. But how wide? Under what might be called "radical pluralism" we would so characterize the deliberations of Members of the Public as to allow for just about any evaluative standard that rational agents have endorsed – including, say, those who value the suffering of others and subjugating them. But this cannot be correct, for some limits are implicit in the very idea of public justification of a morality. Our aim in seeking public justification is to treat others as free and equal moral persons while also claiming moral authority over them. We are moral persons seeking justified mutual authority (§§2.3, 3.4). If each can be confident that all other moral persons, from their own distinctive evaluative perspectives, also have reason to accept common authoritative requirements, the moral claims of all are consistent with the Principle of Moral Autonomy (§12.3b), and so we respect the moral autonomy of others. Suppose, though, Alf seeks to justify rule x to Betty by appealing to her standard Σ_B, which leads her to endorse x. But suppose also that Alf believes that Σ_B is not an intelligible basis for endorsing x: he simply cannot understand how there is a sound deliberative route from Σ_B to x. He cannot see how Σ_B is a standard relevant to endorsing x. In this case, if Alf demands that Betty comply with x because she endorses it on the basis of Σ_B, he has no assurance from his own first-person perspective that she actually has a reason to comply (§12.4a). A plausible conception of evaluative pluralism must accept what we might call "mutually intelligible evaluative pluralism" at the level of Members of the Public. Our deliberators see themselves as deeply disagreeing about the basis for evaluating proposed moral rules but acknowledge that the basis of others' evaluation is intelligible and is relevant to the justificatory problem. As Isaiah Berlin might say, the range of plausible pluralism in the evaluative standards of Members of the

Public is limited by the "common human horizon."[32] One way of thinking of this is that most of the disagreements of Members of the Public will be about how some Σ relates to the evaluation of x (e.g., whether it is outweighed by other evaluative standards) rather than whether it is a bona fide standard relevant to the evaluation of moral rule x. This restriction is bolstered by empirical research that indicates that the main source of our disagreements is not about *what* is valuable, but about what is *more* valuable. According to Milton Rokeach, Americans largely agree in affirming a set of thirty-six values; what they differ on is "the way they organize them to form value hierarchies or priorities."[33]

In the Deliberative Model all Members of the Public share a list of evaluative standards that are agreed to be intelligible as grounds for deliberating. Now while they generally agree on what constitutes a good standard they do not always do so. We do not wish to go so far as to suppose that each endorses all the evaluative standards of others, or even that each thinks all the standards of others would be warranted at higher levels of deliberation. But each must accept that the standards of others are warranted at least at the minimum requisite level and that all can see the intelligibility of employing these standards when thinking about the justification of a moral rule. This, I think, is simply to say that each can genuinely see the standards of others as providing reasons for the evaluation of moral rules; to attribute a reason to a person is to suppose her deliberations are intelligible and relevant to the enterprise of justifying a moral rule. To attribute reasons to others is partly an interpretive enterprise, and to interpret is to make sense of what the other is doing. I cannot (successfully) interpret your action in a way that renders it unintelligible. Thus the very idea of reasonable pluralism – a pluralism based on reasons – implies an intelligible pluralism. Not only must reasons be intelligible, they must be relevant to the justification of the social practice of morality. Certainly we must exclude, for example, evaluative standards that disvalue the very idea of morality, value immoral acts qua immoral acts, disvalue conformity to justified moral rules, or value forcing people

---

[32] See my *Contemporary Theories of Liberalism*, chap. 2.
[33] See Milton Rokeach, The Nature of Human Values p. 110; Milton Rokeach, "From Individual to Institutional Values," p. 208. See my *Value and Justification*, p. 209.

to conform to unjustified moral rules. "My reason for endorsing this is that it is a bad rule, and I like bad rules" probably does not qualify as a sufficient reason of any moral agent, but even if it did it is not relevant to the justification of social morality. "I am a burglar and I have a reason to keep on burglaring" could, perhaps, be a sufficient reason for some to act, but that too is irrelevant to the justification of a moral rule against theft.

Our real – or, at a minimum our first – problem is the nature of a publicly justified social morality among boundedly rational moral persons committed to the moral enterprise, and who confront each other as deeply disagreeing on the ends of life and the ultimate justification of each other's foundational commitments, and yet who conceive of each other as reasonable and intelligible (though often deeply wrong-headed). Such people do not include pure egoists, though many Members of the Public put great weight indeed on their own interests and plans; neither do they include monomaniacs who are solely committed to one and only one value, such as one who cares about nothing but counting blades of grass, or his stamp collection. Such persons are the stuff of philosophical stories and objections, but in many ways they are beyond (or at the edge of) the common human horizon. In the end we should have something to say about such people, but we only confuse ourselves if we think moral inquiry commences with them. The general problem of social morality under pluralism among moral persons who confront each other as intelligible agents is severe enough; even those who think a crucial job is what we say to the Nazi should at least allow that what we say to good-willed intelligible others is an important first step.

It must be emphasized that these constraints on intelligibility are imposed on the model by "you and me," who are seeking to philo-sophically reflect on the problem of public justification. In answer-ing our question, "how far can we stretch intelligibility?" (or "how wide a pluralism are we to admit in the Deliberative Model?") we can learn from Rawls' remarks on arriving at the correct description of the original position: "In searching for the most favored description of this situation we [you and I] work from both ends. We begin by describing it so that it represents generally shared and weak conditions. We then see if these conditions are strong enough to yield a significant set of principles. If not, we look for further premises equally reasonable."[34] Without accepting the details of Rawls' account,[35] we can conceive of the development of the Deliberative Model as an iterative procedure. In constructing the Deliberative Model we start out with a very broad range of moral persons who disagree, and construct Members of the Public as idealized representations. We then see what sorts of moral rules can be justified to them. We then may go back and consider those value systems that stretch intelligibility, which we have not yet modeled. We shall want to inquire whether these persons are committed to the moral enterprise and treating others as free and equal; if they are, we must see whether we can model any remotely intelligible Member of the Public to represent them. If we can see how some such persons might be described, we may iterate our deliberative model to determine whether the results radically change. Do we find that our justified social morality is fundamentally transformed in a way that is manifestly unacceptable (say, it shrinks to a very small core or even disappears)? If we find this, we may conclude that we have reached the limits of the reconciliation of reasonable pluralism with a morality and free and equal persons, and must confront the conclusion that, in the end, moral relations with such persons is not possible. To include them would radically, and unacceptably, reduce the scope of social morality. And this, of course, would be a great cost to us. It would impair social morality's ability to perform the core function of structuring our social life. On the other hand, to exclude moral persons is also a terrific cost: our moral relations with such people would be transformed into the relations that obtain between us and those who are not capable of moral autonomy (§12.3*b*) such as the psychopath. We may treat them as strategic partners, patients to be

---

[34] Rawls, *A Theory of Justice*, p. 18.

[35] Rawls' account depends on the idea of reflective equilibrium – of which I am skeptical as a general method, or criterion, of justified moral belief. See my *Justificatory Liberalism*, pp. 101–108. The reader may note that in one respect I am suggesting the reverse of Rawls' procedure. Commencing with a more constrained model with stronger assumptions about the range of intelligible pluralism, we then see what happens when we relax the constraints. I consider proposals for yet stronger constraints in §14.4*c*.

helped, or dangers to be contained – but not as fellow participants in a moralized social life. The moral emotions and the practice of blame would no longer be appropriately directed at them. Whether we – you and I – bear these costs depends on the intelligibility of those excluded, and the extent to which their inclusion undermines our social morality.

(c) The Shared Reasons Requirement Rejected

In our Deliberative Model, then, Members of the Public evaluate proposed moral rules on the basis of mutually intelligible, but diverse, evaluative standards. The model supposes that Member of the Public Alf may base his evaluation of a proposed rule on a reason R that Betty will deny is a good reason; while she acknowledges that R is a reason for Alf, it is not a reason for her. We must be careful to distinguish their agreement about intelligible reasons from their disagreements about good reasons (both ideas are implicit in the very idea of reasonable pluralism). I can see that you are reasoning in an intelligible, relevant, and competent manner, even though I do not endorse the reasons and standards on which you deliberate. I have thus far been concerned with the worry that the mutual intelligibility requirement may be too restrictive: perhaps we should include those value systems that are barely intelligible, or strike us as barely human (such as our person who cares about nothing but his stamp collection). We wish to extend the range of admissible evaluative standards as far as possible. However, some press from the opposite direction: they wish to further restrict the admissible evaluative standards. The hope, perhaps, is that if we do so, the model will yield (to paraphrase Rawls, §14.4*b*) a more "significant" set of justified moral rules. Thus a number of theorists of public reason insist that we must endorse a shared reasons requirement, according to which a reason R can enter into public justification only if all Members of the Public endorse R as a good reason.[36] In our model the reasons of deliberators are based on their

---

[36] This can be seen as either a basic requirement of the justification of moral rules, principles, and laws, or as a constraint that applies to all exercises of public reason, including political discourse. This expansive view is defended by, for example, Stephen Macedo in "In Defense of Liberal Public Reason: Are Slavery and Abortion Hard Cases?" p. 35. I criticize this expansive version of the

evaluative standards, so let us translate the idea of shared reasons
into that of shared evaluative standards.[37] We can distinguish three
versions of this requirement, ordered from weakest to strongest.

> *Shared Standards*: Members of the Public must reason from a
> common set of evaluative standards. Although they disagree
> on the ordering of these standards, they agree on the set to be
> ordered. Thus Alf never appeals to a standard Σ that Betty
> does not also endorse.
> *Shared Ordering:* Members of the Public not only share a set of
> standards, but order them in the same way.
> *Identical Evaluative Sets:* Members of the Public share the same
> trade-off rates in all complex decisions (they have identical
> indifference maps; §9.4*b*).

On the Identical *Evaluative Sets* formulation, not only must
Members of the Public share the same standards, but they must
share all victorious (or undefeated) reasons for choice (§13.3). So on
the Identical *Evaluative Sets* formulation there is no disagreement at
all once we have properly specified the reasons on which Members
of the Public deliberate, and assuming that they share the same
information set (so that they agree how to map proposals on to
their identical indifference maps). As Rawls says of parties to his
original position, the reasoning of one person is the same as the
reasoning of any other, and so "each is convinced by the same
arguments."[38] This is manifestly an extraordinarily strong requirement and entirely does away with the idea of pluralistic reasoning.
It is hard to even see how to adequately model this idea in any
vaguely realistic way: actual people differ in all sorts of subtle ways
in their trade-off rates. Indeed, research indicates that people often
first devise trade-off rates between x and y when they begin to
confront new choices between them; if one never had to choose,
one may well have no trade-off rates of the relevant considera-

---

requirement in some detail in "The Place of Religious Belief in Liberal Public
Reason."
[37] I shall remain agnostic as to whether evaluative standards are to be understood
as themselves reasons, or the basis of our reasons for ranking moral rules.
[38] Rawls, *A Theory of Justice*, p. 120.

tions.[39] It is thus hard to even know what it means to claim we all must have the same trade-off rates, since many of us do not yet have any trade-off rates between some considerations. In any event, it is hard to see how we can make progress in understanding how people who disagree can live together by assuming that, in justificatory contexts, we are identical. The Shared Ordering formulation is, at first glance, more plausible; we might model Members of the Public as sharing a gross ordering of evaluative standards, but not the trade-off rates. Now to be sure, the idea of a simple gross ordering makes sense when we are selecting different options from a feasible set, as, for example, in the Members of the Public's choice of one moral rule from a set of competing candidates. However, it makes much less sense to see a person's basic evaluative system – the grounds on which she ranks candidate moral rules – as itself a gross ordering of considerations. Once we realize that people's actual decisions involve complex trade-off rates, trading off multiple values and principles, rules, and so on, the idea of a "shared ordering" of evaluative standard Σ_1 over Σ_2 loses its meaning. It tells us very little to say, for example, that everyone, say, ranks fidelity to duty above family values. Brutus (§9.4*b*) favored duty over his family in many cases, but not even he always favored duty. To talk about "ordering" one's evaluative standards is simply a useful shorthand for a system of trade-off rates that can be generated out of orderings.[40] If, though, we mean by "sharing an

---

[39] See Philip Tetlock, "Coping with Trade-offs." See also Fred D'Agostino, *Incommensurability and Commensuration*, and S. I., Benn, *A Theory of Freedom*, chap. 3.

[40] In the discussion of complex decision functions (§9.4*b*) I employed indifference curve analysis, which only relies on ordinal information about choices over bundles. I do not wish to imply by this that somehow people really "think ordinally." Utility theory can model a person's all-things-considered reasons without modeling her mental deliberative processes. There is strong reason to doubt that we actually process evaluative information ordinally. John Pollock has convincingly shown that binary preference relations (i.e., ordinal reasoning) cannot be basic to the way humans value. Assuming (unrealistically) that states of the world are characterized by simply 300 two-valued parameters of which only sixty are value-laden, and employing a number of assumptions to decrease the possible number of value rankings, Pollock estimates that this would still require 10^{18} different binary preferences, which is more than current estimates of the entire storage capacity of the human brain. If we increase the number of value-laden properties in the world to 300, the number of binary preferences required is twelve times greater than the number of particles on the universe! Pollock's point

ordering" that Members of the Public share an entire system of trade-off rates, we are back to the Identical Evaluative Sets formulation.

Most plausible is the weakest version – Shared Standards. This only requires that each Member of the Public endorses every Σ in the sense that Σ enters into her own deliberations or is somehow acknowledged by her as genuinely justificatory. On the Shared Standards formulation, Members of the Public disagree on the relative importance of the various considerations and so trade them off in very different ways. In the end, I would conjecture that there is not a great practical difference between a deliberative model based on the Shared Standards view and that of mutual intelligibility; for both, the crux of or evaluative disagreements is the different trade-off rates reasonable individuals employ between their generally shared evaluative standards. Still, Shared Standards is a stronger condition: it imposes a significant further restraint on the standards relevant to public justification. Indeed, Shared Standards implies a strong right of Member of the Public Alf to veto the use of Betty's Σ_B in her own deliberations about whether x is justified to her. If Alf does not endorse Σ_B, then he has a right to block Betty from employing it in her own deliberations. This surely is objectionable, even if he cedes a similar veto to her. One of our actual moral problems – perhaps not the fundamental problem, but a serious one nonetheless – is that under conditions of real cognitive limitations we sometimes face intractable disputes among competent reasoners about the status of evaluative standards, such as religious considerations. Citizens of faith insist that they could not possibly evaluate moral rules without knowledge of their religious convictions and are certainly not willing to accord others a veto over whether they may do so.[41] Proponents of shared reasons requirements typically insist that because shared reasons must be

---

is that given our cognitive limitations, humans must store value judgments in analog forms involving continuous variables. Pollock, *Thinking about Acting*, pp. 25–30.

[41] For arguments along these lines, see Nicholas Wolterstorff, "The Role of Religion in Political Issues"; Michael Perry, *Love and Power*, esp. chaps, 1 and 2; Kent Greenawalt, *Religious Convictions and Political Choice* and his *Private Consciences and Public Reasons*.

secular reasons religious standards are excluded.[42] To simply say, as does Macedo, that religious citizens must "grow up" and refrain from relying on their controversial reasons does not advance our confidence that all moral persons have sufficient reasons to conform to our social morality.[43] And that, we must always remember, is why in the end we are interested in public justification.

Some such as Steven Wall endorse the shared reasons requirement as an implication of the very concept of a reason, or at least a reason relevant to moral judgment. According to Wall, if R is a reason for me to, say, rank moral rule x above moral rule y; and if you disagree with my ranking; and after reflection I still affirm it, then I must judge that "a fully rational version of yourself" would accept my judgment about what is the better moral rule. So I must suppose that you did not, really, have a reason to rank y above x. And, Wall insists, "I must reject the construal" of the justificatory public that "limits idealization to . . . [less than full rationality]."[44] Now if we understand full rationality simply in terms of affirming the reasons that there are (§13.1), and Wall is saying that he knows the reasons that there are, his claim that a fully rational other will agree with him is analytic. But we have rejected the idea that a person necessarily possesses the reasons that there are, or that apply to her (§13.1). If Wall is making a substantive claim that, in fact, given our understanding of fully rational people, they would always agree on sufficient reasons, then his claim is false, for we have seen that it is a myth that fully rational persons must agree (§13.2). In any event, real humans simply have no access to anything approaching the degree of warrant that Wall appears to be supposing that he possesses, that is, once he has reaffirmed the judgment he has grounds to suppose that his view simply must be correct. The practice of social morality and our reasoning within it occurs among normal humans; it is the reasons that they have that count if our relations with them are to be characterized by freedom and equality. It is this with which the Deliberative Model is concerned.

---

[42] See, for example, Robert Audi, *Religious Commitment and Secular Reason*, pp. 86–100 and "Liberal Democracy and the Place of Religious Argument in Politics."

[43] Macedo, "In Defense of Liberal Public Reason," p. 35.

[44] Steven Wall, "On Justificatory Liberalism," p. 135.

(d) Principles of Sincerity

Jonathon Quong has recently insisted that in Rawlsian theory "public reasons" must be "shared reasons."[45] Quong's argument is, essentially, that the mutual intelligibility requirement is not sufficient for bona fide public justification. "It is imperative not merely that each citizen accept a given political decision, but rather that they have good reasons to do so. By stipulating that the arguments we offer to others when engaged in public reasoning must be sincere, we acknowledge that the aim is to find principles and policies that each citizen has good reason to endorse."[46] This reasoning leads Quong to adopt what he calls a "principle of justificatory sincerity" (PJS) "according to which A may only endorse X if the following are true (and vice versa for B):"

(1) A reasonably believes he is justified in endorsing X,

(2) A reasonably believes that B is justified in endorsing X.

Quong believes that this sincerity principle deems nonjustificatory a case in which Alf endorses a moral rule solely on reason R_A and Betty endorses it solely on R_B, where it is the case that Alf does not think R_B is a good reason (it is not a reason that he holds), and Betty does not think R_A is a good reason. Quong asks us to

Consider things from A's point of view. A believes he is justified in endorsing X for non-public [i.e., not shared] reason R_A, but because his reason is non-public, he knows it cannot serve as a justification for B. Additionally, A believes that the non-public reason which explains why B endorses X, R_B, is unsound. That is, A does not believe that R_B justifies X. R_B we can assume, is drawn from B's comprehensive doctrine, a doctrine that A rejects as unjustified. Assuming there are no other considerations that speak in favour of X, then A cannot endorse X without violating PJS. The same obviously applies when we consider things from B's point of view. [47]

The idea is that because Alf believes that Betty's comprehensive doctrine is "unjustified," and because R_B is derived from that comprehensive doctrine, he must believe that R_B is unsound. But if

---

[45] Quong, *Liberalism without Perfection*, chap. 9.
[46] Ibid.
[47] Ibid. Notation slightly altered.

it is unsound, then it would be insincere for Alf to appeal to R_B in justifying a common moral or political requirement. This coheres with what I have already said about intelligibility (§14.4*b*). If Alf is to base a claim to moral authority over Betty on moral rule x, he must be assured that he sees how she has a reason to endorse x. Quong is certainly correct that some sort of principle of sincerity is presupposed by public justification.[48] There are, though, a number of different levels of warrant at which such a principle might operate. Thus we can distinguish a number of principles of sincerity. We might say that Alf can sincerely appeal to R_B in a public justification only if

(A) Alf believes[49] that (*i*) he would be warranted in endorsing R_B (i.e., he would endorse R_B if he completed all possibly relevant reasoning – see §13.3) and (*ii*) so would Betty if she completed such reasoning.

(B) Alf believes that, at the level of deliberation engaged in by Members of the Public (*i*) he would have sufficient reason to endorse R_B and (*ii*) so would Betty.

(C) Alf believes that that, at the level of deliberation engaged in by Members of the Public, (*i*) Betty would have sufficient reason to endorse R_B and (*ii*) as a Member of the Public, Alf could see this as intelligible and relevant, though he does not endorse it.

(D) Alf believes that, at the level of deliberation engaged in by Members of the Public, Betty would have sufficient reason to endorse R_B, whether or not he, as a Member of the Public, could see this as intelligible and relevant.

Clearly (A) is unacceptable. As bounded reasoners, we have very little idea of what our, much less another's, fully warranted beliefs would be. Alf has a grasp of his sound beliefs and evaluative standards at some level of deliberation but it almost certainly is well short of full warrant. Moreover even if Alf did have a belief about

---

[48] See my *Justificatory Liberalism*, pp. 199ff.

[49] We might also invoke Quong's stronger condition of reasonable belief, or a weaker condition than belief, such as "Alf has no reason to doubt that . . . . " There are many different principles of justificatory sincerity.

what his and Betty's fully warranted views would be, for him to employ these as a test of the acceptable standards of Betty almost certainly would detach some of the justificatory reasons of Betty from the reasons she has, and we have already seen how such detached reasons cannot fulfill the requirements of our moral practices (§13.1). Should we, then, accept principle (B), an epistemically accessible version of Quong's PJS? According to (B) in the practice of moral justification, one can appeal to a reason only if it is a sufficient reason for both you and the other. Now two considerations pose insuperable barriers to this notion of sincerity. We have seen that justification and warrant are path-dependent (§13.2*d*). This is so even at full rationality, but it is manifest and pervasive at more accessible levels. Because of this, at the level of warrant characterizing Members of the Public, it will often be the case that Alf has within his evaluative system a defeater for R_B that is not present in Betty's system. Consequently, he must conclude that while he is not justified in appealing to R_B as a ground for X, Betty is justified in doing so. But if so, it is not objectionably insincere for Alf to hold that Betty's endorsement of X on the grounds on R_B is justificatory – as indeed it is in her evaluative system. It is defeated in his system, but his system does not determine what is justified for her to believe. Add to this a second consideration: the Public includes diverse reasoners (say, Kohlberg's stages 2–3 to 6; §13.5). Principle (B) allows Members of the Public at one stage to veto the reasons employed by those operating at others. Stage 6 Alf would not see some of Betty's stage 4 reasons as warranted at his level, so he could not see her, as a fellow Member of the Public, as having sufficient warrant for her views (and Betty could veto some of Alf's, which are not confirmed in her deliberations). Rather than a principle of sincerity, we seem to have a principle that allows vetoing the reasonable considerations of others, manifesting disrespect for them as fellow moral agents.

There is good reason to conclude that principle (C) properly specifies the conditions under which Alf is not being objectionably insincere. He accepts that at as real, and so bounded, reasoners, both his and Betty's beliefs and evaluative standards are path-dependent and defeasible. Both have engaged in the relevant degree of deliberation, and so possess the relevant degree of justification for their beliefs and evaluative standards. Alf is not taking advantage of any clear mistakes or errors: ex hypothesi, at the appropriate level of deliberation R_B is justified for Betty. To be sure, Alf may think she is ultimately wrong, and at a higher level of warrant her view would be defeated, but this does not make his appeal to R_B objectionably insincere. Consider: I believe that virtue theory is an erroneous account of basis of social morality, and I believe that at some level of deliberation this can be shown. Yet I believe that my colleagues who are virtue theorists have considerable warrant for their beliefs. Now suppose that I am deliberating with one of these colleagues about the proper rule governing, say, property, and I point out that, on grounds of her virtue theory, rule x is to be ranked as superior to rule y. I believe that she has sufficient warrant for her beliefs at this level of deliberation, and so for her endorsement of x (over y). I have respected her moral autonomy and have appreciated that on these difficult matters highly competent reasoners have conflicting beliefs. No insincerity, manipulation, or deception is involved in our relations: I treat her as a free and equal person with her own store of warranted beliefs at this level of deliberation, which quite properly guide her as a rational agent. And, importantly, the rational reactive attitudes are sustained. Should she violate $x's$ requirements, I can accurately claim that as a competent moral agent she has accessible warranted reasons to conform to it.

An interesting question is whether we should endorse (C) or (D). Some may think there is no real distinction between the two: if Members of the Public hold that others have sufficient reasons for their beliefs and standards at the appropriate level of deliberation, then they must see the standards and beliefs of the others as relevant and intelligible. If so, this is a welcome result: it would imply that the requirement of mutual intelligibility (§14.4b) is entailed by the very idea of endorsement by Members of the Public. Suppose, though, that there is a distinction. After all, insofar as the rationality of the Members of the Public is characterized procedurally (§13.3), we cannot be certain of the substantive outcome of mutual intelligibility. If so, (D) looks attractive, as it does not involve any "veto" rights: so long as R_B is confirmed in Betty's deliberations at the

appropriate level, appeal to it is justificatory. In contrast, principle
(C) grants a weak veto to Alf: if he simply cannot see how R_B and
relevant, he cannot view it as justificatory. It may seem that even
this weak veto betokens disrespect for Betty as a free and equal
moral person. We must keep in mind, however, that the
Deliberative Model is meant to help us think about justified rules in
our actual moral practices. In our actual moral life it borders on
incoherence to simultaneously hold that one is giving the other a
justificatory reason and that it this is unintelligible as a relevant
reason. The principle of sincerity expressed by (C) is entirely
appropriate. Unless it is met Alf must be uncertain about the
justificatory force of his appeal to R_B – it is a mystery to him how
this could be taken as of justificatory relevance to x by Betty. We
have real doubts whether Alf's appeal to R_B is a sincere exercise in
reason giving – even he cannot really see how it is an exercise in
reason giving. Note that a plausible principle of sincerity confirms
our characterization of the evaluative standards to be employed in
the Deliberative Model.

But this is a modest principle of sincerity, falling well short of
the shared reasons view. It is especially striking that Rawlsians
such as Quong, who have so impressed upon us the importance of
reasonable pluralism, seem so perplexed by pluralistic reasoning.
The important question for justification is whether, given our
understanding of the degree of warrant that a certain sort of activity calls for, we accept that the beliefs of the other are undefeated in
her system and can see her deliberations and standards as intelligible. To deny that others have reasonable evaluative standards,
justified beliefs, and reasons that I do not share, and with which I
disagree, deeply misconceives our real predicament as severely
cognitively bounded reasoners.

15 Proposals

15.1 MODELING LEGISLATION IN THE REALM OF ENDS

At the outset (§2.4), I depicted the solution to the fundamental justificatory problem in Kantian terms: "A rational being belongs to the

realm of ends as a member when he gives universal laws in it while also himself subject to these laws. He belongs to it as sovereign when he, as legislating, is subject to the will of no other."[50] Supposing each Member of the Public proposes a rule that thus models her role as a Kantian legislator: she takes on the role of lawgiver. If a law that binds all is also willed by all, moral freedom and moral authority are reconciled. The proposal-based model thus reflects this basic Kantian insight.

An immediate worry occurs. Our concern is whether normal moral agents can appreciate reasons to endorse morality. That is ambitious enough: surely it is fanciful to think that each person can be a self-legislator of morality.[51] Understanding morality as self-legislated in this way is characteristic of highly sophisticated (Kohlbergian stage 6 reasoning); to model moral deliberation in this Kantian manner appears manifestly inconsistent with the idea that the public justification of social morality must be accessible to the reasoning of normal moral agents. How can we specify the Deliberative Model in this Kantian-inspired way and yet hold that the resulting justification will be accessible?

Once again it is of the utmost importance to keep clearly in mind the distinction between the philosophical perspective and that of real agents. Our philosophical worry is whether you and I have sufficient reason to suppose that social morality meets the Principle of Public Justification; we construct an idealized model for thinking through this problem. It is never to be claimed that this model is itself highly accessible; what is important for the model is that it never supposes in *its* modeling of people's reasons to endorse a morality that they have reasons that are not accessible to them.

We need not suppose that proposing moral rules is within the competency of all Members of the Public. It is the reasons to

---

[50] Immanuel Kant, *Foundations of the Metaphysics of Morals*, p. 52 [Akademie, 433–4].

[51] "These steps from a minimal to a more adequate conception of morality (i.e., to a conception which at least begins to square with what we nowadays vaguely understand by the word) may easily encourage abstract exaggerations and distortions in moral philosophy. For instance, the necessary truth that the members of a moral community in general acknowledge some moral claims upon them may be exaggerated into the idea of a self-conscious choice or adoption of the principle of those claims, So everyone appears, grandly but unplausibly, as a moral self-legislator." Strawson, "Social Morality and Individual Ideal," pp. 10–11.

endorse, or refrain from endorsing, that are central to public justification, and it is these that must be accessible to normal moral
agents. However, if our model is to dispel our reflective worries
about the justification of our morality, we must be assured that all
plausible candidates have been canvassed. Although more conventional reasoners may focus simply on our current rules, either
accepting, rejecting, or proposing minor changes, post-conventional
reasoners (such as the readers of this book) may insist that adequate moral deliberation must cast its net much more widely. More
sophisticated reasoners may hold that they have most reason to
advance rules that are indeed acts of self-legislation based on moral
theories (§13.5). By allowing each Member of the Public to propose
a rule, post-conventional reasoning is permitted in the Deliberative
Model; those whose reasons endorse significant departures from
the current rule make their proposal to all.

15.2 CONSTRAINTS ON PROPOSALS

In fixing the choice set for the Deliberative Model we (you and I,
seeking to inquire whether our morality is publicly justified) must
restrict our thinking to rules that qualify as bona fide moral
proposals. A rule that prescribed "Give Alf a present on
Christmas!" simply would not qualify *as* a moral rule, even if
everyone had reason to endorse it. Although by the time he
formulated the famous original position model in *A Theory of Justice*
the parties themselves no longer offer proposals, Rawls (following
Baier, Hare, and other) holds that the alternatives with which they
are presented must meet certain constraints on "the choice" of all
ethical principles. Such formal constraints are especially appropriate for a proposal-based choice set, for they identify criteria for
acceptable proposals. These constraints are not ad hoc: they specify
features that proposals must have for you and me to consider them
as serious candidates for a justified rule in social morality.

(a) Generality
Rawls insists that proposals must be general. "That is, it must be
possible to formulate them without the use of what would be

intuitively recognized as proper names or rigged definite descriptions."[52] Many have thought that this requirement is a critical formal device that goes a long way toward a regulatory regime characterized by nondiscrimination and justice. Rousseau, for example, argued that

> when the whole people decrees for the whole people, it is considering only itself. . . . In that case the matter about which the decree is made is, like the decreeing will, general. . . .
>
> When I say that the object of laws is always general, I mean that law considers subjects *en masse* and actions in the abstract, and never a particular person or action. Thus the law may indeed decree that there shall be privileges, but cannot confer them on anybody by name. It may set up several classes of citizens, and even lay down the qualifications for membership of these classes, but it cannot nominate such and such persons as belonging to them. . . .
>
> In this view, we at once see that it can no longer be asked . . . whether the law can be unjust, since no one is unjust to himself.[53]

Scanlon too believes that the generality requirement is closely tied to ensuring fair principles.[54] Now while edicts that manifestly violate generality such as Bills of Attainders (which name particular persons) are apt to be unfair, the task of employing generality as a way to guarantee, or produce, fairness seems extraordinarily difficult. As the passage from Rousseau illustrates, rules very often identify classes and roles; they can even identify privileges. Parent, child, wife, husband, speaker, seller, buyer, renter, borrower, teacher, worker, farmer, citizen, alien – all specify roles, and general rules regulating those roles can be grossly unfair; and as evaluators of rules we know our likely and possible role identities. Some wrongful acts can only be committed against women, and we now all see that if men devise the rules, generality and oppression are entirely consistent. Although he acknowledged the ways that fairness has been sought through generality, Lon Fuller advanced a much more modest justification of generality, namely, the

---

[52] Rawls, *A Theory of Justice*, p. 113. Rawls notes that his view most closely follows Baier's in Chapter VIII of *The Moral Point of View*.

[53] Rousseau, *The Social Contract*, p. 192 (Book II, chap. 6).

[54] Scanlon, *What We Owe Each Other*, pp. 206–13.

requirement that regulation "must be [achieved through] rules of some kind, fair or unfair as they may be."[55] As we have already seen, generality is a mark of rules (§8.1): they seek to regulate specific actions through general descriptions. Regulation via rules prevents some types of unfairness, but it allows a great deal as well. Generality is a very modest device in our search for fairness. Nonetheless, the very idea of a moral order implies regulation of conduct through general requirements.

(b) Weak Publicity

Baier proposed what we might think of as a *weak publicity condition*, requiring that "moral rules must be taught to all children," and so all would know what the rules are. As Baier says, social morality is for everybody.[56] Such weak publicity is absolutely essential for the rules of social morality to perform their job of coordinating a mutually beneficial social existence. Rules that are too complex to be reliably taught to children could not be followed by the population in general. A social morality composed of abstract principles that required sophisticated philosophical reasoning to be applied simply cannot form the basis of a shared public morality; neither could a social morality that required sophisticated case-by-case moral judgment. Perhaps such moral theories apply to some aspects of moral discourse, but insofar as the cognitive demands far outstrip the abilities of normal moral agents, they cannot provide the framework of our shared social existence. Consequently, Baier's teachability requirement is a constraint on all proposals.

Rawls' publicity condition is stronger: justified moral principles must be publicly known to be such.[57] We might distinguish *strong* and *complete* publicity. With strong publicity the reasons justifying morality are accessible to all; with complete publicity the fact of strong publicity is common knowledge. These publicity conditions – especially, I think, strong publicity – are at the core of a justified social morality; and as Samuel Freeman has shown, Rawls' attempt to ensure that the justification of principles was public in

---

[55] Lon Fuller, *The Morality of Law*, p. 47.
[56] Baier, "The Point of View of Morality"; Baier, *The Moral Point of View*, pp. 195–200. See also Gert, *Morality: A New Justification of the Moral Rules*, p. 148.
[57] Rawls, *A Theory of Justice* p. 115.

demanding ways was a key factor in the evolution of his thought.[58] A morality that meets the strong publicity condition is one that free and equal people can readily see as providing them with reasons to comply; it does not confront them as an alien social demand by the powerful or the dead hand of tradition, but as an expression of their deepest values and commitments. It is a great advantage of our Deliberative Model that it provides the foundation for strong publicity; any rule justified by the model will be one that all normal moral agents have sufficient accessible and mutually intelligible reasons to endorse (§14.4). This, though, does not ensure complete publicity, for all having sufficient reasons that withstand scrutiny does not ensure that it is public knowledge that all have such reasons. Building public justification on the accessible reasons of each is nevertheless a critical first step in arriving at complete publicity. Although securing strong and complete publicity are important goals, they are not themselves constraints on proposals: we require at this stage only weak publicity. The first – but only the first – step in achieving fuller levels of publicity is to solve our deliberative problem. As we shall see in Chapter VII, when a society achieves a free moral equilibrium, each has reason to suppose that all others have sufficient reason for endorsing its moral rules.

(c) Conflict Resolution and Claim Validation

Rawls follows Baier in requiring that moral rules (or principles) order competing claims. That the key role of a morality is to adjudicate conflicting claims was presented in Rawls' first essay, "Outline of a Decision Procedure for Ethics," and continued through his later work. Rawls held that we view ourselves as "self-authenticating sources of valid claims,"[59] and so the fundamental task was not to show that our claims are valid[60] but to arrive at a

---

[58] Samuel Freeman, "The Burdens of Justification: Constructivism, Contractualism and Publicity."

[59] Rawls, *Justice as Fairness*, p. 23. The importance of this idea of self-authentication is easily overlooked in Rawls' thinking. It first appeared in his 1951 paper "An Outline of a Decision Procedure for Ethics," which conceived of ethics as adjudicating the claims of individuals, which he clearly saw as self-authenticating. See section 5 of that paper.

[60] Hence, because of this, parties to Rawls' original position are not required to

justified way to publicly order them when they conflict. This
expresses Rawls' Expansive View of a free and equal person (§2.1) –
one whose very nature is such as to advance valid claims on others.
This is puzzling, for to advance a self-authenticating claim on
others is not to respect their moral autonomy, for it implies that
others are bound by moral claims they cannot authenticate through
their own reason. The supposition of equal moral freedom requires
that one's moral claims be validated by those to whom they are
addressed. If so, the point of moral rules cannot be to order valid
claims, but to resolve, or even better, avoid disagreement about
what are our valid claims. The task of moral rules is to provide an
ordered moral life, and to do that the rules must point the way to
commonly acceptable ways of acting, avoiding innumerable
conflicts about what is to be done. This means that, as Baier
stressed, to some extent a moral rule must contain, at least implicitly, some priority claims, such as "Lying to someone is preferable
to doing him serious harm."[61] To learn a moral rule is also to learn,
at least for typical cases, an implicit trade-off rate to resolve
standard types of conflicts.

(d) Rules as Requirements
If rules are to resolve disagreements in this way they must be more
than mere guidelines: they must provide very weighty reasons to
act. A proposed rule is presented as providing a requirement for
action that typically overrides one's aims, values, and goals (§9.2).
This is weaker than the finality condition imposed by Baier and
Rawls, according to which the rules of morality are conclusive in
the sense that they are the final court in human reasoning.[62] It also
must be remembered that moral rules are social rules: the proposals, then, are for a certain requirement to be accepted as a social
rule, and so a requirement that would be generally acted on by the
relevant public.

---

advance justifications for their claims, as Rawls argues in "Kantian Constructivism," p. 334.
[61] See Baier, *The Moral Point of View*, p. 170.
[62] Rawls, *A Theory of Justice*, p. 113; Baier, *The Moral Point of View*, abridged edn., p.
vii.

(e) Universalizability as Reversibility

Moral principles, held Rawls, must be "universal in their application. They must hold for everyone in virtue of their being moral persons."[63] Now Strawson recognized that this common requirement is in conflict with an account of social morality such as I have defended here, which connects morality and the rules of one's society:

We might simply drop the idea of moral rules as universally binding on men as men. Or we might say that though there was something in this idea, it was absurd to try to apply it directly and in detail to the question of what people were required to do in particular situations in particular societies. And here we might be tempted by another manœuvre, which we should note as a possible one even if we do not think that it, either, is altogether satisfactory. We might be tempted to say that the relevant universally applicable, and hence moral, rule, was that a human being should conform to the rules which apply to him in a particular situation in a particular society. Here universality is achieved by stepping up an order.[64]

Whatever the merits of this maneuver, it is clear that in the sense of the *range of subjects* who are subject to a certain rule, the Baier–Strawson account I have been developing does not invoke universalization as a constraint on moral rules. However, at the core of most universalization requirements is not, I think, unlimited population of application but the necessity of reversibility. In explaining how universalization applies to moral reasoning, Hare famously considers a parable from Matthew XVIII: 23–33:

Therefore is the kingdom of heaven likened unto a certain king, which would take account of his servants. And when he had begun to reckon, one was brought unto him, which owed him ten thousand talents. But forasmuch as he had not to pay, his lord commanded him to be sold, and his wife, and children, and all that he had, and payment to be made. The servant therefore fell down, and worshipped him, saying, Lord, have patience with me, and I will pay thee all. Then the lord of that servant was moved with compassion, and loosed him, and forgave him the debt. But the same servant went out, and found one of his fellow servants, which

[63] Rawls, *A Theory of Justice*, p. 113.
[64] Strawson, "Social Morality and Individual Ideal," p. 6.

owed him an hundred pence: and he laid hands on him, and took him by the throat, saying, Pay me that thou owest. And his fellow servant fell down at his feet, and besought him, saying, Have patience with me, and I will pay thee all. And he would not: but went and cast him into prison, till he should pay the debt. So when his fellow servants saw what was done, they were very sorry, and came and told unto their lord all that was done. Then his lord, after that he had called him, said unto him, O thou wicked servant, I forgave thee all that debt, because thou desiredst me: Shouldest not thou also have had compassion on thy fellow servant, even as I had pity on thee?

On Hare's adaptation (which loses a good deal from the King James Bible), A owes money to B, and B owes money to C, and there is a law that creditors may have debtors imprisoned. B may wish to imprison A because he cannot pay her, so she assents to the personal prescription, "Let me have A imprisoned." But if she is proposing this as a moral rule, the prescription is not simply singular, but one that applies to all (within its range of application) and so to herself. If she advocates the moral rule "Imprison debtors!" she must assent to the universal prescription "Creditors: imprison debtors!" and since she is in debt to C, she must endorse C having her imprisoned.[65] Even if she is not in debt, of course, the point is that she must genuinely endorse being imprisoned should she become a debtor.

Genuine moral proposals must be universalizable in this crucial sense: a person's advocacy must not depend on her knowledge that she will only occupy specific roles or positions. As Kohlberg recognizes, reversibility is at the heart of both Hare's and Rawls' versions of "universal prescriptivism" – moral judgments are in "equilibrium" only if they continue to be asserted when the prescriber changes roles or positions (puts herself in the other party's shoes).[66] Rawls' "veil of ignorance" device, according to which one chooses in ignorance of one's social position, gender, race, and so on, is intended to force his model's purely rational self-interested agents to make such reversible judgments. Or, as Rawls puts it in *Political Liberalism*, the parties to his deliberative model

---

[65] R. M. Hare, *Freedom and Reason*, pp. 90–1.
[66] Kohlberg, *The Philosophy of Moral Development*, pp. 190–201.

are forced by lack of knowledge to employ their rationality in a "reasonable" manner, namely, they are "ready to propose" principles that specify terms of cooperation that all can accept since they make reversible judgments.[67] Rawls goes to great lengths to derive a specific form of reversible reasoning, leading to a unique choice for all parties, from the principles of rational choice for certain types of choices under uncertainty (i.e., his famous maximin principle). Universalization as reversibility, however, is much broader than this version employed by Rawls' model. It is critical in thinking about what constitutes a fair proposal, though, despite Hare's and Rawls' hope, different individuals, because they employ different evaluative standards, will advance conflicting reversible proposals: different proposals may be in equilibrium.

A person's proposal is in equilibrium if she asserts it even when she evaluates it from her occupancy of each of the roles and positions it identifies, and understands the duties and obligations involved in each. This does not require her to try to think what her view would be if she had other people's evaluative standards, as if she became them.[68] Not only do we not expect anyone to have such knowledge of the evaluative standards of others, but she is apt to disagree with those standards in many ways. Her proposal will be in equilibrium if, given her own evaluative standards, she continues to affirm it when she imagines herself, with her evaluative standards, confronting all the different demands the rule could make on her. Only proposals in equilibrium in this way can be considered as adequately fulfilling the office of universal lawgiver. When proposals are not in equilibrium the proposer is simply advancing a rule with an eye to advantaging a specific social position or role.

(f) A Modest Common Good Requirement
No one can reasonably expect other Members of the Public to endorse a moral rule that undermines their good. This is to not say that the only important consideration is a person's good, or that

---

[67] Rawls, *Political Liberalism*, pp. 49–50. Note that Rawls continues to refer to a proposal condition even though by this time he has dropped this from his deliberative model.
[68] Cf. Hare, *Freedom and Reason*, chap. 7.

acceptable proposals must best promote the good of all. People may care about things other than their good, but it would not be reasonable to propose a moral rule that one conceived as hostile or threatening to the good of some other Members of the Public. Reflect again on the case of the slave where we have a good case that slavery is important to the social order (§12.3*b*). The social benefits would still be insufficient as a ground for attributing her sufficient reasons to internalize the slavery rule and experience guilt should she violate it. The rule requires her to sacrifice her core interests. As I have argued, it is very hard to see how we can rationally expect others to internalize such ultra-strong require-ments (§§9.2*a*; 12.3). We are, to be sure, rule followers who come to care for rules, even when this can require setting aside our values and concerns (§§11.4, 21.1), but this is quite different from coming to care for a rule that is the enemy of one's good.

Baier agrees that "moral rules must be for the good of everyone alike,"[69] but thinks a common good requirement is too strong. In their actual operation the rules may work out to the advantage of some but not others. His example is a pay raise to miners, which helps the miners but not others.[70] This, though, is not a moral rule, but a policy. If we think of moral rules such as telling the truth, refraining from harming others, respect for personal property, respect for privacy, and so on, we do not suppose that the opera-tion of any of these rules is basically hostile to anyone's good. We must distinguish episodic sacrifices called for by the rule (which are the very raison d'être of social morality) from a general threat posed by the rule to one's good.[71] One of the great moral impacts of Victorian literature was to effectively call into doubt the legitimacy of many moral rules about property by depicting them as threat-ening the very lives of the poorest. If this was the case, however useful such rules might have been, they were the enemies of some Members of the Public, and could not be part of social morality of morally autonomous persons.[72]

[69] Baier, *The Moral Point of View*, p. 200
[70] Ibid., p. 201.
[71] As Baier stresses, ibid., p. 314.
[72] On property, see sections 18.3, 24 below.

The common good requirement, then, is that each Member of the Public has an undefeated reason (at least at the level of adequate deliberation) to believe that her proposal poses no threat to the good of any Member of the Public. Of course we disagree about what is to the good of others, and so goodwilled Members of the Public will disagree in what they see as necessary to meet this requirement. Some will have more perfectionist accounts, others more subjective. However, we have also come to agree on some basic ingredients of a person's good, such as protection of her bodily integrity, basic liberties to make her decisions about most of the important aspects of her life, control over basic resources needed to live a life, and so on. A rule that severely undermines a person's ability to secure these elements of her good is surely not one that we can reasonably hold she has sufficient reasons to endorse. Of course, even idealized Members of the Public may be wrong in their judgment that their proposed rule does not threaten anyone's good; we do not suppose that they have detailed knowledge of each other's evaluative standards. However, they do have knowledge of the basic idea of what is good for a person. It is on the basis of this knowledge that they are to exercise their responsibilities as legislators in the realm of ends.

16 Evaluating Proposals and the Problem of Indeterminacy

16.1 RANKINGS OF MEMBERS OF THE PUBLIC

(a) Modeling Sufficient Reasons and Incomplete Rankings
In our Deliberative Model Members of the Public confront a choice set composed of all proposals that satisfy the constraints on moral rules. As we have seen, we need not expect actual members of the public to engage in such legislating activity; the aim is to satisfy "you and me," from the philosophical perspective, that we have considered a set of proposed rules that, first, fulfills important criteria for being genuinely moral and, second, reflects the evaluative standards of diverse Members of the Public. The public justification of a social morality need not suppose that all competent

moral agents can perform this complex legislative task, though neither can we prohibit proposals from those able to formulate them. What the public justification of a social morality does require is that both normal and more sophisticated reasoners have sufficient reasons to endorse its moral rules. We now, then, turn to the evaluation of proposals by Members of the Public, whose reasons to endorse must be accessible to their counterpart actual agents.

We wish to model deliberation about the sufficient reasons of Members of the Public from a fairly large choice set. Rather than requiring the cognitively demanding task of considering the entire set as it were, all at once, suppose that, employing her evaluative standards, each Member of the Public makes pairwise comparisons of proposals. Deliberating about proposals x and y, each consults her own evaluative standards to decide which is better – that is, which better satisfies her evaluative standards. Building on pairwise choice provides a cognitively realistic understanding on the choice set: rather than asking an evaluator to examine all options, or asking the vague and ill-defined question of whether she has reason to endorse x, our question is always "Do you have sufficient reason to endorse x over y?" Assume that our deliberator decides that she does; we can say that she prefers x to y. The concept of a "preference" will allow us to more formally model the choice of the deliberators, but unless we are extremely careful it will lead to a basic misunderstanding of the nature of the model. As I remarked earlier (§9.4b), "preference" is often understood as a type of psychological state akin to a desire or a liking as in the phrase "that is just a mere preference for that result." On this view, preferences lie behind choices: they do not simply formally model them, they explain them. I have argued that there are good reasons to avoid this noncomparative sense of "preference," but for now the crucial point is that appeal to the idea of a preference to model a choice in no way commits us to its use. To say that an agent prefers x to y is just to say that x is more choice worthy: it is not to say that it is more choice worthy *because* she prefers it.[73]

We wish to construct for each Member of the Public an ordinal ranking of proposals through preferences that meet the conditions

---

[73] See further S. I. Benn and G. W. Mortimore, "Technical Models of Rational Choice." See also my *On Philosophy, Politics, and Economics*, chap. 2.

of consistent choice: asymmetry of preferences, symmetry of indifference, reflexivity of preference, and transitivity of strict preference. As we saw in section 4.3, there is some debate about the transitivity requirement, but I argued that there is strong reason to maintain transitivity of strict preference: it should be part of a moderately idealized conception of rational agency. To be sure, there is evidence that actual agents make intransitive choices, experiencing "preference reversal."[74] My claim, though, is not that normal agents always make transitive choices, but that as a requirement of consistent choice, transitivity of strict preference is accessible: it is part of real rationality.[75]

The deep problem of a realistic public reason model is that, at the level of warrant that we can expect of even our idealized Members of the Public, it is simply wrong that they will always be able to generate a complete ordering of the set of proposals. We have seen that sometimes, perhaps often, the reasons a person has at the appropriate level of warrant are indeterminate; a person may have two competing reasons, neither of which defeats the other (§13.3). Given that, she may have an undefeated reason to rank x above y, and an undefeated reason to rank y above x. At this level of deliberation, the system of beliefs and evaluative standards may be indeterminate: she has no sufficient reason to decide that one option is more choice worthy. As I stressed (§13.2), a great attraction of the myth of full rationality was that it promised to make all decision and choice problems determinate, so that we could easily suppose that fully rational agents would always be able to answer the question "is x better than y, worse than y, or tied with y?" Once we have abandoned that myth, we must confront the basic fact that at the level of warrant that we can impose on even our idealized agents, they will often be unable to answer this question. Given this, we cannot simply postulate a complete ranking of the proposals – that would be simply to suppose determinacy at lower levels of warrant than full rationality, and that cannot be right. Any

---

[74] See. e.g., Paul Slovic, "The Construction of Preference," pp. 491ff; Jack L. Knetsch, "The Endowment Effect and Evidence of Nonreversible Indifference Curves."

[75] The point here is that we should not infer from the fact that certain sorts of reasoning errors are common that normal agents do not have sufficient reasons to endorse the correct norm. See my *Justificatory Liberalism*, chap. 4.

modeling that seeks to stay within the bounds of real rationality must accept that there will be "unresolved conflict" within rational agents about pairwise comparisons.[76] Can we develop a formal model for choice under such indeterminacy?[77]

It is important to realize that the standard social choice conception of indifference does not apply to one who cannot make up his mind.[78] Indifference is based on the R relation according to which xRy means that x is at least as good as y. So if xRy and yRx, then xIy; that is, if x is at least as good as good as y, and y is at least as good as x, then they are equally good – indifferent. So if a Member of the Public has accessible reasons such that she has sufficient reason to conclude that x and y are equally good, then xIy. Here "indifference" means "equally good." This, though, is not a person who cannot make up his mind. Sen nicely brings out the distinction between the standard concept of indifference and that of indeterminacy (or inconclusiveness) by two interpretations of the problem of "Buridan's ass": the donkey who was precisely midway between two haystacks and could not decide whether to turn right (x) to eat from one or left (y) to eat from others, and ended up dying of starvation (z).

The less interesting, but more common, interpretation is that the ass was indifferent between the two haystacks, and could not find any reason to choose one haystack over the other. But since there is no possibility of a loss from choosing either haystack in the case of indifference, there is no deep dilemma here either from the point of view of maximization or that of optimization. The second – more interesting – interpretation is that the ass could not rank the two haystacks and had an incomplete preference over this pair. It did not, therefore, have any optimal alternative, but both x and y were maximal – neither known to be worse than any of the other

---

[76] See Isaac Levi, *Hard Choices*, p. 84.

[77] We can see the attractions of postulating a common way of evaluating proposals, such as Rawls' maximin principle, which requires each person to evaluate all proposals in terms of how well she would fare under them should she occupy the least advantaged roles. But that, of course, is simply another way of bracketing the fact that real agents have very different bases for their evaluations of the framework for social cooperation.

[78] See Sen, *Collective Choice and Social Welfare*, p. 3; John Craven, *Social Choice*, p. 14.

alternatives. In fact, since each was also decidedly better for the donkey than its dying of starvation z, the case for a maximal choice is strong.[79]

Given this, standard utility theory cannot show that there is a rational choice to be made from the set; on the standard interpretation our Members of the Public will not hold xPy, or yPx, or xIy. But suppose, like Buridan's ass, where z is $\{\neg x, \neg y\}$ our Member of the Public has a sufficient reason to judge that xPz and yPz. If so, if he is unable to choose from the set $\{x, y\}$ he does not choose to avoid alternative z – that is, he chooses neither. Buridan's ass' predicament is the same as that of our Member of the Public who has arrived at the decision that his reasons point to endorsing either x or y, but not both, but both are better than some third alternative, z. At this stage of his deliberation he is stuck at the conclusion that he does not have sufficient reason to judge that x is at least as good as y, and he does not have sufficient reason to judge that y is at least as good as x, though he does have sufficient reasons to conclude that both are better than z.

Our concern, it will be recalled, is how to model rational choice given such incomplete orderings. (Because our concern is modeling, the answer is a little technical.) Sen's R^+ relation, the completed extension of R, is of help. According to R^+, xR^+y if and only if $\neg(yPx)$.[80] The completed extension R^+ holds that x is not worse than y if and only if y is not preferred to x. If x is not less choice worthy than y, then xR^+y, and if y is not less choice worthy than x, then yR^+x. As Sen shows, the R^+ can convert incompleteness relations into indifference relations, thus constructing a complete ordering out of indecisiveness.

Sen views the R^+ relation as a construct, a way to mimic a complete preference order with an incomplete one characterized by indecisiveness over some options. It cannot, he warns, be attributed to agents.[81] Sen understands preferences as elements in delibera-

---

[79] Sen, "Maximization and the Act of Choice," p. 184. See also Eliaz and Ok, "Indifference or Indecisiveness? Choice-Theoretic Foundations of Incomplete Preferences."

[80] Sen, "Maximization and the Act of Choice," pp. 185ff.

[81] Some accounts seek to identify rational choices under incompleteness by attributing to agents a distinct "indecisiveness" preference relation and developing a more complex utility theory to accommodate it. See, for example, Eliaz and Ok,

tions but there is reason to favor an alternative view according to which preferences are a summary of a person's reasons to choose.[82] A person's reasons to choose determine the choice worthiness of options, and we can develop a preference ordering from this that describes her best choice and allows us to construct a mathematical representation of it. On this conception of utility theory, the preference relations we employ are those that best model a person's reasons to choose, and what best model them in any specific case will depend upon our aims and assumptions. It would indeed be erroneous generally to characterize incomplete preferences in terms of indifference. Consider Sen's "assertive incompleteness" in which *in principle* we know the relation is $\neg(xPy)$ & $\neg(yPx)$ & $\neg(xIy)$, which we can contrast to "tentative incompleteness," in which the person has not yet been able to rank the alternatives.[83] The former is essentially what Raz understands as incommensurability,[84] and it would certainly be unacceptable to employ R^+ to derive a complete ordering via indifference. If a person insists that x and y are noncomparable, we cannot say that he is indifferent between them. But the case of "tentative incompleteness," especially in the context of the Deliberative Model, is importantly different. Reflect on a rational version of Buridan's ass, who is deliberating about whether to endorse a rule x ("turn right to eat") or y ("turn left to eat"). The ass has not continued deliberation far enough to arrive at a warrant for either choice, though it believes that if it continued to deliberate it would have a warrant for opting for x or y, but certainly not both. At this point the ass cannot conclude whether xRy and/or yRx, but has concluded that xPz (where z is not turning) and yPz. Sen is right; only an ass would insist that because it cannot decide on whether xRy and/or yRx, it cannot compare the options, and so we must model it as having no reason to choose from the maximal set

---

"Indifference or Indecisiveness?" and Efe Ok, "Utility Representation of an Incomplete Preference Relation." For a classic paper on the problem, see Robert Aumann, "Utility Theory without the Completeness Axiom."

[82] See my *On Philosophy, Politics, and Economics*, chap. 2.

[83] Sen's "tentative incompleteness is what I have called "inconclusiveness," while his "assertive incompleteness" is what I have described as "indeterminacy." See my *Justificatory Liberalism*, pp. 151–4 and section 13.3 above.

[84] Raz, "Value Incommensurability: Some Preliminaries."

$\{x, y\}$.[85] The important thing is not to get stuck with z! Here it is entirely appropriate to interpret the relation between x and y in terms of an indifference relation where x is not more choice worthy than y, y is not more choice worthy than x, they are not equal, but choosing from $\{x,y\}$ is more choice worthy than z. In Sen's terms, $\{x,y\}$ form the maximal set for $\{x,y,z\}$ and the ass (as well as our Members of the Public) have sound reasons to choose from the maximal set.

In what follows I shall suppose R^+ completed preference orderings. That is, when a Member of the Public's reasons are inconclusive between options, we shall model this as a type of indifference between x and y. As a consequence, with this indifference relation we must weaken the transitivity requirement to quasi-transitivity according to which there is transitivity of strict preference [if (xPy) & (yPz), then (xPz)]; however, indifference need not be transitive.[86] That is, even if Alf is indifferent between w and x (because he is tentatively indecisive), and he is indifferent between x and y (because he is tentatively indecisive), he need not be indifferent between w and y (he need not be indecisive in his judgment about them). This is a slight weakening of transitivity, but preserves the crucial intuition about the rationality of strict preference.[87]

---

[85] Raz's view is very different, seeing incommensurability as an opening for choice. See *Engaging Reason*, chap. 3.

[86] See Sen, *Collective Choice and Social Welfare*, p. 491; Sen, "Maximization and the Act of Choice," pp. 185–6.

[87] Those wary of the proposal can avail themselves of an alternative way to complete tentatively indecisive orderings: that is, as overcomplete orderings. Suppose again that a Member of the Public's inconclusive reasoning has arrived at the conclusion of our ass. We might complete his ordering by making it over-complete, holding that he holds xPy, yPx, and xIy. Of course this would make him strictly inconsistent, and it looks senseless to attribute these preferences to actual rational persons. But we might, as it were, break the person into several parts, completed in all possible ways, giving rise to different rankings of proposed principles. The effect is to increase the model's population by adding each different completion as a distinct ordering. This would ensure that if the rule passes the test of public justification it is certainly justified, for no matter how the person completed his ordering, the test would be passed. The drawback is that, perhaps, we are making it even more difficult for any proposed candidate rule to pass the test as we have increased the public, and perhaps the diversity of its orderings. And, counterintuitively, those who have reached no judgment on the matter receive, as it were, additional representation in the Public; the more tentative you are, the more you are represented. That seems a very odd result. See Sen, *On Ethics and Economics*, p. 66. For a discussion, see my *Contemporary Theories of*

(b) Diversity of Rankings of Proposals
Given deep pluralism of the evaluative standards on the basis of
which each ranks the proposals, there will be similar pluralism in
the rankings of the proposals. Because the basis for judging moral
requirements is diverse, so too will be the evaluations of moral
requirements. Deep moral disagreement is the inevitable result of
deep evaluative pluralism in our Deliberative Model. Indeed,
anything but the strongest version of the shared reasons requirement would allow disagreement in rankings (§14.4*c*), and we have
seen that these requirements are too restrictive. Once we introduce
more plausibility into the Deliberative Model, we must suppose
great disagreement among the Members of the Public in their
rankings of proposed rules. Recall that our model (*i*) allows deep
pluralism into the deliberations of Members of the Public, bounded
only by the requirement of mutual intelligibility of evaluative standards (§14.4*b*), (*ii*) understands each Member of the Public as
having a complex system of standards characterized by a trade-off
rate among the various elements (i.e., an indifference map; §9.4*b*),
and (*iii*) allows that the required level of warrant for Alf to have a
sufficient reason R is within the bounds of Alf's understanding
(§§13.3–5). Given all of this, our Deliberative Model must suppose
that the Members of the Public will have very different ideas as to
what constitutes the optimal (best) moral rule. Even if most of
conventional reasoners end up endorsing the current rule, post-
conventional reasoners will almost surely have different ideas as to
what rule best satisfies their relevant evaluative standards. Our
question is this: given all of this disagreement, is there anything we
can say about the range of proposals that Members of the Public
will find acceptable?

16.2 DENYING AUTHORITY TO A RULE

(a) The State of Nature in Traditional Social Contract Theory
Based on her relevant and intelligible evaluative standards, we
model each Member of the Public as comparing each pair of
proposals $\{x,y\}$, and holds either xPy, yPx, or xIy (based on the R^+

relation). These preference relations model an individual's reasons in terms of pairwise evaluations: does she have reason to endorse x over y (or, we might say, is y rejectable in favor of x)? Given that Members of the Public have R^+ completed orders, one of these relations holds between every pair of proposals (§16.1a). Now consider the pair $\{w,x\}$. Betty's (as a Member of the Public) sufficient reasons allows us to model her as having one of these preference relations, and so we can model her judgments of choice worthiness between them, but we might wonder whether in some cases, though she prefers w to x she holds that both are in some sense unacceptable. Of course, both w and x are to be rejected in relation to higher-ranked proposals, but Betty might complain that these two alternatives are, as it were, so objectionable to her that though she has reasons to endorse w over x, she does not in some sense really have sufficient reasons to endorse either. They are, she might say, both unacceptable, even if one is better than the other. (One reason why we should not equate "preference" with "desire" is that one can have a preference between two options one loathes.) Given the plural basis of the parties' deliberation, we cannot preclude that Alf, some other Member of the Public, will advance proposals that Betty finds objectionable in this way. To be sure, given that all are reasoning on the basis of evaluative standards that all accept as relevant to moral deliberation, and further that all Members of the Public hold that their proposals conform to the formal constraints on moral rules, there will not be out-and-out dictatorial, selfish, or manifestly oppressive proposals. Yet their differences in evaluative standards can still lead some to propose moral rules that others find strictly unacceptable. For example, when deliberating about rules concerning freedom of religion, Alf may sincerely propose (w) a rule of freedom of thought and exercise, though with an obligation to support (at least financially) a single national Church, on the grounds that this will promote community spirit and dampen sectarian conflicts. As an adherent of a particular faith, Betty may insist that such a rule is strictly unacceptable.

On the face of it, Betty looks as if she is appealing to a noncomparative notion of rejectability. She is not saying that w is the worst option (z may be even worse), but even if she holds that

$w\mathbf{P}z$, she looks like she is claiming that w is absolutely rejectable on its own merits. As I have argued, this is an ill-formed choice; to know whether she really has reasons to refrain from endorsing it – whether, we might say, it is "absolutely unacceptable" – we still must have some idea of the opportunity costs of this rejection, that is, what option this leaves her with. What is the relevant alternative to which it is inferior? It may seem, perhaps, that we can avoid this search by invoking the idea of "option regret" in which Betty regrets that she must choose from this choice set. If she regrets that she must choose from $\{w,x\}$ we might say she finds the choice strictly unacceptable. But as D'Agostino notes, option regret is "nearly ubiquitous."[88] Some may regret having to choose from a set that does not include their first-ranked option, but this hardly shows that all other sets are to be rejected as unacceptable. Suppose Betty is deliberating between $\{v,y\}$, proposals that are well down in her ranking – say twentieth or twenty-first. Even if she regrets that in the end she may have to choose among this lower-ranked pair, that does not mean that either is, in some sense, absolutely unacceptable.

In traditional social contract theory, the idea of the state of nature provides a way to model the idea of an "absolutely unacceptable" proposal without abandoning the idea of a defined choice set: if any proposal is ranked below continued life in the state of nature (z), an agent would have no reason to "sign the social contract." Even if $w\mathbf{P}x$, if $z\mathbf{P}w$ then w (and by transitivity, x) is to be rejected as an unacceptable social contract. This is an appealing idea. Suppose Betty insists that w is "simply unacceptable" and Alf disagrees. One of the things he may seek to do is to show that, while flawed, w performs the core tasks of social morality. "If you reject w and we fail to agree on a moral rule," he may say to Betty, "we will be left with a purely instrumentalist basis for social cooperation, and we have seen (here he invokes the analysis of Chapter II) that this will gravely reduce your ability to pursue your ends." The argument is by no means irrelevant or silly. We can understand the long-standing appeal in social contract theory

---

[88] D'Agostino, *Incommensurability and Commensuration*, p. 31.

of defining a state of nature baseline, so that we have a point by which improvements can be measured in justificatory discourse. Without a "no agreement point," how can we know whether an agreement is rational? Nevertheless, the attempt to model life without the agreement – the state of nature – is hopelessly controversial. Any modeling would have to present a case for what would be, as it were, the next best world to that without some moral rule from the choice set. We would need to have a good idea of the opportunity costs of rejecting all moral rules on the matter and to know that we would have to know the next best situation. And here the controversy blooms. Would it be a social world of more or less stable instrumentalist conventions, nonmoral social norms, a precarious scheme of social cooperation? These are the cruxes of long-standing debates of social philosophy (we ask our students, "whose description of the state of nature is more accurate: Hobbes, Locke, or Rousseau?"). I believe that recent social philosophy shows that, generally, without moral rules there would be less stable social cooperation backed up by considerable threats of punishment for deviating from the nonmoral norms, but of course this would differ whether, say, we are confronting essentially Prisoners' Dilemmas or Assurance Games. In any event, in any specific case modeling the next best situation will be highly conjectural.

(b) Rejection on the Grounds of the Formal Constraints
Consider a tale of two post-conventional reasoners, James and John Stuart Mill. James Mill held that women did not need a vote because their interests were adequately protected by their fathers or husbands.[89] There is no reason to believe that he was insincere, or out to oppress women, or was not convinced that his judgment was reversible (if he were a woman, he would see the wisdom in his proposal). Like all of us on many occasions, he simply failed to appreciate the good of others and the ways rules impact their evaluative standards. Although many women entertained evaluative standards that agreed with the elder Mill, many did not. As his son, John, made clear in the *Subjection of Women*, despite the sincere

---

[89] James Mill, *An Essay on Government*, p. 45.

though ultimately selfish convictions of most men, many of the social rules of the nineteenth century oppressed women in ways that most men were unable to grasp, but large numbers of women did. When John evaluated his father's proposals in terms of the constraints on moral rules – such as nonoppression – he concluded that they failed.

Both James and John were goodwilled, post-conventional moral agents. But James' proposal, which he made in good faith and, in his view, advanced the good of all, was seen by his son as manifestly failing to take seriously the good of some. As a post-conventional moral reasoner, John must have sufficient reasons to endorse a proposal as genuinely moral; if he is to employ it in his relations with others, John cannot think that it fails to be adequately general, public, is sufficiently clear in its requirements, or that it adequately meets the common good and reversibility conditions (§15.2). Even though James would have concluded it did, this cannot be enough for John; he cannot have reason to grant moral authority to a rule that fails to meet the minimum conditions for a genuinely moral rule. In the Deliberative Model, then, although each proposal seeks to conform to the constraints on ethical rules, given self-bias and limited imagination there can be no assurance that the proposed rule meets the constraints in the eyes of all. Thus one ground for refusing to grant authority to a rule is that, according the evaluative standards of a Member of the Public, it fails to adequately meet the constraints on moral rules, especially the requirements of the common good and reversibility. Of course we need not think of the complaint in these formal terms. What is important is the complaint of women that the rules of Mill's society were hostile to their good. And John would complain that the rule fails reversibility: if he were a women, he certainly would not be able to endorse proposals that fail to take the concerns of women seriously. One cannot accord moral authority to such rules: some rules are such that they could not have the authority of morality.

I have stressed that both James and John were post-conventional reasoners. There is no expectation that all normal agents must apply these tests; as Kohlberg stresses, reversibility reasoning is most characteristic of stage 6 agents, generally the smallest group in a population (§§12.2, 15.2*e*). Recall, though, that basic to our life as reasoners is the way in which more sophisticated reasoners can contribute knowledge to their fellows, without their fellows having to replicate their reasoning (§13.4). Our post-conventional Members of the Public thus serve the entire Public; by refusing to grant moral authority to rules that fail to adequately meet the relevant requirements, we will see that they eliminate proposals that are objectionable as genuinely moral rules.

(c) Rejection Based on the Excessive Costs of Moralization

The authority of social morality has both great benefits and costs. It allows a moral life based on mutual authority and mutual respect while providing the basis of social order and relations of trust.[90] However, as I have stressed, social morality is by no means costless; we give others standing to demand actions of us, we open ourselves to censure for failure to comply. Our actions become the business of others. And, importantly, we internalize the rule and feel guilty when we do not comply. We come to care about the rule as itself worthy of being followed even at the cost to our ends and plans, and engage in self-punishment and reproach when we fail to live up to it. One of the great merits of both Baier's and Gauthier's work is their keen appreciation that morality is not a costless way to organize our common life. Too often moral philosophers suppose that morality, with its attendant practices of guilt, blame, and punishment, is an unmitigated blessing, of which we just cannot get enough. The Victorians certainly had too much of it, submitting to wide-ranging moral regulation of their sexual lives and much of their personal lives. In different ways, Neitzsche and Freud were reactions to this hypermoralization of life. At some point a good-willed person, deliberating on his evaluative standards, will come to the conclusion that, given some proposed rule and its attendant costs, he does not have sufficient reason to endorse this serious, and sometimes costly, human practice. One may hold that, while some other moral rule over this area of social life is justified, for this rule the costs of moralization are simply too great. Perhaps one concludes that "the strains of commitment" of a proposed rule

---

[90] On the importance of trust to the social order and our personal relations, see Marek Kohn, *Trust: Self-Interest and the Common Good.*

would be excessive: a person may conclude that he could not generally live up to its demands, so he would constantly feel guilty were he to internalize it. Or he may think, inspired by Freud, that too many others would feel guilt-ridden, and so such a rule would, overall, make people's lives worse. Thus he might "reasonably reject" such a rule.[91] And he is apt to have severe doubts whether such a rule could become a social rule, actually followed by the group.

More radically, some may conclude that no rule over some area of social life is justified. Suppose we are considering, say, the morality of smoking. It has recently been argued that smoking is becoming "moralized,"[92] and some, such as James Q. Wilson, seem to think that such addictions are immoral.[93] Others may insist that we have a moral right to smoke, so a high tax that discouraged people from smoking violates their right (in the same way as would a tax for attending church). Others, though, may simply think that no rule about this matter is called for. We may be in the realm of unappealing personal habits, but in this view invoking moral authority in any way is simply unwarranted.

In this latter case the rejecter asserts that we all have what Hobbes called a "blameless liberty" (to smoke).[94] Let us say that you and I have mutual blameless liberty to ϕ if and only if neither of us has a duty to ϕ or a duty to refrain from ϕ-ing.[95] Should others exercise this blameless liberty to smoke, resentment on your part would be inappropriate, as you have no standing to complain (you may still be annoyed or disgusted). This is just like the textbook case of two individuals, each seeing a dollar bill ahead on the sidewalk. Both have a blameless liberty to try to pick up the dollar, and so see each other simply as competitors; neither has a duty to refrain from seeking to pick it up first. What, though, if in

[91] Brian Barry, *Justice as Impartiality*, pp. 61–7; Rawls, *A Theory of Justice*, pp. 153–4.
[92] Paul Rozin, "The Process of Moralization."
[93] See Wilson, *The Moral Sense*, pp. 94–5. I consider Wilson's views in more depth in my "Sentiments, Evaluations, and Claims."
[94] Hobbes, *The Elements of Law, Natural and Politic*, p. 71 (Part I, chap. 16, §6). See further my *Value and Justification*, pp. 281–92.
[95] This is H. L. A. Hart's "bilateral character of liberty rights," which he contrasts to Wesley Hohfeld's "unilateral" characterization of a liberty. See Hart, "Legal Rights," pp. 166–7.

competing for the dollar I shoot you? H. L. A. Hart emphasized that blameless liberties occur within a "protective perimeter" of other rights.[96] One has a blameless liberty to try to pick up the dollar first but not to harm the other in the attempt; the blameless liberty is embedded in rules that limit the manner in which one can exercise it. Now when I think through whether on some matter I shall endorse the authority of a moral rule or endorse no rule – a blameless liberty where there is no obligation, claim, or duty on the matter – I must know this "protective perimeter," for only then do I know the bounds of the liberty. Recall the idea of an order of justification (§14.3). We must first turn our attention to fundamental matters, carving out, as it were, the basic rights and duties, and identifying the core of the protected sphere, extending outward to other rules the justification of which assumes as given the more basic moral rules. In the next chapter I shall defend what I believe is the quintessential liberal order of justification, which commences with rights of agency and claims against harms and moves outward to other rights and duties. Of course, this order is not strict and clear, but the idea of first justifying the basic rights of the person, and then supposing these in subsequent justificatory discourse (taking them as "fixed points," as it were) is so common that it is easily overlooked. This is the moral parallel to political theory, where we first fix our attention on constitutional essentials, and then reflect on the justification of other matters with these parameters fixed. When Victorian authors depicted the horrors of late nineteenth-century capitalism, they called into question property rules by showing that they led to violations of more fundamental norms – against severe harm and impairment of agency. And when feminists pointed to the injustice of sexual discrimination in university appointments they were questioning the established rights of those participating in certain types of associations on the grounds that they conflicted with basic principles of equal liberty to pursue an occupation of one's own choice (§17). To be sure, in such instances we arrive at a new appreciation of the more fundamental claims when we come to see how less fundamental rules come into

---

[96] Hart, "Legal Rights," pp. 171–2.

conflict, but this does not obviate the importance of distinguishing basic and less basic features of our social morality.

Holists, we have seen, are wrong to suppose that we can consider everything at once, but Scanlon is entirely correct that the justification of one principle takes place against the background of holding others fixed. Only working with some idea of an order of justification can adequately respond to both these insights. Now this means that in an evaluation of whether to reject the authority of a rule on some matter, its place in the order of justification is of fundamental importance. To deny authority to rules concerning basic rights of the person is a grave matter indeed, for it would commit one to a regime of blameless liberty about basic aspects of agency. This is not to say that a goodwilled agent would never come to deny authority to some proposed rule, but the only plausible grounds of rejection would be on the grounds of failure to conform to the constraints on moral rules. These constraints are powerful tools for criticizing basic moral rules. As Hare, Rawls, and Baier all stressed, reversibility, publicity, and the common good are at the heart of our moral thinking and criticism. When we move to less foundational issues, however, where there is a strong "protective perimeter" in place, denying the authority of a rule will be a far less grave matter, and so rejection on the basis of over-moralization will become more prevalent.

There is another reason that it is crucial to secure the core rights – the protective perimeter. Stephen Darwall has recently shown with great care the intimate relation between the status of having dignity and that of having the standing to make moral demands on others. "Dignity," Darwall reminds us, "is not just a set of requirements with respect to persons; it is also the authority persons have to require compliance with those requirements by holding one accountable for doing so."[97] The idea of having dignity is in part that one has a standing to insist that others not treat one in certain ways. A being that was treated with great care, so that its aims were always considered by others in their deliberations and its freedom of action protected, still would be without dignity if it had no standing to itself make determinations of what is owed to it, and

---

[97] Darwall, *The Second-Person Standpoint*, p. 14.

to demand what is its due. As Darwall says, there is "a set of requirements" upon which one's dignity depends, and one must have authority to demand compliance with those. This, though, does not mean – as I think the Expansive View of freedom and equality implies (§2.1) – that our dignity demands we have a standing claim in all matters to be treated in ways that we cannot reasonably reject. Sometimes, thank goodness, morality simply is silent.

(d) Blameless Liberty as the Default

To treat another as free and equal is, as Rawls says, to lay no claim to moral authority over him – except that which he himself (as a Member of the Public) endorses. This implies that blameless liberty is the default: a person must have reason to endorse the authority of a moral rule. There is thus an asymmetry between Alf, who claims that he has moral authority over Betty, and Betty who denies the authority of the rule. Alf's claim is justified only if Betty has reasons to endorse the authority; Betty's claim is justified simply if there are no reasons. She does not have to provide a case for rejecting Alf's claim to authority – she is *free* and equal. He must provide a case that he has authority over her. Fundamental to seeing others as free and equal is to refrain from asserting moral authority over them without justification. But only Alf is asserting any claim to moral authority. To see, as do some,[98] Alf and Betty's justificatory burdens as symmetric (call this the "symmetry thesis") is to say that Betty is under an equal burden to show Alf that his claim to authority over her is ungrounded as he is to show her that it is well grounded. If there are no reasons on either side, according to the symmetry view, neither Alf's nor Betty's position is vindicated. Although this may be consistent with a sort of moral equality between them (anyone's claims to moral authority over anyone else is prima facie valid), it is not consistent with seeing Betty as morally free, for she is hostage to Alf's belief that he has moral authority over her, even when his authority is not justified from her point of view.

[98] See Wall, "On Justificatory Liberalism."

From the perspective of moral justification, the default position must be that one is not under the moral authority of another. We begin by supposing that free and equal persons have no authority over each other, and so it is authority that must be justified: the failure of justification is the failure to justify authority over each other. Suppose Alf goes ahead and holds that his proposed rule establishes a valid moral requirement such that Betty is under an obligation, say, not to smoke. To be sure, he may go ahead and judge that in his view "Betty does wrong" but, because he has failed to justify his demand he does not address Betty's practical reasoning and the moral emotions are undermined. He cannot say that as a Member of the Public she endorses his antismoking rule, and so she has reason to do as he demands, and so guilt on her part for lighting up would be inappropriate, as would blame, resentment, and indignation on his part. But as I have stressed, these are fundamental to people's conceptions of a moral rule, as opposed to a merely personal conviction about what others must do (§10). Alf, in effect, has a personal norm that condemns this activity (based, say, on a supposed insight into perfectionist moral truths to which, apparently, other Members of the Public do not have access) but his norm is unable to perform the job of a moral rule in our actual social-moral practice. On the other hand, Betty makes no moral claims on him in this regard; her non-claim is entirely consistent with the failure to justify. And that is why there is indeed a deep asymmetry between their justificatory positions.

Steven Wall objects to this view of morality. Drawing on Samuel Scheffler's work, he argues that "morality is pervasive."[99] To say that morality is "pervasive" can either be a sort of metaphysical thesis about the nature of morality (i.e., on the correct view of morality, it is the sort of thing that applies to each and every human action) or a thesis about the pervasiveness of one's moral authority over another. As I have been at pains to point out, social morality is only concerned with the latter. Like so much else, whether morality is pervasive (in the metaphysical sense) is one of the things about which the Public disagrees. Given that Wall

---

[99] Wall, "On Justificatory Liberalism,"p. 312; Samuel Scheffler, *Human Morality*, chap. 2.

invokes the symmetry thesis just discussed,[100] I believe that he is endorsing the pervasiveness of moral authority of one person over another: he holds that there is a standing requirement such that, in order to have a blameless liberty, you must have good reasons that show others that you have a blameless liberty to act on your own (nonmoral) ends.[101] If you do not have such reasons, you cannot claim to have a blameless liberty. Others may not be able to show that you have a duty, but according to his symmetry thesis, this does not let you off the moral hook: it just shows that the moral issue is unresolved. Now to reject this version of the "pervasiveness of morality" is just to reject the pervasiveness of others' authority over me to instruct me what morality requires. If I thought I had a moral obligation in this matter, then as a Member of the Public I would acknowledge those reasons; even if the duty could not be justified to others, I would still be apt to act on it as a personal norm (i.e., not part of social morality) that defines my own first-person understanding of decent action. In the difficult case on which we are focusing, someone says to me that I must justify to her that I am not under a duty, where I can see no duty. And I ask, "whence did she receive this standing to so direct me?" Taking the role of sovereign she claims authority to grant me moral permissions over my actions: "apply to me, and I can grant you a moral permission to act as you see fit based on my view of morality." As a free and equal Member of the Public I must refuse to acknowledge her first-person aspirations to sovereign standing to so interpret morality and so direct my actions. When no claims to interpersonal moral authority can be justified, we are, of necessity, left with moral no-authority – blameless liberty.

16.3 THE SOCIALLY ELIGIBLE SET

(a) Kantian Legislation and the Pareto Rule
In his evaluation of a proposed rule, then, Alf (a Member of the Public), on the basis of his evaluative standards, may deny

---

[100] Wall, "On Justificatory Liberalism," pp. 129ff.
[101] This is the view that Susan Wolf disputes and which Scheffler endorses. See her "Moral Saints," p. 436.

authority to some proposed moral rules, either because as he
understands it, it fails to conform to the constraints on moral rules,
or on the grounds of the costs of moralization. We can say that all
proposals that are so rejected are *ineligible* in Alf's ranking. They are
ineligible because he cannot accept claims to moral authority based
on such rules. It follows that for Alf {blameless liberty R^+ such a
rule}. That is, he does not have reason to endorse this rule over no
moral authority at all. This is not to say that he rejects the rule as,
say, a useful social convention or as a coordination device: *Alf does
not necessarily reject following it, but be does refuse to accord it authority
over him or internalize it as a rule of morality.* Now a rule that is in any
Member of the Public's ineligible set is a socially ineligible rule.
Any rule that is in the ineligible set of any Member of the Public is
such that at least one free and equal person does not have reason to
endorse the authority of its claims. The socially eligible set, then,
consists in all those proposals that are unanimously ranked by all
Members of the Public as strictly preferred to blameless liberty –
that is, rules that all have reasons to endorse as authoritative. We
thus must eliminate as a possible moral rule among "citizens of the
realm of ends" any proposed moral rule that is in the ineligible set
of any Member of the Public. Only rules that everyone holds are
better than no moral authority are in the socially eligible set. For us
to appeal to a moral rule outside the socially eligible set in our
relations with the rejecter would be insisting on standards of judgment that, as a free moral person, the rejecter cannot accept as legitimate: she cannot will them to be universal laws regulating all
Members of the Public. One thing we might mean by the inability
to will a law – or its rational rejectability – is that we cannot see it as
superior to a blameless liberty.

We can further reduce the socially eligible set by (again) invoking the Pareto rule. If all Members of the Public prefer x to y, then
we can say that the Public prefers x to y.[102] If y is in this way Pareto-
dominated by x – if everyone prefers x to y – we can eliminate y on
the grounds that it is a nonoptimal choice. If everyone holds that x
is better than y, then the morality should be x rather than y. Acting

---

[102] The initial identification of the socially eligible set can be understood as itself an
application of the Pareto Rule: x is in the socially eligible set if for all Members of
the Public {x P a blameless liberty}. See section 16.3*b*.

on y would manifest a sort of collective irrationality: even though everyone sees it as inferior to x, we follow it anyway. This allows us to identify a socially *optimal eligible* set of moral rules: no proposed rule in the set is ineligible in anyone's ranking, nor is it dominated by any other member of the set. Now there are three possibilities: (*i*) the socially optimal eligible set (and, so the eligible set) is null; (*ii*) it is a singleton; or (*iii*) it comprises a maximal set with no optimal (best) element.

Re (*i*): sometimes the optimal set certainly will be null, in which case no moral rule on this matter is publicly justified. Some may think that it will always be null: some Members of the Public will deem every proposal ineligible because in *their* eyes it fails to meet the constraints on moral rules or its costs exceed the benefits for *them*. I shall argue in the next chapter that in relation to many rules (say, concerning the most basic matters), the socially optimal eligible set will not be null. Social morality is fundamental to social life, and each person has strong commitment to moral practices sustaining her moral emotions and, indeed, her own moral dignity, as well as protecting her basic good. The proposals all seek to conform to the specified constraints, including being goodwilled attempts to meet the reversibility and weak common good requirements. As we have seen, this does not ensure that they will do so in the eyes of all, but we should not imagine that Members of the Public are sorting through a variety of palpably self-interested bargaining ploys. Denying moral authority to basic moral rules is a grave matter indeed. Members of the Public would do so only when confronted by rules that, in their view, palpably fail to adequately perform their tasks. Conventional Members of the Public are apt to endorse moral regulation of areas of social life that are presently governed by rules; post-conventional thinkers will be more critical but will also be more reflective about why social morality is necessary on basic matters of social life and the good of persons.

Re (*ii*): Kant, Hare, and Rawls all believed that if we set up the constraints on moral legislation properly, the optimal eligible set will be a singleton. Only one rule can meet the constraints on right, properly understood. However, in our model, reasonable pluralism is taken seriously: Members of the Public are applying their interpretations of the test on the basis of different evaluative standards and beliefs. There is no reason to suppose that, except at a very abstract level (§17), the results of the application of the same tests, by different Members of the Public, on the basis of different evaluative standards, will yield the same answer. As we saw, having diverse evaluative standards, they will rank the proposals differently on the basis of these standards. There is no reason to suppose that, out of all this diversity, Members of the Public will converge on the same proposal.

Re (*iii*): this leaves us with a maximal set of more than one proposal without an optimal element. After we have seen that the set will not be null, this is the only plausible outcome. In this sense, the outcome is indeterminate: from the perspective of Members of the Public there will be a large socially maximal set, with no option socially better than any other, but all of which are better than proposals outside the optimal eligible set.

Invoking, as we have done, the Pareto Principle may strike some as suspicious in a Kantian-inspired analysis, as it is often associated with forms of welfarism and ordinalist utilitarianism. However, as Rawls recognized in "Justice as Fairness," the Pareto Principle is ideally suited to a Kantian deliberative model because it approves only of alternatives upon which there is rational consensus, with this being understood in terms of pairwise consensus. Kantian legislation is simply a theory of moral legislation by rational consensus. The drawback of the Pareto Principle is not that it is in any way in tension with Kantianism or a public reason justification, but that it is typically indeterminate: it is a strict test for rational consensus, and so it is not apt to identify a single best option among a diverse public. Thus Rawls' first version of his social contract argument, which relied on the Pareto Principle, was seen by both his critics, and Rawls himself, as indeterminate insofar as it could not select a uniquely best option.[103] If we wish to generate a collective moral deliberation situation with a determinate choice, we must specify the motivations and information sets of the parties

---

[103] See Rawls, "Distributive Justice," p. 136. The indeterminacy of the Pareto Principle in Rawls' first formulation of his contract is stressed by Robert Paul Wolff, *Understanding Rawls*, p. 51. On the indeterminacy of the principle, see Russell Hardin, *Indeterminacy and Society,* chap. 4.

in a detailed way so that they all reason the same and will choose the same point on the Pareto frontier (the strongest version of the Shared Reasons Requirement, along with an assumption about identical information sets such that each not only shares the same indifference map but also agrees where to place each rule on it), would do the trick [§14.4c]). Thus the path that led to *A Theory of Justice*: its strengths and weakness are well known. Although Rawls began by posing a problem of collective choice, ultimately, as he tells us, the problem is reduced to the reasoning of a single person. If we exclude "knowledge of those contingencies which set men apart . . . ," then since "everyone is equally rational and similarly situated, each is convinced by the same arguments."[104] Now I do not maintain that this exercise never has value: as we shall see in section 17, it can help to imagine abstracted agents who agree on some matter of great importance. On the other hand, we shall also see that under conditions of evaluative pluralism, such a mental experiment has far weaker implications for public justification than many have hoped.

(b) A Preliminary Assessment: The Benefits of a Modest Model

At this point the reader may be disappointed: we have employed a fairly detailed model, only to arrive at the conclusion that there is no clear answer to our fundamental question of what morality is publicly justified. A lot of work for a little result, it might be thought. This understandable reaction both underestimates the importance of what we have already discovered and the enlightening results that we shall be able to generate in the next few chapters. At this juncture, three conclusions should be stressed.

First, if our current rule is not in the socially eligible set, it fails to be publicly justified in a strong sense, and if it is not in the socially optimal eligible set, Members of the Public do not have, let us say for now, fully sufficient reasons to endorse it (I return to this issue in Chapter VII). Despite the lack of determinateness of the model, we have a clearer idea of what it means for a rule to fail to be publicly justified. This is no mean result.

---

[104] Rawls, *A Theory of Justice*, pp. 17, 120.

Second, the modesty of our results thus far follows from the greater realism of the model compared to versions of contractualism with which we are acquainted. To be sure, it idealizes, but this idealization is rooted in real concerns and competencies, and importantly it places at center stage the fundamental problem that we disagree about the relevant importance of the standards for evaluating moral rules. Because the model is not, as it were, formulated with the aim of getting a determinate result, we are in a position to distinguish clearly derivable results from problems yet to be resolved.

And this is because, *third*, the principles that we have employed to reduce the size of the choice set are as uncontroversial as possible. Given that public justification requires the endorsement of all Members of the Public, we have employed only criteria that directly follow from our shared concept of morality and the Deliberative Principle of Public Justification. In this regard it is worth pointing out that the decision rule that we have employed comes as close as possible to being a counterexample to Arrow's theorem. As is well known, Arrow showed that, given a social choice over three or more options (with two or more people choosing), there is no procedure for producing a social ranking of the options that (*i*) is guaranteed to produce a complete and transitive social ordering and (*ii*) meets a set of reasonable conditions: universal domain, monotonicity, nonimposition, Pareto optimality, independence of irrelevant alternatives, and nondictatorship.[105] The

---

[105] This is one statement of the conditions; they can be reduced. Some rough definitions: (1) *Universal Domain*: There is a transitive social ordering for every possible set of individual preference profiles; (2) *Monotonicity*: An individual's changing her evaluation from {y is better than x} to {x is better than y} cannot itself make x socially less preferred than y; (3) *Nonimposition*: The social ordering is always a function of individual orderings; (4) *Pareto optimality*: If everyone prefers x over y, the social ordering ranks x over y; (5) *Independence of Irrelevant Alternatives*: The social preference between x and y must depend only on individuals' preferences between x and y and cannot be affected by the presence or absence of some third alternative, z; (6) *Nondictatorship*: There is no person whose individual ordering over every pair of options is decisive for the social ordering. For a statement of the formal proof, see my *On Philosophy, Politics, and Economics*, pp. 154–64, which follows Sen, *Collective Choice and Social Welfare*, chap. 3*. For a different version, see Dennis Mueller, *Public Choice III*, 582–6, who follows William Vickery's formulation. Wulf Gaertner goes through several versions of the proof, including

rule that we have employed in identifying the socially optimal eligible set is equivalent to what Sen has called the Pareto-extension rule, according to which xR^+y if and only if y is not Pareto-superior to x.[106] That is, x is not worse than y if and only if y is not preferred by everyone to x. Clearly, we have employed this rule in our reduction of the socially eligible set; all those options that are Pareto-superior to some members of the eligible set were determined to be socially preferred to those (nonoptimal) elements; we were left with the members of the optimal eligible set, for all pairs $\{x,y\}$ of which it is true that xR^+y and yR^+x. The Public is thus indifferent between all members of the socially optimal eligible set; they prefer any member of the optimal eligible set to all members of the non-optimal eligible set. We can now see that the eligible set itself is defined in terms of a Pareto rule: for every member of the eligible set, everyone prefers it to no moral authority at all.

Interestingly, Sen has shown that the Pareto-extension rule meets all of Arrow's conditions except transitivity, for which (as we saw in §16.1*a*) it substitutes quasi-transitivity (transitivity of strict preference but not of indifference).[107] Thus, as Sen points out, by adopting quasi-transitivity we turn Arrow's impossibility theorem into a possibility result: all the conditions are now met. This is worth stressing: it is important that our Pareto procedure not only correctly models Kantian legislation but it also meets all of Arrow's conditions while generating a quasi-transitive social ordering. In a literature that has spawned a variety of highly controversial deliberative and choice models, this is a refreshing result.

(c) The Absence of a Compelling More Determinate Method

The Pareto-extension rule generates a lot of indifference – which is again just to say that it is indeterminate, identifying in our case a large maximal set. Traditionally social contract theory has sought to reduce the eligible social contracts to a single option. There, is however, no method for reducing the socially optimal eligible set to a singleton that is not highly controversial. An implication of

Blackorby, Donaldson, and Weymark's graphical formulation, in *A Primer in Social Choice Theory*, chap. 2.
[106] Sen, "Maximization and the Act of Choice," p. 185.
[107] Sen, *Collective Choice and Social Welfare*, pp. 48–9.

Arrow's theorem is that there is no aggregation system for generating a social ranking of options that dominates the alternatives in the sense that it is best on all criteria for a good choice procedure: all possible procedures violate some reasonable condition.[108] Members of the Public who disagree in their rankings of Arrow's conditions (nondictatorship, nonimposition, weak monotonicity, etc.) will thus disagree in their ranking of different choice procedures. Assuming that there are six conditions, there are 720 different orderings. Alf's ranking of possible aggregation procedures will depend on his ranking of the importance of the conditions. Although Arrow's theorem is sometimes radically interpreted as showing that there is no fair or coherent system of aggregation, we need make no such radical claim. The crucial point is that there will not be consensus on which system is best since Members of the Public will disagree about the relative importance of the conditions, and no system satisfies all.

For example according to the Borda method of aggregation a proposal's score is determined by summing up its ranks; for each first-placed ranking it receives one point; for each second, two, and so on. The option with the lowest point total wins. Borda cannot yield a cycle (an intransitive result, according to which (xPy) & (yPz) & (zPx)), but can violate the independence condition: even if no one changes her preference between $\{x,y\}$, under Borda the social preference can sometimes be xPy, and other times yPx, depending on whether a third option is being considered. Those who think that it is more important to avoid intransitive results and who are not worried about the arbitrariness involved in violating the independence of irrelevant alternatives are thus apt to rank Borda highly. In contrast, others think Borda's violation of independence shows that it is arbitrary (the social preference between x and y depends on the absence or presence of third option, z); if they are not as worried about the possibility of cycles of social preference will prefer Condorcet voting, according to which the social preference between $\{x,y,z\}$ is determined by a series of pairwise

---

[108] Strictly, Arrow's theorem only applies to procedures that seek to devise a social ranking of the option. However, procedures that simply seek to choose one element from the set (a choice rule, rather than a ranking function) are subject to similar problems. See my *On Philosophy, Politics, and Economics*, pp. 164–71.

votes (i.e., to order {*x,y,z*} we take pairwise majority votes between {*x,y*}, {*x,z*}, {*y,z*}). Condorcet voting is often considered the most majoritarian way to choose among three or more alternatives. Another condition that many find compelling is (weak) monotonicity: it should never be the case that voting *for x* can lead to *x*'s defeat. (It should never be the case that Alf can truly say, "If only I hadn't voted for *x*, it would have won!") The single-transferable vote system, employed in elections to Australia's House of Representatives, violates this condition. Those who think this is a basic requirement of rational aggregation will place such procedures low in their ranking.[109]

The important point here is that since no preference aggregation procedure X even weakly dominates all the others,[110] evaluative diversity will again manifest itself, and Members of the Public will arrive at different orderings of the possible selection procedures. Now this result, which follows from Arrow's theorem, would seem to mean that we have no way to employ a procedure to select from the optimal eligible set, because no procedure can itself be publicly justified as optimal. There is no uncontroversial way to provide a determinate commensuration of our unconstrained diverse rankings by developing an aggregation method that rationally and fairly transforms individual rankings into a publicly justified social ranking.[111] There are a number of such functions, but all are flawed, and there is no reason to suppose that rational and reflective people will converge on one.

There is a debate as to how much this matters in actual democratic politics. We know that equally reasonable, flawed, procedures *can* produce different results; the debate concerns how often they do so in real politics.[112] But the certain knowledge that

[109] In William Riker's eyes, "Theoretically . . . one should, on technical grounds, reject all nonmonotonic systems, though practically compromise may be appropriate." *Liberalism against Populism*, p. 51. Riker provides a still-excellent explanation of the points made in this paragraph. See *Liberalism against Populism*, chaps. 4 and 5.

[110] X weakly dominates Y if it always does at least as well as Y at meeting each condition and sometimes does better.

[111] This is one of D'Agostino's main points in *Incommensurability and Commensuration*.

[112] Compare William Riker, *Liberalism against Populism*, chap. 1 and see Gerry Mackie, *Democracy Defended*.

(*a*) no system dominates the others in terms of meeting all the rational criteria for systems of aggregation and (*b*) that different systems *can* produce different results is sufficient for us to conclude that Members of the Public could not unanimously prefer any alternative to the Pareto-extension rule that would reduce the degree of indeterminacy. Only if all possible reasonable procedures were guaranteed to arrive at the same result could Members of the Public put aside their disagreements about the virtues of different aggregation methods. From the perspective of the theory of rational aggregation, the problem as to what aggregation method to employ is indeterminate. And I have only touched on the diversity of possible "social welfare functions" – ways of taking individual utility and generating a social welfare function.[113]

Bargaining theory offers an alternative way of selecting from the eligible set, but it is even more controversial.[114] The crux of bargaining theory is that there is some procedure that takes the utility functions of the parties as inputs and generates some rational compromise solution. In *Morals by Agreement* David Gauthier relied on the principle of minimax relative concession drawn from the Kali–Smorodinsky bargaining solution,[115] which essentially seeks to split the difference between the claims of individuals. We compute each party's minimal claim (the least she would take rather than simply walking away from the agreement), her maximal claim (the most she could get consistent with the other party getting his minimal claim), and then for any possible agreement α, compute the ratios between what a party gets under α and her maximal claim: the aim is to select the agreement that minimizes the relative concession made by the party who conceded the most. Thus if α is selected by the minimax relative concession rule, we can say to the party who had the greatest relative concession under α "Yes, you made the greatest concession under α, but for all alterative agreements there was someone who would have made an even larger concession." As with aggregation methods, bargaining theory is controversial insofar as there are multiple bargaining theories that give different solutions. Most decision theorists today accept the

---

[113] See Dennis Mueller, *Public Choice III*, chap. 23.
[114] See further Philip Pettit, *The Common Mind*, pp. 291ff.
[115] I also relied on it in my *Value and Justification*, pp. 346ff, 443ff.

Nash bargaining solution, though it has some counterintuitive consequences.[116] R. B. Braithwaite, in his application of game theory for moral philosophers, also advanced a bargaining solution.[117] More fundamentally, there is good reason to conclude that bargaining theory is itself inherently indeterminate.[118] Rawls objected on other grounds. In "Justice as Fairness" Rawls rejected formal bargaining theory such as that proposed by Braithwaite on the grounds that threat advantage is relevant to the final bargain, and "To each according to his threat advantage is hardly a principle of fairness."[119] Thus, while Rawls clearly saw the choice problem as one that involved a sort of bargaining or compromise, he insisted that formal game theoretic approaches were inappropriate.[120]

The deeper worry, though, is whether compromise is really at the heart of public justification.[121] On the one hand, it may seem obvious that reasonable parties seeking to live together must exercise the virtue of meeting others halfway (i.e., splitting the difference).[122] And if we are negotiating over, say, the common fruits of joint labor in which we cannot adequately track individual contributions, making a "reasonable" claim on the output will involve some tendency to concede to others their share, and this manifests a tendency to compromise. Indeed, when Rawls and Scanlon explain their core concept of a "reasonable" person, they are apt to use as a quintessential example of *un*reasonable behavior hard bargaining, in which one employs a superior bargaining situation so that one does not show a disposition to compromise.[123] However, when we take a broader view and understand public justification as deliberation about whether one's evaluative standards endorse a rule, the claim that the heart of the endeavor is about compromise looks dubious. To say that public justification involves splitting the difference between what a religious person believes is justified and

---

[116] Although Binmore endorses Nash's solution, he acknowledges that the case for it is "not entirely overwhelming." Binmore also nicely brings out how it can depart from other solutions. *Natural Justice*, chap. 2.

[117] For a nice account of the contrast, see Brian Barry's *Theories of Justice*, chap. 1.

[118] See Robert Sugden, "Contractarianism and Norms."

[119] Rawls, "Justice as Fairness," p. 58n.

[120] Ibid., p. 57.

[121] As I mistakenly thought in *Value and Justification*, pp. 343ff.

[122] Rawls, *Political Liberalism*, p. 253.

[123] Ibid, p. 48; Scanlon, *What We Owe Each Other*, p. 192.

what an ardent secularist holds to be supposes that living according to one's evaluative standards is like claiming a share of a common product, to be negotiated away. I hasten to add that this does not mean that when living under common rules a "reasonable" person will insist that the rules must be best from his evaluative viewpoint; we know that living with others involves accommodation to the fact that they have different standards, and we may have to accept that the justified rule is not the one we would have chosen if we were dictator. Chapter VII shows how such accommodation is consistent with our status as free and equal moral persons and does not at all involve a fundamental disposition to compromise. But for now the crucial point is that while such accommodation to the reality of pluralism is necessary, this does not show that public justification is centrally about the correct compromise concerning how much the moral rules we live under reflect our basic normative convictions, as if they were pots of money to be divided up, or negotiation aims to be haggled over.

CONCLUSION

In this chapter I have presented a Deliberative Model of public justification. The aim of the Deliberative Model is to translate a difficult justificatory problem into a more tractable deliberative one, in which we can identify the core features of the justificatory problem and provide a more disciplined framework for thinking about public justification. In thinking about the model, two sets of contrasts must be kept clearly in mind. First, we must always take care to locate the philosophical perspective of "you and me." We are engaging in a highly reflective endeavor: we wish to know what would be required for a moral rule to be justified, and in particular, whether the moral rules of our society are justified. In thinking this through we may appeal to specialized ideas such as theories of rationality and social choice theory. Our aim is to model the second perspective – normal and (more sophisticated) moral agents – to see what reasons they can be said to have, and how, given the reasons they have, a moral rule may be publicly justified. In this model we distinguish our second pair of perspectives – that of Member of the Public as proposer and as endorser. As a proposer we attribute a Member of the Public with the ability to grasp, and conform to, the constraints on moral rules, including the common good and reversibility constraints. To be sure, many normal agents do not seek to perform the role of moral legislator, and there is no reason a publicly justified morality must insist that each does so (here, then, we depart from Kant). But we must allow that a wide variety of rules are considered, for many moral agents – especially those post-conventional reasoners occupying chairs of philosophy – will advance their proposals. Members of the Public all, though, occupy the role of evaluators of proposals insofar as each has reasons to endorse or reject them. The model makes this idea of endorsability more tractable by reducing it to pairwise comparisons: "is x to be endorsed or rejected in favor of y?" Each also must at some point make the judgment that she does not have sufficient reason to accord some rule z, moral authority over her. This is not an especially refined capacity restricted to philosophical reflection: when normal agents reject existing rules as mere taboos, superstitions, or the results of oppressive tradition they are, in effect, doing this. If our concern is to justify moral authority, we must suppose at some point that there is insufficient reason for according some rule (and demands based on it) authority. Such a rule manifestly fails the test of public justification. The set of rules that all Members of the Public have some reason to accept as authoritative yields what I have called a socially eligible set. We then employed our Pareto-extension rule to identify a socially optimal eligible set.

All this has been regrettably formal and abstract. It is time to turn to more substantive matters.

VI

The Rights of the Moderns

First ask yourself, Gentlemen, what an Englishman, a Frenchman, and a citizen of the United States of America understand today by the word "liberty."

For each of them it is the right to be subjected only to the laws, and to be neither arrested, detained, put to death or maltreated in any way by the arbitrary will of one or more individuals. It is the right of everyone to express their opinion, choose a profession and practice it, to dispose of property, and even to abuse it; to come and go without permission, and without having to account for their motives or undertakings. It is everyone's right to associate with other individuals, whether to discuss their interests, or to profess the religion which they and their associates prefer, or even simply to occupy their days or hours in a way which is most compatible with their inclinations or whims. Finally, it is everyone's right to exercise some influence on the administration of government, either by electing all or particular officials, or through representations, petitions, demands to which authorities are more or less required to pay heed.

Benjamin Constant, "The Liberty of the Ancients Compared
with that of the Moderns"

The previous chapter introduced a deliberative model, which took seriously the cognitive limits of Members of the Public and, especially their diverse bases for evaluating proposed moral rules. The result, we saw, was that when a rule is justified, we will typically be left with what Sen calls a large "maximal set": everything in the set is preferred to other proposals, but the Public, as a group, is indifferent among the members of the set. There is compelling reason to choose from within the maximal set but, without introducing controversial choice mechanisms, there seems no way to settle on a single option.

This chapter explores two partial solutions to the problem of indeterminacy, both concerning the idea of individual rights – the rights that Constant called the "liberty of the moderns." These solutions are "partial" because they serve only to narrow the maximal set over core questions of social morality; we have a much better idea of the contours of the set, but they still do not provide a way to identify one option. That is the task of the next chapter.

17 Arguments from Abstraction and the Claims of Agency

17.1 A DOUBLE ABSTRACTION STRATEGY

Recall the Kantian–Rawlsian two-step procedure discussed in section 3.1. Faced with a diversity of ends and values, we might seek to abstract away from this diversity to discover some common basis for evaluation of moral rules. We might bracket our disagreements and identify some shared perspective, which provides the grounds for shared reasoning. As Rawls points out, our aim would be to exclude from the deliberation "contingencies which set men at odds."[1] The success of an argument from abstraction depends on three key claims.

(*i*) Most obviously there must be a shared perspective that identifies a common basis of evaluation. The aim is to show that once we abstract to a certain shared perspective, we share pretty much identical evaluative sets (§14.4*c*).

(*ii*) This perspective must identify especially important shared evaluative standards; it will be of little avail to identify a shared perspective that does not capture really important evaluative standards. We must, as Rawls says, "give very great and normally

---

[1] Rawls, *A Theory of Justice*, p. 17.

overriding weight" to evaluative standards of the shared stand-point.[2]

(*iii*) Related to this point, it must be the case that the deliberative conclusions are not overturned as the process of abstraction is undone and Members of the Public are again understood to be guided by their full set of evaluative standards. What was simply "freestanding" must, if it is to be fully justified, serve as a "module" that fits into each free and equal rational moral person's set of evaluative criteria. In the end, to publicly justify must be to justify in terms of all the relevant evaluative standards. We wish to structure common moral life on terms that everyone – considering all that she holds to be important and relevant – has sufficient reason to endorse.

It is, I think, a serious mistake to think that Rawls' basic notion of justification changed from *A Theory of Justice* to *Political Liberalism*, replacing the focus on shared reasoning in the original position with justification as "overlapping consensus" – that all reasonable evaluative systems overlap on the basic liberal principles. Rather, the core idea throughout his work is the argument from abstraction in the original position,[3] but Rawls increasingly worried that as the abstraction is undone and people come to know their comprehensive conceptions of value, their devotion to the principles might be "overridden" (§3.2). Full knowledge of evaluative standards may change what is validated from the perspectives of citizens. Hence Rawls' claim that under "full" justification the normative importance of the pro tanto argument from abstraction is preserved (i.e., condition iii is met). Let us, then, call this third requirement the *stability of abstract justification under full justification*. This requirement is immensely important: unless the conclusion of the argument from abstraction can be affirmed in light of a rational and reflective free and equal moral person's full set of evaluative criteria, the abstract justification will be defeated by these other elements of her evaluative set. A theory that is grounded on the importance of evaluative pluralism can bracket some disagreements as a device within the theory to help us see where agreement

---

[2] Rawls, *Political Liberalism*, p. 241.
[3] See here D'Agostino, *Incommensurability and Commensuration*, p. 100.

is possible and progress might be made, but ultimately this agreement only provides Members of the Public with sufficient reasons to endorse a proposed rule if, given all their relevant evaluative standards, it is to be endorsed.

A second abstraction characteristic of Rawls' original position is that we focus on the justification of abstract principles rather than rules. I argued in section 14.3 that principles are too vague and too subject to interpretive controversy to provide an effective framework for cooperation; they are not the ultimate aim of public justification. However, they can help us delimit our justificatory problem: if Members of the Public could agree on some abstract principles, and if these were stable under full justification, they would at least have narrowed their problem to the justification of rules that are adequate interpretations of the already justified principles.

17.2 THE PERSPECTIVE OF AGENCY

In a world in which the reasonable pluralism of evaluative standards is accepted as a fact of life, an important and basic part of our self-conception is our status as agents. This need not be the case in all social orders. In more homogeneous orders, basic to everyone's conception may be that of being a Roman Catholic; or in traditionally differentiated but rigid orders one's self-conception may be largely defined by one's socially endorsed role – a serf, a cobbler, a monk, or a lord of the manor. In pluralistic orders, in which identities and roles are constantly challenged and open to revision, even those who endorse tradition cannot help but see this as a choice of theirs – an exercise of their agency. We employ roles not as an alternative to agency but as a way to express and manage our presentation to others.[4] The perspective of agency forces itself on us, and we are unable not to see ourselves as agents, whose actions are properly determined by our own deliberations. To be an agent is to be what Stanley Benn calls a "natural person":

---

[4] See Erving Goffman, *The Presentation of Self in Everyday Life*.

The use of expressions such as "decision making," "making a choice," "forming an intention," suggest a kind of creativity in personal causation, in which the relation between agent and the processes initiated by his decision is more like that between a potter and his pot or an architect and his plan than like the relation between a skidding car and the resulting accident. . . .

. . . It is this consciousness of one's own thought as the prolegomenon to intended action that underlies a person's conviction that he makes decisions – that, unlike skids or lightning strikes, they do not just happen to him.[5]

Agency is so basic to our understanding of the self that, as Benn indicates by the term "natural personality," we have a hard time seeing non-agents as persons: we describe those without a sense of their own agency as having personality disorders. R. D. Lang depicted schizoid personalities as those who understood their activity and choices as other-controlled, and so the "true self" was detached from its own life, its activities directed by a stereotyped script that was determined by others.[6] Clifford Geertz's description of the traditional Balinese shows how alien non-agent persons are to us. At least according to Geertz, the traditional Balinese conceive of themselves not as agents making choices but as social actors playing well-defined, socially constructed parts. "Balinese conceptions of personhood," concludes Geertz, "are – in our terms anyway – depersonalizing."[7]

We should not infer from this that we are all therefore committed to an ideal of "personal autonomy" in which we engage in "rational scrutiny of and deliberation about our projects and goals."[8] An agent may be guided by superstitious beliefs, be totally unreflective about his commitments, have conflicting desires and inconsistent beliefs, or live according to traditional rules simply because he has been brought up to. All these traits are consistent with being an agent – one who sees his actions as following from

---

[5] Benn, *A Theory of Freedom*, p. 91.
[6] See Laing, *The Divided Self*, chap. 6.
[7] Geertz, "Person, Time and Conduct in Bali," p. 390.
[8] Emily Gill, *Becoming Free: Autonomy and Diversity in a Liberal Polity*, p. 23.

his own deliberations (based, to be sure, on unreflective, traditional, or superstitious considerations).

Steven Wall advances a "perfectionist" conception of "personal autonomy" according to which it is an "ideal of people charting their own course through life, fashioning their character by self-consciously choosing projects and taking up commitments from a wide range of eligible alternatives, and making something out of their lives according to their own understanding of what is valuable and worth doing."[9] In a similar vein, Joseph Raz maintains that "[t]he autonomous person is one who makes his own life," while Robert Young tells us that "[t]he fundamental idea in autonomy is that of authoring one's own world."[10] Although these formulations are by no means identical, all identify autonomy with being the author of one's life. An autonomous life is chosen by the agent rather than, say, dictated by tradition; most articulations of this ideal require a wide range of choices through which "one makes something" out of one's life.

Personal autonomy as self-authorship is a controversial ideal that is not shared by all Members of the Public. The self-authorship metaphor points to an aesthetic view of life in which one's life is a creation and the agent the artist. The metaphor is not misleading; such conceptions of autonomy are offered by "perfectionist liberals."[11] The very idea of perfection indicates a quasi-artistic attitude toward one's life, as a work to be perfected. It hardly seems that all normal moral persons are committed to such a view. Consider one whose goals are entirely focused on bringing about states of affairs that do not include the perfection of human beings, but say, the protection of nature or advancing scientific discovery. The latter may involve the perfection of human nature (the former may well call for thwarting it), but the point is that these goals are not about

---

[9] Wall, *Liberalism, Perfectionism and Restraint*, p. 203. Cf. Gerald Dworkin: "What makes an individual the particular person he is is his life-plan, his projects. In pursuing autonomy, one shapes one's life, one constructs its meaning. The autonomous person gives meaning to his life." *The Theory and Practice of Autonomy*, p. 31.

[10] Raz, *The Morality of Freedom*, p. 375; Robert Young, *Personal Autonomy: Beyond Negative and Positive Liberty*, p. 19.

[11] Raz and Wall, for example.

human nature and its excellences; they concern the production of certain states of affairs that do not make necessary reference to the flourishing of humans.[12] If these states of affairs can be brought about without perfecting human nature, or without a life of self-authorship, that in no way detracts from their value. Agents pursuing such states of affairs are not self-focused; they do not take up an attitude of creative authorship to their lives but possess practical reasons to investigate and change the world in a variety of ways. As such, they are not committed to personal autonomy as self-authorship or perfectionism.

To be sure, the perfectionist can argue that they should be: he can insist that there is a reason for them to care, and they should see it. At the appropriate level of idealization, however, all Members of the Public do not have reasons to pursue this ideal. Members of the Public see themselves as committed to religious and other doctrines that can defeat the claims of such perfectionist autonomy. An environmentalist or scientist is committed to seeing himself as an agent with reasons to act, so he must conceive of himself as an agent; many, though, do not also conceive of themselves as authors or creators of their own lives, seeking to make something out of them through their chosen modes of self-authorship. A self-directed person may not be one who actively affirms a way of life. Agents may fall well short of fully integrated personalities.[13] They may possess nothing so grand as a conception of the good life, much less an examined life: the much-derided beer drinking[14] football fan whose week is, unreflectively, centered around Sunday's Buffalo Bills game is an agent.

Our Buffalo Bills fan alerts us to the fact that not all of us place our status as agents at the core of our self-understanding. For many, that one is a child of Christ may be more fundamental; for others, that one is a part of an ecosystem. But a conception of ourselves as agents is a fundamental aspect of our self-

[12] On the tension between this conception of autonomy and environmental ethics, see my "Respect for Persons and Environmental Values."
[13] Benn, *A Theory of Freedom*, chap. 10.
[14] The implication, perhaps obvious to most academics, is that a wine-drinking fan would achieve an altogether higher level of autonomy.

understanding, and there is no aspect of our identities that is as widely shared and as deeply embedded in who we are.

17.3 FREEDOM AND AGENCY

(a) The Presumption in Favor of Liberty
Suppose, then, that Members of the Public abstract to evaluate proposals simply from the perspective of agency. They deliberate only on the basis of the importance of being an agent – someone who deliberates, makes choices, and whose actions normally are based on those choices. Now this last point is important. An agent is one who understands her action as based on her choices: to choose is not simply an intellectual, but a practical, exercise. As Benn put it (§17.2), an agent is one who sees "one's own thought as the prolegomenon to intended action that underlies a person's conviction that he makes decisions – that, unlike skids or lightning strikes, they do not just happen to him." Further, he is aware of himself as a causal force in the sense that it is his decisions that lie behind his actions. Benn argues that agents will endorse a Principle of Non-interference, or as I shall say:

> *The Presumption in Favor of Liberty*: (1) agents are under no standing moral obligation (in social morality) to justify their choices to others; (2) it is wrong to exercise one's liberty so as to interfere with, block, or thwart the agency of another without justification.[15]

Of course this is, like all principles, vague; crucial ideas such as interfering, blocking, or thwarting agency are subject to interpretive controversy. However, at this point the aim of Members of the Public is not to arrive at moral rules but principles of morality that delimit the range of disagreement and provide the basis for more fine-grained justification.

Now it seems clear that as agents we have a fundamental interest in (1). If I have a moral obligation, we have seen, what I do is the business of others (§11.2). It is not enough to satisfy myself that I have done what I should; others can demand my compliance with

---

[15] Benn, *A Theory of Freedom*, pp. 87–90, chap. 7.

the obligation as they understand it. If we have a standing moral obligation to justify our choices to others – a standing obligation to show that they conform to a code or a script – we would be confronted with precisely the "depersonalized" understanding of the person that Geertz attributes to the Balinese: the self is always masked by the requirements of the code or the script. As an agent, with my own purposes and values which I know, given evaluative pluralism, cannot be endorsed by public reason, I know that I could not justify my action to others on the grounds on which I am acting – that this act serves God's will or advances human perfection. I would have to appeal to some public reason that permits me to act on my own aims and purposes. I must, as it were, apply for public permission to act on my ends. There is no doctrine so bizarre and unappealing that philosophers have not defended it, and the denial of clause (1) is no exception. According to the straightforward act utilitarian, in every action of one's life, one should perform that action that maximizes aggregate utility. Understood as a code of social morality, this means that it is always everyone's business whether one does so. And that you have decided that ϕ is the act that does so has no privileged status; if another is a better calculator of utility and knows your options, in principle her deliberation is the one that should determine your action. One only has permission to act on one's own ends if doing so is the best way (not necessarily determined by you) to maximize aggregate utility – in which case it becomes, like all action, a duty. Every act of one's existence is, in principle, determined by a moral duty with a determinate imperative.

Clause (2) looks more problematic – at least I have found that a number of critics have denied it. Some dispute it on the grounds that "there is no standing duty to justify morally relevant actions."[16] We might interpret this objection in four ways.

(1) If Alf can show that his ϕ-ing, which blocks Betty's agency, is a morally required or permitted action, Alf is under no burden to show that ϕ-ing is justified;

---

[16] Rainer Forst, "Political Liberty: Integrating Five Conceptions of Autonomy," p. 240.

(2) If Alf's ϕ-ing is a morally required or permitted action, there need not be a justification for his ϕ-ing;

(3) If Alf's ϕ-ing is a morally required or permitted action, he need not *have* (as accessible) a justification for ϕ-ing;

(4) If Alf's ϕ-ing is a morally required or permitted action, he need not show Betty he has a justification for ϕ-ing.

Interpretation (1) is not a challenge to the presumption: to show that one has a morally relevant ground for interference simply is to justify one's action, so this does not dispute the presumption. This is important: showing that something is required by social morality simply is showing that one has a public justification for doing it. Neither does interpretation (2) dispute the presumption. If ϕ is required by social morality, then there is, in principle, a justification for ϕ – namely, that it is morally required. Of course its status as morally required must be accessible to Members of the Public. If (2) is interpreted as implying that the morality of an act need not be verified by public reason, then of course it must be rejected, for the reasons I have presented in Chapters IV and V. But this dispute is not about the Presumption in Favor of Liberty but the very relation of social morality and public reason. This point should be stressed. Many of those who dispute the Presumption of Liberty do so on the grounds of a devotion to a first-person perspective on morality (§12.4), according to which if Alf thinks ϕ is morally required he should go ahead and do it whether or not it can be justified to Betty.[17] But, of course, we have seen that unless the relevant rule can be justified to Betty it cannot be part of a moral practice among free and equal persons. Interpretation (3), on the account presented here, is contradictory: if there is a public justification for the status of an act as moral, this justification must be accessible. Accounts of public justification that highly idealized Members of the Public may well have to decide whether to accept or reject (3), since in their view a bona fide public justification may not be accessible to the reason of all, but that is not a concern of ours. The fourth interpretation can be embraced; of course Alf need not always engage in

---

[17] See Wall, "On Justificatory Liberalism."

the demonstration of his justification whenever he acts on the grounds of a justified moral rule.

A much more general challenge might be advanced, namely, that it is simply a fact of life that we often interfere with, block, and thwart each other's agency, and we just have to grow up and get used to it. Unless our agency is protected by a specific right, each has a "blameless liberty" (§16.2c) to block or thwart the agency of others as she wishes, for whatever reason she wishes. If I am the sort who happens to enjoy blocking the agency of others, then doing so is in itself morally unobjectionable (though not, of course, if I do so by violating a specific right). Now in evaluating this general objection we need to put aside cases that are controversial examples of blocking or thwarting, such as a case in which the competition between two individuals, each seeking to act on his ends within his rights, results in one person decreasing the other's options. For example, suppose I buy the last Buffalo Bills ticket because I love the Bills (and worry that they will move to Toronto, so I'd better hurry up and see them), and, as a result, you cannot go to the game. Some may see this as interfering with, or blocking, your agency, while others do not. There is also the question of whether, if this is a blocking, it is justified via a system of property rights. To test the general objection, we need an uncontroversial case of Betty blocking Alf's agency where this action clearly does not fall under a specific right of Alf's (or a duty of Betty's). Benn provides such a case:

Imagine Alan sitting on a public beach, a pebble in each hand, splitting one pebble by striking it with another. Betty, a casual observer, asks him what he is doing. She can see, of course, that he is splitting pebbles; what she is asking him to do is to explain it, to redescribe it as an activity with an intelligible point, something he could have a reason for doing. There is nothing untoward about her question, but Alan is not bound to answer it unless he likes. Suppose, however, that Betty had asked Alan to justify what he was doing or to give an excuse for doing it. Unlike explanations, justifications and excuses presume at least prima facie fault, a charge to be rebutted, and what can be wrong with splitting pebbles on a public beach? Besides, so far as we can tell, Alan is not obliged to account to Betty for his actions. . . .

Suppose Betty were to prevent Alan from splitting pebbles by . . . removing all the pebbles within reach. Alan could now quite properly demand a justification from Betty, and a tu quoque reply from her that he, on his side, had not offered her a justification for splitting pebbles would not meet the case, for Alan's pebble splitting had done nothing to interfere with Betty's actions. The burden of justification falls on the interferer, not on the person interfered with. So while Alan might properly resent Betty's interference, Betty has no ground for complaint against Alan.[18]

Benn's argument here, I think, is ingenious for he does not directly ask us about the morality of Betty's action but whether Alan would be appropriately resentful. To reject the Presumption in Favor of Liberty is to hold not simply that *you* would not resent Betty doing this to *you*, but that resentment on Alan's part would be inappropriate. As we saw in section 12, for resentment to be appropriate it must be the case not only that one holds that the action is wrong but also that the other had reasons to appreciate that it is wrong. Now it is very hard to see how, simply from the perspective of agency, Alan could be criticized for resenting that Betty has thwarted his agency in this way. To be sure, if she had some good reason, Alan could see her action as unobjectionable; but it could not be inappropriate for him, as an abstract agent, to feel resentment at someone who sets about a project of blocking his agency for no good reason, or for malicious reasons. And this not only implies that Alan may appropriately object, but that it is reasonable for him to suppose that Betty could see the wrongness of blocking his agency in this way.

Alan Gewirth advanced a very similar defense of "a general presumption in favor of freedom."[19] In Gewirth's view, insofar as we consider ourselves simply from the abstract perspective of agency, we must consider the aims and purposes of our action as good; we must value those aims and purposes that form the basis of our decision to act. Consequently, we cannot help but claim noninterference to act on these aims and purposes. How could one have no objection to thwarting what one sees as good? Freedom is a proximate necessary condition for acting on one's aims, and one's

---

[18] Benn, *A Theory of Freedom*, p. 87.
[19] Alan Gewirth, *Human Rights: Essays on Justification and Applications*, p. 16.

devotion to one's aims implies a valuing of the necessary conditions to act on one's choices. Now Gewirth himself believed that there was a direct route from this basic claim of agency to a general moral right, via his famous "Principle of Generic Consistency."[20] Gewirth's argument was based on the rational commitments of the "first-person" standpoint (§12.4): from within the first-person standpoint each is committed to (*i*) claiming noninterference with her actions, (*ii*) recognizing that this claim derives from the generic features of human agency as such and so (*iii*) all agents have the same ground for claiming noninterference as one does; thus Gewirth argued that (*iv*) one who claimed the right for herself, but refused to accord it to others, was contradicting herself.[21] Now no such derivation is claimed here; our concern is the evaluative standards that Members of the Public would rely on insofar as they abstract to their status as agents. Steps (*i*)–(*iii*), though, are powerful: to see oneself as an agent – understanding simply the generic features of agency divorced from particular aims and values – is to see oneself as devoted to acting on one's values, ends, and goals, and for that one has reason to claim freedom from interference with one's choices. Gewirth, indeed, not only defends a presumption in favor of freedom, but he insists "[t]his is, moreover, a strong presumption: it requires compliance on the part of all persons so that, without special justification, no one's freedom is to be restricted. There is no similar general presumption in favor of coercion or unfreedom."[22] Gewirth thus advocates a general right to freedom so understood, as a demand of persons as agents.

(b) Autarky

It is sometimes objected that the Presumption in Favor of Liberty is biased because it privileges negative over positive liberty. Here again (§2.4c) we must resist the pressure to take sides in this long-running dispute; our aim must be to sort out the justification for various sorts of liberty claims in our overall account of social order among free people. In a fundamental respect, as I have argued,

[20] Alan Gewirth, *Reason and Morality,* chap. 3.
[21] See ibid., pp. 150–61; *Human Rights,* pp. 20ff.
[22] Gewirth, *Human Rights,* p. 17.

positive liberty as moral autonomy, not negative liberty, is basic in the account. The aim is for each to act freely while conforming to the demands of social morality. Even putting aside for now this foundational commitment to positive liberty aside, the Presumption in Favor of Liberty itself has important implications for types of actions and interventions that are often discussed under the heading of "positive liberty." Recall our "normal" citizen of Oceania, who has been subjected to a system of thought control such that she is unable to think some thoughts, and so unable to even conceive of some choices (§12.3*a*). Here too we have an unjustified blocking and thwarting of a person's agency, in this case by efforts to subvert a person's status as a chooser.

Benn calls a person who meets the minimum condition for self-directed agency "autarchic." "Autarchy is a condition of human normality, both in the statistical sense, that an overwhelming majority of human beings satisfy it, and in the further sense that anyone who fails to satisfy it falls short in some degree as a human being."[23] Failures of autarky include[24]

> *Compulsive and obsessive behavior.* A person in the grip of an obsession has difficulty aligning his actions to his deliberate choices and settled aims; the obsessive desire intrudes and choice seems impossible. As Freud described the compulsive, there is "an ever-increasing indecisiveness, loss of energy, and curtailment of freedom."[25]
>
> *Disassociations of the self from its agency,* such as schizoid personalities. Such persons, we saw, do not understand themselves as agents.
>
> *Severe disruption of deliberative and belief-forming processes,* such as in schizophrenia. Agents understand themselves to base their actions on their deliberations and choices; severe disruption of deliberation undermines this status as deliberation-directed. Less severe disruptions, such as being raised to be terrified of making one's own choices, also thwart a person's agency.

---

[23] Benn, *A Theory of Freedom*, p. 155.
[24] For a much more thorough discussion, see ibid., pp. 156ff.
[25] Freud, *A General Introduction to Psychoanalysis*, p. 230.

"Brainwashing" in the sense of aims and values induced by others that by-pass one's deliberative process, as well as some forms of indoctrination. To act out the values and aims implanted in one by others supplants one's own deliberations and aims with theirs, making one's actions a tool of their deliberations.

To induce any of these conditions constitutes a blocking or thwarting of one's agency and certainly would fall under the Presumption in Favor of Liberty. Indeed, it is difficult to see how these sorts of blocking ever could be justified, for they often have the effect of permanently and severely blocking one's agency. More than that, they undermine moral agency itself and so one's status as a full-fledged participant in the moral order. The most insidious threats to free agency are totalitarian plans (such as the effort to create a "New Soviet Man") that set out to control agents' deliberative processes so as to conform to the regime's values. Still, the claim at this point is only that such thwarting of a person's agency in this way without justification would be wrong, and we would be (and almost always are) rationally indignant when it occurs.

As I said, many of these ways of limiting freedom by undermining agency have been associated with the positive liberty tradition. A person who is subject to some impulse or craving (think here of the compulsive) that he cannot control, Green said, is "in the condition of a bondsman who is carrying out the will of another, not his own."[26] In his famous essay on "Liberal Legislation and Freedom of Contract" Green argued that the sale of alcohol undermined agency, and so there was a case based on freedom for regulating this trade. In our terms, under some conditions such a trade might be considered thwarting another's agency. This cannot be ruled out on principle. We need to know the actual effects of drugs on agency and the degree to which consent is able to be given and justifies the thwarting. I believe that when we do the work and examine the specific drugs, we will conclude that they do not constitute the threats to agency that they are typically depicted

[26] T. H. Green, "On the Different Senses of 'Freedom,'" p. 228.

as posing,[27] but that is a matter of detailed specific deliberation, not a direct implication of the idea of liberty.

However, as Benn stresses, autarky falls well short of "personal autonomy." As we have seen, personal autonomy is a controversial ideal (§17.2); it concerns a critical attitude toward one's beliefs and values, and often some idea that one's life has been reflectively chosen by the agent. The positive liberty tradition typically goes beyond a commitment to freedom as autarky, to conceive of true or complete freedom as attaining such autonomy, or some excellence of agency or life. In his defense of positive liberal legislation, Green went far beyond the worry that some people's agency may be blocked:

We shall probably all agree that freedom, rightly understood, is the greatest of all blessings; that its attainment is the true end of all of our effort as citizens. But when we speak of freedom, we should be careful what we mean by it. We do not mean merely freedom from restraint or compulsion. . . . When we speak of freedom as something to be so highly prized, we mean a positive power or capacity of doing or enjoying something worth doing or enjoying.[28]

This ideal of positive freedom is based on a controversial ideal of what is worth doing: it is not a demand of agency, but of a theory of what constitutes an excellent agent. Again we see how the negative/positive distinction is far too blunt an instrument for analyzing the requirements of a free social order.

(c) The Rights Not to Be Coerced and Deceived
Gewirth sketches a more detailed description of the claims involved in the right to freedom:

This consists in a person controlling his actions and his participation in transactions by his own unforced choice or consent and with knowledge of relevant circumstances, so that his behavior is neither compelled nor prevented by the actions of other persons. Hence a person's right to

---

[27] See Douglas N. Husak, *Drugs and Rights*.
[28] T. H. Green, "Liberal Legislation and Freedom of Contract," p. 199.

freedom is violated if he is subject to violence, coercion, deception, or any other procedures that attack or remove his informed control of his behavior by his own unforced choices. The right includes having a sphere of personal autonomy and privacy whereby one is let alone by others and until he unforcedly consents to undergo their action.[29]

Gewirth rightly stresses that from the perspective of the value of agency, Members of the Public will claim strong rights not to be forced to act against their own choices. This right is not, of course, absolute; coercion that is publicly justified is permissible. But as Gewirth indicates, an agent will advance a strong claim to be free from "violence, coercion, deception, or any other procedures that attack or remove his informed control of his behavior by his own unforced choices." Some deny this and so assert that others need not have justification for forcing you to do as they wish. But as an agent and a Member of the Public, deliberating on what moral principles one can endorse, to endorse as the default a moral permission of others to force you to conform your action to their wishes conflicts with one's core values as an agent, concerned with deliberating, choosing on the basis of one's deliberation, and acting on the basis of one's choices.

Now many insist that a right not to be coerced, or, we might say, a right not to be coerced without public justification – cannot be a basic right, since the idea of coercion is so vague and controversial. The last forty years has witnessed a number of fundamentally divergent accounts of coercion.[30] It is widely agreed that coercion typically involves some sort of threat of harm (§17.4) by which the "coercer" gets (or aims at getting) the "coercee" to do as he wishes, but there is considerable disagreement about what constitutes a threat of harm, whether all such threats are coercive, and so on. Again, we must remind ourselves that our aim here is only to see whether Members of the Public, as agents, would agree on abstract principles and rights of agency; none of the conclusions of public reason at this juncture have the determinacy required for rules that regulate social life. So long as Members of the Public could agree

29 Gewirth, *Human Rights*, pp. 56–7.
30 For an excellent survey, see Scott Anderson's "Coercion."

on paradigmatic cases of coercion, their inability to settle on an overall philosophical account is not a concern. Indeed, philosophical theories that seek to provide a biconditional analysis of a concept (i.e., ϕ is an act of coercion if and only if conditions C_1 . . . C_n are met) are notoriously subject to counter-examples and controversy; we almost always have a far better grasp of the use of an idea than the philosophical analysis of it.

Still, it might be thought that there is a deeper reason to abjure reference to coercion in specifying basic (abstract) rights. At least in some cases coercion presupposes already established moral rights. If I threaten your property unless you conform to my demands, I am coercing you through your property; but this seems to suppose it really is your property. It is plausible to suppose that as one's rights expand through public justification, so do the ways in which others can coerce you. As your rights expand so does the boundary of your moral personality. This idea of the expansion of juridical personhood through rights was central to Kant's analysis of property. To own a thing is not simply to have possession of it, or even stable, secure, recognized possession. It is to enter into a juridical relation such that "any hindrance of my use of it would constitute an injury to me, even when I am not in [physical] possession of it (that is, when I am not a holder of the object)."[31] Once property rights are justified, a threat by the state to take my property is a threat against me: to take my property is to do an injury to me as a juridical person. Without property rights, you only do injury to me by taking my possession if you use force against my person (narrowly construed), or threaten to, when taking it. If I should put it down and walk away, it would be no injury to me for you to take it, and so it would be no threat against my person for you to threaten to take it away under these circumstances.[32] However, if it is my property the injury is done not by reason of physical possession but by an extension of the bounds of my person to include my relation to it. Thus, when you threaten to destroy my property, you

---

[31] Kant, *The Metaphysical Elements of Justice*, p. 45 [Akademie, 249].

[32] To be sure, there may be an intelligible sense in which I still might be said to coerce you: "If you don't do what I want I will pick up your possession the next time you put it down!" Again, though, a general account of coercion (if one is to be had) is not our aim.

make a threat against me, just as surely as if you threatened to hit me.

Although it is correct to say that as one's moral boundaries expand so does the range of possible coercion, it does not follow that all coercion involves a threat to violate the rights of another, and hence coercion is a thoroughly moralized concept.[33] Even in a condition such as Hobbes' state of nature, in which everyone has a blameless liberty to do as he thinks necessary and so no one has claim rights to noninterference, we can sensibly and importantly say that people are coercing each other.[34] Indeed, the idea of replacing such private lawless coercion with public lawful coercion is an important theme in Kant's social contract theory; we have no difficulty understanding the idea of coercion without law and rights.[35] Applying the concept of coercion (and, of course, force) makes sense even in relations among purely "natural persons" – those whom we do not consider bearers of rights.

So at this basic stage of justification, Members of the Public understand the right not to be coerced as a right not to have threats made against one's natural person.[36] (It will expand along with the boundaries of one's moral personhood as justification proceeds.) Coercion against one's natural person is a quintessential instance of interference with agency. As Hayek stressed, coercion is an attempt to supplant one's agency: "coercion occurs when one man's actions are made to serve another man's will."[37] Gewirth recognizes that a right not to be deceived has a similar justification. Lying,

---

[33] See Alan Wertheimer, *Coercion,* pp. 277ff.

[34] I defend this interpretation of Hobbes in *Value and Justification,* pp. 275ff.

[35] Kant's view is complex. Though we have private rights in the state of nature, because there is no impartial judge about their contour, the state of nature also is characterized by an absence of public claims of justice; the idea of the social contract is to establish public justice and rights. *Metaphysical Elements of Justice,* pp. 115–16 [Akademie, 312].

[36] It also, I think, involves a right not to have threats made against what one cares for as a way of interfering with your agency. If Alf threatens to harm Betty's son unless she does as he wishes, he coerces her. Interestingly, if he threatens to destroy her beloved painting – which *he owns* – if she does not agree to move to Australia with him, he still may plausibly be said to coerce her into moving without threatening her person (he threatens to harm his own property), though such "blackmail" may be justified by his ownership.

[37] F. A. Hayek, *The Constitution of Liberty,* p. 133.

censorship of information, propaganda, and fraud all constitute attempts to undermine one's status as an effective agent by altering one's deliberations and choices so as to make choices that conform to the values and deliberations of others, not oneself.[38] Reflecting simply on their status as agents committed to autarkic choice – simply on the values of effective agency – Members of the Public would surely agree on an abstract right not to have their agency shaped by others in these ways.

(d) The Core Status of Freedom of Thought

Liberalism emerged as a distinct political theory calling for freedom of speech and thought. As John Plamenatz observed, freedom of thought "is an idea which emerges slowly in the West in the course of the sixteenth and seventeenth centuries; and yet today, in the eyes of the liberal, it is this liberty which is most precious of all."[39] Now the claim to freedom of thought is a two-sided claim – both internal and external. One the one hand, it is a demand of agents to deliberate freely and not be coerced or conditioned in ways such that one's deliberations and conclusions are determined by others. In this respect, freedom of thought is a fundamental claim of respect for autarky. Those tempted to place Hobbes in the liberal pantheon should remember just how hostile he was to the emergence of this core right of a free person. Hobbes thought that respect for freedom of thought was easily achieved; since belief is not voluntary, but forced on us by our deliberations, "beliefs and unbelief never follow men's commands" and so "a private man has always the liberty (because thought is free) to believe, in his heart."[40] Freedom of conscience, however, prohibits not simply attempts to command belief, but to induce it by constraining and controlling discourse – something which Hobbes certainly advocated, placing as he did the teaching of all doctrines under the authority of the sovereign. "For the actions of men proceed from their

---

[38] This is so even if the lie is to one's advantage, as in a paternalistic deception. Gewirth appeared to think that lying always decreases "one's capabilities for success in action." *Human Rights*, p. 9.

[39] John Plamenatz, *Man and Society*, vol. I, p. 46.

[40] Hobbes, *Leviathan*, p. 338 (chap. 42, ¶11); p. 300 (chap. 37, ¶13). I have greatly benefited from discussions with Shane Courtland on this matter.

opinions; and in the well-governing of opinions, consisteth the well-governing of men's actions, in order to their peace, and concord."[41] Central to freedom of thought is the claim that one's belief-forming process should not be interfered with in ways that circumvent or constrain one's deliberation; thus free speech, allowing free communication of different views, is central to freedom of thought itself. Again, Hobbes denies this; since "freedom of the tongue is but an external thing"[42] we must obey the sovereign's command to profess beliefs. Freedom of thought is also claim to be able to act on one's beliefs and judgments. When Hobbes allows the sovereign to command the outward forms of worship, he again offends against the other, external, side of freedom of conscience, for one's deliberations instruct an agent what to do; to allow her the freedom to deliberate but not to act on her deliberations is not to respect her as an agent, an actor on her beliefs. To be sure, such a claim is defeasible: social morality constitutes a justification for interfering with a person's action grounded on her current deliberations. But this does not undermine freedom of conscience grounding a defeasible claim to so act, and so interference must be justified.

Freedom of conscience is a core liberal right as it sums up the main grounds of free agency, uniting free deliberation and free action. It has a basic place in the order of justification for agents. Appropriately, it is the core right that Rawls' parties endorse in his deliberative original position. Although Rawls specifies a list of rights,[43] including "political freedom of speech and assembly;

---

[41] Ibid., p. 113 (chap. 18, ¶9).

[42] Ibid.

[43] Rawls holds that "there is a general presumption against imposing legal and other restrictions on conduct without sufficient reason." And, he rightly insists, "this presumption creates no special priority for any particular liberty" – it does not serve to identify some liberties as especially important (*Justice as Fairness*, p. 44; see also p. 112). In his 1971 deliberative model Rawls had the parties agreeing on a general principle of liberty: "[E]ach person is to have an equal right to the most extensive basic liberty compatible with a similar liberty for others" (*A Theory of Justice* [1971 edition], p. 60). In the revised edition this was changed to "[E]ach person is to have an equal right to the most extensive scheme of equal basic liberties compatible with a similar scheme of liberties for others" (Rawls, *A Theory of Justice*, p. 53). This change was made in response to a criticism by H. L.

liberty of conscience and freedom of thought [and] freedom of the person, which includes freedom from psychological oppression,"[44] the justification of the entire set of rights is held to be a generalization of the case for freedom of thought or conscience.[45]   Empirical research confirms widespread consensus of actual (i.e., non-idealized) people on an abstract right to freedom of speech, as the top half of Display VI-1 shows. Some researchers take the bottom part of the table to demonstrate the irrelevance of abstract assent to moral rights: when push comes to shove – specific cases – this devotion withers. This skeptical interpretation is not called for. When we focus on an abstract idea, free of specific interpretations and vivid competing considerations, we agree; as the interpretation becomes more specific, agreement turns into dissensus, or sometimes is even largely overturned. But what *is* the status of public buildings – should they be used for Nazi gatherings seeking to overturn democracy? As Rawls himself worried, how much of the rights of toleration extend to the intolerant?[46] What is it to *denounce* the government – is this to encourage unrest? What are the appropriate ways to enforce the law? The strength and weakness of arguments from abstraction is that they focus our attention on general ideas with which we agree, but they mask the disagreement that erupts when we turn to specific interpretations. It is not until the next chapter that we will turn to disagreements in interpretation; our focus here is in identifying the basis for abstract agreement.

A. Hart, questioning the general idea of equal most extensive liberty. See Hart's "Rawls on Liberty and Its Priority."

[44] Rawls, *A Theory of Justice*, p. 53. I consider the other rights Rawls mentions later in this chapter, as their relation to agency is not obviously focused on the demand for liberty.

[45] Rawls, *A Theory of Justice*, p 181.

[46] Ibid., §35.

Abstract Right	Percentage supporting abstract right
I believe in free speech for all no matter what their views might be.	89
People who hate our way of life should still have a chance to talk and be heard.	82
We could never be free if we gave up the right to criticize our government.	89
Unless there is freedom for many points of view to be presented, there is little chance that truth can be known.	86
The idea that everyone has a right to his own opinion is being carried too far these days.	81

Specific Liberties	Percentage supporting specific liberties
Free speech should be granted •to all regardless of how intolerant they are of other people's opinions. •only to people who are willing to grant the same rights of free speech to everyone else.	58
Should government authorities be allowed to open the mail of people suspected of being in contact with fugitives? •No, it would violate a person's right to correspond with his friends. •Yes, as it may help the police catch criminals they have been looking for.	50
Should a community allow the American Nazi party to use its town hall to hold a public meeting? •Yes. •No.	18
If a group asks to use a public building to hold a meeting denouncing the government, their request should be •granted. •denied.	23

DISPLAY VI-1 DIFFERENT SUPPORT FOR AN ABSTRACT RIGHT AND SPECIFIC LIBERTIES

Source: Elliot Turiel, Melainie Killen, and Charles C. Helwig, "Morality: Its Structure, Functions and Vagaries," pp. 162, 164, reporting on the research of H. McCloskey and A. Brill.

17.4 WELFARE, RESOURCES, AND AGENCY

(a) Harm

Gewirth argues that agents must claim, as conditions for their agency devoted to achieving their purposes (which they see as good), not only rights to freedom but to well-being too. A rational agent, Gewirth argues, must regard "his capabilities of action as constituting his own well-being as an agent. . . . It would be contradictory for an agent to hold that certain general abilities and conditions are required for his purpose-fulfilling activity . . . and also hold that these are no part of his well-being."[47] Well-being understood in terms of the conditions for purpose-fulfilling action is thus a necessary good of agents and, so as agents, they must claim a right to such well-being, just as they must claim a right to freedom.[48] Although Rawls' focus is on resources rather than well-being, he models his abstract agent deliberators as devoted to obtaining "primary goods" – goods such as liberty, opportunities, income, and wealth – which are necessary for the successful pursuit of their ends, whatever these ends may be. "They know that in general they must try to protect their liberties, widen their opportunities, and enlarge their means for promoting their aims whatever these are."[49]

"The obligations of an agent with regard to the basic goods of other persons," writes Gewirth, "are at least to refrain from interfering with their having these goods."[50] Interferences with basic goods needed for successful agency are basic harms. Members of the Public as abstract agents would certainly agree with at least one aspect of Mill's harm principle, namely, regarding "actions as are prejudicial to the interests of others, the individual is accountable, and may be subject either to social or legal punishment, if society is of the opinion that one or the other is requisite for its protection."[51] It is not, though, simply society but each agent who must have assurance that her basic welfare interests – bodily integrity, health,

---

[47] Gewirth, *Reason and Morality*, p. 60.
[48] Ibid., p. 61.
[49] Rawls, *A Theory of Justice*, p. 123.
[50] Gewith, *Reason and Morality*, p. 212.
[51] John Stuart Mill, *On Liberty*, p. 292 (chap. V, ¶2).

the absence of severe pain, absence of psychological torture and distress, reasonable security of necessary resources – are not set back severely by the agency of others. Of course, like all abstract moral categories, the contour of our concept of "harm" is subject to dispute,[52] but there is wide consensus on quintessential harms from which morality protects us. A large number of studies have confirmed that children understand harm rules as moral rules – not only cases such as hitting, pushing, and killing, but psychological harms such as ridiculing the disabled.[53]

(b) Rights to Assistance

Gewirth insists that from the perspective of agency, the duties of agents regarding the necessary goods of others would not be restricted to negative duties to refrain from harm. "[W]henever some person knows that unless he acts in certain ways other persons will suffer basic harms, and he is proximately able to act in these ways with no comparable cost to himself, it is his moral duty to prevent these harms."[54] As abstract agents, Members of the Public will realize that their agency can be endangered in innumerable ways, and often the only way to avoid severe harm to the basic goods necessary for agency requires assistance from others – either a service (such as saving a drowning person by throwing her a life preserver) or by providing goods such as food to the starving. So long as the duty to provide the goods would not be apt to endanger agency of the provider as much as absence of honoring the claim would endanger the agency of the claimant, all Members of the Public, deliberating simply on the knowledge that they are agents, would seem to have reason to endorse such a right. "Since every agent has a deep stake in his own basic well-being, he must hold that he has a right to it and that other persons also have this right. He must hence admit that he ought to refrain from interfering with their basic well-being, and where his inaction would interfere, that he ought positively act to protect their well-being without

---

[52] I consider some of these in my *Social Philosophy*, chap. 8.
[53] For a summary of these studies, see Turiel, Killen, and Helwig, "Morality: Its Structure, Functions and Vagaries," p. 174.
[54] Gewith, *Reason and Morality*, p. 217.

comparable harm to himself."[55] This same line of reasoning leads to a general claim for a basic level of welfare or necessary goods as a right of all agents. Following it, Gewirth defends, for example, a human right to relief from starvation held against those who have abundance.[56]

The perspective of agency leads to endorsing some welfare rights. Members of the Public, aware only that they are agents, and of their reasons to maintain their agency and to be successful as agents, would insist not only on the freedom to pursue their agency but also the necessary means. Even libertarians such as Loren Lomasky concur that if an individual is unable to sustain her agency, then she has a claim on those with a surplus.[57] The claims of abstract agency, however, would seem to go much further. Agents, as Members of the Public, would not simply be concerned with maintaining the minimal conditions for agency but also with acquiring the goods for an effective agency – one that is successful in achieving one's aims, ends, and values. Each Member of the Public, deliberating simply on the values of agency, would weigh whether some guarantee of goods or resources would have a net positive impact on her agency, given the risks encountered in social life. Of course this is still highly indeterminate, for it depends on just how much information each knows about herself and her aversion to risk. Still, it certainly looks plausible that some fairly strong welfare rights follow from this perspective.

17.5 THE STABILITY OF ABSTRACT RIGHTS UNDER FULL JUSTIFICATION

Recall the three conditions for a successful argument from abstraction: (*i*) it must identify a common perspective that leads to consensus on certain evaluative standards; (*ii*) this common perspective must be a deep part of everyone's system of evaluative standards; and (*iii*) when the abstraction is lifted, and the deliberators are aware of the full range of their evaluative standards, the conclusion

[55] Ibid., p. 227-28.
[56] Gewirth, *Human Rights*, chap. 8.
[57] Loren Lomasky, *Rights, Persons, and the Moral Community*, p. 126.

reached via abstraction must not be overturned. The first two requirements are satisfied by arguments from agency. Certainly it is a shared perspective and a deep commitment of those in pluralistic societies (§17.2). I have drawn on Gewirth's analysis (§§17.3–17.4) because he is the most successful at abstracting from all considerations except the demands of agency itself, and demonstrating that this perspective gives us a common ground for endorsing claims (again, this conclusion stands apart from his controversial appeal to the Principle of Generic Consistency).

As Rawls came to realize, meeting the third condition is difficult; we must show that, given the full range of reasonable pluralism of evaluative standards, all moral persons still have sufficient reason to endorse the claims of agency. If they do not, then appeal to these claims does not treat some as free and equal; some are subjected to the authority of moral claims that they cannot, as rational moral persons, endorse. We can understand why some followers of Rawls such as Jonathan Quong would like justification to end at the abstracted argument, in which parties only reason on the basis of a shared conception of personhood and its demands (§14.4d). To do this, however, is to ignore the motivating reason for the entire public reason project: because the use of our reason leads us to disagree on the relevant standards of evaluation we must discover what can be endorsed by the reason of all. To declare irrelevant to justification the evaluative standards on which we disagree is to ignore the problem, not solve it.

I think it is quite clear that the abstract freedom demands of agency are stable under full justification. The motivating problem of our project – the project of Rousseau and Kant – is that free and equal moral persons require that the demands of social morality be confirmed by their reason. When others seek to claim authority over them – to instruct them in what they must do – a free person insists that she is an equal interpreter of the demands of morality, and *her* understanding of morality is the one that should guide *her* action. Only a publicly justified social morality can satisfy this claim of each and every free and equal moral person. But note that this is itself a quintessential claim of agency – it is a demand for free *moral* agency. The free and equal person insists that her reasons, as determined by her deliberation, determine what she ought to do; her reason is for her the definitive judge of what she, as a moral agent, must do. She understands herself as a self-directed moral agent, and only a moral practice that gives her sufficient reasons will suffice. This is not simply an abstracted feature of her set of reasons that might be overturned under full justification, for to be a free moral person is to, all things considered, demand reasons for one's compliance with morality. A free moral person demands reasons to endorse moral requirements and, if there are sufficient reasons, she normally has a reason to comply with the moral demands and constrain the pursuit of her ends and purposes (§9.4*b*).

Hence all Members of the Public are already committed to the full justification of their status as free and equal moral persons and the claims for equal moral freedom that this entails. And so, they already have full justification for the claims of free moral agency. Now it might be conjectured that Members of the Public are fully justified in making claims on the basis of their free moral agency but not on the basis of free agency in general. In a society of rational evaluative pluralism, however, in determining whether he can freely endorse a moral rule, a rational moral person consults his evaluative standards, seeking to determine whether the moral rule conforms to them. Rational moral persons, then, are committed to more than simply free moral action; they are committed to their evaluative standards, and ensuring that moral demands are endorsed by them. They understand these standards as providing them with reasons to judge and to act, and so the claims of free agency include the freedom to act on these evaluative standards. In his argument for freedom of thought and speech, Rawls supposes that deliberators have (unknown) moral and religious obligations that they must honor.[58] To conceive of oneself as under an obligation to conform to one's evaluative standards is certainly possible, but even without the talk of obligation, Members of the Public recognize a fundamental commitment to their own evaluative standards, which, they hold, should shape their action. And there can be no public way to distinguish actions that are genuinely based on "deep" evaluative standards from "mere"

---

[58] Rawls, *A Theory of Justice*, p. 181.

personal goals and desires.[59] There is great disagreement about evaluative standards and their ordering; individuals have a fundamental and fully justified interest in acting according to their own deliberations and reasons about their standards, and what they call for. Because of this, they must – not simply as abstract agents but as actual persons – deem it appropriate to object to unwarranted interferences that thwart them from acting on their standards, especially those that involve the threat of force against their persons (and so simultaneously threaten their basic conditions for acting on their standards).

The intimate tie between free moral agency and free agency generally is summed up by the common good requirement: a moral rule that can be endorsed by all free moral agents must be consistent with the common good of all, at least in the minimal sense of not itself posing a threat to anyone's good (§§9.2a, 15.2f). Free and rational moral agents must consider how their overall systems of values, goals, and ends will fare under a proposed moral rule, and so they cannot have good reason to embrace a moral rule that poses a threat to what they care for. This common good requirement not only includes freedom to act on one's aims, goals, and purposes but also protection from basic harms. There cannot, I think, be any doubt that a principle prohibiting basic harms (a strong yet defeasible principle) is fully justified. Rules against harms are part of all moral systems and are among the rules that children first recognize as necessary to social life.[60] In pluralistic cultures with strong commitment to the perspective of agency, harm rules are apt to focus on protection of the basic goods for effective agency.

Gewirth believes that the common good requirement of morality justifies not only rules against harm but also duties of assistance.[61]

---

[59] Cf. Josuha Cohen, "Democracy and Liberty," where he seeks to single out for protection "deeply held" and "substantial reasons." For a critical discussion of Cohen's proposal, see my *Contemporary Theories of Liberalism*, pp. 129–31.

[60] See Shaun Nichols, *Sentimental Rules*, pp. 141–7; Turiel, Killen, and Helwig, "Morality: Its Structure, Functions and Vagaries," p. 174; Richard Schweder, Manamohan Mahapatra, and Joan G. Miller, "Culture and Moral Development," p. 50.

[61] Gewirth holds that "every transaction must be for the good of the recipient as well as the agent" but adds "[a] transaction is for the common good of its participants if it respects the good of each participant." *Reason and Morality*, p. 211.

Recall that in his view, "whenever some person knows that unless he acts in certain ways other persons will suffer basic harms, and he is proximately able to act in these ways with no comparable cost to himself, it is his moral duty to prevent these harms." This strong duty of assistance is not stable under full justification. Fundamental to many people's evaluative systems is a strong devotion to principles of desert. Desert is not – or, at least it certainly need not be – simply a positive notion, in the sense that one can deserve benefits for contributing to a common good, or for creating something, or for being prudent. One can also deserve bad things – for undermining the common good, for destroying value, or for being imprudent. Of course there is disagreement about this: Members of the Public will hold different views of desert and its importance, and some may reject the entire idea.[62] But desert does not have to be embraced by all; it is a *defeater* if to Betty, a Member of the Public, when taken together, the argument for a positive right to assistance AND her concept of desert is a sufficient reason to reject the right of assistance. If the concept of desert is a defeater in any Member of the Public's evaluative system for the right, then the right is not publicly justified.

It might be claimed that Betty's counterproposal, that there be no right of assistance to the undeserving, fails the reversibility test (§15.2e): if *her* agency were endangered, then she would claim the right to assistance even if she was undeserving. If this was true we could dismiss her objection; it is only because she knows that she is unlikely to be a recipient of the duty that she rejects the claim. While this may be the case with some who reject a claim of the undeserving for assistance, it is surely not universally so. All of us who have taught problems of distributive justice know that some of the most voracious objections to unqualified assistance come from some of our poorest students, who believe that those who are not deserving have no call on others. They are quite adamant that responsibility for one's welfare or well-being is up to the

---

[62] On normal agents' understandings of desert, see, e.g., David Miller, "Distributive Justice: What People Think"; Bert Overlaet, "Merit Criteria as Justification for Differences in Earnings." On how people's judgments are affected when considering general and specific questions, see Shaun Nichols and Christopher Freiman, "Is Desert in the Details?"

individual. We need not, though, resort to impressionistic evidence. Recent empirical investigation of European attitudes of whether individuals (or government) should take more responsibility for welfare showed the expected correlation with social class (.134) and income (.037);[63] these are significant but by no means overwhelming. When more sophisticated techniques are employed, it was found that

[i]n the case of social class [which was the strongest predictor], raising one's class level from the lowest to highest possible value while holding all other variables constant generates a 9.6 percent increase in the probability of the respondent preferring that people should take more responsibility for the provision of welfare. Following social class, income (6.1 percent) has the second largest relative effect, followed by education (2.2 percent), gender (1.3 percent), and employment status (1.2 percent).[64]

These findings indicate that deliberative models such as Rawls' are correct in supposing that in deliberations about welfare provision individuals are concerned with "what's in it for me?"[65] But even if, a la Rawls' veil of ignorance, knowledge of class and income that affects people's deliberations is excluded, indeed even if each supposes that everyone is in the lowest (as opposed to the highest) social class, this would increase the probability of a person's support for welfare provision by (I think we can reasonably say "only") 9.6 percent; having them also suppose that they were in the lowest (as opposed to having them assume they were in the highest) income group increases the probability favoring government rather than individual responsibility for welfare by another 6.1 percent.

We may wish to dismiss the support of many lower-class and lower-income individuals for individual responsibility for providing welfare as an instance of false consciousness ("they have been indoctrinated into this attitude!") but talk of indoctrination aside,

[63] Karl C. Kaltenthaler and Stephen J. Ceccoli, "Explaining Patterns of Support for the Provision of Citizen Welfare," p. 1053. Given the way the variables were defined, there were negative correlations in the study.

[64] Ibid., p. 1054.

[65] Kaltenthaler and J. Ceccoli, "Explaining Patterns of Support for the Provision of Citizen Welfare," p. 1054.

these agents are autarkic. Perhaps one might say they are not fully autonomous and reflective, but that is irrelevant, since autonomy is itself a controversial character ideal (§17.2); the justificatory public cannot be restricted to the autonomous, any more than it can be restricted to people who do not have strong convictions about desert. Once such Members of the Public are fully cognizant of their full set of evaluative standards, they will not (as free and equal people) have sufficient reasons to endorse a strong right to assistance that does not account for what a person deserves – and, of course, there is great disagreement about what this amounts to. If someone needs assistance because of decisions of hers for which she is held to be responsible, those with strong commitments to desert are apt to think it is unjustified for her to claim a right to assistance from others, even if they could provide such assistance at low cost to themselves.

It might seem that all Members of the Public would concur on a principle to vitiate the effects of brute luck in the distribution of goods: "Give people what they deserve, but do not allow basic goods to be distributed simply on the basis of brute luck" – luck which is not the outcome of a deliberate gamble, but simply the outcome of a process uncontrolled by the individual, about which the individual never decided to make any deliberate gambles.[66] How could a reasonable Member of the Public not agree to this? Hayek has long argued that such anti-luck sentiment is inconsistent with the operation of markets. "Reward for merit is reward for obeying the wishes of others in what we do, not compensation for the benefits we have conferred upon them by doing what we thought best."[67] In the market, Hayek argues, although one's reward depends partly on how much others benefit from your actions, a good deal of luck is also involved. An entrepreneur may gain because she was in the right place and the right time, and so able to perceive a way to satisfy others' wants. In the market, two entrepreneurs may have tried equally hard, done everything in their power, and one entirely failed and the other was a great

---

[66] On the distinction between "option" luck and "brute" luck, see Ronald Dworkin, *Sovereign Virtue: The Theory and Practice of Equality*, pp. 73ff.

[67] F. A. Hayek, *The Constitution of Liberty*, p. 100.

success. It is not the case that such luck is simply about the way a "deliberate gamble" works out; the luck may be that the entrepreneur's local situation was such that she had possibilities of gain that were simply unknowable by others. Again, one need not endorse Hayek's analysis; the question is whether it is an unreasonable view that must be excluded from the justificatory public – and it is hard to see how such a claim can plausibly be made. If it is not excluded, it operates as a defeater of proposals that the distribution of agency goods should compensate for brute luck.

Even if we focus simply on "deliberate gambles," people's attitudes differ greatly. To some extent, one's degree of risk aversion affects whether one is in favor of assistance by others. "The more risk accepting a person is, the more likely they will believe that individuals should take greater responsibility in providing for themselves."[68] On the other hand, there are worries that protecting people against risk incurs a "moral hazard," providing incentives to take risky actions. There is evidence that in response to measures that reduce risks, people adjust their behavior and take on additional risks. In Sweden, for example, it was found that drivers with studded snow tires drive faster than drivers with regular tires when the roads are icy, but not when they are dry.[69] Those employing an economic model of behavior are apt to be especially worried that comprehensive rights to necessary goods will encourage a higher level of risk taking relating to those goods, and so a redistribution of the costs of risks from the agent to others. Although, say, health care provision often has been enacted on the grounds that everyone's basic welfare interests should be protected, experience has shown that the careless or reckless make inordinate demands on health care systems. Because welfare provision is funded by all, those who are more careful may end up paying a good deal for the recklessness of others. Flood relief is another example. When floods occur, both private individuals, organizations, and the government typically respond by assisting the victims of floods. But as flooding

---

[68] Kaltenthaler and J. Ceccoli, "Explaining Patterns of Support for the Provision of Citizen Welfare," p. 1054.
[69] Steven E. Rhodes, *An Economist's View of the World*, p. 57.

recurs – say, in the floods plain of the Mississippi River – the "rescuers" increasingly complain that people ought not to be allowed to, foolishly, rebuild in these flood-prone places. In these sorts of cases we see that what starts out as provision of necessary goods ends up with calls for regulation of foolish behavior that makes costly "rescue" necessary. Often, to reduce these moral hazards, regulations are introduced to discourage this potentially costly and risky action, but then worries about infringement of agency freedom arise.

There are other potential reasonable objections to assuring goods that we cannot canvass here.[70] This is not to say that no duties of assistance could be fully justified. Consider a duty that required us to rescue another (*i*) from extreme danger to her crucial welfare interests when (*ii*) the imperiled person is not responsible for her plight and (*iii*) is not in a position to easily extricate herself from her predicament, while (*iv*) we are in the position to effectively do so at (*v*) no or very low cost or risk to ourselves. It is hard to see how reasonable agents, who understand that unexpected and extreme threats to life, limb, and property arise and can destroy one's ability to pursue one's values and goals, would have defeaters of such a minimal duty.[71] It is also hard to see, though, how a much more extensive right to assistance can go undefeated under full justification among a public deliberating on a diverse set of evaluative standards.

It must be stressed that this in no way precludes the public justification of a welfare state, or even a more egalitarian redistributive state. Our question here is whether an extensive right to assistance is justified at, as it were, the "ground level" of basic claims

---

[70] One interesting problem is that it is often surprisingly difficult to predict whether attempts to increase basic goods actually do so. Suppose we improve access to medical care, and so hospitals. People will thus be encouraged to undergo more procedures, but all hospital stays have a non-negligible risk of harm through error. One study concludes that one patient in a hundred is negligently injured; as people enter hospitals for increasingly minor procedures, the number of those "unnecessarily" injured will increase. According to one estimate, avoidable injuries in hospitals cause twice as many deaths each year as highway accidents. See Edward Tanner, *Why Things Bite Back*, p. 42.

[71] This is what Judith Thomson has called "Minimally Decent Samaritanism." See her "A Defense of Abortion."

of agency. Rawls thought so. Although in his principles that were agreed to in his original position deliberative model, agency freedom had priority, a strong principle of economic redistribution, requiring that individuals be secured a bundle of resources that satisfy their basic needs, was also justified as part of the fundamental claims of free and equal agents. But we know that free and equal agents deeply disagree on questions of distributive justice and whether the person herself or others should have responsibility for protecting the individual's welfare. To assert that this is a matter of consensus for all reasonable and rational free and equal people under full justification is either simply implausible, or stipulative, deeming a wide range of individuals in Western societies to be unreasonable. These are complex and contentious issues; a claim that they have been resolved because there really is no reasonable dispute about them and that the level of consensus of reasonable agents on them is akin to that on freedom of speech is simply not credible. We must resist the temptation to insist that what we care for most is a moral fundamental beyond reasonable rejection. Whatever strong rights people have to the provision of goods is not an implication of the claims of agency itself or the idea of the basic claims of reasonable and rational free and equal persons, but involves difficult and controversial issues about the justification of an overall scheme of property and proper public policy – issues that are essentially matters for settlement in the political arena, in which individuals who reasonably disagree on these matters can adjudicate their differences. I defer them until Chapter VIII. In contrast, there is wide and deep consensus on agency freedom and abstract rights not to be harmed. Evidence indicates that ordinary reasoners – children as well as adults – are widely agreed on the moral standing of basic freedoms and prohibitions of harm, just as they disagree on so many matters of distributive justice. These are the fundamental claims of agency and are basic in the order of justification among agents such as ourselves.

17.6 THE LIMITS OF ARGUMENTS FROM ABSTRACTION

Arguments from abstraction help us make progress on our justificatory problem. Given the central importance of agency, some abstract rights of agency are fully publicly justified. We have grounds for concluding that all Members of the Public endorse under full knowledge of their evaluative standards abstract freedom rights and protection from harm. The limits of arguments from abstraction also should be clear. We are faced with essentially the same problem we encountered at the end of Chapter V, though over a narrower range of issues. Given that these principles are all abstract, they must be interpreted – translated into moral rules – before they can perform their crucial social function of providing a framework for social cooperation. As Rex Martin notes, "rights are fairly determinate things."[72] But then we are again faced with a version of the deliberative problem: selecting a publicly justified interpretation of the abstract principle. If the interpretation is to be publicly justified, it must be endorsed by all free and equal moral persons. Our Deliberative Model, though, indicates that it is unlikely in the extreme that a specific interpretation would be so endorsed. Suppose each Member of the Public proposes an interpretation of an abstract right, such as the right to freedom of speech. Given her evaluative standards, Betty will rank some specifications of this right as superior to others. If, say, she has strong religious commitments, she may well think that freedom of speech is strongly linked to freedom of conscience, while Alf may conceive of it more as a device to facilitate the exchange of opinions so as to arrive at better justified views that render one a more successful agent. And Charlie may be a Freudian who thinks that a crucial desideratum is to avoid severe neuroses that impair autarky, so that free speech must protect free information about, and depictions of, a wide range of sexual matters. Betty does not have sufficient reason to endorse Alf's "social epistemological" interpretation over hers, and she very likely does not think much of Charlie's preferred interpretation; neither of them has sufficient reason to endorse Betty's over theirs. All, let us suppose, have reason to live by one of the interpretations rather than under no freedom of speech principle at all, for all three have acknowledged the importance of an abstract right of freedom of speech. We again confront the problem of a maximal set with no agreed-upon optimal

---

[72] Rex Martin, *A System of Rights*, p. 25.

element: they see reason to select from the maximal set, but the choice from within it is, from the perspective of the Members of the Public, indeterminate.

We cannot exclude the possibility that an interpretation may be strictly unacceptable to some Members of the Public (Betty may certainly have severe doubts about Charlie's Freudian proposal). A proposal might, in the opinion of a Member of the Public, be such a bad interpretation of the abstract right of freedom of speech that it does hardly anything to secure the core interests and concerns of agency that are being interpreted, or else it severely and unnecessarily attacks her own evaluative standards. This certainly should not be a commonplace, since all are devoted to these core interests and all agree that it is of the first importance that the basic claims of agency be secured. To end up with a null set of eligible interpretations would be a moral disaster for the agency of all. And we must remember that the constraints on proposals still apply, including reversibility and the weak common good requirement (§15.2). Members of the Public are thus confronted by a set of socially *optimal eligible interpretations* of an abstract justified right, just as they were confronted by a socially optimal eligible set of possible rules, x, y, z. We have compelling reason to think that the set would be neither null nor a singleton. Their justificatory problem is narrowed (regarding a range of issues, only rules that are interpretations of the abstract right are now proposed, and they agree on the central importance of having a socially eligible set), but there is no reason to suppose it will have an agreed-upon optimal element.

18 Jurisdictional Rights

18.1 THE FUNCTIONS OF RIGHTS

The previous section was concerned with the rights of agency as basic protections from interference, manipulation, and invasion, as well as assurances that certain assistance will be provided or goods supplied. One important function of rights is to protect us, to specify claims that we have against others that they must not do some things to us, or that they must provide us with something.

This, though, is not the only function of rights. The history of thinking about the concept of rights, like the history of the philosophical analysis of so many concepts, has been dominated by the search for "a theory" of rights that supplies necessary and sufficient, or at the very minimum interesting necessary conditions, for a conceptually correct statement that "Entity X has a right to ϕ" or "Entity X has a right that entity Y ϕ."[73] The long-running debate between "choice" and "interest" theories of rights was (for the most part) predicated on the supposition that each identified a necessary condition for a sound claim that "Entity X has right R." An advocate of the will (or choice) theory would typically insist that X must be capable of choice, or exercising her will, and R must somehow be responsive to X's choices. Thus H. L. A. Hart insisted that babies and animals did not have rights (though, of course they can be wrongly treated).[74] In contrast, Mill and others have upheld an account of rights as necessarily protecting important interests.[75] Given that babies and animals have interests, they can be rightholders: thus the common claim that a fetus has a right to life, though of course it cannot choose whether to exercise it.

There is, though, little reason to think that we can identify even enlightening necessary conditions for a concept such as "rights," employed in diverse practices such as abstract theory ("The right of nature, which writers commonly call *jus naturale*, is the liberty each man hath to use his own power as he will himself for the preservation of his own nature"),[76] practical ethics ("the rights of trees"), political discourse ("the rights of a people to self-determination"), the law and jurisprudence ("a right to a fair trial"), games such as American football ("loss of the right to repeat the down"), arguments with a jealous spouse ("she had no right to look at you that way!"), and complaints against life ("after all the problems I've had, I have a right to some happiness in my old age"). In any event, I shall put aside this search for "a theory" of rights. My concern is to analyze a crucial function of rights that is distinct from simple

---

[73] For the most recent, and a sophisticated, attempt, see Leif Wenar, "The Nature of Rights."
[74] Hart, "Are There Natural Rights?" p. 181.
[75] Mill, *On Liberty*, p. 276 (chap. IV, ¶3).
[76] Hobbes, *Leviathan*, p. 79 (chap. 15, ¶1).

protection of interests or respect for the will – the jurisdictional function.[77] I do not claim that all well-formed rights must be jurisdictional, or that justifications of specific rights cannot combine jurisdictional considerations with the importance of choice or protecting interests. I do not present the jurisdictional analysis as a *theory* of rights at all, at least if by "theory" we mean an account that identifies necessary conditions for a well-formed right claim.

18.2 RIGHTS AND DEVOLUTION

Fred D'Agostino has advanced a subtle and empirically sophisticated analysis of the problem (which is our problem) of "commensurating" diverse values, of finding ways that people with diverse orderings of standards can come to some sort of social agreement. Typically, the problem of the "incommensurability" of values is seen as a metaphysical problem about the very nature of values, an epistemological problem about our lack of access to the correct ways to compare multiple dimensions of value, or a conceptual problem about vagueness.[78] D'Agostino approaches it as a practical problem: what devices can we employ to achieve some sort of agreed-upon social ordering or outcome when we are faced with irresolvable differences in the individual ordering of values? We have just explored one "device" D'Agostino analyzes: abstracting to a common perspective where our orderings converge.[79] He considers another way in which individuals with deep disagreements in their ordering of evaluative standards may nonetheless share a common moral framework: "[i]n effect, we say that in a society with *n* individual members, there are *n* separate spheres in which an answer . . . may be sought, each of which is, in theory, inviolable and particular to the individual who occupies it."[80] If we partition the moral space in this way, for each and every

[77] This function of rights has been stressed by Eric Mack, "In Defense of the Jurisdiction Theory of Rights." He shows that it does not collapse into either the choice or interest theories.
[78] For examples of these approaches, see the essays in Ruth Chang's edited volume, *Incommensurability, Incomparability, and Practical Reason.*
[79] D'Agostino, *Incommensurability and Commensuration*, p. 100.
[80] Ibid., p. 105. See also my *Justificatory Liberalism*, pp. 199ff.

person there is some part of the moral space over which her evaluative standards have public standing. In that part of the moral space controlled by a person, her evaluative standards are sovereign, and others must respect those standards in that space.

Let us return to our original problem: we have a dispute about some possible moral rule, which we can understand as providing a social moral regulation of some "social space," and so our problem is how to regulate that space – what moral requirements we are to share that instruct us in how to act in various parts of that space. Kant and Rousseau conceive of the problem of moral legislation as finding a common way of regulating the moral decision space. We can think of this as a centralizing response (which is implicit in Kant's understanding of a *law*). And it may seem implicit in the very idea of a *rule*. Under conditions of deep evaluative diversity, as we saw in Chapter V, this centralizing response is apt to lead to indeterminacy of justification. If we take as inputs a large body of diverse standards and seek to generate a single type of conduct that is required of all, we are unlikely to succeed. If we are to adequately cope with these "burdens of justification" we cannot rely solely – or even mainly – on centralizing responses to public justification. Rather than seeking a uniform way to regulate the moral space, we must partition it. We can devolve authority over different parts of it to different individuals.

Such partitioning yields a system of jurisdictional rights. Hart pointed out that some rights grant the rightholder "authority or sovereignty in relation to some specific matter."[81] Jurisdictional rights are individualized spheres of moral authority in which the rightholder's judgment about what is to be done provides others with moral reasons to act. A regime of jurisdictional individual moral rights is thus a form of public justification – or perhaps it is better understood as a way to settle the problem of public justification in such a way that in the future it is no longer a collective problem. Benjamin Constant, I think, saw this in his famous lecture, "The Liberty of the Ancients Compared with That of the Moderns." Constant noted that the liberty of the ancients consisted of "exercising collectively, but directly, several parts of the complete

[81] Hart, "Are There Natural Rights?" p. 184.

sovereignty."[82] For the ancients, freedom manifested itself as a centralized, collective activity. In contrast, the moderns conceive of freedom in terms of individualized spheres in which a person's own evaluative standards hold sway, such as freedom of association and religion, the right to "choose a profession and practice it, to dispose of property, and even to abuse it; to come and go without permission, and without having to account for their motives or undertakings."[83]

18.3 THE RIGHT OF PRIVATE PROPERTY

John Gray once noted how private property rights economize on collective justification:

The importance of several [i.e., private] property for civil society is that it acts as an enabling device whereby rival and possibly incommensurable conceptions of the good may be implemented and realized without any recourse to any collective decision-procedure. . . . One may even say of civil society that it is a device for securing peace by reducing to a minimum the decisions on which recourse to collective choice – the political or public choice that is binding on all – is unavoidable.[84]

Private property rights are quintessentially jurisdictional. To own property is to have a sphere in which one's evaluative standards have great authority for others. A property owner has extensive moral powers within the sphere of his property. If a church is owned by the Roman Catholics, it can insist that those who enter must conform to a wide range of its controversial standards. Within a large range of discretion, they can determine these standards: they can insist that certain language not be used, that those who enter engage in certain actions, and even that they make certain professions of belief. And they have the power to change these requirements. The rights and responsibilities of those in a Hustler Club are rather different, as are those in a university seminar room.

[82] See Benjamin Constant, "The Liberty of the Ancients Compared with that of the Moderns," p. 311.
[83] Ibid., p. 311.
[84] John Gray, *Post-Enlightenment Liberalism*, p. 314.

In all cases the owner has the power to grant liberties, impose obligations and conditions, or waive them on the basis of her own evaluative standards. Although in the public realm one possesses simply one controversial set of evaluative standards among others, within the sphere of one's property one's evaluative standards have moral authority over others.

A deeply pluralistic social order can effectively cope with many of its disagreements about what evaluative standards to adopt by establishing a system of private property. As Jeremy Waldron observes, private "[o]wnership . . . expresses the abstract idea of an object being correlated with the name of some individual, in relation to a rule which says that society will uphold that individual's decision as final when there is any dispute about how the object should be used."[85] Ownership establishes the authority of the owner over other persons in respect to what is owned. Although a person owns a part of the natural or social world, the authority of ownership implies that other agents must defer to the owner in disputes about the use of that which is owned and the conditions for its use. The decision of the owner is normally determinative for others.

Many have insisted, however, that the ideas of private property and ownership are anachronistic. Although in a simpler world it was possible and important to identify "the" owner of, say, a piece of real property, today the concept of property has disintegrated into a list of separable rights, liberties, and powers.[86] Drawing on the classic analysis of A. M. Honoré, let us say that a person (Alf) has full ownership of ρ if Alf has[87]

(1) *Right of Use*: Alf has a right to use ρ, that is,
   (a) Alf has liberty to use ρ, and
   (b) Alf has a claim that others not interfere with his use of ρ.
(2) *Right of Exclusion* (or possession): Others may use ρ if and only if Alf consents, that is,

---

[85] Jeremy Waldron, *The Right to Private Property*, p. 47.
[86] Thomas C. Grey, "The Disintegration of Property."
[87] A. M. Honoré, "Ownership." See also Frank Snare, "The Concept of Property" and Lawrence C. Becker, *Property Rights*, chap. 2.

(a) If Alf consents others have a liberty to use ρ;

(b) If Alf does not consent others have a duty not to use ρ.

(3) *Right to Compensation*: If someone damages or uses ρ without Alf's consent, then Alf has a right to compensation from that person.

(4) *Rights to Destroy, Waste, or Modify*: Alf may destroy ρ, waste it, or change it.

(5) *Right to Income*: Alf has a right to the financial benefits of forgoing his own use of ρ and letting someone else use it.

(6) *Absence of Term*: Alf's rights over ρ are of indefinite duration.

(7) *Liability to Execution*: ρ may be taken away from Alf for repayment of a debt.

(8) *Power of Transfer*: Alf may permanently transfer (1)–(7) to specific persons by consent.

We could add some rights to this list for an even fuller notion of ownership, but (1)–(8) spell out a fairly complete notion of ownership. If Alf has rights (1)–(8) over ρ, he is the owner in a full-fledged sense. But, today we find these various "incidents" divided in complex ways. One may sell his right to live in a house, put it in trust (in which case the trustee no longer has the right to use it uneconomically), sign over to a historic commission the right to change the exterior or agree to a covenant with one's neighbors about acceptable exterior colors, and so on. Thomas Grey asks:

When a full owner of a thing begins to cede various rights over it – the right to use for this purpose tomorrow, for that purpose next year, and so on – at what point does he cease to be the owner, and who then owns the things? You can say that each one of many right holders owns it to the extent of the right, or you can say that no one owns it.[88]

To think about what sort of ownership is required to cope with the burdens of public justification, recall that given the problem of evaluative pluralism, we can see that each Member of the Public has a fundamental interest in instituting a system whereby the natural and social world is divided into different jurisdictions in

---

[88] Grey, "The Disintegration of Property."

which the evaluative standards of the "owner" – the rightholder –
will be determinative. There are three dimensions along which
such a system of property rights can be "strong." (*i*) A strong property right may simply be defined as full ownership. For each ρ
which is held as property there may be someone who has the full
set of ownership rights over it. In the above passage Grey stresses
that in this sense current systems of property rights are not very
strong: ownership is often far short of full ownership. (*ii*) Property
systems are strong in another sense if whatever property rights
(whatever "incidents" in the above list) that Alf holds regarding ρ,
these rights (liberties or powers) are not easily overridden by other
moral and political claims. Libertarians sometimes seem to suppose
that if ρ is owned it must be impossible to justifiably override the
owner's rights; this would be a maximally strong, or absolute right
to property. A system could still have strong property rights, but
overriding them with good reasons may be justifiable. If, though,
overriding was easily justifiable in most cases, the system would
fail to be strong on this dimension even if people generally had the
full set of ownership rights. (*iii*) The system assigning property
rights is strong qua extensive insofar as for any decision about any
social or natural asset or object ρ there will be some individual or
non-governmental group that has authority over it, though different incidents may be held by different private actors. Thus systems
that do not allow the private ownership of natural resources or
productive assets fail to be strong in this respect.

Members of the Public will endorse a system of property rights
that tends toward being strong in the last two senses: rights that are
not easily overridden and that are extensive, including private
property in capital assets. Whereas Constant identified the right to
"to dispose of property, and even to abuse it" as one of the rights of
the moderns, in Rawls' gloss on the rights of the moderns, private
property has at best a minor role. In some places Rawls includes
among the liberties of the moderns "basic" rights of property, while
at other times no mention at all is made of property. In any event,
Rawls maintains that "while a right to property in productive
assets is permitted, that right is not a basic right but subject to the

requirement that, in existing conditions, it is the most effective way to meet principles of justice."[89] Rawls thus holds that a form of market socialism is justifiable.[90] Now suppose that Rawls' restriction of private property to "personal property" means simply private property in consumer goods but not in residences or buildings. In a regime in which everyone is a renter from the state, the state's policies determine what a person is entitled to do in her home, from decorating to cohabitating with others; whether she is given liberties, and what they may be, or whether her freedom is restricted – all this is a decision of a social authority. Given the pervasiveness of reasonable pluralism, these directives will, at best, manifest the evaluative standards of some rather than others. Without the private ownership of residences and buildings, the ability of each to have a sphere in which her standards are sovereign is drastically reduced. As we saw above (§17.3d, Display VI-1), most believe that freedom rights are restricted in public buildings; if all buildings are public, the freedom rights of dissenting groups are almost certain to be severely curtailed. If we allow ownership of structures, then we will have property markets, and the opportunities to make profit by investment arises.

Suppose we permit some markets and private investments, but, as has been done by some socialist states, prohibit people from hiring more than a handful of others. As we saw in the earlier quote, for Rawls whether or not we should do so simply depends on what is the "best" way to achieve economic justice. The clear implication is that whether we allow private property in productive assets is simply an instrumental question that has no intrinsic relevance to justice. What is, I think, remarkable about this, is that although Rawls seeks to reply to "Marx's critique of liberalism,"[91] his account of economic systems misses perhaps the most profound of Marx's criticism of the economic order of his time – that laborers worked merely to live rather than lived to work. Work becomes "not the satisfaction of a need but a mere means to satisfy needs

---

89 Rawls, *Justice as Fairness*, p. 177. Rawls includes property at *Political Liberalism*, p. 5, and *Justice as Fairness*, p. 2; he omits it at *A Theory of Justice*, p. 195; *Justice as Fairness*, p. 144; and *Political Liberalism*, p. 299.
90 Ibid., pp. 137–8.
91 Ibid., p. 176ff.

external to it."[92] One understanding of the human good is productive work. Now valued work is varied, from artisanship to team work, but it also involves organization, personal initiative, and innovation in production. Entrepreneurship is itself a form of human flourishing (in some ways, a thought more akin to Marx than to Rawls). Start-ups, innovation, risk taking, organizing groups to solve problems and implement new ideas – all these are not simply ways to produce the stuff to be distributed according to "economic justice": they are basic to the evaluative standards of some Members of the Public.[93] To exclude all these personal ideals about what is worth doing in life on the grounds that by adopting a socialist system we have the purported best means to arrive at an abstract theory of justice unacceptably constrains the ability of many to lead lives in which their fundamental values hold sway over some parts of their life.

But, it will almost certainly be pressed, doesn't this simply mean that the workers will be unable to have *their* values hold sway during their working lives? Much depends on who we mean by "the workers" and what constitutes "prevention." J. S. Mill favored firms jointly managed by the workers and owned collectively by them (but workers were not to own individual shares, so they could not take their investment in the firm with them when they left, or sell it).[94] He believed that in the short term such firms could co-exist with capitalist firms, although over the long term Mill thought that capitalist firms would wither away, as the workers opted for the democratic life of cooperative firms. "[T]here can be little doubt that the status of hired labourers will gradually tend to confine itself to the description of workpeople whose low moral qualities render them unfit for anything more independent: and that the relation of masters and workpeople will be gradually superseded by partnership, in one of two forms: in some cases,

---

[92] Karl Marx, *Economic and Philosophical Manuscripts of 1844* ["Estranged Labour"], p. 74.

[93] An investor in the "Impossible Project," a firm seeking to bring Polaroid film back into production, said to the founder: "I have looked all your team in the eye and none of them is in here for the money. They are in here to make it happen." *Financial Times*, August 15/16, 2009, Life and Arts Section, p. 15.

[94] Mill, *Principles of Political Economy*, Book IV, chap. 8.

association of the labourers with the capitalist; in others, and perhaps finally in all, association of labourers among themselves."[95] Mill was right that the master–servant relation is a basic element of capitalism.[96] As R. M. Coase and his followers have effectively shown, the "master and servant" relation is a source of efficiency in the hierarchical firm, reducing transaction costs.[97] Now if firms with the master/servant relation are more efficient, they generally will be able to offer higher wages than competing cooperative firms and so, contrary to Mill's expectations, successfully compete against cooperatives for workers. Although worker cooperatives have managed to survive in some environments, they generally have not been able to effectively compete against capitalist, hierarchical firms. We must remember that the promotion of personal autonomy is not part of social morality (§§17.2, 17.3b). Contrary to Mill, who personally embraced a perfectionist ideal of personal autonomy, we cannot say that there is anything morally suspicious about a worker exchanging some personal autonomy for higher wages, shorter working hours, or the prospect of advancement. A proponent of worker cooperatives may insist that just because capitalist firms are often more attractive to real-world workers, they effectively "prevent" the flourishing of worker-managed cooperatives, and so workers who value their autonomy should take precedence; there should be regulations that hinder the rise of firms based on the master–servant relation. Such pleas cannot be honored in a free and diverse society; they seek to inhibit competing ways of life in the name of a rationally controversial evaluative standard. "We cannot have what we value if the others act on what they value, since our option will be insufficiently popular, so we must inhibit people from going over to our competitors." Small cities such as Duluth, Minnesota, can make precisely the same claim about the attractiveness of the Minneapolis–Saint Paul job

---

[95] Mill, *Principles of Political Economy*, p. 769 (Book 4, chap.7, §4).

[96] For characterizations of capitalism that make it central, see Talcott Parsons' "Introduction" to Max Weber, *The Theory of Social and Economic Organization*, p. 51; Niehans, *A History of Economic Theory*, p. 144; Karl Marx, *Capital*, chap. 14, §5.

[97] See R. M. Coase, *The Firm, the Market and the Law*, chap. 2; Oliver E. Williamson, *The Economic Institutions of Capitalism*. See also P. J. D. Wiles, *Economic Institutions Compared*, pp. 69ff, chap. 6.

market, which drains Duluth of its young. According to the Presumption in Favor of Liberty (§17.3a) people need not justify acting on their own evaluative standards; in contrast, project and plans that can only succeed by limiting others from acting as they see fit require justification.

I have thus far said little about strong property rights in the most common (our first) sense – if one is an owner, one is a "full" owner. No doubt over some property such extensive ownership will be important, but so long as an exchange of rights is possible, individuals can accrue customized jurisdictions that best suit their evaluative standards.[98] Indeed, the "disintegration" of property is *required* by a concern for evaluative pluralism as it allows individuals to secure those domains that best suit their understanding of what is important. However, because it is impossible to fully specify contractual rights, and to leave a right regarding ρ unspecified is essentially a decision that it remain common property and so subject to conflicting evaluative standards, some notion of residue ownership is required in an effective system of property jurisdictions.

18.4 PRIVACY AND OTHER RIGHTS

(a) The Dimensions of Privacy
Jurisdictional rights are not exhausted by private property. Mill's defense of a "self-regarding sphere" in which "the individual is sovereign" is the classic liberal case for individual jurisdictions.[99] Such a sphere is composed not simply of property rights (in fact, Mill has little to say about property in *On Liberty*), but crucially, of privacy rights too. To be sure, privacy and property rights overlap.[100] If we think of privacy of places such as hotel rooms, houses, and clubs, claims to privacy can be understood as quasi-property rights: rights to use and exclude. So too with privacy of information. To say that information is private is to say that you have

---

[98] This alerts us to be the danger of supposing that control and not transfer (and so income through exchange) is crucial to justified ownership. Cf. Waldron, *The Right to Private Property*, pp. 43ff; John Christman, *The Myth of Property*, esp. Part I.
[99] Mill, *On Liberty*, Chap. 1, ¶9.
[100] See Stephen R. Munzer, *A Theory of Property*, pp. 90–8.

control over its use and dissemination, again giving one a quasi-property right over it. Like property rights, privacy rights are a complex bundle of liberties, claims, immunities, and powers.[101]

PRIVACY AS AN IMMUNITY. A fundamental aspect of the claim that one has a sphere of privacy is that within this sphere what one does is not the business of others. As we have seen, when something is a matter of morality, it is everyone's business – everyone has standing to demand that we conform to the moral rules (§11.2). When a matter is subject to legislation, it is the state's business. A claim to a private sphere is a claim that one has an immunity against assertion of social authority to regulate matters within the sphere. As Benn points out in his detailed analysis of privacy, a sphere in which one is immune to the demands of others is fundamental to the liberal tradition.

The totalitarian claims that everything a person does and is has significance for society at large. He sees the state as the self-conscious organization of society for the well-being of society; the social significance of our actions and relations overrides any other. Consequently, the public or political universe is all-inclusive, *all* roles are public, and every function, whether political, economic, artistic, or religious, can be interpreted as a public responsibility. [102]

A sphere of privacy is a claim that parts of our lives are immune to social demands. Within this sphere we are free to act on our own evaluative standards; we can rest assured that we shall not be subject to purported justifications of intrusions. When it is claimed that reproductive decisions are a private matter, for instance, it is being claimed that this matter is not, and cannot be, subject to authoritative demands from others, or society at large.

PRIVACY AS A CLAIM. *On Liberty's* defense of a self-regarding sphere can be read mainly as a defense of the immunity of an individual from the authority of society. Actions in that sphere, Mill argues, are not subject to punishment, either by the formal

---

[101] This subsection draws on Benn's detailed analysis in *A Theory of Freedom*, chaps. 14 and 15.
[102] Ibid., p. 289.

mechanism of the law or informal social sanctions. We have already seen that Mill conceives of liability to blame (and punishment) as analytically tied to obligation (§11.3*b*), so the self-regarding sphere is a sphere in which one is free from the obligations of social morality and the law, and which neither social morality nor the law is empowered to regulate. Thus individuals have an immunity from imposition of obligations on them in this sphere. Now this means that in a juridical sense what others do is not our business, but Mill also thought that in a nonauthoritative manner we *should* make the doings of others our business:

Though doing no wrong to anyone, a person may so act as to compel us to judge him, and feel to him, as a fool, or as a being of an inferior order: and since this judgment and feeling are a fact which he would prefer to avoid, it is doing him a service to warn him of it beforehand, as of any other disagreeable consequence to which he exposes himself. It would be well, indeed, if this good office were much more freely rendered than the common notions of politeness at present permit, and if one person could honestly point out to another that he thinks him in fault, without being considered unmannerly or presuming. We have a right, also, in various ways, to act upon our unfavourable opinion of any one, not to the oppression of his individuality, but in the exercise of ours. We are not bound, for example, to seek his society: we have a right to avoid it (though not to parade the avoidance), for we have a right to choose the society most acceptable to us. We have a right, and it may be our duty, to caution others against him, if we think his example or conversation likely to have a pernicious effect on those with whom he associates. We may give others a preference over him in optional good offices, except those which tend to his improvement. In these various modes a person may suffer very severe penalties at the hands of others, for faults which directly concern only himself: but he suffers these penalties only in so far as they are the natural, and, as it were, the spontaneous consequences of the faults themselves, not because they are purposely inflicted on him for the sake of punishment.[103]

Mill was an exceptionally strong-willed and willing to defy social expectations. For the rest of us, it is intimidation to suffer "severe penalties" at the hands of others in the form of their avoidance of us on the grounds that they disapprove of our sexual proclivities,

---

[103] Mill, *On Liberty*, p. 278 (chap. IV, ¶5).

our tastes in literature, the diseases that we have contracted, or our regular attendance at Buffalo Bills games. And if we thought that we would get a good "talking to" from our disapproving friends or employer, this would be a very significant deterrent to acting on our standards. Over some aspects of our life, we need a stronger interpretation of the claim that what we do is not other people's business – we must possess a moral claim that certain information about us not be disseminated without our approval, and that many of our activities be shielded from the public gaze. As Hubert Humphrey remarked, "We act differently if we believe we are being observed. If we can never be sure whether or not we are being watched and listened to, all our actions will be altered and our very character will change."[104]

PRIVACY AS A POWER. Privacy rights are not simply on/off claims that we can either insist upon or waive; they give us a large degree of control over what aspects of our life are made available, and to whom, and for what purposes. Privacy rights give us "the ability to maintain the state of being private or to relax it, and to the degree that, and to whom, one chooses."[105] Information may be shared with a limited number of people for specific purposes (as with medical records) or it may be shared with those with whom we are doing business (as with confidential business records). We may (or at least some of us) license others to use our image for profit, or we may go on Facebook and tell everything to 2,447 "friends." Privacy rights allow us to manage what others do and do not know about us. We can consult our evaluative standards to decide when they are served by sharing with some, or all, and when they are enhanced by restricting the flow of information about us. Privacy allows us to determine whether our evaluative standards are best served by private, semiprivate, or fully public performances.

(b) Freedom of Association
Other rights also perform the critical function of identifying a sphere in which our evaluative standards either publicly hold

[104] Quoted in Stanley I. Benn, "Privacy, Freedom and Respect for Persons." p. 241.
[105] Benn, *A Theory of Freedom*, p. 266.

sway, or it is publicly acknowledged that we are free to act on our standards without others being empowered to inquire and to judge. Freedom of association is fundamental to each having a sphere in which she may participate in the construction of a social world that corresponds to the demands of her evaluative standards. Many of our evaluative standards are social: their success requires the participation of others. As we saw earlier, under some conditions standards that require the mandatory participation of others may thwart public justification (§18.3). But many social evaluative standards can be satisfied by associations of like-minded others who, at least in some parts of their lives, devise rules and practices that are based on values and goals that can be achieved only by common projects and undertakings. Indeed, it has been powerfully argued that to take pluralism seriously leads to the fundamental role of voluntary associations in a free society.[106] As should be apparent by this juncture, if we are all to live as free and equal, society as a whole cannot be devoted to the pursuit of a set of values or a "comprehensive conception of the good." A free society cannot be what Michael Oakeshott calls an "enterprise association," a collective project devoted to achieving specific values, goals, or projects.[107] But if a society is to adequately satisfy the various evaluative standards of its members, it must allow for a diverse range of such enterprises within it: places where people arrange their common affairs by devotion to common projects and shared aspirations.

It is important to stress that I am not maintaining that all of our common moral requirements – indeed, not all of moral rights – are inherently jurisdictional. We have already seen that the rights of agency, including rights against being harmed, can be more adequately seen as common basic protections; and even the rights of privacy have this protective, as well as a jurisdictional function. The point to be stressed is that the obstacles to a robust common morality that treats all as free and equal are severe, and a critical project of liberal public reason must be to show that the challenge

---

[106] See John W. Chapman, "Voluntary Association and the Political Theory of Pluralism."

[107] Michael Oakeshott, *On Human Conduct*, essay II.

posed by these obstacles can be met. Jurisdictional rights, I maintain, are crucial to doing so.

18.5 WHAT SCHEME OF RIGHTS?

As Gray correctly claimed, a system of rights reduces to a "minimum" the recourse to collective choice (§18.3). However, no system of jurisdictional rights can do away with collective justification. Most important for our purpose is that we require collective moral justification to partition the moral decision space in some particular way. We cannot do without a common view about which of the large set of potential partitioning systems we shall live under. Of course, not all systems of jurisdictional rights pass the test of public justification. For the first two hundred years of its existence, American society upheld a system of jurisdictional rights in which the moral domains of some whites included the lives and bodies of African Americans. To say that a system of jurisdictional rights is necessary to adequately cope with the burdens of justification is not to claim that any such system will suffice. No such system may justifiably violate the basic rights of agency. Some partitions of the moral space clearly fail the test of the public justification. On the other hand, it seems that a number of schemes of rights will be acceptable to all Members of the Public, though they will disagree about the ordering (our problem of a maximal set with no optimal element once again confronts us; §16.3). It looks as though we are back where we began, with moral disagreement and indeterminacy, though again with a narrowed set of options. We must now turn to grapple with this fundamental problem of the indeterminacy of public justification.

CONCLUSION

In this chapter I have explored how a regime of rights can help us lessen the burdens of public justification in a society characterized by extensive reasonable pluralism. Arguments from abstraction allow us to identify those core demands of agency itself, rights to freedom and protection from harm, manipulation, and invasion. In a society in which all are deeply committed to understanding themselves as agents with aims and reasons to act, these are the fundamental rights in the order of justification. They must be assumed as given when we grapple with further justificatory problems.

What Constant called the liberties of the moderns is one of the great modern discoveries. It provides a framework for a common morality that reconciles deep differences in our evaluative standards by devolving moral authority to individuals, giving each a sphere in which her evaluative standards have authority. A regime of rights is the key to solving Rousseau's fundamental problem: reconciling freedom and social order. Rousseau did not appreciate this, and neither do many of his contemporary followers, who are enamored with the "liberties of the ancients" – collective decisions (or commensuration) to reach joint judgments about socially endorsed evaluative standards. A current fascination in contemporary political theory is "deliberative democracy" – a diverse family of views favoring enlarging the scope of democratic decision making based on widespread public deliberation aiming at consensus.[108] In this view the regulative ideal "is agreement of conviction on the basis of public reasons uttered as assessed in public discourse."[109] Even Rawls came to embrace some version of this doctrine.[110] Apparently we are still held captive by the highly idealized picture in our mind's eye of the Athenian polis: why can't we again be like that? (Was it ever like that?)

The attempt to emulate in practice a romantic image of the past can only lead to authoritarianism and oppression. Deliberative democracy supposes that our differences in evaluative standards are, as it were, only on the surface. Once we reason together and talk things through, deliberative democrats hold that our value orderings will be transformed;[111] the range of disagreement will so radically narrow that the problems of social commensuration will become fairly insignificant, if not vanish altogether. Surely, though,

---

[108] The core work here has been done by Jürgen Habermas. See his "Popular Sovereignty as Procedure."

[109] Gerald J. Postema, "Public Practical Reason: Political Practice," p. 356.

[110] Rawls declares himself to be a "deliberative democrat" in "The Idea of Public Reason Revisited, p. 772.

[111] See Jon Elster, "The Market and Forum," pp. 10–11.

this is a fantastic claim; in the end deliberative democrats acknowledge that we must cut off discussion and take a vote, but then the majority is subjugating others to their judgment in the name of public reason – reason that is not shared by the dissenting minority. And we know that there is nothing uniquely correct about the outputs of any actual voting procedures. Once we accept that our disagreements are widespread and deep – that the range of possible value orderings is essentially unlimited – democratic procedures simply are not up to the task of collective commensuration (again we come back to Arrow-like problems, §16.3c).

I have argued that our commitment to treating others as free and equal moral persons implies a commitment to the public justification of our moral claims. Given reasonable evaluative diversity, the public justification of a social morality must, somehow, take these reasonably diverse standards and arrive at a common, justified morality. The burdens of justification are weighty. A regime of rights helps solve the commensuration problem by devolving moral authority. Thus I have upheld the liberty of the moderns – understood as a system of individual rights – over the liberty of the ancients, which stressed collective decision making as the primary mode of public commensuration.

VII

Moral Equilibrium and Moral Freedom

> Living as members of society and dependent for the satisfaction of most of our needs on various forms of cooperation with others, we depend for the effective pursuit of our aims clearly on the correspondence of the expectations concerning the actions of others on which our plans are based with what they really will do. This matching of the intentions and expectations that determine the actions of different individuals is the form which order manifests itself in social life. . . . [The] . . . authoritarian connotation of the concept of order derives . . . from the belief that order can be created only by forces outside the systems (or "exogenously"). It does not apply to an equilibrium set up from within (or "endogenously").
>
> F. A. Hayek, *Rules and Order*

> The law is the creation of the authoritative decisions of society, that is, its officials, its legislators, and judges. In relation to the making and applying of the law, though, the members of a legal order are merely its subjects. . . . .By contrast, a society's morality is the joint product of the moralities of its individual members. As far as its content is concerned, individual members are its joint makers, not merely its subjects.
>
> Kurt Baier, *The Rational and the Moral Order*

The previous chapter examined two "devices of public reason" – approaches to public justification that help us cope with the diversity of evaluative standards, those individual bases for reasoning about the acceptability of moral rules. One device is to abstract away from our many disagreements to our fundamental common evaluative standards as agents. The rights of agency are, I argued, basic in the order of justification because agency is basic to our conception of who we are. However, as we saw, it does not follow that every moral right or claim that we would make from the abstracted perspective of agency is one that we have sufficient reason to make, all things considered. Nevertheless, we can identify certain abstract rights to which, all things considered, moral persons are committed. The other device of public reason is the idea of jurisdictional rights, which I believe is one of the most important modern innovations in moral life. Rather than insisting that the question "what is the right thing to do?" must be answered by a common judgment about the correct evaluative standards to apply in specific situations, in a culture of tolerance we often devolve moral authority, providing to each a sphere in which her evaluative standards have public standing.

These are the critical insights of the liberal tradition about how to arrive at a publicly justified moral order among free and equal moral persons who reasonably disagree on the basis for evaluating that order. However, as I stressed throughout the previous chapter, they provide us with only general or abstract principles or guidelines, not with the sorts of rules that can provide the basis for firm mutual expectations about, as Hayek says in an epigraph to this chapter, what people will really do. The fundamental problem now becomes how we move from abstract principles to an actual ordered social life (and is there no possibility for such order except on this basis of abstract principles?). We normally think that when faced with a set of maximal options (among which, in some sense, society is "indifferent"), we must socially decide on a procedure that allows us to justifiably select from the set. This, we will see, in the next chapter, is the method of political adjudication. However, as Hayek and Baier both stress in our lead quotations, the moral order (at least for the most part) is not created by an imposed political decision; it is, or at least can be, an internal equilibrium. In this chapter I seek to show how this can be so, and how such an equilibrium respects the status of each as a free and equal moral person. Thus we will arrive at a nonpolitical solution to Rousseau's fundamental problem, with which we began: "how each, while uniting himself with all, may still obey himself alone, and remain as free as before?"

19 Coordinating on a Morality

19.1 THE PROCEDURAL JUSTIFICATION REQUIREMENT

Even after we have employed our two devices of public reason we are left with optimal eligible sets (or in Sen's terms, "maximal sets"; §§16.1a, 16.3). Arguments from abstraction justify some rights to freedom of thought and speech, freedom of occupation, protection from harm, and so on, but these are abstract and general ideas, the interpretation of which is the subject of great controversy. After having concluded the argument from abstract agency, we must again resort to the Deliberative Model: our Members of the Public propose specific interpretations of these abstract rights (and rank the proposals). For the reasons we canvassed in section 16.3 they again will be left with an optimal eligible set that is neither null nor a singleton. As I indicated in section 17.6, the argument here for a nonempty eligible set is especially compelling; these rights are fundamental to our agency itself, so failure to justify any specific right as eligible would be a moral disaster. So too with jurisdictional rights; the great liberal insight is that there is little prospect for a publicly justified moral order unless each can be given a significant sphere in which her evaluative standards have authority to shape her social relations.

When faced with a substantive disagreement about what is best, but each also having a strong reason to select some member of the maximal set, it is natural to suppose we should resort to a choice procedure. Exhausting, as it were, substantive public reasoning about what rule (interpretation) is best, we might pick out one element of the optimal eligible set via some social choice procedure. However, the same reasoning that showed that there was no aggregation method (more determinate than our Pareto-extension rule) that is uncontroversially best also shows why there is no procedure to which all would agree (§16.3c). We are back to the same problem in a different guise. We can see now why Arrow-like analyses are such a threat to the public justification project when we allow great diversity in the basis for evaluation: there is no method to select from the eligible set that is uncontroversially the best. Public justification thus would appear to come to a halt; we confront a large optimal eligible set and can proceed no further.[1] No wonder Rawlsians end up bracketing evaluative diversity, supposing that the reasoning of Members of the Public is identical (§§14.4c–d).

We have been led to our justificatory dead-end by an apparently compelling principle, to wit:

> *The Procedural Justification Requirement*: That process O selects option x from the optimal eligible set cannot show that x is uniquely publicly justified unless O itself is uniquely publicly justified.

The Procedural Justification Requirement seems uncontroversial. The Members of the Public could select a unique x from the optimal set by drawing straws to see which option is selected, but this would justify the selection of x only if drawing straws was the publicly justified procedure. If some Member of the Public ranked drawing straws below summing the ranks of each proposal (the Borda count; see §16.3c), relying on drawing straws rather than employing the Borda count could not be justified to her. She has sufficient reason to hold that summing ranks, and not drawing straws, is the way to proceed. Thus, imposing x on her would fail to treat her as free and equal; she would be subjected to the authority of the proponents of drawing straws.

Despite its apparent obviousness, the Procedural Justification Requirement is misguided. There can be a procedure O, which uniquely selects x from the optimal eligible set, and although O is not itself publicly justified, each Member of the Public, consulting only her own evaluative standards, has sufficient reason to act on x. If this is so, then x solves the fundamental problem; each adopts rule x as the moral rule to be followed, and each has sufficient reasons to do so. Thus x's authority is consistent with the freedom and equality of all. That is the main lesson of this chapter.

---

[1] This is the compelling lesson of Fred D'Agostino's analysis in *Incommensurability and Commensuration*, especially chaps. 1 and 2.

19.2 MODELING COORDINATION

(a) A 2 × 2 Toy Game Analysis

When confronting the problem of indeterminacy of public justification caused by the diversity of evaluative standards, theories of public reason have responded in two ways. Either (*i*) the troublesome evaluative diversity is essentially eliminated and/or (*ii*) some powerful philosophical or decision-theoretic device is employed that breaks through the disagreement and yields a determinate solution. Suppose, however, that our Members of the Public refuse to take either of these routes (because some object). Having exhausted the resources of deliberation, and (as a group) unconvinced by new innovations in decision theory, suppose the Members of the Public stop deliberating and, embracing their results (the socially optimal eligible set),[2] they begin to interact. Since they were deliberating about some area of social life, suppose that they interact in that area – though of course they will have some disagreement about the contours of that area, since we can expect that different members of the optimal eligible set will identify different boundaries. At this point our members of the public face an impure coordination game along the lines of Display VII-1.

Betty

	x	*y*
Alf *x*	2 / 1	0 / 0
y	0 / 0	1 / 2

DISPLAY VII-1 A TOY COORDINATION GAME

We are assuming that *x* and *y* are alternative moral requirements in the socially optimal eligible set. The numbers in the matrix refer to ordinal utility, with high numbers indicating highly ranked options. It is crucial to stress that by "utility" I simply mean a measure of the ranking of the options based on each person's

---

[2] Henceforth, unless explicitly noted otherwise, "optimal eligible set" and "eligible set" refer to the social sets.

evaluative standards. Utility does not mean "self-interest," nor is it an independent value; it is simply a summary measure of how well an option satisfies the evaluative standards (Σ) of the individual as Member of the Public (§9.4d). The uncoordinated outcomes indicate no shared moral rule on this issue. Looked at *ex ante*, Betty's evaluative standards give her reason to endorse rule x; Alf's lead him to endorse y. *Ex ante*, Betty does not have reason to accept y over x, nor does Alf have reason to accept x rather than y. They do, however, have reason to coordinate on either of the two requirements rather than none at all. That is, they have reason to coordinate on some member of the optimal eligible set (recall the lesson of Buridan's ass; §16.1a). Should Alf and Betty find themselves at x/x neither would have reason to unilaterally change his or her action. Given each of their evaluative standards, they would have the most reason to act on rule x. Should they instead find themselves at y/y, each would then have most reason (given his or her evaluative standards) to act on y. Note that in neither case is any party induced by some external consideration to conform to a requirement that is not, from his or her perspective, optimal: *consulting simply his or her own evaluative standards, each has decisive reason to freely endorse whichever moral requirement they have coordinated on.* At x/x Betty can demand that Alf conform and, consulting only his own evaluative standards, he will have a reason to conform, and at y/y Alf can demand conformity to y, and Betty will have reason to act on it – and this even though, from the initial deliberative perspective, neither had reason to act on the other's preferred moral requirement.[3] In our 2 × 2 game Members of the Public converge on one member of the optimal eligible set, both of which are Nash equilibria. Every element of the optimal eligible set is a Nash equilibrium; having arrived at some coordinated morality that is within the optimal eligible set, no Member of the Public has reason to unilaterally change her "move" – to unilaterally act on another rule in the set. It is important to stress that in making this decision, she consults only her own set of evaluative standards and

---

[3]   Again, we should not be misled by the language of "preference." To prefer x to y is simply to rank x over y for purposes of choice; in our terms one's evaluative standards indicate reason to rank x over y – this is all that is implied by saying one has a preference for x over y. See sections 9.4b, 16.1a.

does that which *best* satisfies her standards. She is not bound by prior agreement to coordinate or a desire to compromise; as in the Deliberative Model, she consults only her full set of relevant evaluative standards and performs the act that best satisfies them.

(b) The Kantian Coordination Game: An N-Person Iterated Toy Game

A one-shot two-person game can give us some insight, but it is clearly an inadequate way to model the selection of a moral rule from the optimal eligible set. The relevant coordination problem is not a single-play game, but an iterated game. We have a number of encounters with others, and each can be understood as a play in a series of impure coordination games. Recall that in an iterated game a person's utility (again, remember this is defined solely in terms of her evaluative criteria) is a combination of her utility in this play, plus her expectations for utility in future games (§6.1). Thus a person might sacrifice utility in one play to induce play in future moves that will yield her a more favored result. Moreover, it is certainly the case that in iterated games the play can move from one equilibrium to another. Peter Vanderschraaf and Brian Skyrms have shown how taking turns on each of the two equilibria emerges in iterated two-person impure coordination games.[4]

However, in large *N*-person impure coordination games with a large number of potential equilibria, a "taking turns" solution is practically impossible. In such large *N* iterated games a bandwagon effect takes over. To intuitively see the driving force behind bandwagon effects, let us assume for ease of exposition a cardinal utility measure (10 = best, 0 = no coordination) in a game with just two equilibria and nine players, as in Display VII-2:

	A	B	C	D	E	F	G	H	I
x	2	3	4	5	6	7	8	9	10
y	10	9	8	7	6	5	4	3	2

DISPLAY VII-2: DIFFERENT EVALUATIONS OF TWO MORAL RULES

If player A coordinates with another player on his preferred moral requirement (*y*), he ranks that option as satisfying his evaluative

---

[4] Peter Vanderschraaf and Brian Skyrms, "Learning to Take Turns."

standards to degree 10; if they coordinate on x he scores the outcome as 2. If he fails to coordinate – he acts on, say, y while the other acts on x – they each get 0. Of course at this point he cannot claim that his rule has authority over another unless the other also "plays" it. Indignation, resentment, and so on would be inappropriate responses by an x-player confronting a person who plays y; the x player must admit that the y player does not have sufficient reason to act on x.[5] So there is a morality that treats each as a free and equal person only when two players meet who endorse the same rule, for then both hold that this is the moral rule (from the optimal eligible set) that they both have sufficient reasons to endorse.

Now what is a Member of the Public to do given these differences in evaluative standards? Consider a simple-minded but illustrative policy. Each begins play by employing her favored requirement in all her interactions (except for player E who flips a coin and, given the flip, acts on the y requirement). Again, if a player coordinates with another player on the same requirement, each gets her coordination payoff in Display VII-2; otherwise each player receives 0 since they fail to coordinate (and so there is no basis for moral claims between them). At the close of each round a player compares the score she received in that round with what she would have received if all others had played just as they did, but she played the opposite. If the opposite play would have resulted in a higher score (i.e., her relevant evaluative standards would have been better satisfied), she changes her move. Assuming that each player meets every other player once in the first round, we have the payoffs in Display VII-3.

In round 2, player F, given her own evaluative criteria, should switch her allegiance to y; if F had played y in round 1, she would have received 25 (5×5) rather than 21. Once F switches from x to y in round 2, at the end of round 2 player G will find that she would have done better (24 rather than 16) by changing to y, so G then will also change to y. And once G also has changed to y, players H and I will also do so. We quickly reach an all-y equilibrium.

---

[5] For simplicity, I suppose that the different rules call for different actions, say ϕ and not-ϕ.

Partner→	A	B	C	D	E	F	G	H	I	Total
Player A	–	10	10	10	10	0	0	0	0	40
Player B	9	–	9	9	9	0	0	0	0	36
Player C	8	8	–	8	8	0	0	0	0	32
Player D	7	7	7	–	7	0	0	0	0	28
Player E	6	6	6	6	–	0	0	0	0	24
Player F	0	0	0	0	0	–	7	7	7	21
Player G	0	0	0	0	0	8	–	8	8	24
Player H	0	0	0	0	0	9	9	–	9	27
Player I	0	0	0	0	0	10	10	10	–	30

DISPLAY VII-3 N-PERSON KANTIAN COORDINATION GAME, ROUND 1

It is crucial to realize that the all-y equilibrium is not reached through a collective decision procedure. Because in our example the entire process began with E's toss of a coin, it may seem as if we have simply assumed that a toss of the coin is a justified procedure for identifying a specific equilibrium. This, of course, would simply beg the question: how did we come to view *this* procedure as publicly justified? The Kantian Coordination Game is important because we can see how, contrary to the Procedural Justification Requirement, a social process that is not itself justified can yield a unique publicly justified outcome. The upshot of the first stage of Kantian public justification (Chapters V and VI) was that y is eligible as a binding, moral, requirement; and according to the second, iterated interaction, stage, each Member of the Public has sufficient reason (simply given her own evaluative standards) to follow y over every other member of the optimal eligible set as the common binding requirement. It cannot be stressed too much that the Members of the Public do not see themselves as bound by the result of the process, as if they had agreed to adopt that member of the optimal eligible set identified by a random procedure, or as if there is an independent justification for employing this iterated procedure. Although a random element begins the process, each acts simply on her own standards and does what she has most reason to do given the free actions of others.

19.3 THE INCREASING RETURNS OF SHARED MORAL
REQUIREMENTS

The Kantian Coordination Game is, of course, still terribly over-simplified, depending on a rather dumb decision rule and an assumption that all players meet all others an equal number of times.[6] And of course we have supposed a certain population distribution. It is by no means inevitable that the Public must converge on a common rule. If in Display VII-2 the entire population was evenly divided between A-type and I-type utility functions, the population could settle into a "polymorphic" equilibrium, with A-types always playing y and I-types always playing x. Note that this is much more likely to occur with populations split into largely noninteracting groups and where each group ranks the other's alternative as only marginally better than no coordination at all. This raises the possibility of a publicly justified "multicultural" society, with each group having different moral codes. One segment could gravitate to an x equilibrium, while another to y. However, this is most unlikely to occur about matters of basic rights when there is significant interaction between the groups. Supposing that the two moralities are incompatible in some case (one prescribing "ϕ!" and the other "not-ϕ!"); those from the different communities would be left without a common social morality in their interactions, a great loss to their evaluative standards.

Despite its obvious limitations, The Kantian Coordination Game brings out a crucial feature of moral life among free and equal persons with a commitment to respecting each other's status: the increasing returns of coordinating on a common understanding of moral requirements. We can think of each Member of the Public as having two distinct morality-related desiderata: (*i*) to act on the moral requirement that best satisfies her evaluative standards and

---

[6] As Brian Skyrms shows, if players can detect other players with complementary utility functions, the analysis of the game is different. See his *Evolution of the Social Contract*, chap. 1. There has not been a great deal of work modeling what equilibrium will emerge in iterated impure coordination games; some experiments cast doubt on whether any simple mechanism, such as the most "salient" solution, will be adopted. See Morton D. Davis, *Game Theory* pp. 133–5. On uncertainty in coordination games, see Fernando Vega-Rodondo, *Economics and the Theory of Games*, pp. 188ff.

(*ii*) to act on moral requirements that are embraced by others, so that in her interactions she can make moral demands that respect their equality and moral freedom. Other things equal, a Member of the Public has reason to seek a common moral life that conforms to (*i*), but as more and more other free and equal persons come to act on some member of the optimal eligible set, the second desideratum comes increasingly into play (even for those such as person I who sees it as much less important than acting on her favored rule). Accepting the moral rules that others do, so long as it is in the optimal eligible set, comes to be the actual way in which each Member of the Public can best satisfy her entire set of evaluative standards.

Formally, converging on a common morality is an instance of increasing returns: the larger the percentage of the population that comes to embrace a certain moral requirement, the more reason others have to also embrace it.[7] As we see in Display VII-2, some people's evaluative standards may strongly favor an alternative moral rule (consider person I), yet so long as everyone places significant importance on acting as others do (the second desideratum), our Members of the Public still end up coordinating: as more and more adopt an alternative, even those who strongly favor another option come on board. As one option (perhaps simply because of some random event) becomes slightly more popular than the others, people will gravitate to that option (as it stands the best chance of universal acceptance), and we witness a bandwagon effect based on the increasing returns. This dynamic is illustrated in Display VII-4.

As we can see, starting out with a population evenly split between advocates of *x* and of *y*, random events can lead the population to all *x* or all *y* equilibria. Which equilibrium emerges will be path dependent: at time zero there is no reason that one or the other should emerge as the *unanimously selected choice*. Chance events, people's reactions to what they perceive as the favored option, the publication of *A Theory of Justice* in 1971 – any can lead

---

[7] The path-breaking work on increasing returns was done by W. Brian Arthur. See his *Increasing Returns and Path Dependency in the Economy*. For the more technically minded, the increasing returns arise from network effects: one's use of a rule has positive externalities for others.

Members of the Public to converge on one member of the optimal eligible set. But once they have arrived at such a convergence, each Member of the Public, consulting only her own evaluative standards, will freely act on the moral requirement in equilibrium. For our purposes what is crucial is that the contingent and accidental way in which large groups can come to coordinate on a common practice is no bar to there being a determinate morality that all can endorse given their evaluative criteria *once it has been arrived at.*

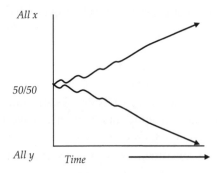

DISPLAY VII-4 INCREASING RETURNS DYNAMICS[8]

19.4 FREEDOM, FAIRNESS, AND EQUILIBRIUM

(a) How a Free Morality is Chosen
According to the Basic Principle of Public Justification (§14.1), a moral imperative based on a moral rule is an authoritative requirement of social morality only if each normal moral agent has sufficient reasons to (*i*) internalize the rule, and (*ii*) hold that the rule requires acts of this type in these circumstances. To respect another as a free and equal moral person is to address moral imperatives to another only if it meets these conditions. As I stressed at the outset (§2.1), this conception of what it is to treat another as free and equal is less expansive than that often associated with Kantian approaches that accord each a fundamental right to be

[8] Adapted from Arthur, *Increasing Returns and Path Dependency in the Economy*, p. 3.

treated only in ways one can endorse, or not reasonably reject. The justification for relying on the Restricted View – in which to respect others as free and equal involves only a constraint on what types of moral authority claims one advances – is not simply that it is a more modest claim, but that the Restricted View is the conception of freedom and equality implicit in the core features of our moral practices (§12.3c). Rather than, as it were, deciding on independent grounds what conception of freedom and equality to endorse, we look to the social morality in which we are participants and seek to understand what its structure and presuppositions give us reasons to endorse. Now on the Restricted View, the type of moral equilibrium I have been sketching is one that respects the moral freedom and equality of all. Positive freedom (§§2.4c, 12.3c) requires that when a person acts on a moral rule she is acting on her own sufficient reasons; the authority of morality is not overriding her reasons based on her evaluative standards – it is expressing them. This is precisely what occurs at the type of equilibrium I have been analyzing. Each Member of the Public, when confronted by a moral demand consults only her own evaluative standards and sees that acting on this moral demand is the thing that best satisfies those standards. No alternative action – either acting on an alternative rule in the optimal eligible set, or no rule at all – better satisfies those standards that are the basis of her deliberation.

That each acts on her own reasons when a rule is an equilibrium solution, of course, does not mean that each acts on the rule she most prefers. That, we have seen, is impossible. If a free agent could legitimately control the actions of others, then she would choose the rule that bests satisfies her evaluative standards and require that all coordinate on it. With a rule in equilibrium, she best satisfies her standards *given what others are doing*. In our Kantian Coordination Game we stipulate that no one is violating the conclusions of public reason as thus far articulated – each acts on some member of the optimal eligible set. And we have also assumed that a person issues an authoritative prescription only when she meets another who shares her rule, so no one claims unjustified moral authority over others. As a free and equal person this is all she can demand of others – to act within public reason and claim no unjustified moral authority over her. She cannot claim a further right to dictate how they should act within those constraints. Given their exercise of their own freedom, and her aim of coordinating with them, she must take into account what they will do (as they must take account of what she will do). Her freedom is not the freedom of an asocial agent who is free simply when she does what she thinks best regardless of what others do, but the freedom of a social moral agent who considers what her evaluative standards deem is the best thing to do *given* what others justifiably do on the basis of their own standards. We can think of this as a Social Realm of Ends populated by free and equal persons with diverse evaluative standards. When a person takes this perspective, she sees that she is free when she acts on a moral rule that is in equilibrium.

The choice of a moral rule in a Social Realm of Ends is not a collective "we" choice; the group, *as a group*, does not choose its moral rules.[9] Nevertheless, a moral rule in equilibrium is a social fact that arises from the interdependent choices of its members. As interdependent individuals, we choose our moral rules — at least, if we are lucky enough to actually possess bona fide moral rules. In the end, this is a real choice of actual people; not a hypothetical choice, or one dictated by impartial reason. To be sure, it is the choice of social creatures, who must take into account what others are doing, and cannot dictate to the group their preferred rule (although, if they are moral philosophers they will probably do their best to). Importantly, although the rule is chosen by members of society, taken individually in their interdependent interactions, and unless some rule was so chosen by the society there would be no effective morality, the authority of the morality does not depend on each and every person choosing the rule. Once society has chosen a rule, if the rule in equilibrium is also a member of the optimal eligible set, *we have created through our actual interdependent choices what impartial reason could not deliver: a uniquely justified rule.* For once the rule is in social equilibrium (and is a recognized social norm), then all have conclusive moral reason to act on this rule rather than any other in the optimal eligible set. Thus, having created a justified rule through our interdependent choices, we can

<hr>

[9] Cf. Gilbert, *A Theory of Political Obligation*, Part II.

then insist that all conform to this rule, for all free and equal persons now have conclusive reason to conform to this rule, rather than any other: it is the one that best fulfills the evaluative standards of each. That genuine moral authority is created by our choices does not entail that one who holds out, refusing to choose our rule, escapes the moral authority of our justified social-moral rule. In this fundamental sense, a free society consents to the moral rule to which we are all bound, even those who have not consented.

Filmer long ago pointed out that, the "plausible and dangerous" notion that all are free and equal appears to require that each and every person consents to authority, but of course it is impossible to imagine that all do so. And, Filmer insisted, it is not enough to say that the majority, even the overwhelming majority, have consented: "universal consent" is required.[10] This has always been the Achilles' Heel of consent theory.[11] On the account advanced here, the consent of the overwhelming majority — their actual choices in selecting a rule from the optimal eligible set — does have the power to bind the rest. Once society has chosen a rule through its joint actions it becomes the sole rule that is uniquely rationally justified: it then is the one rule that all have reason to endorse. It is the only rule that all can endorse and that is able to provide the basis of shared moral life in which all are treated as free and equal. Each, consulting only her set of relevant values, ends, and moral ideals, has reason to act on that rule over any alternative. What was *ex ante* indeterminate, is, through the choices of moral agents, *ex post* uniquely justified.

(b) Fairness and Equilibrium

It may seem that this result is unfair. Think about Display VII-2: the Kantian Coordination Game's outcome is produced by E's flipping a coin, and so deciding to act on *y*: person A ends up with his "10" payoff in every interaction thereafter, while person I forever ends up with her "2" payoff. This seems manifestly unfair: why should

---

[10] Filmer, *The Anarchy of a Limited or Mixed Monarchy*, pp. 140ff. Cf. Locke's claim that in civil society "the *Majority* have a Right to act and conclude the rest." *Second Treatise*, §95.

[11] See Gilbert, *A Theory of Political Obligation*, chap. 5.

A get all of what she wants and person I end up with her minimum payoff? Moreover, this seems inconsistent with what we know about stable equilibria in ultimatum games (§7.4): as we saw, if in such games the Proposer gives herself the lion's share, leaving the Disposer with her absolute minimum, the Disposer will reject the offer. So won't person I reject person A's offer?

Let us first turn to the more formal point, and then to the general worry about fairness. The formal point, relying on experimental data about ultimatum games, is not especially compelling. It is easy to be misled by the formal depiction of "utility" in our Kantian Coordination Game in terms of cardinal numbers, as if the results of the game are (as they are in ultimatum games) monetary payoffs that can be split between individuals. When there is a pot of resources to be distributed with no prior claims by any participants, then fair distribution of resource norms come into play, and so someone may well "punish" a distributor who violates those norms – the punisher (the Responder) refuses to take a small offer, leaving both of them worse off. But this characterization does not apply to the Kantian Coordination Game. The utility numbers are not interpersonally comparable; we cannot, as it were, transfer some amount of utility from person A to person I. To say that the cardinal utility is not interpersonally comparable is to say that unless we tell a great deal more complicated story, it cannot be inferred that if person A receives a utility of 10 from coordination on y, and person I receives 10 from coordinating on x, they receive the same utility from getting their first choices.[12] Utility, we must recall, is simply a measure of how well a person's standards are satisfied, measured on an arbitrary scale specifying numbers (0, 10) to indicate minimum and maximum satisfaction. Thus understood, utility is not a transferable good subject to distributive norms. Moreover, we saw in section 7.4, while results in ultimatum games are often interpreted as indicating a preference for equal distributions of gains, a more compelling hypothesis is that Responder's

---

[12] Ken Binmore insists that "the problem isn't at all that making interpersonal comparisons is impossible. On the contrary, there are an infinite number of ways this can be done." (*Natural Justice*, p. 121). This is too strong, for there may be an infinite number of mathematical formulas for doing it but yet none might be justified. Certainly, though, the mere derivation of cardinal functions for each person does not tell us whether there is a plausible interpersonal function.

refusal of low offers is an act of punishment for norm violation. But insofar as our interactions are searching for a mutually acceptable norm (from a mutually acceptable set), it is inappropriate to punish others for failing to conform to a norm that, *ex hypothesi*, you admit they do not have good reason to endorse. Of course it still might be argued that, appropriate or not, "losers" do punish "big winners." But this returns us to whether this is indeed a distributional issue.

More important, it is not generally the case that in large-scale interactions people punish those who are more satisfied with the social equilibrium than are they. Many of us who are not enamored of Windows freely use it, and we do not begrudge the fact that some of our fellows actually *like* Windows and so get "so much more utility" (whatever that might mean) from using it. In fact, almost every aspect of large-scale cooperation involves an equilibrium that some "like" much more than others. Consider the standard idea of consumer's surplus, as in Display VII-5 below.

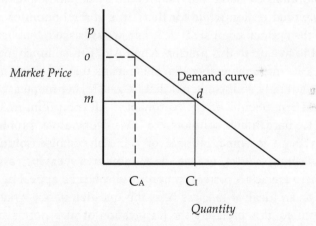

DISPLAY VII-5 REPRESENTATION OF CONSUMERS' SURPLUS

In Display VII-5, we see that at quantity d of production, the market price is m. Now consumer C_I is the marginal consumer: for her, the marginal benefits of purchase of the good at m just equal the costs; if the price was greater than m she would not purchase it. But all other consumers of the good at m pay less for the good than they are willing to pay. Consider C_A. He would pay price o for the good, but because the equilibrium price is m, he receives a pure benefit of $o\text{-}m$; he would pay o, but only has to pay m. This is his consumer's surplus (the total consumer surplus for all consumers is defined by the area $m\text{-}d\text{-}p$). In contrast C_I receives no consumer surplus at all. Yet, at price m both C_A and C_I, consulting only his or her own utility, freely purchase the good. This is a much closer analog to our Kantian Coordination Game than is the ultimatum game. First, it is a large-scale interaction in which the equilibrium is produced by the choices of numerous people. More important, the differences are not a difference in the division of a monetary pool to be distributed, but differences in how well the outcomes satisfy the person's own standards. Just as people do not demand that C_A give up some of his "unfair" gains to C_I, so too those who are happiest with a moral order are not asked to give up some of their "unfair" gains to those who are less happy with it.[13]

But morality, it may well be insisted, is different: here there must be an equal, or at least fair, distribution of "utility gains." In our Kantian Coordination Game, a moral rule x may be justified though it is Alf's favored option while for Betty it is at the bottom of her ranking of the optimal eligible set. Is it fair, we are asked, that Betty is expected to live up to this practice when Alf "gets so much more out of it?" (we must remember that this means that his standards much more strongly endorse it, not that he gets higher monetary or welfare benefits). Should not a "reasonable" Alf compromise? We are back to bargaining solutions to the deliberative problem (§16.3c): is there is some rational or fair compromise solution between clashing views of the best morality? Leaving aside whether there is such a correct compromise solution, appealing at this point to an ideal of fairness begs the question about what is morally justified; it is precisely the justification of such norms that is being considered. What is fair is an issue *within* morality: it cannot be employed to adjudicate between rival views *of* morality that include different conceptions of fairness. So too is it suspicious to appeal to the notion of the "reasonable." As used in contemporary political theory, the notion of the "reasonable" tries to link the very idea of moral sensibility to a disposition to compromise.

---

[13] Monopolists can extract some of the consumer surplus, but this is seldom done in the name of fairness.

Someone who is not willing to meet others "halfway"[14] displays a failure of moral sensibility. But this is dubious: compromise is not always a good, and it certainly is not always demanded in virtue of a person's devotion to a moral life. That each Member of the Public accepts that some option z is in the optimal eligible set only if each and every free and equal person has sufficient reason to accord z moral authority on the basis of her own evaluative standards, and that all the elements in the set satisfy the formal constraints on moral rules (§15.2) already shows that all Members of the Public have a commitment to respect the standards of others and do not press for moral rules that some cannot freely endorse.

Of course, it may be argued that given our evaluative standards, we do share a meta-norm that identifies a standard of fairness regulating the distribution of the degree to which a rule satisfies the evaluative standards of each. If so, this can be integrated into the account as a more demanding notion of what constitutes the eligible set. Commencing with my looser notion of an optimal eligible set, we could then see that people's evaluative standards converge on a meta-theory of moral justification that justifies a more constrained criterion of the eligible set. That would be an extra level of justification within the account. I am now skeptical that such a meta-norm can be justified.[15] Consider a long-standing issue in political philosophy. Some criticize liberal claims to be a neutral political doctrine (i.e., not favoring any conception of the good in the justification of rules and laws) on the grounds that since liberals fare so much better under liberalism than do, say, conservatives, liberalism is objectionably tilted against (i.e., unfair toward) the conservative who does not get as much out of liberal society as do liberals. On this view, any moral code will be especially biased toward those whose values converge with it and will be biased against those whose values chafe. But to seek such meta-fairness between value systems looks not only contentious but a recipe for the instability of public justification. To see this, suppose that at time t_1 society has the ordering in Display VII-6.

---

[14] Rawls, *Political Liberalism*, p. 253.

[15] My account in *Value and Justification* erroneously adopted a bargaining solution at this point, pp. 439–75. Loren Lomasky pointed the error out long ago; I was far too slow in seeing it.

A	B	C	D
x	z	x	z
y	y	y	y
z	x	z	x

DISPLAY VII-6 INITIAL ORDERINGS OF ELEMENTS IN THE OPTIMAL ELIGIBLE SET

Based on Display VII-6, the meta-fairness doctrine might identify y as the fair proposal: either of the others would leave half the Members of the Public with their lowest ranked option.[16] Now we know that as people live under a system of rules, many who may have been initially critical come to embrace it; normal reasoners have a tendency to prefer the status quo,[17] though some (for example, political philosophers) have a tendency to oppose it. So at t_2 we are apt to have

A	B	C	D
y	y	y	z
x	z	x	x
z	x	z	y

DISPLAY VII-7 LATER ORDERINGS OF ELEMENTS IN THE OPTIMAL ELIGIBLE SET

Now three Members of the Public, who have come to embrace the status quo, receive their first choice, and D, the critic, receives his last choice. If we are committed to the meta-fairness norm, it seems that we must once again look for a fair compromise. But surely this cannot be correct. It is a great and important thing, not a cause of regret, that when living under a justified scheme people come to better appreciate its virtues and become increasingly devoted to it;

---

[16] It is easy to see that y can be recommended by a minimax relative concession rule (see §16.3c). To make things obvious, assume cardinal utilities between 2 and 0. Under y the maximum concession anyone must make is 1; x and z require a maximum concession of 2. For an ordinalist exposition, see my *Value and Justification*, pp. 439ff.

[17] See, for example, Jonathan Baron and James Jurney, "Norms against Voting for Coerced Reform."

this is a crucial source of moral stability.[18] It represents no cosmic unfairness that once moral persons live under a justified system of rules most come to embrace it and see that it serves their evaluative standards. More than that, our evaluative standards themselves are transformed when we witness how a mutually acceptable cooperative scheme of agency and other rights allows all to follow their deepest convictions while treating their fellows as free and equal moral persons. It would be crazy to think that somehow morality itself required us to overturn this stability in the interests of meta-fairness and making sure that we are always meeting others half-way.

Normative ethical theory is not, as it were, constructed from scratch. We are not in a state of nature, nor are we thinking for the first time what our moral life should look like. We have been formed in a moral order, our standards reflect such a moral order, and we know the virtues and vices of our order better than alternative orders. Seldom do we find ourselves at Display VII-6; if we are fortunate enough to have a publicly justified rule, we are already at Display VII-7. We certainly need to know whether our rule is in the eligible set (and perhaps whether it is optimal; §21.3c), but we should not worry about whether our morality correctly splits the difference between Members of the Public, as if we are playing a large numbers division of resources game. Distributive justice is part of morality; moral justification, however, is not itself a case of distributive justice.

20 The Evolution of Morality

20.1 SOME EVOLUTIONARY FEATURES OF THE ACCOUNT

(a) A Slow Progression, and Repeated Experience of the Inconveniences of Transgressing
Our Kantian Coordination Game constitutes, at a minimum, a sort of possibility theorem that a publicly justified outcome can be

---

[18] See Rawls, *A Theory of Justice*, §§71–2.

reached via a process that has not itself been publicly justified.[19] Thus we – you and I – are justified in rejecting the Procedural Justification Requirement (§19.1) and its skeptical conclusion that public justification must grind to a halt before we have justified rules specific enough to provide the basis for social cooperation. Coordination on a morality can occur even though no procedure of coordination has itself been publicly justified. Our analysis of how Members of the Public might come to coordinate on a morality also suggests, though, that the process of arriving at a publicly justified morality may well be a social evolutionary one, in which people gradually come to coordinate on a common set of moral rules. Hume certainly thought that a moral convention grows through "a slow progression, and by our repeated experience of the inconveniences of transgressing it."[20] And, as David Lewis stressed, conventions are coordination equilibria; so on our account a publicly justified moral rule constitutes a Lewisian convention.[21] If the Kantian Coordination Game is more than a mere possibility, but captures at least some aspects of actual social processes that push in the direction of moral equilibrium, it provides an outline of a certain social evolutionary conception of moral justification.

The proposal that the model may help us understand aspects of the actual evolution of moral rules is bolstered by the fact that we can weaken the assumptions – allowing for agents whose actions do not track their idealized Member of the Public counterpart – and still get a similar result. Suppose that we take an actual group, and divide it into two subgroups that are roughly equal: the Moralists and the Simple Coordinators. The Moralists reliably recognize elements of the socially eligible set, S; they act like Members of the Public. In contrast the Simple Coordinators either have no special concern with morality, or they simply have a fuzzy idea of the contours of S. They also have only a vague idea of what rules would best satisfy their values (we can think of Simple Coordinators as those who have a harder time tracking what their

---

[19] Compare the Kantian Coordination Game to Nozick's invisible hand account of the rise of the state in *Anarchy, State and Utopia*. One function Nozick's analysis serves is as a possibility theorem, allowing him to reject the anarchist claim that a legitimate state is impossible.

[20] Hume, *Treatise of Human Nature*, p. 490.

[21] David Lewis, *Convention: A Philosophical Study*, esp. chap. 1.

counterpart Member of the Public would judge). Simple Coordinators do, though, see the advantage of coordination with others:
they are aware of the confusion and disorder produced by contradictory moral demands. Simple Coordinators will coordinate on
any moral rule, in or out of S. In contrast, a Moralists deems
granting moral authority to a rule outside S (the socially eligible
set) as certainly no better than having no moral rule at all. It fails
the test of being an eligible moral rule, yet to adopt it as moral rule
allows that others can insist that one conforms to it, rebuke one for
failing to conform, and one is to internalize it and feel guilty for not
conforming to it. Display VII-8 presents a basic coordination game
between a Moralist and a Simple Coordinator.

Simple Coordinator

		x in S	*z not in S*
Moralist	*x in S*	1 2 0	0 0
	z not in S	0 0	1 0

DISPLAY VII-8 A MORE REALISTIC KANTIAN COORDINATION GAME WITH A STRICT
AND A NONSTRICT NASH EQUILIBRIUM

In this game the Moralist thinks coordination on z is no better than
failure to coordinate. In Display VII-8 coordinating on x is a strict
Nash equilibrium – playing x is each person's uniquely best
response to the play of the other. In contrast, z/z is a non-strict Nash
equilibrium: although the Moralist cannot improve his utility by
unilaterally changing his move, for him playing x *is just as good of a
response*. We can see the shortcomings of this equilibrium: Moralist
has no more reason to play z than he does x. If he is playing x he
has no reason to switch and play z if the Simple Coordinator does
so. Given that he thinks x is in S while z is not, we would in fact
expect him to prefer unilaterally acting on x to coordinating on z,
thus yielding a game with only one Nash equilibrium, at x/x, as in

Display VII-9. We thus see that a large enough group of Moralists can move the entire group to an equilibrium within the eligible set.

Simple Coordinator

		x in S	*z not in S*
		1	0
	x in S		
Moralist		2	1
		0	1
	z not in S		
		0	0

DISPLAY VII-9 A MORE REALISTIC KANTIAN COORDINATION GAME WITH ONE NASH EQUILIBRIUM

Some worry about the practical import of game theoretic models employing the concept of Nash equilibrium because they doubt whether real people actually play Nash equilibria. In many contexts, Nash equilibrium solutions require a tremendous amount of information; each player must have correct knowledge of the moves of all the other players. For Alf and Betty to be in a Nash equilibrium, each must be making the best move (given his or her own utility function), given the move made by the other. But that means that each must know the moves of all other players. In large N-person interactions, this may seem to require an incredible amount of common knowledge. However, there is much more reason to suppose that a Nash equilibrium adequately models individual action in evolutionary, iterated settings in which individuals can gradually learn the moves that others make. Individuals can slowly learn what others are doing, and adjust their moves. There is reason to think that people do play Nash equilibria in evolutionary interactions.[22]

---

[22] On the common knowledge requirements of Nash equilibrium, see Herbert Gintis, *The Bounds of Reason*, chap. 8. For a defense and elaboration of Nash equilibrium in evolutionary analysis, see George J. Mailath, "Do People Play Nash Equilibrium? Lessons from Evolutionary Game Theory." Mailath shows that Nash equilibrium can be translated as a type of evolutionary stable state in evolutionary processes. See also Herbert Gintis, *Game Theory Evolving*, chap. 7; Brian Skyrms, *The Evolution of the Social Contract*, chap. 4.

I think that, indeed, our abstract model of how coordination on a morality may occur alerts us to important ways in which our social morality has evolved, and how this evolutionary process may itself be justificatory. We need to be careful, though, for social evolutionary accounts of morality make a number of different claims, some of which our analysis endorses, while others we must reject. Rather than simply endorsing the broad idea of a "socially evolutionary account" of the justification of morality, we would do better to examine the distinct claims advanced by evolutionary accounts and consider their place in our overall account of a moral order of public reason. In this section I consider some of the evolutionary claims that a theory of real public reason endorses; section 20.2 examines some of the aspects of social evolutionary accounts of morality that are not endorsed.

(b) Contingent History Can Be Justificatory

A purely descriptive social evolutionary account of morality holds that the moral rules we have ended up with are a matter of actual historical events, and so are in that sense contingent. Think of the way the signing of the Magna Carta in the thirteenth century has affected the thinking about the specification of liberties, and the means to best protect them, in English-speaking countries. Or, to take another example, consider the influence on the moral thinking of English-speaking (and some other) peoples of the idea that a man's home is his castle. As Blackstone put it, "And the law of England has so particular and tender a regard to the immunity of a man's house that it styles it his castle and will never suffer it to be violated with impunity; agreeing herein with the sentiments of antient Rome, as expressed in the words of Tully: '*quid enim sanctius, quid omni religione munitius, quam domus uniuscujusque civium?*'"[23] In 1998 Justice Scalia cited this doctrine in a concurring opinion, arguing against dissenters who would see (and thereby weaken) the right not to be searched as simply an aspect of the general right to expectations of privacy.[24] Appealing to the idea

---

[23] William Blackstone, *Commentaries on the Laws of England*, vol. 2, p. 233. ["What more sacred, what more strongly guarded by every holy feeling, than a man's own home?"]

[24] Concurring opinion in 525 US 83, *Minnesota v. Wayne Thomas Carter* (1998).

that one's house is one's castle, some American state governments have justified the use of deadly force against presumed house breakers.[25] These of course are legal and not directly moral matters, but they clearly track the moral consciousness of many; this ancient English doctrine has had a tremendous effect in our understanding of the relation of privacy, property, and the extent of the authority of a person in his home.[26] Social evolutionary accounts stress that these actual facts – a codification of a particular doctrine at a particular time – can shape the moral equilibrium for centuries.

If reasonably goodwilled people interact over a longish period of time, seeking to find mutually acceptable norms of interactions, they can come to converge on a common rule x, and this fact – that they have converged on *this* morality rather than that – itself can provide a public justification for x. That is, the fact that *this* rule is the one we have converged upon may show why x is publicly justified. In our Kantian Coordination Game there is no correct answer to the problem of which element to select from the optimal eligible set. But the actual interactions of what we might call a group of predominantly moderately goodwilled people – people who are primarily concerned about living according to their own standards (§14.4), but not through oppression and authoritarianism – can lead to a solution to the problem. Indeed, even less than such moderately goodwilled individuals could find a solution: if each is devoted to her evaluative standards, and is willing and able to resist those who impose norms that disregard them, they still can achieve a series of interactions that may lead to the selection of an eligible morality. This, though, means that normative ethics, understood as an inquiry into the justification of our social morality, cannot tell us what is true morality without appeal to the actual facts about the moral equilibrium we have reached. This, in turn means that the distinction between "true" and "positive morality" is not hard and fast. We thus have vindicated a major and, in many philosophers' eyes, controversial thesis of the Baier–Strawson View (§10.4). True and positive morality are not simply overlapping: that

---

[25] Chris Bury and Howard L. Rosenberg, "A Man's Home Is His Castle, and He Can Defend It."

[26] For a critical analysis, see Jeannie Suk, *At Home in the Law: How the Domestic Violence Revolution Is Transforming Privacy.*

a morality is positive can be one of the ingredients in *making* it true (see further §21.1).

(c) The Path-Dependency of Justification

Evolution, including social evolution, is path dependent.[27] Suppose that a time t_1 (in environment E_1) a society selects rule x over w; at time t_2 (in environment E_2), it selects y over x and finally at a later time it selects z over y. That it ends up with z is apt to be dependent on the path the society has followed and what options were advanced at what times. It is entirely possible that if the first choice had been between w and z, w might have eliminated z, and z never would have appeared again; in that case society might have ended up with the y rule.

Path dependence surely characterizes a publicly justified social morality. We must coordinate on a morality – moderately good-willed people need to find some rule that all can employ in their social relations. When changes occur in a society, new problems arise, or its members come to doubt aspects of its current morality, the content of its positive morality is apt to exercise great influence on the revised morality. Consider, for example, debates about a woman's reproductive rights. Those who have become convinced that our social morality has been unjustified on this matter because it does not allow a sufficient sphere of jurisdiction for women to decide, often seek to justify rights by appeal to privacy (as did the Supreme Court in *Griswold v. Connecticut*),[28] rights of ownership, or rights to the control over one's body. These are fundamental rights in our liberal society, and showing that reproductive rights are part of them would have great import. But by including reproductive rights in these already articulated individual rights, the shape and nature of social morality about reproductive issues are greatly affected. For example, decisions about abortion may be seen as almost exclusively under the women's jurisdiction. Compare this to a society that has developed strong family-based jurisdictions; here the equilibrium on these matters might gravitate to rules that, while

---

[27] For a nice discussion of path dependency in the context of cultural evolution, see Douglas Glen Whitman, "Hayek Contra Pangloss on Evolutionary Systems," pp. 55ff.

[28] 381 U.S 479 (1965).

providing reproductive freedom, give biological fathers greater authority. Moral innovations and change work with what the current morality is, and so even attempts at reform are deeply influenced by the moral status quo. Philosophers who advocate radical moral change, urging a revolution in our society's morality, should not be surprised that their work has little practical import; new moral equilibria are apt to be arrived at via some pretty clear path from current rules. This is not to be regretted; it is an important tool of social convergence.

(d) Efficient Causes and Sustaining Justifications

The path dependence of justified morality also alerts us to another feature of actual justified morality: why the moral rule was originally adopted may have little relevance to its current justification. Consider the rules about civility and gentlemanly behavior, which were originally introduced in part to solidify class distinctions and mark off the gentle from the working classes. They were not simply social and class distinctions, but moralized ones; certain sorts of moral behavior were held to be inaccessible to the lower classes. Although these class-based rules were not publicly justified, they became the basis for more generalized and justifiable norms of civility and nonoffensive behavior. No doubt many of our current rules were simply imposed on society by the powerful; one would have to be extraordinarily naïve not to appreciate that features of our positive morality have been shaped by unjustified power. But as with our belief systems, what is ultimately important are not efficient causes but sustaining reasons.[29] Most individuals acquire many of their lifelong moral beliefs to please parents or peers; the original cause of adopting the beliefs – the efficient cause – surely was not justificatory.[30] But in revising their belief systems, individuals can and do come to new, and sound, justifications that sustain these old beliefs; that, indeed, is what much moral development is all about. So too with social morality: even those rules that were unjustifiably imposed upon the society can serve as equilibrium solutions under new conditions.

---

[29] See further my *Justificatory Liberalism*, pp. 19–28.
[30] These attitudes are basic to Kohlberg's conventional levels of moral reasoning.

To some this will seem objectionably unfair. Only rules with perfect (i.e., entirely legitimate) pedigrees, they insist, can serve as a basis for a justified morality; otherwise, past power can determine the shape of our current social morality. And how can power affect the justification of morality? Quite properly, though, we accept that unjustified power has had important influences on even the most justified political systems; trace the history of any regime back a bit, and we will see that some of its features are the result of unjustified power. But we do not expect that the entire history of a regime must be pure for its present institutions to be justified. Even if the United States Senate was partly a device of the elite to make sure the masses did not exercise too much control, the Senate as it is now constituted may well be justifiable. But, of course, we would not have the Senate as it is now constituted without these earlier, not entirely admirable, influences. So too with our morality. An evolutionary account of our morality stresses history, but it is not a "historical entitlement" view, which insists that justified moral change can occur only via justified steps from an initial justified situation.[31] Of course, violations of morality are always wrong, but that a rule originally became current on unjustified grounds does not preclude its eventually being the focus of a justified equilibrium.

Members of the Public are certain to make proposals that were originally introduced into society on questionable grounds. Just why certain rules and ideas were originally introduced (such as a man's house is his castle) is highly conjectural, and certainly most will not be aware of these aspects of the history of ideas. To be sure, some of the more sophisticated reasoners will be aware, and they may rank a proposal lower because of its questionable history. Only in the most extreme cases, though, would this lead them to have sufficient reasons to deem an option ineligible; to do that means that the option is so unacceptable as to have no moral authority, and so one ranks it as no better than the absence of moral authority – a most serious conclusion. And, of course, any proposal in the optimal eligible set can serve as an equilibrium choice in a society of free persons.

[31] The model here, of course, is Robert Nozick's view in *Anarchy, State and Utopia*.

20.2 CONTRASTS TO HAYEK'S MORE RADICAL SOCIAL EVOLUTIONARY THEORY

A realistic account of public reason must acknowledge that a social equilibrium on a member of the optimal eligible set provides the basis for each to conform to a social morality while she still obeys only herself. This equilibrium is not only explanatory but justificatory; it does not simply explain why we arrive at a common morality, but that we have reached it justifies this morality (this rule) over other members of the optimal eligible set. How we have arrived at this rule is a combination of contingent history, moral ideas, happenstance, and the exercise of power. The route to it is path dependent. All these are important aspects of a social evolutionary account of justified morality, and all should be endorsed.

An account of morality integrating these features is a genuinely evolutionary theory, though of course not Darwinian. Hayek repeatedly warns us against equating all evolutionary theories with the Darwinian account of biological evolution.[32] Theories of social evolution were advanced in the eighteenth century, including Adam Smith's account of the evolution of language and Ferguson's essay on the development of civil society.[33] It was only in the Social Darwinism of the late nineteenth century that theories of social evolution were presented as a social application of Darwin's account of biological evolution; and even in the late nineteenth and early twentieth centuries there were important theories of non-Darwinian social evolution.[34] And, of course, more recently

---

[32] See, for example, Hayek, *Rules and Order*, p. 22; Hayek, *The Fatal Conceit*, pp. 23ff. Even though Hayek so often and so clearly distinguished his view from Social Darwinism (which he opposed), the charge that he was a Social Darwinist can still be found in the literature. See, for example, Ellen Frankel Paul, "Liberalism, Unintended Orders, and Evolutionism," and David Miller, "The Fatalistic Conceit." For those who rightly reject this characterization of Hayek, see Whitman, "Hayek contra Pangloss on Evolutionary Systems," and Geoffrey M. Hodgson, *Economics and Evolution: Bringing Life Back into Economics*, pp. 161–2.

[33] Adam Smith, "Considerations Concerning the First Formation of Languages"; Adam Ferguson, *An Essay on the History of Civil Society*.

[34] A good example of a Social Darwinist is William Graham Sumner; see, for example, his essay "Socialism." Herbert Spencer is often cited as a paradigmatic Social Darwinist, but his early writings on social and moral evolution are not Darwinist. See, for example, his *First Principles* and *Principles of Sociology*. Even at the turn of the twentieth century there was great debate about the relation of

sociologists such as Boyd and Richerson (§7.2) have presented rich models of genetic-cultural coevolution.

Although Hayek manifestly did not advocate Social Darwinism – he actually postulated a conflict between cultural and biological evolution[35] – the structure of his theory of social evolution has affinities with the structure of Darwinian accounts. Hayek's view of social evolution is *selectionist:* it specifies a mechanism according to which certain social traits are selected in a competitive environment over others. A selectionist theory explains the rise of trait X_α (entity X with feature α) by identifying at least one mechanism according to which in some past environment E, mechanism M selected X_α over some X_β. Hayek is often criticized for not identifying "the" selection mechanism, but an adequate selectionist theory need not rely on a single mechanism. Darwin himself proposed both natural and sexual selection as mechanisms, and these apparently can work in opposite directions. Biologists are still debating whether sexual selection can select for traits such as male bird feathers that do not render the male fitter to survive in its environment and may actually result in traits that render it less fit to survive. For Darwin, one selection mechanism involves differential survival rates: those Xs with α have a higher probability of survival than those with β. A non-Darwinian social evolutionary selectionist theory also could be based on, say, differential social growth rates, and differential group prosperity. "The rules of conduct have," Hayek thus writes, "evolved because the groups who practiced them were more successful and displaced others. They were rules that, given the environment in which men lived, secured that a greater number of the groups or individuals who practiced them would survive."[36] Hayek also tells us that a comparative increase of wealth and

social evolution (which was a widely embraced doctrine) to Darwinism. For "left-wing" anti-Social-Darwinist evolutionists, see David G. Ritchie, *Darwinism and Politics,* and L. T. Hobhouse, *Social Evolution and Political Theory.* Hobhouse develops his cooperative theory of social evolution in works such as *Mind in Evolution* and *Development and Purpose.* The important twentieth-century anthropologist Morris Ginsberg was a disciple of Hobhouse.

[35] See his "Epilogue" to *The Political Order of a Free People.*

[36] Hayek, *Rules and Order,* p. 18. See also Hayek, *The Fatal Conceit,* p. 25. Hayek here is unclear whether he is advocating individual or group selection; both play a role in his theory. See above section 7.2.

population are means of evolutionary selection.[37] An evolutionary account of customs, he holds, must show the "distinct advantages by those groups that kept to such customs, thereby enabling them to expand more rapidly than others and ultimately to supersede (or absorb) those not possessing similar customs."[38] Those who are wealthier will be able to expand and fend off external threats, and their culture may come to dominate others. We also would expect them to attract immigration; Hayek suggests that this *attractor* trait is probably more important than internal population growth.[39]

My aim here is not to evaluate these claims but to emphasize that the account presented in this chapter is not selectionist. I have not postulated any mechanism such that orders that converge on a justified morality have some selection advantage over those that do not. We can remain agnostic about whether such a mechanism exists (it would be nice to think it did). However, we cannot remain agnostic about another core claim of Hayek's theory of moral evolution. He writes:

To understand our civilisation one must appreciate that the extended order resulted not from human design or intention but spontaneously: it arose from the unintentional conforming to certain traditional and largely *moral* practices, many of which men tend to dislike, whose significance they usually fail to understand, whose validity they cannot prove, and which have nonetheless fairly rapidly spread by means of an evolutionary selection – the comparative increase of population and wealth – of those groups that happened to follow them.[40]

Apparently Hayek holds that, being the outcome of the evolutionary selection mechanism, the rules we have are *good rules*, having survived a competition with other candidates. And that would show why we should take account of the rules in our decisions: they are good moral rules. One interpretation of Hayek's doctrine, then, is that if a moral rule has evolved as part of our moral order, then we have good reason to follow this rule. Having evolved as part of the complex order would be sufficient to give us good

---

[37] Hayek, *The Fatal Conceit*, p. 6. See also Hayek, *Rules and Order*, pp. 3, 17.

[38] Hayek, *The Fatal Conceit*, p. 43.

[39] Hayek, *The Political Order of a Free People*, p. 159.

[40] Hayek, *The Fatal Conceit*, p. 6. Emphasis in original.

§20 *The Evolution of Morality* 421

reason to follow the rule or principle. Call this the evolutionist's *Sufficiency Claim*. To see our way to an evaluation of this claim, let us begin by granting:

> (*i*) Given some selection mechanism *M*, our current system of moral rules has been selected (in a competition with other orders over the course of history).

Claim (*i*) itself does not provide us with reasons to follow a moral rule selected by *M*. Suppose we accept that *M* has selected moral rule *x*. We can now step back and consider whether *x* is mere superstition, or whatever. That evolved rules might be very bad is the moral of H. G. Wells' *Time Machine*: the rules by which the Morlock and Eloi lived (Morlocks fed, clothed, and then ate the Eloi) had indeed evolved in a long process of cultural (and biological) evolution, but we can see that they are deeply objectionable. Some might object. Perhaps the Morlock and Eloi norms are immoral *to us, given our evolved morality*. We can reject the rules of the Morlock and Eloi in the light of our evolved morality, but we cannot (nor can the Eloi) reject in toto our (their) own morality, though some bits of it can be rejected in the light of other parts. Hayek is attracted to this view; we can consider the adequacy of some moral rule only in light of the "givenness" of the others, and only an ill-advised rationalism would radically question the overall outcome of social evolution.[41] He writes:

It is the submission to undesigned rules and conventions whose significance and importance we largely do not understand, this reverence for the traditional, that the rationalistic type of mind finds so uncongenial, though it is indispensable for the working of a free society. It has its foundation in the insight which David Hume stressed and which is of decisive importance for the antirationalist, evolutionary tradition – namely, that the "rules of morality are not the conclusions of our reason." Like all other values, our morals are not a product but a presupposition of reason, part of the ends which the instrument of our intellect has been developed to serve.

[41] Hayek, *The Constitution of Liberty*, p. 63.

At any one stage of our evolution the system of values into which we are born supplies the ends which our reason must serve.[42]

Since our reason is itself the product of social evolution, it does not give us an Archimedean point from which to stand outside of cultural evolution and evaluate its outcomes. However, even if morality and reason are the product of some process M, it does not follow that reason, having developed, cannot evaluate M. As Anthony O'Hear rightly points out, once our capacities have evolved through M, they may develop and be exercised in ways that M would never select.[43] Even if, say, our intelligence was selected for as a way to obtain better food in competition with other primates, our intelligence could now lead us to go on a hunger strike against the mistreatment of other primates at the local zoo. After all, that Hayek criticizes the rationalist for calling traditional morality into question rather suggests that such questioning can be done; and indeed we can stand a long way back from our present moral practices and quite coherently ask whether any of them are justified – whether any of them give us good reasons to act.

In order for a rule x to be justified just because it has been selected by M, an additional claim is necessary:

(*ii*) M-selected rules such as x are worthy.

It is crucial to realize that (*ii*) does not follow from (*i*). One can accept that our present moral rules are produced by M and conclude that M is a nasty process that gives rise to nasty rules. If we are going to embrace the rules selected by M as not simply our society's positive morality, but as the rules of true morality, we must have reason to think that M-selected rules tend to conform to our conception of worthy rules. It is not enough, though, to provide some analysis according to which our society's principles or rules are worthy; if the aim is to employ evolution as a justificatory method, our confidence in their worthiness must depend on the fact that M produced them.

If we are to accept the Hayekean account, we need to suppose that being M-selected is something like a sufficient reason to

---

[42] Ibid., p. 63.
[43] O'Hear, *Beyond Evolution*, p. 214.

believe that our current rules are worthy. Hayek and other advocates of evolutionary ethics make much of the ways that evolved moral rules help us solve coordination problems and, of course, I too have argued that it is of fundamental importance to secure a mutually beneficial cooperative social order (Chapters II and III). Let us grant the very strong assumption that we know:

(*iii*) M tends to select good rules of type Q (say, coordination rules), which are, upon reflection, a good thing.

It still is not clear, though, whether being selected by M, or being a Q-type rule, is what is really justificatory. If we have independent grounds for determining what are and are not Q-type rules, the contribution to justification of the fact that a rule was selected by M looks minor. Our reflective attitude, which allows us to stand back a long way from our specific culture and language, now commends a specific rule x, because it is a Q-type rule, and that is a good thing. But if we already know that the rule is a Q-type rule, then we already know that it is a worthy rule. How, though, does the fact that it is selected by M figure into the story? Does the fact that it coordinates *and* was selected by M make it even more justified than if, say, it helped coordinate but was not selected by M? The fact that it was selected by M would certainly add extra justification to the story if we accepted:

(*iv*) M-selected rules tend to promote cooperation, though we cannot know this by inspecting each rule.

On this view, M-selection is about the only good evidence we have that a rule is of type Q. This evidential claim, though overstated in claim (*iv*), has some merit. Often we cannot directly know the function a rule performs, and so we can only infer the function from that fact that it was selected by, and survived in, a cooperative social order. That a rule has survived in a society for a long period of time is some evidence that it serves a useful social function.[44] This, though, falls far short of the Sufficiency Claim for two reasons. *First*, because of path dependence, that a rule was selected for and survived in previous environments certainly does not entail

[44] "The generality of a practice is in some cases a strong presumption that it is, or at all events was, conducive to laudable ends." Mill, *The Subjection of Women*, p. 263 (chap 1, ¶5).

that it now is socially useful. What M selects in a pre-industrial economy need not be selected by M in a post-industrial one. If social change is rapid, formerly useful rules may now be dysfunctional. *Ex hypothesi*, they were selected by M as more worthy than some competitors at t, but if $t + 1$ is very different, there is not a strong presumption that the rules are more worthy now. The upshot is that even if we make the strong assumption that the selection mechanism inherently selects rules we consider worthy, if social change is rapid we cannot conclude that our current rules are worthy unless social evolution also occurs very rapidly.[45]

Second, and more important, there are oppressive ways of achieving social cooperation, as evinced by our tale of the Morlock and Eloi; there was cooperation between them, but the Eloi's role was to be food. As Strawson stressed, the mere fact that a rule is instrumental to social life does not show that all have reason to act on it (§11.1*a*). Our moral concern is not simply to have rules that allow cooperation but to have cooperation that respects all as free and equal moral persons. Consequently, there are insuperable difficulties in defending any version of the Sufficiency Claim (i.e., just because a rule has been selected by evolution it is a morally justified rule). We must evaluate our evolved rules from the perspective of public reason: we must seek to determine whether the outcome of the social evolutionary process is within the optimal eligible set. Moral justification simply cannot be inferred from any social evolutionary process. However, though social evolution is not sufficient for moral justification, it is necessary; public reason gives a critical perspective on the evolved rules of our society, but it does not have within it the resources to determine our social morality.

21 The Testing Conception

21.1 TESTING THE STATUS QUO

"A society's morality," says Baier, "is or involves that part of its mores which purport to pass the appropriate test of acceptabil-

---

[45] On Richerson and Boyd's analysis, cultural evolution is adaptive when environments are changing moderately quickly. *Not by Genes Alone*, chap. 4.

ity."[46] The "test" a moral claim must pass, he famously argues, "in order to be called true" is acceptability from the moral point of view.[47] This is precisely correct. We confront a current moral rule, x, in our society that is widely observed – it is an actual social rule ("a more") and so is actually followed by a large proportion of society (§10.2) – and we wish to test whether it is acceptable from the perspective of free and equal moral persons, modeled as our Members of the Public. The Deliberative Model explicates the moral point of view, and what is acceptable is any option in the optimal eligible set. That is the test. If x is in the optimal eligible set, then x as a current social rule is now the basis of a moral equilibrium: a rule that has been converged upon and can be freely followed, and whose authoritative nature can be acknowledged by each while consulting only her own evaluative standards. A rule of our social morality that is validated from the moral point of view is thus one that solves Rousseau's fundamental problem. Following it, we remain free. Of course we do not have the freedom of dictators, who see themselves as free only if everyone else does as they command. It is the freedom of a social being, in a world of other social beings exercising their own freedom within the constraints of real public reason.

Now some may be unsettled that moral theory thus understood "privileges the status quo." If an existing rule is within the optimal eligible set, it is publicly justified for that reason – just because it is the existing rule. Surely, it may be thought, the justification of moral rules from the moral point of view should be characterized by the neutrality constraint.[48] A collective choice rule should be neutral between alternatives insofar as neither alternative has a built-in advantage, and so the labels attached to the proposal ("the status quo," a "revision of the status quo") cannot matter. For example, a rule that a two-thirds decision is required to pass a proposal – otherwise it fails – violates neutrality: it is *biased in favor of the status quo*. The rationale behind the neutrality condition is that we do not want our social decision-making procedure to work to

---

[46] Kurt Baier, *The Rational and the Moral Order*, p. 212.
[47] Kurt Baier, *The Moral Point of View*, pp. 183–4.
[48] See K. O. May, "A Set of Independent, Necessary and Sufficient Conditions for Simple Majority Rule."

the advantage of some options ("no change from the status quo")
and to the disadvantage of others ("change the status quo"). Under
the two-thirds rule, the decision-making rule favors those people
with conservative preferences and places an extra obstacle in front
of those with reformist preferences.

In the context of the public justification of a social morality, this
defense of neutrality fails to appreciate that an eligible rule that is
also the status quo has moral properties that other eligible rules do
not. There is a relevant difference to which our moral theory must
be sensitive. We are not simply "preferring" the status quo; we are
choosing an option that has the crucial, additional, moral property
of being an equilibrium such that all have reason to act on it, and
so, uniquely, I treat you as a free and equal moral person when I
demand that you conform to it. When an eligible rule is also a
current rule, a very large proportion of the population employs it.
As we saw (§19.2*b*), a Member of the Public (and so, each of us) has
two types of reasons to act on a rule in the optimal eligible set: (*i*)
reasons based on how highly this rule ranks in her own eligible set,
and (*ii*) reasons to achieve a common morality that allows each to
treat others as free and equal while also asserting morally authoritative prescriptions. Now as on almost all matters, reasonable free
and equal persons disagree on the relative importance of these two
reasons. It is important to stress that for all its oversimplicity, the
Kantian Coordination Game models this disagreement. Given the
increasing returns of shared moral requirements (§19.3), once the
large part of society has converged on some rule, even those who
place great importance on reasons of type (*i*) and relatively less
importance on reasons of type (*ii*) will come to converge on the
shared rule. For once society converges on an equilibrium, an individual will consult his own evaluative standards and see that he
can best satisfy them by acting on the equilibrium. So to continue to
act on his preferred rule (type *i* reasons) when society has
converged on another assures that he will be denied moral relations
with others on these matters.

Recall (§10.1), that for a moral rule to have de jure authority – to
authoritatively order our moral relations – it must not simply be
justifiable but must also in some way be effective and acknowledged. A justifiable rule that only one person looks to as

authoritative in her social relations provides no social and moral authority at all. The upshot of Chapters II and III is that our rule-governed social morality must perform a critical function. As participants in social morality we are not simply engaged in an intellectual activity of arriving at a catalog of correct moral judgments; we are individuals living lives devoted to diverse ends and are participating in a framework that provides an ordered, yet also free, social existence. This requires settled empirical expectations about the expected rule-governed actions of our fellows (§10.2). If we compare two rules in the optimal eligible set, one that is now currently acknowledged and one that is not, only the former now does what we require a moral rule to do: provide an authoritative basis for interpersonal moral demands.

Social recognition is especially important for a regime of jurisdictional rights (§18). Jurisdictional rights are complexes of privileges, claims, immunities, and powers; recall that as H. L. A. Hart saw it, such rights define a sphere in which the rightholder has "authority or sovereignty in relation to some specific matter."[49] If, as with property rights, the individual possesses moral powers over others – the normative status to change another's moral obligations, including imposing duties on him, such as an obligation to genuflect before the tabernacle – these powers must be recognized by others if they are to perform their function. Moral powers identify a sphere effectively only when one's evaluative standards hold sway to the extent that they are socially recognized. Just as with the jurisdictions of governments, our rights define the contours of our jurisdictions to the extent that they are socially recognized. T. H. Green thus was correct about at least a class of rights: a right is "a power claimed and recognized as contributory to a common good."[50] To the extent that the function of rights is to localize moral authority by dispersing moral powers, they cannot fulfill this function if they are not generally recognized. If there are no recognized rights, we are in a state akin to civil war, each side seeking to construct its own preferred spheres of authority. But, as Green

---

[49] H. L. A. Hart, "Are There Natural Rights?" p. 184. Compare Mill, *On Liberty*, p. 224 (chap. 1, ¶11).

[50] See Green, *Lectures on the Principles of Political Obligation*, §99. See also Rex Martin, "T. H. Green on Individual Rights and the Common Good," pp. 49–50.

observes, in situations like this, there really is no sovereignty at all (§10.1). Rights as powers (dispersed moral authority) are thus partly defined by recognition. Without general recognition, no authority exists. "A mere claim to have a right," R. E. Ewin points out, "settles nothing if it is not, in the end, accepted by the relevant community."[51] Again, this is not an illicit bias toward the status quo: it is a moral task that can be performed only by a currently recognized scheme of jurisdictions.

21.2 HUMAN RIGHTS AS TRANSCENDENT PRINCIPLES

On Green's account, to be a right holder requires that one's jurisdiction is recognized by others. This "rights recognition thesis" has not only been controversial, but it has also been largely dismissed.[52] W. D. Ross provides a typical rebuttal:

Now it is plainly wrong to describe either legal or moral rights as depending for their existence on recognition, for to recognize a thing (in the sense in which "recognize" is used here) is to recognize it as existing already. The promulgation of a law is not the recognition of a legal right, but the creation of it, though it may imply the recognition of an already existing moral right. And to make the existence of a *moral* right depend on its being recognized is equally mistaken. It would imply that slaves, for instance, acquired the moral right to be free only at the moment when a majority of mankind, or of some particular community, formed the opinion that they ought to be free, i.e., when the particular person whose conversion to such a view changed a minority into a majority changed his mind. Such a view, of course, cannot consistently be maintained.[53]

Let us leave aside the details of Green's own account, as well as debates about the semantics of "recognition."[54] On the analysis

---

[51] R. E. Ewin, *Liberty, Community and Justice*, p. 41.
[52] See Peter P. Nicholson, *The Political Philosophy of the British Idealists*, pp. 83ff. For relatively rare, sympathetic treatments, see Rex Martin, *A System of Rights*; Derrick Darby, "Two Conceptions of Rights Possession."
[53] W. D. Ross, *The Right and the Good*, p. 51. Ross is explicitly responding to Green.
[54] As Ross indicates, often for a person to recognize something (say, the house in which he was born) implies that the thing already exists and that *then* the person recognized it for what it is. Thus for Ross and most rights theorists, it makes perfect sense to say that society is failing to recognize a person's moral rights: the

developed here, a slave society is certainly subject to deep moral criticism as it fails to respect the abstract rights of agency (§17). As we saw, these are abstract claims or principles that persons must be protected against blocking and thwarting their agency, and claims not to be harmed in basic ways. I stressed that these abstract rights must be interpreted into more specific rules and requirements before they can perform their functions of providing a framework for cooperation among free and equal persons; but they always serve as a basis for moral criticism of societies that fail to have any adequate (i.e., acceptable to all Members of the Public of the relevant society) scheme to interpret these abstract rights. If there is no eligible interpretation of an abstract right of agency, a society's social morality is deeply flawed. In a straightforward sense, such societies fail to respect human rights and are properly subject to censure. However, while appeals to such abstract rights provide a ground for censure, they are not sufficient for the sort of specified moral claims that an ongoing order of public reason requires. We can say that the society is unjust, and it must institute reforms so that it adequately interprets the abstract rights of agency.[55] But until the right is interpreted (either within the social order or by international institutions to which the relevant political order is subject), there is not as yet an effective scheme of agency rights. Both Green and Ross are correct: a slave society has no regime of rights because there is no social recognition *and* we can appeal to nonrecognized rights to condemn the society and insist upon reform.

I earlier allowed that there may be some traditional societies in which persons do not conceive of themselves as self-directed agents (§17.2). My aim was to stress that persons-as-agents is a historical

---

rights are there, but people do not recognize them, as they might fail to recognize true genius. Green's model of recognition, however, is akin to a chair at a meeting who, *in recognizing* a speaker *creates a status*; to recognize that someone has the floor *is to give* him the floor. We have two models of recognition available to us: acknowledging a status and creating a status. Green cannot be charged with a simple confusion about the way "recognition" works; it works in two ways. For a general defense of Green's account, see my "The Rights Recognition Thesis: Defending and Extending Green."

[55] This will usually involve claims that the political order institutionalizes an effective scheme of rights. I consider the moral tasks of the political order in Chapter VIII.

and contingent conception and cannot be presumed to be a necessity of human nature. That said, in our current world it would be most unwise to identify some cultures as based on conceptions of the persons that do not place self-directed agency at their core. In all large-scale societies the conception of persons as self-directed agents is current and spreading; you and I act at our moral peril if, on the basis of uncertain evidence, we conclude that some peoples or groups do not conceive of themselves in this way. The Great Society is now a worldwide society, and its participants conceive of themselves as such agents (§14.3). The morality of agency is thus today a universal, transcendent morality: all true moralities must accommodate the basic claims of agency (§10.4*d*). We may truly say that the claims of agency are human rights.

Jurisdictional rights, we have seen, are necessary devices of public reason in social orders characterized by deep evaluative pluralism. In an important respect they are less basic than agency rights; we barely can imagine a social order today that is not composed of agents, but it is often said that some social orders are far less evaluatively diverse than others. Those in the Western cultures often suppose that other societies display great cultural and religious homogeneity. We must be cautious about endorsing such views. It is extraordinarily easy to conceive of other societies as uniform and one's own as diverse.[56] And some of the intellectual elites of these societies, seeking to reject Western values including its pluralism, may encourage the perception that they possess a unity of culture lacking in the West. These are difficult issues that certainly cannot be resolved here. I simply sound a note of caution in supposing that the jurisdictional rights so critical to public justification under pluralistic conditions – private property, privacy, and freedom of association – are unimportant in non-Western societies. Women, minority religions, ethnic minorities, and various urban populations often manifest an understanding of what is valuable and important that is at odds with the majority, and certainly departs from the stereotypical image of the "non-

---

[56] It is also easy to see past societies as much more homogeneous than they were. Communitarians who look back to less pluralistic days often ignore deep cleavages in these societies. See Derek L. Phillips, *Looking Backwards: A Critical Appraisal of Communitarian Thought.*

Western." While care and sensitivity to difference are required, jurisdictional rights have a compelling claim to the status of transcendent morality, though eligible schemes of jurisdictional rights are apt to be broader than the set of eligible agency rights.

To be sure, all this presupposes that non-Westerners are also free and equal persons, and so Rousseau's fundamental problem is theirs too. Their status too demands that the moral order be one that all have sufficient reason to endorse. Rawls, however, holds that there may be decent non-Western societies in which not all persons are regarded as free and equal;[57] if so, then the basic requirements of public justification would not apply. I do not insist that this is impossible, but again we have reason to be skeptical. We have seen that the concept of oneself as an agent who has one's own aims, and so who objects to unwarranted intervention, is closely tied to conceiving of oneself as a free and equal moral person (§17.5). Just as an agent believes that she has a claim that her actions be based on her deliberations, free and equal moral agents insist that their moral obligations be confirmed by their own deliberations. Agency, I have suggested, is now properly deemed a universal self-conception, and so grounds a conception of human rights as agency rights. Once the idea of oneself as an independent agent properly acting on one's own deliberations has taken root, the foundation is provided for conceiving of oneself as a free moral agent in one's moral relations. One sees one's deliberations as instructing one as to what one should do, and so one sees moral authority as something one must confirm. This is not inconsistent with seeing oneself as under the authority of religious superiors. Just as a Roman Catholic remains free and equal when her evaluative standards lead her to accept the moral authority of the Pope, so too can those in non-Western societies have standards that give them reasons to defer to the moral authority of local religious scholars and teachers. Agents, though, see their actions and beliefs, including their acceptance of moral authority, as being *theirs* and following from their own understanding of the normative world. The rise of the world of agents is inevitably accompanied by the rise of free moral persons. Our world may contain cultures

[57] Rawls, *The Law of Peoples*, p. 71.

comprised of large groups who are not moral persons, just as it may contain groups of non-agents. The abstract possibility cannot be denied. However, given our lack of knowledge about others, our tendencies to oversimplify their worldviews and to radically over-estimate their cultural homogeneity, the presumption against concluding this is mightily weighty.

When Rawls says that "all persons in a decent hierarchical society are not regarded as free and equal"[58] we may take this as meaning that some societies are based on a decent moral hierarchy; some claim an intrinsic or natural moral authority over others, such that they need not justify to their inferiors their rule over them, or their treatment of them. Now it is tempting to suppose that such a hierarchy of moral authority may in some way be acceptable to the subjugated, and again we cannot deny that this is within the range of human possibility.[59] Consider, though, not a logical or concep-tual possibility, but an empirical finding: Brahmans typically think it is morally right for husbands to beat a disobedient wife.[60] *Perhaps* there is some *possible* "common good" justification; it is within the range of human possibility that the family unit is of central impor-tance to the welfare of all its members, that it must have a leader, that this leader is always the father, and that effective social coop-eration requires that husbands be entitled to beat their wives. We cannot say that any of this is conceptually impossible. When confronted by such actual oppressive practices, however, we would do well to recall Mill's exposé of the claims of men that they possess decent authority to rule over women. A tremendous amount of pressure and indoctrination has gone into perpetuating such a system:

All men, except the most brutish, desire to have, in the woman most nearly connected with them, not a forced slave but a willing one, not a slave merely, but a favourite. They have therefore put everything in practice to enslave their minds. The masters of all other slaves rely, for maintaining obedience, on fear; either fear of themselves, or religious fears. The masters of women wanted more than simple obedience, and they turned the whole

---

[58] Rawls, *The Law of Peoples*, p. 71.
[59] Rawls himself tells us his "remarks about a decent hierarchical society are conceptual." *The Law of Peoples*, p. 75n.
[60] See Shweder, Mahapatra, and Miller, "Culture and Moral Development," p. 50.

force of education to effect their purpose. All women are brought up from the very earliest years in the belief that their ideal of character is the very opposite to that of men: not self-will, and government by self-control, but submission, and yielding to the control of others. All the moralities tell them that it is the duty of women, and all the current sentimentalities that it is their nature, to live for others: to make complete abnegation of themselves, and to have no life but in their affections. And by their affections are meant the only ones they are allowed to have – those to the men with whom they are connected, or to the children who constitute an additional and indefeasible tie between them and a man.[61]

As Mill stressed, despite all the pressure and indoctrination that had gone into seeking to convince women to endorse their subjugated status, it was simply false that all women embraced their subjection. And that is no less true today than in 1869. When confronted by any remotely realistic "decent hierarchical" society that denies some of its members equal freedom "to employ their faculties, and such favourable chances as offer, to achieve the lot which may appear to them most desirable,"[62] it will always be the case in the contemporary world that this hierarchical relation is rejected by some of those denied freedom. Those claiming the status of free and equal persons, resisting their subordination to the unjustified authority of others, have a call on us: they demand only what we suppose is our own due as moral persons – to be guided by one's own reasoning and understanding of the normative world. To reply to them that their subordination is decent, and so they decently can be denied what we view as our most basic claim as a moral person in our social world, manifests a moral superiority and complacence; those demanding to be treated as we demand to be treated can be dismissed because they – but not us – can lead decent yet subjugated lives. Given who we are, we cannot in conscience dismiss a plea of others to be treated as free and equal moral persons, even should they find themselves living among others who might be convinced that their despotic claims are decent.

---

[61] Mill, *The Subjection of Women*, pp. 271–2 (chap. 1, ¶11).
[62] Ibid., p. 272 (chap. 1, ¶13).

That all must be accorded the status of free and equal moral persons, and so all authoritarian moral regimes are to be condemned, does not deny the important truth that different societies have different true moralities. Within the limits of public reason, there are many possible moral equilibria based on many different sets of evaluative standards. As Baier perceptively recognized, the crude distinction between moral universalists, who insist on the same morality for all humans, and moral relativists, who think one society's morality is as good as the next, is woefully inadequate as a basis for understanding the nature of moral truth in different orders. There are many true moralities, but there are many false ones too.

21.3 MORAL CRITICISM AND MORAL REFORM

Let us turn to a person's criticism of the morality of her own society. I do not wish to belittle the importance of criticism of the morality of other social orders; quite the contrary, it is manifestly of great import today. It is, though, an especially vexing problem; it concerns not only questions of moral justification but also epistemic difficulties about knowing the true condition and values of those in other social orders, as well as special problems of the morality of nonmembers intervening in other orders. I have argued that moral criticism of other orders for violating abstract human rights is justified and appropriate; what follows in the way of justified actions is a complex matter indeed. Like many issues of pressing importance, they are pressing because they are so difficult. We can make progress on this issue by trying to better understand the nature of moral criticism and reform within a moral order.

(a) Unjustified Moral Rules That Are Social Equilibria without Punishment
We have thus far been considering the most serious failing of a moral order – that it fails to accord some members their justified abstract rights of agency and jurisdictions. Such orders are oppressive; protections and jurisdictions that are justified among free and equal persons are not respected within that moral order. The

subjugation of women and African Americans represents the two appalling examples within our order of denial of basic agency rights. When confronting such basic oppression, reform is urgent, and appeal to the political order will be necessary (see Chapter VIII). A moral order that denies some their basic claims of agency suffers from widespread loss of authority. Of course, the rules are without authority in our dealings with our oppressed fellows, but the corrosion of moral authority is apt to spread. If the property system is outside the eligible set, so that some are denied their proper opportunity to acquire property, the authority of all property claims comes into question. If one is dealing with a husband who possesses unjustified control of his wife's possessions, or a white shopkeeper who has benefited from the prohibition of African American competitors, the moral authority of these relations, and others that they in turn infect, is undermined. To knowingly benefit from the denial of the basic claims of agency is itself a great moral failing.

Certainly one may not teach these oppressive rules to children as moral rules, for they are not true moral rules, and to teach them would be to deeply implicate oneself in the maintenance of an oppressive social order. To knowingly teach immorality as morality is an awful thing and manifests a betrayal of one's children and the young. It would also be a great moral failing to employ these rules oneself as a basis of authoritative claims; to do so, of course, would be to fail in a most serious way to treat others as free and equal moral persons. Indeed, one surely has some duty to speak out against such oppression, though much here depends on the nature of the specific case. To speak out when doing so endangers oneself or one's family may be admirable, but not required; to speak out when it endangers the oppressed themselves may not even be admirable. Whether or not one should ignore or violate the oppressive rules is yet another and even more complex question. Think about the rules of property ownership in American society during the nineteenth and much of the twentieth century; they clearly were deeply infected by an oppressive social morality. African Americans were often denied the opportunity to acquire property and were denied the full protection of the property they did possess. While the property system – or at least a number of its rules – were thus without moral authority, they still performed critical social tasks, allowing the coordination of expectations necessary for productive activity. All-out rejection of the entire property system – refusing to pay attention to its rules – would have seriously harmed everyone and perhaps done nothing to attain a just society. As the world saw in the first part of the twentieth century, great economic disorder is by no means guaranteed to lead to more just regimes.

This leads us to the important distinction between a rule as a mere social rule and a genuine moral convention.[63] Some conventions about, say, the rights of property and harm to others are necessary to any human society. One way to understand the problems of people in Hobbes' state of nature is that there is no property – "no mine and thine distinct; but only that to be every man's, that he can get; and for as long as he can keep it."[64] There is no common recognition of what "belongs" to anyone. At any moment, someone may try to take what you possess. There cannot be an end to the state of war until each knows what belongs to her and what belongs to others. To secure peace, each person needs to know what she has a right, or a claim, to. Thus it may seem that property is so necessary to social existence that *any* system is better than none at all, and so all property systems are within the eligible set. However, this is to confuse the mere desirability of property as a social convention with a system of property with moral authority. Hobbes provides a plausible argument for coordinating on some system of property and welcoming its rules as coordination rules as compared with the state of nature, but this does not imply validating them as having moral authority. Consider Display VII-10.

Here Alf and Betty are in a state of moral disorder (as was American society under discriminatory social rules). Nevertheless, they may converge on an R_1 social rule as a nonmoral, simply social equilibrium; based on their overall interests, they agree that the current rule is better than no social convention at all, but it is not eligible from the moral point of view because it fails to adequately

[63] See Cristina Bicchieri, *The Grammar of Society*, chap. 1.
[64] Hobbes, *Leviathan*, p. 78 (chap. 13, ¶13).

	Alf	**Betty**
Individual view of eligible moral rights	R_1 (Current right)	R_2
	R_3	R_3
	R_2	
Rankings outside the individual eligible set	No moral right	No moral right
		R_1 (Current right)
	No social rule	No social rule

DISPLAY VII-10 CONVERGENCE ON A BAD DESCRIPTIVE NORM

satisfy Betty's evaluative standards. She cannot grant it moral authority. Given this ordering, the evaluative standards of neither Alf nor Betty endorse simply ignoring the current property rule. Nevertheless, their current system of property is oppressive; they possess no justified property jurisdictions and so fail to respect the abstract moral right of property. There are two options that are eligible to both, R_2 and R_3, but they have thus far failed to coordinate on either.

This is by no means a mere philosophical fancy. One of the most intractable types of injustice is depicted by Display VII-10, where we have coordinated on a bad norm because a bad social rule is better than no social coordination at all. Employing different types of analyses, Robert Richerson and Peter Boyd also show how societies can equilibrate on such bad norms, and moving to acceptable ones can be exceedingly difficult.[65] We can see one reason why: a route to a justified equilibrium that moves us through no social rule at all may be disapproved of by all or, less dramatically, by a majority of those who are oppressed by the current rule. The oppressed themselves may resist moral reform (as it is likely that they will inordinately bear the costs of the breakdown of the social convention). Here, perhaps, only the political order is apt to be an adequate engine of moral reform as it can move us to a new equilibrium much more quickly than informal social processes (§22.2).

[65] Richerson and Boyd, *Not by Genes Alone*, pp. 23ff.

(b) Unjustified Moral Rules That Are Social Equilibria with Punishment
In the cases we have been considering, the unjustified moral rule is
a social convention in equilibrium even when we do not consider
that violators will be punished. The convention itself serves the
interest, though not the morally relevant evaluative standards, of
all. Social orders can become stuck with bad norms in another way:
because violation of the social rule is typically punished, each may
have sufficient reasons to conform simply to avoid punishment.
Cristina Biccchieri analyzes such cases:

> Fear should never be discounted, because there are many cases in which
> one obeys a norm only because neglecting others' expectations and prefe-
> rences will bring about some form of punishment. We may conform with-
> out any intrinsic value to the norm and without finding others' expecta-
> tions legitimate. Some Arab women may observe Muslim sexual mores,
> and Corsican men embrace norms of revenge, for fear of being punished if
> they break the rules. In both cases they may find their community norms
> oppressive and ill-suited to modern life, but whoever speaks first or rebels
> first runs the risk of bearing huge costs. Breaking the rules looks like the
> risky cooperative choice in a social dilemma. Freedom from a bad norm is
> a public good that is often very difficult to bring about.[66]

As Boyd and Richerson show, punishment can stabilize just about
any norm, good or bad.[67] Again, then, social equilibrium does not
imply moral equilibrium, and the fact that a bad norm is in social
equilibrium can make it very difficult to dislodge. Nevertheless,
compared to the cases we discussed earlier (§21.3*a*), moral reform
does not have as steep a hill to climb in these cases because
oppressed individuals have incentives to violate these bad norms
when they can escape detection. Such norms are vulnerable to
attack by an avant-garde who place high value on fidelity to their
evaluative standards and moral justification. In response to their
violations and the example they set, defenders of the status quo
typically are pressed to extend more resources on detection and
punishment; errors and excesses in punishment are apt to induce
further alienation from the norm and convince yet others that as

---

[66] Bicchieri, *The Grammar of Society,* p. 42.
[67] Boyd and Richerson, *The Origin and Evolution of Cultures,* chap. 9.

punishment is impossible to escape, opposition is rational. Of course repression can, and all too often has, succeeded for a very long time, especially when the oppressors have control of the state, but in these cases we can see plausible dynamics that over the long run may lead to overturning the oppressive rule. Victorian sexual mores collapsed with amazing speed; within two generations of Queen Victoria's death, the oppressive and elaborate (and rigidly enforced) code of sexual conduct that dominated much of the nineteenth century was largely forgotten.

(c) Non-Optimal Moral Equilibria

I have been stressing that social equilibrium can occur on moral rules outside the eligible set, and in these cases moral reform – moving society to a moral equilibrium – can be terrifically difficult. Although some will object to this account of an order of public reason on the grounds that the perspective of impartial reason does not yield an unequivocal correct morality, our real and pressing moral problem is that we so often are confident that we are outside the eligible set, but the unjustified rule is fortified by a social equilibrium. A case for moral reform with less urgency is depicted by Display VII-11.

Alf	Betty
z	z
x^*	y
y	x^*
No moral rule	No moral rule

DISPLAY VII-11 A SUBOPTIMAL MORAL EQUILIBRIUM

In Display VII-11, x^* is our current moral rule. Rule x^* is, within this two-member public, Pareto-dominated by z, so x^* is not in the socially optimal eligible set, though it is in the socially eligible set.

Baier observes that "improvements in the society's morality can occur only by changes in the member's morality and these are best brought about by the members' own efforts at convincing one another by their discussions with others (and, of course, by their own critical reflections)."[68] Suppose first that z is a plausible extension or modification of $x^* - x^*$ with a tweak. Alf's understanding of the justifiability of x^* certainly ought to undergo a change, as he has been given a compelling case that free and equal moral persons, employing their evaluative criteria, will endorse z rather than x^*. He must conclude that current morality contains claims that are less than fully justified. Accepting the current rule is in a sense irrational – as always is the case when people select a lower-ranked option. Alf should teach z to his children as something all should aim for; in personal interactions he may make a point of appeal to z, as he has the opportunity for showing that it is justified among free and equal moral persons. In relations with strangers, however, it would be morally presumptuous for him to either (*i*) insist that all others honor this claim or (*ii*) deny the claims of others based on x^* in his interactions with them. For all its inadequacies, x^* is a moral equilibrium in the eligible set, and so despite its inefficiencies it solves Rousseau's fundamental problem: given the actions of others, each, consulting only her own evaluative standards, has reason to act on it.

A more puzzling case occurs if z takes us, as it were, by surprise. It is not a modification of x^* that can lead us to teach x^* in a new way or convince people to adopt a more expansive or restricted version of x^* but, say, the results of a philosophical treatise that has provided a conclusive case for z, a pretty radically new rule. Of course much depends on just how superior z is to the current equilibrium, but the case for moral reform here is much more difficult to make. Having achieved a flawed moral equilibrium, we must question the wisdom of endangering it by seeking a better one to which there is no clear and easy path. The road to moral improvement is uncertain, and there is always the real danger that radical change will simply bring about moral confusion. Appeal to the political order is also of dubious wisdom here for, as we shall see, like all coercive systems it too can impose both bad and good equilibria through punishment. Since no political order is guaranteed to produce an equilibrium result (§22.2), we again run the risk of replacing an imperfect equilibrium with moral disorder.

[68] Baier, *The Rational and the Moral Order*, p. 217.

(d) Moral Innovation

Thus far I have concentrated on three cases of moral criticism and reform: when there is a justified abstract right but no equilibrium on any eligible interpretation, when there is a moral rule outside the eligible set that is in social equilibrium, and when there is a moral rule that is in moral equilibrium but is suboptimal. Another case arises when there is no rule of positive morality over some area in which there is an eligible set. The most obvious case is what we might call the moralization of some aspect of life that has subsequently been a blameless liberty within our "protective perimeter" (§16.2c). Baier provides a general guideline as to when moralization of some type of conduct is appropriate:

> But what are moral questions? . . . [A] question is a moral one if and only if it is one whose being generally answered in accordance with self-anchored reasons [i.e., reasons based on an individual's goals, ends, values, aims, and other personal ideals] would have suboptimal results and which, therefore, should be answered on the basis of reasons which are paramount over self-anchored ones. . . . [R]easons are rightly so regarded if, in an ideal moral order, their generally being so regarded has optimal results, that is, if it results in the maintenance of a state of affairs which is, from every member's point of view, the best thing possible for the members.[69]

This is very close to the upshot of our analysis. If on some matter, each acting on her own ideals and evaluative standards produces a result that, from the perspective of each Member of the Public, is suboptimal (according to her relevant evaluative standards), then we may hold that some authoritative moral rule is to be ranked above no moral authority at all. The model here is mixed motive interactions such as the Prisoners' Dilemma, but the analysis is more general: any question about which Members of the Public conclude on the basis of their relevant evaluative standards that some morally authoritative rules are preferred to a mere liberty is a moral question. Nonmoral action need not be uncoordinated action. As we have seen, even those acting on their blameless liberty may coordinate on a social convention. But Members of the Public may conclude that some such conventions are morally

---

[69] Ibid., p. 282 (note deleted).

objectionable and seek to replace the existing social convention with a moral equilibrium.

In the last fifty years new areas of social life have been moralized. Paul Rozin has documented the moralization of smoking – an activity that surely has gone from a blameless liberty to a morally regulated one.[70] (I pass over the question of whether all this regulation is justified; we must always keep in mind that punishment can produce an equilibrium on bad as well as good rules.) The rise of moral rules about littering is another striking case. Again not only has littering behavior become less common, but there is good evidence that this is social rule-driven. R. Cialdini, C. Kallgren and R. Reno found that about half of those who had no or weak personal standards against littering nevertheless conform to an anti-littering rule when the rule is activated – that is, the relevant conditions for activating the script occur (§10.2).[71]

Moral innovation, like cultural innovation in general, starts with trendsetters who act on their own evaluation of what is best; others tend to copy if doing so seems likely to advance their own standards.[72] At this point, though, the evolution of new rules presents us with a quandary, for the trendsetting behavior may involve punishment and criticism of noncompliers that, at the early stages of the evolution of the new norm, is not justified. Unless the society is already "normatively primed" – unless it has arrived at a state in which all concur that some rule on this matter is justified – trendsetters act unjustly if they punish on the basis of the new norm. Indeed, even if the society is normatively primed for some rule in this area, trendsetters who select one from the eligible set and begin to act and punish based on it still fail to treat others as free and equal, since at the early stages of moral innovation all do not have reason to endorse any specific member of the eligible set.

Is there any way in which new norms can be introduced without a period of trendsetter (and early follower) authoritarianism? The short answer is "yes." Boyd and Richerson show how under some

---

[70] Paul Rozin, "The Process of Moralization."
[71] R. Cialdini, C. Kallgren, and R. Reno, "A Focus Theory of Normative Conduct: A Theoretical Refinement and Reevaluation of the Role of Norms in Human Behavior." See also Bicchieri, *The Grammar of Society*, chap. 2.
[72] See Boyd and Richerson, *The Origin and Evolution of Culture*, Part 1.

conditions group beneficial norms can spread quickly throughout a population without the use of punishment.[73] As they argue, we often do not know what is the best thing to do, but as trendsetters experiment, others tend to copy the successful; in this case rule spreading does not occur via punishment but by a spreading out of copying the successful. If we think of a society spatially distributed, a core group of the new rule trendsetters will do better than their neighbors and thus will be copied by those in close proximity; and these early copiers will in turn be copied by their neighbors, and so on, radiating outward from the core trendsetting group.[74] Importantly, what Baier identifies as the sphere of moral questions requires just the type of moral rule that can spread without trend-setter authoritarianism: where individual action on the basis of personal goals is clearly suboptimal and so others see that trend-setting rule-based cooperative behavior is advantageous and so freely imitate it. This is an important lesson; if we follow Baier in restricting moral issues to, broadly speaking, cases of suboptimality of action based on individual ideals, moral innovation can spread throughout a population without the use of authoritarian punishment.

21.4 THE DANGERS OF UTOPIANISM

Moral reform is usually a matter of extreme urgency. It is a grave matter when our moral order fails to treat some as free and equal – their basic agency rights are disrespected, their jurisdictions are inadequate. Complacency in the face of these serious moral failings is itself a serious moral failing, for our participation in such an order infects us all as we disrespect our fellows in our interactions. Taking seriously the urgency of moral reform in response to these failings is endangered when, as current political philosophy almost obsessively does, we focus on the specification of an "ideal" or "utopia." In his *Law of Peoples,* Rawls declares that "I begin and end with the idea of a realistic utopia. Political philosophy is

---

[73] Ibid., chap. 12.
[74] For a dynamic analysis employing copying the best, see Jason Alexander and Brian Skyrms. "Bargaining with Neighbors: Is Justice Contagious?"

realistically utopian when it extends what are ordinarily thought of as the limits of practical political possibility."[75] A reasonably utopian theory characterizes the just state in terms of what "could and may" exist,[76] at least under favorable historical conditions. Rather than "realistic utopia," David Estlund prefers the label of "aspirational" political theory – one that "sets sound standards that are not met, but could be met, and it tells us how to meet them."[77] There is nothing, of course, objectionable about an aspirational moral or political theory: every moral theory aspires to a social state in which moral standards are better met than they are today. We do not now treat all as free and equal, and we should; this is surely a worthy aspiration.

However, a utopianism that identifies a merely possible, perfectly just condition, far removed from our disagreements and uncertainties, is apt not only to be a distraction, but itself a source of injustice. It is a distraction because it fails to adequately distinguish the most morally urgent reforms from the aspiration for ideal justice. In his famous two principles of justice, Rawls includes respect for a person's basic agency rights and a highly controversial criterion of distributive justice – the difference principle – according to which income, wealth, and the social basis of self-respect are to be distributed in a way that is to the long-term advantage of the least advantaged productive class. To be sure, the basic liberties are said to be prior to the difference principle in the sense that they cannot be sacrificed to secure the favored distribution (they are, as I would say, prior in the order of justification), but both principles are fundamental to the nature of a just society. The result of this utopianism is that a highly controversial principle that Rawls himself devised is elevated to a necessary component of a just society because, on his view, the aim of a theory of justice is to specify a possible society in which justice is fully achieved. Perhaps we could someday achieve Rawls' ideal, but we know that no social order is even close to it, and most have little interest in achieving it. Nevertheless, it is necessary to Rawslian utopian justice, so all societies that fail to meet it (i.e., every existing one) is unjust. Not

---

[75] Rawls, *The Law of Peoples*, p. 6.
[76] Ibid., p. 7.
[77] Estlund, *Democratic Authority*, p. 267.

too surprisingly, Rawls thus condemns as unjust every existing politico-economic order, going so far as to lump the modern welfare state and Soviet-style command economies together as intrinsically unjust.[78] The fact that modern welfare states do better at protecting agency rights than any regimes in history, while Soviet-style systems had a horrendous record, does not apparently count at all.[79] This is an upshot of the utopian aspiration: to fall short is to stand condemned, even if an order falls short on a criterion that only Rawls and his fellow utopianists embrace. Under the influence of this way of thinking, a theory of justice no longer can serve as a basis for identifying urgent reform, for it condemns as unjust all societies that have ever existed – and for all we know all societies that will ever be. And so the moral urgency of reform is undermined: if just about any system that has been or ever likely will be is unjust, how can one sustain moral urgency in the face of injustice?

The utopian aspiration also itself leads to injustice. We deeply disagree about ideal justice. Rawls and his followers have painted a portrait of the fully just society, but it is not the picture of all free and equal persons. For Rawlsians to insist, in the face of the intense and sophisticated disputes about the nature of distributive justice, that all free and equal persons endorse this specific vision as their own ideal simply cannot be accepted as credible.[80] Free and equal persons disagree about ideal moral arrangements. A free social order is possible just because we do not have to agree on the ideal, and no ideal sets the benchmark of justice. Freedom is possible in our nonutopian world because we converge on a moral equilibrium, and truly reasonable moral persons do not condemn it as unjust simply because it falls short of their ideal, since all possible equilibria fall short of some reasonable ideals. In the world in which the demands of justice are defined by a person's realistic utopia, each will condemn the other's conception of justice as unjust. And that is precisely the world of much contemporary

---

[78] Rawls, *Justice as Fairness*, pp. 138ff. The argument here is more complex than I have indicated, since Rawls also relies on his controversial thesis about the protection of political rights. I call this thesis into question in section 24.2 below.

[79] See section 24.2*a*

[80] Rawls apparently also finds it so in *Political Liberalism*, pp. xlviii, 6, 156ff.

moral and political philosophy – a world in which philosophers defend their moral ideals and criticize their colleagues as advocates of injustice. We are all free to paint pictures of our ideal, but it is morally arrogant and irresponsible to elevate them into the requirements of justice itself.

CONCLUSION

In this chapter I have tried to show how we can achieve a free moral order while disagreeing on the ideal moral order. When free and equal moral persons reach an equilibrium within the optimal eligible set, Rousseau's fundamental problem is solved; each can call on the rule as the source of an authoritative prescription while the other has reason to comply, consulting only her own evaluative standards. From the perspective of impartial reason – the moral point of view – no rule in the optimal eligible set is better than any other, yet social processes characterized by the increasing returns of a shared morality can lead us to converge on one rule, which then becomes the uniquely publicly justified rule. In some ways this leads to a social evolutionary account of moral justification, though I have been at pains to point out that it is only evolutionary in a weak sense.

It is typically complained that any evolutionary account illegitimately privileges the status quo. Real public reason does indeed hold that a real moral equilibrium has moral properties that merely possible equilibria do not. It provides the basis for an actual authority based on an actual rule that provides the basis for actual expectations about the nature of our social interactions. There is nothing illegitimate about this; as we saw in Part One, it is necessary for social morality. In an account of real public reason, the aim of moral theory is not to paint pictures of an ideal world but to show how we can achieve a real social morality that meets the test of moral acceptability of the real reason of moral agents. This is not at all the same as moral complacency in the face of immorality and injustice. I have explored cases where there is urgent need for moral reform, and some of the barriers to achieving it.

Some readers will be left unsatisfied. For one, I have not given a catalog of the proper interpretation of the agency rights and jurisdictional rights, or the proper specification of other moral rules. As some critics have asked "what *is* my conception of agency rights or property rights?" These are questions of the utmost importance for our practical reflection and applied work. They are not, though, fundamental to a philosophy of social morality that seeks to show how, under conditions of bounded reason and evaluative diversity, free and equal persons can share a moral authority. For that, the specific interpretations are not important; what is important is that we can achieve an equilibrium on a member of the eligible set.

VIII

The Moral and Political Orders

It is a mistake then to think of the state as an aggregation of individuals under a sovereign – equally so whether we suppose the individuals as such, or apart from what they derive from society, to possess natural rights, or suppose them to depend on the sovereign for the possession of rights. A state presupposes other forms of community, with the rights that arise out of them, and only exists as sustaining, securing, and completing them. In order to make a state there must have been families of which the members recognised rights in each other (recognised in each other powers capable of direction by reference to a common good); there must further have been intercourse between families, or between tribes that have grown out of families, of which each in the same sense recognised rights in the other. . . . That, however, is the beginning, not the end, of the state. When once it has come into being, new rights arise in it and further purposes are served by it.

T. H. Green, *Lectures on the Principles of Political Obligation*

In the last chapter we saw how a moral equilibrium can arise in a society on some member of the optimal eligible set. Our social morality is the outcome of social processes that lead to the social recognition of rights and duties, which provide the basis of an ordered yet free social life. Green rightly criticizes social contract theory's supposition that the political order is the only source of moral authority; for Hobbes it creates the claim rights and duties of citizens, while for Locke it is the only source of social authority by which we can resolve disputes about the proper interpretation of

448

our rights. The Baier–Strawson View of social morality – as well as Green's Hegelian view – do not make this mistake; justified social morality does not reduce to justified law. However, we should not be so impressed by the social basis of moral order that we ignore the importance of the political order. We saw in the previous chapter how a social order can become fixated on a social equilibrium that is outside the eligible set; in such cases moral reform without political authority may be well-nigh impossible. Moreover, in societies confronting rapid changes many socially recognized rights require adjustment or, regarding complex rights such as property, detailed completion by the political order. And, of course, regarding many rights, informal social enforcement may be inadequate, and so the organized coercive authority of the state is necessary. This chapter explores some of the basic relations of the moral and political orders. I have elsewhere dealt with more detailed matters such as legislative procedures and judicial review;[1] here my aim is to understand the nature of a publicly justified political order in light of our understanding of the moral order.

22 The Authority of the State

22.1 SOCIAL CONTRACT THEORY AND THE SUPREMACY OF POLITICAL AUTHORITY

(a) The Comparative Procedural Justification Principle
After his review of the classical social contract theories of Hobbes, Locke, and Rousseau, T. H. Green concluded that "they look only to the supreme coercive power on the one side and to individuals, to whom natural rights are ascribed, on the other" and so "they leave out of sight the process by which men are clothed with rights and duties, and with senses of rights and duties, which are neither natural nor derived from the sovereign power."[2] They ignore the way in which individuals are clothed with moral rights through the evolution of a social morality. For Hobbes, Locke and Kant, our disagreements about the contours of our basic rights and the rules

[1] In my *Justificatory Liberalism*, Part Three.
[2] Green, *Lectures on the Principles of Political Obligation*, §113.

of social life must be adjudicated by the state. It is often not fully appreciated that part of Locke's contract is that all agree that, concerning the interpretation of the law of nature, "all private judgment of every particular Member" must be "excluded" in determining morality.[3] It is the task of government to serve as the umpire and the voice of public reason about what morality requires. The political order becomes the interpreter of the moral order regulating interpersonal actions. To be sure, Locke held that individuals have a right to dissent from the authority of the state when its judgments are clearly outside the eligible set – when it is not offering specifications of basic rights that all can endorse as authoritative. Nevertheless, when it is operating within the eligible set (providing a reasonable adjudication of disputes about the laws of nature), its pronouncements are the sole authoritative decisions, backed by the authority of the community, for the resolution of disputes about the rights. There is no role for social morality as a distinct and independent source of moral authority. As Green stressed, there is nothing between the private individual conscience and the political-moral authority of the state.

The social contract theorist may respond to Green that this direct appeal to the state as the source of social moral authority is not an error, but is based on the claim that the state is the uniquely justified voice of the community. More formally, a defense of traditional social contract theory may appeal to

> *The Comparative Procedural Justification Principle:* If the Members of the Public have available two procedures for selecting from the optimal eligible set, *O* and *P,* and *P* is itself publicly justified while *O* is not, *P* should be employed.

In the last chapter (§19.1) I argued that we have compelling grounds to reject the Procedural Justification Requirement, according to which process *O's* selection of option *x* from the eligible set cannot show that *x* is uniquely publicly justified unless *O* itself is uniquely publicly justified. However, the Comparative Procedural Justification Principle is more modest, holding only that

---

[3] Locke, *Second Treatise,* §88. Compare Kant, *Metaphysical Elements of Justice,* pp. 116-119 [Akademie 312ff]. On Hobbes, see my *Contemporary Theories of Liberalism,* chap. 2.

if the Members of the Public have a choice, they should employ a publicly justified process over one which is not. Appealing to the Comparative Procedural Justification Principle, a Lockean can argue that the state should be the sole source of social-moral authority, adjudicating when an individual's claims have moral standing and when they do not, because the state can be publicly justified through the social contract. Someone who is impressed by the argument for meta-fairness in selecting from the eligible set (§19.4) is apt to press for the comparative principle and agree with the social contract theorist that if political procedures for selecting from the optimal eligible set themselves can be publicly justified, then we might suppose that all Members of the Public concur that it is a reasonably fair way of selecting an option from the optimal eligible set. Given this, what I have termed the error of the social contract tradition may in fact appear to be its strength.

This argument for the priority of political adjudication, though seldom explicitly stated, is a presupposition of contemporary "public reason liberalism." Rawls, for example, quite rightly understands the problem of public reason as arising out of reasonable evaluative pluralism but maintains that the "reason of the public" is the "reason of free and equal citizens," that is, a political public reason.[4] If we embrace the Comparative Procedural Justification Principle, the priority of the political over the social appears to be not an unexamined supposition but a deep fact about the nature of public justification among free and equal persons.

(b) The First Theorem of Liberal Democracy

The appeal to the Comparative Justification Principle supposes that there is some political procedure than can be publicly justified. There is indeed a compelling case that only regimes that qualify as representative democracies will comprise the eligible set of possible political systems. I have elsewhere defended what I have deemed the "first theorem of liberal democracy" – that only law-making procedures that are widely responsive to the judgments of the

---

[4] See Rawls, "The Idea of Public Reason Revisited," §1. A clear feature of the evolution of Rawls' thought was that the problem of justified authority, starting out as a social moral problem in his "Outline of a Decision Procedure for Ethics," and still focused on moral social practices in "Justice as Fairness," eventually became a purely political doctrine in *Political Liberalism*.

citizenry are reliable protectors of basic individual rights.⁵ This is
not to say that democracy is generally a good way of getting at the
moral truth whatever that may be;⁶ the first theorem supposes that
a central concern of the political process is to protect, complete, and
harmonize basic rights of agency and jurisdictions. We have no
reason to think that states without well-respected rights of political
representation, free and frequent elections, and political pluralism
do well at protecting the basis abstract rights. Display VIII-1 is
suggestive.

Score of 1 civil rights & score of 1 on political rights	Score of 1 on civil rights & score of 2 on political rights	Score of 2 on civil rights and score of 1 on political rights
45	**3**	**10**

DISPLAY VIII-1 FREEDOM HOUSE 2008 SCORES (1–7 SCALE)

Display VIII-1, drawing on 2008 data from Freedom House, shows
that of the forty-eight states that scored highest (a score of 1 on a
scale of 1 to 7) on the protection of civil rights (freedom of
expression, freedom of association, rule of law, and personal
rights), forty-five also scored highest on the protection of basic
political rights; the remaining three (they are Monaco, St. Vincent
and the Grenadines, and Taiwan) scored 2. Of the fifty-five states
that scored highest (a score of 1) on the protection of political
rights, all but ten also scored highest on the protection of civil
rights, and the remaining ten states all scored 2 on the protection of
civil rights. This of course is merely indicative; it shows only an
extremely strong correlation in our present world between regimes
that respect both sorts of rights, but it is strikingly impressive
nonetheless. The possibility of an authoritarian regime that respects
civil rights is not instantiated in our world, and we may well
wonder whether it ever has been or will be.

It should be stressed that Constant included political rights
among rights of the moderns. Given the influence of Rawls' gloss
on Constant's distinction, in which political liberties are identified

⁵ *Justificatory Liberalism*, pp. 226ff.
⁶ This is a central claim of David Estlund's *Democratic Authority*.

with the liberties of the ancients,[7] this is often overlooked. Constant was explicit that the liberty of the moderns includes "everyone's right to exercise some influence on the administration of the government, either by electing all or particular officials, or through representations, petitions, demands to which the authorities are more or less compelled to pay heed."[8] For Constant, it will be recalled (§18.2), the liberty of the ancients concerned not simply political rights but also the "collective exercise of sovereignty; in deliberating, in the public square, over war and peace; in forming alliances with foreign governments; in voting laws, in pronouncing judgments, in examining the accounts, the acts, the stewardship of the magistrates; in calling them to appear in front of the assembled people, in accusing, condemning or absolving them."[9] Constant quite rightly recognized that the abstract rights of agency and spheres of individual jurisdictions go hand in hand with rights to political representation.

It might be queried, though, how it can be claimed that only, broadly speaking, democratic regimes are within the eligible set of political procedures when we know that some Members of the Public hold antidemocratic views. Bryan Caplan, a public choice economist, has recently insisted that voters are not only ignorant but systematically irrational, and so claims that democracies systematically choose bad policies.[10] More generally, we have survey evidence that public choice economists are suspicious of majority rule.[11] Now we need to distinguish a case that some forms of democracy (say, a pure form of majority rule) might be outside the eligible set of political procedures, from the view that nondemocracies will be within it; our concern here is the latter. At this point Caplan's main claim, that democracies pursue bad

---

[7] See Rawls, *A Theory of Justice*, pp. 176–7, 195; Rawls, *Justice as Fairness*, p. 143; Rawls, *Political Liberalism*, pp. 396ff.

[8] Constant, "Liberty of the Ancients Compared with That of the Moderns," p. 311.

[9] Ibid., p. 311.

[10] See Bryan Caplan, *The Myth of the Rational Voter*. I consider Caplan's arguments in "Is the Public Incompetent? Compared to Whom? About What?"

[11] Members of the American Economic Association (who are not public choice economists) are more likely to accept than reject the proposition that "simple majority rule is the preferred way to make group decisions," while public choice economists are against it by a ratio of 3 to 1. Robert C. Whaples and Jack C. Heckelman, "Public Choice Economics: Where Is There Consensus?" p. 69.

economic policies, is not to the point (see, however, §25); our concern is the public justifiability of political regimes based on their ability to resolve conflicts about social morality and to complete and protect individual rights. In the order of justification these basic rights are fundamental (§§14.3, 17.3*d*); because they are fundamental in the order of justification, they must be supposed as given in deliberations of the Public on other matters, including the nature of an acceptable political order. When deliberating about political regimes, then, Members of the Public are assumed to take as given that these fundamental agency and jurisdictional rights must be respected by an eligible political regime, and so only regimes that can be plausibly said to be reliable protectors of these rights can be included in the eligible set (even if they do pursue bad economic policies). There is no plausible case that nondemocratic regimes could thus qualify.

(c) The Irrelevancy of the Comparative Justification Principle

As so often in this work, we have arrived at an eligible set, but this does not allow the Members of the Public to settle on a unique electoral rule or a regime type. Some form of democracy, understood as a representative system with rights of participation and political pluralism, is certainly abstractly justified, but Members of the Public will not concur on which system is best.[12] Democracies differ in fundamental ways. Arend Lijphart famously contrasted basic differences in governance between majoritarian and consensual democracies;[13] democracies also differ in whether they are unicameral or bicameral, have proportional representation, are parliamentary or presidential, have a unitary or federal structure, possess a written or an unwritten constitution, have a strong or weak system of judicial review – just to name some of the more obvious factors. Members of the Public will have reasonable differences about how to rank different democratic regimes; there is reasonable dispute both about differences in the effects of electoral

---

[12] Under what conditions this will and will not occur is the crux of the dispute between William Riker and Gerry Mackie. Compare Riker's *Liberalism against Populism* and Mackie's *Democracy Defended*.

[13] See Arend Lijphart, *Democracies: Patterns of Majoritarian and Consensus Government in Twenty-One Countries*.

laws[14] and differences in the likely outputs of different systems (bicameral regimes, for example, are said to make legislation more difficult), as well as disagreements about the intrinsic value of some regimes (some hold, for example, that basic democratic values incline towards proportional representation). Whether we take these issues as a bundle (Members of the Public choose regime types) or divide them up into a series of choices (§23.2*b*), Members of the Public will order the options differently.

As with social morality itself, different societies arrive at different equilibria on these matters, largely on the basis of a path-dependent political history. Just as our justification of abstract agency rights, or abstract jurisdictional rights, is insufficient to yield a publicly justified system of rights, so too is the abstract justification of democracy and its attendant political rights insufficient to yield the justification of a system of governance. Even the United States, which can trace its constitutional structure to an explicit convention, has accrued two hundred years of development, due often to unpredictable social and political events, and the unpredictable responses to them. Public reason does not mandate a specific democratic regime (how could it?). To be sure, those committed to a democracy that secures publicly justified outcomes may well advance proposals for institutional design that, in their view, do a better job than other arrangements (see below, §22.2), but Members of the Public will, of course, disagree about the merits of these proposals. Consequently, the Comparative Justification Principle does not support political authority over informal social authority, for political authority too relies on informal social-moral authority – an evolution of a political-moral culture leading to the selection of one of a wide range of acceptable political systems.

---

[14] For a classic study see Douglas Rae, *The Political Consequences of Electoral Laws*. Of course contemporary political science has much to say about these matters, though it is typically open to reasonable dispute, even among the experts.

22.2 THE PRIORITY OF SOCIAL MORALITY

The proponent of the social contract view, which grants to political processes all social authority to identify an acceptable moral equilibrium, sees law as the preeminent response to moral disagreement. Consider, for example, Jeremy Waldron's well-known argument that law is a response to disagreement about what is best. The law, Waldron argues, can help us to coordinate on a common solution to common problems: it renders one coordination point more salient by attaching sanctions, and so makes it less likely that people will hold out for their favorite outcome. "But before it can do that, the society must have decided which of the coordinative strategies to select as the one to be bolstered in this way. That itself is no mean achievement – and I want to say that it is by embodying that achievement that law commands our respect."[15] The real achievement of the law is to select which coordination point should be sought. Thus, in a way similar to the analysis of Chapter VII on the evolution of a moral convention among goodwilled agents (§19.2a), Waldron believes that law and legal authority can be modeled on an impure coordination game:

We want to act together in regard to some matter M, but one of us thinks it is important to follow policy X while others think it is important to follow policy Y, and none of us has reason to think any of the others a better judge of the merits of M than himself. . . .

   In these circumstances, the following will *not* be a way of settling on a common policy: each does whatever he thinks is important to do about M. We must find a way of choosing a single policy in which [we] . . . can participate despite our disagreements on the merits.[16]

As Waldron understands politics, we debate and discuss the merits and demerits of each of the possible coordination points; since it is an impure coordination game, Alf prefers a different coordination point (x/x) than does Betty (y/y), and so they have something to argue about. However, they each prefer any coordination point to lack of coordination. In essence, then, Waldron argues that we need

---

[15] Jeremy Waldron, *Law and Disagreement*, p. 104.
[16] Ibid., p. 107.

to coordinate on some single reasonable law, even if it is not the one that each of us sees as most reasonable. "*A piece of legislation deserves respect because of the achievement it represents in the circumstances of politics: action-in-concert in the face of disagreement.*"[17]

Waldron is correct that legislation has an attractive feature; it can move us from no equilibrium to equilibrium or, as in Display VIII-2, from a suboptimal equilibrium to an optimal one:

		Group B					
		x^*		y		z	
	x^*		2		0		0
		1		0		0	
Group A	y		0		3		0
		0		2		0	
	z		0		0		4
		0		0		-1	

DISPLAY VIII-2 LEGISLATION: OPTIMAL OR INELIGIBLE?

In Display VIII-2, we have two groups of citizens. Suppose the society is now at x^*/x^*, which is in equilibrium. But we see that y/y is Pareto superior to it. As we saw in the previous chapter (§21.3c), a society can become fixed on a suboptimal equilibrium, and it may be very difficult to dislodge it. Legislation can allow us to break the inferior x^*/x^* equilibrium, and move to the superior y/y moral rule. This is the great advantage of legislation: we can, as it were, collectively and quickly move to a Pareto-superior law. The vice of legislation is just as clear: if group B is bigger than group A, it can also move society from x^*/x^* to z/z. Suppose the voters are not sure of each other's utilities (even Members of the Public do not have this information, much less actual voters), and so the members of B do not know that they are decreasing the utility of group A. Nevertheless, they can easily do so; we can thus see how democracy can move society out of the eligible set as well as move

[17] Ibid., p. 108. Emphasis added.

it into the eligible set or into an optimal equilibrium from a suboptimal one.

Any outcome is possible under legislative systems – including
moving away from the Pareto frontier – because legislation does
not require unanimity. If unanimity were required, and excluding
mistakes on the part of voters about their own evaluative
standards, moves away from the Pareto frontier would be impossible. Unanimity rules, though, have their own severe problems in
actual choice situations, in which time is limited and people engage
in bargaining behavior. Holdouts may seek additional payments to
agree to moves that are already recommended by their own values
and aims. James Buchanan and Gordon Tullock famously argued
that the optimum rule (as in Display VIII-3) is the one that minimizes these two costs: external costs (the tendency of a rule to lead
to legislation that allows some to impose costs on others, such as
the move to z/z above), and internal costs (decision-making costs,
including bargaining, holdouts, etc.).[18]

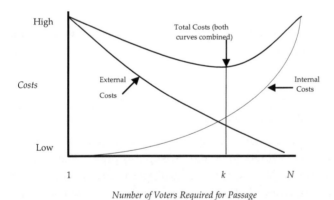

Number of Voters Required for Passage

DISPLAY VIII-3 BUCHANAN'S AND TULLOCK'S COST CURVES

In Display VIII-3 the k rule (requiring less than the entire population) is most efficient. Now, Buchanan and Tullock argue, there is
no reason to think that $k = N/2 + 1$ (i.e., the majority rule). The way

[18] See Buchanan and Tullock, *The Calculus of Consent*, chap. 6; Dennis Mueller, *Public
Choice III*, chap. 4.

the cost curves are drawn in the display, the k rule is between simple majority and unanimity rule.

However, while the k rule is efficient in avoiding legislation moving us outside the eligible set, it will not do as well as majority rule in breaking social equlibria in which society has settled on a point outside the eligible set (§21.3). When we are at such equilibria, perhaps only a small minority is aware that the present social equilibrium is a bad norm, because, say, the present rules interpret an abstract right in a way that is outside their individual eligible sets. If this oppressed group is less than k voters, legislation to move us toward a justified equilibrium may be defeated, even if all the voters are goodwilled, so long as they are not certain of each other's standards. The problem is a common one in selecting reliable procedures: that which does best at avoiding false positives (Buchanan and Tullock's k rule) does not do best in avoiding false negatives (that is, avoiding failure to pass morally required legislation). Majority rule does better at avoiding false negatives, but, as we saw in Display VIII-2, can easily yield false positives (legislation it deems morally justified but which is not).

There is no single correct answer about how to trade off a rule's, or an entire regime's, tendency to make these two sorts of mistakes. If one is convinced that one lives in a deeply unjust society, one may conclude that false negatives are a great worry and so one may favor systems that incline toward majoritarianism. This is not to say, however, that we should ever aim at legislative systems that are strictly neutral between imposing and not imposing laws (§21.1) for, as we shall see (§23.1d), all coercive legislation, even that which improves our system of morality, must overcome a presumption against employing force against persons. If one believes, however, that in general the social morality of one's society passes the test from the moral point of view, there is a strong case for devices that significantly tempers majority rule, either by adopting formal k rules, or systems such as bicameralism that have much the same effects.[19] This last point is of the utmost importance. If we have arrived at a social equilibrium within the optimal eligible set, we should be most reluctant to modify it

---

[19] See Buchanan and Tullock, *The Calculus of Consent,* pp. 237ff.

through the political process. Some may object; the moral equilibrium, they may insist, is not where they would most like it to be. Given their evaluative standards, the current moral equilibrium is, though better than no moral rule at all, not one of their most highly ranked rules. Why, they ask, can they not seek a better outcome through the political process? The answer, I think, is manifest: the political process is a deeply imperfect way to arrive at equilibrium, as it can so easily miss the mark, and move us from a current equilibrium to a moral disequilibrium that, because it is backed by coercive punishment, can be a stable social equilibrium (§21.3*b*). Coercive punishment, we have seen, can make bad as well as good norms stable social equilibria. Because the political process is such an imperfect way to bring about moral equilibrium, a current bona fide moral equilibrium must be respected by the political process.

22.3 MORAL AND POLITICAL AUTHORITY

(a) Over-Individualized Morality and Skepticism of Political Authority
Contemporary legal and political philosophy is often skeptical that the state has authority in the sense that citizens generally have an obligation to obey the law, just because it is the law.[20] Such skeptical views are often described as upholding "philosophical anarchism" as they deny the moral legitimacy and authority of all states; that is, they insist that one never has a moral duty to obey any law on the grounds that it is an authoritative political decision. An inspiration of this line of thinking was Robert Paul Wolff's *In Defense of Anarchism*. Wolff provided a plausible Kantian defense of philosophical anarchism, building on the common view that one's dignity as a rational being is to be an individual, autonomous self-legislator: the law comes from one and applies to one.

---

[20] See, for example, A. John Simmons, *On the Edge of Anarchy*, pp. 248ff; A. John Simmons, "The Anarchist Position"; Joseph Raz, "The Obligation to Obey the Law;" Joseph Raz, *The Morality of Freedom*, chap. 4; Leslie Green, *The Authority of the State*. For a criticism, see Richard Dagger, "Philosophical Anarchism and Its Fallacies." For important recent works challenging the philosophical anarchist position, see George Klosko, *Political Obligations*; Margaret Gilbert, *A Theory of Political Obligation*.

The defining mark of the state is authority, the right to rule. The primary obligation of man is autonomy, the refusal to be ruled. . . . Insofar as a man fulfills his obligation to make himself the author of his decisions, he will resist the state's claim to have authority over him. That is to say, he will deny that he has a duty to obey the laws of the state *simply because they are the laws*. In that sense, it would seem that anarchism is the only political doctrine consistent with the virtue of autonomy.[21]

If we commence with this overindividualized and asocial conception of moral life, political authority immediately becomes troubling; when one enters the political sphere, suddenly the claim is that one no longer must conform to one's own rational moral legislation but must now do as others say. If one's dignity as a moral being is to act on the law as one has autonomously legislated it, to endorse political authority – especially about moral matters – appears to be pure heteronomy, and a betrayal of one's status as a free and equal moral person. Thus it is common for philosophical anarchists to claim that one must always act with fidelity to one's understanding of morality, and this will mean that one cannot also accept a moral obligation to do what the state says independently of one's evaluation of the substantive morality of its commands. We now appreciate the deep error at the heart of this view. Social authority concerning our moral rights and duties does not start at politics; substantive moral requirements are partly determined by social conventions. If the social convention has selected x from the eligible set, then even if one holds that y is the superior moral rule – and even if one is correct about this – the authority of the social convention is such that one has reason to defer. The social decision identifies binding rules.[22] Given that all social morality is based on the common recognition of the authority of certain social rules, we should resist the widely endorsed vision of the morally autonomous self-legislator or moral agent suddenly having to renounce his moral autonomy or free moral agency as he submits to political authority.

---

[21] Robert Paul Wolff's *In Defense of Anarchism*, p. 18. Emphasis in original.
[22] Which, I have stressed, is very different from saying that the social decision procedure is binding. See section 19.1.

I noted earlier Green's observation that social contract theory looks "only to the supreme coercive power on the one side and to individuals, to whom natural rights are ascribed, on the other" (§22.1). This direct jump from the individual with her moral rights[23] to the state invites the challenge of philosophical anarchism, for it suggests that the problem of authority arises only with the state; consequently, philosophical anarchists who believe that the problem of authority cannot be solved only need to refuse to recognize the authority of the state, not social morality itself. By depicting the state as the sole source of authority adjudicating moral differences, social contract theory plays into the hands of the imperious private conscience (§12.4*b*), which sees the moral life in terms of fidelity to its own vision. If we ensconce morality in the first-person point of view – the justified demands of social morality are interpreted as simply the dictates of an individual's conscience – the state's claim to authority unsettles the private conscience, jarring it with the claim that it is only one among others, and that it cannot dictate the terms of shared moral life. "How can the evaluative standards of others ever bind me?" it asks in disbelief. We should not be surprised if, having encouraged the private conscience that it can lay down the requirements of social morality, it is appalled by the idea of a political order in which suddenly its imperious claims are not taken seriously.

(b) Minimal Authority: The Permissible Use of Force

In many contexts we can usefully speak of "political authority" in general; however, when we examine the problem of political authority we find that the general idea is employed to cover several distinct claims. Thomas Christiano has usefully distinguished three "concepts of authority": "legitimate political authority as justified coercion, legitimate political authority as the capacity to impose duties, and legitimate political authority as the right to rule."[24] Christiano rightly stresses that rather than seeking to defend one as

---

[23] Raz makes a similar jump from "ordinary *individual morality*" to "political *authority*," and so he too finds the authority of the state problematic, although somewhat less so than the philosophical anarchists. *The Morality of Freedom,* p. 72, emphasis added.

[24] Thomas Christiano, *The Constitution of Equality,* p. 240.

the uniquely correct understanding of authority, we would do best to examine each and consider how it enters into the overall idea of the authority of the state.

The minimal understanding of the authority of the state[25] is a moral permission to employ force or the threat of force against citizens to enforce its laws (see further §23). On this minimal conception of authority, citizens need not have any corresponding moral obligation to obey the law, or even a moral obligation to acquiesce in the coercion. In this sense, the authority of the state is akin to the authority of a party in Hobbes' state of nature who has a "blameless liberty" to coerce (§16.2c) that does not correlate with duties on the part of others. In deliberating about political institutions, Members of the Public have compelling reasons to endorse some such minimal authority, as they would be well aware that there are some persons in any social order who are not moral persons and so are unable to internalize moral rules – only the threat of punishment can provide them with incentives to obey. In her striking study on noninstitutionalized psychopaths Cathy Spatz Widom found a significant number of psychopaths within the general (noninstitutionalized) population.[26] We have already seen that there is impressive evidence to conclude that psychopaths do not possess the moral emotions or a conception of others as free and equal (§§9.3b, 12.1), and so they do not have reasons to endorse moral rules as authoritative (§13.3). That psychopaths (and others who fail to achieve moral personhood) do not have "the right sort of reasons" (§11.1a) to endorse moral duties does not imply, though, that it would be wrong to coerce them to conform to moral rules. Given our absence of moral relations with them, we have a blameless liberty to act as we see fit. Being restricted to instrumental reasoning, they can often respond to incentives,[27] and so can be given nonmoral reasons to conform. There is no moral reason to refrain from coercing such persons to conform to the moral rules of our social order. More generally, temporary residents within the

---

[25] Except when explicitly stated otherwise, "authority" denotes "legitimate" or "de jure" authority.

[26] Cathy Spatz Widom, "A Methodology for Studying Non-Institutionalized Psychopaths."

[27] Recall that Widom found that they can cooperate in iterated Prisoners' Dilemmas. See her "Interpersonal Conflict and Cooperation in Psychopaths."

boundaries of the state (or those whom, say, our state has temporarily occupied in a war)[28] who, because of deep cultural differences, do not endorse some of our moral rules,[29] nevertheless can be induced through the use of coercion to conform to the moral rules, producing a stable social equilibrium on these rules. It is important to stress that in such a case the temporary residents are under no moral obligation to submit or comply, and so in these areas we do not treat them as moral persons. This cost can be borne with respect to short-term visitors but is unacceptable in a free social order concerning long-term residents.

Leaving aside those who are not moral persons settled within the social order, we may inquire whether Members of the Public would concur that the state may permissibly coerce in order to sustain morally unjustified social conventions. On the face of it, this seems manifestly impossible. If we presently possess a social convention on some rule z, and z is outside the eligible set regarding some abstractly justified right, a social life structured by z fails to treat some as free and equal. Yet, we have also seen that it will often be the case that all Members of the Public prefer a morally unjustified social convention (which, of course lacks moral authority) over no social convention at all (§21.3). Situations have arisen in which the polity is deliberating about the proper moral reform (seeking a political selection of some option in the eligible set), but the debates are protracted and for a considerable time inconclusive. Consider the long struggle not simply for the enfranchisement of women but for their full legal personality, including as owners of property. During the time when it became clear that the property and voting rules were unjustified (i.e., outside the eligible set), they certainly had no moral authority, and citizens had no obligation to comply. But it seems extreme to say that the state was wrong to continue enforcing the right of property or conducting elections according to the unjustified rules. Here are cases where the necessity of some social convention may be so important that, for a protracted time, the state may permissibly employ force to uphold an unjustified one. Certainly there is no algorithm in making such

[28] See Christiano, *The Constitution of Equality*, p. 241.
[29] Let us suppose that such cases can occur. Within a free moral order among strangers characterized by deep evaluative diversity, it is a limiting case.

decisions; just how unjust the law is, and how protracted political inaction is, will be crucial in deciding the permissible limits of coercion to uphold unjustified laws. About these matters Members of the Public will disagree. One thing, though, is clear: the state's permission to coerce is limited. It may coerce to sustain social convergence on justified moral rules, and sometimes even to sustain for a time convergence on unjustified social conventions. But all coercion must be justified (§§17.3c, 23.1), so the state has no *carte blanche* authorization to coerce as it sees fit.

(c) Authority as the Moral Power to Create Rights and Duties
It may seem that minimal political authority is sufficient for the state to perform its crucial tasks of breaking immoral social equilibria and directing settlement to a new one within the optimal eligible set. Recall Waldron's thesis that the state, by use of coercion, makes a specific member of the eligible set salient, and so directs us to that rule (§22.2). Once it directs us to some specific rule x, and once we do coordinate on it, it will provide a moral equilibrium on which all free and equal moral persons have sufficient reasons to act. So it may appear that so long as the state has the moral permission to coerce, it can push us to coordinate on x, and once having so coordinated, that moral equilibrium would ground the moral authority of x. So the state itself need not be the source of any moral authority; it simply facilitates the creation of moral authority through moral equilibrium.

On some matters this may well be sufficient, and this is perhaps one reason that those who claim that the state never has a general authority to impose obligations do little real harm. For once the state has employed coercion to make some "way of acting together" salient, this often will itself provide citizens with reasons to conform to the new equilibrium even if they do not acknowledge the authority of the state to impose an obligation to act on x. The philosophical anarchist may proclaim that he has no moral reason to do as the state directs just because the state directs it, but it still will often be the case that because the state directed us to x and was able to exercise coercion to induce x-action, the philosophical anarchist will then have moral reason to act on x, now a social-moral equilibrium. However, the state does not merely select a clear option such that, once we all understand what it is, we need no further guidance. It innovatively elaborates rights and duties to render operative some especially complex rights, such as the right to property. This elaboration involves developing and articulating the right and, because of the right's complexity, an ongoing system of interpretation to resolve disputes, often giving determinations in hard or unclear cases. The state thus provides detailed and complex legislation about property rights in financial instruments, which involve banking and financial regulations. In all these matters the state exercises authority in the stronger sense of having a moral power; it creates new and complex rights and duties over its citizens, and its ongoing administrative and judicial determinations provide authoritative case-by-case answers for which, by definition, there is no current social equilibrium. We go to court when we cannot decide what the rule is. Moreover, given the complexity of these regulations, they may not be well understood, and given the pace of change, they may be altered quite rapidly (the financial crisis of the years following 2008 is a case in point).

Now it may be tempting to think that here, too, the state is simply pointing us to a new equilibrium, and it is the equilibrium, not the action of the state, that is really the source of our moral reasons to comply. However, when we appeal to these rights and make claims on others, the authority of the state allows us to make the implicit claim that should there be controversy or uncertainty about our claim, there is an authoritative answer that we all have reason to endorse. In the absence of the recognition of the state's authority to articulate and interpret our rights, many of our complex rights are indeterminate. At the time t_1 when we make a claim, there may be no unique answer in public reason as to whether our claim is justified – whether it is really a part of the socially recognized right. If we conceive of the state as simply pointing to a new equilibrium, hoping that the state's determinations at time t_2 will produce a new equilibrium at t_3, our claim at time t_1 is not justified, for it involves matters that will not be settled until time t_3. To accept the authority of the state is partly to accept that at t_1 there is an answer in public reason about what our claim is: the answer arrived at by the interpretive organs of the state.

This recalls the famous controversy between H. L. A. Hart and Ronald Dworkin about hard cases in the law.[30] Roughly, Hart held that in hard cases the legal rule was indeterminate; given the open texture of natural language, there simply was no answer within the rule in certain hard cases, and so the judge had discretion to create new law, extending the rule in a way that was not implicit in previous interpretations. Dworkin replied that while the case for a correct answer was rationally inconclusive, and so we could reasonably disagree, there was a best answer as to what the law required in this case, and the task of the judge was to uncover it. It may seem that we are siding with Dworkin and against Hart here by saying that one's right claim at t_1 is now justified if it will be upheld by the judge at t_2; this suggests that there already is a correct answer – implicit at t_1 – that the judge is seeking to uncover at t_2. But this is not so; both Hart's and Dworkin's views are consistent with the claim that a right claim at t_1 is justified at t_1 if it will be upheld by the judge at t_2. Dworkin holds that the judge upholds the claim at t_2 because the law really justified it at t_1; Hart claims that while the law did not uphold it at t_1, the judge's decision at t_2 validates the claim at t_1. The Hartian account implies ex post justification, while Dworkin's does without this (perhaps odd) idea, simply upholding ex post validation of what was justified at t_1. Both, though, concur that at time t_1 there was a justified claim. As Hobbes recognized, the important point is that without an authoritative interpreter of the law – one whose judgment determines not simply what we will do, but what the law is – in controversial cases we have no justified claims in public reason.

Of course, Members of the Public would not grant the state unlimited authority about how to decide disputes or how to extend and develop rights. As Locke stressed, it is because there is reasonable dispute about the content of our moral rights that we often require a state to interpret and develop them, so its determinations will have authority for us only if they are themselves within the range of reasonable disputes, or within the range of reasonable developments of the rights.[31] In evaluating the exercise of the

---

[30] See H. L. A. Hart, *The Concept of Law*, chap. 7; Ronald Dworkin, *Taking Rights Seriously*, chaps. 1–4.

[31] For a development of this standard, see my *Justificatory Liberalism*, pp. 184ff.

state's authority we ascend to the moral point of view (§21), and we ask whether this exercise of the authority of the state can pass the test of the moral point of view. If it cannot pass the test of the moral point of view the determinations of the state cannot have moral authority. It is important to stress that, as we have seen (§22.3*b*), state coercion to enforce them may nevertheless be justifiable. Thus the authority of the state as source of moral rights and duties is, as should be expected, more circumscribed than its permission to employ coercion.

(d) "The Right to Rule"

Christiano notes that the state's moral power to impose duties does not imply that these duties are owed to it. If we understand political authority as in large part a device of public reason to enforce, interpret, and complete the system of rights, its core moral power is its ability to create moral rules that define our rights.[32] The duties entailed by such rights are not owed to the state but to other members of the moral order. When the state determines our civil rights or our right to property, we owe it to our fellows to respect their rights, which through the state have become socially recognized.[33] In these matters political authority is a collective tool of the public to assist in the construction of a moral order of public reason. We do not owe it to the tool to comply with its determinations, but to those who hold the rights that its determinations specify. Thus understood, the core of the political authority of the state is not its "right to rule" understood as possessing a valid claim upon its subjects to obey its rules, a duty that they owe *to* the authority.[34]

Contrary to the account presented here, Christiano takes the right to rule as

the primary notion of legitimacy while the others are dim reflections of this primary notion. To inquire about the legitimacy of an authority is in the first instance to inquire into its right to make decisions for others. The demand for legitimacy arises when an agent has the power to make

[32] See Rex Martin, *A System of Rights*, especially chap. 1.
[33] See further ibid., pp. 58ff.
[34] Christiano, *The Constitution of Equality*, p. 241.

decisions for others and makes controversial decisions. It is to ask of a person: "who made you the boss?" And if the answer is "my decisions are morally justified," we are likely to think that the question has not been fully answered. If the answer is, "I am an expert on these matters," we are likely to be more satisfied except in the case of political decisions. In the case of political decisions, which are necessarily controversial, the answer we are looking for is not the justification of the decision or a claim to expertise but rather a valid claim on us to respect the status of the decision maker even when we disagree with the substance of the decision.[35]

The account of political authority developed here allows us to answer Christiano's queries without embracing the idea that the core of political authority involves a duty to a political organization. He is quite right that the core question is "who put you in charge?"[36] And because the fundamental moral task of political authority is to define and develop our abstract rights, and from the collective perspective of the Members of the Public there is no uniquely correct determination, it is no answer at all to claim a special insight into the moral truth. It is indeed just because we reasonably disagree that we may require a political determination of our basic rights as well as other moral rules. But the justification of this political authority, with its moral powers to select rights from the eligible set, as well as to interpret and to develop them, does not imply that we owe our obedience to this authority. We owe obedience to our fellows, who have justified moral claims on us based on these rules.

In order to perform its task as selector, interpreter, and developer of our rights and duties, the state requires resources, sometimes monetary, sometimes in terms of our service. Regarding these facilitatory functions, it may be thought that we really do owe a duty to the political organization – to pay our taxes to it, or serve on its juries. But as this last example indicates, even here it is odd to think that we owe the duty to the state, as if we wrong the state by

---

[35] Ibid., pp. 241–2.

[36] Putting the challenge in terms of "who made you the boss?" gets us off on the wrong foot, since being "a boss" is often to occupy an office in an authority structure defined by property rights, where the source of the authority is the right owed to the owner, who either is the boss or has appointed the boss. This leads us in the wrong direction – thinking that the boss' authority is based on a duty owed to her.

refusing to comply. We have a duty to supply resources to the state, and it is within the competency of the state to set (within limits) what is required for it to fulfill its functions, but none of this implies that we owe it to the state to pay our taxes or to serve on juries. That we have a duty to yield resources to the state does not imply that this duty is owed to the state.[37] If the resources are genuinely reasonably required, then they are part and parcel of what is required to respect each other as free and equal persons and to respect their basic rights. And we owe this to each other, not to a political organization or its agents.

22.4 POLITICAL AND MORAL AUTHORITY IN A WORLD OF STATES

Contemporary political philosophy is preoccupied with issues of international and global justice, and whether political and moral justification should be focused at the level of states, international organizations, or a world cosmopolitan order. It should come as no surprise that on the view developed here, there are no ahistorical or definitive answers to many of these questions. The modern state is a device of social and moral order that has been developed from approximately the sixteenth century; its form has been affected by both the medieval order from which it developed and historical, social, and moral developments over the last five hundred years.[38] Although we tend to think of the modern state as a single type of entity, it is a general category for a wide variety of forms of political organization, which have evolved in different ways in response to different circumstances. It is reasonable to maintain that a number of other forms of political organization would be superior, or that it is the best way to politically organize distinct moral orders.

We live in a world of states, though not only of states, as states have created international organizations that have taken over some of their traditional responsibilities. This has gone perhaps furthest in the European Union, but from the World Health Organization to the International Monetary Fund, our world of states is supple-

---

[37] That is, we must distinguish {Duty [to yield resources to the state] owed to others} from {Duty [to yield resources to the state] owed the state}.

[38] For a sustained philosophical examination of the idea of the modern state, see Christopher W. Morris, *An Essay on the Modern State.*

mented by an international order. In a world of states the source of political authority over citizens – the moral power to create rights and duties – ultimately resides in the state. For those fortunate to live in a political order with legitimate authority, one's own state is the determiner of many of one's rights and duties because it is recognized as the de jure authority that actually assists in sustaining the moral order.[39] For those living in such an order, three questions about their relations to those in other political orders must be addressed.

(a) Transnational Social Morality

The heart of our social morality is how we are to treat other participants in the social order, but we should not make the mistake of supposing that the boundaries of our social order are co-extensive with the boundaries of our political society. Our contemporary world of states presents a complex mosaic; many of the basic social rules of cooperation extend across state boundaries. One of Hayek's great insights was that the expansion of the market order to constitute a global order induces moral convergence on basic norms of cooperation among strangers. What Hayek called the "Great Society" is a moral order of anonymous persons that is grounded in their market relations. Recent studies by Joseph Henrich and Natalie Smith support this core idea: expanding markets lead to convergence on rules for fair anonymous interactions. In a fascinating series of experiments Henrich and Smith conducted ultimatum games (§7.4) and public goods games in market and nonmarket societies.[40] They compared the play of

---

[39] This I think, is the proper response to the so-called particularity problem: why is one bound by the authority of one's own state? The answer derives from that to the more basic question: why is one bound by the moral order in which one lives? Once we see that morality itself is "particular" (we have a true morality, but not the only true morality), the mystery of being subject to the authority of one's own state (that under which one lives), and not others, vanishes. See A. John Simmons, *Moral Principles and Political Obligation*, chap. 2.

[40] In public good (or common-pool resources) games, N participants (let us say 10) start out with a common pool of money (to use an example in American dollars, say 100); participants are then given the option in the first round to withdraw a certain amount from the pool (say anything up to $10); any money so withdrawn from the pool by a participant is hers to keep. Say the deductions total x; the experimenter then increases $100-x$ by some amount (50 percent in the Henrich

Americans (UCLA graduate students, undergraduates at the University of Pittsburgh, and students at the University of Arizona), students at Hebrew University, and students at Gadjah University in Indonesia, with the Machiguenga of the Peruvian Amazon and the Mapuche of Southern Chile. Display VIII-4 summarizes their results.

	UCLA	*Ariz*	*Pitt*	*Hebrew*	*Gadjah*	*Machi-guenga*	*Mapuche*
Mean offer	.48	.44	.45	.36	.44	.26	.34
Mode offer	.50	.50	.50	.50	.40	.15	.50/.33
Rejection rate	0	—	.22	.33	.19	.048	.065
Rejection of offers below 20%	0/0	—	0/1	5/7	9/16	1/10	2/12

DISPLAY VIII-4 COMPARISON OF ULTIMATUM GAME IN DIFFERENT SOCIETIES[41]

The American results are very similar; the outcomes of the experiments in Israel and Indonesia show more low offers, and the Israeli data show a lower mean offer.[42] Compared, though, to the two relatively isolated small-scale societies, the variance in the results is

---

and Smith experiments), so the final pool is $1.5(100 - x)$. In the second round this amount is equally distributed among the participants, so in the second round each receives $1.5(100 - x)/10$. If no one withdraws any money in the first round, each ends up with 150/10, or $15; if everyone makes the maximum withdrawal in the first round, each ends up with $10. So, as in a Prisoners' Dilemma, universal cooperation ($15 each) is preferred to universal noncooperation ($10 each). But suppose only one of the ten withdraws in the first round: she will receive her $10 in the first round, and in the second round she will receive $1.5($90)/10$, or $13.5 for a total in both rounds of $23.50. So as in the Prisoners' Dilemma, there is a temptation to cheat; but if all do so each will end up with $10 instead of $15.

[41] Source: Joseph Henrich and Natalie Smith, "Comparative Experimental Evidence from Machiguenga, Mapuche, and American Populations," p. 132. The data from the University of Pittsburgh and Hebrew University are drawn from A. E. Roth, V. Prasnikar, M. Okumo-Fujiwara, and S. Zamir, "Bargaining and Market Behavior in Jerusalem, Ljubljana, Pittsburgh, and Tokyo"; the Gadjah University data are from the low stakes experiment of L. Cameron, "Raising the Stakes in the Ultimatum Game: Experimental Evidence from Indonesia"; University of Arizona data are from E. Hoffman, K. Shachat, and V. Smith, "Preferences, Property Rights and Anonymity in Bargaining Games."

[42] Henrich and Smith question the importance of means and modes in analyzing the results of ultimatum games. "Comparative Experimental Evidence from Machiguenga, Mapuche, and American Populations," pp. 133–4.

slight; in these small-scale societies we see very low rejection rates and a much higher tendency to make low offers. Henrich and Smith also find striking differences in public goods games: the Machiguenga are especially prone to free riding, withdrawing an average of 77 percent of the pooled money in the first round.[43] While both the Americans and the Machiguenga have a number of free riders, the Machiguenga have a consistent tendency to take more for themselves than do the Americans; the key difference is that about a quarter of the Americans are fully cooperative, withdrawing nothing in the first round, while the Machiguenga sample has no full cooperators, and even relatively few who withdraw only 20 percent.[44] Overall, Americans, the Machiguenga, and the Mapuche differ in their views about fairness. When asked the reasons for their offers in ultimatum games, the Machiguenga who did offer 50 percent in ultimatum games cited fairness, as did many Americans; the Mapucche seemed motivated simply by fear that their offers might not be accepted.[45] Henrich and Smith conclude:

In order to exist, modern, industrial, urban centers must have developed norms (behaviors and expectations) to deal effectively with anonymous transactions, and allow people to cooperate in a wide variety of contexts. Market societies are filled with opportunities to "cheat," such that, if most people took advantage of these loopholes, our systems would rapidly crumble. We think that these systems persist because people share sets of re-enforcing norms about how to behave in different contexts, what is "fair" in different contexts, and what to punish. . . . The point is, large-scale, market-based societies could not function without well-coordinated norms for dealing with anonymous, one-shot, monetary interactions. However, there is no reason to expect other societies, where anonymous monetary transactions are recent and rare, to share such norms.[46]

As the market order expands, groups adopt its norms of fairness.[47] Crucial to the adoption of norms regulating the fairness of anonymous market interactions is the core idea of social morality:

---

[43] Ibid., p. 148.
[44] Ibid., p. 149.
[45] Ibid., pp. 144–3.
[46] Ibid., pp. 162–3.
[47] This may be happening with the Machiguenga. Ibid., p. 141.

that morality is everyone's business, and so one can expect that defection from cooperative behavior will be sanctioned even when it is with strangers. The Machiguenga, in contrast, "have little or no expectation of favorable treatment from anonymous persons, no sense of group fairness, and thus no reason to punish."[48] They make little effort to monitor each other's actions, and so third-party punishment is rare, and fair behavior to strangers is not expected. Thus, for example, the Machiguenga have not developed norms about cutting into waiting lines, a basic rule of fairness that unites market societies such as Chile, the United States, and India.[49]

The important point here is that the evolution of a universal, transnational morality is, as Hayek argued, spurred by market relations among strangers. That morality is social does not imply that it is restricted to individual societies. And, of course, even when we do not share specific moral rules with those in other political societies, as free and equal persons we recognize abstract rights as transcendent moral principles (§21.2). Insofar as we see others as free and equal agents with their own goals and values, we hold that their moral and political orders must respect and adequately interpret these abstract rights. Because these rights are better understood as broad principles that must be met – but can be met in a variety of ways – they do not necessarily entail specific duties on others.[50] If they are not adequately implemented, no doubt the prime duty falls on their political order to perform its core task,[51] but all free and equal persons have reason to be concerned about violations and endorse reasonable efforts to address them. As human rights become specified in international law, we are developing a global order in which these abstract principles have at least rudimentary specifications, and so begin to provide the basis of actual correlative duties, though again these are largely duties of states.

[48] Ibid., p. 159.
[49] Ibid., pp. 163–4; Shweder, Mahapatra, and Miller, "Culture on Moral Development," pp. 47ff.
[50] See Joel Feinberg, *Social Philosophy*, pp. 66–7.
[51] See Martin, *A System of Rights*, pp. 87ff.

(b) The Authority of One's Political Order over Others

While we can expect the growth of transnational moral rules following from the expansion of the importance of anonymous market relations, it still remains that many of our moral rules are articulated through the authority of the state. We appeal to the state to provide definite interpretations of our moral principles and rules when social evolution alone cannot perform the task. Let us call this portion of our social morality its *politically articulated element*. Clearly the politically articulated element is crucial for social life; it is because it is so important that the political order is itself essential to the moral order. If, though, the authority of the politically articulated portion of social morality depends on the authority of our state over us, it would follow that our moral relations with those in other political orders will be in an important sense incomplete. In a world of states, even if states perform their moral functions perfectly, our moral relations with those in other political societies will be incomplete.

As with many real problems of actual moral orders, there is no single response to this type of moral incompleteness. Indeed, there is no single answer to whether it is a pressing problem. Under many conditions, incompleteness may pose little difficulty. Suppose that one is visiting another political society, which shares the basic transnational social morality of the Great Society and that is not manifestly oppressive. As they will with its more specific rules of social morality, visitors will, at a minimum, be able to view the laws of the other order as useful social conventions providing the basis for coordination; even if they do not acknowledge its authority over them, they may hold that the political order is justified in coercing to uphold these social conventions (§22.3*b*). More strongly, visitors will be apt to conclude that the moral rules and political determinations of publicly justified orders merit their deference insofar as they would also be justified were they members of these orders. If I am visiting another just political order, I may well conclude that were I to conceive of myself as a member of *this* public, its rules and political determination would be justified to me, and so I have a reason as a free and equal person to endorse them as authoritative – they now provide me with a moral equilibrium. One of the great benefits of public justifications under deep pluralism is that the arrival of new entrants will not typically upset the moral equilibrium, as justification was achieved under conditions of great disagreement. In contrast, public justification in homogeneous societies is apt to be unstable in the light of immigration and generational change, and visitors may find the rules alien and unjustifiable.

The problem of moral incompleteness becomes severe when our aims and activities require that the political determinations of our political order are authoritative for those in others. Consider copyright laws. I may claim that I own the book I am writing – I have intellectual property rights over the product. Suppose that my political order has a publicly justified determination of intellectual property. But my activity may require (say, if I am heavily investing in certain scientific processes) that those in other political orders respect my property claims; I claim that my intellectual property rights are authoritative around the world. Perhaps other orders have roughly similar schemes, and I am content for my rights to vary in different political orders, but I may also hold that some other schemes are inadequate. But, of course, the determinations of my political order do not have authority over others, even should its determination be uniquely correct. As I have stressed, to be an authority is not simply to be justified but in some way socially recognized (§§10.1, 21.2), and the decisions of my order may not be recognized by others. In a world of states, convergence on a common system of authoritative legal rules is typically secured by international treaty, such as the World Intellectual Property Organization Copyright Treaty. If the signatory states are legitimate (in the sense of generally possessing the authority to impose rules and duties on their citizens), the problem of incompleteness can be overcome in this manner. However, deep problems arise in a world in which many states are oppressive. The World Intellectual Property Organization Copyright Treaty has been implemented by the United States and Chinese governments, and the former has pressed the latter to protect the copyrights of United States citizens and corporations. But the Chinese government is oppressive; Freedom House deems it "not free" and it scores very badly on the protection of civil and political rights. Such oppressive states do not have authority (in the sense of creating rights and duties) over their citizens; to employ them to enforce our authority claims is not to treat the citizens of repressive regimes as free and equal. To demand that Chinese citizens comply with a rule that *would* have authority over them *only if* a justified political order imposed it is, in the present conditions, to demand that they comply with unjustified rules.

Societies under oppressive regimes have pressing need for social conventions, so the use of force to implement and enforce them may be permissible. Let us allow that, at least in a variety of circumstances, the regime of the People's Republic permissibly employs force to sustain social cooperation, though its laws are without authority in any stronger sense. Let us further suppose that The World Intellectual Property Organization Copyright Treaty is not palpably unjust – it could have been made authoritative in China by ratification by a justified regime. The question becomes: under these conditions may the government of the United States press the oppressive government of the People's Republic to enforce the treaty as a social convention? This, I think, is the best case that can be made for external pressure to conform: we are supposing that convention is useful to the social order and not inherently unjust. Although clearly the United States would have no claim to have the treaty enforced, perhaps pressure to induce conformity would not be unjustifiable. But this is a limiting case. Because punishment can induce stability on bad norms, regimes that employ punishment without democratic checks are apt to enforce many repressive and manifestly unfair rules. Even though it may be permissible to enforce socially necessary bad norms (§23.3*b*), for a just regime to press a repressive regime to do so for the benefit of the just regime's citizens is to become a party to the continuation of repressive norms to secure goods to one's citizens, and runs the very real risk of one's state becoming an obstacle to respect for the abstract rights of others.[52] These are complex and

---

[52] Thomas Pogge believes that participation in the current world economic order is a harm to those in many other political orders and retards the development of democracy in these orders. His case is premised on a host of disputable claims, both empirical and normative, but he is surely correct that enforcement of, or even tacit support for, unjustified conventions that thwart the development of democracy constitutes a serious harm. See his *World Poverty and Human Rights*, esp. chap. 6.

difficult issues, and a host of perplexing questions confront us. They are themselves matters for the use of public reason in politics; reasonable citizens will disagree about these matters, and there are no definitive answers to be provided by philosophical reflection.

The problems I have been analyzing stem from the aim of securing international conventions in a world in which so many states do not treat their citizens as free and equal, and so have no authority to impose rights and obligations on them. Given these complexities, we can better appreciate the force of Rawls' proposal that liberal states may admit into the "society of people's" some regimes that do not fully respect the fundamental rights of all as free and equal persons (§21.2). If regimes that fail to treat their citizens as free and equal are nonetheless sufficiently "decent" so that, at least in international affairs, they are viewed as possessing genuine authority (qua ability to create duties) over the populations, justified liberal states would be able to extend their authority over peoples ruled by nonliberal regimes through treaties. We would not face the complexities of wrestling with what conventions might be justified and how far we may press for their enforcement; these illiberal states would have the authority to bind their citizens through international treaties. Such an international order would have greater moral completeness, but only because we grant authority to political orders that fail to treat their citizens as free and equal moral agents.

(c) Effects of Our Actions on Those in Other Political Orders
Even if we do not claim authority over those in other political orders, or seek to induce them to enforce unjustified laws, our individual actions and collective policies may violate their rights and harm them. Perhaps the most glaring case is contemporary immigration policy. A great amount of coercion is employed to police the boundaries of states, preventing potential immigrants from entering and forcibly removing them should they succeed in evading border controls. It is hard to see a plausible case that under current laws this coercion can be justified to those who are coerced; we must suppose that basic abstract rights of agency are violated by current immigration policies (§17.3c). That a political society has boundaries and its own system of authority does not give it

permission to coerce nonmembers without justification. Again, there may be multiple ways of correcting such injustices, the merits of which reasonable citizens disagree about. But a free political order cannot simply treat would-be immigrants as though they can be coerced without justification, or that it is enough that the laws be justified within the excluding community. Claims based on the values of national identity or shared communal feelings are certainly relevant to the justificatory problem, but they cannot be decisive under conditions of extensive reasonable pluralism, in which many (citizens and would-be immigrants alike) place little importance on them.

In the future international organizations will perhaps provide authoritative fora for interstate complaints about policies and actions of one order that harm others. The World Trade Organization presently has rules about policies such as subsidies that are seen as harming those in other states; these organizations have been proliferating in response to pressing global problems. In a world in which all states were members, and all states possessed justified authority, it would be easy to see how such organizations could provide international authority, but in a world where 103 states are only "partly free" or "not free"[53] this cannot be supposed. Serious questions arise as to how in the current world such organizations can possess legitimate authority in relation to member states that are without justified political authority over their own populations (and so whose accession to the relevant treaties cannot transfer authority to these organizations)

23 The Justification of Coercive Laws

23.1 THE RIGHT AGAINST LEGAL COERCION

(a) A Simple Case
We have seen that a fundamental claim of agency is a right not to be coerced (§17.3c). As I remarked earlier, the idea of coercion is controversial, and thus so are the contours of this abstract right. We

---

[53] Freedom House, 2008 rankings. Of these 37 are not free. See http://www.freedomhouse.org.

certainly can reasonably disagree about coercion, and I will consider later (§23.3) how these disagreements affect the public justification of coercive legislation. But to help fix the core idea of the right not to be coerced and how it applies to the justification of legislation, let us suppose that we are now considering the justifiability of some law *L*, and let us also suppose for now that it is appropriate to query the justification of an individual law *L*, rather than some smaller question (how much force should the police employ to enforce *L*?), or a larger question of whether, say, entire systems of law should be justified at one go. I shall take up these other issues presently, but for now let us focus on this relatively simple case. By a law I mean a piece of legislation with the penalties attached to noncompliance: that is the object of our deliberation. This of course is also a simplification, but not an implausible one. You and I have often considered and debated specific legislation with our friends and colleagues. To be sure, if we are sophisticated, when deliberating about the justification of a specific law, we are apt not merely to think of its formal text but also the sorts of enforcement measures that the police and other agencies are apt to invoke: a law's coerciveness is not just determined by the formal extent of its penalties, but whether the police will, say, have grounds for harassing ethnic and racial minorities, and our view of how likely this is to happen. However, we cannot introduce all the complications at once. And in a work of abstract philosophy there are many complexities of actual deliberation that we will never get to. Our aim is to see whether we can simplify the problem without making it too unrealistic; if so, the analysis may shed some light on the nature of a real order of public reason.

So, as we might do any day when we open the newspaper, we ask, "is this new legislative proposal justified?" When we ask this question we suppose an already settled scheme of basic liberties and rights (§14.3) – unless, of course, the legislation is about these rights themselves (see §24). Given that these more basic rights and claims are taken as settled, we can say that our law threatens coercion against noncompliers. What makes the proposal – even if it turns out to be justified – morally problematic is that it employs force, or threatens to use force, against the persons of its citizens and residents. Legal restrictions, requirements, and other rules require compliance, and if compliance is not forthcoming the citizen is typically threatened with the use of force *against her person;* she is threatened with loss of freedom, or loss of her property. The police will come, use force against her person, and may imprison her. This, indeed, is a quintessential case of coercion, and let us suppose that on all plausible accounts it constitutes genuine coercion. But as agents we have a right not to be coerced, and this right is fundamental in the order of justification. Thus the coercive proposal must be justified: all Members of the Public must have reason to endorse this legislative claim as overriding their right not to be coerced.

(b) Is Justified Legislation Exempt?

This problem could be overcome if the state had a standing permission to coerce as it sees fit, or that the right to not be coerced has already been interpreted so that the state's threat of force never infringes this right. Call this the *State Exemption Thesis.* A friend of the state may argue that no piece of legislation that it proposes could possibly violate the right not to be coerced, either because the state has already interpreted the right in a way such that it simply cannot be an unjustified coercer, or that the right simply cannot be held against the state – it is the wrong sort of entity to have such a right held against it. Bernard Bosanquet upheld this thesis, arguing that the state acting as a state simply cannot violate basic aspects of individual morality. Strictly speaking, Bosanquet held there could be no rights against the state, for the state embodies the institutionalization of a scheme of rights.[54] Liberalism denies the State Exemption Thesis. It simply is not plausible to think that free and equal people would accord such unlimited authority to any collective organization. We know that even well-intentioned governments can do great wrongs (think of the internment of American citizens of Japanese descent in the Second World War). That government can violate the basic rights of citizens has been the core of liberalism since Locke, and it has held that all arguments for the State Exemption Thesis are implausible.

---

[54] Bosanquet, *The Philosophical Theory of the State,* pp. 284ff and Editors' Introduction, p. xxix.

Andrew Lister objects to the claim that free and equal citizens have a right not to be coerced, or as I have elsewhere put it, there is a standing presumption against coercing a person. As he sees it, if we adopt this view

> we would have to be prepared to say that laws against murder, assault, and rape are only justified because the standing presumption against coercion is successfully rebutted. Yet our belief that such laws are legitimate does not seem to be based on an "on balance" judgment. We do not weigh the benefit of being safe from murder and rape against the cost of losing one's freedom to murder and rape; we do not count frustrated desires to murder and rape as having any value. [55]

Lister concludes, then, that "coercion is not itself bad." It looks as if Lister is holding that a person performing a wrongful action has no claim at all against being coerced. This cannot be right. Take Lister's own example of a law against murder. And take an easy case: where someone has been rightfully convicted for murder and is about to be sentenced and punished. To be sure, we do not think that a cost of punishing this person lies in her frustrated desire to murder – after all, we have not succeeded at frustrating her desire to murder if we are at the point of punishing her. [56] Nevertheless, when the state inflicts punishment on our convicted murderer it will be inflicting great harm on her. When English judges sentenced convicted murderers to death they donned a black sentence cap; the occasion was one of great solemnity. They were about to inflict great harm on her, and officially recognized that we all have a moral reason not to intentionally kill fellow citizens. If the crime was really an undermining defeater [57] of the claim not to be killed – if justified coercion really was not "bad" at all – they would have no reason for any deep regret that they were about to sentence the murderer to death. It would not really harm her at all, at least not

---

[55] Andrew Lister, "Public Justification and the Limits of State Action," p. 164.

[56] We may think that where a person has successfully been deterred from murder by a threat there is a cost of impinging agency – it would have been better if she had freely exercised her agency to do the right thing – but I shall not insist on that. In a case such as this I think it is at least reasonable to conclude that the reason not to coerce has been undermined.

[57] See section 13.3, note 125, on such defeaters.

in any morally significant sense. The judges did, though, see a genuine reason not to inflict a real harm on the murderer, but one that the dictates of justice overrode.[58] And the point has nothing to do with the death penalty: taking away a person's freedom of movement for twenty years, her ability to decide what she will do, and when and how she will do it, is to inflict grievous harms on her. To say that we have *no reason* to refrain from doing this to guilty people – that we have no reason to refrain from inflicting all this harm and suffering – strikes me as manifestly erroneous. Draco (who, we are told, codified the first set of law for Athens) is said to have insisted that even the smallest infractions such as stealing an apple should be punished by death. Draconian laws are wrong because they fail to see any moral reason to refrain from harming the guilty and so inflict excess punishment. Having no moral reasons to weigh against punishing, any punishment seems justifiable. To say that the state always has a moral reason not to threaten its citizens with such harm, and even a moral reason not to inflict it when they do violate the law, strikes me as clearly correct, and an important feature of a just and humane state. If we could only effectively enforce a law against jaywalking by imposing five-year prison sentences, such a penalty still would not be justified.

On the view I am advocating, to say that one has a right not to be coerced allows for the right to be justifiably overridden, as in the case of justified laws. But that a right is overridden does not mean that the reason not to coerce vanishes; that is why even when we justifiably coerce we may do so with a certain regret.[59] However, this way of analyzing justified coercion is not necessary to the general idea that we have a claim not to be forced to do things, or threatened with force, and that a justified law must show that the challenge of this claim can be met. Consider, for example, the view that the right not to be coerced does not limit the justification of legislation on the grounds that if law *L* is justified, it does not violate any rights, and so it does not coerce, for coercion requires

---

[58] In terms of the analysis of section 13.3, the justification is a rebutting defeater of the reason not to kill.

[59] See here Judith Jarvis Thomson, *Rights, Restitution and Risk*, pp. 51ff.

the violation of rights.[60] We might call this the *No Coercion with Justification* thesis. Thus, if law *L* threatens the use of force against my person, but *L* is justified, *L* does not coerce me. It is not clear that this way of redefining coercion will make much difference. Suppose *L* is proposed, and it threatens force against me, and I have a right not to be forced or threatened with force, though of course this right is not absolute, for force may be justified. The question then becomes this: is the threat of force in *L* justified? If it is not justified, then if the state goes ahead and imposes it and violates my rights, it *coerces* me; if it can be justified, and so justifiably infringes my rights, or shows that my rights to do not apply here, then *No Coercion with Justification* holds that it *forces me but does not coerce me*. But the important thing is that one's right not to be forced would in this case still be a constraint on the justification of state action. There is still a reason not to pass the law, and we must show that there is a public justification for overriding this reason.

(c) A Right, Not a Goal

If we each have a right not to be coerced, then an act of coercion that does not justify overriding this right violates our right. Because such a right is abstract, it is perhaps better understood as a principle of social morality the contours of which are open to dispute, but we must remember that it is a principle that states an abstract right claim. Now this abstract right is a claim held against any one, or any organization, that would coerce. Because the State Exemption Thesis must be rejected, this right is held against the state (understood as an artificial moral person) and its officers. The right comes down to this: a coercive law is *pro tanto* wrong (wrong as far as it goes), though should the law be publicly justified, then, of course, not only is it not wrong, but it generally will be authoritative (§§22.3*b*–*c*). Such a right is a restraint on the actions of others;[61]

---

[60] I believe that Lister holds this view. See his "Public Justification and the Limits of State Action."

[61] Nozick calls this a "side constraint," but his discussion suggests that these constraints cannot be overridden, which is not part of my analysis here. See *Anarchy, State and Utopia*, chap. 3. On the stringency of Nozick's rights, see Thomson, *Rights, Restitution, and Risk*, pp. 55ff.

my claim is against their coercive actions. The state wishes to enact *L*, and it must make sure that its case for *L* overrides my right not to be coerced.

In some earlier works I stated the anti-coercion principle in terms of a presumption against coercion – there is standing reason not to coerce a person unless the coercion can be justified.[62] Now although the rights and presumption formulations can be translated into each other, the rights formulation is superior insofar as it is clear that the principle does not specify a goal that coercion be reduced, that unjustified coercion be minimized, or even that unjustified coercion against any specific person be minimized. Rights, as Nozick and Dworkin have taught us, do not specify goals to be pursued, or states of affairs to be obtained, but claims on the actions of others. For an agent to possess a right not to be coerced is to have a claim against one who would coerce him to stop – unless there is a justification for overriding the right. The rights of abstract agency are our basic claims on others to not engage in certain actions toward us.

I stress this because a number of critics have supposed that the presumption against coercion is a principle against creating new net coercion in the world from some baseline of no coercion, or low coercion. Consider, for example, Christiano's interpretation of my case for an anti-coercion principle:

Every departure from the baseline must satisfy a burden of proof while remaining at the baseline need not. In order to have my way, it must either be at the baseline or I must provide justification to others.

....[But] the choice of baseline is likely to be as controversial as any other choice of political principles.

For example, the idea of the minimal state has been proposed as such a baseline solution to conflicts of view over more ambitious conceptions of the role of the state. The reason given for this is that the minimal state involves a smaller state than more ambitious schemes. It seems to limit liberty less than other schemes. The minimal state is a baseline, some might claim, because there is more liberty in it. But this is clearly not generally

---

[62] In *Value and Justification* (pp. 390ff) I employed the idea of a right to liberty, which involved claims not to be coerced. In order to stress just how weak this right is, I sometimes simply referred to a general principle that the state may not coerce a person without justification. See my "On Two Critics of Justificatory Liberalism."

true. It is a matter of the particular circumstances. Some might assert that the minimal state is a baseline because there is more coercion in more ambitious states than in minimal states. But why believe this?[63]

We must distinguish between the following:

Baseline View: state of affairs S does not stand in need of justification; all departures from S do.

Rights View: if there is a right against φ-ing, φ-ing needs to be justified; if φ-ing is not justified, one must not φ.

Christiano and others take the Rights View for a Baseline View, since each says that if we are now in state of affairs S, an action φ (which, by definition, would constitute a departure from S), needs to be justified. The Baseline View says that S has some property such that leaving it needs a special case; the Rights View says that action φ must be justified in all states of affairs. There is no claim on the Rights View that, say, the present baseline has some morally attractive feature, such as Christiano's suggestion that "there is more liberty in it." On the Rights View we might be in a state with very little liberty, or a lot of it, but nevertheless any coercive action in that state (so any departure from it) would have to be justified. Does the Rights View collapse into the Baseline View if we add a second right: a person is free to act as she sees fit without having to justify herself? If we add a presumption in favor of liberty (§17.3a), we can say that acting freely is the moral default (needs no justification) while coercive interference does need justification. But this default does not identify a baseline state of affairs; it distinguishes in any state of affairs those actions that require justification from actions that do not. There is nothing in either right that says that certain states of affairs do not have to be justified, since – like all rights claims – they simply are not principles about the justification of states of affairs.

The right not to be coerced does not entail any goal-based principle about coercion minimization. It cannot be said, for example, that if the state honors the right there will be less rather than more coercion in the world. Suppose we are living in a society in which a number of people defect from the social rules of morality and

[63] Thomas Christiano, "Must Democracy Be Reasonable?" p. 31. Notes omitted.

employ unjustified force against others. Suppose that Draconian laws would do the trick – they would reduce overall coercion, but at a cost of executing some people for trivial defenses. The Rights View holds that such coercion against persons is still unjustified, and so we are prevented from moving from a more to a less coercive world. In the current social world where there is great private coercion, the right not to be coerced (which is honored by the state, let us say, but not by highway robbers) need not minimize the total amount of coercion employed against people. It would be most odd for a Baseline View to endorse this: if we are now in a bad, coercive, social state, why favor it? To be sure, the social contract theorist has insisted that an excellent justification for state coercion is that it often prevents a great deal of private force and coercion, and so additional state coercion may well be justified to achieve a more peaceful social state. Although seeking to reduce private coercion may justify state coercion it does not turn a Rights View into a Baseline conception.

(d) Liberalism and the Rejection of Neutral Legislative Procedures
One reason that Christiano and others confuse the Rights and Baseline views is that they both lead to the rejection of the neutrality constraint on legislative processes; for example, if proposal x is to retain the status quo, and y is to change it, the legislative process must be neutral between x and y in the sense that there must be no built-in advantage to x or y (§21.1).[64] Now the Baseline View clearly violates neutrality if we are in the Baseline state, for according to the Baseline View all moves away from the state (y) must be justified, while staying at it (x) does not. The Rights View may also be interpreted as anti-neutral. As I have been arguing, a right against coercion is a constraint on actions, and on at least one understanding of action, each action moves us to a new social state. Given our right not to be coerced, if the state wishes to enact law L, which would move us to y, but it cannot justify ϕ-ing, it cannot justifiably move us to y. But if the state does not enact any law, we will stay at x. So failure to justify can keep us at x, where a move to y needs to

---

[64] See also here Steffen Ganghof, "Must Democracy Be Supermajoritarian? Justificatory Liberalism and Political Institutions."

be justified. The Rights View rejects the neutrality of the legislative process.

What if there are now, at x, which involves violations of rights? Suppose first that the state is not the violator. Then we are back to the case we considered earlier (§23.1c); that other parties are violating rights does not show that state coercion to halt these violations is necessarily just, so we still might remain at x. Just because rights are being violated, it does not follow in reason that state legislation can justifiably fix the problem. What, though, if the state is itself now doing the violating at x? This, of course, is a reason for it to stop its wrongful action at x, and for the law to be repealed, or for state officials to cease their present way of administering the law. This, though, does not run afoul of the right not to be coerced, since we suppose that repealing a law is not coercive. Suppose we consider a case in which law L is proposed, and while this introduces new coercion, it replaces law K, which was very coercive and unjust. Here it would seem that an anti-coercion principle would insist that the legislative system not be biased against L in favor of K – it must not in any way make it easier to stay with K than enact L. Again, though, rights are not goals. L still must be justified, since L is an act that coerces some people, and these may be different people from those coerced by K. Perhaps the unjust K heavily coerced all drug addicts, and the new L greatly reduces overall coercion for using dangerous drugs but adds certain herbal remedies to the overall category of drugs to be criminally regulated. And suppose that certain citizens, whose livelihood depends on the sale of such remedies, reasonably object that this feature of L is unjust. Can we say that their objections should not be able to defeat L, since L would replace even more unjust activities? We cannot, because rights are not goals, and so it does not follow that the state can justifiably infringe the rights of some citizens to reduce its rights violations elsewhere in the polity. Although given the constraints of time and resources a government devoted to the protection of individual rights will sometimes have to make decisions that trade off the protection of some citizens' rights in order to better secure the rights of others (think of decisions about where to most efficiently employ police), it is simply wrong to think that this translates into the dictum that all

§23 *Coercive Laws* 489

legislation is a means to maximize rights satisfaction, or minimize rights violations.[65] Even if *L* would make the overall system of laws less coercive than *K*, *L* might still not be justified because it would violate some citizens' rights not to be coerced. That the injustice of *K* must be removed does not give the state the right to inflict new injustices.

A free social and political order cannot simply coerce its citizens to improve current morality through a specific law without ensuring that the coercion employed in *this* specific law can be justified to all. And as we have seen, it does not follow that in real conditions any law that moves us to a more just or less coercive set of laws is necessarily justified, for this new law may itself involve unjustifiable coercion. Fixing things by imposing new rights violations may not be justifiable. A political order that treats all as free and equal does not have a goal of achieving justice, such that greater justice for some must justify the imposition of some injustice on others. Those inclined toward consequentialism have always objected to this feature of a regime of rights: a person's rights can stand in the way of a system that better protects rights! Surely this is irrational, if our concern is to best respect rights. As I have been stressing, however, the protection of rights is not a goal but a constraint on actions, including the actions of the state – and this includes the state's aim of rectifying previous injustice. Even the most admirable goals and social reforms may be blocked if they unjustifiably violate some people's rights.

Philosophers inclining toward consequentialism have long asserted that this is highly counterintuitive. Now if we are concerned with real public reason and not appeals to special philosophical insight, a claim that some view is counterintuitive must mean that normal moral agents would obviously find this doctrine bizarre or clearly wrong. But this is not the case. Research shows that ordinary moral reasoners who believe that coercive reform would be beneficial nevertheless sometimes oppose it. When asked to (*i*) judge whether a reform via a coercive norm would be beneficial and (*ii*) whether one would vote for that norm, Jonathan Baron

---

[65] See Philip Pettit, "Non-consequentialism and Political Philosophy" and the discussion in section 9.4*c*.

and James Jurney found that while in the large majority of cases those who answer affirmatively to the first question also do for the second (no surprise there), in a significant number of cases a positive answer to the first is coupled with a negative answer to the second. "Subjects often oppose [coercive] proposals despite the belief that they would improve matters. Forty-five of sixty subjects . . . would not vote for at least one proposal they considered beneficial."[66] And, Baron and Jurney found, a key explanation of refusal to vote for beneficial coercive reform is that the reform would violate rights or norms of fairness.

23.2 WHAT IS TO BE JUSTIFIED?

(a) The Radical Derivative Justification Thesis

I have been supposing that a specific law L needs to be justified. The question arises as to whether "a specific law" is the proper subject of justification.[67] Rawls, acknowledging that "all political power is coercive" holds that

> our exercise of political power is fully proper only when it is exercised in accordance with a constitution the essentials of which all citizens as free and equal may reasonably be expected to endorse in the light of principles and ideals acceptable to their common human reason. This is the principle of liberal legitimacy. To this it adds that all questions arising in the legislature that concern or border on constitutional essentials, or basic questions of justice, should also be settled, so far as possible, by principles and ideals that can be similarly endorsed.[68]

We might interpret this Rawslian doctrine in two ways. Rawls may be (and, I think, is) endorsing the *Restriction of Public Justification Thesis*, according to which the requirement that legislation be justified through public reason is restricted to matters of basic justice and constitutional essentials, apparently leaving much normal legislation simply exempt from the requirements of public

---

[66] Jonathan Baron and James Jurney, "Norms against Voting for Coerced Reform."
[67] Andrew Lister has pressed this question. See his "Public Justification and the Limits of State Action."
[68] Rawls, *Political Liberalism*, p. 136.

justification.[69] Any such restriction must be unacceptable: free and equal persons have a right not to be forced or coerced to do things, and so the claim that there were some acts of coercion that simply do not need to be justified must be wrong. Rawls believes that health care is a constitutional essential, while apparently environmental legislation is not; thus according to the Restriction of Public Justification Thesis, health care legislation would be subject to the requirement of public justification,[70] but an environmental law that, say, closed one's business and deprived one of one's livelihood would not be seen as coercion that must be justified. It is exceedingly difficult to discern a compelling rationale for this.

We might, though, reinterpret the core Rawlsian doctrine – that constitutions and matters of basic justice are the sole focus of public justification – as upholding the *Radical Derivative Justification Thesis*, according to which if (*i*) a constitution *C* regulates when and how all political power is to be exercised and (*ii*) *C* is publicly justified, then (*iii*) all acts of political power, including specific legislative acts, authorized by *C* are themselves publicly justified.[71] The Radical Derivative Justification Thesis does not deny that all laws must be justified, but it insists that law-by-law justification is not

[69] Jonathan Quong attributes this view to Rawls and argues that it is inadequate. See his *Liberalism without Perfection*, chap. 9.

[70] Rawls, *The Law of Peoples*, p. 50.

[71] Rawls, of course, speaks of "legitimacy," not justification. One thing he is doing is pointing out that even though we cannot expect the legislature to always reflect our views about justice, it still may be a legitimate authority. The idea of the eligible set helps us understand this idea: we certainly cannot expect the legislature (or even the constitution) to always conform to our view about what is best or truly just; but we can expect it to at least usually settle within the range of reasonable dispute – the eligible set. An adequate justificatory liberalism would hold that the legitimacy of a regime is partly determined by its tendency to legislate in the eligible set. A regime may certainly be legitimate even though it sometimes legislates outside the eligible set (that is inevitable in any regime), and so the legitimacy of laws differs from their authority. On the other hand, such legitimacy is a function of the tendency to produce authoritative laws. We must, then, distinguish three questions: does the law enact what we think is the correct answer? (is it our idea of justice?) Is the law within the eligible set? (does it have authority?) Does the regime tend to legislate within the eligible set? (does the regime basically do the job we ask of it?) A legitimate state, we might say, is one whose laws have been reached via the proper procedural routes and, while not always just and while not always having authority, do not stray too far from justice. And, in addition, we must keep in mind the distinction between legitimacy as permission to coerce and true political authority. So many distinctions!

the proper way to proceed. We substantively justify a constitution in terms of substantive public reason. Members of the Public evaluate different constitutional structures in their deliberations, and once a constitutional structure has been selected, all its enactments are derivatively justified: they conform to the requirements of a justified constitution, and so are themselves justified.

On the face of it, whether we justify constitutional structures or (directly) specific laws may appear to generate radically different results. Recall that each Member of the Public considers all the proposals and determines whether some proposal is better than no collective choice at all. Suppose, then, that Members of the Public are deliberating about constitutional structures, and various proposals are made, including, say, a constitution that allows perfectionist legislation – perhaps legislation that employs political power to induce us to lead fully secular lives.[72] Now if a Member of the Public was simply to consider whether such a regime was better than no constitutional structure at all, this perfectionist constitution would plausibly be within the eligible set. After all, it would be a great loss not to have a constitutional structure at all: even a religious citizen would prefer a new secular order to the state of nature. Contrast a law-by-law justification. Here a religious citizen would obviously see as ineligible a law that sought to employ coercive political power to induce her to lead a secular life. Thus it seems that whether our secular law is publicly justified will depend on what we have chosen as the objects of justification: laws, constitutions, or something in between.

As stated, this argument greatly exaggerates the difference between the justificatory results of the two perspectives. We must always keep in mind that Members of the Public are not considering whether some social convention shall exist (thus they are not choosing order over chaos), or even whether there will be an organization that simply possesses a moral permission to coerce (minimal authority, §22.3*b*), but whether the laws of the state will have genuine moral authority over citizens (§22.3*c*). So when evaluating a constitutional scheme, a citizen will ask whether she can grant genuine moral authority to the use of political power

---

[72] As the American dollar bill says, the regime aims at "*Novus Ordo Seclorum.*"

employed by this regime. Now crucial to her determination will be the extent to which this constitution will employ political power in such a way that it will coerce her to perform actions that, on the merits of the case, she will have no reason to conform to. That is, one of her core criteria for evaluating a proposed constitution will be its tendency to employ its political power in such a way that she will be coerced to do things that, when she evaluates what she is being forced to do, she will not have sufficient reason to endorse. If it often will force her to do what she concludes unjustifiably violates her socially recognized moral rights and her abstract human rights not to be coerced without good reason, she will deny moral authority to the constitution. We must remember that morality is prior in the order of justification to political structures (§22.2), so Members of the Public will evaluate the proposed political structures in terms of their current moral rights. Members of the Public at the stage of constitutional justification will deny moral authority to a proposed constitution that they reasonably expect to frequently coerce them in a way (that at this stage in their deliberations) they cannot endorse.

Liberal constitutionalism was not meant as a device for regimes to expand their authority over citizens, but as a means for citizens to restrict the authority of the state. Constitutional conventions such as that in Philadelphia in 1787 focused on ways to ensure that the legislative results of the regime would respect citizens' rights; a main debate was between those who thought that procedural restrictions were sufficient and those who believed that substantive guarantees were necessary. Constitutions that would authorize manifestly unjust legislation – such as establishment of a church – were rejected because such laws could not be accepted as acts of genuine authority. For the same reasons, in our example religious citizens could not grant authority to a constitution that regularly employed its power to coerce them or their children to lead secular lives. Because constitutional proposals are evaluated on the grounds of whether they will respect the moral rights already justified, Members of the Public will evaluate them in terms of their prospective results – their tendency to enact unjustified laws. Members of the Public will ask themselves: "how likely is it that this constitutional structure will enact laws outside the eligible set?" Recall that the very point of political authority is to allow us to systematize and develop our system of rights; we only have a reason to endorse an act as authoritative insofar as it performs this critical moral function. A constitution that could be expected, as a matter of course, to authorize laws that either conflict with our morality, or develop it in a way that would be ineligible from the moral point of view, simply could not be seen as having moral authority over us. To be sure, citizens will disagree about just what constitutes legislating "too often" outside the eligible set, and so we must expect that on this, as on all matters, that Members of the Public will disagree. But we should not suppose that focusing justification of regime types or constitutions radically affects what types of laws have authority over us.

This is not to claim that it makes no difference at all whether we focus the deliberations of Members of the Public simply on constitutions or also require that individual laws themselves meet the test of public justification. (As I said, the initial statement of the problem *exaggerated* the difference.) If we think simply of the justification of constitutions in terms of the Radical Justification Derivation Thesis we will base our evaluations of the justifiability of a constitution entirely on our predictions about its range of outputs. When we adopt any law-making structure we must predict to some extent, and so we justify some political procedure as an authoritative way to select from the eligible set, even though we are uncertain how well it will operate. All political authority accepts some version of the Justification Derivation Thesis, for we accept that a law is to some extent justified because it has been enacted in accordance with the appropriate constitutional rules; if the justified political authority legislates L, then it has authority although L^* is equally a member of the eligible set. But the radical version of the thesis holds that if and only if the constitution authorizes L it has authority, and so Members of the Public would be committing themselves to accepting as authoritative whatever a process of uncertain outputs endorses. Since Locke liberals have insisted that free and equal moral persons could not reasonably make this *carte blanche* authorization. They must retain the right to evaluate specific outputs to determine their authority. Again, this is not to say that one evaluates a law's authority simply on the grounds of whether one believes it to be the correct choice, but in terms of whether it is within the eligible set – whether what the state has legislated is within the bonds of reasonable dispute. If the state legislates what is not within the bounds of reasonable dispute, one simply cannot see the state as adequately performing its function. One cannot grant such a law authority over one, even if the use of coercion to enforce it may permissible (§§22.3*b–c*).

(b) What Is "an Issue?"

To say that we cannot simply authorize constitutions and so refuse to consider the justifiability of political outputs on specific issues may seem to beg the question of how we individuate issues. I have been speaking of specific laws as though each law is a different issue, but there could be strong interactive effects between two pieces of legislation, x and y, such that a person's reason to endorse one depends on the status of the other. In this case we may wish to say that there is only one issue at stake. In considering whether x and y are different issues for Alf, the key question is whether his evaluative standards are such that his ranking of the x eligible options is dependent on his ranking of y eligible options. More formally, let x and y be two pieces of legislation;[73] and $\{x_1 \ldots x_n\}$ be the set of proposals regarding x, and $\{y_1 \ldots y_n\}$ the set of proposals regarding y, we can then define:

Justificatory Dependency: Legislation x has justificatory dependence on legislative issue y if and only if

(1) there is some Member of the Public Alf, such that for Alf, if Alf makes his individual decision about the eligible members of $\{x_1 \ldots x_n\}$ in the absence of considering y, his eligible set is $\{x_1 \ldots x_i\}$ whereas if he considers his y eligible set, his x eligible set becomes a different set $\{x_1 \ldots x_k\}$;

(2) The socially eligible set differs depending on whether Alf's set is $\{x_1 \ldots x_i\}$ or $\{x_1 \ldots x_k\}$.

The second clause is important; unless the justificatory dependency of x on y in Alf's evaluative system changes the socially eligible set,

---

[73] I am supposing that lawmaking systems themselves provide the criteria for individuating pieces of legislation.

the issues are not socially dependent on each other. Thus simply because in some people's evaluative system issues are dependent that are treated as independent by the legislative process, this does not imply that the legislative process has in any way gone wrong. The justificatory dependence of these issues in Alf's system must actually affect the socially eligible set. If many people are like Alf, then we might expect a justified legislative process to typically reflect that fact that x is dependent on y. Our aim in constructing a justified lawmaking systems is, as far as possible, for acts of legislation to reflect what citizens understand as distinct and manageable issues. Here, as elsewhere, holistic justification is outside the bounds of real human reason (§14.3). Justified legislative processes respect the order of justification and seek to identify issues that are not, at least for the large majority of citizens, dependent on others. In the end, what constitutes an independent issue is itself part of our political life. One of the ways we come to a fuller understanding of our political disputes is through deliberating about the contours of our disagreements, when some issues can be detached from others, and when this is impossible.

The criterion of legislating only on justificatory independent issues provides critical insight into current forms of democracy that systematically violate it. Current legislative systems objectionably and consistently separate dependent issues by treating expenditure and revenue bills as separate. James Buchanan (inspired by Knut Wicksell) has long insisted on the dangers of citizens not constructing "the bridge between the two sides of the fiscal account."[74] To decide whether to spend without deciding how to fund the expenditure hopelessly distorts the apparent eligible set: if legislators simply reflect on how they would like to spend money, without considering where the money will come from, innumerable projects will seem attractive, and huge amounts of money will be unjustifiably spent (or, rather, huge deficits will result). It is interesting that while many today see this as a classical liberal proposal that should be rejected on basically ideological grounds, Wicksell himself was deeply concerned about social justice and

---

[74] James Buchanan, "Taxation in Fiscal Exchange," p. 141.

fairness in taxation.[75] Just as current legislative procedures separate dependent pieces of legislation, so too do they bundle independent issues. Logrolling and omnibus legislation, inducing bargains and trade-offs appealing to the mere self-interest of the parties, are almost the norm in some democracies. Our concern is the public justification of laws: that voting for a bad law may be instrumental (part of a bargain) in passing a good law does not show the former to be justified. Strikingly, some friends of democracy endorse such bargains as giving everyone a share of the legislative pie (some even go so far as to claim, wildly implausibly, that in the end there will be something like an equal share out of this massive unpalatable concoction).[76] But there is no public justification of political authority as a tool for employing coercion to advance the interests of some at the expense of others. A free and equal person cannot accept that others have moral authority to demand that she submit to their efforts to enrich themselves – and the promise that she too might get to make such demands to enrich herself is hardly justificatory.

23.3 COERCION AND THE LIMITS OF THE LIBERAL STATE

(a) Degrees of Coercion and the Demands of Justification
To determine whether some law L has authority over us, we need to arrive at (*i*) a view about the extent of the eligible set and (*ii*) whether the political process is itself justified and has conformed to its own procedures in selecting some member of the eligible set. Thus far I have been focusing on the second issue; let us now turn to the first – the extent of the eligible set.

Suppose we are reflecting on a debate about some legislative proposal L, which satisfies the criterion of justificatory independence. In our – your and my – thinking about this problem we appeal to the Deliberative Model, supposing Members of the Public to order the proposals, and we wish to know whether L is in the

---

[75] Ernesto Screpanti and Stefno Zamagni, *An Outline of the History of Economic Thought*, p. 222.
[76] Massive, since one thing that usually is not included in these bundles is the one thing that should be – revenue bills.

optimal eligible set. As always, we suppose an R^+ completed ranking (§16.1*a*), and from this we can identify the optimal eligible set
for each Member of the Public: the set of proposals that, given her
evaluative standards, is both undominated and better than no
authoritative law (x_0) at all. Let us then simply focus on each individual's optimal eligible set; call this, for any person i, $\{x_1 \ldots x_i\}$. For
every member of the set, i ranks it as at least as good as no law at
all (i.e., $\forall x: x \in \{x_1 \ldots x_i\}$, xPx_0). This would yield for each an ordinal
utility function, say, with 0 equal to x_0 and the most preferred
element equal to 1. It is absolutely crucial to keep in mind that the
idea of a "utility function" is simply a mathematical representation
of a Member of the Public's ordering of her eligible set. It will help
our analysis to transform each person's simple ordinal ranking of
the alternatives (based on her set of evaluative standards) into
somewhat richer information, as in Display VIII-5, which graphs
Alf's and Betty's ordering of the options. Alf's ordering is x_1Px_2,
x_2Px_3, x_3Px_0, with x_4 being worse than x_0. Betty orders the possible
laws x_2Px_3, x_3Px_1, x_1Px_4, x_4Px_0. The socially eligible set is thus $\{x_1, x_2, x_3\}$.

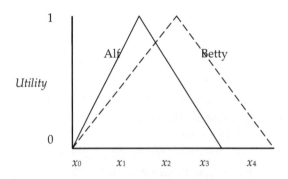

DISPLAY VIII-5 TWO EVALUATIONS OF ELIGIBLE OPTIONS

Now let us reflect on the idea that all coercion must be justified.
If coercion requires justification – if, as S. I. Benn says, one who
coerces others always has a case to answer – then those who engage

in more coercion must have a greater case to answer.[77] The more coercive the law, the greater must be the gains from the law if it is to be justified. A law that instructs all to φ based on the threat of a small fine may be publicly justified while a law instructing all to φ based on a threat of years of imprisonment may not be. To say, however, that a law that coerces to a higher degree requires a higher level of justification must be to say that coercion always has a moral cost that triggers justification, and the higher that cost, the greater must be the law's benefits if it is to be justified.

Coercion limits liberty, and greater coercion limits liberty more. As Feinberg observes:

There is a standing presumption against all proposals to criminalize conduct . . . but the strength of this presumption varies . . . with the degree to which that interest in liberty is actually invaded by the proposed legislation. Invasions of the interest in liberty are as much a matter of degree as invasions of the interest in money, though we lack clear-cut conventional units for measuring them. The interest in liberty *as such* . . . is an interest in having as many open options as possible with respect to various kinds of action, omission, and possession.[78]

A coercive law that closes off only one or two options is, other things equal, less coercive than a law that makes the same threats but closes off many options. Hayek stresses this perhaps more than any recent liberal theorist: "coercion occurs when one man's actions are made to serve another man's will."[79] For Hayek, the more one's choices are restricted to one or a few options – the more the coercer succeeds in getting you to do the thing she seeks – the more you are serving another's will, and so are coerced. On the other hand, if the coercion forecloses few options – say it attaches to a law that simply forbids you to take up one of your many options – you are only minimally subject to the will of another.[80] As Benn points out, coercive laws seek to render some options ineligible by "threaten-

---

[77] Benn, *A Theory of Freedom*, p. 87. Robert Audi further explicates this idea of degrees of coercion in *Religious Commitment and Secular Reason*, pp. 87-8.

[78] Joel Feinberg, "The Interest of Liberty in the Scales," p. 36.

[79] F. A. Hayek, *The Constitution of Liberty*, p. 133.

[80] Hayek actually seems to go so far as to say you are not coerced at all in this case. Ibid., p. 141.

ing penalties for a prescribed action, attaching to it costs which make it significantly less attractive an option than alternative ones."[81] Coercive laws restrict freedom by rendering options considerably less eligible as choices; as the law renders a larger set of actions less eligible in this way, it is more coercive and its costs to liberty increase.

(b) A Simple Model of the Increasing Costs of Coercion

Display VIII-5 models the complete eligible sets of Alf and Betty so all the relevant considerations are expressed in their utility functions. However, since our interest is in seeing how the rising costs of coercion affect justification, let us separate out the costs of coercion from the rest of a person's utility function. That is, for both Alf and Betty let us distinguish (α) his or her evaluation of all the costs and benefits of the law (based, as always on his or her evaluative standards) except for (β) his or her evaluation of the coercive costs of the proposal. Although Alf and Betty may disagree about the concept of coercion, they must agree that the costs increase as coercion increases. Call (α) the Member of the Public's *pro tanto evaluation of the law* and (β) her estimate of *the coercion costs of the law*. It is important that (β) concerns simply the coercion costs imposed *by* the law; we do not count as part of the coercion costs of a law nonstate coercion that might occur under a law or the coercion of other laws. A law that itself imposes low coercion may fail to stop nonstate coercion; a law that imposes greater coercion may do a better job at halting nonstate coercion. But nonstate coercion that is reduced by a law falls under the benefits of that law; if nonstate coercion is rampant under a law that will reduce its *pro tanto* utility.

Display VIII-6 is a very simple model in which Alf and Betty agree about the relative coerciveness of each proposal, as well as the costs of coercion; when the *pro tanto* utility curve of each (α) intersects the coercion cost curve (β), their net utility equals 0. We can see that x_3 still defines the boundary of the eligible set. At x_3 the coercive costs of the law is less than the net benefits for Alf; after point *a*, the costs of the law (measured as always in terms of the

---

[81] Benn, *A Theory of Freedom*, p. 144. See further my *Political Concepts and Political Theories*, pp. 79ff.

satisfaction of his evaluative standards) exceed the benefits, and so he has no reason to endorse x_4. *We see here that as proposals involve higher degrees of coercion, they tend to be dropped from the eligible set because the benefits of the proposal must be greater to justify the l coercion involved.* Thus in this very simple version of the model, we witness a tilt toward the less coercive options.

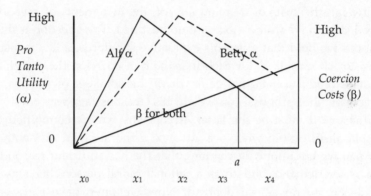

DISPLAY VII-6 UTILITY FUNCTIONS SPLIT INTO TWO PARTS (α AND β)

(c) The Libertarian Dictator Argument

Note that in our simple two-person model, after law x_1 Alf's reasons to accept more coercive proposals decrease. After x_1, it might seem that further increases in coercion cannot be justified to Alf since moving to the right from x_1, the marginal costs of increments of coercion are greater than the marginal benefits for Alf. Indeed, the coercion costs are rising while the benefits are decreasing. If each marginal increase in coercion needs to be justified to everyone, Lister has argued, it looks like the socially eligible set shrinks to just x_1.[82] According to Lister, because justificatory liberalism should be committed to an "incremental version of the public justifiability principle" it is committed to the idea that there be "no excess coercion," and so the least coercive option (in the eligible set) is conclusively justified. In our example, this makes Alf a sort of libertarian dictator. If we range proposals from less to more

[82] Andrew Lister, "Public Justification and the Limits of State Action," pp. 159ff.

coercive, the Member of the Public whose ideal point is first (at the least coercive option) automatically determines the boundary of the eligible set – his ideal point becomes the sole socially eligible option. Lister allows that we may still make a democratic choice, but "only between equally coercive policies unanimously reasonably preferred to less coercive policies."[83]

The libertarian dictator argument turns on the claim that x_2 cannot be justified to Alf because, though the total benefits of x_2 outweigh the costs of coercion for Alf, the increments of coercion needed to move from x_1 to x_2 are not justified. The question is this: should we hold that given his evaluative standards, a law is justified to Alf only if (*i*) for each increment of coercion the marginal costs exceed the marginal gains, or (*ii*) his total set of reasons in favor of the proposal outweigh his reasons against granting authority? It must be the latter. Recall why we are committed to public justification: when we advance a moral claim on another person we are implicitly claiming that she has sufficient reason to do as we demand, and so as a rational moral person, her reason leads her to do as we demand. Now we often have sufficient reasons to comply with rules that involve more coercion than we think is optimal. Recall the basic argument for a moral equilibrium. Considering the member of the eligible set that others have chosen to act on, one consults one's own evaluative standards and decides that, given that they have coordinated on an option in the eligible set, one has sufficient reason to endorse that authoritative rule. But though we can have sufficient reason to endorse these Nash equilibria, they will typically not be our optimal choice. It thus follows that free and equal persons can freely act on nonoptimal options (including those who employ more coercion than one thinks is optimal), so long as the gains (in terms of one's evaluative standards) exceed the costs. And that is true of every member of the optimal set as I have defined it – where the total benefits exceed the total costs.

This, I think, is the truly important point:[84] when engaging in collective justification about a common framework for living, we

[83] Ibid., p. 159.
[84] I reply in more detail to Lister's specific arguments in "On Two Critics of Justificatory Liberalism."

have reason to endorse common rules even when they do not align with our convictions about what is optimal. Suppose we are building a common dwelling, and we all endorse the constraint that each person must agree that the benefits of any proposed plan exceed the monetary costs; the costs must be justified, and the greater the costs, the greater must be the benefits. These are requirements if the participation of each is to be free. As we are discussing our plans, however, the person whose optimal house is the most modest now demands that no expenditure past his optimal amount can be justified since as far as he is concerned his marginal utility begins decreasing at that point; the only decision that the group can make is between houses that cost as much as this lowest price house. But his claim that the building of a larger house cannot be justified to him is belied if others go ahead without him and work on a larger house (that meets the original constraint of total benefits exceeding costs for all) for now he would still join in and freely contribute. (If, however, the total costs exceeded the total benefits, then he would indeed go his own way.) If the cost of the larger house is not justified to him – if he does not have sufficient reason to contribute – then why does he freely continue to contribute? He might grumble that he is not getting his optimal choice, but there is no house that is optimal for all. But, contrary to Lister, that does not mean that we cannot freely live together in anything grander than the most modest of possible structures.

(d) A More Complex Model: Disagreement about Coercion

Our simple model supposes that we agree about the ordering of the proposals from least to most coercive and on the costs of coercion. This is too strong. We disagree about many aspects of coercion, and we reasonably disagree about which laws are more or less coercive. We now need to build into the formal analysis reasonable disagreement about the relation of coercion. Display VIII-7 models the revised situation. In Display VIII-7, Alf's utility functions remain essentially the same; the laws are arranged in *his* order of increasing coerciveness (so his utility functions are single-peaked). Betty holds that the net benefits are highest at x_2, and the costs of coercion are also lowest at x_2. In Display VIII-7, Alf's utility functions remain essentially the same; the laws are arranged in *his* order of increasing coerciveness (so his utility functions are single-peaked). Betty holds that the net benefits are highest at x_2, and the costs of coercion are also lowest at x_2.

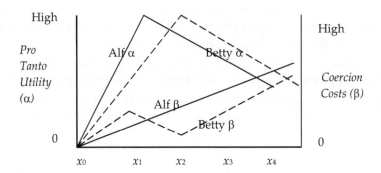

DISPLAY VIII-7 TWO UTILITY FUNCTIONS, DISAGREEING ABOUT THE RELATION OF COERCION AND THE EXTENT OF THE STATE

Note that this weakening of the model's assumptions does not change the result; Alf's judgments of the range of the laws in which the benefits of coercion outweigh the costs are still decisive. It is so because the limits of the eligible set will tend to be determined by those reasonable Members of the Public whose views about the nature of coercion are such that they see it as a steeply increasing cost and are most skeptical about its benefits.

(e) The Influence of Classical Liberal Standards in Public Justification
In the history of political philosophy, such people have been known as classical liberals. Classical liberals such as Mill have long stressed that a central element of their evaluation of a law is its coercive character. This is basic to the argument of *On Liberty* but, importantly, also to Mill's defense of laissez-faire in *The Principles of Political Economy*.[85] Because coercion has such high costs, Mill repeatedly stresses, it should be used sparingly, and only where

---

[85] Mill, *Principles*, p. 938 (Book X, chap. xi, §2). This is the seventh edition.

there is great social benefit to be obtained.[86] To justify legal coercion we must show real necessity, "and there are large departments of life from which it must be unreservedly and imperiously excluded."[87]

The presence in the Public of those with this sort of Millian view pushes the eligible set toward less coercive laws; they will be the first to come to the conclusion that the benefits of increased coercion are less than the additional costs of coercion. They will not be dictators; the optimal eligible set may well contain proposed laws far from their ideal proposal. As long as for everyone the benefits of endorsing the law as authoritative exceed the costs, the law is in the eligible set. It will be important that some matters be regulated by law, and so the conclusion that some proposed law is no better than no authoritative law at all on this matter will not be quickly reached.[88] Indeed, on many basic matters, even Millians may place outside their eligible set only extremely coercive proposals. (It is also important to keep in mind that we are not concerned with strategic and other bargaining behavior, but people's sincere evaluation of whether the reasons for legal regulation outweigh those against.) Nevertheless, insofar as laws can be arranged from least to most coercive, Millian members of the population will move the eligible set in a classical liberal direction.

Some are apt to insist that this is unfair: why should Millians, whose evaluative systems strongly disvalue coercion, have so much influence in public reasoning? Shouldn't they have to compromise with those who think that coercion is relatively benign? As Rawls might say, shouldn't Millians be concerned that their views on coercion be acceptable to others and shouldn't they exercise the virtue of meeting others halfway?[89] We have already, however, rejected such meta-fairness claims in public justification

---

[86] See, for example, Mill's discussion of the proper bounds of moral sanctions in *Auguste Comte and Positivism* pp. 337ff.

[87] Mill, *Principles,* p. 937 (Book X, chap. xi, §2).

[88] We must always keep in mind that the Members of the Public deliberate about whether to accept the law as the basis for justified claims on each other. To say that there is "no law" is not to say that there is no social practice that allows us to coordinate our actions, but that there is no law that grounds justified claims on each other. Again, to say that there is "no law" is not to say that there will be chaos.

[89] Rawls, *Political Liberalism,* p. 253.

(§19.4). Mill's view of the dangers of coercion is manifestly an intelligible and reasonable basis for deliberating about laws; it connects up with a wide range of basic and intelligible human values.[90] To reason in a way that is intelligible to others and relevant to the problem of the justification of laws need not mean that others agree with your reasoning; that is the very point of evaluative pluralism. So there is no good reason to think that Millian anti-coercion values would have been excluded by a plausible specification of the extent of reasonable pluralism in the Deliberative Model. Once the standards of some Members of the Public are acknowledged as a reasonable basis for the evaluation of laws, it is objectionable to add a further requirement that they must seek to meet others halfway or compromise with them to reach an agreement. This is to turn justification and self-legislation into a bargain. Because our Members of the Public are committed to adopting only publicly justified laws, they already are taking account of each other's evaluations and refuse to impose any law not validated by everyone's reasons. Respect for the reasons of others is built into the public justification requirement.

(f) A Critique of the Small State

Because the classical liberal suspicion of coercion is entirely reasonable, and so is a part of the evaluative standards of some Members of the Public, classical liberals exercise an important influence on the range of the eligible set. However, there may seem to be the possibility that their influence could be countered by a critic of the "small state" whose evaluative standards are such that he concludes that laws characterized by low levels of coercion do more harm than good. Consider, for example, Jack's utility function in Display VIII-8 (for simplicity, I assume agreement on the costs of coercion).

---

[90] I try to show just how broad this range is in "Controversial Values and State Neutrality in *On Liberty*."

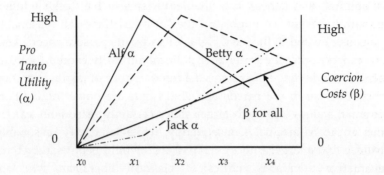

High — Pro Tanto Utility (α)

High — Coercion Costs (β)

Alf α   Betty α

β for all

Jack α

0   0

x_0 x_1 x_2 x_3 x_4

DISPLAY VIII-8 AN ANTI-SMALL STATE UTILITY FUNCTION

For Jack, the costs of coercion exceed the *pro tanto* net benefits until around x_2; when he is included in the Public, the eligible set contracts to $\{x_2, x_3\}$, and importantly, x_1 is now excluded. Suppose that we are justifying a property rights regime (see §24); Jack might hold that a classical liberal state that enforces property rights with a modest provision for the poor imposes coercion costs on the poor that exceed the benefits, and so such a state is not justified in his view. We can easily imagine more radical versions of Jack's position, contending that in no state short of total egalitarianism would the positive values brought about by inegalitarian states compensate for the costs of coercion. What is important about Jack is that he accepts Alf's "Millian" evaluation of the costs of coercion, but nevertheless rejects the least coercive option.

Utility functions such as Jack's are by no means intrinsically unreasonable. Some regimes might employ coercion so selectively and unfairly that even though they employ it sparingly, their laws may be ranked as worse than no law at all by some Members of the Public. The eligible set need not include the least coercive laws for just this reason. However, given the basic place of the rights of the moderns in the order of justification, because the state is necessary for protecting the rights of agency, privacy, and freedom of association, even modest-sized states that perform the job of adequately articulating and developing these core rights typically will have justified authority. Even Jack must acknowledge that a state that performs these basic functions is justified in its use of coercion,

even if on his own evaluative standards such coercion is well short
of optimal. As a general rule, then, criticisms such as Jack's will not
undermine what we might call the "classical tilt" – all reasonable
persons devoted to the basic rights of body, the person, speech, and
so on accept that the benefits of political authority exceed the costs
across a wide range of systems. Given the order of justification, the
basic liberties of the person and civil rights are powerful justifiers
of small states – although larger states certainly reasonably can be
thought to be optimal. Consequently, while some may reasonably
believe that a larger (more coercive) state would better satisfy their
evaluative standards, critics of classical liberalism will not
generally be in the position to reasonably claim that smaller states
do more harm than good. Thus, as Display VIII-9 indicates, even
those who hold that small states are highly coercive will have an
eligible set that goes far toward the small state (Jack's eligible set
ends at *j*).

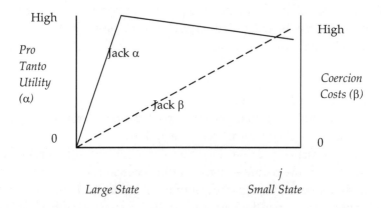

DISPLAY VIII-9 A PRO-LARGE STATE UTILITY FUNCTION (α & B)

24 Private Property and the Redistributive State

24.1 THE FUNDAMENTAL PLACE OF PRIVATE PROPERTY
IN A FREE SOCIAL ORDER

We have seen (§18.3) that the right to private property is fundamental to the jurisdictional solution to the problem of public justification under conditions of evaluative diversity. Private property is
thus justified at an early point in the order of justification; our core
moral problem of how to cooperate under conditions of evaluative
pluralism requires some scheme of private property. Now like all
abstract rights, the right to private property must be interpreted
and developed, but to a far greater extent than other abstract rights,
its definition depends on the state. The centrality of property rights
to economic cooperation and the highly dynamic nature of the
economic system require constant development of property rights
to cover new situations; copyright laws over intellectual property,
patent rights in pharmaceuticals, property rights in financial
instruments, and the regulation of financial transactions – all have
required significant rethinking of the nature and scope of the right
to property. David Schmidtz has stressed that property rights have
always required development due to technological change; at one
point it was granted that one's property right in one's land
extended far above one's land, but the development of aviation
rendered such a right unjustifiable.[91] Because property rights
require constant adjustment, a natural rights theory, which not only
holds (as does Eric Mack),[92] that we have a right to obtain property
but that we have well-specified natural property rights, is simply
implausible. As Kant was well aware, even a basic natural right to
have private property cannot be implemented without a political
order that specifies it, provides the economic institutions for it to be
effective, and so on. Kant held that although we can have a "provisional" right to property in the state of nature, justified rights to
property only become actual in a juridical condition that

---

[91] See David Schmidtz, "Property and Justice."
[92] Eric Mack, "The Natural Right of Property."

determines the shape of property rights.[93] The aim of jurisprudence, Kant says, is to precisely specify "what the property of everyone is"; only in civil society is property adequately guaranteed through public law.[94]

Thus, far more than other basic rights, the political order determines our rights of property. But only within certain bounds. As always, a justified political articulation of an abstract right must be within the eligible set – the set of articulations that all Members of the Public endorse as bona fide interpretations of the right. It is a fundamental mistake to think that because any specific system of property rights is conventional in the sense that property rights require some current convention to specify them, they are purely conventional in the sense that any convention will do as well as any other. Those who make this mistake are apt to insist that since property rights depend on the development of politically formed conventions, the political order cannot offend against them. Liam Murphy and Thomas Nagel, I believe, make this mistake.[95] According to Murphy and Nagel, property rights are simply conventional arrangements defined by governments, so the lawmaking power of government cannot possibly violate them. If the state is in the business of determining the shape of property, it may seem that everything it does – including taxing as it sees fit – is part of this job of specifying property rights. If so, it might appear that nobody could be in a position to argue that the state is taking away his property since until the state specifies it, there really is no effective right to property. There is, in this way of thinking, no Archimedean point outside of the state's determinations of your property rights (or any other rights?) from which to criticize the state's legislation, in particular its revenue legislation, as taking away what is yours, for its decisions determine what is yours.

This conclusion does not follow from recognizing that effective property rights are conventional and depend on the state. All laws are to be justified. This justification occurs against a background of

[93] Kant, *Metaphysical Elements of Justice*, pp. 46ff [Akademie 250ff].

[94] Ibid., 33 [Akademie, 233], 41 [Akademie, 238]. See further Hillel Steiner, "Kant, Property and the General Will," pp. 71ff.

[95] Liam Murphy and Thomas Nagel, *The Myth of Ownership: Taxes and Justice*, pp. 32ff.

one's already justified rights, what I have called the order of justification. Now property rights, if not the most basic rights in the liberal order of justification, are certainly prior to many state laws and policies such as, say, funding museums. Hobbes, Locke, Rousseau, and Kant all recognized that distinguishing "mine" and "thine" is one of the first requisites of an effective social order. In seeking to fund museums, representatives of the state cannot simply say that citizens have no entitlement to their incomes because they, the representatives, determine property rights, and so they may tax for these purposes without justification. "Without us, there would be no property, so you have no property claims against us!" Once property rights have been justified, they form the background for further justifications; they can be justifiably overridden in order to tax, but this must be justified.

24.2 THE INELIGIBILITY OF SOCIALISM

My claim that systems of private ownership are decisively justified (and so socialist systems are outside the eligible set) is apt to appear striking, given that Rawls' canonical formulation of what we might call "public reason liberalism" is hostile to capitalism, and allows socialism. Rawls condemns classical liberalism *and* welfare state capitalism as unjustifiable politico-economic systems.[96] According to Rawls, "laissez-faire capitalism" (or, as he sometimes calls it, "the system of natural liberty") is unjust; its regulative principles would not be agreed to by free and equal persons seeking impartial principles of justice. Because (*i*) it does not require constitutional guarantees of "the fair value" of equal political liberties to ensure that all have real political power (more on this anon) and (*ii*) allows only "a low social minimum" and so does not have institutions in place that aim to maximize the long-term prospects of the least well-off, less advantaged free and equal persons do not have reasons to endorse it. More surprisingly, Rawls holds that even "welfare-state capitalism" fails the test of justifiability. It too allows for inequalities of wealth that, in Rawls' eyes, undermine the fair value of a citizen's political rights. "It permits very large

[96] Rawls, *Justice as Fairness: A Restatement*, pp. 135ff.

inequalities in the ownership of real property (productive assets and natural resources) so that the control of the economy and much of the political life rests in a few hands."[97] Of the five political-economic systems he discusses – laissez-faire capitalism, welfare-state capitalism, state socialism, liberal (market) socialism, and a "property-owning democracy" – Rawls rejects as unjust both systems that he describes as "capitalist." He allows as possible just regimes one form of socialism (market socialism) and a "property-owning democracy" that allows private property but works "to disperse the ownership of wealth and capital, and thus to prevent a small part of society from controlling the economy and, indirectly, political life as well." Indeed, both Rawls and his followers have insisted that the more extreme, "libertarian" versions of the classical view are not genuinely liberal, reinforcing the supposition that a liberalism based on public reason is hostile to substantive liberalisms that endorse wide-ranging limits on government authority.[98]

Let us leave aside for a moment the basic place of private property in the order of justification and suppose that, when deliberating about property rights, Members of the Public are not constrained by the prior justification of the abstract right to private property. Socialist systems would still be outside the socially eligible set. Suppose that Members of the Public are deliberating about property, and all they suppose about the order of justification is that civil and political rights have been justified. Now when deliberating about property rights Members of the Public acknowledge that political and sociological data about the effects of property on these already justified rights is relevant, and perhaps decisive. If, for example, they know that some economic systems tend to undermine the effective establishment of civil rights, this must be relevant and important to their choices. However, to say that it is important for the deliberators to have knowledge of the effects of economic systems on schemes of civil liberty does not itself tell us the rational response of deliberators to such knowledge. Contrast two cases. In case A, a Member of the Public knows that economic scheme S_1 has some small advantage in protecting civil liberties over S_2 in the sense that, given probabilistic information, S_1 has a slightly higher chance of performing a little better in protecting civil liberties than S_2. For example, S_1 may have a higher probability of faster growth rates than S_2, and there may be evidence that, say, richer societies tend to better ensure a right to a fair trial. Even if this were so, some Members of the Public could hold that S_2 still has advantages that more than compensate – say it better conforms to their idea of economic justice. There is nothing unreasonable about such a judgment. On the other hand, in Case B there is evidence that S_2 has a very high probability of doing much worse than S_1 in protecting the broad range of civil liberties, such that it is extremely likely that S_2 will be characterized by widespread violation of civil liberties. Here, given the order of justification, reasonable Members of the Public must reject S_2. It almost certainly will fail to honor already justified civil liberties that are prior in the order of justification, being more closely tied to our basic understanding of the demands of free agency. It would do no good to first insist on a regime of civil liberties and then admit economic systems that have a very high probability of undermining them.

To be sure, there will be many cases between A and B where the probability that an economic system may endanger civil liberty is significant, but not so high that it would be unreasonable for a deliberator to decide that the significant dangers are compensated by perceived benefits. The order of justification does not establish a lexical priority such that no possible costs to a regime of civil liberty could ever be justified by, say, economic benefits. At the same time, rational deliberators must reject economic systems in cases like B, which not only pose some probability, but a very high one, that the core personal and civil liberties will be threatened.

There is compelling evidence that extensive private ownership – including capital goods and finance – is for all practical purposes a requisite for a social and political order that protects civil liberties. It is disturbing that Rawls never appreciates this and simply assumes, on the basis of economic theory, that well-functioning markets can be divorced from "private ownership in the means of production."[99] There has never been a political order characterized

[99] Rawls, *A Theory of Justice*, p. 239.

by deep respect for personal freedom that was not based on a market order with widespread private ownership in the means of production. Display VIII-10, drawn from James D. Gwartney, Robert Lawson, and Seth Norton's *Economic Freedom of the World: 2008 Annual Report*, gives the summary relation between economic freedom (an index summarizing data about a state's extent of personal economic choice; voluntary exchange coordinated by markets; freedom to enter and compete in markets; protection of persons and their property) related to Freedom House's ranking of states that protect civil rights.

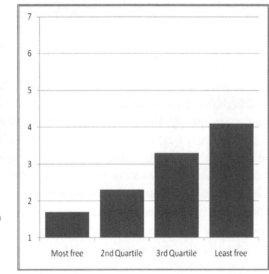

Fraser Institute Economic Freedom Scores
(1st quartile most free; 4th quartile least free)

DISPLAY VIII-10 THE GENERAL RELATION BETWEEN ECONOMIC FREEDOM AND PROTECTION OF CIVIL RIGHTS[100]

As we can see from Display VIII-10, the top quartile of states ranked in terms of economic freedom are the best protectors of civil rights. A further analysis of the data reveal that in 2008, no country rated by Freedom House in category 1 (the highest on Freedom

[100] Adapted from James D. Gwartney and Robert Lawson; with Seth Norton, *Economic Freedom of the World: 2008 Annual Report*, p. 21. Used with permission of the Fraser Institute.

House's 1–7 scale) on protection of civil rights scored less than 50 out of 100 on the Heritage Foundation's score of protection of property rights. No state that does the best job in protecting civil rights scores less than 59 (out of 100) in the Heritage Foundation's ratings of *overall economic freedom*. With the (close) exception of Cape Verde, all states recognized by Freedom House as best protectors of civil rights were classified as free or mostly free in the Heritage House scores. The rankings of Gwartney et al. show a comparable story.[101]

Rawls argues that welfare state capitalism should be grouped along with state socialist systems as socioeconomic arrangements that do not adequately protect the fair value of political rights. Of course it is hard to evaluate Rawls' claim that such systems do worse than his preferred alternatives, since none of his preferred systems have ever existed. As Displays VIII-11 and VIII-12 show, however, in the world as we have known it, the protection of economic liberty and private property is associated with states that do a better job of institutionalizing effective political rights (as well as civil rights). In comparison, Display VIII-12 gives the scores of the remaining state socialist regimes on civil rights, political protection, and economic freedom. The evidence indicates that private property-based regimes that protect property rights and overall economic freedom are the best protectors of civil liberties and, indeed, political rights. Given the evidence, because Members of the Public have a deep commitment to civil liberties, they must reject socialism in favor of private property regimes and, further, must favor private property regimes with considerable economic freedom.

Rawls and his followers appear to have an effective rejoinder. Rawlsians consistently claim that societies with large inequalities in wealth create manifest and extreme dangers to the fair value of political liberties.[102] So even if private property regimes are necessary for protecting civil liberty, private property systems that allow economic inequalities are a grave danger to political liberty. It is seldom appreciated how important this claim is to Rawls' case

---

[101] See Appendix B for the country-by-country breakdown.
[102] Rawls, *Justice as Fairness*, p. 139.

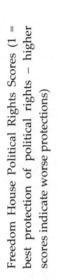
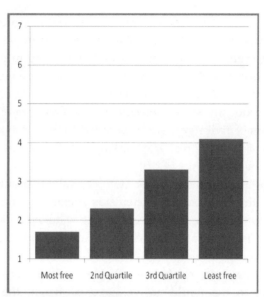

Fraser Institute Economic Freedom Scores
(1st quartile = most economic freedom: 4th quartile = least)

DISPLAY VIII-11   THE GENERAL RELATION BETWEEN ECONOMIC FREEDOM AND
PROTECTION OF POLITICAL RIGHTS[103]

	Civil Rights Score (all "not free")	Political Rights Score (all "not free")	Property Rights Protection Score: Heritage Foundation	Overall Economic Freedom Score: Heritage Foundation
China	6	7	20	53 (*mostly unfree*)
Cuba	7	7	10	28 (*repressed*)
Laos	6	7	10	50 (*mostly unfree*)
Vietnam	5	7	10	50 (*mostly unfree*)
North Korea	7	7	*Not graded*	3 (*repressed*)

DISPLAY VIII-12   CIVIL RIGHTS SCORES AND ECONOMIC FREEDOM IN REMAINING
SOCIALIST STATES[104]

[103] Adapted from Gwartney, Lawson, and Norton, *Economic Freedom of the World: 2008 Annual Report*, p. 21. Digital copy available from www.fraserinstitute.org. Used with permission of the Fraser Institute.

for equality; he believes that inequalities allowed by his "difference principle" – which requires that a just social order must maximize the economic prospects of the least advantaged citizens – might still threaten the fair value of political liberty, and so further equalization may be required.[105] Rawls went so far as to propose a branch of government to readjust property rights, partly to ensure the "fair value" of political liberty.[106] Now while it may simply seem obvious to some that large inequalities of income and wealth undermine the worth of "the least advantaged" citizen's political liberties, this claim is in fact conjectural. Whether citizens have real input – whether their political rights actually have "fair value" – is a matter of complex sociology, involving the features of political culture, including levels of civic participation, institutional structures relating business and governments, the existence of power centers outside of government, levels of overall wealth, and so on. Display VIII-13 shows some of this complexity, charting the relation between income inequality and political rights in selected countries in the Organization for Economic Development and Cooperation (OECD).

Display VIII-13 gives little ground for accepting a strong relation between income inequality and a lesser value of political rights. To be sure, there is some positive correlation: below average income inequality countries always score high or middle on political rights, while above average income inequality countries scored both high and low. The United States, though, scores high on OECD income inequality, but also high on political participation/political pluralism, outperforming more egalitarian countries. In any event, the differences between the Czech Republic, Denmark, France, Japan, and the United States are very slight. The real outliers are Mexico and Turkey, countries that score low on the protection of political

---

[104] Sources: Freedom House, "Freedom in the World 2008: Subscores (Civil Rights)," http://www.freedomhouse.org/template.cfm?page=414&year=2008;   Heritage Foundation 2008 data, "Index of Economic Freedom," http://www.heritage.org/index. Used with permission of Freedom House and the Heritage Foundation.

[105] Rawls, *Political Liberalism*, p. 329.

[106] Rawls, *A Theory of Justice*, pp. 242–51. Rawls also believes that a just society would seek reasonable ways to limit wasteful forms of advertising: "the funds now devoted to advertising can be released for investment or for other useful social ends." *Political Liberalism*, p. 365.

rights and have high income inequality combined with significantly lower overall levels of wealth and income.

	Below Average Income Inequality	Above Average Income Inequality
High Political Pluralism/ Participation Score (16)	Denmark	United States
Middle Political Participation Score (15)	Czech Republic, France	Japan
Lower Political Participation Scores (12-14)		Mexico, Turkey
High Electoral Process Score (12)	Czech Republic, Denmark, France	Japan
Middle Electoral Process Score (11)		United States
Lower Electoral Process Score (10)		Mexico, Turkey
High Functioning Government Scores (11 & 12)	Denmark, Czech Republic, France	United States
Middle Functioning Government Score (10)		Japan
Lower Functioning Government Scores (8–7)		Mexico, Turkey

DISPLAY VIII-13 THE RELATION BETWEEN INCOME INEQUALITY AND EFFECTIVE POLITICAL RIGHTS IN SELECTED OECD COUNTRIES[107]

Perhaps the real danger to political rights is not income, but wealth, inequality. However, measures of income and wealth

[107] Sources: Jean-Marc Burniaux, Flavio Padrini and Nicola Brandt, "Labour Market Performance, Income Inequality and Poverty in OECD Countries," p. 44; Freedom House, "Freedom in the World 2008: Subscores (Political Rights)," http://www.freedomhouse.org/template.cfm?page=414&year=2008.

inequality generally strongly correlate in OECD countries,[108] so we should not expect a great deal of difference. Display VIII-14, employing a different data set of selected OECD countries concerning wealth inequality, arrives at results comparable to those in Display VIII-13.

	Lower Wealth Inequality	Higher Wealth Inequality
High Political Pluralism/Participation Score (16)	Finland, Sweden	United States, Canada
Middle Political Participation Score (15)	Japan, Germany	Australia, Italy
Lower Political Participation Scores (12–14)		Mexico
High Electoral Process Score (12)	Finland, Germany, Japan, Sweden	Australia, Canada, Italy
Middle Electoral Process Score (11)		United States
Lower Electoral Process Score (10)		Mexico
Highest Functioning Government Scores (12)	Finland, Sweden, Germany	Australia, Canada
Higher-Middle Functioning Government Scores (11)		United States, Italy
Middle-Lower Functioning Government Score (10)	Japan	
Lower Functioning Government Scores (8)		Mexico

DISPLAY VIII-14 THE RELATION BETWEEN WEALTH INEQUALITY AND EFFECTIVE POLITICAL RIGHTS IN SELECTED OECD COUNTRIES[109]

[108] Daniela Sonedda, "Wealth Inequality, Income Redistribution and Growth in 15 OECD Countries," p. 21.
[109] Sources: Markus Jänttil and Eva Sierminska, *Survey Estimates of Wealth Holdings in OECD Countries: Evidence on the Level and Distribution*; Freedom House, "Freedom in the World 2008: Subscores (Political Rights)."

In light of Displays VIII-10 to VIII-14, we must view as unfounded the claim that welfare state capitalism, as well as state socialism with a command economy, is unjustifiable partly because it fails to secure the fair value of political liberties.[110] The most we can discover is a modest real correlation between wealth and income inequalities and political right protection scores. Welfare capitalist states such as the United States and the United Kingdom score "1" (the best at protecting rights) and all socialist states "7" (the lowest possible score) on effective political rights. Display VIII-12, of course, does not include market socialist systems, which are one of Rawls' favored alternatives (since none exist). However, the only large-scale market socialist system in history – Yugoslavia under Tito – also repressed civil liberty and political rights. Of course these data are merely indicative, and much work needs to be done, but it is dubious indeed that there is any powerful empirical evidence for a strong relation between economic inequalities and less than a fair value of political liberty. Again, this is not to say that there is no correlation at all, but excluding a whole set of economic arrangements on the basis of a modest correlation over a small range of variance is unjustified.[111] There is good reason to think that in the OECD, the most important variable explaining high political rights scores is simply high wealth and income, and degree of equality is a relatively minor factor.

This knowledge must be relevant to the deliberations of Members of the Public. We suppose that they have already justified civil rights and rights of the person; such rights are basic for all liberals, and so would be prior in the order of justification. Knowing the importance of these rights, when selecting schemes of economic cooperation, the Members of the Public will rank all systems with extensive private ownership and economic freedom as superior to socialist systems. Not only does everything we know about economic prosperity indicate that private ownership is far superior to socialist systems,[112] but, as we have seen, the shared

---

[110] Rawls, *Justice as Fairness*, pp. 137–8.

[111] Much less the claim that such inequalities are simply possible, allowed, or permitted by capitalistic systems. Cf. *Justice as Fairness*, p. 139.

[112] For the relation of economic freedom and income per capita growth, see James D. Gwartney and Robert Lawson; with Seth Norton, *Economic Freedom of the World: 2008 Annual Report*, p. 18.

commitment of all liberals to civil rights provides a decisive reason to rank such systems above socialism. And, we have seen, the Rawlsian counter-claim that, in turn, strong private ownership systems endanger political rights is questionable. Socialist systems would be dominated by private ownership systems and, so, would not be in the optimal set.

24.3 CLASSICAL LIBERALISM, REDISTRIBUTION, AND THE ELIGIBLE SET

Once it has been concluded that systems with private ownership in the means of production (with great economic freedom to invest, start businesses, and so on) are in the optimal eligible set of all Members of the Public, it looks as if the proponent of classical liberalism has won the day. Egalitarian, redistributive proposals will not be in the eligible set of all Members of the Public. We must suppose that some Members of the Public have egalitarian intuitions (evaluative standards), some are welfare statists, while others are more strictly classical liberal. Now the classical liberal Members of the Public are apt to hold that almost every redistributive plan or scheme of social justice is worse than no redistributive/social justice laws at all. It would seem that classically liberal-inclined citizens will rank few if any redistributive laws as better than no laws at all, and so such laws will be excluded from the eligible set. Having secured the abstract right to property through some system of private rights, it would appear that the Public could not go on to institute a redistributive state. Recall that principles of social justice were not stable under full justification (§17.5), so it cannot be held that an abstract principle of social justice has already been justified, and now the task of public justification is to interpret it. It seems, then, that the optimal eligible set will contain only laws with a strong commitment to private ownership and economic freedom.

This argument against the redistributive state succeeds only if the justification of property is not dependent on questions about justified redistribution and/or conceptions of social justice within the evaluative standards of Members of the Public (§23.2*b*). The classical liberal insists that first the Public evaluates schemes of private ownership and *then* it looks at the justification of all redistributive proposals. It is only because the classical liberal first fixed private ownership that she was able to eliminate redistributive proposals. But clearly it is not plausible to see these as even remotely independent issues. The history of debate about economic justice and redistribution has been about the shape of a justified system of private ownership. Many Members of the Public could not possibly evaluate and rank schemes of private ownership unless they know their distributive implications;[113] for many Members of the Public these issues are tightly bound together. Consequently, debates about acceptable systems of property inevitably include debates about the fairness of their resulting distributions.

Although the classical liberal cannot insist that redistributive states or even egalitarian states are outside the set of reasonable proposals, she can invoke our previous result that the boundaries of the eligible set on proposed laws will tend toward the anti-coercion, more limited state views. Classical liberals have a reasonable though, of course, disputed view that highly redistributive states and states with very high levels of taxation are more coercive than less redistributive states. But it may well be objected: how does simply increasing the marginal tax rate increase coercion? Will Wilkinson, a philosopher specializing in public policy matters, poses a challenge:

. . . libertarians and many conservatives often talk about lower taxes as a matter of liberty. But a higher tax isn't more coercive than a lower one. You're either being coerced or you're not. A guy who mugs five people with thin wallets is no less guilty of coercion than a guy who mugs five people with thick wallets. The harm from coercion might be greater if more is taken, but there is no more or less coercion.[114]

Let us begin with a simple contrast between two states with a flat-rate income tax: a low- and a high-rate state. To make the distinction stark, suppose that the low-rate state has a flat rate of 20

---

[113] This is certainly Mill's view in his discussion of private property in Book II of *Principles of Political Economy*.

[114] Will Wilkinson, *http://www.willwilkinson.net/flybottle/2008/05/30/please-discuss/ (The Fly Bottle)*. Wilkinson is suggesting a topic for discussion, and the claim is based on theories of freedom commonly held by classical liberals.

percent and the high-rate state one of 80 percent. Otherwise the tax codes are identical, including both monetary penalties and prison terms. For at least two reasons the high-tax state, other things equal, will be more coercive.

(*i*) As tax rates rise noncompliance will also rise; it is hopelessly utopian not to expect increased noncompliance as tax rates increase. As tax rates rise so does the opportunity cost of voluntarily complying; self-interested citizens have increasingly strong incentives to become noncompliers, and we must assume that in the real world a significant number of citizens will be so motivated. As noncompliance increases the state will increasingly turn its attention to identifying and coercing noncompliers. The amount of money involved will be enormous, and we can expect states to turn increasingly to the criminal law. Something along these lines has occurred in the United States. In the last twenty years the United States Internal Revenue Service developed the concept of a "tax gap" – "the difference between the amount of tax owed and the amount paid."[115] In 2001 the Internal Revenue Service estimated that the tax gap was approximately $312 to $353 billion, resulting from a very significant noncompliance rate of roughly 16 percent.[116] As the tax gap has grown, the Internal Revenue Service has undertaken a "zealous fight" to close the gap, implementing a "Tax Gap Strategy" that involves increased effort to detect violations and enforce criminal law.[117] Tax enforcement thus increasingly comes to stress criminal penalties. The problem clearly is that taxpayers do not at present sufficiently fear detection.[118]

(*ii*) The criminal law seeks to make options ineligible – no longer choice worthy – because of the threatened costs to one's person. Now in our 80 percent rate state, tax policies have the effect of making a large number of options basically ineligible. To be sure, the threat is conditional: if you engage in a range of activities, you

---

[115] Ted F. Brown (Assistant for the Criminal Division of the IRS [1998]), quoted in Liezl Walker, "The Deterrent Value of Imposing Prison Sentences for Tax Crimes," p. 1, note 4.

[116] "Understanding the Tax Gap" (FS-2005-14, March 2005), Internal Revenue Service, http://www.irs.gov/newsroom/article/0,,id=137246,00.html.

[117] Walker, "The Deterrent Value of Imposing Prison Sentences for Tax Crimes," p. 6.

[118] Ibid., p. 7.

must either pay 80 percent to the state or be punished. The state
essentially demands that one pay 80 percent to take up an option,
and threatens one's person if one does not. And indeed a wide
range of options are made less eligible. Market transactions
involving traceable monetary transfers become far less eligible than
informal bartering, leisure activities, writing philosophy, artistic
pursuits, and political activities. By the state's radically increasing
the costs of a wide range of market activities, these are made far
less eligible as a result of the state's power to coerce. If we adopt
Feinberg's metaphor and think of one's options as a series of rail-
road tracks that one might follow, high tax rates make it very difficult to follow a great many; given the costs involved in taking those
routes, they are effectively closed.[119] Of course, one still *can* engage
in these activities if one is willing to pay the 80 percent, but one *can*
still engage in criminal activities if one is willing to pay the penalties.[120]

As a rule, we should expect increases in taxation (and, so generally the redistributive activities of the state) to strongly positively
correlate with increases in coercion.[121] Both the variables I have

[119] Feinberg, "The Interest of Liberty in the Scales," p. 36.
[120] It might be objected that this must be wrong: whereas the criminal law seeks to
render options less eligible in order to deter, an effective tax law (putting aside
sin taxes) must hope that citizens continue with the activity for revenue to be
generated. The will of the state is not for citizens to refrain, but to persist, so they
are not being coerced in Hayek's sense. Coercion thus may seem to require an
intention to deter people from the act, but that is exactly what the state does not
seek to do with taxation – and that is why the state does not close off options but
only makes them more difficult. One who threatens, however, need not wish to
deter, for often enough those making the threat hope that the target will not give
in to the threat. In 1918, for example, Germany issued an ultimatum to the
neutral Dutch, demanding the right to ship materials across their territory and
threatening the Netherlands and Dutch ships in its colonies if their demand was
not met. At the time this threat was seen by many as a pretext, believing that
Germany hoped that the Netherlands would not give in to the threat but instead
would enter the war. What Germany's intentions were did not nullify the coercive threat. See *The New York Times*, April 23 and 28, 1918.
[121] By comparing only flat-tax states I have greatly simplified the analysis. With
variable rate taxation, what constitutes a high-tax country depends on the
combined score on several dimensions. Consider a study of fifteen OECD
countries from 1974 to 1997 (Australia, Belgium, Canada, Denmark, Finland,
France, Germany, Italy, Japan, Netherlands, Norway, Spain, Sweden, the United
Kingdom, and the United States). We might define a high-tax country as one that
has highly progressive rates and high marginal tax rates. On that definition, the

noted – increasing noncompliance and decreasing eligibility of options – are continuous, and we should expect that throughout most of their range the effects noted here will be monotonically related to tax rates. This is not to say that the relation between taxation and coercion is linear; coercion may be insignificant at very low levels of tax and become really oppressive at very high levels. And, of course, the overall relation between the degree of coercion and tax rates may differ depending on historical circumstances. In the Great Depression, for example, an attempt by the state to enforce basic property rights with no significant redistribution against, say, a general population in economic distress might have required a great amount of coercion, while a state that engaged in modest redistribution may well have secured social peace with much less need for threats. We must not succumb to the simple idea that the tax rates and degree of coercion perfectly correlate in all circumstances. Nevertheless, on plausible analysis, classical liberals strongly favored property regimes that typically employ less coercion, while the heavy reliance of the expansive state favored by Rawls and his followers would seem to rely on relatively high levels of taxation, and so favor more coercive states.

Once we get beyond paradigmatic instances of coercion, claims about what constitutes coercion are, notoriously, open to dispute. I stress only that views that link high tax rates with high coercion are reasonable. Thus, those who hold that the coercion costs of redistributive states are high and the benefits relatively low will be the first to conclude that the burdens of justification for these states – the burden of showing that the coercion can be justified to all – cannot be met, and so the more extreme versions are apt to be outside the eligible set. The advocate of the highly redistributive state may simply retort that all small states are outside the eligible set; since they are highly coercive concerning the poor, they too are outside

---

high-tax states are Sweden, the United States, Finland, the United Kingdom, the Netherlands, and Belgium; the low-tax states are Spain, Australia, Norway, Germany, Japan, and Italy. If we define a high-tax state as one that has a high average personal tax rate and a high degree of progressivity, the high-tax rate states are Belgium, Canada, and France; Germany, Norway, and Denmark are low on both dimensions. Sonedda, "Wealth Inequality, Income Redistribution and Growth in 15 OECD Countries," pp. 19–20.

VIII *The Moral and Political Orders*

the eligible set. Recall Jack, who held that a classical liberal state that enforces property rights with a modest provision for the poor imposes coercion costs on the poor that exceed the benefits, and so such a state is not justified in his view (§23.3*f*). Certainly this can sometimes be the case. But we must remember that more limited states secure great benefits when they institutionalize a scheme of basic agency rights and civil liberties. As we saw in section 23.3*f* (see Display VIII-9), because of this, the advocate of the redistributive state still will be committed to seeing great value in smaller states, even if he believes they are more coercive than larger states.

The public justification of the state under conditions of extensive evaluative pluralism tilts toward classical positions. Widespread private ownership will be endorsed by all reasonable Members of the Public as necessary for a free moral order and a secure political one. Property institutions that include significant redistributive elements certainly may be justified, but as they become increasingly coercive they are apt to be judged ineligible by those whose evaluative standards deem coercion to be a great cost, which can be justified only if it brings great benefits. (Again, we must remember to deem a property institution ineligible is not to say that we will have no property convention, but that such a convention has no moral authority.) A liberalism based on a commitment to public justification – a justificatory liberalism – leads not to socialism, or a thoroughgoing egalitarian liberalism, or to libertarianism, but to the more nuanced approach to legislation we find in the fifth book of Mill's *Principles*, allowing that there are a number of tasks that government justifiably performs, but having a strong overall inclination toward less rather than more "authoritative" (i.e., coercive) government.

I have employed both empirical evidence and formal arguments to show why this is so. The basic idea, though, is intuitively clear and compelling. The view I have presented in this discussion rests on five main claims: (*i*) individuals are free and equal; (*ii*) free and equal persons have a moral right not to be forced or coerced without justification; (*iii*) a Member of the Public will hold that the greater her estimates of coercion, the stronger must be the justification; (*iv*) free and equal Members of the Public reasonably disagree on many matters involving degrees of coercion, but many reasonable people believe that large states with high rates of taxation and redistributive institutions are more coercive; and (*v*) only laws that can be justified to all Members of the Public can reconcile coercion with respect for everyone's freedom and equality. Given these commitments a justificatory liberalism must "tilt" against more coercive states, and it must at least be a crucial concern of justificatory liberals that they show that their favored proposals do not employ coercion. For any coercive law, in the evaluation of all Members of the Public its total benefits must outweigh its total costs, including costs of coercion. In my view it is remarkable that this line of reasoning is barely even acknowledged within contemporary justificatory liberalism. Let me offer two explanations of why this is so.

(*i*) At least since Rawls' 1967 essay "Distributive Justice," and certainly in his 1971 *A Theory of Justice*, the main aim of appeal to principles that all free and equal persons can accept has been to justify a certain egalitarian account of distributive justice. Rawls saw that his early formulations of his model led to the indeterminate results I have analyzed here: the parties would endorse (what I have called) an eligible set of economic arrangements, all of which would work in some way to everyone's advantage.[122] Rawls, though, explicitly sought a determinate solution to the deliberative problem; in order to generate a determinate egalitarian result he constrained the reasoning of the parties and the basis of their deliberations so that all reasoned in an identical way.[123] What started out as a collective legislation problem under conditions of disagreement became an account in which everyone cares about the same things and reasons about them in the same way. Even though Rawls continued to describe his account as requiring "unanimous choice,"[124] the essence of a unanimity requirement was lost: the

[122] Rawls suggests that one way to avoid the resulting indeterminacy is "to choose some social position by reference to which the pattern of expectations as a whole is to be judged." From this point on in Rawls' project, the sustained focus is on giving a rationale for why this representative person should be identified with the least advantaged social position. Rawls, "Distributive Justice," p. 137.

[123] "The restrictions on particular information in the original position are, then, of fundamental importance. Without them we would not be able to work out any definite theory of justice at all." Rawls, *A Theory of Justice*, p. 121.

[124] Ibid., p. 121.

outcome of the agreement was no longer in any way limited by deliberators whose reasonable evaluations of the costs are highest and the benefits are lowest. We simply stipulate the correct single motivation to get the result we want, so that the unanimity requirement becomes otiose. Employing such a procedure, the theorist can generate a "unanimity result" justifying any state, even when we know that many reasonable people do not think this is the optimal, or even an eligible, option. Given this, the main contemporary versions of justificatory liberalism see no connection at all between a unanimity requirement and a more limited government. Think how odd this is: we start out with deep respect for freedom, add a unanimity requirement, and we do not get a theory of limited government. Such liberals proclaim that they respect the reasonable concerns of all, and then proceed to specify what these are in ways that allow them to justify precisely the range of government activities they privately endorse. At best, this is remarkably fortuitous.

(*ii*) Those engaged in the contemporary project of showing what systems of property holding can be justified to all have seldom even worried about the use of coercion, or have seldom thought hard about the relation of private property and the protection of basic liberal rights. Indeed, as we have seen, some have explicitly denied that there is *anything* presumptively wrong with coercion, thus rejecting a fundamental liberal idea that runs from Locke through Kant and Mill to contemporaries such as Feinberg, Gewirth, and Benn. Thus an account of liberalism that tells us how important it is to treat persons as free and equal sees no presumption whatsoever against forcing them to do things. Or else, under the guise of constructing an "ideal theory," according to which we suppose perfect compliance with our preferred distributive principles (§21.4), we are licensed to ignore the fact that, say, market socialist regimes would almost surely employ great coercion to prevent people from starting and expanding businesses or would drive commercial activity into black markets, or that governments of such states, controlling all sources of investment, would almost certainly have tremendous political power that would endanger the basic rights of citizens. Thus Rawls can say, without evoking much dissent, that market socialism, which has been institutionalized only by General Tito's repressive Yugoslav state, is within the class of acceptable regimes partly because it *protects* the value of political liberties, whereas a welfare state such as the United Kingdom, which probably protects political rights as well as any regime in history, is clearly unjust because it fails to protect the fair value of political rights. This disregard of political reality has, I think, rendered contemporary justificatory liberalism unreasonably hostile to real-world private property regimes, even including the contemporary welfare state.

25 Further Functions of the State and Practical Paretianism

25.1 THE ABSTRACT ARGUMENT FOR PUBLIC GOODS PROVISION

In the epigraph for this chapter, Green noted that once the state was created to interpret and develop our moral rights, it is available to serve "further purposes." We must distinguish the role of the state as interpreter and protector of social morality from its role as, say, provider of services and goods that are not morally required. This recalls Mill's distinction between the "necessary and the "optional" functions of government:

[T]here must be a specification of the functions which are either inseparable from the idea of a government, or are exercised habitually and without objection by all governments; as distinguished from those respecting which it has been considered questionable whether governments should exercise them or not. The former may be termed the necessary, the latter the optional, functions of government. By the term optional it is not meant to imply, that it can ever be a matter of indifference, or of arbitrary choice, whether the government should or should not take upon itself the functions in question; but only that the expediency of its exercising them does not amount to necessity, and is a subject on which diversity of opinion does or may exist.[125]

---

[125] Mill, *Principles of Political Economy*, p. 800 (Book V, chap. 1, §1). A related distinction is that which James Buchanan draws between the protective functions of the state (which protects the freedom and rights of citizens against invasion by

Let us say that these further or optional functions of government are not necessitated by the abstract rights or moral claims of citizens. Suppose, then, we have in place a scheme of rights and duties, including property rights, and these in general adequately articulate the demands of social morality. Or, at least, let us suppose that the scheme is sufficiently justified that we sometimes confront public policy issues in which justice and morality are not the main criteria of what should be done: the proposed legislation is "optional" rather than morally necessary.

In the work of many economists the chief policy task of government is to correct for market failures, especially the problem of externalities. An externality occurs when some person's consumption or production activity has positive or negative impact on the utility of others (where this impact is not included in the producer's or consumer's cost/benefit calculations).[126] If Alf's activity imposes negative externalities (costs) on Betty, then while as a rational economic agent Alf will engage in it up to the point where *his* marginal benefits equal *his* costs, Alf will not take account of the costs to Betty. But if Alf produces just up to the point where his marginal costs and benefits are equal, and there are additional costs to Betty, it looks as if the total social costs (the costs to Alf and Betty) of Alf's last unit of production will exceed the entire social benefits. Alf has moved them both to a new distribution (with the extra produced unit) which benefits Alf at a cost to Betty.[127] A similar analysis applies to external benefits: if my production benefits you as well as me, then if I stop production when my marginal benefits equal my marginal costs, from a social point of view (which includes the benefits and costs to everyone) the good has been under-produced; social marginal benefits still exceed social marginal costs, since my decision has not taken into account the benefits you receive.

Externalities are a chief source of market failure – where markets fail to produce efficient results. The existence of externalities raises

others) and the productive state, which aims to increase efficiency. See his *The Limits of Liberty* pp. 94–6. See also my *Justificatory Liberalism*, pp. 243–5, 271–4.

[126] See Dennis Mueller, *Public Choice III*, p. 25.

[127] The power of the Coase theorem is its demonstration that, at least in principle, there is still a possibility for Alf and Betty to achieve a Pareto-superior distribution. See Ronald Coase, "The Problem of Social Cost."

the possibility that everyone may approve of a coercive policy as it will make all better off. In thinking about what Members of the Public would approve of in this context, we do not suppose that they are restricted to their morally relevant evaluative standards (§14.4); *ex hypothesi*, they are not considering a moral question but simply their overall sufficient reasons to endorse a policy that secures a good. These reasons may concern their evaluative standards, but we must allow that they may also be largely self-interested. Whereas it is objectionable for a Member of the Public to be single-mindedly self-interested in evaluating moral rules, it surely is acceptable when a policy is justified in terms simply of achieving a Pareto-superior outcome, that is, a policy moving us from social state S_1 to S_2, where no one strictly prefers S_1 to S_2, and at least one person strictly prefers S_2 to S_1. Let us say, then, that in evaluating optional public policies, each Member of the Public considers her unrestricted set of relevant values, Λ (rather than her evaluative standards Σ).[128]

In this light consider the quintessential public goods problem of the "tragedy of the commons" such as fisheries.[129] Many fisheries around the world are overfished, resulting in a depletion of stocks. Now it would probably be to the benefit of fisherman Alf to reduce his catch this year to secure a good yield next year *if he could be confident of obtaining all the future benefits of his reduced yield this year*. But he cannot. If Betty and Charlie fish anyway, the stocks will still be depleted. Alf will have paid a cost but will not gain the full benefits of his restraint. Conversely, Betty and Charlie do not pay the full costs of their overfishing, since the costs of depletion are transferred to other fisherman such as Alf. Thus the fisheries are overfished, and the marginal social costs exceed the marginal benefits. A scheme of property rights that internalized all costs and benefits would be one way to solve the problem.[130] Of course, we have this problem just because property rights over fish in the

---

[128] For now I put aside the degree of warrant that is necessary for λ_x to be a member of some Member of the Public's Λ. I suppose that it is quite modest, lower than what is required to be a member of the morally relevant set of evaluative standards Σ.

[129] See Garret Hardin, *"The Tragedy of the Commons."*

[130] See David Schmidtz, *The Limits of Government: An Essay on the Public Goods Argument*.

ocean are difficult to institutionalize (fish tend to swim around a lot).

Note that this is just the sort of mixed-motive game that led us to the necessity of social morality (§§5–6). Suppose that in the tragedy of the commons case Alf cannot unilaterally have a significant impact on whether the commons will be preserved. One way to model his choices (there are others, depending on our assumptions) is as a multi-person Prisoners' Dilemma in which Alf is playing against "all others," as in Display VIII-15.

		All Others	
		Enough others restrain themselves: the commons is saved	*Not enough restrain themselves: the commons is not saved*
Alf	*Restrain*	Alf gains the good, but has to pay part of the cost for it	Alf pays the cost, but since others don't cooperate, he doesn't get the good
	Doesn't Restrain	Alf gets the good for free	Alf doesn't get the good, but at least he doesn't pay anything

DISPLAY VIII-15 A MULTI-PERSON PRISONERS' DILEMMA

Defection (no restraint) is the dominant strategy; no matter what the rest of society does, Alf does best by not restraining himself. And everyone reasons just as Alf does, and so public goods tend to be undersupplied even if everyone prefers having the public good to not having it.[131]

Now it is tempting to suppose that in all such cases Members of the Public would endorse a coercive policy that restrains each from harvesting so that all may have more in the future. Such a policy

---

[131] There are complexities here. I have put the point simply in terms of a threshold good, but even with public goods without thresholds, rational individuals acting individually will undersupply public goods. Public goods can also be modeled in terms of assurance games.

would benefit all; it provides a means of escape from a Prisoners' Dilemma to a Pareto-superior outcome. Like Hobbes' social contract theory, this familiar idea moves too quickly from the inability of instrumentally rational goal pursuers (reasoning simply strategically) to achieve cooperation to the necessity of the coercive state. As I have argued throughout this work, the persistent error of ignoring the ability of social conventions and norms to solve mixed-motive social interactions (and so secure mutually beneficial cooperation) leads to overemphasizing the role of the state. Recall Green's epigraph to this chapter: between the individual and the state is society. Elinor Ostrom's pathbreaking work has demonstrated that communities of resource users often develop institutions that effectively regulate common pool resource problems without resort to the coercive state.[132] More generally, communities often evolve institutions and norms that solve their cooperation problems without employing the coercive state.[133] Given that state coercion is always a dangerous instrument, which can lead us away from the Pareto frontier as easily as to it, we have good reason to rely on, and respect, endogenously evolved social conventions when they have effectively coped with public goods and common pool problems. Of course the work of Ostrom and others also shows that these conventions do not always evolve or effectively cope with common pool and other problems with public goods characteristics. There are certainly times when the state and its coercive power appear to be the only viable way to cope with some problems. In *these* cases, the provision of public goods is, at least in principle, capable of publicly justifying state coercion.

It was explicitly with reference to state provision of public goods that Knut Wicksell proposed that expenditure and revenue decisions be linked (§23.2*b*). If the claim is that all Members of the Public would endorse the policy, this surely must mean that they would endorse the total package of benefits and costs involved in

---

[132] See Ostrom's now-classic *Governing the Commons: The Evolution of Institutions for Collective Action*. For game theoretic analysis of common pool resource problems, and exploration of its limits, see also Elinor Ostrom, Roy Gardner, and James Walker, *Rules, Games, and Common–Pool Resources*.

[133] See David Schmidtz's important study, *The Limits of Government*. For additional case studies of different problems with different outcomes, see Gary Libecap, *Contracting for Property Rights*.

the mandatory policy over not having the policy. This must include, then, the full costs of the policy, including its taxation costs. Of course citizens will disagree about the relative merits of different packages, so once again we are faced with an eligible set with a number of elements. The provision of policy y supplying public good G is publicly justified if it is a member of the optimal eligible set of G-supplying policies and has been selected by the justified authoritative political process.

Perhaps the policy need not be authoritative. Suppose its aim is simply to supply a good rather than to direct an individual's action. In this case it might be sufficient if the state merely has a moral permission to coerce in order to implement the policy: genuine authority would not be necessary (§22.3b). Perhaps. We need to be cautious, for even policies supplying public goods implicate state authority. First, the state raises funds through its taxation system. Taxation systems that are understood to be without authority are onerous to all. It is relatively easy to cheat on paying taxes; when people see no obligation to pay, they are more apt to cheat, and as people increasingly do so, states adopt increasingly coercive enforcement measures (§24.3), making all worse off. Additionally, almost all policies securing public goods entail coercively enforced regulations, and in mixed-motive games, regulations without authority may require significant coercion. Those who blithely insist that genuine political authority can be replaced by mere permissible coercion may well underestimate the costs of basing policies simply on the threat of force and the amount of force necessary to ensure compliance without obligation.

25.2 QUASI-PUBLIC GOODS AND THE CONSTRAINTS OF PUBLIC JUSTIFICATION

A problem with the abstract argument for state public goods provision is that few goods are purely public. Of special importance to us is that a policy coercively securing a public good is publicly justified only if all Members of the Public rank the package of the coercive policy's costs and benefits above not having the public good. If some Members of the Public do not rank the package above no policy at all, its coercive imposition cannot be publicly justified. We can generalize the problem. Any optional policy on matter Y is publicly justified only if for all Members of the Public, consulting their unrestricted set of values and goals (i.e., Λ), it is the case that for each, the eligible set of Y policies is not empty. If the public is divided into two groups such that for one group Y is nonempty and for the other it is empty, there is no publicly justified policy on Y even if the second group is small.

This is a severe restriction on the range of justifiable public policy. For almost any proposed public policy y, we might suppose that some Member of the Public will conclude that no policy at all is preferred to y, and so y is not in the eligible set as determined by that person's Λ. To paraphrase Nozick, so strong and far-reaching is the requirement of public justification of optional policies that it raises the question of what, if anything, the state and its officials may do.[134] Although there is a compelling public justification of authoritative laws and policies that are required by social morality, it is much less clear how much optional public policy survives the demand for public justification, for it is not at all clear how much "public policy" is genuinely public – actually benefits all. Daniel M. Weinstock suggests that a view such as that which I have defended here leads to "complete state inaction, something which no liberal thinker, not even libertarians like Robert Nozick, ever advocated."[135] Even speed limits, Weinstock argues, would be prohibited, since they "place an obstacle in the way of those who value thrills over safety."[136] Such a radical limitation, says Weinstock, "would be absurdly self-stultifying."[137] He thus presses for a less restrictive conception of public justification. He believes that "a public conception of the good" can be justified. "[S]ubstantive values can constitute part of a conception of public reason when they either are or could be shared by different contending conceptions of the good."[138] Weinstock argues that a value can be appealed to in the public justification of a policy when one of three conditions is met: (*i*) some value λ is shared by all conceptions of

[134] Nozick, *Anarchy, State and Utopia*, p. ix.
[135] Weinstock, "Neutralizing Perfection," p. 47. See also Lister, "Public Justification and the Limits of State Action."
[136] Weinstock, "Neutralizing Perfection," p. 47.
[137] Ibid.
[138] Ibid., p. 55.

the good; (*ii*) some value λ is presupposed by all conceptions of the good, in the sense that all conceptions of the good require λ for their realization; and (*iii*) there is empirical evidence that some actions are required to promote everyone's values. "For example, non-coercive measures promoting physical exercise can ultimately be grounded in the empirically verifiable view that moderate amounts of exercise contribute causally both to the length and to the quality of life, as can the state's mildly coercive policies aimed at making smoking less attractive." [139]

Weinstock's three basic claims are correct. Insofar as all Members of the Public share some value in their Λ, or have sufficient reason for believing empirical propositions that have manifest implications for their values, appealing to such values and claims can enter into the public justification of a policy. However, we cannot move from the claim that (*i*) value λ is embraced by every Member of the Public to (*ii*) λ provides each Member of the Public with a sufficient reason to endorse *y*, the policy recommended by λ. The crucial problem, of course, is that in Λ, the Member of the Public's unrestricted ranking, λ, may be ranked lower than some value that defeats the case of *y*. If this is the case for Alf, he will conclude that his unrestricted set of values gives him reason to *oppose y*, not endorse it. Recall that our main disagreements about the good are not about what is of value, but the relative importance of values (§14.4*b*). Consequently, even if everyone agrees that smoking causes cancer, and that cancer is a very bad thing, Members of the Public clearly disagree about whether the pleasures are worth the risk of death. Given that Members of the Public weigh the relative values of pleasure and safety differently, coercive acts that can be justified only on the grounds that the pleasure does not outweigh the risk to health fail to be publicly

---

[139] Weinstock, "Neutralizing Perfection," p. 55. Mill contrasts "authoritative" laws that require coercion from "unauthoritiative" ones that do not. "It is evident," said Mill, "even at first sight, that the authoritative form of government intervention has a much more limited sphere of legitimate action than the other. It requires a much stronger necessity to justify it in any case; while there are large departments of human life from which it must be unreservedly and imperiously excluded." *Principles of Political Economy*, p. 937 (Bk. V, chap. xi, §2). As Mill recognized, whether there is a significant "unauthoritatve" sphere depends on whether one does not consider the taxation funding such policies a coercive measure that renders the policy itself coercive.

justified. Thus, although the badness of ill health caused by smoking can, as Weinstock says, help to publicly justify a law, that its badness outweighs the goodness of the pleasure of smoking cannot; and without that, no state policies discouraging smoking will be justified.[140]

This same problem applies to any simple appeal to "goods that we all share." There is a long tradition in moral and political philosophy of arguing that since we all agree on what is good, these are impartial considerations. According to Baier, for example:

I take a person's good, what is for his good, to be roughly things such as health, wealth, power, longevity, having friends, about which experience suggests that they are a good thing from anyone's point of view. . . . We are quite confident in saying that everyone prefers being healthy to being sick, that everyone is better able to attain his objectives whatever they may be if he is healthy rather than sick and so on. Nevertheless, even in the case of health what makes it important, really worth caring about, being of value to one, is the central and almost indispensable role it plays in virtually everything one wants to do.[141]

Surely we all – or at least very nearly all – can agree to advance these values or goods. Again, though, to publicly justify an optional policy it is not sufficient to show that we all accept these values or goods, but that there is a trade-off rate or ranking that Members of the Public endorse in their unrestricted set of values (Λ). But one of the ongoing disputes in our society is, for example, the proper way to trade off our interest in making our own choices (the value of liberty) and the good of being healthy. Consider the case of mandatory motorcycle helmet laws. The point of helmet laws is to advance motorcyclists' good by keeping them alive and healthy. From the perspective of that ingredient of their good, it seems to many uncontroversial that motorcyclists have reason to embrace such laws. But many motorcyclists prefer the freedom to choose – to run the risk of a serious accident and brain damage, to ride with

---

[140] This has, I believe, implications for the justifiability of United States drug policy, which is based on certain middle-class value rankings, and which results in policies that place inordinate costs on the poor. See J. Donald Moon, "Drugs and Democracy."

[141] Kurt Baier, "Comments," p. 216.

the wind in their hair – and so resent these laws because they take away their freedom of choice. Now many legislators appear to assert that there is a trade-off rate that all Members of the Public would embrace: it is unreasonable to reject mandatory helmet laws because the health gains outweigh the losses to liberty. To many motorcyclists, however, this is simply the trade-off rate of middle-class, middle-aged people, who are risk-averse. Is it is not clear that it is the motorcyclists who are being unreasonable.

The thought that the public justification constraint absurdly stultifies public policy runs together two different claims: (*i*) if in Alf's unrestricted set of values Λ, the reasons supporting policy *y* are defeated by the reasons for *x*, Alf does not have sufficient reason to endorse *x* over *y* and (*ii*) if Alf ranks *x* over *y*, *y* must be an ineligible public policy. The first claim is quite sound, and it is why mere appeal to Alf's holding a value λ that endorses *y* does not justify the imposition of *y* on Alf. Justification is about the strength of competing reasons, not simply whether one has *some* reason to endorse a policy. But this does not mean that *y* is not included in the eligible set, and so a justified political authority may not impose it. Consider again the case of speed limits. We might think that speed limits could not be publicly justified since some prefer the thrill of speeding to being safe. Suppose, though, we are considering a public policy to build a road, and all concur that many different plans are better than no road at all. In our thrill seeker's unrestricted ordering, we may assume that plans without speed limits are ranked higher than those with speed limits, but many plans with speed limits are preferred to no road at all. (If not, the person probably wants a race track, not a road.) In the rankings of some others, roads without speed limits may well be ineligible, as they may reasonably hold that such roads would be too dangerous to bother building. In this case a strict public justification principle would hold that roads with speed limits can be justified to all.

25.3 PRACTICAL PARETIANISM

A vast amount of public policy is based on a sort of quasi-utilitarianism, in which the total social costs and benefits of a policy are calculated, such that if the total social costs are greater than the total social benefits, the policy is justified.[142] Some individuals are coerced simply to benefit others. To be sure, such aggregately collective action could be genuinely justified if each Member of the Public approved of pursuit of the overall social benefit. But few think this is the case. The pursuit of a great deal of what we call "public" policy simply cannot be endorsed by all Members of the Public.

To avoid this conclusion (i.e., that the Pareto criterion is violated by a proposed uniform public policy) some welfare economists and "Paretian" political philosophers have adopted the Kaldor–Hicks criterion. Suppose we are now presently at social state S_1 and a policy would bring about social state S_2, in which some Members of the Public are worse off (in terms of their Λ, S_2 is ranked lower than S_1). According to the Kaldor–Hicks criterion, the move from S_1 to S_2 satisfies the Pareto test of efficiency so as long as those who gain from the move *could* compensate the losers out of their gains.[143] Suppose Alf is the sole person who has been made worse off by the move from S_1 to S_2 (to make the case simple, assume that everyone else is better off in S_2). Now imagine that after the move to S_2 the gainers transferred enough of their gains to Alf such that he was not worse off; this would bring about a new distribution, S_3, which is indeed Pareto-superior to S_1 because everyone except Alf prefers S_3 to S_1, and Alf is indifferent. We can say, then, that S_2 is Kaldor–Hicks Pareto-superior to S_1 if there is a distribution S_3 that (*i*) could be produced by redistributing the gains made by moving from S_1 to S_2 and (*ii*) S_3 is (in the normal sense) Pareto-superior to S_1. Note the Kaldor–Hicks test says that given (*i*) and (*ii*), S_2 is Pareto-superior to S_1 even though no actual compensation has been paid. Distribution S_3 is that in which compensation actually has been made, but Kaldor–Hicks does not say simply that S_3 is Pareto superior to S_1; it says that S_2 is Pareto-superior to (more efficient than) S_1 even though some people have actually incurred losses by

---

[142] For an accessible overview, see Daniel Hausman and Michael S. McPherson, *Economic Analysis, Moral Philosophy, and Public Policy,* chap. 9.

[143] For examples of contemporary welfarists who rely on this test, see Richard A. Epstein, *Skepticism and Freedom;* Louis Kaplow and Steven Shavell, *Fairness versus Welfare.* This test is also fundamental to much social cost–benefit analysis.

the move from S_1 to S_2. Because S_2 *could* give rise to S_3, and because S_3 *would* be Pareto superior to S_1, S_2 *is* Kaldor–Hicks Pareto-superior to S_1.

This is very odd: the Pareto criterion, which was based on the denial that gains for some can outweigh losses for others, is now employed to justify policies that benefit some at the expense of others.[144] The move from S_1 to S_2 makes some people worse off, yet it is justified as a Pareto improvement. Now if there was some attempt to actually compensate losers – if the state pursued a practical Paretianism that sought an approximation of S_3 – we could say that the policy was practically publicly justified. Of course, the justification would be approximate; given information and transactions costs, all those who gained and lost could not be identified, nor could the precise gains and losses be specified. But actual policy typically is only approximately justified by any cost–benefit analysis; our calculations are always second-best approximations. It is worth stressing, though, that the application of the Kaldor–Hicks test in current policy contexts means that much of the information needed for compensation has already been obtained. Classes of beneficiaries and losers have been identified, and their gains and losses have been calculated. So it is not as if we can have no idea of the affected classes of persons (such as road users, people living around the widened road) and how much they gain and lose; to a significant extent we already have such information but do not use it. Again, the lesson is that practical Paretianism by no means implies the end of useful public policies – at least not those that have Paretian rationales.

Another path to practical Paretianism is through Buchanan–Tullock supermajority rules (§22.2). In the justification of an optional public policy, it cannot be argued that we may presently be at an unjust status quo and so should be suspicious of decision-making systems that, in effect, require large majorities to move us out of it. Here the supposition is that these policies approach Pareto improvements; unless the policy really approximates such improvements, its coercive imposition is unjustifiable. Now it

---

[144] Hausman and McPherson show that the Kaldor–Hicks test only identifies more efficient distributions under restrictive assumptions. *Economic Analysis, Moral Philosophy, and Public Policy,* chap. 9.

might be thought that at best public policies are really quasi-public, being endorsed by the overwhelming majority but not by all, and although compensation to losers may not always be possible and probably never complete, everyone can see the wisdom of allowing public action when a large majority approves it. No one, it may be thought, would wish to live in a society in which a few could block a policy (we must always remember that this problem arises only when compensation is not possible). As Buchanan and Tullock have shown (recall Display VIII-3), the internal costs of a unanimity rule would be high, encouraging holdouts and bluffing. Legislative rules that, in effect, require large majorities to approve of public policies while always seeking to compensate losers constitute the heart of real public reason's theory of justified public policy.

Yet another device of practical Paretianism is to explicitly allow exceptions to public policies that we know some groups do not have reason to endorse. Allowing religious-based exemptions from military or education requirements is, of course, part of the history of American public policy. The United Kingdom also has instituted such exemptions (e.g., Sikhs are exempted by the 1998 Motor Cycles [Protective Headgear] Regulations from the legal requirement to wear motorcycle helmets). Of course, complexities and difficulties arise when a legislative body seeks to craft legislation that allows such exemptions. There are always worries that the possibility of obtaining an exemption may encourage deceit from those who endorse the aims of the legislation but who nevertheless seek the exemption. We confront the endemic worry about free riding on socially usefully policies. Legislators also must consider whether the exemptions are so instituted as to put heavy legal burdens on those who cannot rationally endorse the policy (e.g., requiring complex opt-out procedures), such that there are strong practical incentives for them to submit to unjustified impositions. In some cases it might be fairer to allow blanket opt-outs of entire ranges of policy to some groups.[145] My aim here is not to point to solutions to these important problems but to stress that even when a Member of the Public cannot endorse a public policy, it does not follow that others must do without the policy. As with the

[145] See the very thoughtful treatment of these issues by Lucas Swaine, *The Liberal Conscience.*

European Union, the remaining citizens might reconstitute themselves into a different public (a "core group") on this issue.

Some advocate a different route to practical Paretianism: employ roughly majoritarian legislative rules, but suppose that over a long run of cases, the nature of democratic politics will give all their share of their most preferred quasi-public policies, so that, overall, everyone's interests are advanced through what we might call policy democracy.[146] Buchanan and Tullock demonstrated the fallacy at the heart of this view.[147] In matters of optional public policy we suppose that individuals are very often simply motivated by advancing their own ends (the unrestricted set Λ); if each is subject to a series of majoritarian bargains to advance his interests – sometimes being in the winning majority and sometimes the losing minority – not just the minority, but everyone can lose. So far from being a form of practical Paretianism, this type of democratic policy can lead to strongly Pareto-inferior results, in which everyone is worse off.

To see this, consider a small town of 1,000 that meets to democratically decide on expenditures. Say the town is composed of five equal-sized groups (each has 200 voters):

(*YF*) Young Families who want to spend money to improve the primary schools. They would pay $600 each if they had to purchase the improvements themselves.

(*OW*) Older and Wealthier Citizens, who want to improve the local golf course. They too would pay $600 each if they had to purchase the improvements themselves.

(*YP*) Yuppies, who want to close off the main street and pave it with cobblestones. Again, it is worth $600 to each Yuppy to do this.

(*TC*) Those with Teenage Children, who support improved facilities at the town recreation center: these improvements are worth $600 to each of this group.

---

[146] I believe Christiano holds this general view of democracy. He clearly sees that persistent minorities pose a challenge to this view, since they never get to win. I maintain that *everyone* may lose. See *The Constitution of Equality*, pp. 288ff.

[147] James M. Buchanan and Gordon Tullock, *The Calculus of Consent*, chap. 10. The example in the text is based on their analysis.

(*OR*) Outlying Residents who want to have some side roads paved. These improvements are worth $600 to each Outlying Resident.

Suppose the Young Families put forward their proposal. They need the support of two other groups if the proposal is to pass. Say they agree to trade votes with OW and YP: the Young Families agree to support the proposal of those other two groups in exchange for their support of school improvements. Now each of the families knows that the school improvements are worth $600 to them; but they also know that they will have to support the OW and YO groups when they propose their own plans; they do not wish their total tax bill for all three projects to exceed $600, since that is what their own project is worth to them. Say, then, that they are willing to bear $200 in taxes in support of their own project, $200 to support golf course improvements, and $200 to pay for the Yuppies' paving of the pedestrian mall, for a total of $600. But if everyone in the community is taxed $200 to support school improvements, the community can raise $200 × 1,000, or $200,000 for school improvements. By themselves, the 200 in this group were willing to pay $600, for a total of $120,000. So they seem to get an additional $80,000 worth of improvements for free. So they agree. The coalition is formed, and the measure passes.

At the next meeting the Older and Wealthier group (who favor golf course improvements) put forward their proposal. The Young Families are committed to supporting it, so it already has 400 votes. But they need additional votes. The pro–golf course adults decide to trade votes with the Outlying Residents (good roads are always a good idea). The calculations are precisely the same as with the coalition formed by the Young Families. The pro-golfing adults are willing to bear $200 in taxes in support of their own project, $200 of taxes to support the school improvement they already have voted for, and the $200 they are expecting to pay for paving roads as part of their vote trading with the Outlying Residents. But if everyone in the community is taxed $200 to support the golf course, the community can raise $200 × 1,000, or $200,000 for the improvements. By themselves, the 200 in this group were willing to pay $600, or only $120,000. So they seem also to get an additional $80,000 worth of improvements for free. So they too agree.

Now the Yuppies come forward. They want their paved pedestrian mall. They have the promise of the Young Families, but they need another group's support, so they enlist those with Teenage Children. Another deal is done. Again if everyone is taxed $200, the Yuppies can get $200,000 for their project, even though they would only pay $120,000 if they purchased it privately. Next the families with Teenage Children (TC) advance their proposal. They have the promise of the Yuppies but they need another group's support, so they enlist the Outlying Residents. Another deal is done. Again if everyone is taxed $200 TC can get $200,000 for their project, even though they would pay only $120,000. Finally the Outlying Residents come forward. They already have the promises of the golf course group (OW) and the teenage parents group (TC), so their measure also passes. Display VIII-16 sums up the bargains and total tax rates.

	Coalition Partners	Tax
Young Families (YF)	OW, YP	$200
Older and Wealthier (OW)	YF, OR	$200
Yuppies (YP)	YF, TC	$200
Families with Teenage Children (TC)	YP, OR	$200
Outlying Residents (OR)	OW, TC	$200
Total tax		$1000

DISPLAY VIII-16 MAJORITY VOTING LEADING TO OVEREXPENDITURE ON POLITICALLY SECURED GOODS

Notice that each ends up paying $1,000 even though, if each had purchased the good themselves he would have spent only $600. Because some of the cost could be pushed onto the dissenting minority, each group bought more improvement than they thought worthwhile, ending up with a too-expensive package of improvements. Insofar as each person had more preferred ways to spend the additional $400, each is worse off under this form of collective provision.

The problem is shifting coalitions; as coalitions are reformed adding new members, vote-trading deals proliferate and ever more projects, with ever more taxation, get approved. In the end, this form of democracy exemplifies just the sort of N-person Prisoners' Dilemma that we are seeking to avoid through public policy. All persons or groups can see that it would be good to restrain their efforts to form coalitions for more public spending, since the aggregation of such legislation can lead to the overexpenditure we have just considered. But no group has an incentive to do so. As far as each is concerned, the dominant strategy is to defect on restraint. If others are going to form coalitions to get what they want, the best thing for one to do is to form a coalition to get what one wants. And if others do restrain themselves, again the best thing to do is to form coalitions to secure the quasi-public goods one values. Thus all have an incentive to seek to secure more goods through politics than they really wish to pay for, leading to the type of strongly Pareto-inferior result we have been battling against throughout this work.

CONCLUSION

In this chapter I have examined the relation between the moral and the political orders. While we wish to avoid the mistake of social contract theory of putting the political order at the heart of social morality, we do not want to make the error of undervaluing it. I have argued that the political order is a powerful but dangerous tool; its ability to employ high levels of coercion means that it can quickly move us away from immoral social conventions at which we have been stuck. For the same reason, it can move us to any convention, publicly justified or not. The difference between the classical liberal tradition and what is known as the "new" liberalism is not simply about the justification of property rights but the basic attitude toward state coercion. In his influential statement of the new liberalism, Hobhouse criticized the classical liberal's constant worry that the coercion of the state was a threat to liberty.[148] Today too, many "new" or "egalitarian" liberals simply do not see the worry about using state-backed force; classical liberals understand both that the state's force is both a requirement of a free political order and a serious threat to it. I have argued in

---

[148] L. T. Hobhouse, *Liberalism*, esp. chap. VIII.

this chapter that the costs of coercion require justification, and we can expect a political order of public reason to economize on the use of this dangerous but necessary tool.

Libertarians, on the other hand, err by leaping from a well-founded worry about state coercion to a rejection of almost all (or perhaps even all) state authority. Unless the laws have de jure authority, I have argued, they cannot form the ground of a political order among free and equal persons. Without authority, the laws of the state cannot perform their core function of articulating and protecting our fundamental moral rights. We can think of this critical function of the state as the continuation of moral justification by other means. And only some sort of democratic order can justifiably perform this task.

It is important to distinguish this core task from pure policy functions of the state, where the aim is simply to secure the satisfaction of our goals through collective state action. My remarks on public policy in an order of public reason were regrettably sketchy. My main aim was not to develop a theory of public policy in an order of public reason but to stress how different the justification of such pure policy is from the justification of the core tasks of liberal legislation and, further, to dispel the suspicion that publicly justified policy is ultimately impossible. Admittedly, an order that pursues practical Paretianism will have a far more limited agenda than our current states. To some this shows the error of my approach; many presuppose that political philosophy must in the end justify the range of activities engaged in by our current liberal-like states. The task of political philosophy, however, is not to legitimate current regimes but to examine the conditions under which political coercion can be justified to all, and all can live in a free social and political order.

Concluding Remarks on Moral Freedom and Moral Theory

The philosopher's stone that transforms individual goal pursuit into social restraints on goal pursuit is, like other alchemical projects, enticing but misguided. Large-scale cooperative social orders among anonymous strangers are possible because we are rule followers. Our reason did not produce social order – we did not reason ourselves into being followers of social rules. Rather, the requirements of social order shaped our reason. Although we most certainly are social creatures who have been shaped under norm-guided social life, we need not submit to the demands of the social and moral orders that confront us. To assert one's status as a free moral person is to interrogate claims to moral authority over one; to recognize others as one's moral equals is to reflect on the justifiability of one's own moral demands on them. Social rules provide order and render possible a cooperative social life. They also may oppress, discriminate, and employ social pressure to maintain outdated and unjust practices.

Social-moral rules that pass the test of public justification are endorsed by the reason of all. If moral persons, each devoted to her own goals, ends, and ideals, can endorse the moral rules of the social order as genuinely morally authoritative, each can freely act on the system of social moral authority with which she is confronted. Social freedom does not consist in the freedom to act on one's goals without restraint; a free person subjects herself to moral authority endorsed by her own ends in life and her own standards of acceptable behavior. Justified morality is neither derived from our goals and ideals nor divorced from them. A publicly justified morality serves our ends by limiting our pursuit of them. An order of public reason is not one in which people constantly deliberate and discuss. It is an order that conforms to the reason of all; it is not a process of reasoning or agreement but a rational moral equilibrium that allows each to be an autonomous subject of the moral laws.

Given our status as agents devoted to our own evaluative standards, an order of public reason will secure for all agency rights and core jurisdictions. Thus an order of public reason will be an order of freedom in another sense: not only can each endorse its authority, but these authority claims provide wide-ranging protection for each to act on her evaluative standards and ends, and ensures each a realm in which her evaluative standards have public, moral standing. The full development and protection of this system of rights requires the authority of the democratic state. The political order is needed to complete and reform the moral order, and so we must not be too impressed by the relentless criticisms of the state and its authority pressed by philosophical anarchists and libertarians. But neither should we forget the power of coercive laws to enforce unjustified rules. All states, including democratic ones, have enacted seriously unjust legislation. We must interrogate all claims to authority over us, including that of the state. When law is outside the eligible set, it can have no authority over us. Design and reform of political institutions must seek structures that avoid such enactments.

Many moral philosophers will object; an order of public reason will not be a morally free order because some must submit to moral rules they judge to be authoritative, but far inferior to their own ideal rules. Only if the moral rules of one's society conform to one's ideal social morality, we are told, can one be morally free. This is either deluded, authoritarian, or nihilistic. It is deluded if one thinks that there is such a morality that passes the test of public justification. We confront genuine and often deep moral disagreement, which is not simply due to the fact that some benighted or stupid souls cannot see the truth. In our pluralistic world, rational and goodwilled people will not agree on an ideal moral code or theory of justice. To insist that there is a uniquely just or correct ideal code, a substantive set of rights and duties, or clear distributional norms that are authoritative for all ends up an exercise in moral authoritarianism. Regrettably, much moral philosophy succumbs to the authoritarian temptation, taking up the role of ideal legislator; we are told that our society is unjust – that its norms and laws are without bona fide moral authority – unless it is egalitarian, prioritarian, sufficientarian, libertarian, communitarian, or utilitarian, or that we must do that which best promotes human perfection, flourishing, happiness, welfare, or virtue. Ensconced in his study, the philosopher arrogantly assumes the role of moral legislator, telling us all what is required for true moral authority. Teaching these conflicting moral blueprints, each claiming unique authority over all, we suggest to our students that moral philosophy offers a menu of choices, from which they should select any one they wish, and show on the final that it is uniquely correct. The best are apt to see the implicit lesson – that this babble of mutually depreciatory voices shows that there is no moral truth. Hence the ultimate lesson in nihilism.

To be sure, there is nothing wrong with philosophers painting their personal pictures of ideal moralities and social orders, and sharing them with their colleagues and students. Indeed, it is admirable, for these paintings can move us, and perhaps in the end will produce changes in an order of public reason. Reform of the moral order is often induced by revisions in the evaluative standards of its participants, which may be spurred by the philosopher's depictions of her ideal social morality. But we must not forget that while these ideals are about social morality, they remain personal ideals: they are personal ideals of philosophers about what a social morality should look like. If they are in the eligible set, they may be selected, but they have no authority until they are. As personal ideals, they neither possess moral authority over others, nor does the moral order's failure to conform to them undermine its authority. A true morality may well be within our grasp, and if we achieve it, there is moral freedom for all. The moral philosopher, impressed by her own rectitude, who proclaims that as we move away from her ideal we move away from a justified true morality, becomes the unwitting enemy of a free moral order.

Appendix A

The Plurality of Morality

Perhaps because we are still under the spell of Plato in so many ways, we are apt to suppose there is some single, fairly coherent practice called "morality" about which there are competing accounts or "theories." It is common to hear, for example, that according to "virtue ethics," morality is about the evaluation of character and not – at least not directly and primarily – about the evaluation of acts. Or, as most of us have said in the classroom, deontological theories conceive of morality as centered on acts, not consequences. And it has been claimed that "morality ought to be understood primarily as a matter of what one does or does not do to oneself rather [than] what one does or does not do to others."[1] We assume that these different theories genuinely disagree because they are competing theories of the same thing. If the thing called "morality" is primarily about character, it cannot also be primarily about act evaluations. If the thing called "morality" is primarily a matter about what one does to oneself, it cannot also be primarily a matter about what one does to others. So we often understand our "theories of morality" as competing theories describing and explaining the same phenomenon. Indeed, moral philosophers often identify themselves in terms of the adherence to one or the other theory explaining what morality is all about.

---

[1] Robert B. Louden, *Morality and Moral Theory*, p. 5.

It may seem obvious that from the perspective of some moral theories, this supposition – that we are confronted by a relatively unitary subject matter about which philosophers present sharply different accounts – is grounded in views about the metaphysics of morality. If moral values are to be analyzed as in some way being, or arising out of, "objective values" that, in some straightforward sense (as opposed to the rather thin senses of "real" that many "realists" and "quasi-realists" proffer) are "out there" to be studied, the correct theory is the one that best accounts for these values. (Note how difficult it is to even phrase the point.) Other theories are then simply wrong. Call this the "objectivity thesis." J. L. Mackie, though a harsh critic of the objectivity thesis, nevertheless believed that it was a feature of "ordinary thought" about moral-ity.[2] However, the objectivity thesis is not enough to ground the view that morality is a unitary phenomenon (or a coherent group of phenomena) that applies primarily to character, or to acts, or to interpersonal relations, or to self-perfection, or what have you. To ground the unitary view an objectivist would need to show that "objective" values are such that they primarily concern only character, or acts, or interpersonal relations, and so on. Recall Isaiah Berlin's view that there is "a plurality of values, equally genuine, equally ultimate, above all equally objective; incapable, therefore, of being ordered in a timeless hierarchy, or judged in terms of some one absolute standard."[3] For Berlin, then, plural values are objective – "There is a world of objective values."[4] As Berlin stresses, objectivity by no means implies monism: moral values could be ever so objective, and yet morality might not present a coherent object of study in the sense we have been considering. We may confront an objective realm of moral values that cannot be captured by any unified "moral theory."[5] If morality as a whole is a unitary object of study capable of being accounted for by a single coherent "moral theory," all moral judgments must be of a single type, reducible to single type, or the various types must be capable of

---

[2] J. L. Mackie, *Ethics: Inventing Right and Wrong*, p. 31.

[3] Isaiah Berlin, "Alleged Relativism in Eighteenth-Century Thought," p. 79.

[4] Isaiah Berlin, "The Pursuit of the Ideal," p. 11. On Berlin's conception of objectiv-ity, see my *Contemporary Theories of Liberalism: Public Reason*, pp. 27–31.

[5] Except in the sense of an account of why no unitary explanation or justification of our moral judgments is possible.

being organized into a coherent system.[6] Call this the "monistic thesis." Without the monistic thesis, as Berlin so nicely shows, the objectivity thesis does not support the common claim that morality is primarily about acts, or consequences, or character, or other-regarding acts, or whatever. But observe now that despite initial appearances, the objectivity thesis is not relevant at all, for an anti-objectivist who endorses the monistic thesis still will see all of morality as a unitary and organized subject matter, primarily focusing on acts, or character, or whatever. Our concern is, then, the monistic thesis, not the objectivity thesis.

Michael Gill has convincingly argued that twentieth-century meta-ethics has overwhelmingly supposed the monistic thesis.[7] From G. E. Moore and W. D. Ross, through C. L. Stevenson, R. M. Hare to Alan Gibbard and Michael Smith (and a host of others), twentieth century meta-ethics debated whether "morality" is best explained on realist or nonrealist grounds, whether moral statements are prescriptive, or descriptive, or expressivist, whether moral judgments are simply external or linked to an agent's internal reasons for actions. As Gill shows, so deep is the monistic assumption that when philosophers are confronted with moral statements or practices that do not fit into their favored theory, they claim that these are either "secondary" or perhaps simply bogus. Hare, who, as I argued, advances important insight about the core prescriptive function of social morality (§2.1), aspires to make his analysis fully general: if a person makes a moral judgment that has no practical effect at all on Betty – she says "yes it would be wrong to do that; so what?"– the judgment is a "fraud."[8] Smith uses softer language, saying that such people "do not *really* make moral judgments at all."[9] Yet for David Brink these are genuine, nonmotivating moral judgments: their status as bona fide judgments shows

---

[6] The same point could be framed in terms of plural standards of judgments, or plural basis for evaluation, and so on. At this point seeking too much precision would, I think, be more of a distraction than an aid.

[7] See Michael Gill, "Indeterminacy and Variability in Metaethics" and his "Meta-ethical Variability, Incoherence and Error." I am following Gill's excellent analysis in this paragraph.

[8] R. M. Hare, *Sorting Out Ethics*, p. 119.

[9] Michael Smith, *The Moral Problem*, p. 66.

that Hare's and Smith's "internalism" must be wrong.[10] Underlying the entire debate is supposition that the preferred account must be applicable to all judgments classified as "moral." Thus, for Hare and Smith, if there is a judgment that does not have the necessary internal link to motivation, it is not a genuine moral judgment. To Brink, since there are some genuine judgments that do not have the requisite link, internalism is not the proper account of morality as it does not apply to all moral judgments, thus leading us to externalism.

It is striking that so much of the last one hundred years of moral philosophy has been built on the monistic thesis, yet there is precious little defense of it. On the face it, is seems unlikely that the diverse practices and judgments that we call "moral" should have such a neat, monistic structure. Consider the range of moral judgments and moral evaluations we encounter:

a. Alf claims a right against Betty not to be harmed; they recognize each other as fellow moral agents. The point of the claim is practical: Alf wants Betty to cease harming him.

b. Alf reflects on what duties he owes to nonagents, such as very young children. His point again seems practical.

c. Alf reflects on his duties to protect the environment. His point still seems practical.

d. Betty reads a newspaper and remarks to Alf that the government of a foreign state acted immorally. The main point here may be expressive or descriptive.

e. Alf reflects one evening on the immorality of Athenian imperialist wars. The point here seems neither practical nor expressive.

f. Betty criticizes Alf for being too quick to anger and insensitive to the feelings of others, which she thinks are moral faults. She is evaluating Alf's character, apparently with practical aims, perhaps simply expressively.

---

[10] David Brink, *Moral Realism and the Foundations of Ethics*, pp. 47ff.

g. Alf is a coach of a Little League team, and has to decide whether it is fair to start his son in a playoff game.[11]

h. Nearing his own death, Alf reflects on his deceased father's character as weak and lacking in courage; the point seems neither practical nor expressive.

i. Alf reflects that the outcome of a sporting event was evil because one participant was incompetent.[12]

j. Alf likes to have kinky sex with consenting adults. Betty thinks he is immoral and a pervert.

k. Betty likes to think about kinky sex, and considers herself immoral and a pervert for doing so.

l. Alf likes to think about oppressing others, and has never told anyone of his fantasies. He has never acted on his fantasies and is a longtime member of Amnesty International. He considers himself to be morally flawed because of his fantasies.

m. Over a long period Alf subtly – without coercion or duress – undermines Betty's ability to decide for herself, so that her agency is undermined, and she becomes subservient to him. Charlie reads about this and judges Alf to be evil.

n. Betty decides, all on her own, to live a life of debauchery; she never violates anyone's rights nor asks for anyone's assistance. Alf thinks she has wasted her life – a grave immorality.

o. Alf is deciding whether to take a job, and decides that it would be wrong to do so since the job involves duties that violate *his* ideals.[13] He does not think that all good people must ascribe to these ideals.

p. Alf is sure that it is wrong for women to have less than equal rights in liberal democracies but is uncertain about whether it is wrong in some traditional societies.

[11] See Alan H. Goldman, *Practical Rules: When We Need Them and When We Don't*, p. 27.

[12] See Christine Swanton, *Virtue Ethics: A Pluralistic View*, p. 36.

[13] "George says that *he* cannot accept this [job], since *he* is opposed to chemical and biological warfare. Bernard Williams, "A Critique of Utilitarianism," pp. 97–8, emphasis added.

q. Alf decides that it would be wrong for him to order the torture of a terrorist suspect even though that means he may fail to save the lives of some innocents: the act is intrinsically wrong, perhaps evil.[14]

r. Max Weber tells Alf in *q* to grow up and accept that he must do intrinsically evil things like torture to produce good consequences if he wants to go into politics. *If* he wishes to keep his hands clean, he should keep out of politics.[15]

s. Alf knows that the instrumental returns of voting approach zero so he never votes. It is, he says, irrational. When he conveys this view at a meeting of the American Philosophical Association, the audience is morally shocked. One person in the audience remarks, "I thought you were a good man!"

t. Betty agrees with Alf in *s* that her vote has no consequential effect but believes it is right to vote because it symbolizes her devotion to democracy.

Those upholding the monistic thesis must claim that this diverse list of practices and judgments displays a unity and structure; they all are about the coherent thing called "morality." Some claim that all of these cases are primarily expressive, or prescriptive, or descriptive; or that all are primarily about acts, or consequences, or character. Or perhaps many can be eliminated as illusory cases of morality, so that only the primarily prescriptive, expressive, or descriptive remain. Or we might seek some set of principles that renders them all coherent in a reflective equilibrium.[16] These are all familiar projects; I put them aside in this inquiry. Perhaps the

---

[14] Cf. Michael Walzer, "Political Action: The Problem of Dirty Hands," pp. 166–7.

[15] Max Weber, "Politics as a Vocation," especially pp. 120–3.

[16] For doubts about the usefulness of the widely accepted *method* of "reflective equilibrium," see my *Justificatory Liberalism*, pp. 101–8. See also Millgram, *Ethics Done Right*, p. 10. Sidgwick ultimately despaired of finding "scientific order" in the diversity of our commonsense moral judgments. "We have examined the moral intuitions that present themselves with a *prima facie* claim to furnish independent and self-evident rules of morality: and we have in each case found that from such regulation as the Common Sense of mankind really supports, no proposition can be elicited that, when fairly contemplated, even appears to have the characteristic of a scientific axiom." *The Methods of Ethics,* p. 360. Sidgwick's concern was the content of commonsense morality; my concern has been the forms of activity and concerns over which it ranges.

monistic thesis can be defended, but it is certainly reasonable to remain skeptical. As David Lewis remarked concerning his own account of value, he did not pretend to capture "the one precise sense that the word 'value' bears in pure speech uncorrupted by philosophy, that is heard on the Clapham omnibus." What Lewis says of "value" is true of "morality" and "ethics" – they exhibit "semantic variation and semantic indecision."[17] In this book I seek to develop an account of one type of moral practice. Even here we may be unable to capture the entire semantic content of the practice; but the necessary trimming and selecting will be much more modest than required in grand "theories of morality" and, I hope to show, is justified by the nature of the practice itself. In any event, it is crucial to realize that much of what we call "morality" lies entirely outside the scope of this book.

---

[17] David Lewis, "Dispositional Theories of Value," p. 86. Once again I am indebted to my colleague Michael Gill for pointing me to Lewis's antimonistic supposition. Gill also cites W. D. Falk as skeptical of the monistic thesis.

Appendix B

Economic Freedom in States that Best Protect Civil Rights

Display A-1 on the next page presents comparative data from three databases. The table includes all states that are deemed to best honor civil rights according to Freedom House's 2008 data. (http://www.freedomhouse.org/template.cfm?page=414&year=2008).

The table shows the scores of these states on measures of economic freedom and protection of property rights drawn from (*i*) Gwartney, Lawson, and Norton, *Economic Freedom of the World: 2008 Annual Report*, Digital copy available from www.fraserinstitute.org, www.freetheworld.com and (*ii*) the Heritage Foundation, "Index of Economic Freedom" 2008 data, http://www.heritage.org/Index. (These data are used with permission of Freedom House, the Fraser Institute, and the Heritage foundation.) Note that these data do not include states that do well on measures of economic freedom and protection of property rights but that score low on protection of civil liberties, such as Singapore. Doing reasonably well at protecting property and securing economic freedom is crucial for securing civil liberties — it is clearly not in any way sufficient.

Country	Property and Legal Protection/ Gwartney. Rank (1–141)	Property Rights Protection Score/ Heritage Foundation (100–0)	Economic Freedom/ Gwartney Rank (1–141)	Economic Freedom Score/Heritage Foundation (100–0)
Finland	1	90	14	75
Denmark	2	90	13	79
Norway	3	88	23	69
New Zealand	4	90	3	80
Iceland	5	90	12	77
Austria	7	90	15	71.2
Australia	8	90	8	8
Switzerland	8	90	4	80
Germany	9	90	17	71
Netherlands	10	90	16	77
Sweden	13	90	33	70
Canada	14	90	7	80
U.K.	15	90	5	80
Luxemburg	17	90	21	75
Japan	18	70	27	72
Ireland	19	90	10	82
United States	21	90	8	81
France	22	70	45	65
Estonia	26	90	11	78
Portugal	28	70	47	64
Belgium	30	80	44	72
Chile	31	90	6	80
Barbados	35	90	98	71
Lithuania	37	50	31	70
Costa Rica	39	50	21	65
Spain	40	70	32	70
Hungary	41	70	28	67
Taiwan	42	70	18	71
Greece	43	50	54	70
Italy	48	50	49	62
Israel	49	70	76	66
Czech Rep.	52	70	63	69
Slovenia	57	50	88	61
Poland	62	50	69	60
Ghana	65	50	66	57
Cape Verde	NA	70	NA	59

DISPLAY A-1 ECONOMIC FREEDOM IN STATES THAT BEST PROTECT CIVIL RIGHTS

Bibliography

Alexander, Jason and Brian Skyrms. "Bargaining with Neighbors: Is Justice Contagious?" *Journal of Philosophy*, vol. 96 (November 1999): 588–98.

Alexander, Larry and Emily Sherwin. *The Rule of Rules: Morality, Rules and the Dilemmas of Law*. Durham, NC: Duke University Press, 2001.

Allison, Henry E. *Kant's Theory of Freedom*. Cambridge: Cambridge University Press, 1990.

Anand, Paul. *Foundations of Rational Choice under Risk*. Oxford: Oxford University Press, 1995.

Anderson, Scott. "Coercion." *Stanford Encyclopedia of Philosophy* (Spring 2006 edition), edited by Edward N. Zalta. http://plato.stanford.edu/archives/spr2006/entries/coercion/.

Argyle, Michael. *The Psychology of Interpersonal Behavior*, third edition. Harmondsworth: Penguin, 1978.

Arrow, Kenneth J. "Risk Perception in Psychology and Economics." *Economic Inquiry*, vol. 20 (1982): 1–9.

Arthur, W. Brian. *Increasing Returns and Path Dependency in the Economy*. Ann Arbor: University of Michigan Press, 1994.

Audi, Robert. *The Structure of Justification*. Cambridge: Cambridge University Press, 1993.

"Liberal Democracy and the Place of Religious Argument in Politics." In *Religion in the Public Square: The Place of Religious Convictions in Political Debate*, edited by Robert Audi and Nicholas Wolterstorff. Lanham, MD: Rowman and Littlefield, 1997: 25–33.

Religious Commitment and Secular Reason. Cambridge: Cambridge University Press, 2000.

The Architecture of Reason: The Substance and Structure of Rationality. Oxford: Oxford University Press, 2001.

Aumann, Robert T. "Utility Theory without the Completeness Axiom." *Econometrica*, vol. 30 (1962): 445–62.

Axelrod, Robert. *The Evolution of Cooperation*. New York: Basic Books, 1974.

Baier, Kurt. "The Point of View of Morality." *Australasian Journal of Philosophy*, vol. 32 (1954): 104–35.

 The Moral Point of View: A Rational Basis for Ethics. Ithaca, NY: Cornell University Press, 1958. [Unless explicitly noted, all citations to *The Moral Point of View* are to this edition.]

 The Moral Point of View: A Rational Basis for Ethics, abridged edition. New York: Random House, 1965.

 The Rational and the Moral Order: The Social Roots of Reason and Morality. La Salle, IL: Open Court, 1995.

 "Comments." In *Reason, Ethics, and Society: Themes from Kurt Baier, with His Responses*, edited by J. B. Schneewind. Chicago: Open Court, 1996: 210–86.

Barnett, Randy. *The Structure of Liberty: Justice and the Rule of Law*. New York: Oxford University Press, 1998.

Baron, Jonathan and James Jurney. "Norms against Voting for Coerced Reform." *Journal of Personality and Social Psychology*, vol. 64 (1993): 347–55.

Barry, Brian. *Theories of Justice*. Berkeley: University of California Press, 1989.

 Justice as Impartiality. Oxford: Clarendon Press, 1995.

Becker, Gary. *The Economic Approach to Human Behavior*. Chicago: University of Chicago Press, 1976.

Becker, Lawrence C. *Property Rights: Philosophical Foundations*. London: Routledge & Kegan Paul, 1977.

Benn, Piers. "Freedom, Resentment, and the Psychopath." *Philosophy, Psychiatry & Psychology*, vol. 6 (1999): 29–39.

Benn, S. I. "Personal Freedom and Environmental Ethics." In *Equality and Freedom: International and Comparative Jurisprudence*, edited by Gray Dorsey. Dobbs Ferry, NY: Oceana Publications, vol. 2, 1977: 401–24.

 "Privacy, Freedom and Respect for Persons." In *Philosophical Dimensions of Privacy*, edited by Ferdinand Schoeman. Cambridge: Cambridge University Press 1984: 223–44.

 A Theory of Freedom. Cambridge: Cambridge University Press, 1988.

Benn, S. I. and G. F. Gaus. "Public and Private: Concepts and Action." In *Public and Private in Social Life*, edited by S. I. Benn and G. F. Gaus. New York: St. Martin's Press, 1983: 3–27.

 "Practical Rationality and Commitment." *American Philosophical Quarterly*, vol. 23 (1986): 255–66.

Benn, S. I. and G. W. Mortimore. "Technical Models of Rational Choice." In *Rationality and the Social Sciences*, edited by S. I. Benn and G. W. Mortimore. London: Routledge and Kegan Paul, 1976: 157–96.

Berlin, Isaiah. "Two Concepts of Liberty." In his *Four Essays on Liberty*. Oxford: Oxford University Press, 1969: 149–50.

"Alleged Relativism in Eighteenth-Century European Thought." In *The Crooked Timber of Humanity: Chapters in the History of Ideas*, edited by Henry Hardy. Princeton: Princeton University Press, 1990: 70–90.

"The Pursuit of the Ideal." In *The Crooked Timber of Humanity: Chapters in the History of Ideas*, edited by Henry Hardy. Princeton: Princeton University Press, 1990: 1–19.

Berthoz, Alain. *Emotion and Reason: The Cognitive Neuroscience of Decision Making*, translated by Giselle Weiss. Oxford: Oxford University Press, 2003.

Bicchieri, Cristina. *The Grammar of Society: The Nature and Dynamics of Norms*. Cambridge: Cambridge University Press, 2006.

Bicchieri, Cristina and Alex Chavez. "Behaving as Expected: Public Information and Fairness Norms." *Journal of Behavioral Decision Making*, vol. 23 (2010): 161-178.

Bicchieri, Cristina and Erte Xiao. "Do the Right Thing: But Only if Others Do So." *Journal of Behavioral Decision Making*, vol. 22 (2009): 191-208.

Bickel, Alexander. *The Least Dangerous Branch: The Supreme Court at the Bar of Politics*, 2nd ed. New Haven: Yale University Press, 1986.

Binmore, Ken. *Natural Justice*. Oxford: Oxford University Press, 2005.

Blackburn, Simon. "Practical Tortoise Reasoning." *Mind*, new series, 104 (1995): 695–711.

Ruling Passions. Oxford: Clarendon Press, 1998.

Blackstone, William. *Commentaries on the Laws of England in Four Books*. Philadelphia: J. B. Lippincott, 1893, 2 vols.

Bolton, Gary E. "A Comparative Model of Bargaining: Theory and Evidence." *American Economic Review*, vol. 81 (1991): 1096–136.

Bond, E. J. *Reason and Value*. Cambridge: Cambridge University Press, 1983.

Bonjour, Laurence. *The Structure of Empirical Knowledge*. Cambridge, MA: Harvard University Press, 1985.

Bosanquet, Bernard. *The Philosophical Theory of the State*. In *The Philosophical Theory of the State and Related Essays*, edited by Gerald F. Gaus and William Sweet. Indianapolis: St. Augustine Press, 2001: 1–293.

Boyd, Robert, Herbert Gintis, Samuel Bowles, and Peter J. Richerson. "The Evolution of Altruistic Punishment." In *Moral Sentiments and Material Interests: The Foundations of Cooperation in Economic Life*, edited by Herbert Gintis, Samuel Bowles, Robert Boyd, and Ernst Fehr. Cambridge, MA: MIT Press, 2005: 215–27.

Boyd, Robert and Peter J. Richerson. *Culture and the Evolutionary Process*. Chicago: University of Chicago Press, 1985.

"The Evolution of Indirect Reciprocity." *Social Networks*, vol. 11 (1989): 213–36.

The Origin and Evolution of Culture. Oxford: Oxford University Press, 2005.

Braine, Martin D. S. "On the Relation between the Natural Logic of Reasoning and Standard Logic." *Psychological Review*, vol. 78 (January 1978): 1–21.

Braine, Martin and B. Rumain. "Development of Comprehension of 'Or': Evidence for a Sequence of Competencies." *Journal of Experimental Child Psychology*, vol. 31 (1981): 46–70.

Brandt, Richard. *A Theory of the Good and the Right*. Oxford: Clarendon Press, 1979.

Branscombe, Nyla and Anca M. Miron. "Interpreting the Ingroup's Negative Actions Towards Another Group: Emotional Actions to Appraised Harm." In *The Social life of the Emotions*, edited by Larissa Z. Tidens and Colin Wayne Leach. Cambridge: Cambridge University Press, 2004: 314-35.

Bratman, Michael E. *Faces of Intention*. Cambridge: Cambridge University Press, 1999.

   Intention, Plans and Practical Reason. Stanford, CA: CSLI Publications, 1999.

Brink, David. *Moral Realism and the Foundations of Ethics*. Cambridge: Cambridge University Press, 1989.

Broome, John. "Rationality and the Sure-thing Principle." In *Thoughtful Economic Man*, edited by J. Gay Tulip Meeks. Cambridge: Cambridge University Press, 1991: 74–102.

Brower, Gordon H. and Joseph P. Forgas. "Affect, Memory, and Social Cognition." In *Cognition and Emotion*, edited by Eric Eich, et. al. Oxford: Oxford University Press, 2000: 87–168.

Bryon, Michael, ed. *Satisficing and Maximizing: Moral Theories on Practical Reason*. Cambridge: Cambridge University Press, 2004.

Buchanan, James. *The Limits of Liberty: Between Anarchy and Leviathan*. Chicago: University of Chicago Press, 1975.

   "Taxation in Fiscal Exchange." In *The Collected Works of James M. Buchanan*, vol. I: *The Logical Foundations of Constitutional Liberty*. Indianapolis, IN: Liberty Fund, 1999: 133–49.

Buchanan, James and Gordon Tullock. *The Calculus of Consent*. Ann Arbor: University of Michigan Press, 1962.

Bury, Chris and Howard L. Rosenberg. "A Man's Home Is His Castle, and He Can Defend It." February 1, 2008, http://abcnews.go.com/Nightline/story?id=4272882&page=1.

Caldwell, Bruce. *Hayek's Challenge: An Intellectual Biography of F. A. Hayek*. Chicago: University of Chicago Press, 2004.

Cameron, L. "Raising the Stakes in the Ultimatum Game: Experimental Evidence from Indonesia." *Economic Inquiry*, vol. 37 (1999): 47–59.

Caplan, Bryan. *The Myth of the Rational Voter*. Princeton: Princeton University Press, 2007.

Carlyle, Thomas. *Past and Present*. London: Dent, 1960.

Carroll, Lewis. "What the Tortoise Said to Achilles," *Mind*, new series, vol. 4 (1895): 278–80.

Chang, Ruth, ed. *Incommensurability, Incomparability, and Practical Reason*. Cambridge, MA: Harvard University Press, 1997.

Chapman, John W. "Voluntary Association and the Political Theory of Pluralism." In *NOMOS XI: Voluntary Associations*, edited by J. Roland

Pennock and John W. Chapman. New York: Atheron Press, 1969: 87–118.

Cheng, Patricia W. and Keith J. Holyoak. "On the Natural Selection of Reasoning Theories." *Cognition*, vol. 33 (1989): 285–313.

Cherniak, Christopher. *Minimal Rationality*. Cambridge, MA: MIT Press, 1986.

Christiano, Thomas. *The Constitution of Equality*. Oxford: Oxford University Press, 2008.

"Must Democracy Be Reasonable?" *Canadian Journal of Philosophy*, vol. 39 (March 2009): 1–34.

Christman, John. *The Myth of Property: Toward an Egalitarian Theory of Ownership*. Oxford: Oxford University Press, 1994.

Church, Jennifer. "Morality and the Internalized Other." In *The Cambridge Companion to Freud*, edited by Jerome Neu. Cambridge: Cambridge University Press, 1992: 209–23.

Cialdini, R., C. Kallgren, and R. Reno, "A Focus Theory of Normative Conduct: A Theoretical Refinement and Reevaluation of the Role of Norms in Human Behavior." *Advances in Experimental Social Psychology*, vol. 24 (1990): 201–34.

Coase, Ronald. "The Problem of Social Cost." *Journal of Law and Economics*, vol. 3 (1960): 1–44.

The Firm, the Market and the Law. Chicago: University of Chicago Press, 1998.

Cohen, Gerald A. "Facts and Principles." *Philosophy and Public Affairs*, vol. 31 (2003): 211–45.

Cohen, Josuha. "Democracy and Liberty." In *Deliberative Democracy*, edited by Jon Elster. Cambridge: Cambridge University Press, 1998.

Constant, Benjamin. "The Liberty of the Ancients Compared with that of the Moderns." In *Political Writings of Benjamin Constant*, edited by Biancamria Fontana. Cambridge: Cambridge University Press, 1988: 308–28.

Cooper, William S. *The Evolution of Reason: Logic as a Branch of Biology*. Cambridge: Cambridge University Press, 2001.

Copp, David. *Morality, Normativity and Society*. New York: Oxford University Press, 1995.

Cosmides, Leda. "The Logic of Social Exchange: Has Natural Selection Shaped How Humans Reason? Studies with the Wason Selection Task." *Cognition*, vol. 31 (1989): 187–276.

Cosmides, Leda and John Tooby. "Evolutionary Psychology and the Generation of Culture, Part II. Case Study: A Computational Theory of Social Exchange." *Ethology and Sociobiology*, vol. 10 (1989): 51–97.

Courtland, Shane, "Public Reason and the Hobbesian Dilemma." *Hobbes Studies*, vol. 20 (2007): 63–92.

Craven, John. *Social Choice*. Cambridge: Cambridge University Press, 1992.

Cummins, Denise Dellarosa. "Evidence for the Innateness of Deontic Reasoning." *Mind & Language*, vol. 11 (June 1996): 160–90.

"Evidence of Deontic Reasoning in 3- and 4-year-olds." *Memory and Cognition*, vol. 24 (1996): 823–829.

"The Evolutionary Roots of Intelligence and Rationality." In *Commonsense, Reasoning, and Rationality*, edited by Renée Elio. Cambridge: Cambridge University Press, 2002: 132–47.

Cushman, Fiery. "Crime and Punishment: Distinguishing the Roles of Causal and Intentional Analyses in Moral Judgment." *Cognition*, vol. 108 (2008): 353–80.

Dagger, Richard. "Philosophical Anarchism and Its Fallacies: A Review Essay." *Law and Philosophy*, vol. 19 (May, 2000): 391–406.

D'Agostino, Fred. "Incommensurability and Commensuration: Lessons from (and to) Ethico-Political Theory." *Studies in the History and Philosophy of Science*, vol. 31 (2000): 429–47.

Incommensurability and Commensuration: The Common Denominator. Aldershot, Hampshire: Ashgate, 2003.

D'Agostino, Fred and Gerald Gaus. "Public Reason: Why, What and Can (and Should) It Be?" In *Public Reason*, edited by Fred D'Agostino and Gerald Gaus. Aldershot, UK: Ashgate, 1998: xi–xxiii.

"Contemporary Approaches to the Social Contract" in the *Stanford Encyclopedia of Philosophy*, 2008; http://plato.stanford.edu/entries/contractarianism-contemporary/.

Dancy, Jonathan. *Ethics without Principles.* Oxford: University Press, 2004.

Darby, Derrick. "Two Conceptions of Rights Possession." *Social Theory and Practice*, vol. 27 (July 2001): 387–417.

Darwall, Stephen L. "Two Kinds of Respect. *Ethics*, vol. 88 (October 1977): 36–49.

"Reasons, Motives, and the Demands of Morality: An Introduction." In *Moral Discourse and Practice*, edited by Stephen Darwall, Allen Gibbard, and Peter Railton. Oxford: Oxford University Press, 1997: 305–12.

The Second-Person Standpoint: Morality, Respect and Accountability. Cambridge, MA: Harvard University Press, 2006.

Davis, Morton D. *Game Theory.* Mineola, NY: Dover, 1983.

Dawes, T. Christopher, James H. Fowler, Tim Johnson, Richard McElreath, and Oleg Smirnov. "Egalitarian Motives in Humans." *Nature*, vol. 446 (12 April 2007): 794–96.

De Sousa, Ronald. "Modeling Rationality: Normative or Descriptive?" In *Modeling Rationality, Morality and Evolution*, edited by Peter Danielson. Oxford: Oxford University Press, 1998: 119–34.

Diggs, B. J. "The Common Good as a Reason for Political Action," *Ethics*, vol. 83 (July 1973): 283–93.

Drier, James. "Decision Theory and Morality." In *The Oxford Handbook of Rationality*, edited by Alfred R. Mele and Piers Rawling. Oxford: Oxford University Press, 2004: 156–181.

Dryzek, John. "Democratic Theory." In *The Handbook of Political Theory*, edited by Gerald F. Gaus and Chandran Kukathas. London: Sage, 2004: 143–54.

Dukeminier, Jesse and James E. Krier, eds. *Property*, 5th ed. New York: Aspen, 2002.

Dworkin, Gerald. *The Theory and Practice of Autonomy*. Cambridge: Cambridge University Press, 1988.

Dworkin, Ronald. "The Original Position." In *Reading Rawls*, edited by Norman Daniels. Oxford: Blackwell, 1975: 16–53.

  Taking Rights Seriously. Cambridge, MA: Harvard University Press, 1978.

  Sovereign Virtue: The Theory and Practice of Equality. Cambridge, MA: Harvard University Press, 2000.

Eberle, Christopher J. *Religious Conviction in Liberal Politics*. Cambridge: Cambridge University Press, 2002.

Edwards, Carolyn Pope. "Culture and the Construction of Moral Values." In *The Emergence of Morality in Young Children*, edited by Jerome Kagan and Sharon Lamb. Chicago: University of Chicago Press, 1987: 123–54.

Ekman, Paul. "Biological and Cultural Contributions to Body and Facial Movement in the Expression of Emotions." In *Explaining Emotions*, edited by Amélie O. Rorty. Berkeley: University of California Press, 1980: 103–26.

Ekman, Paul, Wallace V. Friesen, and Phoebe Ellsworth. *Emotion in the Human Face*. New York: Pergamon, 1972.

Eliaz, Kfir and Efe A. Ok. "Indifference or Indecisiveness? Choice-Theoretic Foundations of Incomplete Preferences." *Games and Economic Behavior*, vol. 56 (2006): 61–86.

Elles, Ellery. *Rational Decision and Causality*. Cambridge: Cambridge University Press, 1982.

Elster, Jon. "The Nature and Scope of Rational-Choice Explanation." In *Actions and Events: Perspectives on Donald Davidson*, edited by E. LaPore and B. McLaughlin. Oxford: Blackwell, 1985: 60–72.

  "The Market and Forum." In *Deliberative Democracy: Essays on Reason and Politics*, edited by James Bohman and William Rehg. Cambridge, MA: MIT Press, 1997: 3–34.

Engelmann, Dirk and Urs Fischbacher. "Indirect Reciprocity and Strategic Reputation Building in an Experimental Helping Game," *Institute for Empirical Research in Economics*, University of Zurich, Working Paper 1424–0459 (April 2, 2008).

  Accessed at www.iew.unizh.ch/wp/iewwp132.pdf.

Epstein, Richard. *Skepticism and Freedom*. Chicago: University of Chicago Press, 2003.

Estlund, David. *Democratic Authority*. Princeton: Princeton University Press, 2008.

Ewin, R. E. *Liberty, Community and Justice*. Totowa, NJ: Rowman and Littlefield, 1987.

  Virtues and Rights: The Moral Philosophy of Thomas Hobbes. Boulder, CO: Westview Press, 1991.

Falk, Armin, Ernst Fehr and Urs Fischbacher. "Driving Forces behind Informal Sanctions." IZA Discussion Paper No. 1635 (June 2005). Available at SSRN: http://ssrn.com/abstract=756366.

Fehr, Ernst and Urs Fischbacher. "The Economics of Strong Reciprocity."
    In *Moral Sentiments and Material Interests: The Foundations of Cooperation
    in Economic Life*, edited by Herbert Gintis, Samuel Bowles, Robert
    Boyd, and Ernst Fehr. Cambridge, MA: MIT Press, 2005: 151–91.
    "Modeling Strong Reciprocity." In *Moral Sentiments and Material Interests:
    The Foundations of Cooperation in Economic Life*, edited by Herbert
    Gintis, Samuel Bowles, Robert Boyd, and Ernst Fehr. Cambridge, MA:
    MIT Press, 2005: 193–227.
Fehr, Ernst and Simon Gächter. "Cooperation and Punishment in Public
    Goods Experiments." *American Economic Review*, vol. 90 (Sept. 2000):
    980–94.
    "Fairness and Retaliation: The Economics of Reciprocity." *Journal of Eco-
    nomic Perspectives*, vol. 14 (Summer 2000): 159–81.
Fehr, Ernst and Klaus M. Schmidt. "A Theory of Fairness, Competition,
    and Cooperation." *Quarterly Journal of Economics*, vol. 114 (August
    1999): 817–68.
Feinberg, Joel. *Social Philosophy*. Englewood Cliffs, NJ: Prentice-Hall, 1973.
    "The Interest of Liberty in the Scales." In his *Rights, Justice, and the
    Bounds of Liberty*. Princeton: Princeton University Press, 1980: 30–44.
    Harm to Others. New York: Oxford University Press, 1984.
Ferguson, Adam. *An Essay on the History of Civil Society*, edited by Fania
    Oz-Salzberger. Cambridge: Cambridge University Press, 1996.
Fiddick, Laurence. "Adaptive Domains of Deontic Reasoning." *Philosophi-
    cal Explorations*, vol. 9 (March 2006): 105–16.
Filmer, Robert. "Directions for Obedience to Government in Dangerous or
    Doubtful Times." In *Patriarcha and Other Political Works*, edited by
    Peter Laslett. Oxford: Blackwell, 1949: 231–36.
    "Patriarcha" in *Patriarcha and Other Political Works*, edited by Peter
    Laslett. Oxford: Blackwell, 1949: 49–126.
    The Anarchy of a Limited or Mixed Monarchy. In *Patriarcha and Other Writ-
    ings*, edited by Johann P. Sommervile. Cambridge: Cambridge Univer-
    sity Press, 1991: 131–71.
Fishkin, James S. *Beyond Subjective Morality: Ethical Reasoning and Political
    Philosophy*. New Haven, CT: Yale University Press, 1984.
Foley, Richard. *The Theory of Epistemic Rationality*. Cambridge, MA: Har-
    vard University Press, 1987.
Foot, Philippa. *Virtues and Vices*. Berkeley: University of California Press,
    1978.
Forst, Rainer. "Political Liberty: Integrating Five Conceptions of Auton-
    omy." In *Autonomy and the Challenges to Liberalism*, edited by John
    Christman and Joel Anderson. Cambridge: Cambridge University
    Press, 2005: 226–44.
Fowler, James H., Tim Johnson, and Oleg Smirnov. "Egalitarian Motive
    and Altruistic Punishment." *Nature*, vol. 433 (6 January 2004): E1.
Freedom House. "Freedom in the World 2008,"
    http://freedomhouse.org/.

Freeman, Samuel. "Illiberal Libertarians: Why Libertarianism Is Not a Liberal View." *Philosophy & Public Affairs*, vol. 30 (2001): 105–51.

"The Burdens of Justification: Constructivism, Contractualism and Publicity," *Politics, Philosophy & Economics*, vol. 6 (February 2007): 5–44.

Justice and the Social Contract: Essays on Rawlsian Political Philosophy. Oxford: Oxford University Press. 2007.

Freud, Sigmund. *A General Introduction to Psychoanalysis*, translated by Joan Riviere. New York: Liveright, 1935.

Totem and Taboo, translated by James Strachey. New York: W.W. Norton, 1950.

Civilization and Its Discontents, edited and translated by James Strachey. New York: W.W. Norton, 1961.

Introductory Lectures on Psychoanalysis, translated by James Strachey. Harmondsworth: Penguin Books, 1973.

"Inhibitions, Symptoms and Anxieties" in *On Psychopathology*, edited by Angela Richards, translated by James Strachey. Harmondsworth: Penguin, 1979: 229–315.

"On the Grounds for Detaching a Particular Syndrome from Neurasthenia under the Descriptions 'Anxiety Neurosis.'" In *On Psychopathology*, edited by Angela Richards, translated by James Strachey. Harmondsworth: Penguin, 1979: 33–63.

Friedman, Richard B. "On the Concept of Authority in Political Philosophy." In *Concepts in Social and Political Philosophy*, edited by Richard E. Flathman. New York: Macmillan, 1973: 121–45.

Frijda, Nico H. *The Emotions*. Cambridge: Cambridge University Press, 1986.

Fuller, Lon. *The Morality of Law*, rev. ed. New Haven, CT: Yale University Press, 1969.

Gaertner, Wulf. *A Primer in Social Choice Theory*. Oxford: Oxford University Press, 2006.

Ganghof, Steffen. "Must Democracy Be Supermajoritarian? Justificatory Liberalism and Political Institutions." Manuscript, University of Potsdam.

Gat, Aza. *War in Human Civilization*. Oxford: Oxford University Press, 2006.

Gaus, Gerald F. "Public and Private Interests in Liberal Political Economy, Old and New." In *Public and Private in Social Life*, edited by S. I. Benn and G. F. Gaus. New York: St. Martin's Press, 1983: 183–221.

Value and Justification. Cambridge: Cambridge University Press, 1990.

"Sentiments, Evaluations and Claims." *Criminal Justice Ethics*, vol. 11 (Summer/Fall, 1994): 7–15.

Justificatory Liberalism: An Essay on Epistemology and Political Theory. New York: Oxford University Press, 1996.

"Reason, Justification and Consensus: Why Democracy Can't Have It All." In *Deliberative Democracy*, edited by James Bohman and William Rehg. Cambridge, MA: MIT Press, 1997: 207–42.

"Respect for Persons and Environmental Values." In *Autonomy and Community: Readings in Contemporary Kantian Social Philosophy,* edited by Jane Kneller and Sidney Axin. Albany: SUNY Press, 1998: 239–64.

"Why All Welfare States (Including Laissez-Faire Ones) Are Unreasonable." *Social Philosophy and Policy,* vol. 15 (1998): 1–33.

Social Philosophy. Armonk, NY: M. E. Sharpe, 1999.

Political Concepts and Political Theories. Boulder, CO: Westview, 2000.

"What Is Deontology? Part Two: Reasons for Action." *Journal of Value Inquiry,* vol. 35 (2001): 179–93.

"The Legal Coordination Game." *American Philosophical Association's Newsletter on Philosophy and Law,* vol. 1 (2002): 122–28.

"Goals, Symbols, Principles: Nozick on Practical Rationality." In *Robert Nozick,* edited by David Schmidtz. Cambridge: Cambridge University Press, 2002: 105–30.

"Taking the Bad with the Good: Some Misplaced Worries about Pure Retribution." In *Legal and Political Philosophy,* edited by Enrique Villanueva. Amsterdam: Rodopi, 2002: 339–62.

"Backwards into the Future: Neo-Republicanism as a Post-Socialist Critique of Market Society." *Social Philosophy & Policy,* vol. 20 (2003): 59–91.

Contemporary Theories of Liberalism: Public Reason as a Post-Enlightenment Project. London: SAGE, 2003.

"Dirty Hands." In *The Blackwell Companion to Applied Ethics,* edited by R. G. Frey and Kit Wellman. Oxford: Basil Blackwell, 2003: 169–79.

"Once More unto the Breach, My Dear Friends, Once More: McMahon's Attempt to Solve the Paradox of the Prisoner's Dilemma." *Philosophical Studies,* 116 (2003): 159–70.

"The Place of Autonomy in Liberalism." In *Autonomy and the Challenges to Liberalism,* edited by John Christman and Joel Anderson. Cambridge: Cambridge University Press, 2005: 272–306.

"The Evolution of Society and Mind: Hayek's System of Ideas." In *The Cambridge Companion to Hayek,* edited by Ed Feser. Cambridge: Cambridge University Press, 2006: 232–58.

"The Rights Recognition Thesis: Defending and Extending Green." In *T. H. Green: Metaphysics, Ethics and Political Philosophy,* edited by Maria Dimovia-Cookson and William Mander. Oxford: Oxford University Press, 2006: 208–35.

"Social Complexity and Evolved Moral Principles." In *Liberalism, Conservatism, and Hayek's Idea of Spontaneous Order,* edited by Peter McNamara. London: Palgrave Macmillan, 2007: 149–76.

On Philosophy, Politics, and Economics. Belmont, CA: Thomson-Wadsworth, 2008.

"Reasonable Utility Functions and Playing the Cooperative Way." *Critical Review of International and Social Philosophy.* vol. 11 (June 2008): 215–34.

"Controversial Values and State Neutrality in *On Liberty*." In *Mill's On Liberty: A Critical Guide*, edited by C. L. Ten. Cambridge: Cambridge University Press, 2009: 83–104.

"Is the Public Incompetent? Compared to Whom? About What?" *Critical Review: A Journal of Politics and Society*, vol. 20 (2009): 291–311.

"The Place of Religious Belief in Public Reason Liberalism." In *Multiculturalism and Moral Conflict*, edited by Maria Dimovia-Cookson and P.M.R. Stirk. London: Routledge, 2009: 19-37.

"On Two Critics of Justificatory Liberalism." *Politics, Philosophy and Economics*, vol. 9 (May, 2010): 177–212.

Gaus, Gerald F. and Kevin Vallier. "The Roles of Religious Conviction in a Publicly Justified Polity: The Implications of Convergence, Asymmetry and Political Institutions." *Philosophy & Social Criticism*, vol. 35 (January 2009): 51 –76

Gauthier, David. *The Logic of Leviathan*. Oxford: Oxford University Press, 1969.

Morals by Agreement. Oxford: Clarendon Press, 1986.

"Why Contractrianism?" In *Contractarianism and Rational Choice*, edited by Peter Vallentyne. Cambridge: Cambridge University Press, 1991: 15–30.

"Assure and Threaten," *Ethics*, vol. 104 (July 1994): 690–721.

"Public Reason," *Social Philosophy & Policy*, vol. 12 (1995): 19–42.

"Commitment and Choice: An Essay on the Rationality of Plans." In *Ethics, Rationality, and Economic Behavior*, edited by Francesco Farina, Frank Hahn, and Stefano Vannucci. Oxford: Clarendon Press, 1996: 217–43.

"Rethinking the Toxin Problem." In *Rational Commitment and Social Justice*, edited by Jules Coleman and Christopher W. Morris. Cambridge: Cambridge University Press, 1998: 47–58.

Geertz, Clifford. "Person, Time and Conduct in Bali." In his *The Interpretation of Culture*. New York: Basic Books, 1973: 360–411.

Gert, Bernard. *Morality: A New Justification of the Moral Rules*. Oxford: Oxford University Press, 1988 [revised edition of *The Moral Rules*, 1966].

Gert, Joshua. *Brute Rationality*. Cambridge: Cambridge University Press, 2004.

Gewirth, Alan. *Reason and Morality*. Chicago: University of Chicago Press, 1978.

Human Rights: Essays on Justification and Applications. Chicago: University of Chicago Press, 1982.

Gibbard, Alan. *Wise Choices, Apt Feelings: A Normative Theory of Judgment*. Cambridge, MA: Harvard University Press, 1990.

Gilbert, Margaret. *A Theory of Political Obligation*. Oxford: Clarendon Press, 2006.

Gill, Emily. *Becoming Free: Autonomy and Diversity in a Liberal Polity*. Lawrence: University Press of Kansas, 2001.

Gill, Michael. "Meta-ethical Variability, Incoherence and Error." In *Moral Psychology,* vol. 2: *The Cognitive Science of Morality: Intuition and Diversity,* edited by W. Sinnott-Armstrong. Cambridge: MIT Press, 2008: 387–402.

"Indeterminacy and Variability in Metaethics." *Philosophical Studies,* 145 (2009): 215–34.

Gintis, Herbert. *Game Theory Evolving.* Princeton: Princeton University Press, 2000.

The Bounds of Reason: Game Theory and the Unification of the Behavioral Sciences. Princeton: Princeton University Press, 2009.

Gintis, Herbert, Samuel Bowles, Robert Boyd, and Ernst Fehr. "Moral Sentiments and Material Interests: Origins, Evidences and Consequences." In their edited volume *Moral Sentiments and Material Interests: The Foundations of Cooperation in Economic Life.* Cambridge, MA: MIT Press, 2005: 3–39.

Goffman, Erving. *The Presentation of Self in Everyday Life.* Harmondsworth: Penguin, 1971.

Goldman, Alan H. *Empirical Knowledge.* Berkeley: University of California Press, 1988.

Practical Rules: When We Need Them and When We Don't. Cambridge: Cambridge University Press, 2002.

"The Rationality of Complying with Rules: Paradox Resolved." *Ethics,* vol. 116 (April 2006): 453–70.

Gray, John. *Post-Enlightenment Liberalism.* London: Routledge, 1993.

The Two Faces of Liberalism. Oxford: Polity, 2000.

Green, Leslie. *The Authority of the State.* Oxford: Oxford University Press, 1988.

Green, T. H. *Lectures on the Principles of Political Obligation.* In *Lectures on the Principles of Political Obligation and Other Writings,* edited by Paul Harris and John Morrow. Cambridge: Cambridge University Press, 1986: 13–193.

"Liberal Legislation and Freedom of Contract." In *Lectures on the Principles of Political Obligation and Other Writings,* edited Paul Harris and John Morrow. Cambridge: Cambridge University Press, 1986: 194–212.

"On the Different Senses of 'Freedom' as applied to the Will and the Moral Progress of Man." In *Lectures on the Principles of Political Obligation and Other Writings,* edited by Paul Harris and John Morrow. Cambridge: Cambridge University Press, 1986: 228–49.

Greenawalt, Kent. *Religious Convictions and Political Choice.* New York: Columbia University Press, 1988.

Private Consciences and Public Reasons. New York: Oxford University Press, 1995.

Greene, Joshua D. "The Secret Joke of Kant's Soul." In *Moral Psychology,* vol. 3: *The Neuroscience of Morality,* edited by Walter Sinott-Armstrng. Cambridge, MA: MIT Press, 2008: 35–79.

Greene, Joshua D., Leigh E. Nystrom, Andrew D. Engell, John M. Darely, and Jonathan D. Cohen. "The Neural Bases of Cognitive Conflict and Control in Moral Judgment." *Neuron,* vol. 44 (2001): 389–400.

Greene, Joshua D., R. Brian Sommerville, Leigh E. Nystrom, John M. Darely, and Jonathan D. Cohen. "An fMRI Investigation of Emotional Engagement in Moral Judgment." *Science,* vol. 293 (14 Sept. 2001): 2105–8.

Grey, Thomas C. "The Disintegration of Property." In *NOMOS XXII: Property,* edited by J. Roland Pennock and John W. Chapman. New York: New York University Press, 1980: 69–85.

Gwartney, James D. and Robert Lawson; with Seth Norton. *Economic Freedom of the World: 2008 Annual Report.* Economic Freedom Network. Digital copy available from www.fraserinstitute.org, www.freetheworld.com.

Habermas, Jürgen. "Popular Sovereignty as Procedure." In *Deliberative Democracy: Essays on Reason and Politics,* edited by James Bohman and William Rehg. Cambridge, MA: MIT Press, 1997: 35–66.

Hammond, Peter. "Consequentialist Foundations for Expected Utility." *Theory and Decision,* vol. 25 (1988): 25–78.

Hampton, Jean E. *Hobbes and the Social Contract Tradition.* Cambridge: Cambridge University Press, 1986.

The Authority of Reason. Cambridge: Cambridge University Press, 1998.

Hardin, Garret. "The Tragedy of the Commons." *Science,* vol. 162 (1968): 1243–48.

Hardin, Russell. *Indeterminacy and Society.* Princeton: Princeton University Press, 2003.

Hare, R. M. *Freedom and Reason.* Oxford: Clarendon Press, 1963.

Moral Thinking: Its Levels, Method and Point. Oxford: Clarendon Press, 1981.

Essays in Ethical Theory. Oxford: Clarendon Press, 1989.

Sorting Out Ethics. Oxford: Oxford University Press, 1997.

Harman, Gilbert. *Change in View: Principles of Reasoning.* Cambridge, MA: MIT Press, 1986.

Reasoning, Meaning, and Mind. Oxford: Oxford University Press, 1999.

Harris, Paul L. and María Núñez. "Understanding of Permission Rules by Preschool Children." *Child Development,* vol. 67 (August 1996): 1572–91.

Harsanyi, John C. "Cardinal Welfare, Individualistic Ethics, and Interpersonal Comparisons of Utility." In his *Essays on Ethics, Social Behavior and Scientific Explanation.* Boston: D. Reidel, 1976: 6-23.

"Can the Maximin Principle Serve as a Basis for Morality?" In his *Essays on Ethics, Social Behavior and Scientific Explanation.* Boston: D. Reidel, 1976: 37–63.

Hart, H. L. A. "Are There Natural Rights?" *Philosophical Review,* vol. 64 (April 1955): 175–91.

The Concept of Law. Oxford: Clarendon Press, 1961.

"Rawls on Liberty and Its Priority." In *Reading Rawls*, edited by Norman Daniels. New York: Basic Books, 1974: 223–52.

"Legal Rights." In his *Essays on Bentham: Studies in Jurisprudence and Political Theory*. Oxford Clarendon Press, 1983: 162–93.

Hausman, Daniel and Michael S. McPherson, *Economic Analysis, Moral Philosophy and Public Policy*, 2nd ed. Cambridge: Cambridge University Press, 2006.

Hayek F. A. "The Use of Knowledge in Society." *American Economic Review*, vol. 35 (Sept. 1945): 519–30.

The Counter-Revolution of Science. New York: Free Press, 1955.

The Constitution of Liberty. Chicago: University of Chicago Press, 1960.

"Notes on the Evolution of Systems of Rules of Conduct." In his *Studies in Philosophy, Politics, and Economics*. Chicago: University of Chicago Press, 1967: 66–81.

Rules and Order, vol. 1 of *Law, Legislation and Liberty*. Chicago: University of Chicago Press, 1973.

"The Pretence of Knowledge." In his *New Studies in Politics, Economics and the History of Ideas*. London: Routledge, 1978: 25–34.

The Political Order of a Free People, vol. 3 of *Law, Legislation and Liberty*. Chicago: University of Chicago Press, 1979.

The Fatal Conceit: The Errors of Socialism, edited by W. W. Bartley II. Chicago: University of Chicago Press, 1988.

Heath, Joseph. *Following the Rules: Practical Reasoning and Deontic Constraint*. Oxford: Oxford University Press, 2008.

Henrich, Joseph and Natalie Smith. "Comparative Evidence from Machiguenga, Mapuche, and American Populations." In *Foundations of Human Sociality: Economic Experiments and Ethnographic Evidence from Fifteen Small-Scale Societies*, edited by J. Henrich, R. Boyd, S. Bowles, et al. Oxford: Oxford University Press, 2004: 125–67.

Henrich, Natalie and Joseph Henrich. *Why Humans Cooperate: A Cultural and Evolutionary Explanation*. Oxford: Oxford University Press, 2007.

Hinde, Robert A. *Bending the Rules: The Flexibility of Absolutes in Modern Life*. Oxford: Oxford University Press, 2007.

Hobbes, Thomas. *The Elements of Law, Natural and Politic*, edited by Ferdinand Tönnies. London: Cass, 1969.

De Cive. In *Man and Citizen*, edited by Bernard Gert. New York: Anchor Books, 1972.

Leviathan, edited by Edwin Curley. Indianapolis, IN: Hackett, 1994.

Hobhouse, L. T. *Mind in Evolution*. London: Macmillan, 1901.

Social Evolution and Political Theory. New York: Columbia University Press, 1911.

Development and Purpose. London: Macmillan, 1927.

Liberalism. Oxford: Oxford University Press, 1964.

Hodgson, Geoffrey M. *Economics and Evolution: Bringing Life Back into Economics*. Ann Arbor: University of Michigan Press, 1993.

Hoffman, E., K. Shachat, and V. Smith. "Preferences, Property Rights and Anonymity in Bargaining Games." *Games and Economic Behavior*, vol. 7 (1994): 346–80.

Hohfeld, Wesley. *Fundamental Legal Conceptions as Applied in Judicial Reasoning.* New Haven: Yale University Press, 1919.

Holborow, L. C. "Blame, Praise, and Credit." *Proceedings of the Aristotelian Society*, new series, vol. 72 (1971–2): 85–100.

Holmes, Stephen. *Benjamin Constant and the Making of Modern Liberalism.* New Haven: Yale University Press, 1984.

Honoré, A. M. "Ownership." In *Oxford Essays in Jurisprudence*, edited by A. G. Guest. Oxford: Clarendon Press, 1961: 107–47.

Hooker, Brad and Bart Streumer. "Procedural and Substantive Practical Rationality" in *The Oxford Handbook of Rationality*, edited by Alfred R. Mele and Piers Rawlins. Oxford: Oxford University Press, 2004: 57–74.

Horton, John. "Reasonable Disagreement." In *Multiculturalism and Moral Conflict*, edited by Maria Dimovia-Cookson and P. M. R. Stirk. London: Routledge, 2009: 58–74.

Hume, David. "Of the Original Contract." In his *Essays Moral, Political, and Literary.* Oxford: Oxford University Press, 1963: 452–73.

Treatise of Human Nature, 2nd ed., edited by L. A. Selby-Bigge and L. P. H. Nidditch. Oxford: Clarendon Press, 1976.

Husak, Douglas N. *Drugs and Rights.* Cambridge: Cambridge University Press, 1992.

Izard, Caroll E. *Human Emotions.* New York: Plenum, 1972.

James, Aaron. "Constructing Justice for Existing Practice: Rawls and the Status Quo," *Philosophy and Public Affairs*, vol. 33 (2005): 2–36.

"The Significance of Distribution." In *Reasons and Recognition: Essays for T. M. Scanlon.* Oxford: Oxford University Press, forthcoming.

Jänttil, Markus and Eva Sierminska. *Survey Estimates of Wealth Holdings in OECD Countries: Evidence on the Level and Distribution.* United Nations University, World Institute for Development Economics Research, 2007.

Jeffrey, Richard. *Subjective Probability.* Cambridge: Cambridge University Press, 2004.

Joyce, Richard. *The Evolution of Morality.* Cambridge, MA: MIT Press, 2006.

Kagan, Jerome. *The Nature of the Child.* New York: Basic Books, 1984.

Kaltenthaler, Karl C. and Stephen J. Ceccoli. "Explaining Patterns of Support for the Provision of Citizen Welfare." *Journal of European Public Policy*, vol. 15 (October 2008): 1041–68.

Kant, Immanuel. *Foundations of the Metaphysics of Morals*, translated by Lewis White Beck. Indianapolis: Bobbs-Merrill, 1959.

"What Is Enlightenment?" In *Kant's Political Writings*, edited by Hans Reiss and translated by H. B. Nisbett. Cambridge: Cambridge University Press, 1970.

Critique of Judgment, translated by Werner S. Pluhar. Indianapolis: Hackett, 1987.

The Metaphysical Elements of Justice, 2nd ed., edited and translated by John Ladd. Indianapolis: Hackett, 1999.

Kaplow, Louis and Steven Shavell. *Fairness versus Welfare*. Cambridge, MA: Harvard University Press, 2002.

Kaufmann, Walter. *Without Guilt and Justice*. New York: Peter H. Wyden, 1973.

Kavka, Gregory. "The Toxin Puzzle." *Analysis*, vol. 43 (1983): 33–6.

Keeney, Ralph L. and Howard Raiffa. *Decisions with Multiple Objectives: Preferences and Value Tradeoffs*. Cambridge: Cambridge University Press, 1993.

Kerr, Norbert L. and Cynthia Kaufman-Gilliland. "Communication, Commitment, and Cooperation in Social Dilemmas." *Journal of Personality and Social Psychology* vol. 66 (1994): 513–529.

Keynes, John Maynard. *The General Theory of Employment, Interest and Money*. London: Macmillan, 1974.

Kiehl, Kent. "Without Morals: The Cognitive Neuroscience of Criminal Psychopaths." In *Moral Psychology, vol. 3: The Neuroscience of Morality: Emotion, Brain Disorders, and Development*, edited by Walter Sinnott-Armstrong. Cambridge, MA: MIT Press, 2008: 119–49.

Kliemt, Hartmut. *Philosophy and Economics I: Methods and Models*. Munich: Oldenbourg Verlag, 2009.

Klosko, George. *Democratic Procedures and Liberal Consensus*. Oxford: Oxford University Press, 2000.

Political Obligations. New York: Oxford University Press, 2005.

Knetsch, Jack L. "Endowment Effect and Evidence on Nonreversible Indifference Curves." In *Choices, Values and Frame*, edited by Daniel Kahneman and Amos Tversky. Cambridge: Cambridge University Press, 2000: 171–9.

Kohlberg, Lawrence. "The Child as Moral Philosopher." *Psychology Today*, vol. 4 (September 1968): 24–30.

The Philosophy of Moral Development. New York: Harper and Row, 1981.

"A Reply to Owen Flanagan and Some Comments on the Puka-Goodpaster Exchange," *Ethics*, vol. 92 (April, 1982): 513–28.

Kohlberg, Lawrence and R. Kramer. "Continuities and Discontinuities in Child Development." *Human Development*, vol. 12 (1969): 93–120.

Kohn, Marek. *Trust: Self-Interest and the Common Good*. Oxford: Oxford University Press, 2008.

Korsgaard, Christine M. "The Reasons We Share." In her *The Kingdom of Ends*. Cambridge: Cambridge University Press, 1996: chap. 10.

The Sources of Normativity. Cambridge: Cambridge University Press, 1996.

Kuhn, Thomas S. *The Structure of Scientific Revolutions*, 2nd ed. Chicago: University of Chicago Press, 1970.

Kukathas, Chandran. *The Liberal Archipelago: A Theory of Diversity and Freedom*. Oxford: Oxford University Press, 2003.

Kupperman, Joel J. *The Foundations of Morality*. London: Allen and Unwin, 1983.

Laing, R. D. *The Divided Self.* Harmondsworth: Penguin, 1965.

Larmore, Charles. *The Morals of Modernity.* Cambridge: Cambridge University Press, 1996.

The Autonomy of Morality. Cambridge: Cambridge University Press, 2008.

Lazarus, Richard S. *Emotion and Adaptation.* Oxford: Oxford University Press, 1991.

Levi, Isaac. *Hard Choices: Decision Making under Unresolved Conflict.* Cambridge: Cambridge University Press, 1984.

"Commitment and Change of View." In *Reason and Nature,* edited by José Luis Bermúdez and Alan Miller. Oxford: Oxford University Press, 2002: 209–32.

Lewis, David. *Convention: A Philosophical Study.* Cambridge, MA: Harvard University Press, 1969.

"Prisoner's Dilemma Is a Newcomb Problem." In *Paradoxes of Rationality and Cooperation: Prisoner's Dilemma and Newcomb's Problem,* edited by Richmond Campbell and Lanning Sowden. Vancouver: University of British Columbia Press, 1985: chap. 14.

"Dispositional Theories of Value." In his *Papers in Ethics and Social Philosophy.* Cambridge: Cambridge University Press, 2000: 68–94.

Libecap, Gary D. *Contracting for Property Rights.* Cambridge: Cambridge University Press, 1989.

Lijphart, Arend. *Democracies: Patterns of Majoritarian and Consensus Government in Twenty-One Countries.* New Haven: Yale University Press, 1984.

Lister, Andrew."Public Justification and the Limits of State Action." *Politics, Philosophy, and Economics,* vol. 9 (May 2010): 151–76.

Locke, John. "A Letter Concerning Toleration." In the *Works of John Locke in Nine Volumes,* 12th ed. London: Rivington, 1824: vol. 5.

The Second Treatise of Government. In *Two Treatises of Government,* edited by Peter Laslett. Cambridge: Cambridge University Press, 1960: 285–446.

Lodge, Milton and Charles Taber. "Three Steps Toward a Theory of Motivated Practical Reasoning." In *The Elements of Reason: Cognition, Choice and the Bounds of Rationality,* edited by Arthur Lupia, Matthew D. McCubbins, and Samuel L. Popkin. Cambridge: Cambridge University Press, 2000: 183–213.

Lomasky, Loren. *Rights, Persons, and the Moral Community.* New York: Oxford University Press, 1987.

Louden, Robert B. *Morality and Moral Theory.* Oxford: Oxford University Press, 1992.

Lowenstein, George and Daniel Adler. "A Bias in the Prediction of Tastes." In *Choices, Values and Frames,* edited by Daniel Kahneman and Amos Tversky. Cambridge: Cambridge University Press, 2000: 726–34.

Luce, R. Duncan and Howard Raiffa. *Games and Decisions.* New York: John Wiley, 1957.

Lupia, Arthur, Matthew D. McCubbins, and Samuel L. Popkin, editors. *The Elements of Reason: Cognition, Choice and the Bounds of Rationality.* Cambridge: Cambridge University Press, 2000.

Lycan, William. *Judgment and Justification.* Cambridge: Cambridge University Press, 1988.

Lyons, William. *Emotion.* Cambridge: Cambridge University Press, 1980.

Macedo, Stephen. "In Defense of Liberal Public Reason: Are Slavery and Abortion Hard Cases?" In *Natural Law and Public Reason,* edited by Robert P. George and Christopher Wolfe. Washington, DC: Georgetown University Press, 2000: 11–49.

Mack, Eric. "In Defense of the Jurisdiction Theory of Rights." *Journal of Ethics,* vol. 4 (January–March 2000): 71–98.

"The Natural Right of Property." *Social Philosophy and Policy,* vol. 27 (Winter 2010): 53–78.

Mackie, Gerry. *Democracy Defended.* Cambridge: Cambridge University Press, 2003.

Mackie, J. L. *Ethics: Inventing Right and Wrong.* Harmondsworth: Penguin, 1990.

Mailath, George J. "Do People Play Nash Equilibrium? Lessons from Evolutionary Game Theory." *Journal of Economic Literature,* vol. 46 (September 1998): 1347–1374.

Manktelow, K. I. and D. Over. "Deontic Reasoning." In *Perspectives on Thinking and Reasoning: Essays in Honor of Peter Wason,* edited by Stephen E. Newstead and Jonathan St. B. T. Evans. East Sussex, UK: Lawrence Erlbaum, 1995: 91–114.

Martin, Rex. *A System of Rights.* Oxford: Clarendon Press, 1993.

"T. H. Green on Individual Rights and the Common Good." In *The New Liberalism: Reconciling Liberty and Community,* edited by Avital Simhony and David Weinstein. Cambridge: Cambridge University Press, 2001: 49–50.

Marx, Karl. *Economic and Philosophical Manuscripts of 1844.* In *The Marx-Engels Reader,* 2nd ed., edited by Robert C. Tucker. New York: W.W. Norton, 1978.

Capital. In *Marx/Engels Collected Works,* vol. 1. London: Lawrence & Wishart, 1975–2002.

May, K. O. "A Set of Independent, Necessary and Sufficient Conditions for Simple Majority Rule." *Econometrica,* vol. 10 (1952): 680–84.

McClennen, Edward F. *Rationality and Dynamic Choice.* Cambridge: Cambridge University Press, 1990.

"The Rationality of Being Guided by Rules." In *The Oxford Handbook of Rationality,* edited by Alfred R. Mele and Piers Rawling. Oxford: Oxford University Press, 2004: 222–39.

McDougall, William. *The Energies of Men,* 3rd ed. London: Meuthen, 1935.

McKeever, Sean and Michael Ridge. *Principled Ethics: Generalism as a Regulative Ideal.* Oxford: Oxford University Press, 2006.

McMahon, Christopher. *Collective Rationality and Collective Reasoning.* Cambridge: Cambridge University Press, 2001.

Mill, James. *An Essay on Government*. Cambridge: Cambridge University Press, 1937.

Mill, John Stuart. *On Liberty*. In *The Collected Works of John Stuart Mill*, edited by J. M. Robson, Toronto: University of Toronto Press, 1963: vol. 18: 213–310.

    Principles of Political Economy. In *The Collected Works of John Stuart Mill*, edited by J. M. Robson. Toronto: University of Toronto Press, 1963: vols. 2 and 3.

    The Subjection of Women. In *The Collected Works of John Stuart Mill*, edited by J. M. Robson. Toronto: University of Toronto Press, 1963: vol. 21: 259–340.

    Utilitarianism. In *The Collected Works of John Stuart Mill*, edited by J. M. Robson, Toronto: University of Toronto Press, 1963: vol. 10: 203–59.

Miller, David. "The Fatalistic Conceit." *Critical Review*, vol. 3 (Spring 1989): 310–23.

    "Distributive Justice: What People Think." *Ethics*, vol. 102 (April 1992): 555–93.

Millgram, Elijah. *Ethics Done Right: Practical Reasoning as a Foundation for Moral Theory*. Cambridge: Cambridge University Press, 2005.

Moon, J. Donald. "Drugs and Democracy." In *Drugs and the Limits of Liberalism*, edited by Pablo De Greiff. Ithaca: Cornell University Press, 1999: 133–55.

Morris, Christopher W. *An Essay on the Modern State*. Cambridge: Cambridge University Press, 1998.

Morrow, James D. *Game Theory for Political Scientists*. Princeton: Princeton University Press, 1994.

Mortimore, G. W. "Rational Action." In *Rationality and the Social Sciences*, edited by S. I. Benn and G. W. Mortimore. London: Routledge and Kegan Paul, 1976: 93–110.

Mueller, Dennis. *Public Choice III*. Cambridge: Cambridge University Press, 2003.

Munzer, Stephen R. *A Theory of Property*. Cambridge: Cambridge University Press, 1990.

Murphy, Liam and Thomas Nagel. *The Myth of Ownership: Taxes and Justice*. New York: Oxford University Press, 2002.

Nichols, Shaun. *Sentimental Rules: On the Natural Foundations of Moral Judgment*. Oxford: Oxford University Press, 2004.

    "After Incompatibilism: A Naturalistic Defense of the Reactive Attitudes." *Philosophical Perspectives*, vol. 21: Philosophy of Mind (2007): 406–27.

    "Emotions, Norms, and the Genealogy of Fairness." *Politics, Philosophy & Economics*, vol. 9 (August 2010): 275–96.

Nichols, Shaun and Christopher Freiman. "Is Desert in the Details?" *Philosophy and Phenomenological Research*, forthcoming.

Nicholson, Peter P. *The Political Philosophy of the British Idealists*. Cambridge: Cambridge University Press, 1990.

Niehans, Jürg. *A History of Economic Theory: Classic Contributions, 1720–1980*. Baltimore: Johns Hopkins University Press, 1990.

Nietzsche, Friedrich. *Beyond Good and Evil*, translated by Walter Kaufmann. New York: Vintage Books, 1966.

Nozick, Robert. *Anarchy, State, and Utopia*. New York: Basic Books, 1974.
Philosophical Explanations. Oxford: Clarendon Press, 1981.
"Newcomb's Problem and Two Principles of Choice." In *Rationality in Action*, edited by Paul K. Moser. Cambridge: Cambridge University Press, 1990: 207–34.
The Nature of Rationality. Princeton: Princeton University Press, 1993.

Nunner–Winkler, Gertrude and Beate Sodian. "Children's Understanding of Moral Emotions." *Child Development*, vol. 59 (October 1988): 1323–38.

Oakeshott, Michael. "Rationalism in Politics." In his *Rationalism in Politics and Other Essays*, expanded ed. Indianapolis: Liberty Press, 1991: 5–42.
On Human Conduct. Oxford: Clarendon Press, 1975.

O'Hear, Anthony. *Beyond Evolution: Human Nature and the Limits of Evolutionary Explanation*. Oxford: Oxford University Press, 1997.

Ok, Efe A. "Utility Representation of an Incomplete Preference Relation." *Journal of Economic Theory*, vol. 104 (2002): 429–49.

Okasha, Samir. *Evolution and Levels of Selection*. Oxford: Clarendon Press, 2006.

Ostrom, Elinor. *Governing the Commons: The Evolution of Institutions for Collective Action*. Cambridge: Cambridge University Press, 1990.

Ostrom, Elinor, Roy Gardner, and James Walker. *Rules, Games, and Common Pool Resources*. Ann Arbor: University of Michigan Press, 1994.

Overlaet, Bert. "Merit Criteria as Justification for Differences in Earnings." *Journal of Economic Psychology*, vol. 12 (1991): 689–706.

Page, Scott E. *The Difference: How the Power of Diversity Creates Better Groups, Firms, Schools, and Societies*. Princeton: Princeton University Press, 2007.

Pareto, Vilfrado. *Manual of Political Economy*, edited by Ann S. Schwier and Alfred N. Page, translated by Ann S. Schwier. London: Macmillan, 1971.

Parfit, Derek. "Rationality and Reasons." In *From Action to Value: Exploring Practical Philosophy*, edited by Dan Egonnsson et al. Aldershot: Ashgate, 2001: 18–39.

Parsons, Talcott. "Introduction." In *The Theory of Social and Economic Organization* by Max Weber, translated by A. M. Henderson and Talcott Parsons. New York: Free Press, 1947.
The Social System. London: Routledge and Kegan Paul, 1965.

Paul, Ellen Frankel. "Liberalism, Unintended Orders and Evolutionism." *Political Studies*, vol. 36 (1988): 251–72.

Perry, Michael. *Love and Power*. New York: Oxford University Press, 1992.

Pettit, Philip. "The Prisoner's Dilemma Is an Unexploitable Newcomb Problem." *Synthese*, vol. 76 (July 1988): 123–34.

"Consequentialism." In *A Companion to Ethics*, edited by Peter Singer. Oxford: Blackwell, 1991.

The Common Mind: An Essay on Psychology, Society, and Politics. Oxford: Oxford University Press, 1993.

"Non-consequentialism and Political Philosophy." In *Robert Nozick*, edited by David Schmidtz. Cambridge: Cambridge University Press, 2002: 83–104.

Rules, Reasons, and Norms. Oxford: Oxford University Press, 2002.

Phillips, Derek L. *Looking Backwards: A Critical Appraisal of Communitarian Thought*. Princeton: Princeton University Press, 1993.

Piaget, Jean. *Logic and Psychology*. Manchester: Manchester University Press, 1953.

The Moral Judgment of the Child, translated by Marjorie Gabain. New York: Free Press, 1965.

Pincione, Guido and Frenando Tesón. *Rational Choice and Democratic Deliberation: A Theory of Discourse Failure*. Cambridge: Cambridge University Press, 2006.

Plamenatz, John. *Man and Society*. London: Longman's, 1973, 2 vols.

Pogge, Thomas. *World Poverty and Human Rights*. Oxford: Polity, 2002.

Pollock, John L. *Contemporary Theories of Knowledge*. Totowa, NJ: Rowman and Littlefield, 1986.

Thinking about Acting: Logical Foundations for Rational Decision Making. New York: Oxford University Press, 2006.

Postema, Gerald J. "Public Practical Reason: Political Practice." In *NOMOS XXXVII: Theory and Practice*, edited by Ian Shapiro and Judith Wagner DeCrew. New York: New York University Press, 1995: 345–85.

Prichard, H. A. "Does Moral Philosophy Rest on a Mistake?" In his *Moral Obligation: Essays and Lectures*. Oxford: Oxford University Press, 1949: 1–17.

Prinz, Jesse J. *The Emotional Construction of Morals*. Oxford: Oxford University Press, 2007.

Prinz, Jesse J. and Shaun Nichols. "Moral Emotions." In the *Oxford Handbook of Moral Psychology*, edited by J. Doris and S. Stich. Oxford: Oxford University Press, 2010: 111–148.

Quong, Jonathan. *Liberalism without Perfection*. Oxford: Oxford University Press, 2010.

"Three Disputes about Public Reason: Commentary on Gaus and Vallier,"
www. publicreason.net/wp-content/PPPS/Fall2008/JQuong1.pdf.

Rachels, James. *The Elements of Moral Philosophy*, 3rd ed. New York: McGraw-Hill, 1999.

Rachels, Stuart. "Counterexamples to the Transitivity of Better Than." *Australasian Journal of Philosophy*, vol. 76 (March 1998): 71–83.

Rae, Douglas. *The Political Consequences of Electoral Laws*. New Haven: Yale University Press, 1971.

Rashdall, Hastings. *The Theory of Good and Evil*. Oxford: Oxford University Press, 1907, 2 vols.

Rawls, John. *A Theory of Justice.* Cambridge, MA: Harvard University Press, 1971, rev. ed. 1999. [References in text are to 1999 edition unless explicitly stated otherwise.]

    Political Liberalism. New York: Columbia University Press, 1996.

    "Distributive Justice." In *John Rawls: Collected Papers,* edited by Samuel Freeman. Cambridge, MA: Harvard University Press, 1999: 130–53.

    "The Idea of Public Reason Revisited." In his *The Law of Peoples.* Cambridge, MA: Harvard University Press, 1999: 129–80.

    "Justice as Fairness." In *John Rawls: Collected Papers,* edited by Samuel Freeman. Cambridge, MA: Harvard University Press, 1999: 47–72.

    "Kantian Constructivism in Moral Theory." In *John Rawls: Collected Papers,* edited by Samuel Freeman. Cambridge, MA: Harvard University Press, 1999: 303–58.

    The Law of Peoples. Cambridge, MA: Harvard University Press, 1999.

    "An Outline of a Decision Procedure for Ethics." In *John Rawls: Collected Papers,* edited by Samuel Freeman. Cambridge, MA: Harvard University Press, 1999: 1–19.

    "Themes in Kant's Moral Philosophy." In *John Rawls: Collected Papers,* edited by Samuel Freeman. Cambridge, MA: Harvard University Press, 1999: 497–528.

    Lectures on the History of Moral Philosophy, edited by Barbara Herman. Cambridge, MA: Harvard University Press, 2000.

    Justice as Fairness: A Restatement, edited by Erin Kelly. Cambridge, MA: Belknap Press of Harvard University Press, 2001.

    Lectures on the History of Political Philosophy, edited by Samuel Freeman. Cambridge, MA: Harvard University Press, 2007.

Raz, Joseph. "Reasons for Actions, Decisions, and Norms." In his *Practical Reasoning.* Oxford: Oxford University Press, 1978: 128–43.

    "Value Incommensurability: Some Preliminaries." *Proceedings of the Aristotelian Society,* vol. 86 (1986): 117–34.

    The Morality of Freedom. Oxford: Clarendon Press, 1986.

    "Facing Up: A Reply." *Southern California Law Review,* vol. 62 (1988–1989): 1152–79.

    "Facing Diversity: The Case of Epistemic Abstinence." *Philosophy & Public Affairs,* vol. 19 (1990): 3–46.

    Engaging Reason: On the Theory of Value and Action. Oxford: Oxford University Press, 1999.

    Practical Reason and Norms, 2nd ed. Oxford: Oxford University Press, 2000.

    "The Obligation to Obey the Law." In his *The Authority of Law: Essays on Law and Morality,* 2nd ed. New York: Oxford University Press, 2009: 233–49.

Reiman, Jeffrey. *Justice and Modern Moral Philosophy.* New Haven, CT: Yale University Press, 1990.

Rhodes, Steven E. *An Economist's View of the World.* Cambridge: Cambridge University Press, 1985.

Richerson, Peter J. and Robert Boyd. *Not by Genes Alone: How Culture Transformed Human Evolution*. Chicago: University of Chicago Press, 2005.

"The Evolution of Free Enterprise Values." In *Moral Markets: the Critical Role of Values in the Economy*, edited by Paul J. Zak. Princeton: Princeton University Press, 2008: 107-141.

Ridge, Michael. "Hobbesian Public Reason," *Ethics*, vol. 108 (April 1998): 538-68.

Riker, William. *Liberalism against Populism*. Prospect Heights, IL: Waveland Press, 1988.

Riley, Jonathan. "Justice under Capitalism." In *NOMOS XXXI: Markets and Justice*, edited by J. Chapman and J. R. Pennock. New York: New York University Press, 1989: 122-62.

Riley, Patrick. "On Kant as the Most Adequate of the Social Contract Theorists," *Political Theory*, vol. 1 (November 1973): 450-71.

Rips, Lance J. "Cognitive Processes and Propositional Reasoning." *Psychological Review*, vol. 90 (1983): 38-71.

Ritchie, David G. *Darwinism and Politics*. London: Swan Sonnenschein, 1891.

Rokeach, Milton. *The Nature of Human Values*. New York: Free Press, 1973.

"From Individual to Institutional Values." In his *Understanding Values*. London: Collier Macmillan, 1979.

Rolls, Edmund T. *Emotion Explained*. Oxford: Oxford University Press, 2007.

Rorty, Amélie O. "Explaining Emotions." In her *Explaining Emotions*. Berkeley: University of California Press, 1980: 103-26.

Rosenberg, Alexander. *Philosophy of Social Science*, 2nd ed. Boulder, CO: Westview, 1995.

Rosenberg, Milton J. "Cognitive Structure and Attitudinal Affect." *Journal of Abnormal and Social Psychology*, vol. 53 (1956): 367-72.

"An Analysis of Affective-Cognitive Consistency." In *Attitude, Organization and Change*, edited by Milton J. Rosenberg and Carl I. Hovland. New Haven: Yale University Press, 1960: 15-64.

Ross, Lee and Richard E. Nisbet. *The Person and the Situation*. Philadelphia: Temple University Press, 1991.

Ross, W. D. *The Right and the Good*. Oxford: Clarendon Press, 1930.

Roth, A. E., V. Prasnikar, M. Okumo-Fujiwara, and S. Zamir. "Bargaining and Market Behavior in Jerusalem, Ljubljana, Pittsburgh, and Tokyo: A Experimental Study." *American Economic Review*, vol. 81 (1991): 1068-95.

Rousseau, Jean-Jacques. *A Discourse on Political Economy*. In *The Social Contract and Discourses*, translated with an Introduction by G. D. H. Cole. London: J. M. Dent, 1973: 115-54.

The Social Contract. In *The Social Contract and Discourses*, translated with an Introduction by G. D. H. Cole. London: J. M. Dent, 1973: 3-124.

Rozin, Paul. "The Process of Moralization." *Psychological Science*, vol. 10 (May 1999): 218-21.

Sandler, Todd. *Economic Concepts for the Social Sciences.* Cambridge: Cambridge University Press, 2001.

Sayre-McCord, Geoffrey. "Criminal Justice and Legal Reparations as an Alternative to Punishment." In *Legal and Political Philosophy*, edited by Enrique Villanueva. Amsterdam: Rodopi, 2002: 307–38.

Scanlon, Thomas. *What We Owe Each Other.* Cambridge, MA: Harvard University Press, 1998.

   Moral Dimensions: Permissibility, Meaning, Blame. Cambridge, MA: Belknap Press of Harvard University Press, 2008.

Schauer, Frederick. *Free Speech: A Philosophical Approach.* Cambridge: Cambridge University Press, 1982.

   Playing by the Rules. Oxford: Clarendon Press, 1991.

   "Rules and the Rule of Law." *Harvard Journal of Law and Public Policy*, vol. 14 (1991): 645–94.

Scheffler, Samuel. *Human Morality.* Oxford: Oxford University Press, 1992.

Schmidtz, David. *The Limits of Government: An Essay on the Public Goods Argument.* Boulder, CO: Westview Press, 1991.

   Rational Choice and Moral Agency. Princeton: Princeton University Press, 1995.

   "Property and Justice." *Social Philosophy and Policy*, vol. 27(Winter 2010): 79–100.

Schroeder, Mark. "Hybrid Expressivism: Virtues and Vices." *Ethics*, vol. 119 (January 2009): 257–309.

Schwab, David and Elinor Ostrom. "The Vital Role of Norms and Rules in Maintaining Open Public and Private Economies." In *Moral Markets: the Critical Role of Values in the Economy*, edited by Paul J. Zak. Princeton: Princeton University Press, 2008: 204-227.

Schwartzman, Micah. "The Completeness of Public Reason," *Politics, Philosophy and Economics*, vol. 3 (2004): 191–220.

Screpanti, Ernesto and Stefno Zamagni. *An Outline of the History of Economic Thought*, 2nd ed., translated by David Field and Lynn Kirby. Oxford: Oxford University Press, 2005.

Sen, Amartya. *Collective Choice and Social Welfare.* San Francisco: Holden-Day, 1970.

   "The Impossibility of a Paretian Liberal." *Journal of Political Economy*, vol. 78 (Jan.–Feb. 1970): 152–57.

   "Choice, Orderings and Morality." In *On Practical Reason*, edited by Stephen Körner. New Haven, CT: Yale University Press, 1974: 54–76.

   "Liberty, Unanimity, and Rights." *Economica*, New Series 43 (Aug. 1976): 217–45.

   "Rights and Agency," *Philosophy & Public Affairs*, vol. 11 (1981): 3–39.

   On Ethics and Economics. Oxford: Basil Blackwell, 1987.

   "Internal Consistency of Choice." In his *Rationality and Freedom.* Cambridge, MA: Harvard University Press, 2002: 121–57.

   "Maximization and the Act of Choice." In his *Rationality and Freedom.* Cambridge, MA: Harvard University Press, 2002: 159–205.

Shafer-Landau, Russ. "Moral Rules." *Ethics*, vol. 107 (July 1997): 584–611.

Moral Realism: A Defence. Oxford: Oxford University Press, 2003.

Shapiro, Scott J. "The Difference That Rules Make." In *Analyzing Law: New Essays in Legal Theory*, edited by Brian Bix. Oxford: Oxford University Press, 1998: 33–62.

Sher, George. *Beyond Neutrality: Perfectionism and Politics*. Cambridge: Cambridge University Press 1997.

Shweder, Richard, Manamohan Mahapatra and Joan G. Miller. "Culture and Moral Development." In *The Emergence of Morality in Young Children*, edited by Jerome Kagan and Sharon Lamb. Chicago: University of Chicago Press, 1987: 1–83.

Sidgwick, Henry. *Outlines of the History of Ethics for English Readers*. London: Macmillan, 1925.

The Methods of Ethics, 7th ed. Chicago: University of Chicago Press, 1962.

Simmons, A. John. *Moral Principles and Political Obligation*. Princeton: Princeton University Press, 1979.

"The Anarchist Position." *Philosophy & Public Affairs* 16 (Spring 1987): 269–79.

On the Edge of Anarchy: Locke, Consent, and the Limits of Society. Princeton: Princeton University Press, 1993.

Simon, Herbert. "From Substantive to Procedural Rationality." In *Philosophy and Economic Theory*, edited by Frank Hahn and Martin Hollis. Oxford: Oxford University Press, 1979: 65–85.

Reason in Human Affairs. Stanford, CA: Stanford University Press, 1981.

Skyrms, Brian. *Evolution of the Social Contract*. Cambridge: Cambridge University Press, 1996.

The Stag Hunt and Evolution of Social Structure. Cambridge: Cambridge University Press, 2005.

Slovic, Paul. "The Construction of Preference." In *Choices, Values, and Frames*, edited by Daniel Kahneman and Amos Tversky. Cambridge: Cambridge University Press, 2000: 489–502.

Smith, Adam. "Considerations Concerning the First Formation of Languages." In the *Glasgow Edition of the Works and Correspondence of Adam Smith*, vol. IV: *Lectures on Rhetoric and Belles Lettres*, edited by J. C. Bryce. Indianapolis: Liberty Fund, 1985.

Smith, John Maynard. "The Evolution of Behavior." *Scientific American*, 239 (1978): 176–92.

Smith, Michael. *The Moral Problem*. Oxford: Blackwell, 1994.

"Internal Reasons." In his *Ethics and the A Priori*. Cambridge: Cambridge University Press, 2004: 17–42.

Smith, Vernon L. *Bargaining and Market Behavior: Essays in Experimental Economics*. Cambridge: Cambridge University Press, 2000.

Snare, Frank. "The Concept of Property." *American Philosophical Quarterly*, vol. 9 (April 1972): 200–206.

Sobel, John Howard. "Not Every Prisoner's Dilemma Is a Newcomb Problem." In *Paradoxes of Rationality and Cooperation: Prisoner's Dilemma and Newcomb's Problem*, edited by Richmond Campbell and Lanning

Sowden. Vancouver: University of British Columbia Press, 1985: chap. 16.

Taking Chances: Essays on Rational Choice. Cambridge: Cambridge University Press, 1994.

Sober, Elliot and David Sloan Wilson. *Unto Others: The Evolution and Psychology of Unselfish Behavior*. Cambridge: Harvard University Press, 1998.

Solum, Lawrence B. "Constructing an Ideal of Public Reason." *San Diego Law Review*, vol. 30 (Fall 1993): 729–63.

Sonedda, Daniela. "Wealth Inequality, Income Redistribution and Growth in 15 OECD Countries." Royal Economic Society Annual Conference (2003) Royal Economic Society, 21, http://ideas.repec.org/e/pso158.html.

Spencer, Herbert. *First Principles*. London: Murray, 1862.

Principles of Sociology. New York: D. Appleton, 1896.

Stein, Edward. *Without Good Reason: The Rationality Debate in Philosophy and Cognitive Science*. Oxford: Clarendon Press, 1996.

Steiner, Hillel. "Kant, Property and the General Will." In *The Enlightenment and Modernity*, edited by Norman Geras and Robert Walker. New York: St. Martin's, 2000.

Sterba, James P. "Completing the Kantian Project: from Rationality to Equality." *Proceedings and Addresses of the American Philosophical Association*, vol. 82 (2): 47–83.

Sterelny, Kim. "The Return of the Group." In his *The Evolution of Agency and Other Essays*. Cambridge: Cambridge University Press, 2001: 81–106.

Strawson, P. F. "Freedom and Resentment," *Proceedings of the British Academy*, vol. 48 (1962): 187–211.

"Social Morality and Individual Ideal," *Philosophy*, vol. 36 (1961): 1–17.

Sugden, Robert. "Contractarianism and Norms." *Ethics*, vol. 100 (July 1990): 768–86.

"The Contractarian Enterprise." In *Rationality, Justice, and the Social Contract*, edited by David Gauthier and Robert Sugden. New York: Harvester Wheatshaft, 1993: chap. 1.

Suk, Jeannie. *At Home in the Law: How the Domestic Violence Revolution Is Transforming Privacy*. New Haven, CT: Yale University Press, 2009.

Sullivan, Roger J. *Immanuel Kant's Moral Theory*. Cambridge: Cambridge University Press, 1989.

Sumner, William Graham. "Socialism." In *On Liberty, Society, and Politics: The Essential Writings of William Graham Sumner*, edited by Robert C. Bannister. Indianapolis: Liberty Fund, 1992.

Swaine, Lucas. *The Liberal Conscience*. New York: Columbia University Press, 2006.

Swanton, Christine. *Virtue Ethics: A Pluralistic View*. Oxford: Oxford University Press, 2003.

Talisse, Robert B. *Democracy after Liberalism: Pragmatism and Deliberative Politics*. London: Routledge, 2005.

Tanner, Edward. *Why Things Bite Back*. London: Fourth Estate 1996.
Taylor, Gabriele. *Pride, Shame, and Guilt: Emotions of Self-Assessment.* Oxford: Clarendon Press, 1985.
Thaler, Richard H. "The Ultimatum Game." *Journal of Economic Perspectives*, vol. 2 (Autumn, 1988), No. 4: 195–206.
Tetlock, Philip. "Coping with Trade-offs: Psychological Constraints and Political Implications." In *The Elements of Reason*, edited by Arthur Lupia, Matthew McCubbins, and Samuel Popkin. Cambridge: Cambridge University Press, 2000: 239–63.
  Expert Political Judgment: How Good Is It? How Can We Know? Princeton: University of Princeton Press, 2005.
Thomson, Judith Jarvis. "A Defense of Abortion." *Philosophy and Public Affairs*, vol. 1 (Fall 1971): 47–66.
  Rights, Restitution and Risk. Cambridge, MA: Harvard University Press, 1986.
Tuomela, Raimo. *The Philosophy of Social Practices: A Collective Acceptance View*. Cambridge: Cambridge University Press, 2002.
Turiel, Elliot. *The Development of Social Knowledge: Morality and Convention.* Cambridge: Cambridge University Press, 1983.
Turiel, Elliot, Melainie Killen, and Charles C. Helwig. "Morality: Its Structure, Functions and Vagaries." In *The Emergence of Morality in Young Children*, edited by Jerome Kagan and Sharon Lamb. Chicago: Chicago University Press, 1987: 155–243.
Tversky, Amos and Daniel Kahneman. "Rational Choice and the Framing of Decisions." In their edited collection *Choices, Values and Frames*. Cambridge: Cambridge University Press, 2000: 209–23.
Vanberg, Viktor J. *Rules and Choice in Economics*. London: Routledge, 1994.
Vanderschraaf, Peter. *Learning and Coordination: Inductive Deliberation, Learning, and Convention* (New York: Routledge, 2001).
  "War or Peace?: A Dynamical Analysis of Anarchy," *Economics and Philosophy*, vol. 22 (2006): 243–79.
  "Covenants and Reputations." *Synthese*, vol. 157 (2007): 167–95.
Vanderschraaf, Peter and Brian Skyrms. "Learning to Take Turns." *Erkenntis*, vol. 59 (2003): 311–46.
Vega-Rodondo, Fernando. *Economics and the Theory of Games*. Cambridge: Cambridge University Press, 2003.
Vellman, J. David. *The Possibility of Practical Reason*. Oxford: Clarendon Press, 2000.
von Neumann, John and Oskar Morgenstern. *Theory of Games and Economic Behavior*. Princeton: Princeton University Press, 1972.
Voorhoeve, Alex. "Heuristics and Biases in a Purported Counterexample of the Acyclity of 'Better Than,'" *Politics, Philosophy and Economics*, vol. 7 (2008): 285–99.
Waldron, Jeremy. *The Right to Private Property*. Oxford: Clarendon Press, 1988.
  Law and Disagreement. Oxford: Oxford University Press, 1999.

Walker, Liezl. "The Deterrent Value of Imposing Prison Sentences for Tax Crimes." *New England Journal of Criminal and Civil Confinement*, vol. 26 (Winter 2000).

Wall, Steven. *Liberalism, Perfectionism and Restraint*. Cambridge: Cambridge University Press, 1998.

"On Justificatory Liberalism." *Politics, Philosophy and Economics*, vol. 9 (May 2010): 123–50.

Walzer, Michael. "Political Action: The Problem of Dirty Hands," *Philosophy and Public Affairs*, vol. 2 (1973): 160–80.

Wason, P. C. "Reasoning about a Rule." *Quarterly Journal of Experimental Psychology*, vol. 20 (1968): 273–81.

Wason, P. C. and P. N. Johnson-Laird. *The Psychology of Reasoning: Structure and Content*. London: B. T. Batsford, 1972.

Weber, Max. "Politics as a Vocation." In *From Max Weber*, edited and translated by H. H. Gerth and C. Wright Mills. New York: Oxford University Press, 1946: 77–128.

Economy and Society: An Outlines of Interpretive Sociology, edited by Guenther Roth and Claus Wittich. New York: Bedminster Press, 1968, three volumes.

Weinstock, Daniel M. "Neutralizing Perfection: Hurka on Liberal Neutrality," *Dialogue*, vol. 38 (1999): 45–62.

Wenar, Leif. "The Nature of Rights." *Philosophy and Public Affairs*," vol. 33 (2005): 223–52.

Wertheimer, Alan. *Coercion*. Princeton: Princeton University Press, 1987.

Whaples, Robert C. and Jack C. Heckelman. "Public Choice Economics: Where Is There Consensus?" *American Economist*, vol. 49 (Spring): 66–78.

Whitman, Douglas Glen. "Hayek contra Pangloss on Evolutionary Systems." *Constitutional Political Economy*, vol. 9 (1998): 450–66.

White, Mark D. "Can *Homo Economicus* Follow Kant's Categorical Imperative?" *Journal of Socio-Economics*, vol. 33 (2004): 89–106.

Widom, Cathy Spatz. "Interpersonal Conflict and Cooperation in Psychopaths." *Journal of Abnormal Psychology*, vol. 85 (1978): 330–34.

"A Methodology for Studying Non-Institutionalized Psychopaths." In *Psychopathic Behavior: Approaches to Research*, edited by R. D. Hare and D. Schalling. New York: Wiley, 1978: 71–84.

Wiles, P. J. D. *Economic Institutions Compared*. New York: John Wiley, 1977.

Williams, Bernard. "A Critique of Utilitarianism." In *Utilitarianism: For and Against*, by J. J. C. Smart and Bernard Williams. Cambridge: Cambridge University Press, 1973: 75–150.

"Internal and External Reasons." In his *Moral Luck*. Cambridge: Cambridge University Press, 1981: 101–13.

"Internal Reasons and the Obscurity of Blame." In his *Making Sense of Humanity and Other Philosophical Papers, 1982–1993*. Cambridge: Cambridge University Press, 1995: 35–45.

Williamson, Oliver E. *The Economic Institutions of Capitalism*. New York: Free Press, 1985.

Wilson, James Q. *The Moral Sense*. New York: Free Press, 1993.

Wolf, Susan. "Moral Saints." *Journal of Philosophy*. vol. 79 (August 1982): 419–39.

Freedom within Reason. Oxford: Oxford University Press, 1990.

Wolff, Robert Paul. *In Defense of Anarchism*. New York: Harper & Row, 1970.

Understanding Rawls: A Reconstruction and Critique of A Theory of Justice. Princeton: Princeton University Press, 1977.

Wolterstorff, Nicholas. "The Role of Religion in Political Issues." In *Religion in the Public Square: The Place of Religious Convictions in Political Debate*, edited by Robert Audi and Nicholas Wolterstorff. Lanham, MD: Rowman and Littlefield, 1997.

Wright, Derek. *The Psychology of Moral Behavior*. Harmondsworth: Penguin, 1971.

Young, L., Nichols, S., and Saxe, R. "Investigating the Neural and Cognitive Basis of Moral Luck: It's Not What You Do But What You Know." *European Review of Philosophy*, (Special Issue on Psychology and Experimental Philosophy, edited by J. Knobe, T. Lombrozo and E. Machery), forthcoming.

Young, Robert. *Personal Autonomy: Beyond Negative and Positive Liberty*. London: Croom-Helm, 1986.

Zamir, Shmuel. "Rationality and Emotions in Ultimatum Bargaining." *Annales d'Économie et de Statistique*, no. 61 (January–March 2001): 1–31.

Index